SECOND CANADIAN EDITION

ADVERTISING & PROMOTION

AN INTEGRATED MARKETING COMMUNICATIONS PERSPECTIVE

George E. Belch
San Diego State University

Michael A. Belch
San Diego State University

Michael A. Guolla
University of Ottawa

McGraw-Hill
Ryerson

Toronto Montréal Boston Burr Ridge, IL Dubuque, IA Madison, WI New York
San Francisco St. Louis Bangkok Bogotá Caracas Kuala Lumpur Lisbon London
Madrid Mexico City Milan New Delhi Santiago Seoul Singapore Sydney Taipei

Dedicated to my wonderful family
Teresa, Louise, Daniel, and Nicholas

Advertising & Promotion
An Integrated Marketing Communications Perspective
Second Canadian Edition

Statistics Canada information is used with the permission of the Ministry of Industry, as Minister responsible for Statistics Canada. Information on the availability of the wide range of data from Statistics Canada can be obtained from Statistics Canada's Regional Offices, its World Wide Web site at http://www.statcan.ca, and its toll-free access number 1-800-263-1136.

ISBN: 0-07-093985-3

1 2 3 4 5 6 7 8 9 10 QD 0 9 8 7 6 5

Printed and bound in the United States of America.

Care has been taken to trace ownership of copyright material contained in this text; however, the publisher will welcome any information that enables them to rectify any reference or credit for subsequent editions.

Executive Sponsoring Editor: Lynn Fisher
Sponsoring Editor: Kim Brewster
Developmental Editor: Andrew Simpson
Senior National Sales Manager: Megan Farrell
Marketing Manager: Charlotte Liu
Manager, Editorial Services: Kelly Dickson
Supervising Editor: Joanne Limebeer
Copy Editor: Erin Moore
Senior Production Coordinator: Jennifer Wilkie
Permissions Research: Karen Becker, Andrew Simpson
Page Layout: Greg Devitt
Cover Design: Greg Devitt
Cover Photo: Alan Marsh/Firstlight.ca
Printer: Quebecor Printing Dubuque, Inc.

National Library of Canada Cataloguing in Publication Data

Belch, George E. (George Eugene)
    Advertising & promotion: an integrated marketing communications perspective / George E. Belch, Michael A. Belch, Michael A. Guolla -- 2nd Canadian ed.

First Canadian ed. written by George E. Belch ... [et al.]. Includes bibliographical references and index.
ISBN 0-07-093985-3
1. Advertising--Textbooks. 2. Sales promotion--Textbooks. 3. Communication in marketing--Textbooks.
I. Belch, Michael A. II. Guolla, Michael Angelo

HF5823.B38 2005   659.1   C2005-900976-4

Contents in Brief

iii

Contents

iv

PART 3
ARTICULATE THE MESSAGE

☐☐☐☐☐☐☐☐

Contents

PART 5
STRENGTHEN THE MESSAGE

☐☐☐☐☐☐☐☐

Contents

☐ CHAPTER 15
Direct Marketing — 442

☐ CHAPTER 16
Internet and Interactive Media — 462

PART 6
IMPLEMENT AND CONTROL THE IMC PLAN

☐☐☐☐☐☐☐☐

ix

☐☐
☐☐
☐☐
☐☐
☐☐
☐☐
☐☐
☐☐
☐☐
☐
☐
☐
☐
☐

Preface

The Changing World of Advertising and Promotion

Nearly everyone in the modern world is influenced to some degree by advertising and other forms of promotion. Organizations in both the private and public sectors have learned that the ability to communicate effectively and efficiently with their target audiences is critical to their success. Advertising and other types of promotional messages are used to sell products and services as well as to promote causes, market political candidates, and deal with societal problems. The field of advertising and promotion has changed tremendously with recent advancements in technology coupled with adaptations of organizations and their agencies to meet the needs of many different target audiences.

For decades, the advertising strategy for a national brand involved creating one or two commercials that could be run on network television, a few print ads that would run in general interest magazines, and some sales promotion support such as coupons or premium offers. However, in today's world there are a myriad of media outlets—print, radio, specialty TV channels on cable and satellite delivery services, and now the Internet—competing for consumers' attention. Marketers are looking beyond the traditional media to find new and better ways to communicate with their customers. They no longer accept on faith the value of conventional advertising placed in traditional media.

A number of factors are fueling this evolution in marketing communications. The audiences that marketers seek, along with the media and methods for reaching them, have become increasingly fragmented. Advertising and promotional efforts have become more regionalized and targeted to specific audiences. Retailers have become larger and more powerful, forcing marketers to shift money from advertising budgets to sales promotion. Marketers expect their promotional dollars to generate immediate sales and are demanding more accountability from their agencies. The Internet is well established as a medium and the online audience is growing rapidly throughout the world. Many companies are coordinating all their communications efforts so that they can send cohesive messages to their customers. Some companies are building brands with little or no use of traditional media advertising. Many advertising agencies have acquired, started, or become affiliated with sales promotion, direct-marketing, interactive agencies, and public relations companies to better serve their clients' marketing communications needs. Their clients have become "media-neutral" and are asking that they consider whatever form of marketing communication works best to target market segments and build long-term reputations and short-term sales.

This text will introduce students to this fast-changing field of advertising and promotion. While advertising is its primary focus, it is more than just an introductory advertising text because there is more to most organizations' promotional programs than just advertising. The changes discussed above are leading marketers and their agencies to approach advertising and promotion from an integrated marketing communications (IMC) perspective, which calls for a "big picture" approach to planning marketing and promotion programs and coordinating the various communication functions. To understand the role of advertising and promotion in today's business world, one must recognize how a firm can use all the promotional tools to communicate with its customers.

Changes to the Second Canadian Edition

A number of changes have been undertaken in the creation of the second Canadian edition.

- **A Continuing Emphasis on Integrated Marketing Communications** This edition continues to place a strong emphasis on approaching the field of advertising and promotion from an integrated marketing communications perspective. It shows how the various elements of an organization's promotional mix are combined to develop a total marketing communications program that sends a consistent message to customers. More attention is also given to setting communication objectives for IMC programs. The importance of specific communication objectives for each target audience and the importance of unique messages that resonate for each target audience are given greater attention. This approach helps establish a unique brand position for each target audience while maintaining the overall market position of the brand. Collectively, these ideas allow for individual components of the IMC program, such as advertising or sales promotion, to have their own communication objectives that contribute to the overall communication objectives of the entire IMC program.

- **New Chapter Opening Vignettes** *All* of the chapter opening vignettes in the second Canadian edition are new and were chosen for their currency and relevance to Canadian students. They demonstrate how various companies and advertising agencies use advertising and other IMC tools. They also provide interesting insights into some of the current trends and developments that are taking place throughout Canada.

- **New and Updated Perspectives** All of the boxed items focusing on specific examples of how companies are using integrated marketing communications are new or updated, and provide insight into many of the most current and popular advertising and promotional campaigns being used by marketers. The IMC Perspectives also address interesting issues related to advertising, sales promotion, direct marketing, and marketing on the Internet. Nearly all of the boxed items focusing on global and ethical issues of advertising and promotion are new.

- **Canadian Examples** The field of advertising and promotion changes very rapidly. Wherever possible, the statistical information presented in tables, charts, and figures throughout the text have been updated. The most current Canadian trade literature was reviewed to ensure that this text reflects the most current perspectives on advertising, promotion, and the rapidly evolving area of integrated marketing communications in Canada. Many new Canadian examples and ads throughout the book have been added. *Advertising & Promotion* is the most contemporary text on the market, offering students as timely a perspective as possible.

- **Clear Decision Focus** Chapter 1 features a clear planning framework and identifies the content of an IMC plan. This framework is followed more closely throughout the text. The major parts of the text are organized and given a title that corresponds to the steps in the IMC plan as noted in a previous section. Further, within many chapters, a clear distinction is made between the type of decisions that a marketer or advertiser makes versus the information they use to formulate the decision. This approach makes it easier for students to understand the key decisions that need to be made for a successful IMC plan.

Organization of This Text

This book is divided into six major parts. In Part One, "Understand Integrated Marketing Communications" we examine the role of advertising and promotion in marketing and introduce the concept of integrated marketing communications. Chapter 1 provides an overview of advertising and promotion and its role in modern marketing. The concept of IMC and the factors that have led to its growth are discussed. Each of the promotional mix elements is defined and an IMC planning model shows the various steps in the promotional planning process. This model provides a framework for developing the integrated marketing communications program and is followed throughout the text.

In Part Two, "Connect Consumers to IMC," we cover the various theories and models to understand consumer behaviour in the context of marketing communication in order to perform a promotional program situation analysis. Chapter 2 covers the stages of the consumer decision-making process. The focus of this chapter is on how advertisers can use an understanding of buyer behaviour to develop effective communication that is directed to specific target audiences. Chapter 3 examines various communication theories and models of how consumers respond to advertising messages and other forms of marketing communication.

These first sections of the text provide students with a solid background in the areas of IMC planning, consumer behaviour, and communication. This lays the foundation for the remaining sections as we discuss the development of the integrated marketing communication program.

In Part Three, "Articulate the Message," we consider how firms develop objectives for their integrated marketing communications programs and how to translate those objectives into meaningful messages. Chapter 4 stresses the importance of knowing what to expect from advertising and promotion, the different types of communication objectives, characteristics of good objectives, and problems in setting objectives. Chapter 5 explores various ways advertisers try to position their brands through effective communication. Chapter 6 discusses the planning and development of the creative strategy and advertising campaign. In Chapter 7 we turn our attention to ways to execute the creative strategy and some criteria for evaluating creative work. Chapter 8 discusses ways to measure the effectiveness of various elements of the integrated marketing communications program, including methods for pretesting and posttesting advertising messages and campaigns.

In Part Four, "Deliver the Message," we explore the various ways of getting the message to the target audience. Chapters 9 through 12 cover media strategy and planning and the various advertising media. Chapter 9 introduces the key principles of media planning and strategy, and examines how a media plan is developed. We have also integrated the discussion of various methods for determining and allocating the promotional budget into this chapter. Chapter 10 discusses the strengths and limitations of broadcast media, as well as issues regarding the purchase of radio and TV time and audience measurement. Chapter 11 considers the same issues for the print media (magazines and newspapers). Chapter 12 examines the role of out-of-home and support media.

In Part Five, "Strengthen the Message," we continue the IMC emphasis by examining other promotional tools that are used in the integrated marketing communications process. Chapter 13 examines the area of sales promotion, including both consumer-oriented promotions and programs targeted to the trade (retailers, wholesalers, and other middlemen). Chapter 14 covers the role of public relations in IMC. Chapter 15 looks at the rapidly growing areas of direct marketing. This chapter examines database marketing and the way by which companies communicate directly with target customers through various media. Chapter 16 provides a detailed discussion of interactive media and marketing on the Internet and how companies are using the World Wide Web as a medium for communicating with customers. We discuss how this new medium is being used for a variety of marketing activities including advertising, sales promotion, and even the selling of products and services.

In Part Six, "Implement and Control the IMC Plan," we explore two issues for IMC program success. Chapter 17 describes how firms organize for advertising and promotion and examines the role of ad agencies and other firms that provide marketing and promotional services. A discussion of how ad agencies are selected, evaluated, and compensated, as well as the changes occurring in the agency business are included. The text concludes with Chapter 18, a discussion of the regulatory, social, ethical, and economic environments in which advertising and promotion operate.

Chapter Features

The following features in each chapter enhance students' understanding of the material as well as their reading enjoyment.

Chapter Objectives

Objectives are provided at the beginning of each chapter to identify the major areas and points covered in the chapter and guide the learning effort.

> ### CHAPTER OBJECTIVES
>
> - To review the various elements of the promotional mix: advertising, sales promotion, public relations, direct marketing, Internet marketing, and personal selling.
>
> - To introduce the concept of integrated marketing communications (IMC) by considering its evolution, growth, importance, and a broader view.

Chapter Opening Vignettes

Each chapter begins with a vignette that shows the effective use of integrated marketing communications by a company or ad agency or discusses an interesting issue that is relevant to the chapter. These opening vignettes are designed to draw the students into the chapter by presenting an interesting example, development, or issue that relates to the material covered in the chapter.

Jays Field a New Positioning

As the Toronto Jays baseball team attempted to reclaim its on-field glory years of the late 1980s and early 1990s, culminating in two successive World Series titles, it also faced the task of attracting an entirely new audience of baseball fans with its current communication plan. In 2002, its attendance figures placed Toronto's Major League Baseball team in the bottom 20 percent after setting records 10 years ago.

While many cited a variety of reasons for the decline such as a less-competitive team, the players' strike of 1994 along with the negative perceptions associated with no World

more than 10 percent from 1.6 million to 1.8 million. Furthermore, viewership of Jays' televised games was up 30 percent especially among women and those in the 18–35 demographic and registered visitors to the Jays website rose by 150 percent. For 2004, the Jays continued with the Baseball North theme but evolved the original positioning from "It's a Different Kind of Game Up Here" to "You've Got to See These Guys Play."

The communication campaign included additional price promotion for tickets and extensive product placement of the brand in a Martin Short

IMC Perspectives

These boxed items feature in-depth discussions of interesting issues related to the chapter material and the practical application of integrated marketing communications. Each chapter contains these insights into the world of integrated marketing communications.

IMC PERSPECTIVE   Chapter 14 | Public Relations   14–2

A Clear PR Message for Labatt Sterling

The content of a message is a critical advertising decision as well as a significant public relations decision as seen by the recent launch of Labatt Sterling, a beer containing just 2.5 grams of carbohydrates. The increasing health concerns of consumers and the introduction of specialized, brand name diets has resulted in low-carbohydrate niche products in a variety of food categories and beer was no exception in the latter part of 2003.

According to Ipsos-Reid, a leading market research firm, 80 percent of all Canadians believed a low-carb diet could be part of their efforts

consume. This approach appeared better than claiming carbohydrates are a problem and Sterling is a low-carbohydrate solution.

To communicate this critical message, Labatt turned to public relations through many media interviews that generated over 20 million impressions across Canada. A television spot supported the public relations a few months later, but success had already been achieved with the initial part of the campaign. With only public relations communicating its message, Labatt sold 85,000 six-packs in the first week, causing shortages in three provinces. It obtained 1 percent of the

Ethical Perspectives

These boxed items discuss the moral and/or ethical issues regarding practices engaged in by marketers and are also tied to the material presented in the particular chapter.

Key Terms

Important terms are highlighted in boldface throughout the text and listed at the end of each chapter with a page reference. These terms help call students' attention to important ideas, concepts, and definitions and help them review their learning progress.

Chapter Summaries

These synopses serve as a quick review of important topics covered and a very helpful study guide.

Discussion Questions

Questions at the end of each chapter give students an opportunity to test their understanding of the material and to apply it. These questions can also serve as a basis for class discussion or assignments.

Support Material

With this support package, you and your students receive everything from the basic supplements to the latest in educational technologies. Check it out for yourself.

Lecture Preparation, Assessment, and Presentation Tools

Instructor's CD-ROM. The CD-ROM includes all of the necessary Instructor supplements, including:

- **Instructor's Manual.** The thoroughly revised Instructor's Manual includes Chapter Overviews, Chapter Objectives, Chapter and Lecture Outlines, Teaching Suggestions, Answers to Discussion Questions, and Additional Discussion Questions and Answers (not shown in text).

- **PowerPoint® Presentation and Digital Assets.** These incorporate a high-quality photo and art program, including figure slides, commercials, product shots, advertisements, and advertising-in-practice shots.

- **Computerized Test Bank.** This test bank contains 3,000 questions categorized by topic and level of learning (definitional, conceptual, or application). The instructor-friendly format allows easy selection of questions from any part of the text, boxed materials, and cases. The program allows you to select any of the questions, make changes if desired, or add new questions—and quickly print out a finished set customized to your course.

Video Case Studies. A unique series contemporary advertising cases (both Canadian and international) is available on VHS and DVD and from the Online Learning Centre.

Online Technology

Online Learning Centre
This robust book-specific website at www.mcgrawhill.ca/ college/belch includes resources for both instructors and students. For the instructor, we offer downloadable supplement materials. Students have a 24/7 study centre to keep them up-to-date, to provide examples for application, and to prepare for tests.

Instructor Centre
- Instructor's Manual
- PowerPoint®—Includes concept screens, art from the text, and notes on other digital assets available in the PowerPoint® Presentations.

- CBC Videos
- Video Case Solutions
- Bessies Showreel (Canadian Television Commercial Festival)
- *Marketing Horizons* Newsletter
- Notes for using the Advertising Campaign Planner

Student Centre
- Chapter Objectives
- Multiple Choice Quizzes
- Internet Exercises
- Video Cases
- Web Links
- Glossary
- Access to *Marketing Magazine*
- Marketing Plan
- Σ-STAT
- Study To Go
- PowerWeb (optional package)
- *Globe and Mail* Headlines
- Career Profiles & Planning
- Advertising Campaign Planner

New Online IMC Campaign Builder

An online template demonstrates how to build and design a comprehensive Integrated Marketing Communications (IMC) plan, enabling students to achieve a keen awareness and understanding of the decisions, issues, and activities involved in developing such a plan. In the creation of their own first-rate IMC plan, students will apply the fundamental concepts they have learned and gain an appreciation for the complexity of a complete IMC plan.

Online Course Options

The material in *Advertising & Promotion* can be used with instructor-generated online learning sites. Any online platform, including WebCT and Blackboard, is compatible with the text's material. There are two basic options here: a course companion website or an online course where the material is fully or partially delivered via a course website.

McGraw-Hill's PageOut course website tool enables you to create a course website where you can post your syllabus, case solutions, course information updates, test results, and other key material. You can include links to McGraw-Hill's Online Learning Centre content, add links to important resources, and maintain student results in the online gradebook.

Superior Service

Service takes on a whole new meaning with McGraw-Hill Ryerson and *Advertising & Promotion*. More than just bringing you the textbook, we have consistently raised the bar in terms of innovation and educational research—both in marketing and in education in general. These investments in learning and the education community have helped us to understand the needs of students and educators across the country, and allowed us to foster the growth of truly innovative, integrated learning.

Integrated Learning

Your Integrated Learning Sales Specialist is a McGraw-Hill Ryerson representative who has the experience, product knowledge, training, and support to help you assess and integrate any of our products, technology, and services into your course for optimum teaching and learning performance. Whether it's using our test bank software, helping your students improve their grades, or putting your entire course online, your *i*Learning Sales Specialist is there to help you do it. Contact your local *i*Learning Sales Specialist today to learn how to maximize all of McGraw-Hill Ryerson's resources!

*i*Learning Services Program

McGraw-Hill Ryerson offers a unique *i*Services package designed for Canadian faculty. Our mission is to equip providers of higher education with superior tools and resources required for excellence in teaching. For additional information, visit www.mcgrawhill.ca/highereducation/*i*services.

Teaching, Learning & Technology Conference Series

The educational environment has changed tremendously in recent years, and McGraw-Hill Ryerson continues to be committed to helping you acquire the skills you need to succeed in this new milieu. Our innovative

Teaching, Learning & Technology Conference Series brings faculty together from across Canada with 3M Teaching Excellence award winners to share teaching and learning best practices in a collaborative and stimulating environment.

Acknowledgments

This second Canadian edition represents a tremendous amount of work that would not have become a reality without the assistance and support of many other people. Authors tend to think they have the best ideas, approach, examples, and organization for writing a great book. But I quickly learned that there is always room for our ideas to be improved on by others. A number of colleagues provided detailed, thoughtful reviews that were immensely helpful in making this a better book.

I would like to thank the following reviewers who provided valuable feedback and helped shape the content of the second Canadian edition: Michael Conyette, *Northern Lights College*; Jim Sherritt, *University of Northern British Columbia*; Allen Richert, *Confederation College*; Dwight Dyson, *Centennial College*; Bev Holoboff, *Northern Alberta Institute of Technology*; Tammy Kiss, *College of the Rockies*; Steve Janisse, *St. Clair College*; Christina Clements, *Humber College*; Stephen Ash, *Acadia University*; Joe Freeburn, *British Columbia Institute of Technology*; MaryLouise Huebner, *Seneca College*.

I would also like to acknowledge the cooperation I received from many people in the business, advertising, and media communities. The second Canadian edition contains several additional ads, illustrations, charts, and tables that have been provided by advertisers and/or their agencies, various publications, and other advertising and industry organizations. Many individuals took time from their busy schedules to provide us with requested materials and gave us permission to use them. A special thanks to all of you.

A manuscript does not become a book without a great deal of work on the part of a publisher. Various individuals at McGraw-Hill Ryerson have been involved with this project over the past year. My sponsoring editor, Kim Brewster, provided valuable guidance and encouragement to complete the revision successfully. A special thanks goes to Andrew Simpson, my developmental editor, for his continuous hard work and appropriate reminders to stay on schedule. Thanks also to Joanne Limebeer for doing a superb job of managing the production process. I also want to acknowledge the outstanding work of Karen Becker and Andrew Simpson for their help in obtaining permissions for many of the Canadian ads that appear throughout the book. I'd also like to recognize and thank Darren Hick for his work during the review process and Erin Moore for her conscientious editing that made the book a more enjoyable read. Thanks to the other members of the production team for all their hard work on this edition.

I'd like to thank Anne Marie Webb-Hughes of British Columbia Institute of Technology, who contributed to Chapters 16 and 17.

I would like to acknowledge the Dean of the School of Management at the University of Ottawa, Micheál Kelly, who supported my involvement in this project right from the start.

I'd like to extend my appreciation to my current and previous students who have given me the opportunity to develop my ideas. It is very gratifying to know that you enjoy my teaching and are using your new-found knowledge in the business world.

On a personal note, my kids, Louise, Daniel, and Nicholas, have been very supportive during this time-consuming and hectic process of working on the text. Their interest and encouragement have been very inspiring. All my love and gratitude goes to my wife Teresa who has helped me tremendously during this and all my academic pursuits.

Michael Guolla

About the Author

Michael Guolla is an assistant professor at School of Management of the University of Ottawa. He completed his Ph.D. in Business Administration with a concentration in Marketing at the University of Michigan (Ann Arbor) and received his Honours in Business Administration from the Richard Ivey School of Business at the University of Western Ontario. Dr. Guolla has published articles in academic journals, proceedings of scholarly conferences, and management journals in the areas of customer satisfaction, innovation, marketing strategy, and business marketing. He has also written many cases.

Professor Guolla's most recent teaching includes promotion management, services marketing, and marketing research. He has previously taught at Richard Ivey School of Business, the Michigan Business School, and at Queen's Business School.

1

Integrated Marketing Communications

CHAPTER OBJECTIVES

- To review the various elements of the promotional mix: advertising, sales promotion, public relations, direct marketing, Internet marketing, and personal selling.

- To introduce the concept of integrated marketing communications (IMC) by considering its evolution, growth, importance, and a broader view.

- To examine how various marketing and promotional elements must be coordinated to communicate effectively with the IMC perspective.

- To summarize a model of the IMC planning process and examine the steps in developing a marketing communications program.

Fashionable Success for L'Oréal Canada

L'Oréal Canada, recognized as *Marketing Magazine's* Marketer of the Year, built its L'Oréal Paris, Maybelline, and Garnier brands through innovative use of advertising, sales promotion, sponsorship, public relations, and Internet marketing in 2003. Faced with constraints of key marketing activities decided at the brand headquarters of Paris, New York, and Tokyo, L'Oréal Canada created a Canadian identity for its primary consumer brands. As a result, L'Oréal Canada attained superior response from young consumers who it had not targeted previously and achieved outstanding sales growth compared to other cosmetics firms.

L'Oréal Canada started well with its Maybelline sponsorship of the Quebec reality show *Star Académie* during the winter of 2003. Approximately 40 percent of all Quebecers witnessed the final episode and provided L'Oréal Canada with extensive visibility and vaulted it to the number two known brand in the province! As part of the campaign, Maybelline tweaked its famous slogan to fit the star theme of the hit television show, allowed its make-up artists to interact with the public on the Internet, organized autograph sessions in shopping malls with contestants that had been eliminated, and continued its advertising message on other media like radio.

During the summer of 2003, L'Oréal Paris sponsored the hit show *Canadian Idol*. In addition to

regular commercials and highlighted presence on the website for *Canadian Idol*, the show featured sponsorship announcements and on-air promotions that linked consumers to interactive, stylish fun on the L'Oréal Paris website. Consumers reacted positively as seen in the follow-up survey of women; almost all felt the L'Oréal Paris sponsorship was appropriate, 75 percent appreciated the beauty tips communicated on the show and more than half could connect L'Oréal Paris to *Canadian Idol* without any prompting. Sales growth topped 30 percent during the promotional communication and easily surpassed the 25-percent objective.

Established promotional efforts continued to put L'Oréal Canada at the forefront of Canadian marketers with positive publicity. Its interactive campaign in honour of International Women's Day provided much needed money for the Canadian Women's Foundation's Economic Development Fund. Promotional support for other fashion and arts events permitted L'Oréal Canada to keep its high profile. And to help facilitate these media communications, L'Oréal Canada worked with pharmacy retailers to deliver contest promotions and much needed communication at the point of sale.

Sources: Chris Powell, "Idol Worship," *Marketing Magazine*, November 10, 2003; Danny Kucharsky, "Because You're Worth It," *Marketing Magazine*, February 9, 2004.

As the opening vignette illustrates, large companies like L'Oreal Canada use advertising and other promotional techniques such as websites, direct marketing, sales promotion, public relations, and event sponsorship to effectively communicate. In fact, finding the right combination of marketing communication tools is a critical decision for small and large firms, private and public organizations, and those marketing goods, services, or ideas. Complicating this decision is an uncertain environment featuring the fragmentation of mass markets, the introduction of new technology, the emergence of global markets, and changes in consumer buying behaviour.

In response to this new landscape, many companies recognize that their promotional tools need to be linked or connected appropriately to effectively communicate with their current and prospective customers. This emerging trend is known as *integrated marketing communications*. Companies now develop their promotional plans with the recognition that each communication tool retains its unique communication effect and that the combination of communication tools contribute to the overall communication effect of the brand or organization,

This opening chapter introduces you to the topic of marketing communications. It briefly describes the different promotional or marketing communication tools available for marketers. Next, we illustrate the relatively new idea of integrated marketing communications. We then turn our attention to the contents of a promotional plan as a way of orienting you to the perspective and organization of this text.

MARKETING COMMUNICATIONS

Marketing is defined as "the process of planning and executing the conception, pricing, promotion, and distribution of ideas, goods, and services to create exchanges that satisfy individual and organizational objectives."[1]

The marketing function in an organization facilitates the exchange process and the development of relationships by carefully examining the needs and wants of consumers, developing a product or service that satisfies these needs, offering it at a certain price, making it available through a particular place or channel of distribution, and developing a program of promotion or communication. These four Ps—product, price, place (distribution), and promotion (marketing communications)—are elements of the **marketing mix**. The basic task of marketing is combining these four elements into a marketing program to facilitate the potential for exchange with consumers in the marketplace.

The primary focus of this book is one element of the marketing mix: promotion, or marketing communications. **Promotion** has been defined as the coordination of all seller-initiated efforts to set up channels of information and persuasion to sell goods and services or promote an idea.[2] While implicit communication occurs through the various elements of the marketing mix, most of an organization's communications with the marketplace take place as part of a carefully planned and controlled promotional program. The basic tools used to accomplish an organization's communication objectives are often referred to as the **promotional mix** (Figure 1–1).

FIGURE 1–1 ☐☐☐☐ Elements of the promotional mix

The Promotional Mix

Advertising | Direct marketing | Internet marketing | Sales promotion | Public relations | Personal selling

Traditionally the promotional mix has included four elements: advertising, sales promotion, public relations, and personal selling. However, in this text we view direct marketing as well as interactive media as major promotional-mix elements that marketers use to communicate with their target audiences. Furthermore, while either term is suitable, promotion or marketing communications, many marketers are using the latter since the tools are linked to achieve specific communication objectives. We now review the definition of each tool and summarize its role more clearly.

ADVERTISING

Advertising is defined as any paid form of nonpersonal communication about an organization, product, service, or idea by an identified sponsor.[3] The *paid* aspect of this definition reflects the fact that the space or time for an advertising message generally must be bought. An occasional exception to this is the public service announcement (PSA), whose advertising space or time is donated by the media.

The *nonpersonal* component means advertising involves mass media (e.g., TV, radio, magazines, newspapers) that can transmit a message to large groups of individuals, often at the same time. The nonpersonal nature of advertising means there is generally no opportunity for immediate feedback from the message recipient (except in direct-response advertising). Therefore, before the message is sent, the advertiser must consider how the audience will interpret and respond to it.

Advertising is the best-known and most widely discussed form of promotion, probably because of its pervasiveness. It is also a very important promotional tool, particularly for companies whose products and services are targeted at mass consumer markets. There are several reasons why advertising is such an important part of many marketers' promotional mixes. First, it can be a very cost-effective method for communicating with large audiences. For example, during a television season, prime-time network television reached 85 percent of Canadians on a daily basis. A recent cost per thousand households reached was estimated to be approximately $18.00.[4]

Second, advertising can be used to create brand images and symbolic appeals for a company or brand, a very important capability for companies selling products and services that are difficult to differentiate on functional attributes. For example, since 1980 Absolut has used creative advertising to communicate its vodka as an upscale, fashionable, sophisticated drink and to differentiate it from other brands. The advertising strategy has been to focus on two unique aspects of the product: the Absolut name and the distinctive shape of the bottle (Exhibit 1–1). Most of the print ads used in this long-running international campaign are specifically tailored for the magazine or region where they appear. The campaign, one of the most successful and recognizable in advertising history, has made the Absolut brand nearly synonymous with imported vodka. While many other spirits sales have declined significantly over the past two decades, Absolut sales have increased substantially in North America.[5]

A third feature of advertising is its ability to strike a responsive chord with consumers when differentiation across other elements of the marketing mix is difficult to achieve. Popular campaigns can be leveraged into successful promotional programs. For example, Eveready used the popularity of its Energizer Bunny campaign to generate support from retailers in the form of shelf space, promotional displays, and other merchandising activities (Exhibit 1–2). Consumer promotions such as in-store displays, premium offers, and sweepstakes feature the pink bunny. Pictures of the Energizer Bunny appear on Energizer packages to ensure brand identification and extend the campaign's impact to the point of purchase. Eveready has extended its marketing efforts to include tie-ins with sports marketing and sponsorships.

Exhibit 1–1 Creative advertising has made Absolut a popular brand of imported vodka

Exhibit 1–2 Eveready used the popularity of its pink bunny campaign to generate support from retailers

Finally, advertising is a flexible tool that can be used for many industries (e.g., cars versus soft drinks), situations (e.g., new products versus established products, as in Exhibit 1–3), and target audiences (e.g., new customers versus loyal customers). Furthermore, marketers advertise to the consumer market with national and retail/ local advertising, which may stimulate primary or selective demand. For other markets, they use business-to-business, professional, and trade advertising. Figure 1–2 describes the most common types of advertising.

Exhibit 1–3 The goals of this milk campaign are to change the image of milk and increase sales of the product

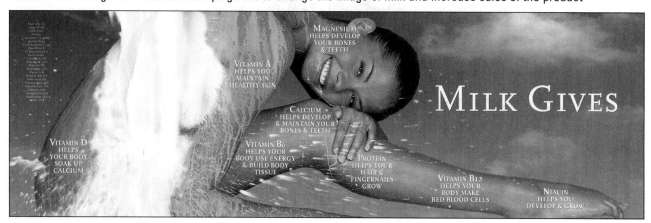

ADVERTISING TO CONSUMER MARKETS

FIGURE 1–2
Classifications of
advertising
☐ ☐ ☐ ☐ ☐

National Advertising

Advertising done by large companies on a nationwide basis or in most regions of the country. Most of the ads for well-known companies and brands that are seen on prime-time TV or in other major national or regional media are examples of national advertising. The goals of national advertisers are to inform or remind consumers of the company or brand and its features, benefits, advantages, or uses and to create or reinforce its image so that consumers will be predisposed to purchase it.

Retail/Local Advertising

Advertising done by retailers or local merchants to encourage consumers to shop at a specific store, use a local service, or patronize a particular establishment. Retail or local advertising tends to emphasize specific partronage motives such as price, hours of operation, service, atmosphere, image, or merchandise assortment. Retailers are concerned with building store traffic, so their promotions often take the form of direct action advertising designed to produce immediate store traffic and sales.

Primary versus Selective Demand Advertising

Primary demand advertising is designed to stimulate demand for the general product class or entire industry. Selective demand advertising focuses on creating demand for a specific company's brands. Most advertising for various products and services is concerned with stimluating selective demand and emphasizes reasons for purchasing a particular brand.

An advertiser might concentrate in stimulating primary demand when, for example, its brand dominates a market and will benefit the most from overall market growth. Primary demand advertising is often used as part of a promotional strategy to help a new product gain market acceptance, since the challenge is to sell customers on the product concept as much as to sell a particular brand. Industry trade associations also try to stimulate primary demand for their members' products, among them cotton, milk, orange juice, pork, and beef.

ADVERTISING TO BUSINESS AND PROFESSIONAL MARKETS

Business-to-Business Advertising

Advertising targeted at individuals who buy or influence the purchase of industrial goods or services for their companies. Industrial goods are products that either become a physical part of another product (raw material or component parts), are used in manufacturing other goods (machinery), or are used to help a company conduct its business (e.g., office supplies, computers). Business services such as insurance, travel services, and health care are also included in this category.

Professional Advertising

Advertising targeted to professionals such as doctors, lawyers, dentists, engineers, or professors to encourage them to use a company's product in their business operations. It might also be used to encourage professionals to recommend or specify the use of a company's product by end-users.

Trade Advertising

Advertising targeted to marketing channel members such as wholesalers, distributors, and retailers. The goal is to encourage channel members to stock, promote, and resell the manufacturer's branded products to their customers.

SALES PROMOTION

Sales promotion is generally defined as those marketing activities that provide extra value or incentives to the sales force, distributors, or the ultimate consumer and can stimulate immediate sales. Sales promotion is generally broken into two major categories: consumer-oriented and trade-oriented activities.

Consumer sales promotion is targeted to the ultimate user of a product or service and includes couponing, sampling, premiums, rebates, contests, sweepstakes, and various point-of-purchase materials (Exhibit 1–4). These promotional tools encourage consumers to make an immediate purchase and thus can stimulate short-term sales. *Trade sales promotion* is targeted toward marketing intermediaries such as wholesalers, distributors, and retailers. Promotional and merchandising allowances, price deals, sales contests, and trade shows are some of the promotional tools used to encourage the trade to stock and promote a company's products.

Promotion and *sales promotion* are two terms that often create confusion in advertising and marketing. As noted, promotion is an element of marketing by which firms communicate with their customers; it is a term that is synonymous with all the marketing communications outlined in Figure 1–1. However, many practitioners use the term sales promotion to mean the incentives directed towards either consumers or the trade (retailers, wholesalers) to stimulate sales. We follow this logic in this book. Promotion is used in the broader sense to refer to the various marketing communications activities of an organization, and sales promotion is used to refer to the incentives.

PUBLIC RELATIONS

Another important component of an organization's promotional mix is public relations. When an organization systematically plans and distributes information in an attempt to control and manage its image, it is engaging in a function known as public relations. **Public relations** is defined as "the management function which evaluates public attitudes, identifies the policies and procedures of an individual or organization with the public interest, and executes a program of action to earn public understanding and acceptance."[6] Public relations uses a variety of tools —including special publications, participation in community activities, fundraising, sponsorship of special events, and various public affairs activities—to enhance an organization's image. Organizations also use advertising as a public

Exhibit 1–4
Coupons are a popular consumer sales promotion tool

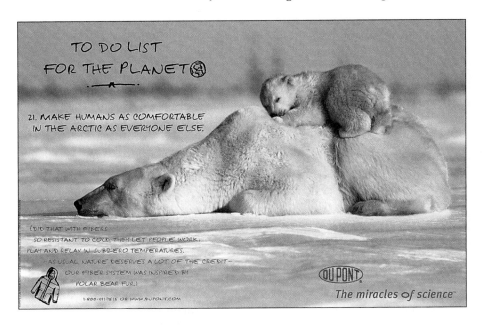

relations tool. For example, Exhibit 1–5 shows a corporate ad for DuPont, which shows how the company uses science to make life better.

Publicity refers to nonpersonal communications regarding an organization, product, service, or idea not directly paid for or run under identified sponsorship. The message reaches the public in the form of a news story, editorial, or announcement about an organization and/or its products and services. Like advertising, publicity involves nonpersonal communication to a mass audience, but unlike advertising, publicity is not directly paid for by the company. The company or organization attempts to get the media to cover or run a favourable story on a product, service, cause, or event. Tools used to gain publicity include news releases, press conferences, feature articles, photographs, films, and videotapes.

An advantage of publicity over other forms of promotion is its credibility. Consumers generally tend to be less skeptical toward favourable information about a product or service when it comes from a source they perceive as unbiased. For example, the success (or failure) of a new movie is often determined by the reviews it receives from film critics, who are viewed by many moviegoers as objective evaluators. Another advantage of publicity is its low cost, since the company is not paying for time or space in a mass medium such as TV, radio, or newspapers. While an organization may incur some costs in developing publicity items or maintaining a staff to do so, these expenses will be far less than those for the other promotional programs.

Traditionally, public relations and publicity have been considered more supportive than primary to the marketing and promotional process. However, many firms have begun making PR an integral part of their predetermined marketing and promotional strategies. PR firms are increasingly touting public relations as a communications tool that supports many of the functions of conventional advertising and marketing.[7]

DIRECT MARKETING

One of the fastest-growing sectors of the Canadian economy is **direct marketing**, in which organizations communicate directly with target customers to generate a response and/or a transaction. Direct marketing includes telemarketing and call centres, direct mail, mail-order catalogues, and direct-response ads in various broadcast and print media. Traditionally, direct marketing has not been considered an element of marketing communications since it had distinct objectives, strategies, and tactics.

Exhibit 1–6
Energy uses direct advertising to promote its product line

However, we view direct marketing as an important component of a firm's marketing communications program since it is connected to many other communication tools.

Direct-marketing tools are used by companies that distribute their products to consumers directly and by companies that distribute their products through traditional distribution channels or their own sales force. Companies spend large amounts of money each year developing and maintaining databases containing the addresses and/or phone numbers of present and prospective customers. They use telemarketing to call customers directly and attempt to sell them products and services or qualify them as sales leads. Call centres are used to respond to customer inquiries or concerns. Marketers also send out direct-mail pieces ranging from simple letters and flyers to detailed brochures, catalogues, and videotapes to give potential customers information about their products or services. Direct-marketing techniques are also used to distribute product samples and other promotional items. In addition, marketers use **direct-response advertising**, whereby a product is promoted through an ad (e.g., television or print) that encourages the consumer to purchase directly from the manufacturer (Exhibit 1–6).

Direct marketing has become very popular over the past two decades, owing primarily to changing lifestyles, particularly the increase in two-income households. This has meant more discretionary income but less time for in-store shopping. The availability of credit cards, toll-free phone numbers, and reliable delivery services has facilitated the purchase of products from direct marketing tools. This evolution has made shopping more convenient for consumers and has led to a tremendous growth of direct marketing.

INTERNET MARKETING

We are currently experiencing a dynamic and revolutionary change in marketing. This change is being driven by advances in technology and developments that have led to dramatic growth of communication through interactive media, particularly the Internet. **Interactive media** allow for a back-and-forth flow of information whereby users can participate in and modify the form and content of the information they receive in real time. Unlike traditional forms of marketing communications such as advertising, which are one-way in nature, these new media allow users to perform a variety of functions such as receive and alter information and images, make inquiries, respond to questions, and, of course, make purchases. The interactive medium that is having the greatest impact on marketing is the Internet, especially through the component known as the World Wide Web, however interactive media also include CD-ROMs, kiosks, and interactive television.

While the Internet is changing the ways companies design and implement their entire business and marketing strategies, it is also a marketing communications tool in its own right. Thousands of companies, ranging from large multinational corporations to small local firms, have developed websites to promote their products and services, by providing current and potential customers with information. Other firms develop websites to entertain or communicate more emotionally with their clientele. In fact, as part of a complete IMC program that included advertising, sales promotion, events, and public relations, Guinness beer used the Internet to help initiate the Guinness Party of Canada, a pseudo-political organization dedicated to making St. Patrick's Day a national holiday. Interested drinkers could join via the website and keep track of the results of Guinness's efforts.[8] The Internet is a medium that can be used to execute all the elements of the promotional mix. In addition to advertising on the Web, marketers offer sales promotion incentives such as coupons, contests, and sweepstakes online, and they use the Internet to conduct direct marketing, personal selling, and public relations activities more effectively and efficiently. For example, Exhibit 1–7 shows an ad for Lands' End promoting the fact that consumers can now shop and purchase interactively through the company's website.

Exhibit 1–7
Lands' End uses a website as part of its direct-marketing efforts

PERSONAL SELLING

The final element of an organization's promotional mix is **personal selling**, a form of person-to-person communication in which a seller attempts to assist and/or persuade prospective buyers to purchase the company's product or service or to act on an idea. Personal selling involves direct contact between buyer and seller, either face-to-face or through some form of telecommunications such as a telephone. This interaction gives the marketer communication flexibility; and the seller can see or hear the potential buyer's reactions and tailor the message to the customer's specific needs or situation. In this book, we do not devote any material to personal selling since many college/university programs have separate courses. An important point to keep in mind is that the message from sales people should be consistent with what is communicated from the other promotional tools.

PARTICIPANTS IN THE PROMOTIONAL PROCESS

Thus far we have identified the major promotional tools that marketers use. To understand the context in which promotional decisions are made, we identify the participants of the promotional process (Figure 1–3). Overall, there are five major

FIGURE 1–3 ☐ ☐ ☐ ☐   Participants in the promotional process

11

groups: the advertiser (or client), advertising agencies, media organizations, specialized communication services, and collateral services. Each group has specific roles in the promotional process.

The advertisers, or **clients**, have the products, services, or causes to be marketed, and they provide the funds that pay for advertising and promotions. The advertisers also assume major responsibility for developing the marketing program and making the final decisions regarding the advertising and promotional program to be employed. The organization may perform most of these efforts itself, either through its own advertising department or by setting up an in-house agency.

However, many organizations use an **advertising agency**, an outside firm that specializes in the creation, production, and/or placement of the communications message and that may provide other services to facilitate the marketing and promotions process. Many large advertisers retain the services of a number of agencies, particularly when they market a number of products. More and more, ad agencies are acting as partners with advertisers and assuming more responsibility for developing the marketing and promotional programs.

The primary function of **media organizations** is to provide information or entertainment to their subscribers, viewers, or readers. But from the perspective of the promotional planner, the purpose of media is to provide an environment for the firm's marketing communications message. The media must have editorial or program content that attracts consumers so advertisers and their agencies will want to buy time or space with them. While the media perform many other functions that help advertisers understand their markets and their customers, a medium's primary objective is to sell itself as a way for companies to reach their target audiences with their messages effectively.

Specialized marketing communications services include direct marketing agencies, sales promotion agencies, interactive agencies, and public relations firms. These organizations provide services in their areas of expertise. A direct-response agency develops and implements direct-marketing programs, while sales promotion agencies develop promotional programs such as contests and sweepstakes, premium offers, or sampling programs. Interactive agencies are being retained to develop websites for the Internet and help marketers as they move deeper into the realm of interactive media. Public relations firms are used to generate and manage publicity for a company and its products and services as well as to focus on its relationships and communications with its relevant publics.

Other firms provide **collateral services**, the wide range of support functions used by advertisers, agencies, media organizations, and specialized marketing communications firms. These individuals and companies perform specialized functions the other participants use in planning and executing advertising and other promotional functions. They include marketing research companies, package design firms, consultants, media buying services, photographers, printers, video production houses, and event marketing services companies.

INTEGRATED MARKETING COMMUNICATIONS

For many years, the promotional function in most companies was dominated by mass media advertising. Companies relied primarily on their advertising agencies for guidance in nearly all areas of marketing communication. Most marketers did use additional promotional tools, but sales promotion and direct marketing agencies as well as package design firms were generally viewed as auxiliary services and often used on a per-project basis. Public relations agencies were used to manage the organization's publicity, image, and affairs with relevant publics on an ongoing basis but were not viewed as integral participants in the marketing communications process.

Consequently, many marketers planned and managed the different promotional tools as separate practices, with different budgets, different views of the market, and different goals and objectives. Most recently, companies now recognize that the wide range of promotional tools must be coordinated to communicate effectively and present a consistent image to its target audiences. For instance, Kraft Canada entered an agreement with Rogers Media to share food and lifestyle information to many print, television, and online audiences. A dedicated website, thingstocelebrate.com, consumer promotions, and vignettes on OMNI television enhanced this communication. Each of these promotional tools allowed Kraft to reach a unique target audience to offer a customized message. For example, the magazine *Today's Parent* featured articles and profiles of Canadians working to reduce child obesity that complimented Kraft's emphasis of healthy eating in response to research indicating that consumers expected food companies to be more responsible in their promotions.[9] We now turn to the topic of integrated marketing communications and discuss its evolution, growth, importance, and a broader view of IMC.

THE EVOLUTION OF IMC

During the 1980s, many companies realized the need for a strategic integration of their promotional tools. These firms began moving toward the process of **integrated marketing communications (IMC)**, which involves coordinating the various promotional elements and other marketing activities that communicate with a firm's customers.[10] As marketers embraced the concept of integrated marketing communications, they began asking their ad agencies to coordinate the use of a variety of promotional tools rather than relying primarily on media advertising. Companies also began to look beyond traditional advertising agencies and use other types of promotional specialists to develop and implement various components of their promotional plans. Many agencies responded to the need for coordinating the promotional tools by acquiring PR, sales promotion, and direct marketing companies and touting themselves as IMC agencies that offer one-stop shopping for all of their clients' promotional needs.[11]

A task force from the American Association of Advertising Agencies (the "4As") developed one of the first definitions of integrated marketing communications that focuses on the process of using all forms of promotion to achieve maximum communications impact:

> a concept of marketing communications planning that recognizes the added value of a comprehensive plan that evaluates the strategic roles of a variety of communication disciplines—for example, general advertising, direct response, sales promotion, and public relations—and combines these disciplines to provide clarity, consistency, and maximum communications impact.[12]

Many companies have adopted an IMC perspective. They see it as a way to coordinate and manage their marketing communications programs to ensure that they give customers a consistent message about the company and/or its brands. For these companies, the IMC approach represents an improvement over the traditional method of treating the promotional tools as virtually separate activities. However, as marketers become more sophisticated in their understanding of IMC, they recognize that it offers more than just ideas for coordinating all elements of the marketing communications program. IMC Perspective 1–1 illustrates how Allstream altered its corporate identity with various IMC tools. Some academics and practitioners have questioned whether the IMC movement is just another management fad.[13] However, the IMC approach is proving to be a permanent change that offers significant value to marketers.[14]

Allstream's New Corporate Identity

Moving to a new corporate identity is a challenging marketing communications task to say the least, yet Allstream demonstrated success as it shed its old name, AT&T Canada. In a three-phase rollout strategy designed to initiate its major target audiences, Allstream used many IMC tools to effectively show that it was a leading national communication solutions provider in the highly competitive Canadian telecommunications industry. The new name was designed to illustrate the value that its customers could create through Allstream's unique communication solutions and responsive service.

The first phase featured an emphasis on the Allstream name, its connection to the old AT&T Canada, and its strength as a major firm in the Canadian telecommunications industry to its current customers and employees. The second phase focused on Allstream's ability to deliver its products and services with customer success stories and new product announcements across multiple media (i.e., newspapers, magazines, radio, online, electronic outdoor boards). Just prior to the launch, Allstream involved all employees in the communications process to get their commitment to act as positive ambassadors during the crucial first steps. In fact, sales representatives called all customers on launch day and senior executive called their counterparts at Allstream's most important 150 accounts.

Allstream also interacted with its current customers through billing inserts, newsletters, and special links on its website. It also employed many direct marketing avenues to tailor specific messages to well identified segments of its customer base so that each type of customer received information pertaining to their needs in a customized manner. To cap it off, Allstream invited customers to one of 10 customer appreciation events held throughout the country to help ensure their continued loyalty.

Sources: Michelle Warren, "Allstream Speaks with Its Customers," *Marketing Magazine*, October 27, 2003; John Mcleod, "More Than Bits and Bytes," *Marketing Magazine*, November 3, 2003.

REASONS FOR THE GROWTH OF IMC

The IMC approach to marketing communications planning and strategy is being adopted by both large and small companies and has become popular among firms marketing consumer products and services as well as business-to-business marketers. One example of the pervasiveness of IMC in Canada is the Canadian Marketing Association (CMA), a professional body for individual and company members. Previously known as the Canadian Direct Marketing Association, it changed its name and mandate because of the growth and convergence of all aspects of marketing communication and the increased importance of managing brands through communications. This may take some time, as a considerable amount of its professional activities still concern direct marketing. The Association of Canadian Advertisers (ACA), a professional body for about 100 member companies, claims it has always maintained a clear IMC perspective without a belief in the dominant role of any particular promotional discipline; however, it has not paid considerable attention to direct marketing. Whatever the future holds for these associations, it is clear that both are on an IMC path.[15] There are a number of reasons why marketers are adopting the IMC approach, notably, planning efficiency and effectiveness, consumer adoption of new technology and media, and innovative marketing practices.

Planning Efficiency and Effectiveness   One reason for IMC growth is that marketers understand the value of strategically integrating the various communication functions rather than having them operate autonomously. By coordinating their marketing communications efforts, companies can avoid duplication, take advantage of synergy among various promotional tools, and develop more efficient and effective marketing communications programs. Advocates of IMC argue that it is one of the easiest ways for a company to maximize the return on its investment in marketing and promotion.[16]

Consumer Adoption of Technology and Media   The move to integrated marketing communications also reflects an adaptation by marketers to consumer adoption of technology and media. For example, cable TV and digital satellite systems have vastly expanded the number of channels available to households. Some of these channels offer 24-hour shopping networks; others contain 30- or 60-minute direct response appeals known as infomercials, which look more like TV shows than ads. Every day more consumers are surfing the Internet's World Wide Web. Online services such as AOL Canada provide information and entertainment as well as the opportunity to shop for and order a vast array of products and services. Marketers are responding by developing websites where they can advertise their products and services interactively as well as transact sales, such as at WestJet's website shown in Exhibit 1–8.

Even as new technologies and formats create new ways for marketers to reach consumers, they are affecting the more traditional media. Television, radio, magazines, and newspapers are becoming more fragmented and reaching smaller and more selective audiences. A recent survey of leading U.S. advertising executives on trends that will shape the industry into the next century identified the segmentation of media audiences by new media technologies as the most important development.[17] Marketers are also facing the problem of consumers being less responsive to traditional advertising. They recognize that many consumers are turned off by advertising and tired of being bombarded with sales messages. These factors are prompting many marketers to look for alternative ways to communicate with their target audiences.

Innovative Marketing Practices The integrated marketing communications movement is also being driven by factors that change the relative emphasis of all promotional tools.[18]

- *A shifting of marketing dollars from media advertising to other forms of promotion, particularly consumer and trade-oriented sales promotions.* Many marketers feel that traditional media advertising has become too expensive and is not cost-effective.
- *A movement away from relying on advertising-focused approaches, which emphasize mass media such as network television and national magazines, to solve communication problems.* Many companies are turning to lower-cost, more targeted communication tools.
- *A shift in marketplace power from manufacturers to retailers.* Due to consolidation in the retail industry, large retailers are using their clout to demand larger promotional fees and allowances from manufacturers, a practice that often siphons money away from advertising. Moreover, new technologies such as checkout scanners give retailers information on the effectiveness of manufacturers' promotional programs, leading marketers to shift their focus to sale promotions that produce short-term results.
- *The rapid growth and development of database marketing.* Many companies are building databases containing customer names; geographic, demographic, and psychographic profiles; purchase patterns; media preferences; credit ratings; and other characteristics. Marketers are using this information to target consumers through a variety of direct-marketing methods rather than relying on mass media.
- *The rapid growth of the Internet, which is changing the very nature of how companies do business and the ways they communicate and interact with consumers.* The Internet is an *interactive* medium that is becoming an integral part of communications strategy, and even business strategy, for many companies.

Exhibit 1–9

Many non-profit organizations use advertising to meet their marketing objectives

16

IMPORTANCE OF IMC

As noted, companies are changing the ways they market and promote their products and services by using whatever contact methods offer the best way of delivering the message to their target audiences. A successful IMC program requires that a firm find the right combination of promotional tools and techniques, define their role and the extent to which they can or should be used, and coordinate their use. While this prescription sounds good, there are two compelling reasons why IMC has become very important for most firms.

Consumer's Point of View As a marketer, it is important to keep concepts distinct so that you can communicate with other people within your organization or other organizations when making decisions. For example, if you are planning a sales promotion, it is useful to refer to it as a sales promotion so that everyone involved can discuss its merits appropriately and allocate the sales promotion expenditure within the correct budget. Do we have the right sales promotion (i.e., coupon versus bonus pack)? Is the incentive strong enough to encourage the target audience to switch to our brand? Consumers, on the other

Exhibit 1–10
Dell Computer recognizes the importance of developing relationships with customers

hand, receive many exposures from many different brands, each using many different promotional tools. In fact, consumers receive so many exposures that they have the habit of often referring to any promotional tool as "advertising." Given this situation, the need for planning with an IMC perspective becomes imperative. All the elements of the promotional campaign have to be carefully linked in some manner so that the message is clear and does not misrepresent the brand.

The various marketing communication tools used by TD Canada Trust, discussed in IMC Perspective 1–2, shows how marketers are using an *integrated marketing communications* approach to reach their customers. TD Canada Trust runs advertising in a variety of media including television, radio, magazines, newspapers, and billboards as well as on the Internet. Banner ads on the Internet and in other media encourage consumers to visit the TD Canada Trust website (www.tdcanada-trust.com), which provides updated information about the company's products and services. Publicity for TD Canada Trust is generated through press releases and PR activities. TD Canada Trust runs a number of sales promotions to generate extra sales. Recently it has offered cash prizes and cruises as prizes for engaging in various transactions.

Collectively, all of these promotional tools have a strong communication effect, however, it is unlikley that consumers can recall the exact source of the messages over time. Despite this, TD Canada Trust's success with its rebranding indicates the importance of a well planned communications strategy that carefully considers consumers' responses to many tools.

Relationship Marketing   Today, most marketers are seeking more than just a one-time exchange or transaction with customers. The focus of market-driven companies—and many non-profit organizations (Exhibit 1–9)—is on developing and sustaining *relationships* with their customers. This has led to a new emphasis on **relationship marketing**, which involves creating, maintaining, and enhancing long-term relationships with individual customers as well as other stakeholders for mutual benefit.[19]

This relationship focus is generally more profitable since it is often more cost-effective to retain customers than to acquire new ones. Furthermore, these retained customers tend to buy more products or expand their purchases to other products that an organization offers. Marketers are giving more attention to the *lifetime value* of a customer because studies have shown that reducing customer defections by just 5 percent can increase future profit by as much as 30 to 90 percent.[20] Exhibit 1–10 shows an ad

Rebranding Using IMC in the Banking Industry

The TD Bank and Canada Trust merger of February 1, 2000, brought about one of the most ambitious marketing communication challenges ever witnessed in Canada. It needed to manage three different brands: Canada Trust, Toronto-Dominion Bank, and the newly formed TD Canada Trust with its own corporate logo. The success of this venture resulted in TD Canada Trust being recognized as Marketer of the Year by *Marketing Magazine* for the year 2001.

A key element of the marketing communication was the focus on customer service in all its promotional tools. Customer service was a hallmark differentiator for Canada Trust over the years as it had successfully carved out a niche in the competitive "banking" industry. A large, green, leather chair was the primary visual to capture the promise of this benefit, and the slogan "Banking can be this comfortable" reinforced the message and provided a simple reminder to consumers. As Dominic Mercuri, senior vice-president of advertising and marketing notes, "We are trying to drive home that, at TD Canada Trust, the customer, the individual, is our main focus and that they can count on comfort in their financial dealings with us."

Both the chair and the slogan became focal points of the in-print (magazines and newspapers) and television advertising. In fact, the two shades of green that signify TD Canada Trust and the chair were predominantly displayed on posters and floor decals in Toronto's Union Station. And these colours and the visuals from the print ads were reproduced on the first page of the company's website.

As part of the transition launch, a personalized direct-mail piece was sent to each of the nearly 4 million Canada Trust customers. The number of pieces and the customized nature of the message required 24-hour shifts of printing over 29 days! While a 20-percent increase in customer calls for clarification was expected, TD Canada Trust experienced only a 3-percent increase. Employee commitment and understanding was an integral part of the transition as TD Canada Trust launched extensive internal marketing communications campaign that featured a live presentation, video, and "Brand Library" packages for the more than 19,000 employees.

On October 27, 2001, public relations offered an interesting twist during the implementation of the transition. A short-term problem of the bank's computer systems not working due to an unusual hardware glitch resulted in TD Canada Trust immediately issuing an apology ad that appeared in major Canadian newspapers on October 29 and 30.

The rebranding efforts faced an uphill battle since they occurred during a particularly competitive year in the banking industry that featured many new marketing communications campaigns. CIBC attempted to position itself in their ads as a "responsive" bank for Canadians. The Royal Bank of Canada changed its name to RBC Financial Group and focused on the bank as a place for customers to fulfill their dreams, signified by a glowing yellow box in its television and print ads. One competitor jumped at the opportunity to take advantage of a realignment of products across the two merging firms. Scotiabank attempted to attract dissatisfied Canada Trust customers who could no longer use their MasterCard line of credit since TD was affiliated with VISA.

Sources: Lesley Young, "Taking Marketing to the Bank," *Marketing Magazine*, February 11, 2002; Lesley Young, "Comfort and Joy," *Marketing Magazine*, December 17, 2001; Chris Daniels, "Tech Glitch Forces Apology Ads," *Marketing Magazine*, November 5, 2001; Leslie Young, "Banks' Ads Pledge Customer Care," *Marketing Magazine*, October 8, 2001; *Marketing Magazine*, August 6 and 14, 2001.

for Dell Computer, a company that recognizes the importance of developing long-term relationships with its customers. Relationship marketing makes IMC planning imperative as well. Marketers must recognize which tools within the promotional mix are enhancing the relationship. And since their customers are involved so closely with the firm, the need for consistency becomes even more critical.

A BROADER VIEW OF IMC

Advocates of the IMC concept, such as Don Schultz of Northwestern University, argue for an even broader perspective that considers *all sources of brand or company contact* that a customer or prospect has with a product or service.[21] Schultz and others note that integrated marketing communications calls for a "big-picture" approach to planning marketing and promotion programs and coordinating the various communication functions. It requires that firms develop a total marketing communications strategy that recognizes how all of a firm's marketing activities, not just promotion, communicate with its customers.

Consumers' perceptions of a company and/or its various brands are a synthesis of the bundle of messages they receive or contacts they have, such as media advertisements, price, package design, direct marketing efforts, publicity, sales promotions, websites, point-of-purchase displays, and even the type of store where a product or service is sold. This broader view of IMC seeks to have all of a company's marketing and promotional activities project a consistent, unified image to the marketplace. It calls for a centralized messaging function so that everything a company says and does communicates a common theme.

Extending this broader view, Tom Duncan and Sandra Moriarty have developed a communication-based marketing model that emphasizes the importance of managing *all* corporate or brand communications, as they collectively create, maintain, or weaken the customer and stakeholder relationships that drive brand value.[22] Messages can originate at three levels—corporate, marketing, and marketing communications—since all of a company's corporate activities, marketing mix activities, and marketing communications efforts have communication dimensions and play a role in attracting and keeping customers.

At the corporate level, various aspects of a firm's business practices and philosophies, such as its mission, hiring practices, philanthropies, corporate culture, and ways of responding to inquiries, all have dimensions that communicate with customers and other stakeholders and affect relationships. At the marketing level, as was mentioned earlier, companies send messages to customers and other stakeholders through all aspects of their marketing mixes, not just promotion. Consumers make inferences about a product on the basis of elements such as its design, appearance, performance, pricing, service support, and where and how it is distributed.

At the marketing communications level, Duncan and Moriarty note that all messages should be delivered and received on a platform of executional and strategic consistency in order to create coherent perceptions among customers and other stakeholders. This requires the integration of the various marketing communication messages and the functions of various promotional facilitators such as ad agencies, public relations firms, sales promotion specialists, package design firms, direct response specialists, and interactive agencies. The goal is to communicate with one voice, look, and image across all the marketing communications functions and to identify and position the company and/or the brand in a consistent manner.

A broader view of IMC that includes the other marketing mix variables (i.e., product, price, distribution) is beyond the scope of the promotional planning perspective of this text despite their importance. For example, the communication effect of other marketing mix variables can be seen in the recent decision of prestigious cosmetic and fragrance firms distributing their products in drug stores like Shoppers Drug Mart.[23] The question arises as to whether these brands maintain their high-end profile while being sold in a beauty boutique adjacent to pharmacy and personal care products, in a retail environment that also includes aisles of snack foods. Since other elements of the marketing mix have important implications for promotional communication, we briefly review these decisions that you have previously learned to remind you of their extensiveness and highlight their communication role (Figure 1–4).

FIGURE 1–4
Examples of typical
marketing decisions
☐☐☐☐☐

Product Decisions	Price Decisions	Distribution Decisions
Physical Good	Price Level	Channel Type
Features or Attributes	Price Policy	Channel Policy
Quality Level	Discount	Type of Intermediary or Reseller
Package Design	Allowance	Type of Location/Store
Accessories	Flexibility	Service Level
Service		
Installation		
Instructions		
Warranty		
Corporate Name/Identification		
Brand Name/Identification		

Communication Role of Product Decisions   An organization exists because it has some product, service, or idea to offer consumers, generally in exchange for money. This offering may come in the form of a physical product (such as a soft drink, pair of jeans, or car), a service (banking, airlines, or legal assistance), a cause (United Way, March of Dimes), or even a person (a political candidate). The product is anything that can be marketed and that, when used or supported, gives satisfaction to the individual.

Product planning involves many decisions suggesting that a *product* is not just a physical object; it is a bundle of benefits that satisfies the needs of consumers. The needs may be purely functional, or they may include social and psychological benefits. The term **product symbolism** refers to what a product or brand means to consumers and what they experience in purchasing and using it.[24] For products with strong symbolic features, the social and psychological meaning may be more important than functional utility.[25] For example, designer clothing such as Versace, Gucci, and Ferragamo is often purchased on the basis of its symbolic meaning and image, particularly by teenagers and young adults. Advertising plays an important role in developing and maintaining the image of these brands (Exhibit 1–11).

EXHIBIT 1–11
Advertising for designer
clothing

The more visible product decisions, quality, branding, packaging, and even the company standing behind it all contribute to consumers' perceptions.[26] In a broader IMC view, advertising, branding, and packaging are all designed to portray the product as more than just a bundle of attributes. All are coordinated to present an image of the product that extends well beyond its physical attributes. For example, an important role of advertising in respect to branding strategies is creating and maintaining **brand equity**, which can be thought of as an intangible asset of added value or goodwill that results from the favourable image, impressions of differentiation, and/or the strength of consumer attachment to a company name, brand name, or trademark. Brand equity allows a brand to earn greater sales volume and/or higher margins than it could without the name, providing the company with a competitive advantage. The strong equity position a company and/or its brand enjoys is often reinforced through advertising. For example, Rado watches command a premium price because of their high quality as well as the strong brand equity they have developed through advertising (Exhibit 1–12).

Packaging also has a significant communication role. This has arisen because of the self-service emphasis of many stores and the fact that more and more buying decisions are made at the point of purchase. The package is often the consumer's first exposure to the product, so it must make a favourable impression and communicate information on how to use the product, divulge its composition and content, and satisfy any legal requirements regarding disclosure. Moreover, many firms design the package to carry a sales promotion message such as a contest, sweepstakes, or premium offer.

Many companies view the package as an important way to communicate with consumers. Notice the effective use of the instructions on the Listerine package shown in Exhibit 1–13. Besides offering value-added attributes beyond the product itself, the packaging gives Listerine a unique way to convey the claim that its oral care strips dissolve instantly. Design factors such as size, shape, colour, and lettering all contribute to the appeal of a package and can be as important as a commercial in determining what goes from the store shelf to the consumer's shopping cart. Many products use packaging to create a distinctive brand image and identity. The next time you walk by a perfume counter, stop to look at the many unique package designs (see Exhibit 1–14). Packaging can also serve more functional purposes. For

Exhibit 1–12
Rado creates strong brand equity through advertising

Exhibit 1–13
Listerine communicates through effective packaging

Exhibit 1–14
The packaging creates product image

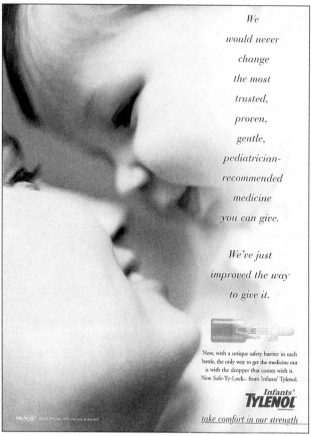

Exhibit 1–15
Packaging may also add product benefits

Exhibit 1–16
Some products compete on the basis of quality rather than price

example, Tylenol's Safe-Ty-Lock bottle protects children from consuming the medicine when they shouldn't (Exhibit 1–15). One Canadian example of a package redesign playing a critical role in the communication of the brand is Polar Ice Vodka, which is trying to take on the North American market. Previously, the bottle had sloping shoulders that did not contribute to the brand's character. Its replacement has an ovoid shape with sharp-edged shoulders. The front now has clear vinyl so that consumers can see the product, and the back has black vinyl to give the bottle a depth perspective.[27]

Communication Role of Price Decisions The *price* refers to what the consumer must give up to purchase a product or service. While price is discussed in terms of the dollar amount exchanged for an item, the cost of a product to the consumer includes time, mental activity, and behavioural effort.[28] Price planning involves fewer decisions and it communicates a significant product attribute. Moreover, it also communicates the economic cost to consumers for all of the product benefits combined. Advertising and promotion play a key role in reinforcing a consumer's belief that the product's benefit or quality accurately indicates the price decisions (Exhibit 1–16). The relationship among price, product quality, and advertising was examined in one study using information on 227 consumer businesses from the PIMS (Profit Impact of Marketing Strategies) project of the Strategic Planning Institute.[29] The study concluded that pricing and advertising strategies go together. High relative ad expenditures should accompany premium prices, and low relative ad expenditures should be tailored to low prices.

Communication Role of Distribution Decisions **Marketing channels**, the place element of the marketing mix, are "sets of interdependent organizations involved in the process of making a product or service available for use or consumption."[30] Planning for a distribution strategy involves many decisions related to marketing channels.

The distribution strategy should also take into consideration the communication objectives and the impact that the channel strategy will have on the IMC program. Stewart and colleagues discuss the need for "integrated channel management," which "reflects the blurring of the boundaries of the communications and distribution functions."[31] Consistent with the product and pricing decisions, where the product is distributed will send a communications message. Does the fact that a product is sold at Holt Renfrew convey a different message regarding its image than if it were distributed at Wal-Mart? If you think about it for a moment, the mere fact that the product is distributed in these channels communicates an image about it in your mind. Stewart gives examples of how channel elements contribute to communications—for example, grocery store displays, point-of-purchase merchandising, and shelf footage. The distribution channel in a well-integrated marketing program serves as a form of reminder advertising as the consumer recognizes the brand based on previous advertising exposure.

PLANNING FOR INTEGRATED MARKETING COMMUNICATIONS

In developing a promotional strategy, a company combines the promotional mix elements, balancing the strengths and limitations of each, to produce an effective promotional campaign. **Promotional management** involves coordinating the promotional mix elements to develop a controlled, integrated program of effective marketing communications. The marketer must consider which promotional tools to use and how to combine them to achieve its marketing and promotional objectives. Companies also face the task of distributing the total promotional budget across the promotional mix elements. What percentage of the budget should they allocate to advertising, sales promotion, public relations, direct marketing, interactive marketing, and personal selling? For example, in its first major promotional campaign in many years, Melitta Coffee increased its budget substantially and selected three IMC tools (Figure 1–5).

Companies consider many factors in developing their promotional mixes, including the type of product, the target market, the buyer's decision process, the stage of the product life cycle, and the channels of distribution. For example, companies selling consumer products and services generally rely on advertising through mass media to

FIGURE 1–5 □□□□ Melitta Coffee campaign

Budget:	$1.8 million (previous year $50,000)
Target:	Women 25–54
Advertising Message:	Everyday indulgence
Advertising Media:	Radio (Vancouver, Calgary, Toronto, Montreal) Television (Prime, Deja View, Mystery, Cool TV, W) Print (*Canadian Living, Coup de Pouce, Canadian Grocer*) March to May, and September to December
Sales Promotion:	Product placement on *Me, My House and I* Contest supported by *Spectacular Spas* television show and newspaper Gift Basket giveaway June to August
Internet:	MochaSofa/Mokasofa.com

We've been a secret too long.

Sure, you know about Honeywell in the home — thermostats, security systems, air cleaners. But our control technology is also...

In Space...guiding space flights and keeping satellites in orbit.
In the Air...helping aircraft navigate and fly safely.
In Industry...boosting productivity while protecting the environment.
In Products...improving performances of appliances, automobiles and other every-day items used at home and work.

Visit our web site to learn the rest of our "secrets"!

Honeywell
www.honeywell.com

Home and Building Control · Industrial Control · Space and Aviation Control

Exhibit 1–17
Business-to-business marketers such as Honeywell use advertising to build awareness

communicate with ultimate consumers. Alternatively, business-to-business marketers, who generally sell expensive, risky, and often complex products and services, more often use personal selling. Business-to-business marketers such as Honeywell do use advertising to perform important functions such as building awareness of the company and its products, generating leads for the sales force, and reassuring customers about the purchase they have made (Exhibit 1–17).

The marketing communications program is generally developed with a specific purpose in mind and is the end product of a detailed marketing and promotional planning process. As with any business function, planning plays a fundamental role in the development and implementation of an effective promotional program. The individuals involved in promotion design a **promotional plan** that provides the framework for developing, implementing, and controlling the organization's integrated marketing communications programs and activities. Promotional planners must decide on the role and function of the specific elements of the promotional mix, develop strategies for each element, and implement the plan. Promotion is but one part of, and must be integrated into, the overall marketing plan and program.

These planning characteristics are particularly important in order to allow firms to have joint marketing efforts of two brands. For example, Sprint Canada's "Red is Smarter" campaign to launch an alternative home phone service teamed up with Fido wireless to offer a telecommunication bundle.[32] Clearly, such marketing efforts require careful internal planning to coordinate and integrate the communications with another firm. We see a similar need for IMC planning in Global Perspective 1–3 when more partners are involved in complex promotional communication situations. A model of the IMC planning process is shown in Figure 1–6. The remainder of this chapter presents a brief overview of the steps involved.

REVIEW THE MARKETING PLAN

The first step in the IMC planning process is to review the marketing plan and objectives. Before developing a promotional plan, marketers must understand where the company (or the brand) has been, its current position in the market, where it intends to go, and how it plans to get there. Most of this information should be contained in the **marketing plan**, a written document that describes the overall marketing strategy and programs developed for an organization, a particular product line, or a brand. Marketing plans can take several forms but generally include five basic elements:

1. A detailed situation analysis that consists of an internal marketing audit and review and an external analysis of the market, company, consumer, competition, and macro-environment.
2. Specific marketing objectives that provide direction, a time frame for marketing activities, and a mechanism for measuring performance.
3. A marketing strategy and program that include selection of target market(s) and decisions and plans for the four elements of the marketing mix.
4. A program for implementing the marketing strategy, including determining specific tasks to be performed and responsibilities.
5. A process for monitoring and evaluating performance and providing feedback so that proper control can be maintained and any necessary changes can be made in the overall marketing strategy or tactics.

For most firms, the promotional plan is an integral part of the marketing strategy. Thus, the promotional planners must know the roles advertising and other promotional mix elements will play in the overall marketing program. The promotional plan is developed similarly to the marketing plan and often uses its detailed information. Promotional planners focus on information in the marketing plan that is relevant to the promotional strategy.

24

FIGURE 1–6 □□□□ An integrated marketing communications planning model

ASSESS THE MARKETING COMMUNICATIONS SITUATION

After the marketing plan is reviewed, the next step in developing a promotional plan is to conduct the situation analysis. In the IMC program, the situation analysis focuses on those factors that are relevant to development of a promotional strategy. Like the overall marketing situation analysis, the promotional program situation analysis includes both an internal and an external analysis.

FIGURE 1–6 (concluded)
An integrated marketing communications planning model
☐ ☐ ☐ ☐ ☐

Review the Marketing Plan
Focus on market, company, consumer, competitive, and environmental information
Examine marketing objectives, strategy, and programs
Understand role of promotion within marketing plan

Assess the Marketing Communications Situation
Internal analysis
    Relative strengths and weaknesses of products/services
    Previous promotional programs
    Brand image
    Promotional organization and capabilities
External analysis
    Customer behaviour analysis
    Competitive analysis
    Environmental analysis

Determine IMC Plan Objectives
Establish IMC communication objectives
Establish IMC behaviour objectives

Develop IMC Programs
For advertising, sales promotion, public relations, direct marketing, and Internet marketing:
    Set specific communication and behaviour objectives for each IMC tool
    Determine budget requirements
    Develop relevant message strategy and tactics
    Select suitable media strategy and tactics
Investigate integration options across all five programs

Implement and Control the IMC Plan
Design all promotional materials internally or with agencies and buy media space/time
Measure promotional program results/effectiveness and make adjustments

Internal Analysis   The **internal analysis** assesses relevant areas involving the product/service offering and the firm itself. The internal analysis assesses the relative strengths and limitations of the product or service; the product's unique selling points, attributes or benefits; its packaging, price, and design; and so on. This information is particularly important to the creative personnel who must develop the advertising message for the brand.

Since the firm is planning a new promotional plan, it is imperative that a review of the firm's previous promotional programs is undertaken. Specifically, the objectives, budgets, strategies, and tactics of all promotional mix elements should be closely examined to understand the strengths and limitations. Furthermore, if the firm has utilized marketing research to track the results of previous programs, this information needs to be examined closely.

Another aspect of the internal analysis is assessing the strengths and limitations of the firm or the brand from an image perspective. Often the image the firm brings to the market will have a significant impact on the way it can advertise and promote itself as well as its various products and services. Companies or brands that are new to the market or those for whom perceptions are negative may have to concentrate on their images, not just the benefits or attributes of the specific product or service. On the other hand, a firm with a strong reputation and/or image is already a step ahead when it comes to marketing its products or services.

Touring Canada in a Porsche

If you're going to tour the rugged terrain of the Canadian Rockies, you might as well do it in a Porsche at top speed. So thought the marketing executives of the famous German automaker as they joined forces with the Canadian Tourism Commission (CTC), Travel Alberta, and the makers of *Top Speed*, an IMAX movie that examined the science and thrills of speed.

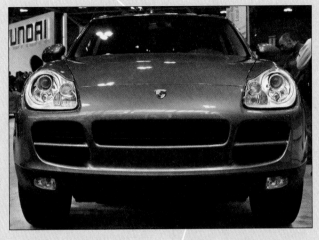

Looking for a break-through approach to launch the Cayenne, Porsche decided to feature the new sport utility vehicle in an exhilarating film shown on an eight-storey high screen to communicate the feeling of driving a Porsche and the exciting image of the company. Porsche viewed the film as a premiere opportunity to go beyond basic product placement as part of it $23-million launch of the Cayenne in North America. The CTC and Travel Alberta entered the picture and convinced Porsche and the filmmakers that the Kananaskis region near Banff National Park in Alberta would be an ideal location to display the car and exhibit the essence of speed.

Brand identification of Travel Alberta was featured on all promotional materials for the movie and included a prominent position on the film's website. At each of the 42 international cities that showed the film, Travel Alberta distributed its own promotional material and brochures of various tour operators that offer trip packages to Canada.

In addition to distributing promotional material, the CTC received 10 pages of advertising and editorial support touting Canada as a travel destination in Porsche's customer magazine. It also wooed Porsche to consider Canada as a location for its prestigious travel club, an exclusive event costing individuals $5,000 for the privilege to drive various Porsche models and relax at five-star hotels.

This was not the first time the CTC ventured with non-traditional partners to promote Canada as a destination for travellers. It previously invited automotive journalists to drive Maserati automobiles throughout Canada thus paving the way for published stories extolling the virtues of Canadian travel. And it did one better as *Electronic Arts* produced an online *Top Speed* game that invited avid visitors to drive the "Kananaskis Country" route. With activities like these, it seems that organizations will use any kind of IMC tool and key partnerships to reach more and more selective audiences.

Source: Paul Ferriss, "Rubber Tire Tourism," *Marketing Magazine*, February 17, 2003.

Reviewing the capabilities of the firm and its ability to develop and implement a successful promotional program, and the organization of the promotional department, the analysis may indicate the firm is not capable of planning, implementing, and managing certain areas of the promotional program. If this is the case, it would be wise to look for assistance from an advertising agency or some other promotional facilitator. If the organization is already using an ad agency, the focus will be on the quality of the agency's work and the results achieved by past and/or current campaigns.

Figure 1–7 is a checklist of some of the areas one might consider when performing analyses for promotional planning purposes. Addressing internal areas may require information the company does not have available internally and must gather as part of the external analysis.

FIGURE 1-7 ☐☐☐☐ Areas covered in the situation analysis

Internal Factors	External Factors
Assessment of firm's promotional organization and capabilities	**Customer behaviour analysis**
Organization of promotional department	Who buys our product or service?
Capability of firm to develop and execute promotional programs	Who makes the decision to buy the product?
Determination of role and function of ad agency and other promotional facilitators	Who influences the decision to buy the product?
Assessment of firm's previous promotional programs	How is the purchase decision made? Who assumes what role?
Promotional objectives	What does the customer buy? What needs must be satisfied?
Promotional budgets and allocations	Why do customers buy a particular brand?
Promotional mix strategies and programs	Where do they go or look to buy the product or service?
Results of promotional programs	When do they buy? Any seasonality factors?
Assessment of firm or brand image	What are customers' attitudes toward our product/service?
Assessment of relative strengths and weaknesses of product/service	What social factors might influence the purchase decision?
What are its key attributes and benefits?	Do the customers' lifestyles influence their purchase decisions?
Does it have any unique selling points?	Do demographic factors influence the purchase decision?
Are the package and label consistent with the brand image?	**Competitive analysis**
	Who are our direct and indirect competitors?
	What key benefits and positioning are used by our competitors?
	What is our position relative to the competition?
	How big are competitors' promotion budgets?
	What promotion strategies are competitors using?
	Environmental analysis
	Are there any current trends or developments that might affect the promotional program?

External Analysis The **external analysis** focuses on factors such as characteristics of the firm's customers, market segments, competitors, and environment as shown in Figure 1–7. An important part of the external analysis is a detailed consideration of customers' characteristics and buying patterns, their decision processes, and factors influencing their purchase decisions. Attention must also be given to consumers' perceptions and attitudes, lifestyles, and criteria for making purchase decisions. Often, marketing research studies are needed to answer some of these questions. A key element of the external analysis is an assessment of the market. The attractiveness of various market segments must be evaluated and the segments to target identified.

The external phase of the promotional program situation analysis also includes an in-depth examination of both direct and indirect competitors. While competitors were analyzed in the overall marketing situation analysis, even more attention is devoted to promotional aspects at this phase. Focus is on the firm's primary competitors: their specific strengths and limitations; their segmentation, targeting, and positioning strategies; and the promotional strategies they employ. The size and allocation of their promotional budgets, their media strategies, and the messages they are sending to the marketplace should all be considered.

DETERMINE IMC PLAN OBJECTIVES

An important part of this stage of the promotional planning process is establishing communication goals and objectives. In this text, we stress the importance of distinguishing between communication and marketing objectives. **Marketing objectives** refer to what is to be accomplished by the overall marketing program. They are often stated in terms of sales, market share, or profitability.

Communication objectives refer to what the firm seeks to accomplish with its promotional program. They are often stated in terms of the nature of the message to be communicated or what specific communication effects are to be achieved. The promotional planner must think about the process consumers will go through in responding to marketing communications. Communication objectives may include creating awareness or knowledge about a product and its attributes or benefits; creating an image; or developing favourable attitudes, preferences, or purchase intentions. Communication objectives should be the guiding force for the overall marketing communications strategy and the objectives for each promotional mix area. Behaviour objectives in terms of trial purchase or repeat purchase may be defined along with the communication objectives.

As these objectives are determined, some attention is given to the promotional budget. Two basic questions are asked at this point: What will the promotional program cost? How will these monies be allocated? Ideally, the amount a firm needs to spend on promotion should be determined by what must be done to accomplish its communication objectives. In reality, promotional budgets are often determined using a more simplistic approach, such as how much money is available or a percentage of a company's or brand's sales revenue. At this stage, the budget is often tentative. It may not be finalized until specific promotional mix strategies are developed.

DEVELOP IMC PROGRAMS

Developing the IMC program is generally the most involved and detailed step of the promotional planning process. As discussed earlier, each promotional mix element has certain strengths and limitations. At this stage of the planning process, decisions have to be made regarding the role and importance of each element and their coordination with one another. As Figure 1–6 shows, each promotional mix element has its own set of objectives and a budget and strategy for meeting them. Decisions must be made and activities performed to implement the promotional programs and evaluate performance to make any necessary changes.

For example, the advertising program will have its own set of objectives, usually involving the communication of some message or appeal to a target audience. A budget will be determined, providing the advertising manager and the agency with some idea of how much money is available for developing the ad campaign and purchasing media to disseminate the ad message.

Two important aspects of the advertising program are development of the message and the media strategy. Message development, often referred to as *creative strategy*, involves determining the basic message the advertiser wishes to convey to the target audience. This process, along with the ads that result, is to many students the most fascinating aspect of promotion. *Media strategy* involves determining which communication channels will be used to deliver the advertising message to the target audience. Decisions must be made regarding which types of media will be used (e.g., newspapers, magazines, radio, TV, billboards) as well as specific media selections (e.g., a particular magazine or TV program). This task requires careful evaluation of the media options' strengths and limitations, costs, and ability to deliver the message effectively to the target audiences.

Once the message and media strategies have been determined, steps must be taken to implement them. Most large companies hire advertising agencies to plan and produce their messages and to evaluate and purchase the media that will carry their ads. However, most agencies work very closely with their clients as they develop the ads and select media, because it is the advertiser that ultimately approves (and pays for) the creative work and media plan.

A similar process takes place for the other elements of the IMC program as objectives are set, an overall strategy is developed, message and media strategies are determined, and steps are taken to implement them. While the marketer's advertising agencies may be used to perform some of the other IMC functions, they may also hire other communication specialists such as direct marketing and interactive and/or sales promotion agencies, as well as public relations firms.

IMPLEMENT AND CONTROL THE IMC PLAN

It is important to determine how well the promotional program is meeting communications objectives and helping the firm accomplish its overall marketing goals and objectives. The promotional planner wants to know not only how well the promotional program is doing but also why. For example, problems with the advertising program may lie in the nature of the message or in a media plan that does not reach the target market effectively. The manager must know the reasons for the results in order to take the right steps to correct the program.

This final stage of the process is designed to provide managers with continual feedback concerning the effectiveness of the promotional program, which in turn can be used as input into the planning process. As Figure 1–6 shows, information on the results achieved by the promotional program is used in subsequent promotional planning and strategy development.

PERSPECTIVE AND ORGANIZATION OF THIS TEXT

Traditional approaches to teaching advertising, promotional strategy, or marketing communications courses have often treated the various elements of the promotional mix as separate functions. As a result, many people who work in advertising, sales promotion, direct marketing, or public relations tend to approach marketing communications problems from the perspective of their particular specialty. An advertising person may believe marketing communications objectives are best met through the use of media advertising; a promotional specialist argues for a sales promotion program to motivate consumer response; a public relations person advocates a PR campaign to tackle the problem. These orientations are not surprising, since each person has been trained to view marketing communications problems primarily from one perspective.

In the contemporary business world, however, individuals working in marketing, advertising, and other promotional areas are expected to understand and use a variety of marketing communications tools, not just the one in which they specialize. Ad agencies no longer confine their services to the advertising area. Many are involved in sales promotion, public relations, direct marketing, event sponsorship, and other marketing communications areas. Individuals working on the client or advertiser side of the business, such as brand, product, or promotional managers, are developing marketing programs that use a variety of marketing communications methods.

30

The purpose of this book is to provide you with a thorough understanding of the field of advertising and other elements of a firm's promotional mix and show how they are combined to form an integrated marketing communications program. The book is organized around six major parts to facilitate this goal.

Part I, "Understand Integrated Marketing Communications," is comprised of this chapter only. Its purpose is to familiarize you with the basic tools of IMC and how they relate to marketing. This chapter has given a brief description of IMC and the content of a promotional plan.

To plan, develop, and implement an effective IMC program, those involved must understand consumer behaviour and the communications process. We focus on consumer behaviour and the target audience decision, and summarize various communication response models in Chapters 2 and 3 respectively. Combined, these two chapters constitute Part II, "Connect Consumers to IMC." Its purpose is to give you a conceptual foundation for developing the subsequent set of decisions of an IMC plan.

The heart of marketing communication lies in what we are trying to say. Part III, "Articulate the Message," concerns a number of decisions firms make to put together a persuasive message. Chapter 4 builds on the communication models of the previous chapter and explains how to set communication objectives to achieve the desired communication effects. Perhaps the most exciting aspects of IMC are discussed in Chapters 5, 6, and 7 where we illustrate the brand positioning strategy, creative strategy, and creative tactics decisions that result in vibrant and exciting ads. Chapter 8 examines how to measure advertising effectiveness, which also sets the stage for understanding how to assess the effects of all IMC tools.

Part IV, "Deliver the Message," explores the key media strategy and media tactics decisions in Chapter 9 and the six traditional media choices (i.e., television, radio, magazines, newspapers, out-of-home, and support) within Chapters 10, 11, and 12. Collectively, Parts III and IV provide a foundation for the advertising tool within the IMC program.

Our interest turns to the other areas of the promotional mix—sales promotion, public relations, direct marketing, and Internet marketing—in Part V, "Strengthen the Message." Each tool is explored in its own chapter and related to communication objectives as done in the advertising chapters.

The book concludes with Part VI, "Implement and Control the IMC Plan." We discuss how firms organize for IMC and make decisions regarding ad agencies and other firms that provide marketing and promotional services. Finally, the text concludes with an examination of advertising regulation and the ethical, social, and economic effects on an organization's advertising and promotional program.

SUMMARY

Advertising and other forms of promotion are an integral part of the marketing process in most organizations. The elements of the marketing mix are the product or service, price, place (distribution), and promotion.

Promotion is the communication function of marketing. It is accomplished through a promotional mix that includes advertising, personal selling, public relations, sales promotion, direct marketing, and interactive/Internet marketing. The inherent advantages and disadvantages of each of these promotional mix elements influence the roles they play in the overall marketing program. In developing the promotional program, a marketer must decide which tools to use and how to combine them to achieve the organization's marketing and communication objectives.

For many years, the promotional function in most companies was dominated by mass-media advertising. However, more and more companies are recognizing the importance of integrated marketing communications, coordinating the various marketing and promotional elements to achieve more efficient and effective communication programs. A number of factors underlie the move toward IMC by marketers as well as ad agencies and other promotional facilitators. Reasons for the growing importance of the integrated marketing communications perspective include a rapidly changing environment with respect to consumers, technology, and media. The IMC movement is also being driven by changes in the ways companies market their products and services. A shift in marketing dollars from advertising to sales promotion, the rapid growth and development of database marketing, and the fragmentation of media markets are among the key changes taking place.

Promotional management involves coordinating the promotional mix elements to develop an integrated program of effective marketing communication. The model of the IMC planning process in Figure 1–6 contains a number of steps: review the marketing plan, assess the marketing communications situation, determine IMC plan objectives, develop IMC programs, and implement and control the IMC plan.

32

KEY TERMS

marketing, *4*
marketing mix, *4*
promotion, *4*
promotional mix, *4*
advertising, *5*
sales promotion, *8*
public relations, *8*
publicity, *9*
direct marketing, *9*

direct-response
   advertising, *10*
interactive media, *10*
personal selling, *11*
clients, *12*
advertising agency, *12*
media organizations, *12*
specialized marketing communications services, *12*

Collateral services, *12*
integrated marketing com-
   munications (IMC), *13*
relationship marketing, *17*
product symbolism, *20*
brand equity, *21*
marketing channels, *23*
promotional
   management, *23*

promotional plan, *24*
marketing plan, *24*
internal analysis, *26*
external analysis, *28*
marketing objectives, *29*
communication
   objectives, *29*

DISCUSSION QUESTIONS

1. Consider all the marketing communication tools (i.e., advertising, sales promotions, public relations, direct marketing, Internet marketing, and personal selling) that are used to market a new car that a graduating student might be expected to buy. Explain why each tool would be effective or would not be effective to create awareness.

2. What is the most important communication tool for each of the following brands: Molson Canadian, Bell Mobility, Nortel Networks, Government of Canada? Give a good reason for each.

3. From your perspective as a consumer, what Canadian brand (other than those discussed in the chapter) has had the most suc-cessful IMC plan during the past year or so?

4. Many sales promotions often look like ads these days. Why might this be occurring?

5. The various classifications of advertising to consumer and business-to-business markets are shown in Figure 1–2. Choose one category of advertising to consumer markets and one to the business-to-business market, and find an ad that is an example of each. Discuss the specific goals and objectives each company might have for the ads you have chosen.

6. Discuss the role integrated marketing communications plays in relationship marketing. How might the customization of adver-tising and other forms of marketing communication be possible?

7. Discuss the role of direct marketing as an IMC tool, giving attention to the various forms of direct marketing.

8. Analyze the role of the Internet in the integrated marketing communications program of a company. Discuss how the Internet can be used to execute the various elements of the promotional mix.

9. Why is it important for those who work in the field of advertising and promotion to understand and appreciate all various integrated marketing communications tools, not just the area in which they specialize?

Consumer Behaviour and Target Audience Decisions

CHAPTER OBJECTIVES

- To understand the role consumer behaviour plays in the development and implementation of advertising and promotional programs.

- To understand the consumer decision-making process and how it varies for different types of purchases.

- To understand various internal psychological processes, their influence on consumer decision making, and implications for advertising and promotion.

- To understand the similarities and differences of target market and target audience.

- To understand the various options for making a target audience decision for marketing communications.

Teen Market Comes Alive

What do Caboodles cosmetics, *Fuel* magazine, and video dance parties all have in common? In their own way, each is part of a growing trend of teens having greater purchasing power through increased financial resources or greater autonomy in the final decision. Whether it's young girls wearing the latest cosmetic styles to express themselves, young boys reading about electronic games, dancers trying new products at a school event, or students deciding what they need for going back to school, the trend is clear, teen consumers are a substantial market in need of understanding of their consumer behaviour if marketers are to be successful in the future.

Caboodles cosmetics of New Westminster, B.C., cracked North America's $13-billion beauty market with its colourful and zany products and achieved sales of $52 million in just five years, all the while expanding internationally. Its success can be attributed to the sheer size of the potential market and the girls' shopping habits. There are approximately 30 million girls aged 14 to 19 in North America and they each have over $100 per week in disposable income. Teens go to the mall on a weekly basis and plan to buy something half the time, and when they do they spend an average of $60 per trip. Three-quarters of the girls use lip products and a nearly equal number are loyal to the brands they buy. It seems Caboodles tapped into a unique market niche with it products, allowing girls to express their personality rather than improving their beauty. In fact, Caboodles will discard a print ad if, as a test, it looks as good if Caboodles puts a competing name on it like Revlon, L'Oréal, or Covergirl instead of its own name!

Reaching teens through a media other than television is an elusive task, however the increased purchasing power of this market has yielded magazines. *What* is published six times per year and is distributed free of charge to 1,300 high schools with coverage of 250,000 copies per issue. Directed to both boys and girls, the magazine features music, entertainment, sports, and teen-oriented articles. Taking a cue from the success of *Maxim*, the lifestyle magazine for men, *Fuel* offers teen-age boys articles on gaming, sports, music, electronics, and clothing and is one of a handful of magazine directed to this market in North America. It has taken time, but advertisers recognize that boys shop and exhibit strong brand loyalty just like girls do and are slowly adopting this kind of media to influence their behaviour. In addition to magazines, advertisers have also targeted teens during video dance parties at high schools. For example, L'Oréal hosted on-stage hairstyling contests to demonstrate its products while Sony tested new PlayStation II games.

Sources: Eve Lazarus, "Caboodles Rule," *Marketing Magazine*, January 20, 2003; Kathleen Martin, "Boys Read," *Marketing Magazine*, January 20, 2003; Lauren Sherman, "Dancing Into the Hearts of Teens," *Marketing Magazine*, January 20, 2003.

The companies described above reveal that the development of effective marketing communication programs begins with understanding why consumers behave as they do. For example, the motives for purchasing, attitudes, and lifestyles need to be understood before effective promotion strategies can be formulated.

It is beyond the scope of this text to examine consumer behaviour in depth. However, promotional planners need a basic understanding of consumer decision making, factors that influence it, and how this knowledge can be used in developing promotional strategies and programs. This chapter addresses these topics and concludes with a summary of the options a promotional planner has for the initial decision, the target audience for an ad or promotional campaign.

AN OVERVIEW OF CONSUMER BEHAVIOUR

A challenge faced by all marketers is how to influence the purchase behaviour of consumers in favour of the product or service they offer. For companies like American Express, this means getting consumers to charge more purchases on their AmEx cards. For BMW, it means getting them to purchase or lease a car; for business-to-business marketers like Canon or Ricoh, it means getting organizational buyers to purchase more of their copiers or fax machines. While their ultimate goal is to influence consumers' purchase behaviour, most marketers understand that the actual purchase is only part of an overall process.

Consumer behaviour can be defined as the process and activities people engage in when searching for, selecting, purchasing, using, evaluating, and disposing of products and services so as to satisfy their needs and desires. For many products and services, purchase decisions are the result of a long, detailed process that may include an extensive information search, brand comparisons and evaluations, and other activities. Other purchase decisions are more incidental and may result from little more than seeing a product prominently displayed at a discount price in a store. Think of how many times you have made impulse purchases in stores.

Marketers' success in influencing purchase behaviour depends in large part on how well they understand consumer behaviour. Marketers need to know the specific needs customers are attempting to satisfy and how they translate into purchase criteria. They need to understand how consumers gather information regarding various alternatives and use this information to select among competing brands. They need to understand how customers make purchase decisions. Where do they prefer to buy a product? How are they influenced by marketing stimuli at the point of purchase? Marketers also need to understand how the consumer decision process and reasons for purchase vary among different types of customers. For example, purchase decisions may be influenced by the personality or lifestyle of the consumer.[1] Notice how the ad shown in Exhibit 2–1 reflects the life of the target audience member.

The conceptual model in Figure 2–1 will be used as a framework for analyzing the consumer decision process. We will discuss what occurs at the various stages of this model and how advertising and promotion can be used to influence decision making. We will also examine the influence of various psychological concepts, such as motivation, perception, attitudes, integration processes,

Exhibit 2–1
Mountain Equipment Co-op appeals to the active lifestyle

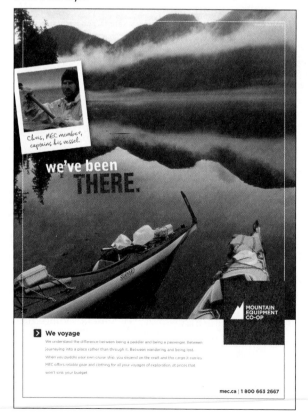

FIGURE 2–1 ☐☐☐☐ A basic model of consumer decision making

A. Stages in the Consumer Decision-Making Process

Need recognition → Information search → Alternative evaluation → Purchase decision → Postpurchase evaluation

B. Relevant Internal Psychological Processes

Motivation → Perception → Attitude formation → Integration → Satisfaction

and satisfaction. The five-stage decision process model of Figure 2–1 views the consumer as a problem solver and information processor who engages in a variety of mental processes to evaluate various alternatives and determine the degree to which they might satisfy needs or purchase motives. This model is a form of cognitive learning. Consumer learning has been defined as "the process by which individuals acquire the purchase and consumption knowledge and experience they apply to future related behaviour."[2] There are other perspectives regarding how consumers acquire the knowledge and experience they use in making purchase decisions. However, this model is the most widely accepted and managerially useful.

THE CONSUMER DECISION-MAKING PROCESS

As shown in Figure 2–1, the consumer's purchase decision process is generally viewed as consisting of stages through which the buyer passes in purchasing a product or service. This model shows that decision making involves a number of internal psychological processes. Motivation, perception, attitude formation, integration, and satisfaction are important to promotional planners, since they influence the general decision-making process of the consumer. We will examine each stage of the purchase decision model and discuss how the various subprocesses influence what occurs at this phase of the consumer behaviour process. We will also discuss how promotional planners can influence this process.

NEED RECOGNITION

Figure 2–1 shows that the first stage in the consumer decision-making process is **need recognition**, which occurs when the consumer perceives a need and becomes motivated to enter a decision-making process to resolve the felt need.

Need recognition is caused by a difference between the consumer's *ideal state* and *actual state*. A discrepancy exists between what the consumer wants the situation to be like and what the situation is really like. A goal exists for the consumer, and this goal may be the attainment of a more positive situation from a neutral state. Or, the goal could be a shift from a negative situation, and the consumer wishes to be at a neutral state.

Sources of Need Recognition   The causes of need recognition may be very simple or very complex and may result from changes in the consumer's current and/or desired state. These causes may be influenced by both internal and external factors.

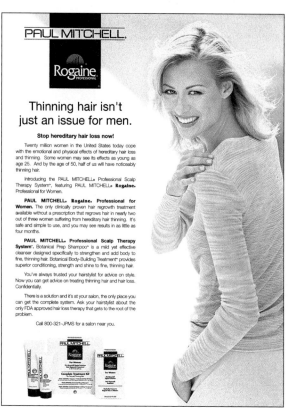

Exhibit 2–2
Rogaine helps women recognize hair loss problems

Exhibit 2–3
This ad for Baby Orajel shows that baby teeth have special needs

Out of Stock   Need recognition occurs when consumers use their existing supply of a product and must replenish their stock. The purchase decision is usually simple and routine and is often resolved by choosing a familiar brand or one to which the consumer feels loyal.

Dissatisfaction   Need recognition is created by the consumer's dissatisfaction with the current state of affairs and/or the product or service being used. For example, a consumer may think her ski boots are no longer comfortable or stylish enough. Advertising may be used to help consumers recognize when they have a need to make a purchase. The Rogaine ad shown in Exhibit 2–2 helps women realize that hair thinning is not just a man's problem.

New Needs/Wants   Changes in consumers' lives often result in new needs and wants. For example, changes in one's financial situation, employment status, or lifestyle may create new needs. As you will see, when you graduate from college and begin your professional career, your new job may necessitate a change in your wardrobe. (Good-bye blue jeans, hello business suits.)

Not all product purchases are based on needs. Some products or services sought by consumers are not essential but are nonetheless desired. A **want** has been defined as a felt need that is shaped by a person's knowledge, culture, and personality.[3] Many products sold to consumers satisfy their wants rather than their basic needs.

Related Products/Purchases   Need recognition can also be stimulated by the purchase of a product. For example, the purchase of a new camera may lead to the recognition of a need for accessories, such as additional lenses or a carrying case. The purchase of a personal computer may prompt the need for software programs or upgrades.

Marketer-Induced Need Recognition   Another source of need recognition is marketers' actions that encourage consumers not to be content with their current state or situation. Ads for personal hygiene products such as mouthwash, deodorant, and foot sprays may be designed to create insecurities that consumers can resolve through the use of these products. Marketers change fashions and clothing designs and create perceptions among consumers that their wardrobes are out of style. The Orajel ad in Exhibit 2–3 demonstrates the special needs of children's baby teeth to stimulate need recognition. Marketers also take advantage of consumers' tendency toward *novelty-seeking behaviour*, which leads them to try different brands. Consumers often try new products or brands even when they are basically satisfied with their regular brand. Marketers encourage brand switching by using advertising and sales promotion techniques that encourage consumers to reconsider their current consumption habits.

New Products   Need recognition can also occur when innovative products are introduced. For example, the Rogers ad shown in Exhibit 2–4 introduces a new camera phone that allows the user to do more than ever before. Marketers' attempts to create need recognition among consumers are not always successful. Consumers may not see a need for the product the marketer is

38

selling. A main reason many consumers were initially reluctant to purchase personal computers was that they failed to see how it fulfilled their needs. One way PC manufacturers successfully activated need recognition was by stressing how a computer helps children improve their academic skills and do better in school.

CONSUMER MOTIVATION

Marketers recognize that while need recognition is often a basic, simple process, the way a consumer perceives a purchase situation and becomes motivated to resolve it will influence the remainder of the decision process. For example, one consumer may perceive the need to purchase a new watch from a functional perspective and focus on reliable, low-priced alternatives. Another consumer may see the purchase of a watch as more of a fashion statement and focus on the design and image of various brands. To better understand the reasons underlying consumer purchases, marketers devote considerable attention to examining **motives**—that is, those factors that compel a consumer to take a particular action.

Hierarchy of Needs One of the most popular approaches to understanding consumer motivations is based on the classic theory of human motivation popularized many years ago by psychologist Abraham Maslow.[4] His **hierarchy of needs** theory postulates five basic levels of human needs, arranged in a hierarchy based on their importance. As shown in Figure 2–2, the five needs are (1) *physiological*—the basic level of primary needs for things required to sustain life, such as

Exhibit 2–4
Rogers introduces a camera phone

FIGURE 2–2
Maslow's hierarchy of needs

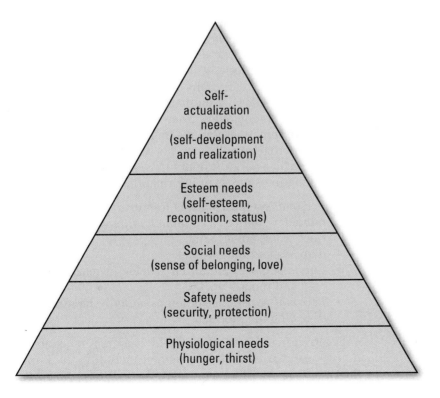

Self-actualization needs (self-development and realization)

Esteem needs (self-esteem, recognition, status)

Social needs (sense of belonging, love)

Safety needs (security, protection)

Physiological needs (hunger, thirst)

Exhibit 2–5

Pampers appeals to needs for love and belonging in this ad

food, shelter, clothing, and sex; (2) *safety*—the need for security and safety from physical harm; (3) *social/love and belonging*—the desire to have satisfying relationships with others and feel a sense of love, affection, belonging, and acceptance; (4) *esteem*—the need to feel a sense of accomplishment and gain recognition, status, and respect from others; and (5) *self-actualization*—the need for self-fulfillment and a desire to realize one's own potential.

According to Maslow's theory, the lower-level physiological and safety needs must be satisfied before the higher-order needs become meaningful. Once these basic needs are satisfied, the individual moves on to attempting to satisfy higher-order needs such as self-esteem. In reality, it is unlikely that people move through the needs hierarchy in a stairstep manner. Lower-level needs are an ongoing source of motivation for consumer purchase behaviour. However, since basic physiological needs are met in most developed countries, marketers often sell products that fill basic physiological needs by appealing to consumers' higher-level needs. For example, in marketing its wipes, Pampers focuses on the love between parent and child (social needs) in addition to the gentleness of the product (Exhibit 2–5).

While Maslow's need hierarchy has flaws, it offers a framework for marketers to use in determining what needs they want their products and services to be shown satisfying. Advertising campaigns can then be designed to show how a brand can fulfill these needs. Marketers also recognize that different types of consumers have different need levels. For example, a young single person may be attempting to satisfy social or self-esteem needs in purchasing a car, while a family with children will focus more on safety needs. Jeep used ads like the one in Exhibit 2–6 to communicate that its cars meet the security needs of consumers with children.

INFORMATION SEARCH

Exhibit 2–6

Jeep uses an appeal to security needs

The second stage in the consumer decision-making process is *information search*. Once consumers perceive a need that can be satisfied by the purchase of a product or service, they begin to search for information needed to make a purchase decision. The initial search effort often consists of an attempt to scan information stored in memory to recall past experiences and/or knowledge regarding various purchase alternatives.[5] This information retrieval is referred to as **internal search**. For many routine, repetitive purchases, previously acquired information that is stored in memory (such as past performance or outcomes from using a brand) is sufficient for comparing alternatives and making a choice.

If the internal search does not yield enough information, the consumer will seek additional information by engaging in **external search**. External sources of information include:

- *Personal sources*, such as friends, relatives, or co-workers.
- *Marketer-controlled (commercial) sources*, such as information from advertising, salespeople, or point-of-purchase displays and the Internet.
- *Public sources*, including articles in magazines or newspapers and reports on TV.
- *Personal experience*, such as actually handling, examining, or testing the product.

Determining how much and which sources of external information to use involves several factors, including the importance of the purchase decision, the effort needed to acquire information, the amount of past experience relevant, the degree of perceived risk associated with the purchase, and the time available. For example, the selection of a movie to see on a Friday night might entail simply talking to a friend or checking the movie guide in the daily newspaper. A more complex purchase such as a new car might use a number of information sources—perhaps a review of *Road & Track, Motor Trend*, or *Consumer Reports*; discussion with family members and friends; and test-driving of cars. At this point in the purchase decision, the information-providing aspects of advertising are extremely important. IMC Perspective 2–1 demonstrates how markets try to influence the information consumers receive during their external search.

PERCEPTION

Knowledge of how consumers acquire and use information from external sources is important to marketers in formulating communication strategies. Marketers are particularly interested in (1) how consumers sense external information, (2) how they attend to various sources of information, (3) how this information is interpreted and given meaning and (4) how the information is retained. These four processes are all part of **perception**, the process by which an individual receives, attends to, interprets, and stores information to create a meaningful picture of the world.[6] Perception is an individual process; it depends on internal factors such as a person's beliefs, experiences, needs, moods, and expectations. The perceptual process is also influenced by the characteristics of a stimulus (such as its size, colour, and intensity) and the context in which it is seen or heard. Selectivity occurs throughout the four stages of the consumer's perceptual process. Perception may be viewed as a filtering process in which internal and external factors influence what is received and how it is processed and interpreted. The sheer number and complexity of the marketing stimuli a person is exposed to in any given day require that this filtering occur. **Selective perception** may occur within all four stages of the perceptual process, as shown in Figure 2–3.

Sensation   **Sensation** is the immediate, direct response of the senses (taste, smell, sight, touch, and hearing) to a stimulus such as an ad, package, brand name, or point-of-purchase display. Perception uses these senses to create a representation of the stimulus. Marketers recognize that it is important to understand consumers' physiological reactions to marketing stimuli. For example, the visual elements of an ad or package design must be designed so that consumers sense their existence. This is one reason why many TV ads start with a particular sound effect or noise.

   Marketers sometimes try to increase the level of sensory input so that their advertising messages will get noticed. For example, marketers of colognes and perfumes often use strong visuals as well as scent strips to appeal to multiple senses and attract the attention of magazine readers. Some advertisers have even inserted microcomputer chips into their print ads to play a song or deliver a message. **Selective exposure** occurs as consumers choose whether or not to make themselves available to information. For example, a viewer of a television show may change channels or leave the room during commercial breaks.

FIGURE 2–3   ☐☐☐☐   The selective perception process

What's the Buzz?

Consumers have long had a love-hate relationship with advertising. We enjoy watching music- and celebrity-laden commercials that are often more entertaining, humourous, or interesting than the programs they are sponsoring. We purchase magazines such as *Glamour*, *Vogue*, and *GQ*, which contain more ad pages than articles. But many consumers are tired of being bombarded with sales messages and are turned off by advertising. This is especially true of Generation Y, the age cohort born between 1979 and 1994, which is 60 million strong. The Generation Y cohort is three times the size of its Gen X predecessor, and its members

constitute the biggest group to hit the U.S. market since the 72 million baby boomers, who are their parents. Having grown up in an even more media-saturated, brand-conscious world than their parents did, they respond to advertising differently and prefer to encounter marketing messages in different places or from different sources.

Marketers recognize that to penetrate the skepticism and capture the attention of the Gen Ys they have to bring their messages to these people in a different way. To do so, many companies are turning to a stealth-type strategy known as *buzz marketing*, whereby brand come-ons become part of popular culture and consumers themselves are lured into spreading the message. Marketers are turning their brands into carefully guarded secrets that are revealed to only a few people in each community. Each carefully cultivated recipient of the brand message becomes a powerful carrier, spreading the word to yet more carriers, who tell a few more, and so on. The goal of the marketer is to identify the trendsetters in each community and push them into talking up the brand to their friends and admirers. As the senior vice president at Bates U.S.A., who developed a buzz campaign for Lucky Strike cigarettes, notes, "Ultimately, the brand benefits because an accepted member of the social circle will always be far more credible than any communication that could come directly from the brand."

A number of marketers have used buzz marketing successfully. Rather than blitzing the airways with 30-second commercials for its new Focus subcompact, Ford Motor Company recruited 120 trendsetters in five key markets and gave them each a Focus to drive for six months. According to Ford's marketing communications manager, who planned

and implemented the program, "We weren't looking for celebrities. We were looking for the assistants to celebrities, party planners, disc jockeys—the people who really seemed to influence what was cool." The recruits' duties were simply to be seen with the car, to hand out Focus-themed trinkets to anyone who expressed an interest in the car, and to keep a record of where they took the car. The program helped Ford get the Focus off to a brisk start, selling 286,166 units in its first full year.

Vespa motor scooter importer Piagio U.S.A. hired a group of attractive models to find the right cafes in and around Los Angeles and to interact with people over a cup of coffee or iced latte and generate buzz for the European bikes.

Even ad agencies that are heavily invested in traditional brand-building techniques acknowledge that buzz marketing has become a phenomenon. Malcolm Gladwell's book *The Tipping Point: How Little Things Can Make a Big Difference*—which describes how a small number of consumers can ignite a trend, if they're the right ones—has become must reading among ad agency personnel. The chairperson and CEO of Grey Global Group notes, "Everybody has read *The Tipping Point* and is trying to figure out the underground streams to reach consumers. Everybody is experimenting with it." For example, Reebok conducted more than 1,000 interviews to identify young Canadian women who were trendsetters among their peers. The company then gave 90 of these women a pair of $150 U-Shuffle DMX cross-trainers to get the funky shoes on the feet of these urban trendsetters. The product seeding campaign helped make the product-line launch one of the most successful in the company's history.

Some experts note that the growing popularity of buzz marketing could well spell its downfall. If everyone does it, it will no longer be buzz; it will simply be obscure and annoying advertising. And when consumers recognize that every company is trying to create a buzz for its brand, they are likely to be turned off to the technique. By then, of course, marketers will have found another stealth way to deliver their sales messages.

Sources: Garry Khermouch and Jeff Green, "Buzz Marketing," *BusinessWeek*, July 30, 2001, pp. 50–56; "Firms Reap Fruits of Product Seeding," *The Montreal Gazette*, September 11, 2001, p. D6.

Selecting Information   Sensory inputs are important but are only one part of the perceptual process. Other determinants of whether marketing stimuli will be attended to and how they will be interpreted include internal psychological factors such as the consumer's personality, needs, motives, expectations, and experiences. These psychological inputs explain why people focus attention on some things and ignore others. Two people may perceive the same stimuli in very different ways because they select and attend to messages differently. An individual's perceptual processes usually focus on elements of the environment that are relevant to his or her needs and tune out irrelevant stimuli. Think about how much more attentive you are to advertising for personal computers, tires, or stereos when you are in the market for one of these products.

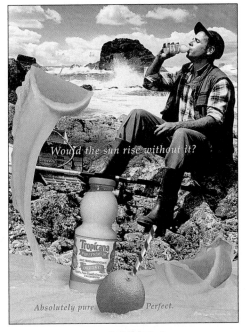

Would the sun rise without it?

Absolutely pure.   *Perfect.*

Selective attention occurs when the consumer chooses to focus attention on certain stimuli while excluding others. One study of selective attention estimates the typical consumer is exposed to nearly 1,500 ads per day yet perceives only 76 of these messages.[7] Other estimates range as high as 3,000 exposures per day. This means advertisers must make considerable effort to get their messages noticed. Advertisers often use the creative aspects of their ads to gain consumers' attention. For example, some advertisers set their ads off from others by showing their products in colour against a black-and-white background (Exhibit 2–7). Marketers also place ads in certain times or locations so that consumers will notice them more easliy. For example, a consumer may pay more attention to a commercial that is heard alone at home than to one heard in the presence of friends, at work, or anywhere distractions may be present. If advertisers can isolate a particular time when the listener is likely to be attentive, they will probably earn his or her undivided attention.

Exhibit 2–7
Tropicana attempts to create attention with this ad

Interpreting the Information   Once a consumer selects and attends to a stimulus, the perceptual process focuses on organizing, categorizing, and interpreting the incoming information. This stage of the perceptual process is very individualized and is influenced by internal psychological factors. The interpretation and meaning an individual assigns to an incoming stimulus also depend in part on the nature of the stimulus. For example, many ads are objective, and their message is clear and straightforward. Other ads are more ambiguous, and their meaning is strongly influenced by the consumer's individual interpretation.

Even if the consumer does notice the advertiser's message, there is no guarantee it will be interpreted in the intended manner. Consumers may engage in **selective comprehension**, interpreting information on the basis of their own attitudes, beliefs, motives, and experiences. They often interpret information in a manner that supports their own position. For example, an ad that disparages a consumer's favourite brand may be seen as biased or untruthful, and its claims may not be accepted.

Retaining the Information   The final stage of the perceptual process involves the storage of the information in short-term or long-term memory. Consumers may make mental notes or focus on some aspect of an advertising message to ensure that they will not forget, thus permitting easy retrieval during the information search stage. **Selective retention** means consumers do not remember all the information they see, hear, or read even after attending to and comprehending it. Advertisers attempt to make sure information will be retained in the consumer's memory so that it will be available when it is time to make a purchase. **Mnemonics** such as symbols, rhymes, associations, and images that assist in the learning and memory process are helpful. Many advertisers use telephone numbers that spell out the company name and are easy to remember. Eveready put pictures of its pink bunny on packages to remind consumers at the point of purchase of its creative advertising.

Subliminal Perception   Advertisers know consumers use selective perception to filter out irrelevant or unwanted advertising messages, so they employ various creative tactics to get their messages noticed. One controversial tactic advertisers have been accused of using is appealing to consumers' subconscious. **Subliminal perception** refers to the ability to perceive a stimulus that is below the level of consciousness. Psychologists generally agree it is possible to perceive something without any knowledge of having seen it. The possibility of using hidden persuaders such as subliminal audio messages or visual cues to influence consumers might be intriguing to advertisers but would not be welcomed by consumers. The idea of marketers influencing consumers at a subconscious level has strong ethical implications. The use of subliminal techniques is *not* a creative tactic we would recommend to advertisers.

ALTERNATIVE EVALUATION

After acquiring information during the information search stage of the decision process, the consumer moves to alternative evaluation. In this stage, the consumer compares the various brands or products and services he or she has identified as being capable of solving the consumption problem and satisfying the needs or motives that initiated the decision process. The various brands identified as purchase options to be considered during the alternative evaluation process are referred to as the consumer's *evoked set.*

The Evoked Set   The evoked set is generally only a subset of all the brands of which the consumer is aware. The consumer reduces the number of brands to be reviewed during the alternative evaluation stage to a manageable level. The exact size of the evoked set varies from one consumer to another and depends on such factors as the importance of the purchase and the amount of time and energy the consumer wants to spend comparing alternatives.

The goal of most advertising and promotional strategies is to increase the likelihood that a brand will be included in the consumer's evoked set and considered during alternative evaluation. Marketers use advertising to create *top-of-mind awareness* among consumers so that their brands are part of the evoked set of their target audiences. Popular brands with large advertising budgets use *reminder advertising* to maintain high awareness levels and increase the likelihood they will be considered by consumers in the market for the product. Marketers of new brands or those with a low market share need to gain awareness among consumers and break into their evoked sets.

Evaluative Criteria and Consequences   Once consumers have identified an evoked set and have a list of alternatives, they must evaluate the various brands. This involves comparing the choice alternatives on specific criteria important to the consumer. **Evaluative criteria** are the dimensions or attributes of a product or service that are used to compare different alternatives. Evaluative criteria can be objective or subjective. For example, in buying an automobile, consumers use objective attributes such as price, warranty, and fuel economy as well as subjective factors such as image, styling, and performance.

Evaluative criteria are usually viewed as product or service attributes. Many marketers view their products or services as *bundles of attributes*, but consumers tend to think about products or services in terms of their *consequences* instead. J. Paul Peter and Jerry Olson define consequences as specific events or outcomes that consumers experience when they purchase and/or consume a product or service.[8] They distinguish between two broad types of consequences. **Functional consequences** are concrete outcomes of product or service usage that are tangible and directly experienced by consumers. The taste of a soft drink or a potato chip, the acceleration of a car, and the clarity of a fax transmission are examples of functional consequences. **Psychosocial consequences** are abstract outcomes that are more intangible, subjective, and personal, such as how a product makes you feel or how you think others will view you for purchasing or using it.

Marketers should distinguish between product/service attributes and consequences, because the importance and meaning consumers assign to an attribute are usually determined by its consequences for them. Moreover, advertisers must be sure consumers understand the link between a particular attribute and a consequence. For example, the Callaway ad in Exhibit 2–8 focuses on the consequences of using the new Callaway golf club, such as more distance and lower scores.

Product/service attributes and the consequences or outcomes consumers think they will experience from a particular brand are very important, for they are often the basis on which consumers form attitudes and decide among various choice alternatives.

ATTITUDES

Attitudes are one of the most heavily studied concepts in consumer behaviour. According to Gordon Allport's classic definition, "attitudes are learned predispositions to respond to an object."[9] More recent perspectives view attitudes as a summary construct that represents an individual's overall feelings toward or evaluation of an object.[10] Consumers hold attitudes toward a variety of objects that are important to marketers, including individuals (celebrity endorsers such as Tiger Woods or Michael Jordan), brands (Cheerios), companies (Microsoft), product categories (beef, pork, tuna), retail stores (The Bay, Sears), or even advertisements (the Energizer bunny ads).

Attitudes are important to marketers because they theoretically summarize a consumer's evaluation of an object (or brand or company) and represent positive or negative feelings and behavioural tendencies. Marketers' keen interest in attitudes is based on the assumption that they are related to consumers' purchase behaviour. Considerable evidence supports the basic assumption of a relationship between attitudes and behaviour.[11] The attitude-behaviour link does not always hold; many other factors can affect behaviour.[12] But attitudes are very important to marketers. Advertising and promotion are used to create favourable attitudes toward new products/services or brands, reinforce existing favourable attitudes, and/or change negative attitudes.

PURCHASE DECISION

At some point in the buying process, the consumer must stop searching for and evaluating information about alternative brands in the evoked set and make a *purchase decision*. As an outcome of the alternative evaluation stage, the consumer may develop a **purchase intention** or predisposition to buy a certain brand. Purchase intentions are generally based on a matching of purchase motives with attributes or characteristics of brands under consideration. Their formation involves many of the personal subprocesses discussed in this chapter, including motivation, perception, and attitude formation.

A purchase decision is not the same as an actual purchase. Once a consumer chooses which brand to buy, he or she must still implement the decision and make the actual purchase. Additional decisions may be needed, such as when to buy, where to buy, and how much money to spend. Often, there is a time delay between

EVEN IN TODAY'S VOLATILE MARKET, THERE IS SUCH A THING AS A SAFE TECHNOLOGY INVESTMENT.

Exhibit 2–8
This ad emphasizes the positive consequences of using Callaway golf clubs

45

the formation of a purchase intention or decision and the actual purchase, particularly for highly involved and complex purchases such as automobiles, personal computers, and consumer durables.

For nondurable products, which include many low-involvement items such as consumer package goods, the time between the decision and the actual purchase may be short. Before leaving home, the consumer may make a shopping list that includes specific brand names because the consumer has developed **brand loyalty**—a preference for a particular brand that results in its repeated purchase. Marketers strive to develop and maintain brand loyalty among consumers. They use reminder advertising to keep their brand names in front of consumers, maintain prominent shelf positions and displays in stores, and run periodic promotions to deter consumers from switching brands. Maintaining consumers' brand loyalty is not easy. Competitors use many techniques to encourage consumers to try their brands, among them new product introductions and free samples. Marketers must continually battle to maintain their loyal consumers while replacing those who switch brands.

Purchase decisions for nondurable, convenience items sometimes take place in the store, almost simultaneous with the purchase. Marketers must ensure that consumers have top-of-mind awareness of their brands so that they are quickly recognized and considered. These types of decisions are influenced at the actual point of purchase. Packaging, shelf displays, point-of-purchase materials, and promotional tools such as on-package coupons or premium offers can influence decisions made through constructive processes at the time of purchase.

INTEGRATION PROCESSES

A key part of the purchase decision stage is the way consumers combine information about the characteristics of brands. **Integration processes** are the way product knowledge, meanings, and beliefs are combined to evaluate two or more alternatives.[13] Analysis of the integration process focuses on the different types of *decision rules* or strategies consumers use to decide among purchase alternatives.

Consumers often make purchase selections by using formal integration strategies or decision rules that require examination and comparison of alternatives on specific attributes. This process involves a very deliberate evaluation of the alternatives, attribute by attribute. When consumers apply such formal decision rules, marketers need to know which attributes are being considered so as to provide the information the consumers require.

Sometimes consumers make their purchase decisions using more simplified decision rules known as **heuristics**. Peter and Olson note that heuristics are easy to use and are highly adaptive to specific environmental situations (such as a retail store).[14] For familiar products that are purchased frequently, consumers may use price-based heuristics (buy the least expensive brand) or promotion-based heuristics (choose the brand for which I can get a price reduction through a coupon, rebate, or special deal).

One type of heuristic is the **affect referral decision rule**,[15] in which consumers make a selection on the basis of an overall impression or summary evaluation of the various alternatives under consideration. This decision rule suggests that consumers have affective impressions of brands stored in memory that can be accessed at the time of purchase. How many times have you gone into a store and made purchases based on your overall impressions of the brands rather than going through detailed comparisons of the alternatives' specific attributes?

Marketers selling familiar and popular brands may appeal to an affect referral rule by stressing overall affective feelings or impressions about their products. Market leaders, whose products enjoy strong overall brand images, often use ads that promote the brand as the best overall (Exhibit 2–9).

POSTPURCHASE EVALUATION

The consumer decision process does not end with the purchase. After consumption, the consumer assesses the level of performance of the product or service. The postpurchase evaluation process is important because the feedback acquired from actual use of a product will influence the likelihood of future purchases. Positive performance means the brand is retained in the evoked set and increases the likelihood it will be purchased again. Unfavourable outcomes may lead the consumer to form negative attitudes toward the brand, lessening the likelihood it will be purchased again or even eliminating it from the consumer's evoked set.

Consumers engage in a number of activities during the postpurchase evaluation process. They may seek out reassurance and opinions from others to confirm the wisdom of their purchase decision, lower their attitudes or opinions of the unchosen alternative, deny or distort any information that does not support the choice they made, or look for information that does support their choice. An important source of supportive information is advertising; consumers tend to be more attentive to advertising for the brand they have chosen.[16] Thus, it may be important for companies to advertise to reinforce consumer decisions to purchase their brands.

Exhibit 2–9
Market leaders such as Labatt can appeal to consumer affect

SATISFACTION

The most significant psychological concept during the postpurchase evaluation process is satisfaction. A leading expert in satisfaction research has recently defined **satisfaction** as a judgment that consumers make with respect to the pleasurable level of consumption-related fulfillment.[17] The notion of fulfillment implies that a consumer's goal has been achieved (i.e., needs met), and that the fulfillment is "judged with reference to a standard." Thus, consumers make a comparison between the consumption outcome and some other referent.

Consumers can make many comparisons. One is to compare the level of product performance to the expectations of the product that consumers had prior to purchase. Satisfaction can occur when the consumer's expectations are either met or exceeded whereas dissatisfaction results when performance is below expectations. Consumers can also compare the product performance to some absolute standard of quality to perceive satisfaction or dissatisfaction.

Another aspect of satisfaction is **cognitive dissonance**, a feeling of psychological tension or postpurchase doubt that a consumer experiences after making a difficult purchase choice. Dissonance is more likely to occur in important decisions where the consumer must choose among close alternatives (especially if the unchosen alternative has unique or desirable features that the selected alternative does not have).

Marketers must recognize the importance of the postpurchase evaluation stage. Dissatisfied consumers not only are unlikely to repurchase the marketer's product but may also spread negative word-of-mouth information that deters others from purchasing the product or service. The best guarantee of favourable postpurchase evaluations is to provide consumers with a quality product or service that always meets their expectations. Marketers must be sure their advertising and other forms of promotion do not create unreasonable expectations their products cannot meet.

Marketers have come to realize that postpurchase communication is also important. Some companies send follow-up letters and brochures to reassure buyers and reinforce the wisdom of their decision. Many companies have set up toll-free numbers for consumers to call if they need information or have a question or complaint regarding a product. Marketers also offer liberalized return and refund policies and extended warranties and guarantees to ensure customer satisfaction. Some have used customers' postpurchase dissatisfaction as an opportunity for gaining new business.

VARIATIONS IN CONSUMER DECISION MAKING

We have reviewed the consumer decision-making process with respect to individual purchases. However, variations in this process arise depending upon the type of purchase and whether the individual is making the decision with other people. We now discuss these two variations in the consumer decision-making process.

TYPES OF DECISION MAKING

The preceding pages describe a general model of consumer decision making. But consumers do not always engage in all five steps of the purchase decision process or proceed in the sequence presented. They may minimize or even skip one or more stages if they have previous experience in purchasing the product or service or if the decision is of low personal, social, or economic significance. To develop effective promotional strategies and programs, marketers need some understanding of the problem-solving processes their target consumers use to make purchase decisions.[18]

Many of the purchase decisions we make as consumers are based on a habit known as **routine problem solving** or routine response behaviour. For many low-priced, frequently purchased products, the decision process consists of little more than recognizing the need, engaging in a quick internal search, and making the purchase. The consumer spends little or no effort engaging in external search or alternative evaluation.

Marketers of products characterized by a routine response purchase process need to get and/or keep their brands in the consumer's evoked set and avoid anything that may result in their removal from consideration. Established brands that have strong market share position are likely to be in the evoked set of most consumers. Marketers of these brands want consumers to follow a routine choice process and continue to purchase their products. This means maintaining high levels of brand awareness through reminder advertising, periodic promotions, and prominent shelf positions in retail stores.

Marketers of new brands or those with a low market share face a different challenge. They must find ways to disrupt consumers' routine choice process and get them to consider different alternatives. High levels of advertising along with sales promotion efforts in the form of free samples, special price offers, high-value coupons, and the like may encourage consumers to reconsider their habit or routine choice.

A more complicated decision-making process may occur when consumers have limited experience in purchasing a particular product or service and little or no knowledge of the brands available and/or the criteria to use in making a purchase decision. They may have to learn what attributes or criteria should be used in making a purchase decision and how the various alternatives perform on these dimensions. For products or services characterized by **limited problem solving** or **extended problem solving** marketers should make information available that will help consumers decide. Advertising that provides consumers with detailed information about a brand and how it can satisfy their purchase motives and goals is important. Marketers may also want to give consumers information at the point of purchase, through either displays or brochures. Distribution channels should have knowledgeable salespeople available to explain the features and benefits of the company's product or service and why it is superior to competing products.

The Fidelity Investments ad in Exhibit 2–10 is a good example of how advertising can appeal to consumers who may be engaging in extended problem solving when considering retirement investing. Notice how the ad communicates with consumers who know little about how to purchase this product. The ad also makes more detailed information available by offering a toll-free number and a website.

GROUP DECISION MAKING

Think about the last time you attended a party. As you dressed for the party, you probably asked yourself (or someone else) what others would be wearing. Your selection of attire may have been influenced by those likely to be present. This simple example reflects one form of impact that groups may exert on your behaviour.

A group has been defined as "two or more individuals who share a set of norms, values, or beliefs and have certain implicitly or explicitly defined relationships to one another such that their behavior is interdependent."[19] Groups are one of the primary factors influencing learning and socialization, and group situations constitute many of our purchase decisions.

A **reference group** is "a group whose presumed perspectives or values are being used by an individual as the basis for his or her judgments, opinions, and actions." Consumers use reference groups as a guide to specific behaviours, even when the groups are not present.[20] In the party example, your peers—although not present—provided a standard of dress that you referred to in your clothing selection. Likewise, your college classmates, family, and co-workers, or even a group to which you aspire, may serve as referents, and your consumption patterns will typically conform to the expectations of the groups that are most important to you.

Marketers use reference group influences in developing advertisements and promotional strategies. The ads in Exhibits 2–11 and 2–12 are examples of *aspirational* reference groups (to which we might like to belong) and *disassociative* groups (to which we do not wish to belong), respectively.

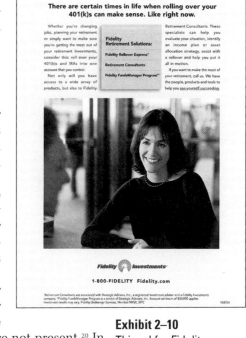

Exhibit 2–10
This ad for Fidelity Investments shows how marketers can appeal to consumers engaging in extended problem solving

Exhibit 2–11
These ads are examples of aspirational reference groups

Exhibit 2–12
This ad represents a disassociative reference group

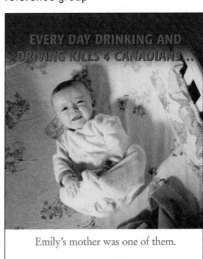

FIGURE 2–4

Roles in the family decision-making process

☐ ☐ ☐ ☐ ☐

The initiator. The person responsible for initiating the purchase decision process; for example, the mother who determines she needs a new car.

The information provider. The individual responsible for gathering information to be used in making the decision; for example, the teenage car buff who knows where to find product information in specific magazines or collects it from dealers.

The influencer. The person who exerts influence as to what criteria will be used in the selection process. All members of the family may be involved. The mother may have her criteria, whereas others may each have their own input.

The decision maker(s). That person(s) who actually makes the decision. In our example, it may be the mother alone or in combination with another family member.

The purchasing agent. That individual who performs the physical act of making the purchase. In the case of a car, a husband and wife may decide to choose it together and sign the purchase agreement.

The consumer. The actual user of the product. In the case of a family car, all family members are consumers. For a private car, only the mother might be the consumer.

In some instances, the group may be involved more directly than just as a referent. Family members may serve as referents to each other, or they may actually be involved in the purchase decision process—acting as an individual buying unit. As shown in Figure 2–4, family members may assume a variety of roles in the decision-making process.[21] As the example indicates, there can be group interaction at every stage of the consumer decision-making process since various members take on a role.

Each role has implications for marketers. First, the advertiser must determine who is responsible for the various roles in the decision-making process so that messages can be targeted at that person (or those people). These roles will also dictate media strategies, since the appropriate magazines, newspapers, or TV or radio stations must be used. Second, understanding the decision-making process and the use of information by individual family members is critical to the design of messages and choice of promotional program elements. In general, to create an effective promotional program, a marketer must have an overall understanding of how the decision process works and the role that each group member plays. IMC Perspective 2–2 discusses communication to children and the influencing role they have on family purchases.

TARGET AUDIENCE DECISION

We reviewed the consumer decision-making process since marketers need to thoroughly understand the behaviour they are trying to influence through their promotional plans. Moreover, marketers also try to understand consumers as much as possible since an IMC plan, IMC program (e.g., advertising campaign), or ad is directed to a particular target audience, which is usually a primary decision made prior to any other communication decision.

Recall that the information and decisions of a marketing plan are key inputs for all promotional plan decisions. In addition, the direction of the target audience decision is derived from the segmentation and target market decisions of the marketing plan. The process of developing and implementing the target market decision is summarized in Figure 2–5. How promotion decisions fit within an organization's marketing strategy and programs is also highlighted.

This model consists of four major components: the organization's situation analysis, the target market process, the marketing program development (which includes the promotional mix), and the target market. As the model shows, the marketing process begins with the development of a marketing strategy and analysis in which the company decides the product or service areas and particular markets where it wants to compete. The company must then coordinate the various elements of the

Communicating to Kids

Communicating to kids is a fascinating part of some marketer's lives. According to Statistics Canada there are 5.8 million Canadian children 14 years and under. And while it can be expected that many of these children "act their age," there is a growing trend of some kids getting older at a younger age. Some children are physically maturing at an earlier age, some pre-teens exhibit teenage-like behaviour, others have increased responsibility in their lives, and it seems all of them have increased disposable income. Consequently, children enter product categories at an earlier age than previously thought possible (i.e., cellphones), explore digital media, participate in complex purchase decisions, or make purchase decisions for their parents.

With increased involvement, marketers are using some interesting approaches to understand the consumer behaviour of children. Many marketers are using more direct and interactive marketing research techniques that have led to innovating communication practices. Levi's combined with MuchMusic on a contest micro website where consumers can make their own version of a song that is featured in TV ads. To follow up on the theme in an integrated manner, representatives organize spontaneous karaoke sessions and give participants free merchandise. Kellogg went a step further in 2000 and actually made the target audience the brand's managers, who had a say in how the brand would be communicated (i.e., ad, packaging) and other marketing decisions such as the product's colour. Examples of IMC tools that cosmetic firms use to reach teenage girls include samples, sponsorship, advertising with key spokespersons, websites with exclusive passwords, and interactive contests.

Not only are children the recipients of advertising messages for their own purchases, it seems children are so informed that they are key influencers on products such as family vacations (64 percent), home electronics (56 percent),

and automobiles (17 percent). In fact, research indicates that children know between 300 and 400 brand names by the age of 10 and influence up to $20 million in Canadian household expenditures, and that parents generally agree to children's requests. Furthermore, television appears to be the main source of the increased brand knowledge. For example, RadioShack planned to reach children as influencers in the purchase of micro remote-control cars by placing two ads on YTV and Teletoon prior to airing them on regular television channels.

As marketers respond to this evolving consumer behaviour, the guidelines for communicating to children may be put to the test. Canada is a world leader in developing standards, policies, and educational initiatives for responsible advertising to children. In the 1970s, Canadian advertisers and broadcasters instituted the Broadcast Code for Advertising to Children, which ensured that all advertising directed to children would take into account the special needs and vulnerabilities of children. The Concerned Children's Advertisers is a non-profit association of Canadian companies and various partners who work together to deliver advertising messages and other communication devices to support children in their understanding of themselves and the role of media in their lives. Combined, these Canadian efforts are the envy of the rest of the world and many countries would like to see the Canadian standards become institutionalized globally.

Sources: Beth Hitchcock, "Thank Heaven for Little Girls," *Marketing Magazine*, January 1/8, 2001; Sunni Boot, "The Lolita Syndrome," *Marketing Magazine*, January 1/8, 2001; Cathy Loblaw, "The Whole World Is Watching," *Marketing Magazine*, August 6, 2001; Marlene Milczarek, "Voices Carry," *Marketing Magazine*, August 6, 2001; Chris Powell, "Under the Influence," *Marketing Magazine*, February 16, 2004.

FIGURE 2–5 □□□□ Marketing and promotions process model

marketing mix into a cohesive marketing program that will reach the target market effectively. Note that a firm's promotion program is directed not only to the final buyer but also to the channel or "trade" members that distribute its products to the ultimate consumer. These channel members must be convinced there is a demand for the company's products so they will carry them and will aggressively merchandise and promote them to consumers. Promotions play an important role in the marketing program for building and maintaining demand not only among final consumers but among the trade as well.

The target market is the focus of the firm's marketing effort, and specific sales, market share, and profitability objectives are set according to where the company wants to be and what it hopes to accomplish in this market. The method by which marketers do this (presented in Figure 2–6) is referred to as the **target market process** and involves three basic steps: segment the market, select a target market, and determine the market positioning strategy of one's product or service. The selection of the target market (or markets) in which the firm will compete is an important part of its marketing strategy and has direct implications for its advertising and promotional efforts. Specific communication objectives are derived and the promotional mix strategies are developed to achieve these objectives. Thus, different objectives may be established, different budgets may be used, and the promotional mix strategies may vary, depending on the market selected.

As we introduced this section, perhaps you noticed that we used the terms target market and target audience. We concur with a recent perspective[22] that suggests promotional planners should make a careful distinction between these concepts since

FIGURE 2–6
The target market process
□□□□□

an advertising plan or IMC plan is one part of the overall marketing plan. The **target market** is the group of consumers for which an overall marketing program is directed towards. The **target audience** is a group of consumers for which the advertising campaign, for example, is directed towards. Conceptually, these targets are interdependent but their distinction allows planners the ability to make more effective promotional decisions with enhanced precision.

In this section, we review the concepts of market segmentation and target market selection to fully understand the context and options for the target audience decision. We begin by summarizing the ways marketers can segment the market in order to select a target market. We then conclude with the options and guidelines for making the target audience decision.

MARKET SEGMENTATION

To identify a target market , the marketer identifies the specific needs of groups of people (or segments), selects one or more of these segments as a target, and develops marketing programs directed to each. This approach has found increased applicability in marketing for a number of reasons, including changes in the market (consumers are becoming much more diverse in their needs, attitudes, and lifestyles); increased use of segmentation by competitors; and the fact that more managers are trained in segmentation and realize the advantages associated with this strategy. Perhaps the best explanation, however, comes back to the basic premise that you must understand as much as possible about consumers to design marketing programs that meet their needs most effectively. Furthermore, as marketers establish a common ground with consumers, the more effective they will be in addressing these requirements in their communications programs and informing and/or persuading potential consumers that the product or service offering will meet their needs.

Marketers competing in nearly all product and service categories are constantly searching for ways to segment their markets in an attempt to better satisfy customers' needs (Exhibit 2–13). The remainder of this section discusses ways to approach this task and make the final segmentation decision.

As shown in Figure 2–7, several methods are available for segmenting markets. Marketers may use one of the segmentation variables or a combination of approaches. Consider the market segmentation strategy that might be employed to market snow skis. The consumer's lifestyle—active, fun-loving, enjoys outdoor sports—is certainly important. But so are other factors, such as age (participation in downhill skiing drops off significantly at about age 30) and income (Have you seen the price of a lift ticket lately?), as well as marital status. Let us review the basis for segmentation and examine some promotional strategies employed in each.

Geographic Segmentation In the **geographic segmentation** approach, markets are divided into different geographic units. These units may include nations, provinces, states, counties, or even neighbourhoods. Consumers often have different buying habits depending on where they reside. To address this, advertisers might use different IMC tools or advertising messages.

Demographic Segmentation Dividing the market on the basis of demographic variables such as age, sex, family size, education, income, and social class is called

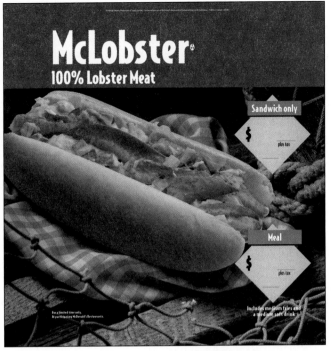

Exhibit 2–13
McDonald's offers a variety of products in different geographic markets

FIGURE 2–7 □ □ □ □ Examples of market segmentation variables

Main Dimension	Segmentation Variables	Typical Breakdowns
Customer Characteristics		
Geographic	Region	West, Central, East
	City size	Under 10,000; 10,000–24,999; 25,000–49,999; 50,000–99,999; 100,000–249,999; 250,000–499,999; 500,000–999,999; 1,000,000 or more
	Metropolitan area	Census Metropolitan Area (CMA); etc.
	Density	Urban; suburban; small town; rural
Demographic	Gender	Male; female
	Age	Under 6 yrs; 6–11 yrs; 12–17 yrs; 18–24 yrs; 25–34 yrs; 35–44 yrs; 45–54 yrs; 55–64 yrs; 65–74 yrs; 75 yrs plus
	Race	Asian; Black; Hispanic; Indian; White/Caucasian; etc.
	Life stage	Infant; preschool; child; youth; collegiate; adult; senior
	Birth era	Baby boomer (1949–1964); Generation X (1965–1976); baby boomlet/Generation Y (1977–present)
	Household size	1; 2; 3–4; 5 or more
	Residence tenure	Own home; rent home
	Marital status	Never married; married; separated; divorced; widowed
Socioeconomic	Income	<$15,000; $15,000–$24,999; $25,000–$34,999; $35,000–$49,999; $50,000–$74,999; $75,000+
	Education	Some high school or less; high school graduate; some college or university; university/college graduate; etc.
	Occupation	Managerial and professional specialty; technical, sales, and administrative support; service; farming, forestry, and fishing; etc.
Psychographic	Personality	Gregarious; compulsive; introverted; aggressive; ambitious; etc.
	Lifestyle	Activities, interests, opinions
	Values	Actualizers; fulfilleds; achievers; experiencers; believers; strivers; makers; strugglers
	Culture	Ethnic; social
	Social class	Low middle class; upper middle class; etc.
Buying Situations		
Outlet type	In-store	Department; specialty; outlet; convenience; supermarket; superstore/mass merchandiser; catalogue
	Direct	Mail order/catalogue; door-to-door; direct response; Internet
Benefits sought	Product features	Situation specific; general
	Needs	Quality; service; price/value; financing; warranty; etc.
Usage	Usage rate	Light user; medium user; heavy user
	User status	Nonuser; ex-user; prospect; first-time user; regular user
Awareness and intentions	Product knowledge	Unaware; aware; informed; interested; intending to buy; purchaser; rejection
Behaviour	Involvement	Minimum effort; comparison; special effort

demographic segmentation. For example, the Alberta Securities Commission targeted young adults aged 24–35 who had very little knowledge of investing and had a perceived need for financial advice as indicated by market research. Print and radio ads directed interested consumers to an education link on the Commission's website. A second phase of the advertising message featured links on Web portals that also highlighted a contest.[23]

While demographics may still be the most common method of segmenting markets, it is important to recognize that other factors may be the underlying basis for homogeneity and/or consumer behaviour. The astute marketer will identify additional bases for segmenting and will recognize the limitations of demographics.

Psychographic Segmentation Dividing the market on the basis of lifestyle, personality, culture, and social class is referred to as **psychographic segmentation**. Each of these variables can be the basis for segmentation.

Lifestyle Many consider lifestyle the most effective criterion for segmentation. The determination of lifestyles is usually based on an analysis of the activities, interests, and opinions (AIOs) of consumers. These lifestyles are then correlated with the consumers' product, brand, and/or media usage. For many products and/or services, lifestyles may be the best discriminator between use and nonuse, accounting for differences in food, clothing, and car selections, among numerous other consumer behaviours.[24]

Psychographic segmentation has been increasingly accepted with the advent of the values and lifestyles (VALS) program. Although marketers employed lifestyle segmentation long before VALS and although a number of alternatives—for example, PRIZM—are available, VALS remains one of the more popular options. Developed by the Stanford Research Institute (SRI), VALS has become a very popular method for applying lifestyle segmentation. VALS 2 divides Americans into eight lifestyle segments that exhibit distinctive attitudes, behaviours, and decision-making patterns.[25] SRI believes that when combined with an estimate of the resources the consumer can draw on (education, income, health, energy level, self-confidence, and degree of consumerism), the VALS 2 system is an excellent predictor of consumer behaviours. A variety of companies, including Mercedes and Eastman Kodak, have employed the VALS 2 program. Campbell's Soup embarked on a new campaign in 2000 to position the soup as a "lifestyle" choice.

Personality Borrowing from psychological theory, we are interested in consumers' personality traits—the relatively enduring characteristics of one's personality that leads people to respond in a reasonably consistent manner. Often, such characteristics like introvert versus extrovert are used to describe a group of consumers more precisely.

Culture The broadest and most abstract of the external factors that influence consumer behaviour is **culture**, or the complexity of learned meanings, values, norms, and customs shared by members of a society. Cultural norms and values offer direction and guidance to members of a society in all aspects of their lives, including their consumption behaviour.

Marketers must also be aware of changes that may be occurring in a particular culture since it could be the basis for effective segmentation. Marketing researchers monitor these changes and their impact on the ways companies market their products and services. IMC Perspective 2–3 demonstrates how some Canadian firms target their communications to specific ethnic cultures.

While marketers recognize that culture exerts a demonstrable influence on consumers, they often find it difficult to respond to cultural differences in different

Canada's Mosaic Population

Approximately 4 million Canadians are visible minorities in a country with about 31 million citizens. Some experts believe that significant retail growth will come from this sizable group of Canadians, especially considering that immigration accounted for more than half of the population growth between the two most recent census tabulations of 1996 and 2001. And as all good marketers know, segmenting the market using this valuable characteristic can be profitable if brands are looking to target a more specific audience.

The largest minority group in Canada is Chinese at 1.1 million. Research suggests that Chinese consumers are interested in luxury brands more than any other ethnic group and use luxury brands as a way of displaying their economic achievement, seek status through products significantly more than white Canadians, and purchase extensively on the Internet. Noting these ideas and the fact that 70 percent of all Chinese children study a musical instrument, the Toronto Symphony Orchestra (TSO) looked to this segment as a source of attracting new customers and tailored a communications offering of advertising, public relations, and promotional incentives in the Chinese language. After its initial success, the TSO continued with even more customized communication including Chinese brochures, designing part of its website in Chinese, advertising in Chinese media, and offering a slogan that fits the Chinese culture more specifically, and even setting up a hot-line in both Cantonese and Mandarin. The TSO expanded these ideas to similar communication programs in other languages such as Italian, Russian, and Korean.

And the TSO is not the only firm targeting the Chinese community. A Rona store in Vancouver experienced similar success with customized communication to Chinese consumers that increased sales so much that the store received a hardware retailer of the year award. However, Rona's main office had yet to customize its national brand advertising for distinct ethnic markets as it preferred to keep a consistent message through translation of uniform advertising messages.

On the other hand, Wal-Mart recently offered its commercials in Italian, Portuguese, Spanish, Cantonese, Mandarin, and Southeast Asian languages on various specialty ethnic channels. The ads show real customers speaking about their Wal-Mart experiences in their own language. This appears to go a step beyond Zellers' effort of dubbing its English ads into other languages.

While slightly smaller at 900,000, Canadians from India and other nearby South Asian countries present another sizable ethnic segment that has its own unique characteristics that marketers attempt to attract. For example, Telus adapted a television ad that included monkeys by changing the background music such that the meaning of the message more closely fit Indian culture and adding a combination of English and Hindi known as "Hinglish." In addition, Telus changed the animal theme in its ad for camera phones for the Indian market since the national campaign showed pigs, an unappealing animal in that culture.

Sources: Eve Lazarus, "Building Better Relationships," *Marketing Magazine*, May 19, 2003; Chris Daniels, "Shopping Mosaic," *Marketing Magazine*, May 17, 2004; Loretta Lam, "Music to Ethnic Ears," *Marketing Magazine*, May 19, 2003; Michelle Warren, "Telus, Fat Free Tailor Indian Ad Effort," *Marketing Magazine*, November 17, 2003; Judy Waytiuk, "Discounter Diversity," *Marketing Magazine*, May 19, 2003.

markets. The subtleties of various cultures are often difficult to understand and appreciate, but marketers must understand the cultural context in which consumer purchase decisions are made and adapt their advertising and promotional programs accordingly.

For example, Bell Mobility rang in the Chinese New Year early in 2004 with an advertising and promotion campaign directed to Asian customers in Western Canada, the first of many specific communication efforts to appeal to a large group of potential customers. To resonate with the people of this culture more significantly, Bell Mobility introduced new creative messages to celebrate the Year of the Monkey. It also edited existing television ads to include scenes reflecting Asian lifestyle more accurately while also translating ads into Cantonese and Mandarin.[26]

Within a given culture are generally found smaller groups or segments whose beliefs, values, norms, and patterns of behaviour set them apart from the larger cultural mainstream. These **subcultures** may be based on age, geographic, religious, racial, and/or ethnic differences. A number of subcultures exist within Canada. These racial/ethnic subcultures are important to marketers because of their size, growth, purchasing power, and distinct purchasing patterns. Marketers develop specific marketing programs for various products and services for these target markets.

Other types of subcultures are also targeted through promotional communication. For example many major brands including Honda Civic, RadioShack, Adidas Canada, and Athletes World target those within the hip-hop culture. The firms have included the hip-hop culture in their television ads and marketing events.[27]

Social Class Virtually all societies exhibit some form of stratification whereby individuals can be assigned to a specific social category on the basis of criteria important to members of that society. **Social class** refers to relatively homogeneous divisions in a society into which people sharing similar lifestyles, values, norms, interests, and behaviours can be grouped. While a number of methods for determining social class exist, class structures in Canada are usually based on occupational status, educational attainment, and income. For example, sociologists generally agree there are three broad levels of social classes in North America: the upper (14 percent), middle (70 percent), and lower (16 percent) classes.[28]

Social class is an important concept to marketers, since consumers within each social stratum often have similar values, lifestyles, and buying behaviour. Thus, the various social class groups provide a natural basis for market segmentation. Consumers in the different social classes differ in the degree to which they use various products and services and in their leisure activities, shopping patterns, and media habits. Marketers respond to these differences through the positioning of their products and services, the media strategies they use to reach different social classes, and the types of advertising appeals they develop.

With smaller Canadian households (2.5 persons) and rising disposable household income, marketers of premium products find that the middle-class consumers behave as upper-class consumers for selective purchases. A sizable group of middle-class consumers who cannot afford premium or luxury goods for all their purchases are "trading-up" for items such as clothing, home furnishings, or alcohol.[29] As a profile variable for target audience decisions, social class offers potential for expanding a brands market.

Benefit Segmentation In purchasing products, consumers are generally trying to satisfy specific needs and/or wants. They are looking for products that provide specific benefits to satisfy these needs. The grouping of consumers on the basis of attributes sought in a product is known as **benefit segmentation** and is widely used.

Consider the purchase of a wristwatch. While you might buy a watch for particular benefits such as accuracy, water resistance, or stylishness, others may seek a

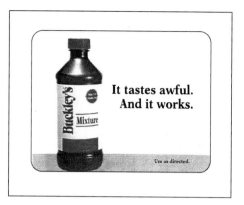

Exhibit 2–14
Buckley's stresses the benefit of its superior cough remedy.

different set of benefits. Watches are commonly given as gifts for birthdays, Christmas, and graduation. Certainly some of the same benefits are considered in the purchase of a gift, but the benefits the purchaser derives are different from those the user will obtain. Ads that portray watches as good gifts stress different criteria to consider in the purchase decision. The next time you see an ad or commercial for a watch, think about the basic appeal and the benefits it offers.

Another example of benefit segmentation can be seen in the cough remedy market. Some consumers want a product with fever reliever (NeoCitran); others prefer one that helps them to sleep (NyQuil). Buckley's offers that their cough mixture "tastes awful and it works" (Exhibit 2–14).

Behaviouristic Segmentation   Dividing consumers into groups according to their usage, loyalties, or buying responses to a product is **behaviouristic segmentation**. For example, product or brand usage, degree of use (heavy versus light), and/or brand loyalty are combined with demographic and/or psychographic criteria to develop profiles of market segments. In the case of usage, the marketer assumes that nonpurchasers of a brand or product who have the same characteristics as purchasers hold greater potential for adoption than nonusers with different characteristics. A profile (demographic or psychographic) of the user is developed, which serves as the basis for promotional strategies designed to attract new users. For example, teenagers share certain similarities in their consumption behaviours. Those who do not currently own a Sony Discman are more likely to be potential buyers than people in other age groups.

Another way of viewing behaviouristic segmentation is to examine the specific situation in which consumers plan to use the product or brand since it directly affects their perceptions, preferences, and purchasing behaviours.[30] Two types of **situations** may be relevant: the specific usage situation and the purchase situation.

Usage refers to the circumstance in which the product will be used. For example, purchases made for private consumption may be thought of differently from those that will be obvious to the public. Furthermore, purchases made for oneself versus for others as gifts offer another way to view consumer markets. The *purchase* situation more directly involves the environment operating at the time of the purchase. Time constraints, store environments, and other factors guide consumers' behaviour, which opens the door for inventive ways of segmenting the market.

TARGET MARKET SELECTION

As we have seen, a number of alternative segmentation approaches may be used. Each time a specific segment is identified, additional information is gathered to help the marketer understand this group. For example, once a specific segment is identified on the basis of benefits sought, the marketer will examine lifestyle characteristics and demographics to help characterize this group and to further its understanding of this market. Behaviouristic segmentation criteria will also be examined. In the purchase of ski boots, for example, specific benefits may be sought—flexibility or stiffness—depending on the type of skiing the buyer does. All this information will be combined to provide a complete profile of the skier.

Promotional planners will refer to the segmentation approach used in the marketing plan. The market segmentation may be based on demographics so the target market could be men between the ages of 18–24 or women between 25–44. And, it may be incumbent upon the planner to perform additional research to develop a more complete profile. Alternatively, the market segmentation used in the marketing plan could employ one variable as a starting point and offer additional variables to further define the target market as seen in the ski boots example.

From a promotional perspective, managers must consider whether the target segment is substantial enough to support individualized strategies. More specifically, they consider whether this group is accessible. Can it be reached with a communications program? For example, you will see in Chapter 9 that in some instances there are no media that can be used to reach some targeted groups. Or the promotions manager may identify a number of segments but be unable to develop the required programs to reach them. For example, the firm may have insufficient funds to develop the required advertising campaign. The more marketers segment the market, the more precise is their understanding of it. But the more the market becomes divided, the fewer consumers are in each segment. Thus, a key decision is: How far should one go in the segmentation process?

A number of companies now offer research services to help marketing managers define their markets and develop strategies targeting them. The VALS and PRIZM systems discussed earlier are just a few of the services offered; others use demographic, socioeconomic, and geographic data to cluster consumer households into distinct "microgeographic" segments. Whether these microunits meet the criteria for useful segmentation is determined by the user of the system. A national company might not attempt to define such small segments, but it could be useful for companies operating within one city or geographic area.

While we have given a couple of promotional implications indicating the degree to which marketers may segment the market, similar arguments hold true for the other marketing mix variables. However, another issue arises as to which segmentation variable is used first and which others are used as additional profile variables. The answer to this question is the art of marketing; the insight individuals see in the information to understand the market impeccably. With the addition of the next part, target audience options, the process becomes clearer.

TARGET AUDIENCE OPTIONS

We now turn our attention to the Rossiter and Percy (R&P) perspective of identifying and selecting the target audience for promotional communication.[31] R&P state that the primary and most logical factor for initially defining a target audience is the current behaviour of consumers. The importance of this factor is critical since it is the individual decision of each customer to purchase a brand that dictates a firm's total sales. Furthermore, this behaviour is a manifestation of a consumer's attitude towards the brand. Thus, in setting the direction for any IMC plan or component of an IMC plan (i.e., advertising), the manager must have a clear idea of the customer status of the target audience. Essentially, this decision hinges on a key question. Is the communication directed towards current customers or non-customers? As we discuss these ideas, we will use the term **focal brand** to indicate the brand that a manager is responsible for.

For customer groups, the manager has the opportunity to direct communications to **brand loyal customers** who regularly buy their firm's products. Recent marketing strategies (i.e., relationship marketing discussed in Chapter 1) and communication strategies regularly focus on a firm's current customers to ensure that customers maintain their current purchasing and consumption behaviour. As we noted in Chapter 1, it is generally very profitable to maintain a stable core of current customers. From a communication standpoint, it suggests that we do not have to advertise as often or we do not have to have as many sales promotions. However, we still see campaigns directed towards current loyal customers. For example, The Movie Network ran an eight-week television, radio, and outdoor campaign in early 2004 that was entirely devoted to its current subscribers base.[32]

To put this idea into another context we highlight the fact that one-third of all Canadians do not drink beer at all and that 74 percent of all Canadian beer drinkers claim they are loyal to their favourite beer.[33] This raises the question as to whether beer company ads should target their loyal customers and ensure future purchases by strengthening the loyalty with relevant messages, or target the remaining customers who claim they are not loyal to a specific beer.

Favourable brand switchers are a second customer group highlighted by R&P. These customers buy the focal brand but also buy other brands within a given relevant time period for the product category. For some product categories, consumers habitually purchase from a few favourites or those brands within their evoked set. These types of purchases may occur for many reasons. Consumers often face different purchase situations (e.g., own purchase versus gift). Sometimes certain moods influence brand choice. Whatever the motivation or external influencing factor, consumers adjust their purchases accordingly. While a manager would dearly love to have all customers be truly loyal, favourable brand switchers are an important source of purchases and are loyal to a degree. For these reasons, marketers would like to communicate directly with these consumers so that the focal brand remains in the evoked set. Alternatively, continued communication may influence stronger loyalty in the future.

Returning to our beer example, it turns out that Canadian beer drinkers may not be strongly aligned to one beer, as 30 to 40 percent will switch brands if a promotional offer coincides with an advertising message.[34] In reality, it appears many Canadian beer drinkers are loyal to their favourite beer to a degree, but they also will include it along with other brands, thereby categorizing themselves as favourable brand switchers.

Communication directed to non-customers are the focus of much advertising and promotion. R&P identify three key groups: **new category users**, **other brand switchers**, and **other brand loyals**. New category users, as the name implies, are those customers that are not purchasing within a product category. For example, after graduating from college or university many young adults begin to enter numerous categories partly because they have the income but also because they are at a stage of their life when new or latent needs emerge. Many advertisers attempt to court this target audience since many of these consumers are potentially ready to make a purchase. Marketers believe that steady communication may entice these customers to their brand when the time comes for these consumers to actually purchase.

Other brand switchers are like the previous group in that they purchase a few different brands within a category. However from a manager's perspective, they are fundamentally different, as they are not purchasing the focal brand. This is a challenging target audience, as the focal brand needs to break into consumer's evoked set and within the brands that these consumers are currently purchasing. This is a formidable task but still the focus of a considerable amount of advertising and promotion.

For example, Coffee Crisp recently started advertising on television after a 10-year hiatus. As the brand manager noted, "Because Coffee Crisp hasn't been advertised for so many years, we haven't brought in a new generation of Coffee Crisp consumers." Naturally, many young consumers were eating other brands of chocolate bars, so Coffee Crisp faced the challenge of appealing to these other brand switchers with a taste alternative. Research showed that Coffee Crisp "owned" the coffee association in the chocolate bar market and with a generation of young coffee drinkers that frequent cafes, the brand had a good opportunity to improve sales with its new ads. In fact, the room for growth is impressive as the famous bar that was once ranked number one or two in Canada, had fallen to number five with a lack of advertising for so many years.[35]

R&P's final group for target audience selection concerns other brand loyals. As this implies, these consumers purchase only one other brand and are completely loyal. It is difficult to say how much advertising and promotion expenditures are directed to these types of consumer across many industries. Logically, it would be very difficult to break the strongly held behaviour in which these consumers currently engage. Nevertheless, this is still a potential target that a firm may wish to establish communication objectives with and deliver some form of advertising and promotion.

After prioritizing the target audience in terms of customer status, R&P argue that other factors such as lifestyle or demographics are added on. For example, one clever ad by Tide detergent shows a child, sitting in a highchair, who has just finished eating a bowl of spaghetti. The child is naturally very messy, and the headline reads, "The day I switched to Tide." It appears that this message is targeted towards other brand switchers or other brand loyals who have a particular family-centred lifestyle. Thus, in order to truly define a target audience, the behavioural variable needs to be combined with other variables.

Another example from a broader perspective is warranted. Many companies target a younger demographic. We may read in the press that they are targeting an 18- to 24-year-old demographic. While this may be true, often an inherent behavioural variable is implied. Sometimes it is more like a new category user because young adults start to consume new categories of products as they mature. Other times, it is more like favourable brand switchers in an attempt to make these consumers exhibit stronger loyalty. The underlying point is that a communication message has to resonate with the target audience based on their current behaviour, whether they buy the brand or not, and some other key variable.

Thus far we have spoken of the target audience, which is the group an ad or a promotional campaign is directed towards, versus the target market, which is the segment the entire marketing mix is directed towards. The difference between target audience and target market can be seen in a recent campaign for Imodium Quick Dissolve tablets, a diarrhea remedy. The campaign tried to reach Canadian vacationers to foreign countries who do not want to be inconvenienced with this unfortunate gastronomic ailment. The secondary target audience was frequent business travellers who may have overlooked being prepared for their discomfort and who could not afford to miss important meetings. Combined together, it appears that Imodium is trying to reach new category users. Imodium used humour to cleverly point out the need for the product with a message, "Visit the country, not just its restrooms," and visuals of various facilities used throughout the world. Naturally, the product has other consumers, and how this product is positioned in the marketplace versus competing products is relevant, but clearly, Imodium has selected a certain part of the market to speak within this campaign that is a sub-set of the overall target market.[36]

SUMMARY

This chapter introduced you to the field of consumer behaviour and examined its relevance to promotional strategy. Consumer behaviour is best viewed as the process and activities that people engage in when searching for, selecting, purchasing, using, evaluating, and disposing of products and services to satisfy their needs and desires.

A five-stage model of the consumer decision-making process consists of need recognition, information search, alternative evaluation, purchase, and post-purchase evaluation. Internal psychological processes that influence the consumer decision-making process include motivation, perception, attitude formation and change, and integration processes. The decision process model views consumer behaviour primarily from a cognitive orientation.

KEY TERMS

consumer behaviour, *36*
need recognition, *37*
want, *38*
motives, *39*
hierarchy of needs, *39*
internal search, *40*
external search, *40*
perception, *41*
selective perception, *41*
sensation, *41*
selective exposure, *41*
selective attention, *43*
selective comprehension, *43*
selective retention, *43*

mnemonics, *43*
subliminal perception, *44*
evaluative criteria, *44*
functional consequences, *44*
psychosocial
    consequences, *45*
purchase intention, *45*
brand loyalty, *46*
integration processes, *46*
heuristics, *46*
affect referral decision rule,
    46
satisfaction, *47*
cognitive dissonance, *47*

routine problem solving, *48*
limited problem solving, *48*
extended problem solving, *48*
reference group, *49*
target market process, *52*
target market, *53*
target audience, *53*
geographic
    segmentation, *53*
demographic
    segmentation, *55*
psychographic
    segmentation, *55*
culture, *55*

subcultures, *57*
social class, *57*
benefit segmentation, *57*
behaviouristic
    segmentation, *58*
situations, *58*
focal brand, *59*
brand loyal customers, *59*
favourable brand
    switchers, *60*
new category users, *60*
other brand switchers, *60*
other brand loyals, *60*

62

DISCUSSION QUESTIONS

1. Explain how consumers might engage in each of the processes of selective perception described in the chapter. Provide examples.

2. A number of factors may lead to problem recognition among consumers. Discuss the various causes of problem recognition, and give an example of each.

3. Explain the concept of an *evoked set*. Why is this concept important to marketers? Give examples of an evoked set, and how marketers might attempt to influence consumers to gain consideration.

4. Jerry Olson and J. Paul Peter define two broad categories of evaluative consequences. Describe each of these and provide examples.

5. Describe how cultural differences might impact viewers' perceptions of advertisements. Provide examples.

6. In the text it was indicated that families may influence the consumer decision-making process. Describe how various family members may assume the different roles described in Figure 2–4. Also explain how these roles might change depending upon the product under consideration.

7. Some marketers contend that demographics is not really a basis for segmentation but is a descriptor of the segment. Discuss examples to support both positions.

8. A number of approaches to segmentation have been cited in the text. Provide examples of companies and/or brands that employ each in their promotional communications.

9. In what situations is the target audience and the target market the same? In what situations is the size of the target audience larger or smaller than the target market?

10. When defining a target audience for communications, why is it a good idea to use consumer behaviour with respect to your brand as the primary variable before using other variables such as demographics or lifestyle?

3

Communication Response Models

CHAPTER OBJECTIVES

- To understand the basic elements of the communication process and the role of communications in marketing.

- To examine various communication response models.

- To analyze the response processes of receivers of marketing communications, including alternative response hierarchies and their implications for promotional planning and strategy.

- To examine the nature of consumers' cognitive processing of marketing communications.

- To summarize an integrative communication response model from a theoretical and managerial perspective.

Jungle Adventure in Calgary

You've heard the expression: "It's a jungle out there" and in Calgary it really is true with the Calgary Zoological Society's new Destination Africa attraction, a wildlife and plant exhibit that includes conference facilities and educational programs. The TransAlta Rainforest and the African Savannah represents the main parts of the exhibit and each reflects an authentic African multi-sensory experience (e.g., sight, sound, smell, feeling). The zoo communicated the idea "A visit to Destination Africa is the next best thing to going to Africa." Naturally, it faced a tremendous communication challenge to lead consumers during a complete process of understanding the message from a unique source through various channels of communication in the face of competing messages from other forms of education or entertainment.

The zoo began "monkeying around" by placing monkey decals on billboards and doors of businesses and stores throughout the city. Nobody quite knew what was up with the monkeys until the official launch a short while later. Media relations explained that it was part of the new exhibit and that anyone could play the "Spot the Monkey" contest by logging on and identifying a monkey location. The prize was a trip to Toronto to see the musical *The Lion King*. Full communication occurred a few days later with TV, radio, newspaper ads, and billboards. Consumers could experience Africa at a fraction of the cost, time, and effort!

And what about success? Others recognized the quality of the message. Alberta Tourism presented the zoo with the Alta Award for Marketing Excellence. The Trans-Canada Advertising Agency Network recognized the annual pass campaign with a Best in Show award. The International Association of Amusement Parks and Attractions selected the zoo for Best of Show–Print Media and the Brass Ring Award for Best in Class–Outdoor Advertising! Attendance was up 83 percent from the previous year during the first three months, substantially higher than planned. Sales of various passes were also up substantially. It seems consumers really did understand the message and took the action the zoo expected.

Source: Larry R. Bannerman, "A Roaring Success," *Marketing Magazine*, March 8, 2004.

The function of all elements of the integrated marketing communications program is to communicate. An organization's IMC strategy is implemented through the various communications it sends to current or prospective customers as well as other relevant publics. Organizations send communications and messages in a variety of ways, such as through advertisements, brand names, logos and graphic systems, websites, press releases, package designs, promotions, and visual images. Thus, those involved in the planning and implementation of an IMC program need to understand the communications process. Marketers must understand how consumers will perceive and interpret their messages and how these reactions will shape consumers' responses to the company and/or its product or service.

This chapter reviews the fundamentals of communication and examines various perspectives and models regarding how consumers respond to advertising and promotional messages. Our goal is to demonstrate how valuable an understanding of the communication process can be in planning, implementing, and evaluating the marketing communications program.

To achieve this, the chapter takes an historical perspective to illustrate how academics and practitioners have evolved in their thinking to understand how advertising works. We begin with a basic model of communication to illustrate the complexity of the communication process. Next, we turn our attention to the response process of consumers that is explained by both traditional and alternative models. The more recent topic, cognitive processing of communications, is the third approach examined. Finally, we summarize with a framework that illustrates the current state of the art of advertising.

A Basic Model of Communication

Communication has been variously defined as the passing of information, the exchange of ideas, or the process of establishing a commonness or oneness of thought between a sender and a receiver.[1] These definitions suggest that for communication to occur, there must be some common thinking between two parties and information must be passed from one person to another (or from one group to another). As you will see in this chapter, establishing this commonality in thinking is not always as easy as it might seem; many attempts to communicate are unsuccessful.

The communication process is often very complex. Success depends on such factors as the nature of the message, the audience's interpretation of it, and the environment in which it is received. The receiver's perception of the source and the medium used to transmit the message may also affect the ability to communicate, as do many other factors. Words, pictures, sounds, and colours may have different meanings to different audiences, and people's perceptions and interpretations of them vary. Marketers must understand the meanings that words and symbols take on and how they influence consumers' interpretation of products and messages. This can be particularly challenging to companies marketing their products in foreign countries, as discussed in Global Perspective 3–1.

Over the years, a basic model of the various elements of the communication process has evolved, as shown in Figure 3–1.[2] Two elements represent the major participants in the communication process, the sender and the receiver. Another two are the major communication tools: message and channel. Four others are the major communication functions and processes: encoding, decoding, response, and feedback. The last element, noise, refers to any extraneous factors in the system that can interfere with the process and work against effective communication.

SOURCE/ENCODING

The sender, or **source**, of a communication is the person or organization that has information to share with another person or group of people. The source may be an

B.C. Hemlock Producers Branch Out

How can Canadian wood producers get its message of better quality hemlock understood by Japanese construction industry members? Enter Mai-no-umi, a 165-cm, 120-kg Japanese Sumo wrestler who has taken on and beaten much larger opponents and has achieved hero-like status as an underdog who performs. The Coastal Forest and Lumber Association (CFLA), an association designed to assist the marketers of many British Columbia wood producers, recently cast this unlikely spokesperson to demonstrate the strength of Canadian Tsuga, a new brand name for Hemlock grown in Canada and distributed in Japan.

B.C.'s share in Japan dropped from 38 percent in 1995 to 26 percent in 2002 due to competition from Europe and Russia. Since hemlock is one of B.C.'s most critical forest products and Japan is a critical foreign market beyond North America, it proved to be a communication challenge to change the negative perceptions of the strength of the wood. Research indicated that Japanese builders considered B.C. hemlock as weak and did not perceive any difference between it and American hemlock. In fact, Japanese referred to all hemlock as Bei Tsuga, Bei meaning American and Tsuga the Latin name for hemlock. With scientific research supporting that Canadian hemlock had the greatest bending stiffness and the greatest nail-holding grip compared to any other species, CFLA had to figure out a way to communicate this so that members of the Japanese construction industry would believe in the superior strength of the product.

Communication featured a new brand name, Canada Tsuga, and a red logo depicting a Japanese house with a red maple leaf placed between the two words of the brand name. Advertising in engineering and architectural journals reached the key decision makers, but the full effect and understanding of the message occurred with the Sumo spokesperson adopted in the past year. CFLA clearly linked the strength of a Sumo to the strength of the product. "We are saying, just as you have the strength of the Sumo and the technical attributes of his game, you have the strength of our Canada Tsuga and the technical attributes of our product."

As a result, Canada Tsuga became the preferred brand for post-and-beam construction in Japan with the Canadian market share climbing 2 percent in the past year. CFLA executives attributed most of this performance to the education and marketing campaigns implemented.

Source: Eve Lazarus, "Branching Out," *Marketing Magazine*, October 20, 2003.

individual (say, a salesperson or hired spokesperson, such as a celebrity, who appears in a company's advertisements) or a nonpersonal entity (such as the brand or organization itself). Because the receiver's perceptions of the source influence how the communication is received, marketers must be careful to select a communicator the receiver believes is knowledgeable and trustworthy or with whom the receiver can identify or relate in some manner.

FIGURE 3–1 ☐☐☐☐ A model of the communication process

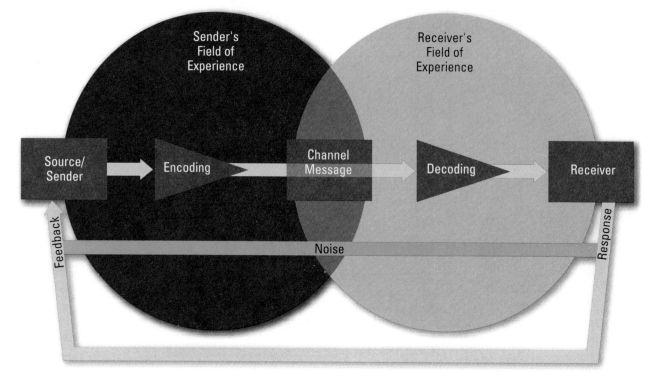

The communication process begins when the source selects words, symbols, pictures, and the like, to represent the message that will be delivered to the receiver(s). This process, known as **encoding**, involves putting thoughts, ideas, or information into a symbolic form. The sender's goal is to encode the message in such a way that it will be understood by the receiver. This means using words, signs, or symbols that are familiar to the target audience. Many symbols have universal meaning, such as the familiar circle with a line through it to denote no parking, no smoking, and so forth. Many companies also have highly recognizable symbols—such as McDonald's golden arches, Nike's swoosh, or the Coca-Cola trademark—that are known to consumers around the world.

MESSAGE

The encoding process leads to development of a **message** that contains the information or meaning the source hopes to convey. The message may be verbal or nonverbal, oral or written, or symbolic. Messages must be put into a transmittable form that is appropriate for the channel of communication being used. In advertising, this may range from simply writing some words or copy that will be read as a radio message to producing an expensive television commercial. For many products, it is not the actual words of the message that determine its communication effectiveness but rather the impression or image the ad creates. Notice how Spellbound perfume in Exhibit 3–1 uses only a picture to deliver its message. However, the product name and picture help communicate a feeling of attraction and fascination between the man and woman shown in the ad.

To better understand the symbolic meaning that might be conveyed in a communication, advertising and marketing researchers have begun focusing attention on **semiotics**, which studies the nature of meaning and asks how our reality—words, gestures, myths, signs, symbols, products/services, theories—acquire meaning.[3] Semiotics is important in marketing communications since products and brands acquire meaning through the way they are advertised and consumers use products and brands to express their social identities. Consumer researcher Michael Solomon notes: "From a semiotic perspective, every marketing message has three basic compo-

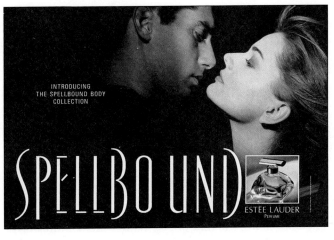

Exhibit 3–1
The image projected by an ad often communicates more than words

nents: an object, a sign or symbol, and an interpretant. The object is the product that is the focus of the message (e.g., Marlboro cigarettes). The sign is the sensory imagery that represents the intended meanings of the object (e.g., the Marlboro cowboy). The interpretant is the meaning derived (e.g., rugged, individualistic, American)."[4]

Marketers may use individuals trained in semiotics and related fields such as cultural anthropology to better understand the conscious and subconscious meanings the nonverbal signs and symbols in their ads transmit to consumers. For example, Levi Strauss & Co.'s agency, TBWA/Chiat/Day, hired a cultural anthropologist to help it better understand the image and meaning of clothing and fashion among young consumers. As part of the process, the agency research team recruited hip-looking young people in the streets of the East Village section of New York City, an area picked because they felt it is the best reflection of today's youth life. Those chosen were handed a piece of red cardboard and a white marker and asked to "write down something you believe in; something that's true about you or your world." The process provided the agency with insight into the teen market and was the impetus for an ad campaign featuring teenagers holding placards inscribed with their philosophical messages.[5] Exhibit 3–2 shows the thinking behind the various elements of one of the ads used in the campaign as explained by Sean Dee, the director of the Levi's brand.

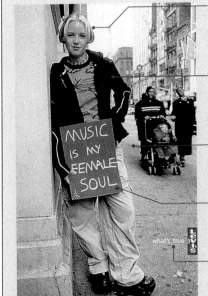

THE MODEL: A premed student at New York University
"We wanted people who are not defined by what they do but by what they are. We chose her because she looks like a Levi's type. She's young. She has her own point of view. She's sexy, but in an understated way. She's not trying too hard. She's definitely got something about her."

THE CLOTHES: Levi's cargo pants, her own T-shirt, zip-up sweatshirt, combat boots, and accessories
"It's important that she wore what she wanted. We're not trying to create a Levi's uniform; that wouldn't be very 'real.' We didn't use a professional stylist or a hairdresser; that wouldn't be real."

THE SETTING: Manhattan's East Village
"We picked New York City because it's the best reflection of today's youth life. We drove around the grittiest parts of the city. The people in the background [of this image] give it a street feel; it's obviously not staged in a studio."

THE STATEMENT: "Music is my female soul"
"It's hard for people to believe, but the [language] came totally from the kids; there was no prompting.... We liked the music theme [in this statement] because we do a lot to promote original music; we see music as being *the* voice of the young people."

THE TAG LINE: "What's true"
"The challenge with youth marketing these days is not to dictate to kids. This [line] is both a statement and a question. Is what we're saying true? Or is it a declaration? It works because it's provocative and ambiguous."

Exhibit 3–2
Semiotic analysis is used to describe the various elements of this Levi's ad

Some advertising and marketing people are skeptical about the value of semiotics. They question whether social scientists read too much into advertising messages and are overly intellectual in interpreting them. However, the meaning of an advertising message or other form of marketing communication lies not in the message but with the people who see and interpret it. Moreover, consumers behave on the basis of meanings they ascribe to marketplace stimuli. Thus, marketers must consider the meanings consumers attach to the various signs and symbols. Semiotics may be helpful in analyzing how various aspects of the marketing program—such as advertising messages, packaging, brand names, and even the nonverbal communications of salespeople (gestures, mode of dress)—are interpreted by receivers.[6]

CHANNEL

The **channel** is the method by which the communication travels from the source or sender to the receiver. At the broadest level, channels of communication are of two types, personal and nonpersonal. *Personal channels* of communication are direct interpersonal (face-to-face) contact with target individuals or groups. Salespeople serve as personal channels of communication when they deliver their sales message to a buyer or potential customer. Social channels of communication such as friends, neighbours, associates, co-workers, or family members are also personal channels. They often represent *word-of-mouth communication*, a powerful source of information for consumers.[7]

Nonpersonal channels of communication are those that carry a message without interpersonal contact between sender and receiver. Nonpersonal channels are generally referred to as the **mass media** or mass communications, since the message is sent to many individuals at one time. For example, a TV commercial broadcast on a prime-time show may be seen by 1 million households in a given evening. Nonpersonal channels of communication consist of two major types, print and broadcast. Print media include newspapers, magazines, direct mail, and billboards; broadcast media include radio and television.

RECEIVER/DECODING

The **receiver** is the person(s) with whom the sender shares thoughts or information. Generally, receivers are the consumers in the target market or audience who read, hear, and/or see the marketer's message. The target audience may consist of individuals, groups, niche markets, market segments, or a general public or mass audience (Figure 3–2). Marketers approach each of these audiences differently.

FIGURE 3–2
Levels of audience aggregation
☐☐☐☐☐

The target audience may consist of *individuals* who have specific needs and for whom the communication must be specifically tailored. This often requires person-to-person communication and is generally accomplished through personal selling. Other forms of communication, such as advertising, may be used to attract the audience's attention to the firm, but the detailed message is carried by a salesperson who can respond to the specific needs of the individual customer. Life insurance, financial services, and real estate are examples of products and services promoted this way.

A second level of audience aggregation is represented by the *group*. Marketers often must communicate with a group of people who make or influence the purchase decision. For example, marketers may have one message and medium directed towards parents who are the deciders and another towards children who are the influencers.

Marketers look for customers who have similar needs and wants and thus represent some type of market segment that can be reached with the same basic communication strategy. Very small, well-defined groups of customers are often referred to as *market niches*. They can usually be reached through personal selling efforts or highly targeted media such as direct mail. The next level of audience aggregation is *market segments*, broader classes of buyers who have similar needs and can be reached with similar messages using a variety of relevant media.

Marketers of most consumer products attempt to attract the attention of large numbers of present or potential customers (*mass markets*) through mass communication such as advertising or publicity. Mass communication is a one-way flow of information from the marketer to the consumer. Feedback on the audience's reactions to the message is generally indirect and difficult to measure. TV advertising, for example, lets the marketer send a message to many consumers at the same time. But this does not mean effective communication has occurred. This may be only one of several hundred messages the consumer is exposed to that day. There is no guarantee the information will be attended to, processed, comprehended, or stored in memory for later retrieval. Even if the advertising message is processed, it may not interest consumers or may be misinterpreted by them. Studies by Jacob Jacoby and Wayne D. Hoyer have shown that nearly 20 percent of all print ads and even more TV commercials are miscomprehended by readers.[8]

Decoding is the process of transforming the sender's message back into thought. This process is heavily influenced by the receiver's frame of reference or **field of experience**, which refers to the experiences, perceptions, attitudes, and values he or she brings to the communication situation. For effective communication to occur, the message decoding process of the receiver must match the encoding of the sender. Simply put, this means the receiver understands and correctly interprets what the source is trying to communicate. As Figure 3–1 showed, the source and the receiver each have a frame of reference (the circle around each) that they bring to the communication situation. Effective communication is more likely when there is some *common ground* between the two parties. (This is represented by the overlapping of the two circles.) The more knowledge the sender has about the receivers, the better the sender can understand their needs, empathize with them, and communicate effectively. Advertisers spend millions of dollars every year to understand the frames of reference of the target audiences who receive their messages. They also spend much time and money pretesting messages to make sure consumers understand and decode them in the manner the advertiser intended.

While this notion of common ground between sender and receiver may sound basic, it often causes great difficulty in the advertising communications process. Marketing and advertising people often have very different fields of experience from the consumers who constitute the mass markets with whom they must communicate. Most advertising and marketing people are university-educated and work and/or reside in large urban areas such as Toronto or Montreal. Yet they are attempting to develop commercials that will effectively communicate with millions of consumers who have never attended university, work in blue-collar occupations, and live in rural areas or small towns. Another factor that can lead to problems in establishing common ground between senders and receivers is age.

NOISE

Throughout the communication process, the message is subject to extraneous factors that can distort or interfere with its reception. This unplanned distortion or interference is known as **noise**. Errors or problems that occur in the encoding of the message, distortion in a radio or television signal, or distractions at the point of reception are examples of noise. Perhaps the foremost distraction is advertising clutter whereby the receiver is confronted with many competing messages.

Noise may also occur because the fields of experience of the sender and receiver don't overlap. Lack of common ground may result in improper encoding of the message—using a sign, symbol, or words that are unfamiliar or have different meaning to the receiver. The more common ground there is between the sender and the receiver, the less likely it is this type of noise will occur.

RESPONSE/FEEDBACK

The receiver's set of reactions after seeing, hearing, or reading the message is known as a **response**. Receivers' responses can range from nonobservable actions such as storing information in memory to immediate action such as dialing a toll-free number to order a product advertised on television. Marketers are very interested in **feedback**, that part of the receiver's response that is communicated back to the sender. Feedback, which may take a variety of forms, closes the loop in the communications flow and lets the sender monitor how the intended message is being decoded and received.

Because advertisers are not in direct contact with the customers, they must use other means to determine how their messages have been received. While the ultimate form of feedback occurs through sales, it is often hard to show a direct relationship between advertising and purchase behaviour. So marketers use other methods to obtain feedback, among them customer inquiries, store visits, coupon redemptions, and reply cards. Research-based feedback analyzes readership and recall of ads, message comprehension, attitude change, and other forms of response. With this information, the advertiser can determine reasons for success or failure in the communication process and make adjustments.

Successful communication is accomplished when the marketer selects an appropriate source, develops an effective message or appeal that is encoded properly, and then selects the channels or media that will best reach the target audience so that the message can be effectively decoded and delivered. Since these decisions must consider how the target audience will respond to the promotional message, the remainder of this chapter examines the process by which consumers respond to advertising and other forms of marketing communications.

THE RESPONSE PROCESS

Perhaps the most important aspect of developing effective communication programs involves understanding the *response process* the receiver may go through in moving toward a specific behaviour (like purchasing a product) and how the promotional efforts of the marketer influence consumer responses. To explain the response process we now review two types of response hierarchy models—traditional and alternative.

TRADITIONAL RESPONSE HIERARCHY MODELS

A number of models have been developed to depict the stages a consumer may pass through in moving from a state of not being aware of a company, product, or brand to actual purchase behaviour. Figure 3–3 shows four of the best-known response hierarchy models. While these response models may appear similar, they were developed for different reasons.

The **AIDA model** was developed to represent the stages a salesperson must take a customer through in the personal selling process.[9] This model depicts the buyer as passing successively through attention, interest, desire, and action. The salesperson must first get the customer's attention and then arouse some interest in the company's product or service. Strong levels of interest should create desire to own or use the product. The action stage in the AIDA model involves getting the customer to make a purchase commitment and closing the sale. To the marketer, this is the most important stage in the selling process, but it can also be the most difficult. Companies train their sales reps in closing techniques to help them complete the selling process.

Perhaps the best known of these response hierarchies is the model developed by Robert Lavidge and Gary Steiner as a paradigm for setting and measuring advertising objectives.[10] Their **hierarchy of effects model** shows the process by which advertising works; it assumes a consumer passes through a series of steps in sequential order from initial awareness of a product or service to actual purchase. A basic premise of this model is that advertising effects occur over a period of time. Advertising communication may not lead to immediate behavioural response or purchase; rather, a series of effects must occur, with each step fulfilled before the consumer can move to the next stage in the hierarchy. As we will see in Chapter 4, the hierarchy of effects model has become the foundation for objective setting and measurement of advertising effects in many companies.

The **innovation adoption model** evolved from work on the diffusion of innovations.[11] This model represents the stages a consumer passes through in adopting a

FIGURE 3–3 □□□□ Models of the response process

Stages	Models			
	AIDA model[a]	Hierarchy of effects model[b]	Innovation adoption model[c]	Information processing model[d]
Cognitive stage	Attention	Awareness	Awareness	Presentation
				Attention
		Knowledge		Comprehension
Affective stage	Interest	Liking	Interest	Yeilding
		Preference		
	Desire	Conviction	Evaluation	Retention
Behavioural stage			Trial	
	Action	Purchase	Adoption	Behaviour

Exhibit 3–3
Sampling or demonstration programs encourage trial of new products such as disposable contact lenses

new product or service. Like the other models, it says potential adopters must be moved through a series of steps before taking some action (in this case, deciding to adopt a new product). The steps preceding adoption are awareness, interest, evaluation, and trial. The challenge facing companies introducing new products is to create awareness and interest among consumers and then get them to evaluate the product favourably. The best way to evaluate a new product is through actual use so that performance can be judged. Marketers often encourage trial by using demonstration or sampling programs or allowing consumers to use a product with minimal commitment (Exhibit 3–3). After trial, consumers either adopt the product or reject it.

The final hierarchy model shown in Figure 3–3 is the **information processing model** of advertising effects, developed by William McGuire.[12] This model assumes the receiver in a persuasive communication situation like advertising is an information processor or problem solver. McGuire suggests the series of steps a receiver goes through in being persuaded constitutes a response hierarchy. The stages of this model are similar to the hierarchy of effects sequence; attention and comprehension are similar to awareness and knowledge, and yielding is synonymous with liking. McGuire's model includes a stage not found in the other models: retention, or the receiver's ability to retain that portion of the comprehended information that he or she accepts as valid or relevant. This stage is important since most promotional campaigns are designed not to motivate consumers to take immediate action but rather to provide information they will use later when making a purchase decision.

Each stage of the response hierarchy is a dependent variable that must be attained and that may serve as an objective of the communication process. As shown in Figure 3–4, each stage can be measured, providing the advertiser with feedback regarding the effectiveness of various strategies designed to move the consumer to purchase. We review issues of measuring advertising effectiveness in Chapter 8 after discussing all decisions relating to an advertising campaign. The information processing model may be an effective framework for planning and evaluating the effects of a promotional campaign.

IMPLICATIONS OF THE TRADITIONAL HIERARCHY MODELS

The hierarchy models of communication response are useful to promotional planners from several perspectives. First, they delineate the series of steps potential purchasers must be taken through to move them from unawareness of a product or service to readiness to purchase it. Second, potential buyers may be at different stages in the hierarchy, so the advertiser will face different sets of communication problems. For example, a company introducing an innovative product like Zenith's high-definition television (HDTV) may need to devote considerable effort to making people aware of the product, how it works, and its benefits (Exhibit 3–4). Marketers of a mature brand that enjoys customer loyalty may need only supportive or reminder advertising to reinforce positive perceptions and maintain the awareness level for the brand.

Effectiveness tests   **Steps in persuasion process**

Effectiveness tests	Steps in persuasion process
Circulation	Exposure
Listener, reader, viewer recognition	Attention
Recall, checklists	Comprehension
Brand attitudes, purchase intent	Message acceptance/ yielding
Recall over time	Retention
Inventory, point-of-purchase consumer panel	Purchase behaviour

FIGURE 3–4
Methods of obtaining feedback in the response hierarchy
☐ ☐ ☐ ☐ ☐

Exhibit 3–4
Advertising for innovative new products such as HDTV must make consumers aware of their features and benefits

75

Third, the hierarchy models can also be useful as intermediate measures of communication effectiveness that could guide future communication decisions. The marketer needs to know where audience members are on the response hierarchy. For example, research may reveal that one target segment has low awareness of the advertiser's brand, whereas another is aware of the brand and its various attributes but has a low level of liking or brand preference.

For the first segment of the market, the communication task involves increasing the awareness level for the brand. The number of ads may be increased, or a product sampling program may be used. For the second segment, where awareness is already high but liking and preference are low, the advertiser must determine the reason for the negative feelings and then attempt to address this problem in future advertising.

As you saw in Figure 3–3, the four models presented all view the response process as consisting of movement through a sequence of three basic stages. The *cognitive stage* represents what the receiver knows or perceives about the particular product or brand. This stage includes awareness that the brand exists and knowledge, information, or comprehension about its attributes, characteristics, or benefits. The *affective stage* refers to the receiver's feelings or affect level (like or dislike) for the particular brand. This stage also includes stronger levels of affect such as desire, preference, or conviction. The *conative* or

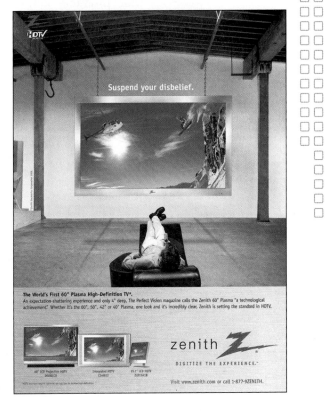

Suspend your disbelief.

The World's First 60" Plasma High-Definition TV®.
An expectation-shattering experience and only 4" deep, The Perfect Vision magazine calls the Zenith 60" Plasma "a technological achievement." Whether it's the 60", 50", 42" or 40" Plasma, one look and it's incredibly clear, Zenith is setting the standard in HDTV.

zenith
DIGITIZE THE EXPERIENCE.™

Visit www.zenith.com or call 1-877-9ZENITH.

behavioural stage refers to the consumer's action toward the brand: trial, purchase, adoption, or rejection.

All four models assume a similar ordering of these three stages. Cognitive development precedes affective reactions, which precede behaviour. One might assume that consumers become aware of and knowledgeable about a brand, develop feelings toward it, form a desire or preference, and then make a purchase. While this logical progression is often accurate, the response sequence does not always operate this way. Over the past two decades, considerable research in marketing, social psychology, and communications has led to questioning of the traditional cognitive → affective → behavioural sequence of response. Several other configurations of the response hierarchy have been theorized.

ALTERNATIVE RESPONSE HIERARCHIES

Michael Ray has developed a model of information processing that identifies three alternative orderings of the three stages based on perceived product differentiation and product involvement.[13] These alternative response hierarchies are the standard learning, dissonance/attribution, and low-involvement models (Figure 3–5).

The Standard Learning Hierarchy In many purchase situations, the consumer will go through the response process in the sequence depicted by the traditional communication models. Ray terms this a **standard learning model**, which consists of a learn → feel → do sequence. Information and knowledge acquired or *learned* about the various brands are the basis for developing affect, or *feelings*, that guide what the consumer will *do* (e.g., actual trial or purchase). In this hierarchy, the consumer is viewed as an active participant in the communication process who gathers information through active learning.

Ray suggests the standard learning hierarchy is likely when the consumer is highly involved in the purchase process and there is much differentiation among competing brands. High-involvement purchase decisions such as those for industrial products and services and consumer durables like personal computers, printers, cameras, appliances, and cars are areas where a standard learning hierarchy response process is likely. Ads for products and services in these areas are usually very detailed and provide customers with information that can be used to evaluate brands and help them make a purchase decision (Exhibit 3–5).

FIGURE 3–5

Alternative response hierarchies: the three-orders model of information processing

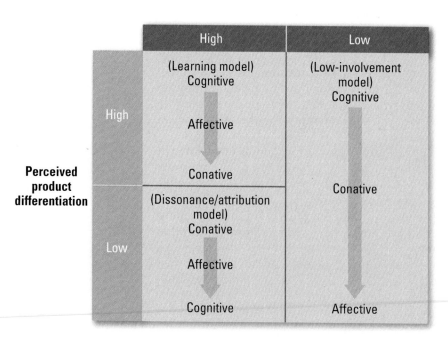

The Dissonance/Attribution Hierarchy A second response hierarchy proposed by Ray involves situations where consumers first behave, then develop attitudes or feelings as a result of that behaviour, and then learn or process information that supports the behaviour. This **dissonance/attribution model**, or do → feel → learn, occurs in situations where consumers must choose between two alternatives that are similar in quality but are complex and may have hidden or unknown attributes. The consumer may purchase the product on the basis of a recommendation by some nonmedia source and then attempt to support the decision by developing a positive attitude toward the brand and perhaps even developing negative feelings toward the rejected alternative(s). This reduces any *postpurchase dissonance* or anxiety the consumer may experience resulting from doubt over the purchase (as discussed in Chapter 2). Dissonance reduction involves *selective learning*, whereby the consumer seeks information that supports the choice made and avoids information that would raise doubts about the decision.

According to this model, marketers need to recognize that in some situations, attitudes develop *after* purchase, as does learning from the mass media. Ray suggests that in these situations the main effect of the mass media is not the promotion of original choice behaviour and attitude change but rather the reduction of dissonance by reinforcing the wisdom of the purchase or providing supportive information. For example, the ad shown in Exhibit 3–6 reinforces consumers' decisions to purchase Michelin tires by showing the number of awards the brand has received for customer satisfaction.

As with the standard learning model, this response hierarchy is likely to occur when the consumer is involved in the purchase situation; it is particularly relevant for postpurchase situations. For example, a consumer may purchase tires recommended by a friend and then develop a favourable attitude toward the company and pay close attention to its ads to reduce dissonance.

Some marketers resist this view of the response hierarchy because they can't accept the notion that the mass media have no effect on the consumer's initial purchase decision. But the model doesn't claim the mass media have no effect—just that their major impact occurs after the purchase has been made. Marketing communications planners must be aware of the need for advertising and promotion efforts not just to encourage brand selection but to reinforce choices and ensure that a purchase pattern will continue.

The Low-Involvement Hierarchy Perhaps the most intriguing of the three response hierarchies proposed by Ray is the **low-involvement hierarchy**, in which the receiver is viewed as passing from cognition to behaviour to attitude change. This learn → do → feel sequence is thought to characterize situations of low consumer involvement in the purchase process. Ray suggests this hierarchy tends to occur when involvement in the purchase decision is low, there are minimal differences among brand alternatives, and mass-media (especially broadcast) advertising is important.

The notion of a low-involvement hierarchy is based in large part on Herbert Krugman's theory explaining the effects of television advertising.[14] Krugman wanted to find out why TV advertising produced a strong effect on brand awareness and recall but little change in consumers' attitudes toward the product. He hypothesized that TV is basically a low-involvement medium and the viewer's perceptual defences are reduced or

Exhibit 3–5
Ads for high-involvement products provide consumers with information to help them evaluate brands

Exhibit 3–6
This ad reinforces the wisdom of the decision to purchase Michelin tires

even absent during commercials. In a low-involvement situation, the consumer does not compare the message with previously acquired beliefs, needs, or past experiences. The commercial results in subtle changes in the consumer's knowledge structure, particularly with repeated exposure. This change in the consumer's knowledge does not result in attitude change but is related to learning something about the advertised brand, such as a brand name, ad theme, or slogan. According to Krugman, when the consumer enters a purchase situation, this information may be sufficient to trigger a purchase. The consumer will then form an attitude toward the purchased brand as a result of experience with it. Thus, in the low-involvement situation the response sequence is as follows:

Message exposure under low involvement →

Shift in cognitive structure → Purchase →

Positive or negative experience → Attitude formation

In the low-involvement hierarchy, the consumer engages in passive learning and random information catching rather than active information seeking. The advertiser must recognize that a passive, uninterested consumer may focus more on nonmessage elements such as music, characters, symbols, and slogans or jingles than actual message content. The advertiser might capitalize on this situation by developing a catchy jingle that is stored in the consumer's mind without any active cognitive processing and becomes salient when he or she enters the actual purchase situation.

Advertisers of low-involvement products also repeat simple product claims such as a key copy point or distinctive product benefit. A study by Scott Hawkins and Stephen Hoch found that under low-involvement conditions, repetition of simple product claims increased consumers' memory of and belief in those claims.[15] They concluded that advertisers of low-involvement products might find it more profitable to pursue a heavy repetition strategy than to reach larger audiences with lengthy, more detailed messages. For example, Heinz has dominated the ketchup market for over 20 years by repeatedly telling consumers that its brand is the thickest and richest. Heinz has used a variety of advertising campaigns over the years, but they all repeat the same basic theme and focus on the consistent quality of the brand (Exhibit 3–7).

As the preceding discussion shows, consumer behaviour and advertising researchers have extensively studied the concept of involvement.[16] Involvement is viewed as a variable that can help explain how consumers process advertising information and how this information might affect message recipients. One problem that has plagued the study of involvement has been agreeing on how to define and measure it. Advertising managers must be able to determine targeted consumers' involvement levels with their products.

Some of the problems in conceptualizing and measuring involvement have been addressed in extensive review by Judith Zaichkowsky. She has noted that although there is no single precise definition of involvement, there is an underlying theme focusing on *personal relevance.*[17] Zaichkowsky developed an involvement construct that includes three antecedents, or variables proposed to precede involvement (Figure 3–6). The first is traits of the person (value system, unique experiences, needs). The second factor is characteristics of the stimulus, or differences in type of media (TV, radio, or print), content of the communication, or product class variations. The third antecedent is situational factors, such as whether one is or is not in the market for a particular product.

The various antecedents can influence the consumer's level of involvement in several ways, including the way the consumer responds to the advertising, the products being advertised, and the actual purchase decision. This involvement theory shows that a variety of outcomes or behaviours can result from involvement with advertising, products, or purchase decisions.

Exhibit 3–7
Advertising promoting taste quality has helped Heinz dominate the ketchup market

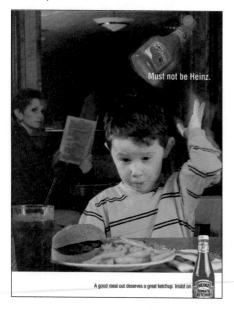

Must not be Heinz.

A good meal out deserves a great ketchup. Insist on HEINZ TOMATO KETCHUP

FIGURE 3–6 □ □ □ □   Involvement construct

INVOLVEMENT = f (Person, Situation, Object)
The level of involvement may be influenced by one or more of these factors.
Interactions among person, situation, and object factors are likely to occur.

IMPLICATIONS OF THE ALTERNATIVE RESPONSE MODELS

Advertising and consumer researchers recognize that not all response sequences and behaviours are explained adequately by either the traditional or the alternative response hierarchies. Advertising is just one source of information consumers use in forming attitudes and/or making purchase decisions. Consumers are likely to integrate information from advertising, other sources, and direct experience in forming judgments about a brand. For example, in a recent study Robert Smith found that advertising can lessen the negative effects of an unfavourable trial experience on brand evaluations when the ad is processed before the trial. However, when a negative trial experience precedes exposure to an ad, cognitive evaluations of the ad are more negative. More recent research has also shown that advertising can affect consumers' objective sensory interpretation of their experiences with a brand and what they remember about it.[18]

The various response models offer an interesting perspective on the ways consumers respond to advertising and other forms of marketing communications. They also provide insight into promotional strategies marketers might pursue in different situations. A review of these alternative models of the response process shows that the traditional standard learning model does not always apply. The notion of a highly involved consumer who engages in active information processing and learning and acts on the basis of higher-order beliefs and a well-formed attitude may be inappropriate for some types of purchases. Sometimes consumers make a purchase decision on the basis of general awareness resulting from repetitive exposure to advertising, and attitude development occurs after the purchase, if at all. The role of advertising and other forms of promotion may be to induce trial, so consumers can develop brand preferences primarily on the basis of their direct experience with the product.

From a promotional planning perspective, it is important that marketers examine the communication situation for their product or service and determine which type of response process is most likely to occur. They should analyze involvement levels and product/service differentiation as well as consumers' use of various information sources and their levels of experience with the product or service. Once the manager has determined which response sequence is most likely to operate, the integrated marketing communications program can be designed to influence the response process in favour of the company's product or service.

COGNITIVE PROCESSING OF COMMUNICATIONS

The hierarchical response models were for many years the primary focus of approaches for studying the receivers' responses to marketing communications. Attention centred on identifying relationships between specific controllable variables (such as source and message factors) and outcome or response variables (such as attention, comprehension, attitudes, and purchase intentions). This approach has been criticized on a number of fronts, including its black-box nature, since it can't explain what is causing these reactions.[19] In response to these concerns, researchers began trying to understand the nature of cognitive reactions to persuasive messages. Several approaches have been developed to examine the nature of consumers' cognitive processing of advertising messages.

THE COGNITIVE RESPONSE APPROACH

One of the most widely used methods for examining consumers' cognitive processing of advertising messages is assessment of their **cognitive responses**, the thoughts that occur to them while reading, viewing, and/or hearing a communication.[20] These thoughts are generally measured by having consumers write down or verbally report their reactions to a message. The assumption is that these thoughts reflect the recipient's cognitive processes or reactions and help shape ultimate acceptance or rejection of the message.

The cognitive response approach has been widely used in research by both academicians and advertising practitioners. Its focus has been to determine the types of responses evoked by an advertising message and how these responses relate to attitudes toward the ad, brand attitudes, and purchase intentions. Figure 3–7 depicts

FIGURE 3–7 ☐ ☐ ☐ ☐   A model of cognitive response

the three basic categories of cognitive responses researchers have identified—product/message, source-oriented, and ad execution thoughts—and how they may relate to attitudes and intentions.

Product/Message Thoughts   The first category of thoughts comprises those directed at the product or service and/or the claims being made in the communication. Much attention has focused on two particular types of responses, counterarguments and support arguments.

Counterarguments are thoughts the recipient has that are opposed to the position taken in the message. For example, consider the ad for Ultra Tide shown in Exhibit 3–8. A consumer may express disbelief or disapproval of a claim made in an ad. ("I don't believe that any detergent could get that stain out!") Other consumers who see this ad may generate **support arguments**, or thoughts that affirm the claims made in the message. ("Ultra Tide looks like a really good product—I think I'll try it.")

The likelihood of counterarguing is greater when the message makes claims that oppose the receiver's beliefs. For example, a consumer viewing a commercial that attacks a favourite brand is likely to engage in counterarguing. Counterarguments relate negatively to message acceptance; the more the receiver counterargues, the less likely he or she is to accept the position advocated in the message.[21] Support arguments, on the other hand, relate positively to message acceptance. Thus, the marketer should develop ads or other promotional messages that minimize counterarguing and encourage support arguments.

Source-Oriented Thoughts   A second category of cognitive responses is directed at the source of the communication. One of the most important types of responses in this category is **source derogations**, or negative thoughts about the spokesperson or organization making the claims. Such thoughts generally lead to a reduction in message acceptance. If consumers find a particular spokesperson annoying or untrustworthy, they are less likely to accept what this source has to say.

Of course, source-related thoughts are not always negative. Receivers who react favourably to the source generate favourable thoughts, or **source bolsters**. As you would expect, most advertisers attempt to hire spokespeople their target audience likes so as to carry this effect over to the message. Considerations involved in choosing an appropriate source or spokesperson will be discussed in Chapter 6.

Ad Execution Thoughts   The third category of cognitive responses shown in Figure 3–7 consists of the individual's thoughts about the ad itself. Many of the thoughts receivers have when reading or viewing an ad do not concern the product and/or message claims directly. Rather, they are affective reactions representing the consumer's feelings toward the ad. These thoughts may include reactions to ad execution factors such as the creativity of the ad, the quality of the visual effects, colours, and voice tones. **Ad execution-related thoughts** can be either favourable or unfavourable. They are important because of their effect on attitudes toward the advertisement as well as the brand.

In recent years, much attention has focused on consumers' affective reactions to ads, especially TV commercials.[22] **Attitude toward the ad** (A → ad) represents the receivers' feelings of favourability or unfavourability toward the ad. Advertisers are interested in consumers' reactions to the ad because they know that affective reactions are an important determinant of advertising effectiveness, since these reactions may be transferred to the brand itself or directly influence purchase intentions. One study found that people who enjoy a commercial are twice as likely as those who are neutral toward it to be convinced that the brand is the best.[23]

Consumers' feelings about the ad may be just as important as their attitudes toward the brand (if not more so) in determining an ad's effectiveness.[24] The

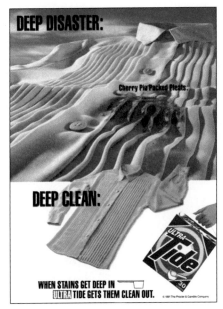

Exhibit 3–8
Consumers often generate support arguments in response to ads for quality products

importance of affective reactions and feelings generated by the ad depend on several factors, among them the nature of the ad and the type of processing engaged in by the receiver.[25] Many advertisers now use emotional ads designed to evoke feelings and affective reactions as the basis of their creative strategy. The success of this strategy depends in part on the consumers' involvement with the brand and their likelihood of attending to and processing the message. Global Perspective 3–2 shows how feelings were an important part of Whirlpool's international campaign.

THE ELABORATION LIKELIHOOD MODEL

Differences in the ways consumers process and respond to persuasive messages are addressed in the simplified **elaboration likelihood model (ELM)** of persuasion, shown in Figure 3–8.[26] The ELM was devised by Richard Petty and John Cacioppo to explain the process by which persuasive communications (such as ads) lead to persuasion by influencing *attitudes*. According to this model, the attitude formation or change process depends on the amount and nature of *elaboration*, or processing, of relevant information that occurs in response to a persuasive message. High elaboration means the receiver engages in careful consideration, thinking, and evaluation of the information or arguments contained in the message. Low elaboration occurs when the receiver does not engage in active information processing or thinking but rather makes inferences about the position being advocated in the message on the basis of simple positive or negative cues.

The ELM shows that elaboration likelihood is a function of two elements, motivation and ability to process the message. *Motivation* to process the message depends on such factors as involvement, personal relevance, and individuals' needs and arousal levels. *Ability* depends on the individual's knowledge, intellectual capacity, and opportunity to process the message. For example, an individual viewing a humourous commercial or one containing an attractive model may be distracted from processing the information about the product.

According to the ELM, there are two basic routes to persuasion or attitude change. Under the **central route to persuasion**, the receiver is viewed as a very active, involved participant in the communication process whose ability and motivation to attend, comprehend, and evaluate messages are high. When central processing of an

FIGURE 3–8
Simplified elaboration likelihood model of persuasion
☐ ☐ ☐ ☐ ☐

Whirlpool Connects with 21st-Century Women

Household appliances are a product category where the advertising has traditionally been pretty bland, with most ads appealing to consumers' rational, functional motives. Television commercials generally would show the capacity of a refrigerator, explain how a washer or dryer works, or tout their reliability; while print ads would feature a shot of the appliance and give a detailed description of how it functions. For example, among the most memorable appliance ads are those from the campaign featuring the Maytag repairman who would wait in vain for a repair call. The campaign was created more than 30 years ago, and the lonely Maytag repairman is still waiting for the phone to ring.

In recent years appliance companies have been focusing on form as well as function and have been touting the design of their products as much as their functionality in their ads. However, one company that has taken a very unique approach to its advertising is Whirlpool, whose "Just Imagine" campaign features Household Goddesses —five ethereal female figures who use water, fire, or air to take control of their environments while promoting various Whirlpool appliances. The campaign is designed to connect with the modern-day "supermoms," working women between the ages of 25 and 54 with children. These women's homes are very important to them; the women are challenged, yet capable of handling a very demanding and busy lifestyle, and they want control of their lives and acknowledgment for all they do and for being very capable. They set new standards and appreciate beauty in their environments. They do not give appliances a great deal of thought until there is a moment of need, such as a broken appliance or a home renovation. Innovation, style, and time saving are all important factors to these women.

The idea for the "Just Imagine" campaign originated in the late 90s in Europe, where Whirlpool was eager to build its brand name and capture a larger share of the appliance market, having acquired the appliance division of the Dutch firm Philips Electronics. The campaign connected well with women in Europe, so in 1999 Whirlpool and its French agency Publicis decided to adapt it to women in the North American market. However, before bringing out the campaign, Whirlpool conducted more than 20 focus groups with women to test their reaction to the goddesses.

According to Whirlpool's manager of brand communication, the ads with the goddesses celebrate the growing power of women in the 21st century. They are aimed at striking an emotional cord with modern-day women, showing them as strong females in control of their environments who can be made even stronger through the latest Whirlpool technology. The mythical figures in the ads include a blue-skinned ice diva who represents the Whirlpool Conquest refrigerator, a silken-robed water nymph who appears in commercials for the Catalyst washer, a heat maiden in cascading red robes who promotes the Senson and Duet dryers, a fire-breathing goddess who helps sell the Speed Cook range, and a flying blonde clean-air angel who extols the virtues of Whirlpool's dehumidifiers and air-conditioners. The goddesses promote many of the innovative features found on Whirlpool appliances, such as a dryer that gently dries clothes in the time it takes to wash them, a washing machine that does not require pretreating because concentrated water and detergent spray through clothes before they are washed, and a refrigerator with more space inside.

The goal of the "Just Imagine" campaign is to use the stylish and dramatic commercials to get consumers to take notice of Whirlpool appliances and make them feel the brand is in tune with their changing needs and values and thus has something more to offer than competing brands. In addition to being in the television commercials, the goddesses appear in print ads, on the Whirlpool website, on company brochures, on billboards on the side of the company's trucks, and in point-of-purchase displays for local retailers. The campaign is the biggest in the appliance maker's history. To many women, using a washing machine or dryer means nothing more than cleaning clothes. However, Whirlpool hopes this campaign will help them feel they are taking control of their lives when they use its appliances.

Sources: "Whirlpool's Worship-Worthy Goddess," *Brand Marketing*, June 2000, p. 33; Katheryn Dranhold, "Whirlpool Conjures Up Appliance Divas," *The Wall Street Journal*, April 27, 2000, p. B14.

Exhibit 3–9
This public relations photo contains peripheral cues, most notably a celebrity endorser

advertising message occurs, the consumer pays close attention to message content and scrutinizes the message arguments. A high level of cognitive response activity or processing occurs, and the ad's ability to persuade the receiver depends primarily on the receiver's evaluation of the quality of the arguments presented. Predominantly favourable cognitive responses (support arguments and source bolsters) lead to favourable changes in cognitive structure, which lead to positive attitude change, or persuasion.

Conversely, if the cognitive processing is predominantly unfavourable and results in counterarguments and/or source derogations, the changes in cognitive structure are unfavourable and *boomerang*, or result in negative attitude change. Attitude change that occurs through central processing is relatively enduring and should resist subsequent efforts to change it.

Under the **peripheral route to persuasion**, the receiver is viewed as lacking the motivation or ability to process information and is not likely to engage in detailed cognitive processing. Rather than evaluating the information presented in the message, the receiver relies on peripheral cues that may be incidental to the main arguments. The receiver's reaction to the message depends on how he or she evaluates these peripheral cues.

The consumer may use several types of peripheral cues or cognitive shortcuts rather than carefully evaluating the message arguments presented in an advertisement.[27] Favourable attitudes may be formed if the endorser in the ad is viewed as an expert or is attractive and/or likable or if the consumer likes certain executional aspects of the ad such as the way it is made, the music, or the imagery. Notice how the public relations photo in Exhibit 3–9 contains several positive peripheral cues, including a popular celebrity endorser and excellent visual imagery. These cues might help consumers form a positive attitude toward the brand even if they do not process the message portion of the ad.

Peripheral cues can also lead to rejection of a message. For example, ads that advocate extreme positions, use endorsers who are not well liked or have credibility problems, or are not executed well (such as low-budget ads for local retailers) may be rejected without any consideration of their information or message arguments. As shown in Figure 3–8, the ELM views attitudes resulting from peripheral processing as temporary. So favourable attitudes must be maintained by continual exposure to the peripheral cues, such as through repetitive advertising.

One reason for explaining how the peripheral route to persuasion works lies in the idea of **classical conditioning**. Classical conditioning assumes that learning is an *associative process* with an already existing relationship between a stimulus and a response. This process is transferred to a **conditioned stimulus** that elicits a **conditioned response** resembling the original unconditioned reaction. Two factors are important for learning to occur through the associative process. The first is contiguity, which means the unconditioned stimulus and conditioned stimulus must be close in time and space. The other important principle is *repetition*, or the frequency of the association. The more often the unconditioned and conditioned stimuli occur together, the stronger the association between them will be.

Learning through classical conditioning plays an important role in marketing. Buyers can be conditioned to form favourable impressions and images of various brands through the associative process. Advertisers strive to associate their products and services with perceptions, images, and emotions known to evoke positive reactions from consumers. Many products are promoted through image advertising, in which the brand is shown with an unconditioned stimulus that elicits pleasant feelings. When the brand is presented simultaneously with this unconditioned stimulus, the brand itself becomes a conditioned stimulus that elicits the

Exhibit 3–10
Lancome associates
itself with moisture

same favourable response. The ad for Lancome in Exhibit 3–10 shows an application of this strategy. Notice how this ad associates Lancome's moisture with the freshness of a rose.

Classical conditioning can also associate a product or service with a favourable emotional state. A study by Gerald Gorn used this approach to examine how background music in ads influences product choice.[28] He found that subjects were more likely to choose a product when it was presented against a background of music they liked rather than music they disliked. These results suggest the emotions generated by a commercial are important because they may become associated with the advertised product through classical conditioning. Kellaris and colleagues also showed that music that was congruent with the message enhanced both ad recall and recognition.[29] Advertisers often attempt to pair a neutral product or service stimulus with an event or situation that arouses positive feelings, such as humour, an exciting sports event, or popular music.

Implications of the ELM The elaboration likelihood model has important implications for marketing communications, particularly with respect to involvement. For example, if the involvement level of consumers in the target audience is high, an ad or sales presentation should contain strong arguments that are difficult for the message recipient to refute or counterargue. If the involvement level of the target audience is low, peripheral cues may be more important than detailed message arguments.

An interesting test of the ELM showed that the effectiveness of a celebrity endorser in an ad depends on the receiver's involvement level.[30] When involvement was low, a celebrity endorser had a significant effect on attitudes. When the receiver's involvement was high, however, the use of a celebrity had no effect on brand attitudes; the quality of the arguments used in the ad was more important.

The explanation given for these findings was that a celebrity may serve as a peripheral cue in the low-involvement situation, allowing the receiver to develop favourable attitudes based on feelings toward the source rather than engaging in extensive processing of the message. A highly involved consumer, however, engages in more detailed central processing of the message content. The quality of the message claims becomes more important than the identity of the endorser.

The ELM suggests that the most effective type of message depends on the route to persuasion the consumer follows. Many marketers recognize that involvement levels are low for their product categories and consumers are not motivated to process advertising messages in any detail. That's why marketers of low-involvement products often rely on creative tactics that emphasize peripheral cues and use repetitive advertising to create and maintain favourable attitudes toward their brand. IMC Perspective 3–3 shows how one firm recently moved to repetitive advertising.

INTEGRATIVE PERSPECTIVES OF COMMUNICATION RESPONSE MODELS

In this final section, we conclude that the traditional communication response models based on a hierarchy or adaptation of a hierarchy are somewhat limited in their ability to explain how advertising works. As the title of this section implies, one needs an integrative perspective of communication that accounts for the different types of responses various consumers have to advertising in a variety of contexts. To accomplish this, we summarize theoretical and managerial approaches for understanding how consumers respond to advertising. The first perspective is concerned with explaining methods for studying or researching how advertising works while the second is concerned with providing guidelines for a planner in making effective promotion decisions.

THEORETICAL APPROACH

Vakratsas and Ambler recently reviewed more than 250 journal articles and books in an effort to better understand how advertising works and affects the consumer.[31] On the basis of their review of these studies, they concluded that although effects hierarchies have been actively employed for nearly 100 years, there is little support for the concept of a hierarchy of effects in the sense of temporal sequence. They note that in trying to understand the response process and the manner in which advertising works, there are three critical intermediate effects between advertising and purchase (Figure 3–9). These include *cognition*, the "thinking" dimension of a person's response; *affect*, the "feeling" dimension; and *experience*, which is a feedback dimension based on the outcomes of product purchasing and usage.

FIGURE 3–9

A framework for studying how advertising works

☐ ☐ ☐ ☐ ☐

TacoTime Goes Mexican

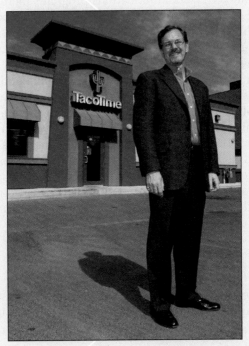

TacoTime is a western-based chain of 112 outlets spanning from Victoria to Thunder Bay that offers tacos and assorted similar foods. Delivered in a quick-service format, a new term for fast food, TacoTime traditionally competed against Burger King, McDonald's, and Wendy's for consumers in the "value meal market." Located in the food courts of malls and drive-through strip malls, TacoTime realized that its current offering had a limited future competing against major chains. And with very little penetration of Taco Bell in western Canada, TacoTime concluded that it could fulfill the need for authentic Mexican food better than any other firm.

Part of the change included adjustments to the menu presentation (e.g., real plates) and retail environment to coincide with the firm's goal to be "the dominant Mexican restaurant chain in Canada." But a significant part of the transformation featured the change in advertising to help clarify consumers' need for authentic Mexican food. The impetus for this emerged from consumer research that highlighted the association of food, sunshine, beaches, and tequila with Mexico. This raised a significant communication opportunity so that consumers would perceive the need for authentic Mexican food and more importantly, think of TacoTime when the idea of eating in a fast-casual dining environment emerged in consumers' decision making. Fast-casual appeared on the horizon in Canada recently as an alternative to quick-service (i.e., fast food) restaurants. Fast-casual had annual growth of 16 percent while quick-service saw a disappointing 2-percent growth, partly a response to consumer perception of less healthy food offerings.

To accomplish this, TacoTime moved away from its normal price and promotion-oriented advertising messages delivered through print and billboard media that occurred two or three times per year. Instead, it chose one main radio station in each city to play its ads many times each day for 48 weeks per year to reach people aged 18 to 49 with a message that focused on the Mexican platters that included salad, rice, and beans ("a real Mexican food experience"). Time will tell whether this communication choice is effective or not, but surely you can't help but think of TacoTime when you want something better than fast food served on wax paper.

Source: Norma Ramage, "TacoTime Dreams Grande," *Marketing Magazine*, March 3, 2003.

The authors conclude that individual responses to advertising are mediated or filtered by factors such as motivation and ability to process information, which can radically alter or change the individual's response to advertising. They suggest that the effects of advertising should be evaluated using these three dimensions, with some intermediate variables being more important than others, depending on factors such as the product category, stage of the product life cycle, target audience, competition, and impact of other marketing-mix components.

Other researchers have been critical of the hierarchy models as well. For example, Hall argues that advertisers need to move away from explicit and implicit reliance on hierarchical models of advertising effects and develop models that place affect and experience at the centre of the advertising process.[32] The implication of these criticisms is that marketers should focus on cognition, affect, and experience as critical variables that advertising may affect. However, they should not assume a particular sequence of responses but, rather, engage in research and analysis to better understand how advertising and other forms of promotion may affect these intermediate variables in various product/market situations.

Those responsible for planning the IMC program need to learn as much as possible about their target audience and how it may respond to advertising, along with other forms of marketing communication. For example, William Weilbacher has noted that marketing communications programs include more than just advertising.[33] Consumers are continually immersed in brand-sponsored communications that include public relations, a broad range of sales promotion activities, websites, direct marketing, event sponsorships, movie and TV show product placements, and other forms of marketing communication. He argues that hierarchy models must move beyond just explaining the effects of advertising and consider how, and with what effects, consumers synthesize information from all the various integrated marketing communications activities for a brand. The various communication models presented in this chapter provide insight into how consumers may process and respond to persuasive messages and hopefully help marketers make better decisions in planning and implementing their integrated marketing communications programs.

These suggestions indicate the importance of recognizing cognition and affect in both the processing stage of receiving the advertising message and in the resulting stage after the ad message has been processed. The managerial approach discussed next continues with this idea further.

MANAGERIAL APPROACH

We introduced the Rossiter and Percy (R&P) perspective in Chapter 2 when identifying the options for the target audience decision. A continuation of their

FIGURE 3-10
Processing and communication effects

perspective is a communication response model that takes a managerial view by identifying the responses in terms of the promotional planner's brand for any type of marketing communication decision. Figure 3–10 shows the initial processing stage that highlights the immediate responses to any advertising message. This idea is consistent with the notion of an integrative communication response model summarized by Vakratsas and Ambler. It also distinguishes the brand communication effects that are established more permanently in consumer memory. Overall, R&P summarize five **communication effects** that an ad, advertising campaign, or IMC plan may have on consumers.

- *Category need:* Target audience perception of requiring a product to satisfy a need.
- *Brand awareness:* Target audience ability to recognize and/or recall the brand within the category in sufficient detail to make a purchase.
- *Brand attitude:* Target audience overall evaluation of the brand in relation to its ability to satisfy the reason they want it.
- *Brand purchase intention:* Target audience self-instruction to respond (purchase, purchase-related action) to the brand.
- *Purchase facilitation:* Target audience perception that a marketing factor could affect their purchase or use of the brand.

Communication effect refers to the lasting brand impression that remains with the target audience after the target audience processes the message. The R&P model has a few noteworthy features compared with the previous hierarchy models. First, there is an obvious and clear connection to the purchase of a particular brand. This is apparent with its reference to the brand in three communication effects. It is also seen in the connection to category need, which speaks to the underlying reason why the consumer is motivated to buy the brand and the consumer's understanding of where the brand fits in the market in relation to other brands. Finally, it is observed with the link to purchase facilitation, which highlights the importance of marketers communicating information to make sure the purchase occurs.

The second feature is that the R&P model recognizes brand attitude as a central communication effect. Recall that the other models described previously viewed the entire process (i.e., cognition, affect, behaviour) as reflecting an attitude, and that some models argued that consumers experienced various steps in various orders depending upon the purchase situation. Brand attitude evaluation includes both cognitive and affective components recognizing that each aspect is relevant no matter what the purchase situation.

The third feature of the R&P model is that it views the communication effect with respect to the brand as being distinct from other aspects of the overall response to advertising. It views communication effects as the step between processing (i.e., consumer's responses to the immediate responses of a message) and behaviour (e.g., trial).

The R&P model and some of the other communication response models will be revisited in the next chapter. Promotional planners use a communication response model to determine the communication objectives for advertising and other promotional tools. It is important to base marketing communication decisions on a model and translate them into specific objectives since promotional planners need clear guidance for the remaining marketing communication decisions.

SUMMARY

The function of all elements of the promotional mix is to communicate, so promotional planners must understand the communication process. This process can be very complex; successful marketing communications depend on a number of factors, including the nature of the message, the audience's interpretation of it, and the environment in which it is received. For effective communication to occur, the sender must encode a message in such a way that it will be decoded by the receiver in the intended manner. Feedback from the receiver helps the sender determine whether proper decoding has occurred or whether noise has interfered with the communication process.

Promotional planning begins with the receiver or target audience, as marketers must understand how the audience is likely to respond to various sources of communication or types of messages. Different orderings of the traditional response hierarchy include the standard learning, dissonance/attribution, and low-involvement models.

The cognitive response approach examines the thoughts evoked by a message and how they shape the receiver's ultimate acceptance or rejection of the communication. The elaboration likelihood model of attitude formation and change recognizes two forms of message processing, the central and peripheral routes to persuasion, which are a function of the receiver's motivation and ability to process a message. There are three critical intermediate effects between advertising and purchase including cognition, affect, and experience. Those responsible for planning the IMC program should learn as much as possible about their target audience and how it may respond to advertising and other forms of marketing communications.

KEY TERMS

communication, *66*
source, *66*
encoding, *68*
message, *68*
semiotics, *68*
channel, *70*
mass media, *70*
receiver, *70*
decoding, *71*
field of experience, *71*
noise, *72*

response, *72*
feedback, *72*
AIDA model, *73*
hierarchy of effects model, *73*
innovation adoption model, *74*
information processing model, *74*
standard learning model, *76*

dissonance/attribution model, *77*
low-involvement hierarchy, *77*
cognitive responses, *80*
counterarguments, *81*
support arguments, *81*
source derogations, *81*
source bolsters, *81*
ad execution-related thoughts, *81*

attitude toward the ad, *81*
elaboration likelihood model (ELM), *82*
central route to persuasion, *82*
peripheral route to persuasion, *84*
classical conditioning, *84*
conditioned stimulus, *84*
conditioned response, *84*
communication effects, *89*

DISCUSSION QUESTIONS

1. Discuss the various elements of the communications process. Find an example of an advertising campaign being used by a company and analyze this campaign in terms of these elements of the communications model.

2. Discuss how semiotics can be of value to the field of integrated marketing communications. Select a marketing stimulus such as an advertisement, package, or other relevant marketing symbol and conduct a semiotic analysis of it such as the one shown in Exhibit 3–2.

3. Explain how a company like Home Depot could use the four models of the response process shown in Figure 3–3 to develop IMC strategies for its various products.

4. What is meant by involvement in terms of advertising and consumer behaviour? How might marketers determine the degree of involvement consumers have with their products and services?

5. Select an ad you think would be processed by a central route to persuasion and one where you think peripheral processing would occur. Show the ads to several people and ask them to write down the thoughts they have about each ad. Analyze their thoughts using the cognitive response categories discussed in the chapter.

6. Assume that you are the marketing communications manager for a brand of paper towels. Discuss how the low-involvement hierarchy could be of value in developing an advertising and promotion strategy for this brand.

7. Evaluate the "Just Imagine" campaign for Whirlpool appliances discussed in Global Perspective 3–2. Do you think this campaign will be effective in connecting with the working women Whirlpool is targeting? Why or why not?

8. Find an example of a print ad and evaluate it using the cognitive response model shown in Figure 3–7. Identify the specific types of cognitive responses that the ad might elicit from consumers and discuss why they might occur.

9. Explain what is meant by a central versus peripheral route to persuasion and the factors that would determine when each might be used by consumers in response to an advertisement.

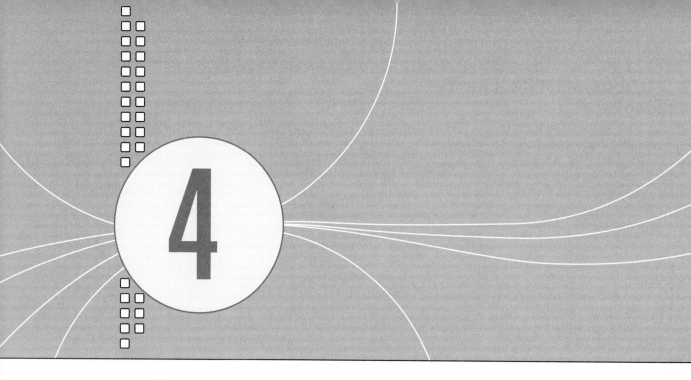

Objectives for the IMC Plan

CHAPTER OBJECTIVES

- To recognize the value of setting specific objectives for advertising and promotion.

- To know the differences between marketing and communication objectives and the issues regarding the use of each.

- To know the historical approaches for setting communication objectives for advertising.

- To understand a comprehensive framework for setting communication and behavioural objectives for all aspects of the IMC plan.

Fun Games by B.C. Lottery

We've heard it all before: "I'll buy a great big house if I win the lottery," "If I win, I'm travelling the world," or "I got my millions, I don't have to work anymore." And so it goes at B.C. Lottery with $1.6 billion in sales that have grown steadily each year from casinos, bingo operations, and lottery games, B.C. Lottery looked to grow its lottery games as its sales had lagged recently compared to the two other gambling alternatives.

Since one-third of all adults in B.C. did not regularly play lotteries, the 15 branded lottery games sold by B.C. Lottery offered varying potential to develop new ad campaigns to attract new users to this mature product category that had brands at different stages in their product life cycle. In particular, three games showed that the B.C. Lottery had distinct objectives for each product in terms of communication, behaviour, and sales.

Super 7 had been launched without extensive advertising causing consumers to have trouble distinguishing it from Lotto 6/49. Ads demonstrating its larger prizes could completely change your life shot Super 7 sales up by 80 percent when the objective had been 30 percent. In contrast, since consumers' understanding of Lotto 6/49 was so well entrenched, it did not

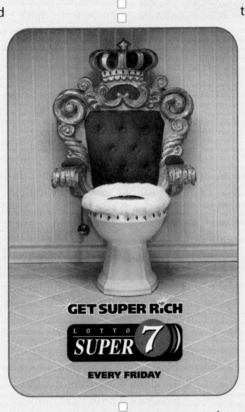

GET SUPER RiCH

LOTTO SUPER 7

EVERY FRIDAY

require extensive advertising for consumers to learn how to play the game or the size of the prizes.

Keno, a lottery game played in bars, topped all lottery products in sales recently despite only 6 percent of all B.C. adults playing the game regularly. However, the challenge appeared daunting to encourage non-users to perceive this social game in a positive light. Many believed it to be something lonely people did to pass the time. B.C. Lottery's objective for its Keno campaign was to get non-users to perceive it less negatively—the managers considered the campaign a success if the non-users had a neutral response after seeing the ads.

The advertising for the Living Large Lottery, a new instant-win game, faced an uphill battle to put a positive spin on the idea of playing the game in the face of many consumers no longer playing instant-win games. Clearly it had to update the attitude of its lapsed users to maintain the sales of this weakening product line.

Source: Eve Lazarus, "More Fun in the Game," *Marketing Magazine*, March 3, 2003.

TODAY
Reduce manufacturing waste going to landfills

TOMORROW
Reduce land going to waste

TOYOTA

Each year Toyota builds more than one million vehicles in North America. This means that we use a lot of resources— steel, aluminum, and plastics, for instance. But at Toyota, large scale manufacturing doesn't mean large scale waste.

In 1992 we introduced our Global Earth Charter to promote environmental responsibility throughout our operations. And in North America it is already reaping significant benefits. We recycle 376 million pounds of steel annually, and aggressive recycling programs keep 18 million pounds of other scrap materials from landfills.

Of course, no one ever said that looking after the Earth's resources is easy. But as we continue to strive for greener ways to do business, there's one thing we're definitely not wasting. And that's time.

www.toyota.com/tomorrow

Exhibit 4–1
The objective of this ad is to demonstrate Toyota's concern for the environment

Many companies have difficulty with the most critical step in the promotional planning process—setting realistic objectives that will guide the development of the IMC program. Complex marketing situations, conflicting perspectives regarding what advertising and other promotional mix elements are expected to accomplish, and uncertainty over resources make the setting of marketing communication objectives "a job of creating order out of chaos."[1] While the task of setting objectives can be complex and difficult, it must be done properly, because specific goals and objectives are the foundation on which all other promotional decisions are made. Budgeting for advertising and other promotional areas, as well as creative and media strategies and tactics, evolve from these objectives. They also provide a standard against which performance can be measured.

Setting specific objectives should be an integral part of the planning process. However, many companies either fail to use specific marketing communication objectives or set ones that are inadequate for guiding the development of the promotional plan or measuring its effectiveness. Many marketers are uncertain as to what integrated marketing communications should be expected to contribute to the marketing program. Furthermore, with the selection of so many different integrated marketing communication tools and target audiences, it is difficult to know how each element of the IMC plan contributes to the complete IMC plan. And it is difficult to know what specific objectives each IMC tool should have to measure their effectiveness (Exhibit 4–1).

Often marketers mistakenly use only marketing objectives to assess whether their advertising and promotion plans were successful. As we know, advertising and promotion are not the only marketing activities involved in generating sales. Moreover, it is not always possible or necessary to measure the effects of advertising in terms of sales. Consider the Forest Products Association of Canada ad shown in Exhibit 4–2. What objectives (other than generating sales) might the company have for this ad? How might its effectiveness be measured?

This chapter examines the nature and purpose of objectives and the role they play in guiding the development, implementation, and evaluation of an IMC program. Attention is initially given to marketing and communication objectives. Then we consider the approaches of setting communication objectives for advertising based on the response models previously discussed in Chapter 3. We then turn our attention to new approaches for setting communication and behavioural objectives for each element of the IMC plan and for the overall IMC plan that will be consistently referred to in Parts Three, Four, and Five of the book.

OBJECTIVE SETTING

VALUE OF OBJECTIVES

Perhaps one reason many companies fail to set specific objectives for their integrated marketing communications programs is that they don't recognize the value of doing so. Advertising and promotional objectives are needed for several reasons, including the functions they serve in communication, planning and decision-making, and measurement and evaluation.

Communications Specific objectives for the IMC program facilitate coordination of the various groups working on the campaign. Many people are involved in the planning and development of an integrated marketing communications program on the client side as well as in the various promotional agencies. The advertising and promotional program must be coordinated within the company, inside the ad agency, and between the two. Any other parties involved in the promotional campaign, such as public relations and/or sales promotion firms, research specialists, or media buying services, must also know what the company hopes to accomplish through its marketing communications program. Many problems can be avoided if all parties have written approved objectives to guide their actions and serve as a common base for discussing issues related to the promotional program.

Planning and Decision Making   Specific promotional objectives also guide development of the integrated marketing communications plan. All phases of a firm's promotional strategy should be based on the established objectives, including budgeting, creative, and media decisions as well as supportive programs such as direct marketing, public relations/publicity, sales promotion, and/or reseller support.

Meaningful objectives can also be a useful guide for decision making. Promotional planners are often faced with a number of strategic and tactical options in terms of choosing creative options, selecting media, and allocating the budget among various elements of the promotional mix. Choices should be made based on how well a particular strategy matches the firm's promotional objectives.

Measurement and Evaluation of Results   An important reason for setting specific objectives is that they provide a benchmark against which the success or failure of the promotional campaign can be measured. Without specific objectives, it is extremely difficult to determine what the firm's advertising and promotion efforts accomplished. One characteristic of good objectives is that they are measurable; they specify a method and criteria for determining how well the promotional program is working. By setting specific and meaningful objectives, the promotional planner provides measures that can be used to evaluate the effectiveness of the marketing communications program. Most organizations are concerned about the return on their promotional investment, and comparing actual performance against measurable objectives is the best way to determine if the return justifies the expense.

Exhibit 4-2
The objective of this ad is to promote the Forest Products Association of Canada's concern for the environment

TYPES OF OBJECTIVES

One difficulty in setting marketing and IMC programs is using the most appropriate objectives for the task at hand. While the IMC program supports the overall marketing program, each should have its own clear objective so that managers can assess where to make corrective decisions if some aspect of the brand's performance is not successful. We turn our attention to marketing and communication objectives and explain how they are related to one another. The distinction of communication objectives and sales objectives is apparent in the beliefs of a Converse All-Star Canada's president who clearly stated that its campaign to launch its new high-performance basketball shoe was not expected to set record sales but to merely reach the right target audience and be recognized as a legitimate brand for consideration.[2]

Marketing Objectives   **Marketing objectives** are generally stated in the firm's marketing plan and are statements of what is to be accomplished by the overall marketing program within a given time period. Marketing objectives are usually defined in terms of specific, measurable outcomes such as sales volume, market share, profits, or return on investment. Good marketing objectives are quantifiable; delineate the target market and note the time frame for accomplishing the goal (often one year). For example, a copy-machine company may have as its marketing objective "to increase sales by 10 percent in the small-business segment of the market during the next 12 months." To be effective, objectives must also be realistic and attainable.

The choice of the type of marketing objective is likely a function of market conditions. A company with a very high market share may seek to increase its sales volume by stimulating growth in the product category. It might accomplish this by increasing consumption by current users or encouraging nonusers to buy the product. A firm in a fast growing market may have market share as its marketing objective since this reflects that it is growing more quickly than its direct competitors. Alternatively, in mature markets with limited growth, firms tend to focus on profit as the key marketing objective. Finally, a firm that faces unique consumer preferences across various geographic markets (i.e., Ontario versus Quebec) may in fact have a separate marketing objective for each region.

Once the marketing communications manager has reviewed the marketing plan, he or she should understand the marketing objectives of the marketing program, how it intends to get there, and the role advertising and promotion will play. Marketing goals defined in terms of sales, profit, or market share increases are usually not appropriate promotional objectives. They are objectives for the entire marketing program, and achieving them depends on the proper coordination and execution of all the marketing mix elements, including not just promotion but also product planning and production, pricing, and distribution. In contrast, many promotional planners approach promotion from a communications perspective and believe the objective of advertising and other promotional mix elements is usually to communicate information or a selling message about a product or service.

Despite this prescription, some managers believe the only meaningful objective for their promotional program is sales. They take the position that the basic reason a firm spends money on advertising and promotion is to sell its product or service. Promotional spending represents an investment of a firm's scarce resources that requires an economic justification. Rational managers generally compare investment options on a common financial basis, such as return on investment (ROI). They believe that monies spent on advertising and other forms of promotion should produce measurable results, such as increasing sales volume by a certain percentage or dollar amount or increasing the brand's market share. These beliefs are partly a result of marketing and brand managers being under pressure to show sales results. They often take a short-term perspective in evaluating advertising and sales promotion programs and look for a quick fix for declining sales or loss of market share.

One problem with sales objectives for promotion is that poor sales results can be due to any of the other marketing mix variables, including product design or quality, packaging, distribution, or pricing. Advertising can make consumers aware of and interested in the brand, but it can't make them buy it, particularly if it is not readily available or is priced higher than a competing brand. As shown in Figure 4–1, sales are a function of many factors, not just advertising and promotion.

Another problem with sales objectives is that the effects of advertising often occur over an extended period. Many experts recognize that advertising has a lagged or **carryover effect**; monies spent on advertising do not necessarily have an immediate impact on sales.[3] Advertising may create awareness, interest, and/or favourable attitudes toward a brand, but these feelings will not result in an actual purchase until the consumer enters the market for the product, which may occur later. A review of econometric studies that examined the duration of cumulative advertising effects found that for mature, frequently purchased, low-priced products, advertising's effect on sales lasts up to nine months.[4] Models have been developed to account for the carryover effect of advertising and to help determine the long-term effect of

FIGURE 4–1
Factors influencing sales
☐ ☐ ☐ ☐ ☐

advertising on sales.[5] The carryover effect adds to the difficulty of determining the precise relationship between advertising and sales.

A third problem with sales objectives is that they offer little guidance to those responsible for planning and developing the promotional program. The creative and media people working on the account need some direction as to the nature of the advertising message the company hopes to communicate, the intended audience, and the particular effect or response sought. As you will see shortly, communication objectives are recommended because they provide operational guidelines for those involved in planning, developing, and executing the advertising and promotional program.

The counter argument to these three points is that sales objectives are appropriate when the above three factors are not relevant. If a marketer is certain that other marketing or environmental factors were not influencing sales, that the carryover effect was not occurring, or that the managers involved did not require guidance, then a sales objective could be plausible. In general, the likelihood of such conditions arising appears quite remote, which necessitates the use of communication objectives as the primary approach for promotional planning purposes. To illustrate this point we will discuss two examples: direct response advertising and the marketing practices of packaged-goods firms.

Direct-response advertising is one type of advertising that typically evaluates its effectiveness on the basis of sales. Merchandise is advertised in material mailed to customers, in newspapers and magazines, or on television. The consumer purchases the merchandise by mail or by calling a toll-free number. The direct-response advertiser generally sets objectives and measures success in terms of the sales response generated by the ad. For example, objectives for and the evaluation of a direct-response ad on TV are based on the number of orders received each time a station broadcasts the commercial. Because advertising is really the only form of communication and promotion used in this situation and response is generally immediate, setting objectives in terms of sales appear appropriate.

However, this is an example where a carryover effect may be working. Consumers receive the ad many times during the campaign and decide not to purchase. During

Manitoba Telecom

Defining your communication objectives and finding the right campaign is an important step in IMC planning, and it looks like Manitoba Telecom Services (MTS) has hit a winner. A wise-talking bison has vaulted MTS to advertising recall of 80 percent and market shares of 98 percent for local access, 90 percent for long distance, 68 percent for cellular service (compared to 29 percent for the next competitor), and 62 percent for Internet access (compared to 23 percent for the next competitor).

Historically a provincial Crown corporation, MTS faced competition for the first time in the 1990s because of deregulation. With a conservative and stuffy image due to its monopoly situation for so many years, the now-public MTS needed to reposition itself in its marketing communications as new products and services emerged along with a growing, technologically oriented younger market. Clearly, MTS had to emphasize awareness as consumers evaluated the products and services of MTS and its competitors; but as importantly, MTS had to ensure that consumers perceived the need for new services and products, and believed that MTS was the firm to purchase from.

Enter Morty the talking bison. As the MTS executives noted, they are using a well-established strategy of having an animal to represent the brand. But in this case, it seems to resonate especially well with the people of Manitoba as the bison is the provincial symbol. In the first 16 months, MTS has run more than three dozen Morty commercials— that's about one new creative execution every two weeks!

Initially, MTS restricted Morty across its IMC tools, but eventually, Morty was the "spokesperson" for all products and services and could be seen in all communications from advertising to direct mail and the company's website. Now when people see a bison, they naturally think MTS. And therein lies concern for the future. As one executive notes, "The challenge in the campaign is to make sure the creative doesn't overpower the message."

And while the campaign acheived its communication objectives successfully, MTS looked to improve its specific product recall in subsequent advertising messages.

Sources: Judy Waytiuk, "Morty Mania," *Marketing Magazine*, March 5, 2001; "Manitoba Telecom Services," *Marketing Magazine*, November 19, 2001.

subsequent campaigns during the year, these consumers have the communication effect of the previous campaign combined with word-of-mouth communication and evaluation considerations. The cumulative impact of all communications can influence the consumer as he or she proceeds through the usual decision-making process. Establishing communication objectives is still a critical step in understanding the effectiveness of the ads once again indicating that sales objectives alone are not sufficient.

We now turn to our second example. Many package-goods companies compete in mature markets with established channels of distribution, stable competitive prices and promotional budgets, and products of similar quality. They view advertising and sales promotion as the key determinants of a brand's sales or market share, so it may be possible to isolate the effects of these promotional mix variables.[6] Many companies have accumulated enough market knowledge with their advertising, sales promotion, and direct-marketing programs to have considerable insight into the sales levels that should result from their promotional efforts. Thus, they believe it is reasonable to set objectives and evaluate the success of their promotional efforts in terms of sales results.

Again, this appears to be a plausible explanation; however, we can surmise a few factors that make the setting of communication objectives an important step for predicting the sales results. Even mature categories have new customers entering the market to which communication effects are important considerations for seeing if these customers are gravitating to one's own or a competing brand. Consumer perceptions of campaign-message changes and promotional-mix alterations may have a delayed effect on sales, and an understanding of consumer psychological reactions (i.e., attitude) may be more immediately forthcoming.

Communication Objectives **Communication objectives** are statements of what the communications will accomplish. In general, objectives are based on one or more consumer response models discussed in Chapter 3. We can speak of communication objectives on three levels depending upon the decision at hand. There are communication objectives for the overall IMC plan. We can also speak of communication objectives for individual IMC tools (i.e., advertising). Often, as was shown in Chapter 1, these communication objectives are referred to as objectives for the particular tool (i.e., advertising objectives). When working in this field, marketers may use either of these terms depending upon their background or company practices. Finally, we can also use the concept of communication objectives for individual elements of a communication tool. For example, when we design an individual print ad, we want to make sure it achieves the communication objectives we set for it.

Irrespective of whether we are speaking of communication objectives for the IMC plan, a particular tool, or a specific ad, **the communication objectives should be based on the particular communication tasks required to deliver the appropriate messages to the specific target audience at a relevant point within the target audience's purchase decision-making process and consumption experience.**

Managers must be able to translate general marketing goals into communication goals and specific promotional objectives. Some guidance in doing this may be available from the situation analysis of the marketing plan, which includes the following:

- The market segments the firm wants to target and the target audiences (customer status, demographics, psychographics, and purchase motives) that the firm wishes to communicate with.
- The product's main features, attributes, benefits, uses, and applications.
- The company's and competitors' brands (sales and market share in various segments, market positioning, competitive strategies, promotional expenditures, creative and media strategies, and tactics).

After reviewing all the information, the promotional planner should see how integrated marketing communications fit into the marketing program and what the firm hopes to achieve through advertising and other promotional elements. The importance of setting communication objectives of a promotional plan that contributes to sales is seen in the Dairyland example. The ad for Dairyland Milk 2 Go in Exhibit 4–3 is part of the company's marketing strategy to increase sales and market share for its chocolate milk by targeting younger consumers who value convenience.

Exhibit 4–3
This ad for Dairyland chocolate milk is part of a campaign designed to increase sales and market share

In some situations, promotional planners may gain insight into the relationship between communication objectives and sales from industry research. Evalucom, Inc., conducted a study of commercials for new products. Some succeeded in stimulating anticipated levels of sales; others did not. Figure 4–2 shows four factors the study identified that affect whether a commercial for a new product is successful in generating sales. For each of these factors, we can see the importance of setting clear communication objectives.

When setting specific communication objectives, promotional planners often are not sure what constitutes adequate levels of awareness, knowledge, liking, preference, or conviction. No formulas provide this information. The promotional manager will have to use his or her personal experience and that of the brand or product managers, as well as the marketing history of this and similar brands. Average scores on various communication measures for this and similar products should be considered, along with the levels achieved by competitors' products. We now turn to various approaches for setting communication objectives that provide guidelines for some of these concerns.

FROM COMMUNICATION RESPONSE MODELS TO COMMUNICATION OBJECTIVES

Over the years, a number of methods have been developed for deciding upon communication objectives for advertising, related tools, and complete IMC plans. We review three approaches from a historical perspective in this section: the DAGMAR model, an application of more comprehensive response hierarchies, and new IMC approaches. We begin with the DAGMAR model that provided guidance for setting advertising objectives. Next we consider an application of the Lavidge and Steiner model discussed in Chapter 3. Then we investigate new IMC approaches that attempt to go beyond the limitations of the traditional response hierarchies.

DEFINING ADVERTISING GOALS FOR MEASURED RESULTS

In 1961, Russell Colley prepared a report for the Association of National Advertisers titled **Defining Advertising Goals for Measured Advertising Results (DAGMAR)**.[7] In it, Colley developed a model for setting advertising objectives and measuring the results of an ad campaign. The major contribution of the DAGMAR model is its

FIGURE 4–2
Factors related to success of advertising for new products
☐ ☐ ☐ ☐ ☐

- **Communicating that something is different about the product.** Successful introductory commercials communicated some point of difference for the new product.
- **Positioning the brand difference in relation to the product category.** Successful commercials positioned their brand's difference within a specific product category. For example, a new breakfast product was positioned as the "crispiest cereal" and a new beverage as the "smoothest soft drink."
- **Communicating that the product difference is beneficial to consumers.** Nearly all of the successful commercials linked a benefit directly to the new product's difference.
- **Supporting the idea that something about the product is different and/or beneficial to consumers.** All the successful commercials communicated support for the product's difference claim or its relevance to consumers. Support took the form of demonstrations of performance, information supporting a uniqueness claim, endorsements, or testimonials.

recognition that communication effects are the logical basis for advertising goals and objectives against which success or failure should be measured. Colley's rationale for communication-based objectives was as follows:

> Advertising's job, purely and simply, is to communicate to a defined audience information and a frame of mind that stimulates action. Advertising succeeds or fails depending on how well it communicates the desired information and attitudes to the right people at the right time and at the right cost.[8]

Under the DAGMAR approach, an advertising goal involves a communication task that is specific and measurable. A **communication task**, as opposed to a marketing task, can be performed by, and attributed to, advertising rather than to a combination of several marketing factors. Colley proposed that the communication task be based on a hierarchical model of the communication process with four stages:

- Awareness—making the consumer aware of the existence of the brand or company.
- Comprehension—developing an understanding of what the product is and what it will do for the consumer.
- Conviction—developing a mental disposition in the consumer to buy the product.
- Action—getting the consumer to purchase the product.

While the hierarchical model of advertising effects was the basic model of the communication response process used in DAGMAR, Colley also studied other specific tasks that advertising might be expected to perform in leading to the ultimate objective of a sale. He developed a checklist of 52 advertising tasks to characterize the contribution of advertising and serve as a starting point for establishing objectives.

CHARACTERISTICS OF OBJECTIVES

A second major contribution of DAGMAR to the advertising planning process was its definition of what constitutes a good objective. Colley argued that advertising objectives should specify a target audience, be stated in terms of concrete and measurable communication tasks, indicate a benchmark starting point and the degree of change sought, and specify a time period for accomplishing the objective(s).

Target Audience An important characteristic of good objectives is a well-defined target audience. The primary target audience for a company's product or service is described in the situation analysis. It may be based on descriptive variables such as geography, demographics, and psychographics (on which advertising media selection decisions are based) as well as on behavioural variables such as customer status (i.e. brand loyal users), usage rate, or benefits sought. This step is critical since the communication effect has to be interpreted from the perspective of the intended receiver.

Concrete, Measurable Tasks The communication task specified in the objective should be a precise statement of what appeal or message the advertiser wants to communicate to the target audience. Advertisers generally use a copy platform to describe their basic message. The objective or copy platform statement should be specific and clear enough to guide the creative specialists who develop the advertising message. According to DAGMAR, the objective must also be measurable. There must be a way to determine whether the intended message has been communicated properly.

Benchmark and Degree of Change Sought   To set objectives, one must know the target audience's present status concerning response hierarchy variables (e.g., awareness) and then determine the degree to which consumers must be changed by the advertising campaign. Determining the target audience's present position regarding the various response stages requires **benchmark measures**. Often a marketing research study must be conducted to determine prevailing levels of the response hierarchy. In the case of a new product or service, the starting conditions are generally at or near zero for all the variables, so no initial research is needed.

Establishing benchmark measures gives the promotional planner a basis for determining what communication tasks need to be accomplished and for specifying particular objectives. For example, a preliminary study for a brand may reveal that awareness is high but consumer perceptions and attitudes are negative. The objective for the advertising campaign must then be to change the target audience's perceptions of and attitudes toward the brand.

Quantitative benchmarks are not only valuable in establishing communications goals and objectives but essential for determining whether the campaign was successful. Objectives provide the standard against which the success or failure of a campaign is measured. An ad campaign that results in a 90-percent awareness level for a brand among its target audience cannot really be judged effective unless one knows what percentage of the consumers were aware of the brand before the campaign began. A 70-percent pre-campaign awareness level would lead to a different interpretation of the campaign's success than would a 30-percent level.

Specified Time Period   A final consideration in setting advertising objectives is specifying the time period in which they must be accomplished. Appropriate time periods can range from a few days to a year or more. Most ad campaigns specify time periods from a few months to a year, depending on the situation facing the advertiser and the type of response being sought. For example, awareness levels for a brand can be created or increased fairly quickly through an intensive media schedule of widespread, repetitive advertising to the target audience. Repositioning of a product requires a change in consumers' perceptions and takes much more time.

ASSESSMENT OF DAGMAR

The DAGMAR approach to setting objectives has had considerable influence on the advertising planning process. Many promotional planners use this model as a basis for setting objectives and assessing the effectiveness of their promotional campaigns. DAGMAR also focused advertisers' attention on the value of using communications-based rather than sales-based objectives to measure advertising effectiveness and encouraged the measurement of stages in the response hierarchy to assess a campaign's impact. Colley's work has led to improvements in the advertising and promotional planning process by providing a better understanding of the goals and objectives toward which planners' efforts should be directed. This usually results in less subjectivity and also leads to better communication and relationships between the client and its agency.

While DAGMAR has contributed to the advertising planning process, it has not been totally accepted by everyone in the advertising field. A number of problems have led to questions regarding its value as an advertising planning tool:[9]

- *Problems with the response hierarchy.* A major criticism of the DAGMAR approach is its reliance on the hierarchy of effects model. The fact that consumers do not always go through this sequence of communication effects before making a purchase has been recognized, and alternative response models have been developed.[10]
- *Practicality and costs.* Another criticism of DAGMAR concerns the difficulties involved in implementing it. Money must be spent on research to establish quantitative benchmarks and measure changes in the response hierarchy. This is costly and time-consuming and can lead to considerable disagreement over method,

criteria, measures, and so forth. Many critics argue that DAGMAR is practical only for large companies with big advertising and research budgets. Many firms do not want to spend the money needed to use DAGMAR effectively.

• *Inhibition of creativity.* A final criticism of DAGMAR is that it inhibits advertising creativity by imposing too much structure on the people responsible for developing the advertising. Many creative personnel think the DAGMAR approach is too concerned with quantitative assessment of a campaign's impact on awareness, brand name recall, or specific persuasion measures. The emphasis is on passing the numbers test rather than developing a message that is truly creative and contributes to brand equity.

COMPREHENSIVE RESPONSE MODEL APPLICATIONS

The DAGMAR model was the impetus for the application of more involved or comprehensive response models for setting communication objectives. Over time, advertising theorists prefer the Lavidge and Steiner hierarchy of effects model, as it is more specific and provides a better way to establish and measure results.[11] Thus, this particular hierarchical model has been used as a basis for analyzing the communication response processes of consumers and has been the foremost application for setting communication objectives.

Figure 4–3 shows the various steps in the Lavidge and Steiner hierarchy of effects model as the consumer moves from awareness to purchase, along with examples of types of promotion or advertising relevant to each step. Recall from Chapter 3 that

Related behavioural dimensions	Movement toward purchase	Example of types of promotion or advertising relevant to various steps
Conative The realm of motives. Ads stimulate or direct desires.	Purchase Conviction	Point-of-purchase Retail store ads Deals "Last-chance" offers Price appeals Testimonials
Affective The realm of emotions. Ads change attitudes and feelings.	Preference Liking	Competitive ads Argumentative copy "Image" copy Status, glamour appeals
Cognitive The realm of thoughts. Ads provide information and facts.	Knowledge Awareness	Announcements Descriptive copy Classified ads Slogans Jingles Skywriting Teaser campaigns

FIGURE 4–3
Effects of advertising on consumers: movement from awareness to action

103

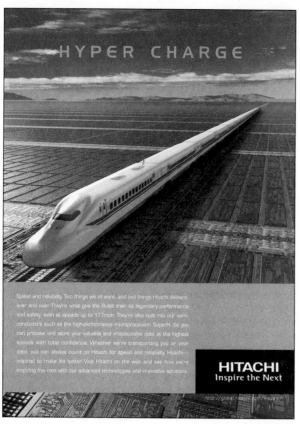

Exhibit 4–4
Hitachi creates an image of speed and reliability

consumers pass through three successive stages: cognitive, affective, and behavioural. As consumers proceed through the three stages, they move closer to making a purchase. Consumers are not expected to respond immediately; rather, advertisers realize they must provide relevant information and create favourable predispositions toward the brand before purchase behaviour will occur. For example, the ad for Hitachi in Exhibit 4–4 is designed to inform consumers of the product's speed and reliability. While it has no call for immediate action, the ad creates favourable impressions about the product so that consumers will consider it when they enter the market for advanced technologies.

Setting communication objectives with a model like this is the same way that a pyramid is built, by first accomplishing lower-level objectives such as awareness and knowledge or comprehension.[12] Subsequent tasks involve moving consumers who are aware of or knowledgeable about the product or service to higher levels in the pyramid (Figure 4–4). The initial stages, at the base of the pyramid, are easier to accomplish than those toward the top, such as trial and repurchase or regular use. Thus, the percentage of prospective customers will decline as they move up the pyramid. Figure 4–5 shows how a company introducing a new brand of shampoo targeted at 18- to 34-year-old females might set its IMC objectives using the communications effects pyramid.

The communication effects pyramid can also be used to determine promotional objectives for an established brand. The promotional planner must determine where the target audience lies with respect to the various blocks in the pyramid. If awareness levels for a brand and knowledge of its features and benefits are low, the communication objective should be to increase them. If these blocks of the pyramid are already in place, but liking or preference is low, the advertising goal may be to change the target markets' image of the brand and move consumers through to purchase.

FIGURE 4–4
Communication effects pyramid

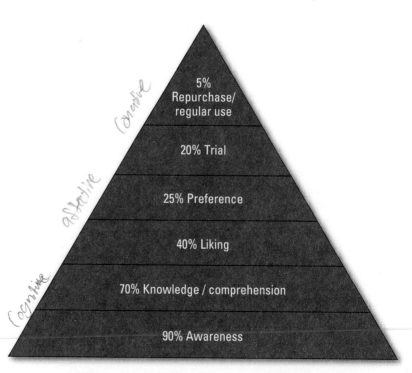

Product: Backstage Shampoo

Time period: Six months

Objective 1: Create awareness among 90 percent of target audience. Use repetitive advertising in newspapers, magazines, TV and radio programs. Simple message.

Objective 2: Create interest in the brand among 70 percent of target audience. Communicate information about the features and benefits of the brand—i.e., that it contains no soap and improves the texture of the hair

Objective 3: Create positive feelings about the brand among 40 percent and preference among 25 percent of the target audience. Create favourable attitudes by conveying information, promotions, sampling, etc.

Objective 4: Obtain trial among 20 percent of the target audience. Use sampling and cents-off coupons along with advertising and promotions.

Objective 5: Develop and maintain regular use of Backstage Shampoo among 5 percent of the target audience. Use continued reinforcement advertising, fewer coupons and promotions

Even though comprehensive response models have been used to set communication objectives for many years, research shows that its acceptance has been limited over time. A 1969 study showed that most advertising agencies did not state appropriate objectives for determining advertising success.[13] Another more recent study found that most of advertisers of their sample did not set concrete advertising objectives, specify objective tasks, measure results in terms of stages of a hierarchy of effects, or match objectives to evaluation measures.[14] The authors concluded: "Advertising practitioners have only partially adopted the concepts and standards of objective setting and evaluation set forth 25 years ago."[15] Finally, another recent study measured the attitudes of chairs, presidents, and other senior managers of business-to-business advertising companies, more than half of the 427 respondents said they did not know whether their advertising was working and less than 10 percent thought it was working well.[16]

A NEW IMC APPROACH

One reason so much attention is given to advertising objectives is that, for many companies, advertising has traditionally been the major way of communicating with target audiences. Other promotional mix elements such as sales promotion, direct marketing, and publicity are used intermittently to support and complement the advertising program.

Another reason is that traditional advertising-based views of marketing communications planning have dominated the field for so long. These approaches are based on a hierarchical response model and consider how marketers can develop and disseminate advertising messages to move consumers along an effects path. This approach, shown in Figure 4–6, is what professor Don Schultz calls inside-out planning. He says, "It focuses on what the marketer wants to say, when the marketer wants to say it, about things the marketer believes are important about his or her brand, and in the media forms the marketer wants to use."[17]

Schultz advocates an outside-in planning process for IMC that starts with the customer and builds backward to the brand. This means that promotional planners study the various media that customers and prospects use, when the marketer's messages might be most relevant to customers, and when they are likely to be most receptive to the message.

A similar approach is suggested by Professor Tom Duncan, who argues that IMC should use **zero-based communications planning**, which involves determining what tasks need to be done and which marketing communications functions should be used and to what extent.[18] This approach focuses on the task to be done and searches for the best ideas and media to accomplish it. Duncan notes that as with a traditional advertising campaign, the basis of an IMC campaign is a big idea. However, in IMC the big idea can be public relations, direct response, packaging, or sales promotion. Duncan suggests that an effective IMC program should lead with the marketing communications function that most effectively addresses the company's main problem or opportunity and should use a promotional mix that draws on the strengths of whichever communications functions relate best to the particular situation.

Both of these views represent how communication objectives should be set within the emerging field of IMC. The next section presents a comprehensive framework for making IMC decisions at all three levels: IMC plan, IMC tool, and an individual element (i.e., print ad). It builds on this IMC vision, retains the key strengths of DAGMAR, and accounts for the limitations of response hierarchies.

SETTING IMC OBJECTIVES

We now turn our attention to the Rossiter and Percy (R&P) perspective of setting objectives. We first introduced the ideas of R&P in Chapter 2 when discussing the guidelines for target audience identification and selection, and in Chapter 3 when summarizing communication response models. An additional feature of their perspective is to provide guidelines for setting behavioural objectives that are based on their view of target audience identification and selection and for setting communication objectives that are based on their view of communication effects.

Compared to the previous approaches of setting communication objectives, the R&P perspective has three main characteristics. First, it is completely consistent with a critical part of the original DAGMAR model. The R&P perspective makes a direct connection between the target audience decision and the type of communication objectives required for each target audience. Secondly, it provides guidelines for communication objectives that are more managerially useful and do not completely rely on a set hierarchy of effects. Finally, it provides guidelines for behavioural or action objectives that are not specified completely in the previous approaches. This step is critical for linking communication objectives and marketing objectives (i.e., sales).

This section will review the options promotional planners should consider when setting behavioural and communication objectives. It will also connect the communication objectives to the various stages of the buyer decision model described in Chapter 2. We include the R&P perspective since it attempts to resolve the limitations of other communication models and approaches for objective setting. Furthermore, the R&P perspective provides guidelines for creative tactics as will be seen in Chapter 7.

OPTIONS FOR BEHAVIOURAL OBJECTIVES

A key part of R&P's approach is to have a clear behavioural objective for each target audience since summating the individual purchasing behaviour of many customers leads to a firm's overall sales. From another perspective, the link between marketing objectives (i.e., sales) and communication objectives (i.e., attitude towards the brands) is behavioural objectives. Advertising and promotion can focus on influencing a particular form of behaviour based on the nature of the advertising message or IMC tool used. We now discuss various types of behavioural objectives.

Trial   A **brand trial purchase** is defined as a consumer's first purchase of a focal brand. For many everyday products, this purchase occurred many years ago; it is probably difficult for you to remember when you purchased your first soft drink or snack food. However, these firms continue to have a **brand trial objective** to some degree as consumers naturally enter the market when they attain a certain age or have income (i.e., allowance from parents). In fact, a brand trial objective is a behavioural objective for almost all firms, but it is not necessarily the primary behavioural objective for all campaigns or all communication tools.

Let's return to the soft drink scenario. It is quite unlikely that you have continued to purchase the same brand of soft drink as the first trial purchase all these years. In fact, many people consume more than one brand of soft drink. Many brand managers are faced with this dilemma. For whatever reason, it is possible that consumers have not purchased a focal brand for a period of time (i.e., perhaps a year). Thus, firms would like consumers to have a new trial experience of the brand. A **brand re-trial purchase** is defined as a consumer's first purchase of a focal brand after some time delay. The length of the delay to focus on when setting a **brand re-trial objective** is a decision the promotion manager makes. It depends upon the purchase frequency of the product, among other factors observed from the situation analysis.

A manager may plan for a brand trial or brand re-trial objective when consumers are purchasing another brand. A **brand-switching purchase** is defined as a consumer's purchase towards a focal brand from some other competing brand. A brand-switching purchase occurs whereby the consumer makes a re-trial purchase of a focal brand and leaves the new favourite. A brand-switching purchase also occurs when the consumer makes a trial purchase of a focal brand from a competing brand. Thus, brand trial or brand re-trial objectives are also known as **brand-switching objectives**.

Now let's put the trial purchase in another perspective, consider the purchase of a cellphone that many young adults presently own. If you have one, what brand did you select and why? How did the advertising and promotion influence this purchase? The cellphone is a different kind of product and likely a somewhat involved purchase for many consumers. Despite this, cellphone companies and service providers had trial objectives as they attempted to attract consumers who did not own such technology. While this is obviously a brand trial purchase, it is also something broader. A **category trial purchase** is defined as a consumer's first purchase in a product category that the consumer has not purchased previously. Marketers of new products, like the cellphone, have a dual challenge of attaining both **category trial objectives** and brand trial objectives.

Repeat Purchase   In the age of relationship marketing and a focus on customer retention, this form of purchase behaviour is most critical. A **repeat purchase** is defined as a consumer's continued purchase of a focal brand within a specified time period. Again, the time factor is at the discretion of the marketer, and once again it is contingent upon purchase frequency of the product or other factors derived from the situation analysis.

Firms can have a **repeat-purchase objective** in many situations. As noted above, marketers desire to have a stable core of customers that remain loyal to the brand. Many firms communicate with these consumers to maintain their positive attitude towards the focal brand. For example, some argue that most of Coca-Cola's advertising and promotions are directed towards its repeat customers. In many product categories, a group of consumers habitually consume two or three brands continuously. For instance, of 15 purchases, over 10 consecutive purchases might be of the focal brand with the remaining five purchases spread across two other brands. This is another situation where a marketer may emphasize a repeat-purchase objective in their communications plan. While this type of consumer does not purchase the focal brand for every single occasion, the consumer is a consistent contributor to the firm's sales and a marketer would want to communicate appropriately to ensure future sales.

The repeat-purchase objective is so pervasive for most organizations. Thus, we identify three alternatives to guide managers in setting their behavioural objectives for IMC: how often to purchase, how much to purchase, and when to purchase.

The first alternative concerns the rate or how often to purchase the brand. This implies that a marketer may set an objective pertaining to consumers purchasing their brand every week instead of every two weeks. This example shows an option where a manager may want to increase the rate of purchase from a "half" product per week to "one" product per week. A second managerial option is to maintain the rate of purchase. While this is a more conservative objective, it is still a viable option in very competitive environments. Finally, a manager may want to decrease the rate of purchase. This option may be viable in unique situations of high demand or with products that have potentially negative consequences (i.e., alcohol).

The amount or how much to purchase each occasion is the second alternative. As this alternative implies, a marketer may set an objective where consumers purchase two products per occasion versus one per occasion. As above, this option is to increase the amount per occasion, but a marketer could still evaluate whether to maintain or decrease the amount per occasion.

The final alternative is the timing or when to purchase. Certain products are seasonal, have a peak in their sales, or can be easily stored. Marketers may have a behavioural objective to influence when consumers will make the purchase. For example, Wendy's restaurant advertises on television in the evening and communicates the fact that its drive-through service stays open late, thus prompting consumers to purchase at a certain time of day. Consistent with the other two alternatives, we can conceive three options: maintain, accelerate, and delay.

An evolution in its message from "Perspective is Everything" to "Don't Miss a Day" signals how the *Globe and Mail* newspaper specified its repeat-purchase objectives over time. Faced with competition from other newspapers, the "perspective" message conveyed one aspect of quality in an attempt to maintain its readership. Recognizing that some readers may not purchase or read its newspaper everyday, the *Globe and Mail* focused its message on increasing the frequency of reading the newspaper in its more recent "day" message.[19]

Purchase-Related Behaviour   Often, communication is designed to encourage a consumer to progress through the decision-making process more smoothly. Or, communication is deemed a necessary part of the process. For example, most people find it imperative to visit a car dealership prior to buying a car. So the focus of some parts of an IMC plan is to have consumers take action that will lead them one step closer to the final destination of a purchase. **Purchase-related behaviour** is an action that consumers take that will lead to a higher probability of purchasing the brand. Many types of purchase-related action exist, but in general, most concern the consumer seeking some amount of information (e.g., visiting a website) about the brand or some kind of experience with the brand (e.g., demonstration, sample). Accordingly, marketers can have many purchase-related behaviour objectives to know whether enough of the target audience is involved with the brand during the decision-making process. For example, the firm can track the number of sales inquiries or requests for samples, or demonstrations to gauge how well it is performing for the objective.

Repeat Consumption   Thus far we have considered repeat purchase as a behavioural objective. Related to this is repeat consumption as a behavioural objective. **Repeat consumption** is defined as the continued consumption of the brand once purchased. Marketers may have a **repeat-consumption objective** when communicating with their current customers who have previously purchased the brand and have the product at their home or work. Some communications have an objective of modifying how often to consume the brand, how much to consume each occasion, and when to consume.

To give an idea of a repeat-consumption objective in action, we will cite two common approaches. Often, food and drink products advertise certain television commercials that show consumption visuals that may prompt consumers to snack or have another beverage. Another approach is to show consumers how to enjoy the product for other uses, or in new or alternative situations.

Milk faces a unique problem of 100 percent trial and 99 percent household penetration, yet its consumption continues to decline. The B.C. Dairy Foundation identified teens and young adults as an audience for a campaign to maintain consumption since research indicated that consumption levels dropped off during the ages of 16–23. Since many of these people still lived at home, the print and television messages: "Don't take your body for granted" and "What would life be like without a body?" tried to ensure that this age group would not stop consuming milk prior to moving out on their own. Exciting outdoor events geared towards this audience attempted to make drinking milk as "cool" as any other beverage![20]

As you can see, the type of purchase and consumption behaviour that firms may try to influence is quite varied. If a firm has multiple target audiences to reach, quite likely it will have to carefully specify the type of behaviour associated with each target audience so that it can develop the most appropriate message and select the most relevant IMC tool. To assist a manager in making these subsequent decisions, it is important to set clear communication objectives.

The Canadian Tourism Commission and Toyota presented an interesting example of a campaign designed to increase repeat consumption. This dual branded message encouraged Canadians to "drive the world's greatest country" in a series of newspaper, television, and radio ads followed by a second wave of Internet and dealer promotions. Since it was assumed that most Canadians had previously taken a road vacation to see various Canadian sites, this campaign attempted to capitalize on the growing trend of domestic travel.[21]

Application   By the end of 2001, approximately one-third of the Canadian population, or 10 million consumers, had a wireless phone, with 2 million of those signing up during 2001. Some sales for companies come from new users, and some sales naturally come from customers who decide to switch for one reason or another. The end of 2001 was a watershed moment as all brands were available across the entire country. Telus had moved east with its purchase of Clearnet, while Fido, Rogers, and Bell Mobility marketed their services in the west. Bell faced the unusual situation of having to operate as a new brand in the west because it was a mature company with a previous monopoly status in the east. The national campaign, "GO," certainly helped the transition when combined with the regional message.

This situation shows many of the above concepts. It shows the importance of defining the target audience initially with a behavioural perspective for marketing communications. It is easier for Bell to move into the new market and attract new users with a trial purchase by establishing an initial brand position with this target audience as opposed to trying to switch consumers from competing brands. In contrast, the "GO" campaign in the east represents a brand re-position as it attempts to switch consumers. Overall, this example shows how an IMC approach is critical as Bell has the challenge of managing at least two target audiences with multiple message and IMC tools.[22]

OPTIONS FOR COMMUNICATION OBJECTIVES

Earlier in this chapter we saw how communication response hierarchy models can be used to formulate communication objectives. The R&P approach is similar since it translates their perspective of communication effects into clear options for managers to set communication objectives. In fact, it offers a number of options for each of the five communication objectives that can be applied to one target audience or multiple target audiences.

These options for communication objectives can be viewed as a universal framework for (i) a specific communication like one print ad or television commercial, (ii) a specific campaign like advertising or sponsorship, and (iii) a complete IMC program that includes all promotional tools. It should be noted that the characteristics of good objectives still retain the characteristics set forth earlier (i.e., specific benchmark with the degree of change sought within a specified time period). Furthermore, the framework is flexible enough to apply the various communication objectives to each stage of the buyer decision-making process. We now turn to summarizing the various options for each communication objective and show this application to the buyer decision process.

Category Need **Category need** pertains to whether the target audience feels the need to purchase within the actual product category. Before describing the three options available for managers, it is useful to understand what we mean by category. Cellphones are a clear product for which some people are consumers and some are not. A cellphone company may try to build demand by convincing new users of the benefits of owning a cellphone versus not owning one. This type of message is likely to be different than the type of message used to convince a current user to switch to another brand when the technology improves with new features. In this example, it is a question of whether the target audience feels their life would be more fulfilled with the product or without it.

Another example of category need occurs with transportation. If you were thinking about buying a "car" upon graduation, your choice may in fact be a truck or a sports utility vehicle. In a broad sense, all vehicles can be used for transportation, but consumers have particular needs that are satisfied more easily with some types or categories of vehicles versus others. A marketer for SUVs may try to communicate in a way so that a target audience will feel the need for an SUV more strongly than the need for a sporty sub-compact, which might be the initial category of product that young consumers would gravitate towards. In this example, it is a question of which distinct yet related category fulfills the target audience's need more completely.

A car purchase is certainly not restricted to one's first purchase and category need is a communication objective managers need to consider as an option when marketing to current car owners. For example, 64 percent of all Canadian minivan owners who bought a new vehicle purchased another minivan in 2000, however this dropped to 48 percent in 2003. In contrast, corresponding numbers rose for large SUVs (e.g., 28 percent to 38 percent) and small cars (e.g., 49 percent to 63 percent). Research suggests consumers "wanted something different" as the most heavily cited reason for changing the type of vehicle.[23] It appears that astute marketers

Maple Leaf Prime™ Naturally* Branded Chicken

Designating a brand name for a commodity like chicken appeared to be the final frontier in food marketing, but that's the recent strategy for Maple Leaf Poultry, a division of Maple Leaf Foods Inc. when it launched M.L. Prime™ Naturally* branded chicken, a 100% vegetable-grain with no animal by products fed poultry. With no initial competition for branded chicken, M.L. Prime™ Naturally* had the jump on competitors in the 1990s when it was initially marketed as M.L. Prime™ chicken, the first national brand of air chilled chicken. Over time, regional producers entered the market with a similar offering. These entrants included brands like Olymel's Flamingo in Quebec, Lilydale Chicken in Western Canada, and Granny's Poultry Co-op in Manitoba, with Loblaw's President's Choice distributed nationally in its many grocery store formats. In July 2001, in response to increased competition, M.L. Poultry, launched Maple Leaf Prime™ Naturally* chicken — a line of chicken that has been raised on 100% vegetable grain feed with no animal by products.

Two earlier creative ads helped to establish the importance of higher quality chicken and to set the stage for consumers to understand that a premium category of chicken existed (i.e., establish category need). One showed a recruiter interviewing a chicken who desired to be a Prime™ Naturally *chicken, while another ad showed chickens working out to strengthen their thighs so that they would be selected. The underlying message had been to communicate that Prime™ Naturally * is better, leaner, and healthier chicken by clearly making a connection between how the product is "produced" to the resulting benefits.

Some market research indicated that the campaign achieved success. During early stages of the advertising, 32 percent of all consumers studied could recall the Prime™ Naturally* chicken without any prompting other than to name a brand of chicken, according to the Chicken Farmers of Canada. It is also the number one branded chicken in Canada in terms of sales according to ACNielsen, an international firm specializing in marketing research.

M.L. Prime™ Naturally* chicken was part of an overall corporate strategy at Maple Leaf Foods to brand its traditional commodity like products. For example, with the success of Prime™ Naturally* chicken, Maple Leaf Pork introduced an all vegetable-grain fed fresh pork product branded as Maple Leaf Medallion™ Naturally**. Using chicken as a template, Maple Leaf Foods planned to establish a premium category for fresh pork and retain a number one position as well. Maple Leaf Foods as a whole continued with this higher quality direction across all corporate branding communications with an umbrella message of "We take care."

Source: Lesley Young, "Plucky Branding," *Marketing Magazine*, October 6, 2003.

* Canada's leading brand of chicken
** Canada's leading brand of pork

anticipate changing needs and adjust their advertising accordingly and introduce category need as an objective when it is appropriate even in existing markets.

We can describe category need in another perspective. Sticking with the transportation theme, public transit services illustrate their benefits by comparing themselves to limitations of commuting with a car. Recent television ads in Montreal featured the message: "Discover Public Transit" by demonstrating how one could not travel quickly on the highways. The irony of the ad existed in its use of "car-like" visuals—travelling freely at great speed—but then coming to a sudden stop due to traffic. Outdoor signs supported the message at precisely the time when drivers would be experiencing the problem and possibly considering an alternative.[24]

In either of these situations or others, a manager has three options with respect to the category need objective:

- *Category need is omitted.* If the need is quite apparent, then it does not need to be the focus of a particular message or campaign.
- *Category need is reminded.* One obvious example of this is reminder advertising (discussed in Chapter 7), where the brand is communicated and the need for the product is communicated clearly. Often, the reminder option of category need is the focus of campaigns for lapsed users.
- *Category need is emphasized* (that is, "sold"). The above two examples (that is, cellphone and vehicle) show two situations where we actively attempt to persuade the target audience to feel the need for the product.

The Swiss Water Decaffeinated Coffee Company required category need as their communication objective as they faced the difficult task of explaining that its process for decaffeinating coffee used water instead of chemicals. Known as the Swiss Water Process, brand name coffees use this approach and highlight the fact on their packages much like the famous "Intel Inside" or the VQA designation on Canadian wines indicating an adherence to quality production. Swiss Water used the message "Decaf without the chemistry" to highlight the difference, yet not scare the target audience towards other products like decaffeinated tea.[25] Thus, a category need objective is usually imperative when competing technologies or substitute products emerge on the market thus creating two subcategories instead of one general category.

Brand Awareness   **Brand awareness** is a universal communication objective. This means that every single point of communication should contribute to a target audience's understanding and knowledge of the brand name. This understanding and knowledge should go even further such that the target audience knows the category that the brand typically competes in when the consumer is in position to make a purchase or some other related action. This stronger interpretation of awareness is important for the brand to be considered in the decision-making process.

Essentially, there are two types of brand awareness:

- *Brand awareness is through recognition.* If the target audience makes a choice at the point of purchase, then simple recognition of past brand messages can be sufficient for brand consideration or purchase.
- *Brand awareness is through recall.* If the target audience feels the need for a product but needs to remember what brands to consider away from the point of purchase, then recall becomes the focus of the campaign.

Naturally, if both forms of brand awareness are relevant, then a manager may have both as awareness objectives.

Brand recall is often referred to as unaided brand awareness when measuring. After its launch in western Canada in 2001, Bell had achieved only 10 percent unaided brand recall. What this means is that when people are thinking about buying a cellphone service, only one in 10 will think of Bell. Obviously, this reduces Bell's chances of having many consumers enter Bell's stores or call to enquire about its services.[26]

Bell Mobility's continued expansion westward included enhanced network and call centre investments along with more intense distribution of Bell World locations and other retail outlets. As expected, brand awareness remained an important communication objective in 2003 when it also launched its new "Making it simple" campaign. With an eye to new customers in the 18–34 age range and an emphasis on quality and innovation, Bell Mobility improved its awareness to 27 percent.[27]

In defining brand awareness we must be careful in distinguishing it from advertising awareness, which concerns itself with whether consumers are aware of a brand's television or print ads. While there is some logical connection between the two, they are not identical. For example, one study pegged Ford's unaided brand awareness at 78 percent but its unaided advertising awareness at 57 percent. Four other major car firms, GM, Chrysler, Toyota, and Honda, also showed a consistent 20-percent difference between the two types of awareness.[28]

Brand Attitude   **Brand attitude** is another universal communication objective. Like brand awareness, every aspect of a firm's IMC program or any particular element, such as a television commercial, should contribute to some aspect of the overall evaluation of the brand from the perspective of the target audience. A logical conclusion to this point is that there should be no such thing as an "awareness campaign," as the campaign should surely influence brand awareness and some aspect of brand attitude.

Since brand attitude is such an important communication objective, prior understanding of the existing brand attitude is a critical guide for each option:

- *Brand attitude is established.* A new target audience that has no awareness and therefore no prior attitude towards the brand generally requires extensive communication so that an attitude is created or established.
- *Brand attitude is maintained.* Often, advertising is performed so that existing attitude levels will remain constant in order to ensure future sales. Stopping communication is one reason for declining sales that have been seen in many examples over time. In contrast, many major advertisers (e.g., Coca-Cola) consistently follow this approach to maintain sales.
- *Brand attitude is increased.* Target audiences who are familiar with the brand and moderately favourable towards the brand can be influenced. For example, we can increase their brand attitude by getting the target audience to believe that the brand delivers better performance on a particular attribute or benefit.
- *Brand attitude is modified.* Similar to the previous option, if the target audience is moderately favourable, we still seek to improve their attitude. However, we modify the brand attitude if no increase is possible. In this option, marketers use a different point of reference in communicating the benefits. Typically, marketers focus on a new consumer motive for purchasing the brand that the target audience will be receptive towards.
- *Brand attitude is changed.* Negative attitudes are difficult to influence, but in some communication situations, the marketer is faced with the challenge of changing the brand attitude for a target audience.

Brand Purchase Intention   There are two fairly simple options for **brand purchase intention** here:

- *Brand purchase intention is assumed.* In situations (i.e., low involvement) where the strength of an intention to purchase is consistent (i.e., highly correlated) with brand attitude, a marketer is not required to include this objective.
- *Brand purchase intention is generated.* In contrast, managers need the target audience to have a plan to purchase a brand in situations of high involvement.

Brand Purchase Facilitation   A proactive interpretation of marketing communication pervades **brand purchase facilitation** by these two options:

- *Purchase facilitation is included.* If the target audience believes that some aspect of the marketing mix is weak or problematic (i.e., availability at certain types of stores), then the marketer should take this into account when designing ads, and offer reassurance, explanation, or information.
- *Purchase facilitation is omitted.* Naturally, this is not a focus of the ad if there are no perceived problems.

Application   Communication objectives seem quite obvious and easy to do sometimes; however, without careful planning, firms can run into difficulties. ITI, a firm that offers private training in information technology, had difficulties with its

113

marketing communications as it grew from a $2-million company in 1995 to a $50-million company in 2000. Because its 10 locations often did their own advertising, ITI claimed, "The brand was all over the map." Essentially, consumers had difficulty knowing what ITI was or where it fit compared to other training and educational institutions (i.e., connection of brand to category). Consumers were confused as to who the program was for (i.e., connection of brand to the user) and what the program offered (i.e., connection of brand to benefits). Despite success so far, ITI was having trouble achieving key category need, brand awareness, and brand attitude communication objectives.

After research, a carefully constructed IMC campaign that had a clear message, and included TV, radio, print, and the Web, resulted in 35,000 calls in 2000 versus 12,000 in 1999. ITI has successfully positioned itself at the high end of private training services of information technology for consumers who have completed university or college. Not only that, it has set the standard for the industry in terms of communication and branding.[29]

COMMUNICATION OBJECTIVES FOR BUYER DECISION STAGES

In Chapter 2, we presented a model of consumer decision making that showed the stages typically experienced when making a purchase. We outlined several steps: need recognition, information search, alternative evaluation, purchase decision, and post-purchase evaluation. One important role of marketing communications is to help the target audience move through theses stages. Marketers require specific communication tools and messages that will resonate with each target audience as they proceed through these stages. We assess this decision-making process for each target audience and make a conclusion as to which communication objectives are most relevant for each stage. Figure 4–7 illustrates how this works.

FIGURE 4–7 ☐☐☐☐ Assessing the consumer decision-making process

Analysis & Conclusions	Need Recognition	Information Search	Alternative Evaluation	Purchase Decision	Post-Purchase Evaluation
Who? (Roles)					
Where? (Location)					
When? (Time, Timing)					
How? (Shopping Behaviour)					
Why? (Key motivator)					
Communication Objectives					
Message Options					
Communication Tool Options					

The analysis occurs in the first six rows where the marketer includes the target audience information and makes a conclusion on the key communication objectives that need to be attained so that the target audience will continue to the next stage. We have addressed some of these ideas already. The first question (Who?) looks at the key participants in the decision. We highlighted these roles in Chapter 2. The next three questions are descriptors of where, when, and how the shopping behaviour will occur. This is based on market research, managerial experience, flashes of inspiration, and assumptions. The key point is that we need to make clear the behaviour that we are trying to influence.

After summarizing these questions, we determine which communication objectives are necessary to ensure that the consumer continues through all stages. For example, what aspect of brand attitude needs to be addressed at the need-recognition stage versus the alternative-evaluation stage? Is recall an awareness objective at the need-recognition stage and recognition an awareness objective at the purchase-decision stage?

Once this assessment has been done, then the marketer can outline preliminary options concerning the types of messages and communication tools that would be most useful. Returning to the first question above, a marketer may decide to have a fun television commercial (e.g., communication tool option) that emphasizes the emotional attachment (e.g., brand attitude) to the product. It should be noted that when identifying some options, the marketer has not fully committed or recommended that this is exactly the plan, but rather that this is the template of analysis for making the final decision.

The Rogers@Home "Download Rigor Mortis" IMC campaign is an excellent example of these concepts. In the spring and fall of 2000, Rogers put together a campaign to attract new users for its high-speed cable Internet service. It featured the humourous result of consumers requiring medical attention after experiencing rigor mortis when they waited for Internet downloads to occur through regular phone lines. The campaign included TV, print, radio, billboards, Web, and direct mail, and resulted in 100,000 new subscribers. As one Rogers executive noted, "I don't think any one piece works entirely on its own. That's what is nice about integrated campaigns; each piece layered on helps build it."

We can now surmise how each IMC tool played a key role in achieving key communication objectives at each stage of the decision-making process. TV worked well at the need-recognition stage, as it generated initial awareness and allowed consumers to easily see the benefit of a new type of Internet service for them (i.e., category need) and understand that Rogers could deliver the key attribute of speed (i.e., brand attitude). Print and Web enhanced the belief that Rogers could deliver the complete service package, as they contained more information (i.e., brand attitude) that consumers would be seeking at the information-search stage. Radio and poster likely reminded consumers to seek additional information (i.e., purchase facilitation) by phoning the company or visiting the website, if the consumer had not done so previously when they were in the purchase-intention stage. Direct mail encouraged consumers to act (i.e., purchase decision).[30]

The rest of this book focuses on how to make IMC plan decisions that are based on the target audience, behaviour objectives, and communication objectives established at the start of the plan. Chapters 5–8 focus on the message, while Chapters 9–15 focus on the communication tools. As we noted at the start of this chapter, content of this framework becomes the key criteria for making all promotional decisions and the criteria by which the results are measured. While all firms may not be able to afford comprehensive studies to assess communication effects, they would benefit from the use of the framework because it provides disciplined thinking before investing in promotion.

SUMMARY

This chapter has examined the role of objectives in the planning and evaluation of the IMC. Specific objectives are needed to guide the development of the promotional program, as well as to provide a benchmark against which performance can be measured and evaluated. Objectives serve important functions as communications devices, as a guide to planning the IMC program and deciding on various alternatives, and for measurement and evaluation.

Objectives for IMC evolve from the organization's overall marketing plan and are based on the roles various promotional mix elements play in the marketing program. Many managers use sales or a related measure such as market share as the basis for setting objectives. However, many promotional planners believe the role of advertising and other promotional mix elements is to communicate because of the various problems associated with sales-based objectives. They use communications-based objectives like those in the response hierarchy as the basis for setting goals. The first approach for this was DAGMAR, which outlined four principles for setting communication objectives for advertising: well-defined target audience, concrete measurable tasks, benchmark with degree of change sought, and a specified time period.

Much of the emphasis in setting objectives has been on traditional advertising-based views of marketing communications. However, many companies are moving toward zero-based communications planning, which focuses on what tasks need to be done, which marketing communication functions should be used, and to what extent. Many of the principles used in setting advertising objectives can be applied to other elements in the promotional mix.

We presented a comprehensive framework for setting behaviour objectives and communication objectives for all levels: IMC plans, individual IMC tools (i.e., advertising) and specific elements (i.e., print ad). The framework identified options for behaviour objectives to guide the formation of communication objectives. It also presented many options for setting communication objectives. The framework was then linked to the buyer decision-making model to see the connection between a consumer's behaviour and a particular brand's objectives.

KEY TERMS

marketing objectives, *95*
carryover effect, *96*
communication objectives, *99*
DAGMAR, *100*
communication task, *101*
benchmark measures, *102*
zero-based communications planning, *105*

brand trial purchase, *107*
brand trial objective, *107*
brand re-trial purchase, *107*
brand re-trial objective, *107*
brand-switching purchase, *107*
brand-switching objective, *107*
category trial purchase, *107*

category trial objective, *107*
repeat purchase, *107*
repeat-purchase objective, *108*
purchase-related behaviour, *108*
repeat consumption, *109*
repeat-consumption objective, *109*

category need, *110*
brand awareness, *112*
brand attitude, *113*
brand purchase intention, *113*
brand purchase facilitation, *113*

DISCUSSION QUESTIONS

1. Discuss the value of setting objectives for the integrated marketing communications program. What important functions do objectives serve?

2. In meeting with your new boss, she informs you that the only goal of advertising and promotion is to generate sales. Present your argument as to why communications objectives must also be considered.

3. What are some of the problems associated with using sales objectives as the only measure of advertising performance? Can you think of any situation where it may be the best and only measure?

4. What are the strengths and weaknesses of using traditional hierarchy models for setting communication objectives?

5. Some claim that promotion is all about communication, so we should only focus on communication objectives and not worry about behavioural objectives. Convince them otherwise.

6. If a firm cannot afford large market research studies to quantitatively assess whether communication objectives have been achieved, why should the firm bother setting communication objectives?

7. How is the framework discussed in the last section similar to and different from setting communications objectives based on the traditional hierarchy models?

8. In what situations would brand awareness be the only communication objective for an advertising campaign?

9. A firm is running a campaign with advertising, sales promotion, and public relations. Why might it have different communication objectives for each IMC tool?

10. Find a print ad and explain what its communication objectives are. Look at the company's website and determine whether the communication objectives are similar or different.

Brand Positioning Decisions

CHAPTER OBJECTIVES

- To review the concepts of market positioning strategy and market position.

- To apply the positioning concept in an advertising context by defining brand positioning strategy and brand position.

- To illustrate how to formulate the brand positioning strategy decision via brand attitude.

- To summarize various brand positioning strategy options and their link to consumer motives.

- To explain the connection between the brand positioning strategy decision and creativity in promotional communication.

Jays Field a New Positioning

As the Toronto Jays baseball team attempted to reclaim its on-field glory years of the late 1980s and early 1990s, culminating in two successive World Series titles, it also faced the task of attracting an entirely new audience of baseball fans with its current communication plan. In 2002, its attendance figures placed Toronto's Major League Baseball team in the bottom 20 percent after setting records 10 years ago.

While many cited a variety of reasons for the decline such as a less-competitive team, the players' strike of 1994 along with the negative perceptions associated with no World Series winner declared, and the competition from other Toronto area professional sports teams, Jays management believed the main problem was too strong a focus on customer retention at the expense of not attracting new customers.

The Baseball North campaign of 2003 changed the image of baseball and the Jays to appeal to a whole host of potential consumers like kids, women, and younger adults, who may not consider baseball as a primary entertainment alternative. The ads provided a Canadian theme to baseball and gave these newer audiences some more light-hearted reasons for going to a baseball game.

Despite a tough tourist season for Toronto, including the SARS epidemic, attendance soared

more than 10 percent from 1.6 million to 1.8 million. Furthermore, viewership of Jays' televised games was up 30 percent especially among women and those in the 18–35 demographic and registered visitors to the Jays website rose by 150 percent. For 2004, the Jays continued with the Baseball North theme but evolved the original positioning from "It's a Different Kind of Game Up Here" to "You've Got to See These Guys Play."

The communication campaign included additional price promotion for tickets and extensive product placement of the brand in a Martin Short film *Lalawood*, and CTV's teen drama *Degrassi: The Next Generation*, along with plans for other shows directed towards children and young adults.

All of the renewed promotional communication was part of a broader marketing program to change the brand from Blue Jays to Jays. The key changes featured a redesigned logo with new colour combination, a fiercer looking bird, and a font that followed baseball tradition more closely. The new brand appeared necessary when most focus group respondents associated losing with the brand created in the mid-1990s.

Sources: Chris Powell, "Blue Jays Make First Foray into Product Placement with New Logo," *Marketing Magazine*, September 15, 2003; *Play Ball*, March 29, 2004.

As the opening vignette implies, advertising and other promotional communication occurs within a marketing strategy. In fact, marketing strategy influences the role of promotion, and promotional communication decisions must be coordinated to support other marketing programs within the marketing mix. Thus, we can understand the contribution promotional communication has towards the overall positioning of the product to selected target markets, or what is known as a market positioning strategy.

However, the promotional communication described in the vignette also had its own unique communication objectives to persuade a very particular target audience to try the product. In this sense, we can understand how various promotional tools and the whole promotional program influences the positioning of a brand to a designated target audience, or what is known as a brand positioning strategy.

Our investigation in this chapter, to understand positioning for both marketing and advertising, continues our earlier discussion in Chapter 2 on the distinction between target market and target audience and our previous point in Chapter 4 on the importance of linking communication decisions with the overall marketing strategy. We begin by reviewing positioning from a marketing strategy perspective since it is an important input for determining how marketers establish the positioning decisions from an advertising perspective. Next, we define brand positioning strategy and illustrate its connection to brand attitude. We then present two methods for defining brand positioning strategy options and summarize the process to make the final decision. We conclude by summarizing the role of creativity in promotional communication to support brand positioning strategy decisions.

MARKET POSITIONING STRATEGY

Any organization that wants to exchange its products or services in the marketplace successfully should have a **strategic marketing plan** to guide the allocation of its resources. A strategic marketing plan usually evolves from an organization's overall corporate strategy and serves as a guide for specific marketing programs and policies.

Recall from Chapter 1 that we emphasized the importance of advertising professionals to use the marketing plan as an important information source when planning for marketing communication decisions. Furthermore, the marketing plan summarizes the situation analysis comprising an evaluation of the company, consumers, environment, market, competition, and the market positioning strategy. More specifically, those creating ads should be familiar with their client's or organization's market positioning strategy and the supporting market and competitive analysis since it gives direction for how a brand should be positioned in the promotion. In this section, we briefly review this analysis and distinguish between market positioning strategy and a firm's resulting market position.

MARKET ANALYSIS

Market analysis should identify alternative market opportunities for existing product lines in current or new markets, new products for current markets, or new products for new markets. **Market opportunities** are areas where there are favourable demand trends, where the company believes customer needs and opportunities are not being satisfied, and where it can compete effectively. A company usually identifies market opportunities by carefully examining the marketplace and noting demand trends and competition in various market segments.

For example, different market segments in the personal computer (PC) industry include the home, education, science, and business markets. These segments can be even further divided. The business market consists of both small companies and large corporations; the education market can range from elementary schools to colleges and universities. A company that is marketing its products in the PC industry must decide in which particular market segment or segments it wishes to compete. This decision depends on the amount and nature of competition the brand will face in a particular market. For example, Apple Computer is firmly entrenched in the education market. Now it is also targeting the business segment, where IBM and Dell are strong competitors. IBM, in turn, has gained market share in the education segment.

COMPETITIVE ANALYSIS

The competitive analysis may range from direct brand competition (which can also include its own brands) to more indirect forms of competition, such as product substitutes. For example, when Lay's introduced Baked Lay's low-fat chips, the product ended up taking away sales from the regular Lay's potato chip brand. At the same time, new consumers were gained from competing brands of potato chips. In addition to having direct potato chip competitors, Lay's faces competition from other types of snack foods, such as pretzels and crackers. One might argue that other low-fat products also offer the consumer a choice and compete with Lay's as well (for example, fruits).

At a more general level, marketers must recognize they are competing for the consumer's discretionary income, so they must understand the various ways potential customers choose to spend their money. For example, sales of motorcycles in North America had declined significantly in the late 1980s and early 1990s. This decline reflected shifting demographic patterns; aging baby boomers are less inclined to ride motorcycles, and the number of 18- to 34-year-old males has been declining. The drop in sales could also be attributed to the number of other options consumers could spend their discretionary income on, including Jet Skis, dirt bikes, home fitness equipment, spas, and home entertainment systems such as large-screen TVs and stereos. Thus, motorcycle marketers like Honda and Harley-Davidson had to convince potential buyers that a motorcycle was worth a sizable portion of their disposable income in comparison to other purchase options. Through successful marketing strategies, the industry was effective in reversing the downturn, increasing sales by over 25 percent by the late 1990s.[1] Changes in lifestyles have also seen changes in the market for trail, running, basketball, and "lifestyle" shoes such as slip-ons (Exhibit 5–1).

Exhibit 5–1
Merrell sees market opportunities for "lifestyle" shoes

MARKET POSITIONING STRATEGY DEFINITION

Positioning has been defined as "the art and science of fitting the product or service to one or more segments of the broad market in such a way as to set it meaningfully apart from competition."[2] A **market positioning strategy** concerns the final decision of the market(s) in which firms wish to compete, combined with the specific elements of the marketing mix that are designed to fulfill the respective needs of the market(s). Typically, firms will write a market positioning strategy statement in their marketing plan to accurately communicate this decision. This statement will be the guiding principle and direction for each of the four areas of decision within the marketing program development phase: product, price, distribution, and marketing communications.

As the firm develops its market positioning strategy, it may consider many combinations of product attributes with varying price levels across different retail outlets. Alternatively, it could evaluate narrow product choices with very wide distribution and a mass advertising appeal. A firm will consider as many feasible options as possible so that it does not miss an opportunity. At this stage, the firm uses its market research and experience wisely to put together a "package of benefits" that will be acceptable to the target market selected in the previous step.

MARKET POSITION DEFINITION

The market naturally reacts to all the marketing programs after they are developed and implemented. It may be very close to what the firm intended or, for many reasons (i.e., competition, aspects of consumer acceptance), it could be quite different. We define this response to be the **market position** of a firm. This distinction signifies that it is not the current or past strategic plans of the marketing managers, but rather the intended or unintended consumer beliefs of the organization's efforts. For example, for a number of years Ford used the phrase "Quality is Job 1" to signal its organization-wide dedication to improving quality. Throughout many of its marketing efforts, Ford had a market positioning strategy of higher quality so that it could compete with Japanese imports that had gained substantial market share in North America. However, it took years before the majority of consumers truly believed that Ford could deliver a quality vehicle, indicating that there had been a tremendous lag between Ford's market positioning strategy and its actual market position.

To expand on these ideas, we will use the Canadian airline industry as an example. As of 2001, Air Canada represented essentially the only full-service national airline. While it has had various ad campaigns over the years, it has always attempted to maintain this full-service position, especially when it faced competition from Canadian Airlines. WestJet, previously a small regional discount carrier, purchased larger, newer jets so that it could offer services for cross-country routes.[3] Advertising now had to maintain its discount market position throughout the country.

We illustrate this situation with a simple market position diagram, recognizing that alternative interpretations may be feasible (Figure 5–1). We graph two axes, high and low service versus high and low price. WestJet and Air Canada are opposite ends of the service spectrum. It appears that both companies have followed some kind of target market process and are putting together the most appropriate marketing program to be successful. While these market positioning strategies appear suitable attempts to successfully deliver needed airline services, time will tell whether consumers truly believe that each occupies the intended market space and has the correct market position in the minds of consumers.

FIGURE 5–1
Hypothetical illustration of market positioning strategy

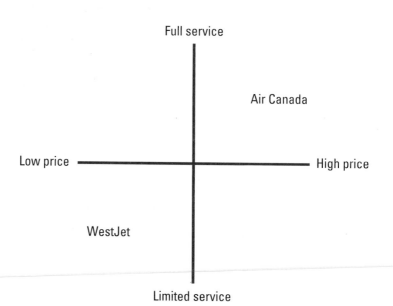

Since promotion is so visible, it is tempting to believe that it alone defines the market positioning strategy. While this may be true in some situations, in most cases, advertising and IMC campaigns typically focus on a particular message that helps the customer understand the product in comparison to other brands *within* a specific product market or category. Furthermore, most ads or other IMC tools speak to a very specific target audience. A bank can have a direct-mail piece to a current customer to obtain a mortgage renewal and focus the message on the ease of continuity and the good follow-up service. Or it may run a TV ad with a message of attractive interest rates and specialized options that may attract customers from competing banks. Since these are obviously different target audiences with different competitive reference points, we need to use the positioning concept appropriately in a communications context that is distinct from positioning in a marketing context. This notion of positioning via marketing communication versus the overall marketing strategy is the topic to which we now turn. We define brand positioning strategy and illustrate how a brand positioning strategy can be developed through the concept of brand attitude.

BRAND POSITIONING STRATEGY

BRAND POSITIONING STRATEGY DEFINITION

Many advertising practitioners consider positioning the most important decision in establishing a brand in the marketplace. David Aaker and John Myers note that the term position has recently been used to indicate the brand's or product's image in the marketplace.[4] Jack Trout and Al Ries suggest that this brand image must contrast with competitors'. They say, "In today's marketplace, the competitors' image is just as important as your own. Sometimes more important."[5] Thus, a **brand positioning strategy**, as used in this text, relates to the intended image of the product or brand relative to a competing brand for a given competitive space as defined by certain product market or category characteristics. The brand positioning strategy is a key decision prior to determining the most effective selling message of the advertising or the IMC. In fact, at some point in the planning process, a brand positioning statement will be written for the appropriate plan.

Now consider your reactions to having seen television commercials or any other communication for any type of product or service. What do you think about the brand, having experienced the message? Do you have positive or negative feelings for the brand? What unique attributes or benefits come to mind when considering the brand? All of these questions pertain to the reactions consumers have to promotions, and constitute what we will refer to as the **brand position**. We need to distinguish between what the firm plans to do with its image versus what the actual image of the brand is, since both occur at different points in time and reside in different locations. The brand positioning strategy is a part of the overall advertising or IMC plan while the brand position exists in the minds of the target audience.

Let us return to our airline example. In the course of developing its discount market positioning strategy, WestJet has a number of options to communicate, of which we will highlight a couple. It could encourage those who never or rarely travel to consider flying since it is now so affordable. Or it may try to convince those who buy the cheapest economy-class tickets (i.e., red-eye flights back east) to buy a WestJet ticket and travel at a more civilized time of the day. In either case, there is a distinct brand positioning strategy decision made to reach each unique target audience. Accordingly, each target audience will have its own unique brand position based on its experiences with the ads and the service.

We continue this idea with a more competitive angle since Air Canada has entered the discount market with Tango. Both WestJet and Tango will compete to be the leader in the discount market, and WestJet may need some elements of their IMC plan to encourage WestJet customers not to switch to Tango or to switch Tango customers to WestJet. These are just a few examples of how WestJet could be using a brand

123

FIGURE 5–2 ☐☐☐☐ Brand position illustration by attributes

FIGURE 5–3 ☐☐☐☐ Brand position illustration by benefits

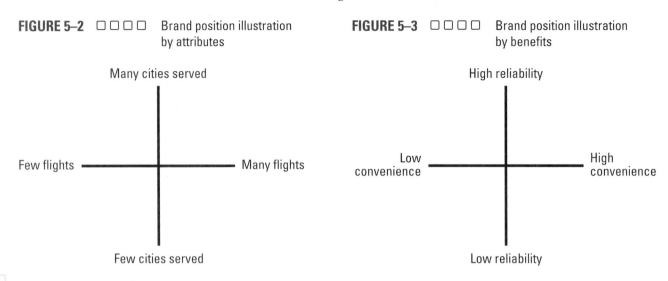

positioning strategy to speak with unique target audiences who are a part of the over-all target market and may be receptive to the overall market positioning strategy.

We now return to our brand position (i.e., consumer perceptions) diagram whereby WestJet and Tango are competing on certain **salient attributes**. Figure 5–2 shows two axes on which the companies *may* compete: frequency of flights and number of cities serviced. We hesitate to locate exactly where both of these firms are, since the discount market is starting to develop. We can also surmise that the airlines *may* be competing on certain **salient benefits** (Figure 5–3) of reliability (i.e., on-time departures, no mechanical delays) and convenience (i.e., check-in, ticket purchase).

Let us turn to another example to illustrate the importance of developing a distinct brand positioning strategy for a new target audience. Sleeman Brewery has maintained an authentic quality position as a microbrewer that makes craft beer (its market position). Much of Sleeman's recent success can be attributed to reaching a core of loyal drinkers in the 35+ age demographic who value its ingredients and brewing methods (brand position). Seeking to grow, Sleeman naturally tried to attract a group of drinkers who were looking to switch as they matured (i.e., aged 25–35). So the issue focused on the appropriate brand positioning strategy to encourage these potential customers to believe that they would now value some of the attributes and benefits of this kind of beer, Sleeman beer in particular. Naturally, the brand positioning strategy that Sleeman used for its new target audience should not alienate the brand position of its loyal drinkers while at the same time maintaining its clear market position. This is quite the challenge and the ads seemed to work.

Sleeman's decided to minimize the use of their long-time spokesperson John Sleeman for their English ads in 2001 while connecting consumption experiences with an attribute of the bottle. The clear glass shows the product clearly such that there is "nothing to hide." Picking up on this idea, the ads symbolically conveyed this with social situations where consumers had "nothing to hide." For example, we do not conceal our true thoughts and feelings when meeting someone. Sleeman continued the theme in 2002 and focused on the fact that the beer does not have a label. It played on the meaning of the word "label" and featured new music groups that had not been signed by a "record label." In both cases, these messages resonate more with a new younger audience.[6] IMC Perspective 5–1 shows another example of brand positioning strategy in the beer market with a similar yet distinct idea in two geographic markets.

Fifty Years of Positioning Labatt 50

Labatt 50 celebrated a company anniversary when it launched in 1950, and from that day forward, the brand revealed a distinct position in different parts of Canada. With unique ad campaigns directed towards each of them throughout the 1960s and 1970s, English Canadians and French Canadians living in Quebec experienced the brand from entirely unique perspectives.

With fewer beer brands in Quebec, considerable investment was placed on Labatt 50 so that it could grow and dominate the market. Second, the brand used a popular culture spokesperson who chatted with various workers about their accomplishments. A well-known comedian at the time, Olivier Guimond represented an ordinary, unpretentious, and charming guy, much like the average Labatt 50 consumer. Accompanied with the slogan: "Lui y connait ça" or "This guy knows…", the brand reached a patriotic status and continued its momentum even with a change in the slogan to a more political tone. At the same time, in contrast, a number of playful ads featuring fun visuals and lots of music dominated English Canadian air-waves. With a wide-range of musical genres, the campaign gave a stylistic feel to the brand. A healthy and adventurous group was seen exploring all parts of Canada and doing all sorts of activities that defined Canada. The end result was that people in Quebec believed Labatt 50 to be a truly Quebec brand, while at the same time, Ontario Labatt 50 drinkers felt the brand was firmly situated within their own province. Even to this day, these beliefs hold true with long-term consumers. However, as the brand slowly declined, the rate was significantly steeper in English Canada where we see a new image emerge.

The present day revival of Labatt 50 builds on its history and continues with more than one brand positioning strategy. A part of the current communication is the redesign of the bottle that has no paper label. Instead, an organic-based polymer ink paint, which can be washed off easily after each use, identifies the brand with a unique image. However, just prior to this, Labatt 50 sales picked up, almost as a "counter-culture" purchase among young consumers. It appears an influential group of young, independent-thinking, urban opinion leaders rediscovered the brand. Picking up on this trend during the launch of the new bottle, Labatt 50 used billboards, illuminated beer signs, beer coasters, and painted delivery trucks with the slogan, "Refuse To Be Labelled." Definitely a low-key approach so as not to fully acknowledge the counter-culture image, yet still retain its street-level orientation, the current brand positioning strategy to this audience has the added feature of not alienating long-term loyal consumers.

Source: Ryan Bigge, "One Beer, Two Solitudes," *Marketing Magazine*, May 5, 2003.

BRAND POSITIONING STRATEGY VIA BRAND ATTITUDE

The previous discussion mentioned the concepts of salient attributes or salient benefits. This notion is based on the idea that consumers may hold a number of different beliefs about brands in any product or service category. However, not all of these beliefs are activated in forming an attitude. Beliefs concerning specific attributes or benefits that are activated and form the basis of an attitude are referred to as **salient beliefs**. Marketers should identify and understand these salient beliefs. They must also recognize that the saliency of beliefs varies among different target audiences, over time, and across different consumption situations. To understand which attributes and benefits to emphasize in advertising, marketers often use a specific model.

Brand Attitude Model Consumer researchers and marketing practitioners have been using multiattribute attitude models to study consumer attitudes for two decades.[7] A **multiattribute attitude model** views an attitude object, such as a product or brand, as possessing a number of attributes that provide the basis on which consumers form their attitudes. According to this model, consumers have beliefs about specific brand attributes and attach different levels of importance to these attributes. Using this approach, an attitude toward a particular brand can be represented as

$$A_B = \sum_{i=1}^{n} B_i \times E_i$$

where A_B = attitude toward a brand
B_i = beliefs about the brand's performance on attribute i
E_i = importance attached to attribute i
n = number of attributes considered

For example, a consumer may have beliefs (B_i) about various brands of toothpaste on certain attributes. One brand may be perceived as having fluoride and thus preventing cavities, tasting good, and helping control tartar buildup. Another brand may not be perceived as having these attributes, but consumers may believe it performs well on other attributes such as freshening breath and whitening teeth.

To predict attitudes, one must know how much importance consumers attach to each of these attributes (E_i). For example, parents purchasing toothpaste for their children may prefer a brand that performs well on cavity prevention, a preference that leads to a more favourable attitude toward the first brand. Teenagers and young adults may prefer a brand that freshens their breath and makes their teeth white and thus prefer the second brand.

Brand Attitude Persuasion Multiattribute models help marketers understand and diagnose the underlying basis of consumers' attitudes. By understanding the beliefs that underlie consumers' evaluations of a brand and the importance of various attributes or benefits, the marketer is better able to develop communication strategies for establishing, maintaining, increasing, modifying, or changing brand attitudes. The multiattribute model provides insight into several ways marketers can influence and persuade consumer attitudes, including:

- Increasing or changing the strength or belief rating of a brand on an important attribute.
- Changing consumers' perceptions of the importance or value of an attribute.
- Adding a new attribute to the attitude formation process.
- Changing perceptions of belief ratings for a competing brand.

The first strategy is commonly used by advertisers. They identify an attribute or benefit that is important and remind consumers how well their brand performs in either case. In situations where consumers do not perceive the marketer's brand as possessing an important attribute or the belief strength is low, advertising strategies may be targeted at changing the belief rating. Even when belief strength is high, advertising may be used to increase the rating of a brand on an important attribute. BMW's "The Ultimate Driving Machine" campaign is a good example of a strategy designed to create a belief and reinforce it through advertising.

Marketers often attempt to influence consumer attitudes by changing the relative importance of a particular attribute. This second strategy involves getting consumers to attach more importance to the attribute in forming their attitude toward the brand. Marketers using this strategy want to increase the importance of an attribute their particular brand has.

The third strategy for influencing consumer attitudes is to add or emphasize a new attribute that consumers can use in evaluating a brand. Marketers often do this by improving their products or focusing on additional benefits or consequences

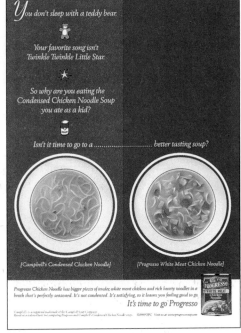

Exhibit 5–2
Panasonic adds a new attribute for customers to consider

Exhibit 5–3
Progresso compares its products to those offered by Campbell's

associated with using the brand. Exhibit 5–2 shows how Panasonic is introducing wireless technology in an attempt to influence consumers' attitudes.

A final strategy marketers use is to change consumer beliefs about the attributes of competing brands or product categories. This strategy has become much more common with the increase in comparative advertising, where marketers compare their brands to competitors' on specific product attributes. An example of this is the Progresso ad shown in Exhibit 5–3, where the company compares what it has to offer to what Campbell's offers.

BRAND POSITIONING STRATEGY OPTIONS

The previous section provided a structured approach for defining brand positioning strategy decisions. In contrast, this section examines the options and the decision-making process. We start by illustrating two approaches for identifying and selecting various options for making the decision and then we present a six-step guide to make sure all aspects of the decision are fully considered.

OPTIONS VIA CONSUMER AND COMPETITION

Brand positioning strategy options can focus on either the consumer or the competition. While both approaches involve the association of product benefits with consumer needs, the former does so by linking the product with the benefits the consumer will derive. The latter approach positions the product by comparing it and the benefit it offers with the competition, as shown in Exhibit 5–4. David Aaker and J. Gary Shansby discuss six brand positioning strategy options: positioning by product attributes, price/quality, use, product class, users, and competitor.[8]

Positioning by Product Attributes and Benefits A common approach to positioning is setting the brand apart from competitors on the basis of the specific characteristics or benefits offered. Sometimes a product may be positioned on more than one

127

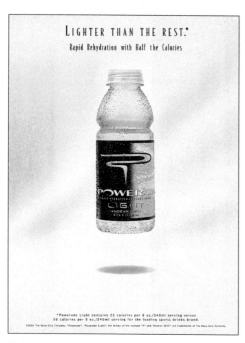

Exhibit 5–4
Positioning that focuses on the competition

Exhibit 5–5
Harvey's positions its hamburgers with a specific attribute

Exhibit 5–6
Lands' End positions its brand as having high quality for the right price

product benefit. Marketers attempt to identify salient attributes (those that are important to consumers and are the basis for making a purchase decision).

For example, the focus of Harvey's advertising message, "Long Live the Grill," emphasizes an attribute regarding how they cook their hamburgers (Exhibit 5–5). Consequently, many consumers can easily interpret a benefit of good taste or better flavour compared with other fast food retailers.[9] By moving towards a specific attribute like this precludes messages regarding other attributes and benefits. Advertisers require good research and reasons for justifying this kind of positioning recommendation.

Positioning by Price/Quality Marketers often use price/quality characteristics to position their brands. One way they do it is with ads that reflect the image of a high-quality brand where cost, while not irrelevant, is considered secondary to the quality benefits derived from using the brand. Premium brands positioned at the high end of the market use this approach to positioning.

Another way to use price/quality characteristics for positioning is to focus on the quality or value offered by the brand at a very competitive price. For example, the Lands' End ad shown in Exhibit 5–6 uses this strategy by suggesting that quality can be affordable. Remember that although price is an important consideration, the product quality must be comparable to, or even better than, competing brands for the positioning strategy to be effective.

Positioning by Use or Application Another way to communicate a specific image or position for a brand is to associate it with a specific use or application. For example, Black & Decker introduced the SnakeLight as an innovative solution to the problem of trying to hold a flashlight while working. A TV commercial showed various uses for the product, while creative packaging and in-store displays were used to communicate the uses (Exhibit 5–7). While this strategy is often used to enter a market based on a particular use or application, it is also an effective way to expand the usage of a product.

Positioning by Product User Positioning a product by associating it with a particular user or group of users is yet another approach. An example would be the Valvoline ad shown in Exhibit 5–8. This campaign emphasizes identification or association with a specific group, in this case, car hobbyists.

Positioning by Competitor Competitors may be as important to positioning strategy as a firm's own product or services. As Trout and Ries observe, the old strategy of ignoring one's competition no longer works.[10] (Advertisers used to think it was a cardinal sin to mention a competitor in their advertising.) In today's market, an effective positioning strategy for a product or brand may focus on specific competitors. Perhaps the best-known example of this strategy was Avis, which positioned itself against the car-rental leader, Hertz, by stating, "We're number two, so we try harder." The PowerAde ad

Exhibit 5–7
Black & Decker shows the various uses of the Snakelight

Exhibit 5–8
Valvoline positions by product user

shown earlier (Exhibit 5–4) is an example of positioning a brand against the competition. When positioning by competitor, a marketer must often employ another positioning strategy as well to differentiate the brand.

Repositioning This positioning strategy involves altering or changing a product's or brand's position. **Repositioning** a product usually occurs because of declining or stagnant sales or because of anticipated opportunities in other market positions. Repositioning is often difficult to accomplish because of entrenched perceptions about and attitudes toward the product or brand. Many companies' attempts to change their positions have met with little or no success.

Exhibit 5–9
This ad is one of a series used in the campaign to reposition Rolling Stone magazine

One extremely successful effort at repositioning was employed by *Rolling Stone* magazine. In an attempt to change advertisers' image of the type of person who reads *Rolling Stone*, the company embarked on an extensive advertising campaign directed at potential advertisers. The ad shown in Exhibit 5–9 is just one example of how this strategy was successfully implemented.

Positioning by Product Class Often the competition for a product comes from outside the product class. For example, airlines know that while they compete with other airlines, trains and buses are also viable alternatives. Via Rail has positioned itself as an alternative to airplanes, citing cost savings, enjoyment, and other advantages. Many margarines position themselves against butter. Rather than positioning against another

129

Surprise! A cup of yogurt
has more potassium than a banana.

One 8 oz. cup of non-fat yogurt has more potassium than a banana, along with
half your daily calcium requirement and many other essential nutrients.* So drink your
milk. Have some yogurt. Enjoy the natural goodness of dairy foods—for life.

Dairy Foods, Good For Life.

America's Dairy Farmers, National Dairy Board ©1991 NDB

Exhibit 5–10
An example of positioning by product class

brand, an alternative strategy is to position oneself against another product category, as shown in Exhibit 5–10.

OPTIONS VIA CONSUMER MOTIVES

The preceding topic summarized the options from a general perspective. However, brand positioning strategy options can also be based on the purchase motivation of the target audience. For instance, as we suggested with the Harvey's attribute positioning, given the content of the ad, the underlying reason for enjoying a grilled hamburger appears to be the taste sensation. However, another perspective is that it could reflect healthier eating (i.e., compared to fried hamburgers) since there is less fat retained in the meat and consequently less fat consumed and a consumer can feel better about oneself and their dietary choices. This connection between the cooking attribute and healthier eating could have been communicated with some subtle changes in the ads of the current campaign. Thus, the attribute positioning still requires the right kind of motivation or reason for purchase demonstrated in the ad to be completely successful.

Keep in mind that the reasons for the Harvey's hamburger purchase are quite distinct, the sensory enjoyment of the hamburger versus the individual accomplishment of eating properly. We highlight these two ideas since they are two of eight basic consumer purchase motives that are more managerially useful to guide the brand positioning strategy decision within Rossiter and Percy's framework we have discussed previously. Figure 5–4 summarizes these motives into two types consistent with psychological theory.

Informational motives are negatively based since the consumer perceives their current consumption situation as some kind of deficit in which the purchase of the product would minimize the shortfall and bring the consumer a neutral or normal state. **Transformational motives** imply consumers perceive their consumption situation as requiring some improvement from a neutral state. Negative and positive oriented motives are consistent with psychological theories of motivation and as you will see when we define each of these motives, two are similar to Maslow's theory, however, there is no implied hierarchy.

Informational Motives Problem removal motives reflect consumption situations where consumers perceive a problem, for example dandruff, and seek a product that resolves the dandruff problem, like anti-dandruff shampoo. Many such products in this category have emphasized this motive in their ads while attempting to highlight its unique attribute or benefit positioning. However, more recent ads for Head and Shoulders in Canada have mentioned the problem while emphasizing how beautiful one's hair feels with their anti-dandruff shampoo, thus reflecting a different primary motive beyond the initial problem removal. Herein lies the reason for

130

FIGURE 5–4
Eight basic consumer purchase motives

Informational Motives	Transformational Motives
Problem removal	Sensory gratification
Problem avoidance	Intellectual stimulation or mastery
Incomplete satisfaction	Social approval
Mixed approach-avoidance	
Normal depletion	

connecting the purchase motive shown in the ad to the brand positioning strategy—it identifies the particular way to communicate effectively with a target audience that the brand has profiled in great detail.

Problem avoidance motives occur when consumers anticipate a problem if they do not take some pre-emptive action through the purchase of a product. Listerine successfully illustrated a problem avoidance motive in its ad messages by colourfully showing how mouthwash superheroes fight germs that cause bad breath. While a positioning by use may be operational, the underlying reason for purchase more precisely defines the overall strategy.

Incomplete satisfaction motives are based on the consumer perceptions that they are not fully satisfied with their current brand choice and are seeking a better product. The Canada food retailer, New York Fries, with 180 outlets in Canada, Australia, and the Middle East, emphasized fresh cut potatoes and cooked to order in a new "Authentically New York" ad message.[11] A positioning on quality, directed towards teens and young adults who purchase high volumes of quick service food, resonates with those who are not completely satisfied with French fries from multiple competing outlets. From another perspective, we can see ads that indicate an incomplete satisfaction motive yet have a positioning by competitor focus. For example, Bell Mobility ran ads inviting Fido users to switch their cell phone provider.[12]

Mixed approach-avoidance motives are active for consumers in purchase situations where they enjoy some elements of a product but dislike other parts and are seeking alternative solutions. WestJet proclaimed itself as a low fare leader in its initial advertising messages. As it developed their service, it also evolved the message to show that it flew more destinations with fun and friendly service.[13] It appears Westjet employed a price/quality brand positioning strategy and its ability to find a competitive niche against Air Canada suggests a mixed approach-avoidance motive, where some consumers liked Air Canada but were seeking a more affordable alternative that had reasonably comparable service levels.

Consumers requiring a product because they have none in stock occurs regularly and so a normal depletion as a reason for purchase is almost an everyday situation, however it is not a viable option for a primary brand positioning strategy. A message focusing on a reminder purchase when a consumer does not have the product is featured in seasonal purchases. For example, gardening products in the spring and back to school supplies in the fall are two obvious ad messages we commonly see. In essence, a normal depletion motive is not a long-term strategy, however it is useful for short-term situations and reaching particular target audiences at a particular point in time to maximize total sales during a year.

Transformational Motives As the term implies, sensory gratification motives are predicated on the product providing a positive experience via one of the five senses. Clearly, this is a valuable approach for indicating purchase in motive for many types of products, but it is important to focus on the right aspect with the right reference point. Encouragement to attend horse racing in Alberta for similar reasons as going to the movies, for the entertainment value, demonstrated a brand repositioning strategy or perhaps positioning by product class to non-users and indicated a sensory gratification motive. Small ads designed like movie ads and placed in the entertainment section of newspapers (versus the sports section to reach current users) provided an entertainment alternative and increased awareness and attendance.[14]

Intellectual stimulation or mastery is an individual motive linked to some element of self-improvement through the purchase of a particular product. Working with their Canadian agency, US Organic Orange Growers sought to develop the Canadian market with the same message "Grown in the U.S.A." that worked well south of the border. Research indicated that Canadians knew that most oranges originated from the U.S., in addition to a few other countries, however, they perceived this attribute with less importance compared to the fact that organic oranges contained 30 percent more vitamin C.[15] Appealing with a health attribute brand positioning strategy, we surmise that improved diet indicates an intellectual stimulation motive as consumers demonstrated their concern for well-being and heightened involvement in their nourishment needs.

Personal recognition is suggested with the social approval motive whereby consumers are motivated to purchase certain product or brands because consumers aspire to be accepted in certain social groups. An anti-smoking message by the Nova Scotia Office of Health Promotion illustrates a social approval motive within the context of positioning towards the product user. The characters from the Canadian cult film *Fubar* provided great tongue-in-cheek reasons to smoke by emphasizing the benefits of body odour and emphysema. The campaign thus positioned non-smoking to non-users of tobacco as something socially desirable.[16]

Competing Positioning Motives Often times, various brands within a product category will compete on a similar motive yet emphasize unique attributes and benefits with a memorable creative campaign. However, we also see instances where the positioning of competing brands will imply different motives. For example, recent ads for Subway focused on health benefits and dietary concerns, implying an intellectual stimulation motive while Mr. Sub and Quiznos ads addressed the "quality ingredients" and "toasted buns" respectively, implying a sensory gratification motive.[17] Subway competed beyond the sub sandwich market (i.e., fast-food hamburger and chicken) and communicated a different and more unique motive from both direct and indirect competitors. The art of positioning and its connection to the creative ad message is challenging and subtle changes must be done with careful consideration to be successful.

BRAND POSITIONING STRATEGY DECISION PROCESS

Having explored the alternative brand positioning strategy options available, the marketer must determine which strategy is best suited for the brand. Essentially, the development of a brand positioning strategy can be broken into a six-step process:[18]

Identify Competitors The marketer must consider all likely competitors, as well as the various effects of use and situations on the consumer.

Assess Consumers' Perceptions of Competitors Once we define the competition, we must determine how they are perceived by consumers. Which attributes are important to consumers in evaluating a product and/or brand?

As you might expect, for many products, they consider a wide variety of attributes or product benefits—most if not all of which are important. Often, consumers are asked to take part in focus groups and/or complete surveys indicating which attributes are important in their purchase decisions.

Determine Competitors' Positions After identifying the relevant attributes and their relative importance to consumers, we must determine how each competitor (including our own entry) is positioned with respect to each attribute. This will also show how the competitors are positioned relative to each other. Consumer research is required to make this assessment.

Analyze the Consumers' Preferences Our discussion of segmentation noted various factors that may distinguish among groups of consumers, including customer versus non-customer, lifestyles, and demographic differences. Each of these segments may have different purchase motivations and different attribute importance ratings. One way to determine these differences is to consider the *ideal brand* or *product*, defined as the object the consumer would prefer over all others, including objects that can be imagined but do not exist.

Make the Brand Positioning Strategy Decision   Going through the first four steps should let us decide which position to assume in the marketplace. Such a decision is not always clear and well defined, however, and research may provide only limited input. In that case, the marketing manager or groups of managers must make some subjective judgments. These judgments raise a number of questions:

- *Is the segmentation approach appropriate?* Positioning entails a decision to segment the market. At this point, managers would re-evaluate or reconsider the previous segmentation decision.
- *Are there sufficient resources available to communicate the brand positioning strategy effectively?* It is very expensive to establish a position. One ad, or even a series of ads, is not likely to be enough. The marketer must commit to a long-range effort in all aspects of the marketing campaign to make sure the objectives sought are obtained. Too often, the firm abandons a position and/or advertising campaign long before it can establish a position successfully. Further, once a successful position is attained, it is likely to attract competitors. It may become expensive to ward off me-too brands and continue to hold on to the brand distinction.
- *How strong is the competition?* The marketing manager must ask whether a position sought is likely to be maintained, given the strengths of the competition.
- *Is the current brand positioning strategy working?* If current efforts are not working, it may be time to consider an alternative brand positioning strategy. But if they are working, a change is usually unwise. Sometimes executives become bored with a theme and decide it is time for a change, but this change causes confusion in the marketplace and weakens a brand's position.

Monitor the Position   Once a brand position has been established, we want to monitor how well it is being maintained in the marketplace. Tracking studies measure the image of the product or firm over time. Changes in consumers' perceptions can be determined, with any slippage immediately noted and reacted to. At the same time, the impact of competitors can be determined.

As we have illustrated in this section, the brand positioning strategy decision is an important requirement for setting the overall strategy for advertising. From this direction, the content of the advertising message, its creative strategy, and tactics can be formulated. Thus, the next step is to ensure that the creativity and the content of the message persuade the target audience appropriately and is consistent with the brand positioning strategy. IMC Perspective 5–2 demonstrates this close connection.

We illustrate this connection between strategy and the creativity and content of the message in the context of advertising since it is so pervasive and familiar to you, and since the general idea process is consistent with other promotional communication tools. The process is consistent whether we are constructing an advertising campaign or a campaign for another promotional communication tool. For example, prior to launching a public relations or publicity campaign, a marketer would specify the positioning of its brand to its intended target audience before deciding upon the exact content of its message and how he or she would creatively present it.

Savin Advertising Connects with Customers

Savin's campaign that launched in 1996 used the tagline "We're going to win you over." The goal of the campaign was to build awareness of and add value to the brand name and to place Savin on the "considered list" of the middle managers who influence or make the copier purchase decisions for their company. A year later Savin launched the second phase of the campaign, which focused on document management and product line attributes, and the tagline evolved into "We've got what it takes to win you over." The first two phases of the campaign leveraged Savin's renewed focus on people, products, and programs and positioned the company as faster and easier to do business with. However, the market was changing rapidly with the emergence of digital technology that offered improved output quality in black and white and colour as well as network connectivity.

Think inside the box.

Think Savin.

The merging of printing and copying functionality changed the marketing focus, as more companies were offering products with similar benefits to the same customers. However, the target audience within companies was shifting. The traditional copier buyer, such as an office manager, was no longer the only person involved in the purchase decision or was losing power to information technology (IT) departments. Moreover, Savin's competitors such as Xerox, Canon, and Hewlet-Packard were seen as the safe choice, and there was still a need to position the company as a viable player in the digital office equipment market.

In 1998 Savin launched the "Alternative to Xerox" campaign. The comparative ads piggybacked off Xerox's efforts to promote new digital copiers and mocked Xerox for wanting to be the "biggest" document company. Savin's ads positioned the company as the "fastest, most responsive and easy to work with name in the business." And since there was a need to reach both existing copier buyers and new customers in the IT space, Savin felt the ad campaign would ring a bell with them. When the comparative campaign began in mid-1998, Savin had a small 2.9 percent share of the U.S. office-copier market, placing it a lowly eleventh out of 14 brands, while Xerox led the industry with a 16.4 percent market share. However, in 1998 and 1999 Savin's growth in sales outpaced that of all major providers of document output systems, and the company nearly doubled its digital sales. The decision to compare Savin to

Xerox built on a successful campaign used 20 years previously that many customers still remembered.

While Savin's comparative campaign was very successful, by 2000, market conditions had changed, causing the company to reconsider its creative strategy. Negative press reports about financial, sales, and marketing issues at Xerox raised concern about using the company as a reference point in Savin advertising and positioning itself as an alternative to the troubled competitor. Also, with the growth of the Internet, intranets, e-mail, and fax machines, the office environment was changing from a "print and distribute" approach to more of a "distribute and print" process. Thus in 2001 Savin decided to take its advertising in a different direction to position the company as an attractive player in the digital office equipment market with its "Think Inside the Box" campaign. The objective of the new creative strategy is to convince decision makers that Savin provides both the advanced digital imaging solutions they need and the customer-focused attitude they want to support all of their network printing and copying requirements. A softening of media costs due to the advertising recession opened the opportunity for Savin to use television advertising for the first time in recent years as part of the campaign, and three 15-second spots were created. The shift to TV makes it possible to broaden awareness of Savin, maximize impact, and generate excitement among its dealer partners. However, creativity was important to enable the spots to break through the clutter, which they have done successfully. Savin is enjoying almost double-digit growth in a category that has experienced a 2-percent annual decline in recent years.

Companies have been responding very favourably to Savin's easy-to-do-business-with philosophy and its ability to provide solutions to all of their printing and copying needs. They also have been responding well to Savin's advertising, which has helped build awareness of the company and position it as a major player in the digital office equipment market.

Sources: Personal correspondence with Louise Stix, Manager of Corporate Communications and Creative Services, Savin Corporation; Raju Narisetti, "Savin Hopes Campaign Will Boost Image," *The Wall Street Journal*, May 19, 1998, p. B10; "Savin Corp. Having Award-Winning Year," *Business Wire*, June 8, 1999.

Upon determining the direction for the communications program, the advertising agency, or the department in the organization responsible for developing ads, focuses on

ADVERTISING CREATIVITY

finding an appropriate creative approach to communicate a message that reinforces the brand positioning strategy. Good advertising creativity can often be central to determining the success of a product or service as it clearly contributes to a strong brand position with its intended target audience. The essence of advertising is its creativity and we now provide a working definition and give you a sense of its importance.

DEFINITION OF ADVERTISING CREATIVITY

For many students, as well as many advertising and marketing practitioners, the most interesting aspect of advertising is the creative side. We have all at one time or another been intrigued by an ad and admired the creative insight that went into it. A great ad is a joy to behold and often an epic to create, as the cost of producing a TV commercial can exceed $1 million. Many companies see this as money well spent. They realize that the manner in which the advertising message is developed and executed is often critical to the success of the promotional program, which in turn can influence the effectiveness of the entire marketing program. Procter & Gamble, Levi Strauss, Nissan, Coke, Pepsi, Nike, McDonald's, and many other companies spend a lot of money each year to produce advertising messages and a lot more to purchase media time and space to run them. While these companies make excellent products, they realize creative advertising is also an important part of their marketing success.

Creativity is probably one of the most commonly used terms in advertising. Ads are often called creative. The people who develop ads and commercials are known as creative specialists. These specialists work for ad agencies that develop ad campaigns or for marketers that handle their own advertising without the help of an agency. Perhaps so much attention is focused on the concept of creativity because many people view the specific challenge given to those who develop an advertising message as being creative. It is their job to turn all of the information regarding product features and benefits, marketing plans, consumer research, and communication objectives into a creative concept that will bring the advertising message to life. This begs the question: What is meant by *creativity* in advertising?

Advertising creativity is the ability to generate fresh, unique, and appropriate ideas that can be used as effective solutions to communications problems. To be *appropriate* and *effective*, a creative idea must be relevant to the target audience. Relevance, as an important characteristic of creativity, has to instantly capture the target audience's attention and generate critical brand associations through specific cognitive and emotional responses. The relevance is even more critical when an advertiser takes into account the selective attention of the target audience. Moreover, the creativity has to crystallize the brand so that it is understood by the target audience, who is also experiencing selective comprehension when faced with many competing promotional messages. Extending this further, the relevance of the creativity to the target audience is critical to establishing an important link to the brand, its benefits, and why the target audience would purchase it. In other words, relevance clearly supports the brand positioning strategy.

Advertising creativity is not the exclusive domain of creative specialists. The nature of the business requires creative thinking from everyone involved in the promotional planning process. Agency people, such as account executives, media planners, researchers, and attorneys, as well as those on the client side, such as marketing and brand managers, must all seek creative solutions to problems encountered in planning, developing, and executing an advertising campaign.

An excellent example of creative synergy between the media and creative departments of an agency, as well as with the client, is seen in the TBWA/Chiat/Day agency and its relationship with Absolut vodka. As discussed in Chapter 1, the creative strategy for the brand plays off the distinctive shape of its bottle and depicts it with visual puns and witty headlines that play off the Absolut name. The agency and client recognized they could carry the advertising campaign further by tailoring the print ads for the magazines or regions where they appear. Absolut's media schedule includes over 100 magazines, among them various consumer and business publications. The creative and media departments work together selecting magazines and deciding on the ads that will appeal to the readers of each publication. The creative department is often asked to create media-specific ads to run in a particular publication.

IMPORTANCE OF ADVERTISING CREATIVITY

Perspectives on what constitutes creativity in advertising differ. At one extreme are people who argue that advertising is creative only if it sells the product. An advertising message's or campaign's impact on sales counts more than whether it is innovative. At the other end of the continuum are those who judge the creativity of an ad in terms of its artistic or aesthetic value and originality. They contend creative ads can break through the competitive clutter, grab the consumer's attention, and have a positive communication effect. Both perspectives indicate the importance of advertising creativity as it either presents a good public exposure or contributes to a brand positioning strategy and ultimately sales.

As you might expect, perspectives on advertising creativity often depend on one's role. A study by Elizabeth Hirschman examined the perceptions of various individuals involved in the creation and production of TV commercials, including management types (brand managers and account executives) and creatives (art director, copywriter, commercial director, and producer).[19] She found that product managers and account executives view ads as promotional tools whose primary purpose is to communicate favourable impressions to the marketplace. They believe a commercial should be evaluated in terms of whether it fulfills the client's marketing and communicative objectives. The perspective of those on the creative side was much more self-serving, as Hirschman noted:

> In direct contrast to this client orientation, the art director, copywriter, and commercial director viewed the advertisement as a communication vehicle for promoting their own aesthetic viewpoints and personal career objectives. Both the copywriter and art director made this point explicitly, noting that a desirable commercial from their standpoint was one which communicated their unique creative talents and thereby permitted them to obtain "better" jobs at an increased salary.[20]

In her interviews, Hirschman also found that brand managers were much more risk-averse and wanted a more conservative commercial than the creative people, who wanted to maximize the impact of the message.

What constitutes creativity in advertising is probably somewhere between the two extremes. To break through the clutter and make an impression on the target audience, an ad often must be unique and entertaining. Research has shown that a major determinant of whether a commercial will be successful in changing brand preferences is its "likability," or the viewer's overall reaction.[21] TV commercials and print ads that are well designed and executed and generate emotional responses can create positive feelings that are transferred to the product or service being advertised. Many creative specialists believe this type of advertising can come about only if they are given considerable latitude in developing advertising messages. But ads that are creative only for the sake of being creative often fail to communicate a relevant or meaningful message that will lead consumers to purchase the product or service.

Everyone involved in planning and developing an advertising campaign must understand the importance of balancing the "it's not creative unless it sells" perspective with the novelty/uniqueness and impact position. Marketing and brand managers or account executives must recognize that imposing too many sales- and marketing-oriented communications objectives on the creative team can result in mediocre advertising, which is often ineffective in today's competitive, cluttered media environment. At the same time, the creative specialists must recognize that the goal of advertising is to assist in selling the product or service and good advertising must communicate in a manner that helps the client achieve this goal.

Another perspective on the issue of creativity is that some Canadian creative people believe that advertising should play an important role in society and be financially accountable. Advertising can have subtle flair and finesse reflecting current social trends and enhance the collective intelligence of society while still cleverly indicating a motive for purchase to ensure a positive investment from a business standpoint.[22] Whether all marketers and agencies agree with this perspective it still highlights the inherent tension between creativity and financial results.

PLANNING CREATIVE STRATEGY

Creative specialists must take all the research, creative briefs, strategy statements, communications objectives, and other input and transform them into an advertising message. Their job is to write copy, design layouts and illustrations, or produce commercials that effectively communicate the central theme on which the campaign is based. Rather than simply stating the features or benefits of a product or service, they must put the advertising message into a form that will engage the audience's interest and make the ads memorable.[23] In this section, we describe the creative challenge, illustrate the creative process, and summarize the end result—the copy platform—when planning for creative promotional communication that supports the brand positioning strategy.

CREATIVE CHALLENGE

The job of the creative team is challenging because every marketing situation is different and each campaign or advertisement may require a different creative approach. Numerous guidelines have been developed for creating effective advertising,[24] but there is no magic formula. As copywriter Hank Sneiden notes in his book *Advertising Pure and Simple*:

> Rules lead to dull stereotyped advertising, and they stifle creativity, inspiration, initiative, and progress. The only hard and fast rule that I know of in advertising is that there are no rules. No formulas. No right way. Given the same problem, a dozen creative talents would solve it a dozen different ways. If there were a sure-fire formula for successful advertising, everyone would use it. Then there'd be no need for creative people. We would simply program robots to create our ads and commercials and they'd sell loads of product—to other robots.[25]

Many creative people follow proven formulas when creating ads because they are safe. Clients often feel uncomfortable with advertising that is too different. Bill Tragos, former chair of TBWA, the advertising agency noted for its excellent creative work for Absolut vodka, Evian, and many other clients, says, "Very few clients realize that the reason that their work is so bad is that they are the ones who commandeered it and directed it to be that way. I think that at least 50 percent of an agency's successful work resides in the client."[26] Many creative people say it is important for markets to take some risks if they want breakthrough advertising that gets noticed.

Not all agree that advertising has to be risky to be effective, however. Many marketing managers are more comfortable with advertising that simply communicates product or service features and benefits and gives the consumer a reason to buy. They see their ad campaigns as multimillion-dollar investments whose goal is to sell

137

the product rather than finance the whims of their agency's creative staff. They argue that some creative people have lost sight of advertising's bottom line: Does it sell?

CREATIVE PROCESS

Some advertising people say creativity in advertising is best viewed as a process and creative success is most likely when some organized approach is followed. This does not mean there is an infallible blueprint to follow to create effective advertising; as we saw earlier, many advertising people reject attempts to standardize creativity or develop rules. However, most do follow a process when developing an ad.

One of the most popular approaches to creativity in advertising was developed by James Webb Young, a former creative vice president at the J. Walter Thompson agency. Young said, "The production of ideas is just as definite a process as the production of Fords; the production of ideas, too, runs an assembly line; in this production the mind follows an operative technique which can be learned and controlled; and that its effective use is just as much a matter of practice in the technique as in the effective use of any tool."[27]

Young's process of creativity is similar to a four-stage approach outlined much earlier by English sociologist Graham Wallas:

1. *Preparation.* Gathering background information needed to solve the problem through research and study.
2. *Incubation.* Getting away and letting ideas develop.
3. *Illumination.* Seeing the light or solution.
4. *Verification.* Refining and polishing the idea and seeing if it is an appropriate solution.

Models of the creative process are valuable to those working in the creative area of advertising, since they offer an organized way to approach an advertising problem. These models do not say much about how this information will be synthesized and used by the creative specialist because this part of the process is unique to the individual. Despite this limitation, the models offer a useful way of describing the creative process.

Preparation, Incubation, and Illumination Stages Only the most foolish creative person or team would approach an assignment without first learning as much as possible about the product or service, the target audience, the competition, and any other relevant **research**. Much of this information would come from the marketing plan and advertising plan, which would give the creative specialist an idea as to the direction of the brand positioning strategy. The creative specialist can acquire background information in numerous ways. Some informal fact-finding techniques have been noted by Sandra Moriarty:

- Reading anything related to the product or market.
- Talking to many people (i.e., marketers, designers, engineers, salespeople, consumers).
- Visits to stores, malls.
- Using the product or service and becoming familiar with it.
- Working in and learning about the business.[28]

Humpty Dumpty saw the importance of research for making advertising and promotion decisions. A brand of potato chips that had seen little change in its communications for some time undertook a comprehensive review of its identity with a market research firm and its advertising agency. The results indicated that while the brand was outdated, old-fashioned, and tired, the teenage target audience would still be receptive to the brand. A key challenge was to find the right creative message that would modify the target's attitude. TV ads led this IMC campaign and the initial two spots communicated taste and flavour attributes while "re-inventing" the Humpty Dumpty character as strong and confident. It appears that consumer were connecting with the brand with shelf space and sales starting to grow.[29]

Creative people use both general and product-specific preplanning input. **General preplanning input** can include books, periodicals, trade publications, scholarly journals, pictures, and clipping services, which gather and organize magazine and newspaper articles on the product, the market, and the competition, including the latter's ads. Another useful general preplanning input concerns trends, developments, and happenings in the marketplace. Information is available from a variety of sources, including local, provincial, and federal governments, secondary research suppliers, and various industry trade associations, as well as advertising and media organizations that publish research reports and newsletters that provide information on market trends and developments and how they might affect consumers. Those involved in developing creative strategy can also gather relevant and timely information by reading Canadian publications like *Marketing* or *Strategy*, and American publications like *Adweek*, *Advertising Age*, and *Brand Week*.

In addition to getting general background research, creative people receive **product/service-specific preplanning input**. This information generally comes in the form of specific studies conducted on the product or service, the target audience, or a combination of the two. Quantitative consumer research includes attitude studies, market structure and positioning studies such as perceptual mapping and psychographic or lifestyle profiles.

Some agencies conduct psychographic studies annually and construct detailed psychographic or lifestyle profiles of product or service users. DDB Needham conducts a large-scale psychographic study each year using a sample of 4,000 U.S. adults. The agency's Life Style Study provides its creative teams with a better understanding of the target audience for whom they are developing ads.

For example, information from its Life Style Study was used by DDB Needham's creative department in developing a recent advertising campaign for Westin. The agency's Life Style Study showed that the younger business travellers the luxury hotel chain was targeting are highly confident, intelligent, assertive, and classy and considered themselves to be a "winner." Rather than using the traditional images that feature buildings and golf courses, the creative team decided to "brand the user" by playing to their ego and reinforcing their strong self-image. The ad campaign used the tagline "Who is he/she sleeping with? Westin. Choose your travel partner wisely" (Exhibit 5–11).

Qualitative research is used to gain insight into the underlying causes of consumer behaviour. Methods employed include in-depth interviews, projective techniques, association tests, and focus groups in which consumers are encouraged to bring out associations related to products and brands (see Figure 5–5). This research is often referred to as motivation research. In general, motivation research is considered important in assessing how and why consumers buy. Focus groups and in-depth interviews are valuable methods for gaining insights into consumers' feelings, and projective techniques are often the only way to get around stereotypical or socially desirable responses.

Focus groups are a prevalent research tool at this stage of the creative process. Focus groups are a research method whereby consumers (usually 10 to 12 people)

Westin Hotels & Resorts
"Male/No Jeans" :30TV ZDNE 6103

(MUSIC: UNDER THROUGHOUT)
(AVO): Broke his neck to get this job...
(MUSIC)
(AVO): ...then broke the corporate sales record.
Even broke the corporate "No Jeans" rule.
Who's he sleeping with?
(MUSIC)
(MUSIC)
Westin.
Choose...
your travel partner wisely.
(MUSIC)
(MUSIC)
(MUSIC)
(MUSIC)

Exhibit 5–11
DDB Needham's Life Style Study provided valuable input in the development of this campaign for Westin

139

FIGURE 5–5

Some of the marketing research methods employed to probe the mind of the consumer

☐☐☐☐☐

In-depth interviews

Face-to-face situations in which an interviewer asks a consumer to talk freely in an unstructured interview using specific questions designed to obtain insights into his or her motives, ideas, or opinions.

Projective techniques

Efforts designed to gain insights into consumers' values, motives, attitudes, or needs that are difficult to express or identify by having them project these internal states upon some external object.

Association tests

A technique in which an individual is asked to respond with the first thing that comes to mind when he or she is presented with a stimulus; the stimulus may be a word, picture, ad, and so on.

Focus groups

A small number of people with similar backgrounds and/or interests who are brought together to discuss a particular product, idea, or issue.

from the target audience are led through a discussion regarding a particular topic. Focus groups give insight as to why and how consumers use a product or service, what is important to them in choosing a particular brand, what they like and don't like about various products or services, and any special needs they might have that aren't being satisfied. A focus group session might also include a discussion of types of ad appeals to use or evaluate the advertising of various companies.

Focus group interviews bring the creative people and others involved in creative strategy development into contact with the customers. Listening to a focus group gives copywriters, art directors, and other creative specialists a better sense of who the target audience is, what the audience is like, and who the creatives need to write, design, or direct to in creating an advertising message.

Since motivation research studies typically use so few participants, there is also concern that they really discover the idiosyncracies of only a few individuals and their findings are not generalizable to the whole population. Still, it is difficult to ignore motivation research in furthering our understanding of consumer behaviour. Its insights can often be used as a basis for advertising messages aimed at buyers' deeply rooted feelings, hopes, aspirations, and fears.

Verification Stage The verification stage of the creative process evaluates ideas generated during the preparation stage, rejects inappropriate ones, refines and polishes those that remain, and gives them final expression. Techniques used at this stage include directed focus groups to evaluate creative ideas/themes; message communication studies; portfolio tests; and evaluation measures such as viewer reaction profiles.

1. Basic problem or opportunity the advertising must address
2. Target audience(s) and behaviour objective(s)
3. Communication objectives
4. Brand positioning strategy statement
5. Creative strategy (creative theme, message appeal, source characteristic)
6. Supporting information and requirements

FIGURE 5–6
Copy-platform outline

☐ ☐ ☐ ☐ ☐

For example, members of the target audience may be asked to evaluate rough creative layouts and to indicate what meaning they get from the ad, what they think of its execution, or how they react to a slogan or theme. The creative team can gain insight into how a TV commercial might communicate its message by having members of the target audience evaluate the ad in storyboard form. A **storyboard** is a series of drawings used to present the visual plan or layout of a proposed commercial. It contains a series of sketches of key frames or scenes along with the copy or audio portion for each scene.

Evaluating a commercial in storyboard form can be difficult because storyboards are too abstract for many consumers to understand. To make the creative layout more realistic and easier to evaluate, the agency may produce an **animatic**, a videotape of the storyboard along with an audio soundtrack. Storyboards and animatics are useful for research purposes as well as for presenting the creative idea to other agency personnel or to the client for discussion and approval. At this stage of the process, the creative team is attempting to find the best creative strategy before moving ahead with the actual production of the ad. The verification stage may conclude with more formal, extensive pretesting of the ad before a final decision is made. Pretesting and related procedures are examined in detail in Chapter 8.

COPY PLATFORM

The end result of the creative process is the written document referred to as copy platform. It specifies the basic elements of the creative strategy and other relevant information that the creative team used. The **copy platform** may have other names depending upon the firm. Essentially, it is plan that summarizes the entire creative approach that is agreed upon by the creative team and the marketing managers.

Figure 5–6 shows a sample copy-platform outline that can be used to guide the creative process. Just as there are different names for the copy platform, there are variations in the outline and format used and in the level of detail included. Copy platforms also include supporting information and requirements (i.e., brand identifications, disclaimers) that should appear in any advertising message to ensure uniformity across various executions of the ads used in a campaign or in meeting any legal requirements.

The first three sections are derived from the marketing plan and prior communications between the creative specialists and brand managers. These sections may be revised slightly during the creative process. The content of these sections were discussed in previous chapters. For example, Chapter 4 showed how the setting of communication objectives requires specifying a well-defined target audience and developing a communication task statement that spells out what message must be communicated to this audience. Determining what problem the product or service will solve or what issue must be addressed in the ad helps in establishing communication objectives for the campaign to accomplish.

At times, creative specialists experience communication problems among the various participants of the creative process. Part of the problem is attributed to creative personnel not actually writing a copy platform. The creative process may be initially described in a series of notes or sketches, and as it evolves through the stages of the creative process, some of the original participants may not be aware of all the changes. Alternatively, the lack of full description leads to misunderstanding of how the sequence of events, for example, would occur in a television commercial. And while it is important to have a written copy platform, it should be brief enough so that all participants could read it quickly and easily and still demonstrate the creativity of the advertising. In the end we can say that the copy platform should (1) be objective, (2) have proper vocabulary, spelling, and grammar, (3) demonstrate logical thinking, (4) be both creative and brief, (5) have specific recommendations, and (6) be viewed as a firm agreement.[30]

Some of the steps of a copy platform are seen in a campaign developed for Polaroid a few years ago. The creative team was faced with the challenge of redefining the relevancy of instant photography and bringing Polaroid cameras out of the closet and back into everyday use. This suggests that the target audience was lapsed users of existing Polaroid instant cameras (and potentially new users of instant cameras) with the intention of generating greater awareness and modifying their attitude. Working with Polaroid's marketing personnel, the agency came up with the idea of focusing on an instant picture as a solution to a problem, an instant tool or "catalyst" to make something happen. The advertising message is designed to give people ideas about how to use their forgotten Polaroid cameras. Thus, a clear brand positioning statement with a specific motive is identified.

The three key decisions of the creative strategy are usually included in the copy platform: creative theme, message appeal, and source characteristics. These are often the responsibility of the creative team or specialist and form the basis of the advertising campaign theme. For Polaroid, the creative idea was "the picture is only the beginning," and the resulting campaign theme built around this idea was "See what develops." The creative strategy was to have each ad in the campaign tell a story in which a Polaroid camera sets off a chain reaction. For example, one of the TV commercials featured a harried architect in a meeting telling his wife on the phone that he can't possibly come home for lunch. But in a sultry voice she tells him to look in his briefcase, saying "I left you something this morning." He pulls out a Polaroid photo, his eyes widen, and he says, "I'll be there in 10 minutes." Another

Exhibit 5–12
The major selling idea behind this Polaroid commercial is that the picture is only the beginning of the story

humourous spot from the campaign shows a dog, wrongfully being scolded for upsetting the trash while an evil-looking cat sneers from the other side of the kitchen. The owner leaves, and the cat goes for the trash once again. However, this time the dog takes a Polaroid snapshot of the cat, astride the trash with a chicken bone in its mouth, and then patiently waits, incriminating photo in mouth, as the door opens and the owner returns. "Oh dear," we hear as the picture fades (Exhibit 5–12). As suggested, these creative examples use a humour appeal with ordinary consumers from the target audience as the source of the message. In this example, we have started to identify the key creative decisions. The next chapter will discuss these fully.

SUMMARY

Promotion plays an important role in an organization's efforts to market its product, service, or ideas to its customers. The marketing process begins with a marketing strategy that is based on a detailed situation analysis and guides for target market selection and development of the firm's marketing program. In the promotional planning process, the situation analysis requires that the marketing strategy be assumed. One of the key decisions to understand from the marketing plan pertains to the target market process, where we segment the market, select a target market, and determine the market positioning strategy.

In many promotional situations, a marketer attempts to communicate with a particular target audience that has been profiled with many segmentation variables. Advertising or any other persuasive message is guided by a company's brand positioning strategy that specifies how it is intending to influence its target audience within a given product category or product-market. The resulting promotions yield a brand position in the minds of the intended target audience. A brand attitude model guides the brand positioning strategy decision. Consumer and competitive approaches for constructing the brand positioning strategy decision provide the advertiser with many ways of constructing and evaluating different options.

The creative development and execution of the advertising message are a crucial part of a firm's integrated marketing communications program. The creative specialist or team is responsible for developing an effective way to communicate the marketer's message to the customer and reinforce the brand positioning strategy. Marketers often turn to ad agencies to develop, prepare, and implement their creative strategy since these agencies are specialists in the creative function of advertising.

The challenge facing the writers, artists, and others who develop ads is to be creative and come up with fresh, unique, and appropriate ideas that can be used as solutions to communications problems. Creativity in advertising is a process of several stages, including preparation, incubation, illumination, and verification. Various sources of information are available to help the creative specialists determine the best creative strategy.

Creative strategy is guided by marketing goals and objectives and is based on a number of factors, including the basic problem the advertising must address, the target audience, behavioural and communication objectives the message seeks to accomplish, and key benefits the advertiser wants to communicate as reflected in the brand positioning strategy. These factors and the creative strategy decisions are generally stated in a copy platform, which is a work plan used to guide development of the ad campaign.

KEY TERMS

strategic marketing plan, *120*

market opportunities, *120*

positioning, *121*

market positioning strategy, *121*

market position, *122*

brand positioning strategy, *123*

brand position, *123*

salient attributes, *124*

salient benefits, *124*

salient beliefs, *125*

multiattribute attitude model, *126*

repositioning, *129*

informational motive, *130*

transformational motive, *130*

advertising creativity, *135*

research, *138*

general preplanning input, *139*

product/service-specific preplanning input, *139*

focus groups, *139*

storyboard, *141*

animatic, *141*

copy platform, *141*

DISCUSSION QUESTIONS

1. Establishing brand image is often difficult for new companies. Explain what these companies must do to establish a strong brand image.

2. More and more business-to-business companies have gone away from purely trade advertising to advertising on consumer media. Is this likely to be a successful strategy? Why or why not?

3. Describe how the market positioning strategy adopted for a brand would need to be supported by all other elements of the marketing mix.

4. What is meant by brand positioning strategy? Discuss the various approaches and give examples of companies or brands that use each approach.

5. What factors would lead a marketer to the use of a repositioning strategy? Find a product or service that has been repositioned recently and analyze the strategy.

6. Assume you have been assigned to work on the advertising campaign for a new soft drink. Describe the various types of general and product-specific pre-planning input you might provide to the creative team.

Creative Strategy Decisions

CHAPTER OBJECTIVES

- To identify three key decisions that comprise a creative strategy: creative theme, message appeal, and message source.

- To explore various approaches used for determining the creative theme that forms the basis of an advertising campaign.

- To summarize the different types of message appeals that advertisers use to persuade their target audience.

- To highlight the source or communicator options a marketer has for a promotional message.

Pfizer's Creative Ads

Pfizer's ad campaigns and its consumer product launches has put it in the forefront of marketing, taking it from being the 27th largest Canadian pharmaceutical company in 1992 to number one! Pfizer's ambitious and innovative marketing programs resulted in it being recognized as Marketer of the Year by *Marketing Magazine* for 2002.

Viagra, of course, was the main attraction as the creative strategy broke new ground with its direct-to-consumer (DTC) ad that showed a smiling middle-aged man who jumps a newspaper vending machine, joins in a kids' basketball game, and frolics down the street while the song "Good Morning" played. The ad, launched in the spring of 2002, closed with the brand name Viagra and a message to talk to your doctor. The song was translated into French to make the ad truly national. A key part of the ad was to communicate that it was not a performance-enhancing drug, but rather something that allowed a man to feel good about himself.

The communication results were simply astounding. Not only did the ad score unprecedented awareness levels, 80 percent agreed or strongly agreed that Viagra projected a positive image and 25 percent of those who had erectile dysfunction (ED) claimed the ad persuaded them to talk to their doctor or partner about the problem or about Viagra. This was especially successful since the ad did not and could not give an explicit description of what Viagra could do medically because of the laws governing Canadian DTC ads. Advertisers could only communicate one or two characteristics; either the brand name or what the product could do, not both. Naturally, with such success the ad was run again in the fall of 2002.

This Viagra ad built on a 2001 ad that showed the difficulty of men speaking about the topic. In the ad, "Doctor's Office" we saw a reluctant man not approach the subject with his doctor. The purpose of this ad was to minimize the stigma attached with such a concern. And somehow this uncomfortable looking character resonated with men as 80 percent of the target audience could recall seeing the ad, nearly double the norm. Even doctors claimed the ad was completely realistic at illustrating the problem they experienced. Later in 2001, another ad, featuring famous hockey player Guy Lafleur, continued with this idea of ED being a frequent problem.

In between the two "Good Morning" campaigns during 2002, Pzifer ran a more informational message called "Straight Goods" that described many facts about ED, again with the idea that men should talk to their doctor. And although this ad had less publicity surrounding it, research indicated that it was the most effective at encouraging patient–doctor discussions.

In 2004, Viagra launched its third branded ad with men of many nationalities singing the song "My Way" while in the shower. This is in the face of significant competition from Cialis and Levitra. Early research suggested that Viagra's ads have a recognizable creative strategy as viewers could identify the ad as a Viagra ad before the presentation of the brand name.

Sources: Lesley Young, "Viagra's Wake-up Call," *Marketing Magazine*, April 1, 2002; Danny Kucharsky, "Pfizer Finds Its Ad Groove," *Marketing Magazine*, February 10, 2003; Editorial, "Marketing ménage à trois," *Marketing Magazine*, April 5, 2004; Lesley Young, "Pfizer's Men Sing for Their Viagra," *Marketing Magazine*, March 8, 2004.

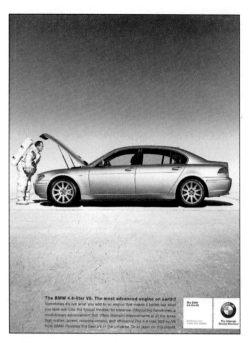

Exhibit 6–1
Excellent advertising helps create an image for BMW automobiles as "the ultimate driving machine"

148

One of the most important components of an integrated marketing communications program is the advertising message. While the fundamental role of an advertising message is to communicate information, it does much more. The commercials we watch on TV or hear on radio and the print ads we see in magazines and newspapers are a source of entertainment, motivation, fascination, fantasy, and sometimes irritation as well as information. Ads and commercials appeal to, and often create or shape, consumers' problems, desires, and goals. From the marketer's perspective, the advertising message is a way to tell consumers how the product or service can solve a problem or help satisfy desires or achieve goals. Advertising can also be used to create images or associations and position a brand in the consumer's mind as well as transform the experience of buying and/or using a product or service. Many consumers who have never driven or even ridden in a BMW perceive it as "the ultimate driving machine" (Exhibit 6–1).

One need only watch an evening of commercials or peruse a few magazines to realize there are a myriad of ways to convey an advertising message. Underlying all of these messages, however, is a **creative strategy** that determines what the advertising message will say or communicate and **creative tactics** for how the message strategy will be executed. In this chapter, we focus on three creative strategy decisions. First, we describe various approaches to determining the big idea that will be used as the central theme of the advertising campaign and translated into attention-getting, distinctive, and memorable messages. Second, we review the many appeals that advertisers use to develop messages designed to persuade consumers. Third, we focus on the key source characteristics that advertisers typically use to gain attention and alter consumers' attitudes. In the next chapter, we will focus on three creative tactics decisions.

Many of you may not be directly involved in the design and creation of ads. However, because creative strategy is often so crucial to the success of the firm's promotional effort, everyone involved in the promotional process should understand the strategic decisions that underlie the development of advertising campaigns and messages, as well as the creative options available to the advertiser. Moreover, as we discussed in the previous chapter, the creativity of promotional messages is critical for brand positioning decisions with which all marketing personnel should be familiar.

CREATIVE THEME

Most ads are part of a series of messages that make up an IMC or **advertising campaign**, which is a set of interrelated and coordinated marketing communication activities that centre on a single theme or idea that appears in different media across a specified time period. Determining the unifying theme around which the campaign will be built is a critical part of the creative process, as it sets the tone for the individual ads and other forms of marketing communications that will be used. A **campaign theme** should be a strong idea, as it is the central message that will be communicated in all the advertising and other promotional activities.

The **creative theme** or **creative idea** is a critical part of a marketing communication program since it must reflect the market positioning strategy and directly communicate the brand positioning strategy to its intended target audience. In this section, we cover three related decisions that comprise the creative theme. First, we discuss various ways to determine the creative theme. Next, we explore the issue of consistency of the creative theme across many parts of the promotional program. We conclude by exploring the importance of unique Canadian creative advertising and its success.

ORIGIN OF CREATIVE THEME

Some advertising experts argue that for an ad campaign to be effective it must contain a big idea that attracts the consumer's attention, gets a response, and sets the advertiser's product or service apart from the competition's. Well-known adman John O'Toole describes the *big idea* as "that flash of insight that synthesizes the purpose of the strategy, joins the product benefit with consumer desire in a fresh, involving way, brings the subject to life, and makes the reader or audience stop, look, and listen."[1] Of course, the real challenge to the creative team is coming up with the big idea to use in the ad. Many products and services offer virtually nothing unique, and it can be difficult to find something interesting to say about them.

While really great ideas in advertising are difficult to come by, there are many big ideas that became the basis of very creative, successful advertising campaigns. A classic example is the "Pepsi generation" theme and subsequent variations like "the taste of a new generation" and "GenerationNext." More recent big ideas that have resulted in effective advertising campaigns include the "Intel inside" campaign for Intel microprocessors that go in personal computers; Nike's "Just do it"; and the "It keeps going and going" theme for Energizer batteries, featuring the pink bunny. It is difficult to pinpoint the inspiration for a big idea or to teach advertising people how to find one. However, several approaches can guide the creative team's search for a creative theme. Some of the best-known approaches follow:

- Using a unique selling proposition.
- Creating a brand image.
- Finding the inherent drama.
- Positioning.

Unique Selling Proposition The concept of the **unique selling proposition (USP)** was developed by Rosser Reeves, former chair of the Ted Bates agency, and is described in his influential book *Reality in Advertising*. Reeves noted three characteristics of unique selling propositions:

1. Each advertisement must make a proposition to the consumer. Not just words, not just product puffery, not just show-window advertising. Each advertisement must say to each reader: "Buy this product and you will get this benefit."
2. The proposition must be one that the competition either cannot or does not offer. It must be unique either in the brand or in the claim.
3. The proposition must be strong enough to move the mass millions, that is, pull over new customers to your brand.[2]

Reeves said the attribute claim or benefit that forms the basis of the USP should dominate the ad and be emphasized through repetitive advertising. An example of advertising based on a USP is the campaign for Trident gum (Exhibit 6–2).The brand's

Exhibit 6–2 This ad uses a unique selling proposition

Because it actually prevents cavities, maybe our gum should have looked like this.

You know how important a toothbrush is in preventing cavities, well you're about to find out how chewing gum can help as well. Trident gum, that is. You see, Trident has Dentec which is proven to prevent cavities. Helping to reduce them not by a little, but quite significantly. By up to 62%* in fact. That's 62% fewer cavities than you would get with a normal oral hygiene program alone. So treat your kids to a good chew, anytime. **Trident. A smile in every chew.**

Exhibit 6–3
Advertising for No Fear creates a unique image for the brand as representing the outer limits of human performance

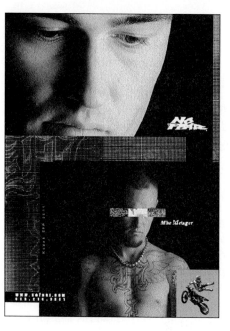

unique attributes make it the only chewing gum with the seal of approval from the Canadian Dental Association.

For Reeves's approach to work, there must be a truly unique product or service attribute, benefit, or inherent advantage that can be used in the claim. The approach may require considerable research on the product and consumers, not only to determine the USP but also to document the claim.

Creating a Brand Image   In many product and service categories, competing brands are so similar that it is very difficult to communicate a unique attribute or benefit. Many of the package-goods products that account for most of the advertising dollars spent are difficult to differentiate on a functional or performance basis. The creative strategy used to sell these products is based on the development of a strong, memorable identity for the brand through **image advertising**.

David Ogilvy popularized the idea of brand image in his famous book *Confessions of an Advertising Man*. Ogilvy said that with image advertising, "every advertisement should be thought of as a contribution to the complex symbol which is the brand image." He argued that the image or personality of the brand is particularly important when brands are similar:

> The greater the similarity between brands, the less part reason plays in brand selection. There isn't any significant difference between the various brands of whiskey, or cigarettes, or beer. They are all about the same. And so are the cake mixes and the detergents and the margarines. The manufacturer who dedicates his advertising to building the most sharply defined personality for his brand will get the largest share of the market at the highest profit. By the same token, the manufacturers who will find themselves up the creek are those shortsighted opportunists who siphon off their advertising funds for promotions.[3]

Image advertising has become increasingly popular and is used as the creative theme for a variety of products and services, including soft drinks, liquor, cigarettes, cars, airlines, financial services, perfume/colognes, and clothing. Many people consume certain brands of these products because of image. The key to successful image advertising is developing an image that will appeal to product users. For example, the sports apparel company No Fear uses this type of advertising to create a unique image for the brand as representing the outer limits of human performance. Ads like the one in Exhibit 6–3 have helped create this image for No Fear.

Finding the Inherent Drama   Another approach to determining the creative theme is finding the **inherent drama** or characteristic of the product that makes the consumer purchase it. The inherent drama approach expresses the advertising philosophy of Leo Burnett, founder of the Leo Burnett agency in Chicago. Burnett said inherent drama "is often hard to find but it is always there, and once found it is the most interesting and believable of all advertising appeals."[4] He believed advertising should be based on a foundation of consumer benefits with an emphasis on the dramatic element in expressing those benefits.

Burnett advocated a down-home type of advertising that presents the message in a warm and realistic way. Some of the more famous ads developed by his agency using the inherent drama approach are for McDonald's, Maytag appliances, Kellogg's cereals, and Hallmark cards. Notice how the Hallmark commercial shown in Exhibit 6–4 uses this approach to deliver a poignant message.

150

LEO BURNETT COMPANY, INC.
AS FILMED AND RECORDED   (4/96)   "Report Card" 2:00
HALLMARK CARDS, INC.
HMHF6359

1. (MUSIC: UNDER THROUGHOUT)

2. MAXX: Hi, Mom, I'm home!
MOM: Hi. Is your coat on the floor?
MAXX: No...

3. MAXX: Can I go over to Lee's house?
MOM: Do you have any homework?
MAXX: Yeah.
MOM: After you finish it you can go.

4. MAXX: Cool.
MOM: Did you turn in your milk money?
MAXX: Yeah.

5. Hey--who moved my lunar module?

6. MOM: Maxx, what's this?
MAXX: Did Amy move my lunar module?
MOM: Maxx?

7. MAXX: It's something from Mrs. Bennett.
MOM: What'd she give you a card for?
MAXX: Cause I was nice to somebody.

8. MOM: Who were you nice to?
MAXX: Scott.
MOM: Who's Scott?

9. MAXX: The boy who comes to school just once in a while cause he's sick.
MOM: Was he at the school play?
MAXX: Nope, can we get an armadillo?

10. MOM: How were you nice to him?

11. MAXX: Well, Mrs. Bennett always has me sit next to him. Scott can't go out for recess and stuff so I stay in and play Yahtzee with him.

12. MOM: I didn't know you were doing that.
MAXX: I like him. It's no big deal. Could I see your card?

13. MAXX: Sure. MOM: (READING): "You didn't have to do what you did. And that's what made it so special." Maxx? Do you know what this means?

14. MAXX: Kinda.
MOM: It means you should be very proud of yourself. I know I am.

15. MAXX: Mom?
MOM: Yeah?
MAXX: You're squooshing me.

Hallmark
When you care enough to send the very best

151

Exhibit 6–5
This ad positions 3M as an innovative company

Positioning   Since advertising is used to establish the brand position in consumers' minds, it can also be the source of the creative theme. Positioning is done for companies as well as for brands. For example, the ad shown in Exhibit 6–5 is part of a campaign designed to reinforce 3M's position as an innovative company. Positioning is often the basis of a firm's creative strategy when it has multiple brands competing in the same market. For example, Procter & Gamble markets many brands of laundry detergent—and positions each one differently.

Trout and Ries originally described positioning as the image consumers had of the brand in relation to competing brands in the product or service category, but the concept has been expanded beyond direct competitive positioning.[5] As discussed in Chapter 5, products can be positioned on the basis of product attributes, price/quality, usage or application, product users, or product class. Any of these can spark a creative theme that becomes the basis of the creative strategy and results in the brand's occupying a particular place in the minds of the target audience. Since brand positioning can be done on the basis of a distinctive attribute, the positioning and unique selling proposition approaches can overlap.

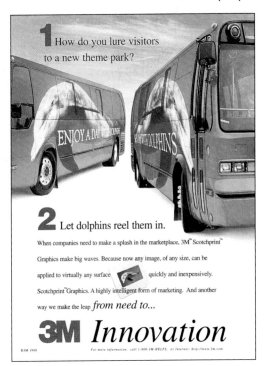

1 How do you lure visitors to a new theme park?

ENJOY A DAY WITH DOLPHINS

2 Let dolphins reel them in.

When companies need to make a splash in the marketplace, 3M™ Scotchprint™ Graphics make big waves. Because now any image, of any size, can be applied to virtually any surface quickly and inexpensively. Scotchprint™ Graphics. A highly intelligent form of marketing. And another way we make the leap *from need to...*

3M *Innovation*

©3M 1998   For more information, call 1-800-3M-HELPS, or Internet: http://www.3m.com

Molson Export returned to its well-established position as an authentic beer in Quebec as the origin for a clever theme. Research indicated that consumers young and old alike still perceived Export as having a strong 100-year history and associated it with classic beer-drinking moments, even though the brand had inconsistent advertising and weak marketing support in recent years. The slogan captured the essence of the repositioning, "Molson Ex. Today's beer since 1903." The first few executions of the creative strategy showed the progression and similarity of Export consumption since its inception. For example, the first spot, "Evolution," says it all as a number of scenes depicted people bringing cases of Export to various parties over the course of time. Using the computer morphing techniques, the images also showed how the labels of the brand had changed.[6]

CREATIVE CONSISTENCY

Consistency in promotional creativity is generally regarded as a key success factor so that the target audience retains the brand position. We explore examples of consistency in the creative theme across time, creative execution, advertising media, promotional tools, and products. The essential point is that when the target audience is exposed to a series of messages across different contexts, the creative theme should not change such that there is a clear reinforcement of the brand positioning strategy. Deviation of the theme allows the possibility that the target audience will process the message alternatively and arrive at a misguided interpretation of the brand.

Consistency Across Time Advertising or communication plans are generally done on an annual basis, thus the creative theme is often short-term in nature. However, the creative themes are usually developed with the intention of being used for a longer time period. While some marketers change their campaign themes often, a successful creative theme may last for years. Figure 6–1 lists the slogans of some enduring ad campaign themes.

A consistent creative theme across time builds on the established awareness of brand's current customers by encouraging continued processing of future advertising messages. Moreover, the familiarity of the creative theme is recognizable to a brand's non-customers when they may be entering the product category or considering switching the purchases.

Pepsi-Cola's campaign in Quebec has starred comedian Claude Meunier for 16 years. The campaign is a unique creative strategy for Pepsi from a worldwide perspective, and it is the longest running campaign and celebrity endorsement in

FIGURE 6–1
Examples of successful long-running advertising campaigns
☐ ☐ ☐ ☐ ☐

Company or Brand	Slogan
Nike	"Just do it."
Allstate Insurance	"You're in good hands with Allstate."
Hallmark cards	"When you care enough to send the very best."
De Beers	"A diamond is forever."
Intel	"Intel inside."
State Farm Insurance	"Like a good neighbour, State Farm is there."
Timex watches	"It takes a licking and keeps on ticking."
Dial soap	"Aren't you glad you use Dial? Don't you wish everyone did?"

the history of the brand. In fact, the relationship is so established that Meunier writes many of the spots and creates the characters he portrays.[7]

Despite this consistent creative theme, Pepsi introduced Patrick, Etienne, Paco, Sebastien and Ivon (first letters spell PEPSI) in a TV ad, as five guys who really, really like Pepsi to continue with its advertising theme of humour, entertainment, and youthful energy. However, this deviation was not the end of Meunier as Pepsi planned on his continued participation.[8]

The Dairy Farmers of Canada took creative consistency of their "spokesperson" to a new level during the past three Olympic Games. For the 1998 Olympics in Nagano, Japan, the cows were in the barn watching the Games. For the 2000 Sydney Summer Games, they were seen on their way to the Olympics. They finally made it by attending events in Salt Lake City during 2002. In fact, they surprised a pair of figure skaters with a bale of hay as a reward at the end of one spot.[9] During the 2004 Summer Games, the cows became little blue animated cows that participated in the actual events.

On the one hand, an advertising campaign that is poorly conceived can be a source of inconsistency. Many companies have solid marketing and promotional plans and spend substantial amounts of money on advertising, yet have difficulty coming up with a creative campaign that will differentiate them from their competitors. For example, Burger King has changed its advertising theme 11 times in the past 15 years and changed agencies six times in search of a campaign that would give the chain a strong identity in the fast-food market (Figure 6–2). During many of these campaigns, market share dropped and franchises were unhappy with the company's inability to come up with an effective campaign.[10]

On the other hand, a good and consistent creative theme is not the only criteria of success. In the late 90s, Nissan asked its agency to change the popular "Enjoy the ride" campaign that was widely praised for its amusing, creative executions but was not helping increase sales.[11] Nissan dealers complained that the ads did not focus enough attention on the product, and in some cases comparisons with the competition were used. However, in late 2002 Nissan launched a new advertising campaign using "Shift" as the umbrella tagline.[12] The new campaign uses a combination of emotional and product-focused ads that are designed to strengthen Nissan's brand

FIGURE 6–2
Burger King advertising themes and agencies

- "We Do It Like You Do It" (1987–1989)
  Agency: NW Ayer

- "Sometimes you gotta break the rules" (1989–1991)

- "Your way. Right away" (1991–1992)

- "BK Tee Vee: I Love This Place" (1992–1994)
  Agency: D'Arcy Masius Benton & Bowles

- "Back to Basics" (1994)
  Agency: UniWorld Group, Inc.

- "Get Your Burger's Worth" (1994–1996)

- "It Just Tastes Better" (1996–1998)

- "Go the Distance—When You Have It Your Way It Just Tastes Better" (1999)

- "Got the Urge" (2000)
  Agency: Lowe Lintas & Partners

- "The Whopper Says" (2001–2002)
  Agency: McCann-Erickson

- "At Burger King, You Got It" (2002–)
  Agency: Amoeba

Exhibit 6–6
In Nissan's new ads, the cars are once again the stars

image while showing its revitalized product line, which includes the new 350Z sports car (Exhibit 6–6).

Consistency Across Executions As we noted above, an advertising campaign features a series of creative executions over time and it is important that marketers ensure that all ads feature a similar "look and feel." Exactly what this entails is a matter of interpretation, but most advertisers and consumers would say they recognize it when they see it. For example, many would say that the creative theme for Absolut vodka is consistent in all of their print ads even though we see the distinctive bottle in many different types of scenes or situations that fit with the specific target audience of the many magazines the ads are placed in.

Kraft Canada has used the same creative theme of an angel consuming Philadelphia cream cheese in the clouds of heaven throughout all of its television executions. This creative approach for communicating the brand's benefits has served it well as a distinctive presentation that is recognizable and consistent with positioning the brand as a tasty and healthy food product.[13]

Consistency Across Media Often a successful creative theme is one that is amenable to more than one media. For instance, the essence of creativity in a print ad is still captured in a follow-up radio ad. Or, the big idea found in a TV commercial transfers to an outdoor billboard. In both cases, the creativity of the initial media is seen in a supportive media—one less central to the primary media, yet still important to continue exposing a similar idea to the target audience.

Consistency Across Promotional Tools Using the advertising creative theme across the various promotional tools is an issue to be resolved. The argument for the same "look and feel" is pervasive. For example, IMC Perspective 6–1 shows how Telus Mobility keeps its nature theme in all of its communications from TV ads to promotional displays to its website and finally all of its public relations and publicity. Action such as this supports the notion that the creative theme for the integrated marketing communication must support the broad market positioning and all brand positioning strategies for its many target audiences.

Consistency Across Products The same kind of use of a consistent theme across all IMC tools is evident in RBC Financial Group's "First" campaign. However, this theme pervades all tools for all of its products and services. And so the campaign's

Telus Can See the Future Clearly

With the takeover of Clearnet Communications in the summer of 2000, Telus had a significant creative decision. What should Telus do with Clearnet's creative use of animals, insects, and flowers in all its marketing communications in Clearnet's famous "The Future Is Friendly" slogan?

Clearnet was an upstart firm offering digital PCS service in the Windsor–Quebec corridor. It had successfully launched its services in the 1990s with an innovative creative that featured various scenes from nature that were associated with the brand's benefits. In one memorable campaign, a frog was seen leaping from a glass jar to freedom. This creative cleverly conveyed the experience of a person who goes completely wireless at home! Clearnet attempted to persuade consumers with a phone line to their house to give it up and move to a completely wireless communication with its PCS product.

The creative concept has been hailed as a simple way to communicate the features and benefits of Clearnet's technology that may appear complex or difficult for new users of advanced technology products and services. Many also believed that the creative offered a unique visual that clearly identified Clearnet and helped it achieve significant brand awareness.

Almost from the start it was obvious that the Clearnet brand name would be discontinued, but many wondered how a recognizable creative that had put Clearnet on the map could possibly whither away. Complicating the issue was the fact that Telus was originally a Western Canada firm whose customers had no direct experience with Clearnet's creative. Likewise, most of Clearnet's customers would be mostly unfamiliar with the new Telus name.

The answer came quickly as Telus used Clearnet's "Disco Duck" for a national ad in January 2001. It was launched during the Super Bowl and an episode of *Survivor*, and the full campaign of TV, print, and billboard started a short time later with a direct-mail follow-up to existing customers. The ad showed two ducks playing catch with an egg to the music of "Sweet Georgia Brown," made famous by the Harlem Globetrotters. When the ducks inevitably drop the egg, it breaks open and the old Clearnet frog quacks. The key message is that two-way wireless e-mail messaging is available to all customers. Clearnet's signature leaf closes the ad, as done previously, but it changes into the new Telus Mobility logo. In an egg shell, we have an established creative attempting to generate key communication effects for a new brand—quite a significant marketing challenge, to say the least.

To complete the transformation, Telus adopted the recognizable purple and green colours and the "The Future Is Friendly" slogan from Clearnet for all six of its business units at the end of 2001. All Telus products and services have the same distinctive and consistent colours and visuals for all its marketing communications. And the website (Telus.com) uses this consistent strategy with the same colours and many of the same characters that have been featured in the advertising messages over the past five years.

Sources: Eve Lazarus, "One Voice," *Marketing Magazine*, December 17, 2001; Lesley Young, "Turning Over a New Leaf," *Marketing Magazine*, February 26, 2001; Lesley Young, "Telus Mobility Spares Dancing Duck," *Marketing Magazine*, February 5, 2001; Lesley Young, "Merger Means End of Clearnet Name," *Marketing Magazine*, August 28, 2000.

consistent theme works on multiple levels. It is positioning the overall firm as an innovative and forward-looking organization. Yet, the campaign adapts well to a variety of purchase and consumption situations for credit or investment products that can be also adjusted depending on whether the target audience is a loyal customer or a potential one that RBC Financial Group is attempting to switch.

CANADIAN CREATIVE THEMES

We now turn our attention regarding creative themes used in Canadian advertising and promotional communication. We begin with a perspective that supports the importance for unique ways of speaking to Canadian consumers. Since many brands are part of a North American or international marketing strategy, there is a tendency to standardize the advertising and promotional message. As further evidence of the importance for Canadian creativity in communication, we highlight recent success stories.

Importance of Canadian Creative Themes The need for unique creative advertising can be found in divergence of values between Canadians and Americans. Decades of consumer research by Environics researcher Michael Adams suggests that while the citizens of North America share similar aspects of society, the underlying values are quite distinct.[14] For example, in 1992, 17 percent of Canadians and 34 percent of Americans agreed that "a widely advertised product is probably a good product," however, in 2000, the percentage for Canadians had remained unchanged while the percentage for Americans had risen to 44 percent.[15] Statistics such as these have led to a profound conclusion.

> Canadians operate by a fundamentally different set of social values than Americans do, and marketers need to be sensitive to these differences. Americans are much more outer-directed, risk-taking, and yet are more concerned with maintaining social order and tradition. In contrast, Canadians are more inner-directed, more security-seeking, and yet are more socially liberal and tolerant of individual diversity. Americans celebrate those who have lived the American Dream—working hard, taking chances and striking it rich—so visual markers of success such as expensive cars, homes and vacations become important indicators of one's status on the social hierarchy. Canadians, on the other hand, believe in greater interdependence, achieving equitable balances, and the "fair" distribution of the wealth of the nation—the Canadian Dream is a strong social safety net. As a result, Canadians are more suspicious of wealth, are less trusting of business and are more skeptical of advertising.[16]

These unique Canadian values influence the motivation for consumption-Canadians buy products for what they can do for us versus what they say about us. Canadians favour experiences over possessions and are less inclined towards conspicuous consumption. For example, Canadians are more likely to believe that a car is basic transportation versus a statement of personal style or image. Therefore, certain types of advertising messages are more palatable for Canadians since the underlying reasons for purchase are more accurately reflected in the dialogue of a commercial or the body copy of a print ad produced by Canadian advertisers.

In fact, one author believes that Canada is truly in an advertising renaissance where agencies are consistently producing world-calibre creative campaigns.[17] Furthermore, the distinctiveness of Canadians derived from this data may be strong evidence for allowing Canadian managers more latitude in developing unique creative messages.[18]

Putting together a creative for Canada can be met with some obstacles. Canadian managers who market U.S. brands in Canada often feel the pressure to run the same campaign in Canada that is being run in the U.S. While this obviously saves on production costs of new ads, it can be more than offset with lower sales due to messages not resonating with Canadian culture. Sometimes firms need to perform specific market research to demonstrate that a unique creative is warranted for the Canadian market. For example, Lever Pond's of Canada felt the U.S. creative for Degree deodorant featuring CEOs and race car drivers would not be acceptable to Canadian consumers. Research was done, a discussion ensued with U.S. managers, and finally a humourous campaign that looked at stressful situations where the dryness benefit of product could be understood. Ironically, the ads in the U.S. barely registered with consumers in follow-up research while the Canadian campaign tested above average.[19]

For RadioShack Canada, their current slogan "You've got questions. We've got answers" appeared less credible in the current information age. Even though their U.S. counterpart continued with the established positioning, RadioShack Canada moved in a new direction with "RadioShack. Just around the corner" during 2003. Since all outlets are within 10 km of 90 percent of all Canadians, the new approach is an accurate depiction of the convenience of shopping. Moreover, the slogan proved flexible with variations such as "Reliability is just around the corner" or "Safety is just around the corner" to fit specific creative messages.[20]

Successful Canadian Creative Themes Historically and recently, insightful and innovative Canadian creative themes demonstrate effective advertising and promotional communication. We take this time to identify the Canadian organizations that recognize creative themes that have been truly outstanding. Specifically, we summarize the CASSIES, the Marketing Awards, the Bessies, and the Extra Awards. We also highlight Canada's performance at the prestigious CANNES competition held in France. IMC Perspective 6–2 shows one successful advertising campaign that has been recognized by many of these awards.

CASSIES Awarded by The Institute of Communication and Advertising (ICA), The Association of Quebec Advertising Agencies, and Publicité Club de Montréal, this recognition is perhaps the most significant in Canada as it identifies Canadian advertising success stories. Initiated in Canada in 1993, the award is based on a similar idea started during the 1980s in the United Kingdom. Originally awarded every second year from 1993 until 2001, the CASSIES are now an annual event.

The CASSIES award recognizes advertising and promotional campaigns that document a direct cause and effect relationship between the campaign and communication and business results. Entrants have to submit the details of their campaign in the form of a business case that summarizes the performance of the brand prior to the campaign and indicates the degree to which the performance has improved. The website, cassies.ca, provides the complete entry requirements, identifies the winners, and contains the actual case history submitted.

The Grand Prix is the single most prestigious award presented each year. It has been won by seven firms since inception; Pepsi in Quebec during 1993, Listerine in Quebec during 1995, Chrysler Minivan for 1997, Sunlight Laundry Detergent in 1999, Molson Canadian for 2001, Diet Pepsi in 2002, and Famliprix in 2003. For 2004, the jury received 94 entries and awarded two gold, ten silver, and six certificates of excellence. Alas, 2004 was the first time no Grand Prix was awarded, and if 2004 is representative of other years, it seems that the CASSIES recognized approximately the top 20 percent of Canadian creative themes entered.

Marketing Awards Sponsored by *Marketing Magazine*, these annual awards identify the top Canadian creative communication launched each year in a number of categories. For example, there is an overall winner for best multimedia campaign, a winner for best single ad and campaign across all major media with television having more awards by various product categories, and awards for non-traditional media, point-of-purchase, and public service announcements.

Recognizing the best of 2003, the 2004 awards saw Bud Light as the overall multimedia winner with other awards going to the B.C. Dairy Foundation, Playland Amusement Park of Vancouver, DDB advertising agency, and the Mini. The best television campaigns included Bud Light, Familiprix, Dominion grocery store, Bud Light for the U.S. market, AGF Funds, Réno-Dépôt, and the Milk Producers of Canada.

Bessies These awards are given by the Television Bureau of Canada (TVB), an organization whose members comprise television stations, networks, and specialty services. The TVB promotes the use of television as an effective media and has an important role as an information resource for its members. The Bessies recognize the best in English TV advertising each year and has been doing so since the early 1960s, shortly after the invention of television (an equivalent award for French TV

157

Hockey Canada Advises Parents to Relax

In the wake of a few high profile incidents of illegal and inappropriate behaviour of parents of minor hockey players, Hockey Canada, the governing body of all local, national. and international hockey, launched a series of TV, radio, and print public service announcements (PSAs) during the fall of 2002. The campaign garnered considerable public reaction as many firms provided considerable media exposure. And a year later, the "Relax, it's just a game" campaign received many awards recognizing its creativity.

The creative theme of the ads conveyed a role reversal between parents and children to highlight the pressures parent place on their children while participating in the sport of hockey. The campaign featured three TV ads. The "Cop" ad shows a child lecturing his father, who has just been pulled over by an officer, that he should "not hold back" and "let him have it." Another boy pressures his father to make a put on a golf course and not to "screw it up" in the "Golf" ad. Finally, after their shopping cart is banged in the "Groceries" ad, a girl yells at her mother to "punch her lights out." The three print and radio ads continued the theme. For example, one print ad showed a boy addressing his parents about babies while they are in bed, and one radio ad had a girl criticizing her mother about the tasteless meatloaf.

From a creative standpoint, many different associations and organizations recognized the campaign's innovativeness. Internationally, the campaign received a Silver Lion at Cannes, two Finalists at the London International Advertising Awards, and a Bronze and Finalist Clio Award in the United States. In Canada, the Canadian Marketing Association named it the best campaign and recognized it for two other Gold awards, *Marketing Magazine* granted the campaign four awards, and the Television Bureau of Canada gave two Gold Bessies. The advertising agency responsible for the campaign, DDB, recognized it with two

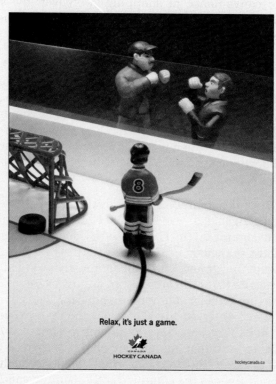

Relax, it's just a game.

HOCKEY CANADA

hockeycanada.ca

of its own Pinnacle Award. The campaign also won nine other design awards.

As it was winning a number of awards for the campaign, the creative message evolved in the fall of 2003 from the more light-hearted role reversal to a stronger emphasis of demonstrating how ridiculous some parents appear when encouraging their child to improve their "game" in three separate TV ads. A mother yells at her daughter for not playing pin-the-tail on the donkey well enough, a father shows his son how to win hide-and-seek by going in the sewer, and a father protests a potato sack race by claiming that another boy is too big and demanding a urine sample. Three print ads showed animated table-top hockey players feeling the effects of a father yelling at his son, a mother throwing coffee at a referee, and two fathers strongly disagreeing in the stands, while a radio ad sounded like a hockey announcer describing a mother causing trouble in the stands.

The second version of the campaign received some awards and continued positive publicity as newspapers continued to write stories. However, it finally received negative publicity on a national scale when Don Cherry criticized the message on *Hockey Night In Canada* during the much-hyped outdoor game played in Edmonton in November of 2003. He was concerned that the ads portrayed hockey parents too negatively and that the vast majority of the parents involved did not mistreat their kids or the referees. It appears the campaign has been successful since its main objectives were to raise awareness of the problem and spark debate among hockey people.

Sources: Lesley Young, "Hockey PSAs Score Big at CMA Awards," *Marketing Magazine*, November 24, 2003; Chris Powell, "PSAs Fight Bad Behaviour in New Ways," *Marketing Magazine*, November 24, 2003; Stan Sutter, "Sour Grapes or Fine Whine," *Marketing Magazine*, January 12, 2004; www.Canadianhockey.ca.

advertising is awarded at La Fête de la Pub). The "Raymond" commercial for Mercedes Benz won best single ad and the Nova Scotia Office of Health won best campaign with their sarcastic "Great Reasons to Smoke" messages.

Extra Awards The Canadian Newspaper Association is similar to the TVB but for daily newspapers. Its Extra Awards recognize outstanding creative advertising in this media by giving ads a gold, silver, bronze, or merit award in nine product categories and types of ads (i.e., local ad, local campaign, national campaign, small-space ad). For 2003, ads for Norske (paper products), Playland Amusement Park, and the Humane Society of Canada won gold, with Norske taking best overall. Ironically, the Norske ads reminded consumers that they were a primary newsprint supplier with a simple message that ran at the top of a blank page along with the signature, "Norske Canada. The world prints on us" and a red tab-like indicator in three separate executions:

- For our product demonstration, please turn the page.
- This isn't a cheap ploy to get you to notice our paper. It's an expensive one.
- We interrupt this newspaper to bring you this newspaper.

CANNES On a global level, the Cannes International Advertising Film Festival is widely considered the most prestigious advertising award competition. The Cannes competition receives entries from agencies around the world hoping to win Lions (the name of the award) in each of the major categories-television; print and poster; online (cyber) advertising, media buying and planning, and direct. Canada has done fabulously at recent Cannes competitions with a total of 51 Lions won from 1998 to 2004, an average of about seven per year. The number of Canadian creatives entered has increased substantially and they are up against 17,000 world-wide competitors.

Canada received 11 Lions in 2004, matching their best performance since 1998, of which eight were in the film category (i.e., TV ads, cinemas ads) and equalling the success of the U.S. and U.K.! Not too bad when the film category alone usually has about 5,000 or 6,000 entries. Just winning one is quite an achievement since there are only about 100 Lions handed out in any given year. However, to top it all off, an ad for Vim was one of three ads considered for the Grand Prix signalling the best film ad in the world!

In the past, some questioned the overall effectiveness of Canadian creativity due to the nature of our culture to not take risks and the fact that many of the brands advertised are part of American or other global brands. However, others contend the increased presence of Canadians in attendance and on the juries of all five categories bodes well for future Canuck creative advertising and their recognition on the international stage. In fact, some argue that countries that have emerged recently with stronger advertising is a result of their advertisers taking the competition more seriously by sending a large contingent of committed creative specialists who learn considerably from international counterparts.[21]

MESSAGE APPEALS

The message or **advertising appeal** refers to the approach used to attract the attention of consumers and/or to influence their attitude toward the product, service, or cause. A message appeal can also be viewed as "something that moves people, speaks to their wants or needs, and excites their interest."[22] The **creative execution** style is the way a particular appeal is turned into an advertising message presented to the consumer. According to William Weilbacher:

> The appeal can be said to form the underlying content of the advertisement, and the execution the way in which that content is presented. Advertising appeals and executions are usually independent of each other; that is, a particular appeal can be executed in a variety of ways and a particular means of execution can be applied to a variety of advertising appeals. Advertising appeals tend to adapt themselves to all media, whereas some kinds of executional devices are more adaptable to some media than others.[23]

159

Exhibit 6–7
Nordica uses a rational appeal to advertise the features of its skis and bindings

As this implies, the message appeal is a creative strategy decision whereas the execution style is more of a creative tactic decision. (We will discuss the tactics in more detail in the next chapter.) One of the advertiser's most important creative strategy decisions involves the choice of an appropriate appeal. Hundreds of different appeals can be used as the basis for advertising messages. We concentrate on five broad appeals: rational appeals, emotional appeals, fear appeals, humour appeals and combined rational and emotional appeals. In this section, we focus on ways to use these appeals as part of a creative strategy and consider how they can be combined in developing the advertising message.

RATIONAL APPEALS

Rational appeals focus on the consumer's practical, functional, or utilitarian need for the product or service and emphasize features of a product or service and/or the benefits or reasons for owning or using a particular brand. The content of these messages emphasizes facts, learning, and the logic of persuasion.[24] Rational-based appeals tend to be informative, and advertisers using them generally attempt to convince consumers that their product or service has a particular attribute(s) or provides a specific benefit that satisfies their needs. Their objective is to persuade the target audience to buy the brand because it is the best available or does a better job of meeting consumers' needs. For example, the Nordica ad shown in Exhibit 6–7 uses a rational appeal to explain the features and benefits of its Beast Synergy System ski collection.

Many rational motives can be used as the basis for advertising appeals, including comfort, convenience, economy, health, and sensory benefits such as touch, taste, and smell. Other rational motives or purchase criteria commonly used in advertising include quality, dependability, durability, efficiency, efficacy, and performance.

The particular features, benefits, or evaluative criteria that are important to consumers and can serve as the basis of a rational appeal vary from one product or service category to another as well as among various market segments.

Weilbacher identified several types of advertising appeals that fall under the category of rational approaches, among them feature, comparative, favourable price, news, and product/service popularity appeals. We also include reminder appeals in this list.

Ads that use a *feature appeal* focus on the dominant traits of the product or service. These ads tend to be highly informative and present the customer with a number of important product attributes or features that will lead to favourable attitudes and can be used as the basis for a rational purchase decision. Technical and high-involvement products often use this advertising approach. This type of appeal can also be used for a service. Notice how the ad shown in Exhibit 6–8 focuses on the various features of the new Jeep Grand Cherokee Overland.

A *comparative appeal* is the practice of either directly or indirectly naming competitors in an ad and comparing one or more specific attributes.[25] A comparative appeal can also be made for different product formats, as shown in Exhibit 6–9. Some studies show that recall is higher for comparative than noncomparative messages, but comparative ads are generally not more effective for other response variables, such as brand attitudes or purchase intentions.[26] Advertisers must also consider how comparative messages affect credibility. Users of the brand being attacked in a comparative message may be especially skeptical about the advertiser's claims.

Comparative appeals may be particularly useful for new brands, since it allows a new market entrant to position itself directly against the more established brands and to promote its distinctive advantages. Direct comparisons can help position a new brand in the evoked, or choice, set of brands the customer may be considering.

Comparative appeals are often used for brands with a small market share. They compare themselves to an established market leader in hopes of creating an association and tapping into the leader's market. Market leaders, on the other hand, often hesitate to use comparison ads, as most believe they have little to gain by featuring competitors' products in their ads.

A *favourable price appeal* makes the price offer the dominant point of the message. Price appeal advertising is used most often by retailers to announce sales, special offers, or low everyday prices. Price appeal ads are often used by national advertisers during recessionary times. Many fast-food chains have made price an important part of their marketing strategy through promotional deals and "value menus" or lower overall prices, and their advertising strategy is designed to communicate this. Many other types of advertisers use price appeals as well.

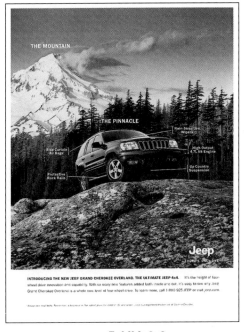

Exhibit 6–8
DaimlerChrysler uses a feature appeal ad to promote its new Jeep® Grand Cherokee Overland

Exhibit 6–9
A comparative appeal across product formats

THERE IS ONLY ONE!

Excedrin® MIGRAINE is now the #1 doctor-recommended brand*
for the relief of migraine pain.

Excedrin MIGRAINE
#1 Doctor Recommended

Exhibit 6–10
This ad promotes the popularity of Excedrin among doctors

News appeals are those in which some type of news or announcement about the product, service, or company dominates the ad. This type of appeal can be used for a new product or service or to inform consumers of significant modifications or improvements. This appeal works best when a company has important news it wants to communicate to its target audience.

Product/service popularity appeals stress the popularity of a product or service by pointing out the number of consumers who use the brand, the number who have switched to it, the number of experts who recommend it, or its leadership position in the market. The main point of this advertising appeal is that the wide use of the brand proves its quality or value and other customers should consider using it. The Excedrin ad in Exhibit 6–10 uses this type of advertising appeal.

A *reminder appeal* has the objective of building brand awareness and/or keeping the brand name in front of consumers. Well-known brands and market leaders often use a reminder appeal which is often referred to as reminder advertising. Products and services that have a seasonal pattern to their consumption also use reminder advertising, particularly around the appropriate period. For example, marketers of candy products often increase their media budgets and run reminder advertising around Halloween, Valentine's Day, Christmas, and Easter.

EMOTIONAL APPEALS

Emotional appeals relate to the customers' social and/or psychological needs for purchasing a product or service. Many of consumers' motives for their purchase decisions are emotional, and their feelings about a brand can be more important than knowledge of its features or attributes. Advertisers for many products and services view rational-based appeals as dull. Many advertisers believe appeals to consumers' emotions work better at selling brands that do not differ markedly from competing brands, since rational differentiation of them is difficult.[27]

The choice between rational or emotional appeal is a challenge and careful consideration must take place to ensure the advertising resonates with the target audience and evokes relevant processing responses connected to the purchase decision or consumption experience. For example, Gaz Métro, the largest natural gas provider in Quebec, repositioned itself to expand sales in the residential market after well establishing itself in the industrial, institutional, commercial sectors. Faced with strong electric power competition from Hydo Quebec, Gaz Métro needed to educate and reassure consumers that natural gas was a secure alternative to electricity when consumers were renovating or upgrading their household energy requirements. While some might have expected Gaz Métro to use a rational argument, they instead used an emotional appeal that showed how comfortable one's home would feel with the seductive blue flame of natural gas in a stunning visually oriented television commercial.[28]

Many feelings or needs can serve as the basis for advertising appeals designed to influence consumers on an emotional level, as shown in Figure 6–3. These appeals are based on the psychological states or feelings directed to the self (such as pleasure or excitement), as well as those with a more social orientation (such as status or recognition).

Advertisers can use emotional appeals in many ways in their creative strategy. Kamp and Macinnis note that commercials often rely on the concept of *emotional integration*, whereby they portray the characters in the ad as experiencing an emotional benefit or outcome from using a product or service.[29] Ads using humour, sex, and other appeals that are very entertaining, arousing, upbeat, and/or exciting can affect the emotions of consumers and put them in a favourable frame of mind. Many TV advertisers use poignant ads that bring a lump to viewers' throats. Hallmark,

Personal States or Feelings	Social-Based Feelings
Safety	Recognition
Security	Status
Fear	Respect
Love	Involvement
Affection	Embarrassment
Happiness	Affiliation/belonging
Joy	Rejection
Nostalgia	Acceptance
Sentiment	Approval
Excitement	
Arousal/stimulation	
Sorrow/grief	
Pride	
Achievement/accomplishment	
Self-esteem	
Actualization	
Pleasure	
Ambition	
Comfort	

FIGURE 6–3
Bases for emotional appeals
□ □ □ □ □

163

AT&T, and Kodak often create commercials that evoke feelings of warmth, nostalgia, and/or sentiment.

Marketers use emotional appeals in hopes that the positive feeling they evoke will transfer to the brand and/or company. Research shows that positive mood states and feelings created by advertising can have a favourable effect on consumers' evaluations of a brand.[30] Studies also show that emotional advertising is better remembered than nonemotional messages.[31]

Mercedes Benz Canada successfully used an emotional appeal in its first Canadian-made television commercial in 2003. Preliminary research indicated that many potential buyers had a very positive attitude towards Mercedes Benz but delayed purchasing for various reasons. Brand associations of Mercedes Benz being "older money and prestige," and "distancing and intimidating," along with consumers feeling they had not "arrived yet" led to a sizable target audience of young consumers who have never bought previously. Enter the positioning message, "Mercedes Benz. You're Ready" along with "The Story of Raymond" that traces the life of one who delays buying ice-cream as a boy and throughout much of his adult life. At the conclusion, we see a few shots of the car and realize the creative is a metaphor for desiring a Mercedes Benz yet postponing the purchase. Subsequent research revealed outstanding levels for emotions, entertainment value, and consumer understanding of the key message. In fact, Mercedes Benz received e-mail and telephone responses from consumers saying the ad spurred them to purchase.[32]

FEAR APPEALS

Fear is an emotional response to a threat that expresses, or at least implies, some sort of danger. Ads sometimes use **fear appeals** to evoke this emotional response and arouse individuals to take steps to remove the threat. Some, like anti-smoking ads, stress physical danger that can occur if behaviours are not altered. Others—like those for deodorant, mouthwash, or dandruff shampoos—threaten disapproval or social rejection.

Before deciding to use a fear appeal–based message strategy, the advertiser should consider how fear operates, what level to use, and how different target audiences may respond. One theory suggests that the relationship between the level of fear in a message and acceptance or persuasion is curvilinear, as shown in Figure 6–4.[33] This means that message acceptance increases as the amount of fear used rises—to a point. Beyond that point, acceptance decreases as the level of fear rises.

This relationship between fear and persuasion can be explained by the fact that fear appeals have both facilitating and inhibiting effects.[34] A low level of fear can have facilitating effects; it attracts attention and interest in the message and may motivate the receiver to act to resolve the threat. Thus, increasing the level of fear in a message from low to moderate can result in increased persuasion. High levels of fear, however, can produce inhibiting effects; the receiver may emotionally block the message by tuning it out, perceiving it selectively, or denying its arguments outright. Figure 6–4 illustrates how these two countereffects operate to produce the curvilinear relationship between fear and persuasion.

A recent study by Anand-Keller and Block provides support for this perspective on how fear operates.[35] Their study indicated that a communication using a low level of fear may be ineffective because it results in insufficient motivation to elaborate on the harmful consequences of engaging in the destructive behaviour (smoking). However, an appeal arousing high levels of fear was ineffective because it resulted in too much elaboration on the harmful consequences. This led to defensive tendencies such as message avoidance and interfered with processing of recommended solutions to the problem.

Another approach to the curvilinear explanation of fear is the protection motivation model.[36] According to this theory, four cognitive appraisal processes mediate the individual's response to the threat: appraising (1) the information available regarding the severity of the perceived threat, (2) the perceived probability that the threat will occur, (3) the perceived ability of a coping behaviour to remove the threat, and (4) the individual's perceived ability to carry out the coping behaviour.

This model suggests that both the cognitive appraisal of the information in a fear appeal message and the emotional response mediate persuasion. An audience is more likely to continue processing threat-related information, thereby increasing the likelihood that a coping behaviour will occur. The protection motivation model suggests that ads using fear appeals should give the target audience information about the severity of the threat, the probability of its occurrence, the effectiveness of a coping response, and the ease with which the response can be implemented.[37]

FIGURE 6–4
Relationship between fear levels and message acceptance
☐ ☐ ☐ ☐ ☐

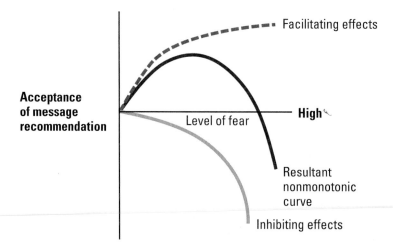

It is also important to consider how the target audience may respond. Fear appeals are more effective when the message recipient is self-confident and prefers to cope with dangers rather than avoid them.[38] They are also more effective among nonusers of a product than among users. Thus, a fear appeal may be better at keeping nonsmokers from starting than persuading smokers to stop.

In reviewing research on fear appeals, Herbert Rotfeld has argued that some of the studies may be confusing different types of threats and the level of potential harm portrayed in the message with fear, which is an emotional response.[39] He concludes that the relationship between the emotional responses of fear or arousal and persuasion is not curvilinear but rather is monotonic and positive, meaning that higher levels of fear do result in greater persuasion. However, Rotfeld notes that not all fear messages are equally effective, because different people fear different things. Thus they will respond differently to the same threat, so the strongest threats are not always the most persuasive. This suggests that marketers using fear appeals must consider the emotional responses generated by the message and how they will affect reactions to the message.

HUMOUR APPEALS

Humourous ads are often the best known and best remembered of all advertising messages. Humour is usually presented through radio and TV commercials as these media lend themselves to the execution of humourous messages. However, humour is occasionally used in print ads as well. IMC Perspective 6–3 shows how Irving Oil used humour in their advertising campaign.

Advertisers use **humour appeals** for many reasons. Humourous messages attract and hold consumers' attention. They enhance effectiveness by putting consumers in a positive mood, increasing their liking of the ad itself and their feeling toward the product or service. And humour can distract the receiver from counterarguing against the message.[40] Critics argue that funny ads draw people to the humourous situation but distract them from the brand and its attributes. Also, effective humour can be difficult to produce and some attempts are too subtle for mass audiences.

Clearly, there are valid reasons both for and against the use of humour in advertising. Not every product or service lends itself to a humourous approach. A number of studies have found that the effectiveness of humour depends on several factors, including the type of product and audience characteristics.[41] For example, humour has been more prevalent and more effective with low-involvement, feeling products than high-involvement, thinking products.[42] An interesting study surveyed the research and creative directors of the top 150 advertising agencies.[43] They were asked to name which communications objectives are facilitated through the appropriate situational use of humour in terms of media, product, and audience factors. The general conclusions of this study are shown in Figure 6–5.

COMBINED RATIONAL AND EMOTIONAL APPEALS

In many advertising situations, the decision facing the creative specialist is not whether to choose an emotional or a rational appeal but rather determining how to combine the two approaches. As noted copywriters David Ogilvy and Joel Raphaelson have stated:

> Few purchases of any kind are made for entirely rational reasons. Even a purely functional product such as laundry detergent may offer what is now called an emotional benefit—say, the satisfaction of seeing one's children in bright clean clothes. In some product categories the rational element is small. These include soft drinks, beer, cosmetics, certain personal care products, and most old-fashioned products. And who hasn't experienced the surge of joy that accompanies the purchase of a new car?[44]

Humour Appeals to the Irvings

Irving Oil, based in St. John, N.B., is a major petroleum refiner and retailer for gas, convenience stores, and home heating, and recently found marketing and humour in its ads to build sales across its many products. With new market research in tow, their new agency set out to tell consumers of eastern Canada something about Irving Oil. Even though it had very high name recognition, many consumers were unsure how Irving Oil was different from the competition.

To complicate matters, K.C. Irving, the founder, and his descendents who now run the company have been historically private and reluctant to draw attention to their business achievements. For example, while donating a recent gift to Acadia University, the Irvings were reluctant to highlight the magnitude of their gift. It seems the Irvings have been comfortable with sticking to the philosophy of making good products and delivering excellent customer service to it customers so that potential customers will be attracted. There almost appeared to be no need for advertising.

A recent print campaign that encouraged homeowners to replace their old furnaces with a new, high efficiency furnace leased from Irving Oil sparked a change. With the intention to let the personality of the company shine through, Irving Oil used self-deprecating humour to present a unique perspective for the firm, entirely unexpected for an oil company. For instance, advertising copy like "My furnace is older than my car. And my car's a Pinto" and "When my furnace was new, it was state-of-the art. Just like my 8-track stereo." The campaign won a CASSIE award and

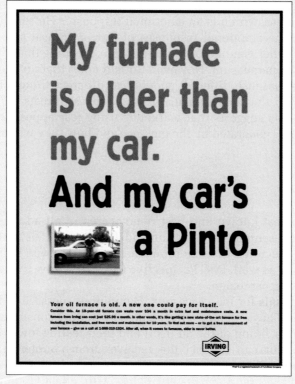

My furnace is older than my car. And my car's a Pinto.

Your oil furnace is old. A new one could pay for itself.

Consider this. An 18-year-old furnace can waste over $34 a month in extra fuel and maintenance costs. A new furnace from Irving can cost just $25.99 a month, in other words, it's like getting a new state-of-the-art furnace for free including the installation, and free service and maintenance for 10 years. To find out more – or to get a free assessment of your furnace – give us a call at 1-888-310-1924. After all, when it comes to furnaces, older is never better.

IRVING

according to a company executive, the program exceeded their very lofty objectives.

Irving Oil used the same print campaign in the New England region of the US and supported it with similar humour in radio ads that featured celebrities from the 1970s to remind consumers the last time they actually thought about their furnace. For example, Erik Estrada, who starred as a police officer in the hit TV series *Chips* suggested that "furnaces were like actors, out of sight, out of mind" all the while giving directions to passing cars.

A similar humourous approach worked for advertising the "World of Taste" coffee sold at the convenience stores of the Irving Oil gas stations. Lines such as, "Any fresher and you'd be sucking on a bean" and "We don't make it like we used to. (You're welcome.)" Radio ads featured customers speaking about their love of the coffee although speaking very quickly due to too much caffeine. Again, another very successful campaign as the company reported that significant coffee sales increased during the campaign and even months later.

While the approach has been a form of humour, the Irvings believe this perspective of communicating with the customer is consistent with an emphasis on customer service that has been the hallmark of their marketing activities since inception. In fact, founder K.C. Irving would clean a customer's window if he happened to be getting gas.

Sources: Kathleen Martin, "The Irvings Find Marketing," *Marketing Magazine*, March 24, 2003; Kathleen Martin, "Bay City Roller Speaks for Irving Oil, *Marketing Magazine*, April 7, 2003.

FIGURE 6–5
Conclusions of the
humour study

☐ ☐ ☐ ☐ ☐

- Humour does aid awareness and attention, which are the objectives best achieved by its use.
- Humour may harm recall and comprehension in general.
- Humour may aid name and simple copy registration.
- Humour may harm complex copy registration.
- Humour may aid retention.
- Humour does not aid persuasion in general.
- Humour may aid persuasion to switch brands.
- Humour creates a positive mood that enhances persuasion.
- Humour does not aid source credibility.
- Humour is generally not very effective in bringing about action/sales.
- Creatives are more positive on the use of humour to fulfill all the above objectives than research directors are.
- Radio and TV are the best media in which to use humour; direct mail and newspapers are least suited.
- Consumer nondurables and business services are best suited to humour; corporate advertising and industrial products are least suited.
- Humour should be related to the product.
- Humour should not be used with sensitive goods or services.
- Audiences that are younger, better educated, upscale, male, and professional are best suited to humour; older, less educated, and downscale groups are least suited to humour appeals.

Consumer purchase decisions are often made on the basis of both emotional and rational motives, and attention must be given to both elements in developing effective advertising. Exhibit 6–11 shows a very clever ad that uses the Freudian concepts of id and superego to suggest that there are both emotional and rational reasons for purchasing the Lexus SC 400 coupe. Sometimes appeals are difficult to interpret and they may be considered a combined rational and emotional appeal as shown in the Altoids ad (Exhibit 6–12).

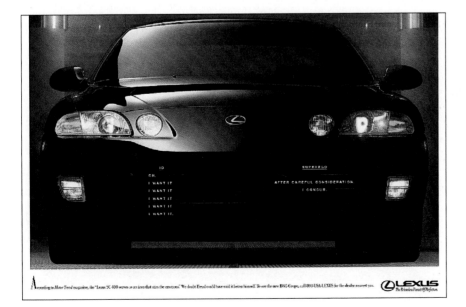

Exhibit 6–11
Lexus addresses both
rational and emotional
appeals in this clever ad

Exhibit 6–12
Altoids uses reminder advertising to build brand awareness

Advertising researchers and agencies have given considerable thought to the relationship between rational and emotional motives in consumer decision making and how advertising influences both. McCann-Erickson Worldwide, in conjunction with advertising professor Michael Ray, developed a proprietary research technique known as *emotional bonding*. This technique evaluates how consumers feel about brands and the nature of any emotional rapport they have with a brand compared to the ideal emotional state they associate with the product category.[45]

The basic concept of emotional bonding is that consumers develop three levels of relationships with brands, as shown in Figure 6–6. The most basic relationship indicates how consumers *think* about brands in respect to product benefits. This occurs, for the most part, through a rational learning process and can be measured by how well advertising communicates product information. Consumers at this stage are not very brand loyal, and brand switching is common.

At the next stage, the consumer assigns a *personality* to a brand. For example, a brand may be thought of as self-assured, aggressive, and adventurous, as opposed to compliant and timid. The consumer's judgment of the brand has moved beyond its attributes or delivery of product/service benefits. In most instances, consumers judge the personality of a brand on the basis of an assessment of overt or covert cues found in its advertising.

McCann-Erickson researchers believe the strongest relationship that develops between a brand and the consumer is based on feelings or emotional attachments to the brand. Consumers develop *emotional bonds* with certain brands, which result in positive psychological movement toward them. The marketer's goal is to develop the greatest emotional linkage between its brand and the consumer. McCann-Erickson believes advertising can develop and enrich emotional bonding between consumers and brands. McCann and its subsidiary agencies use emotional bonding research to provide strategic input into the creative process and determine how well advertising is communicating with consumers. McCann-Erickson used emotional bonding research as the basis for its award-winning "Priceless" campaign for MasterCard International. When the agency took over the account a few years ago, MasterCard was perceived as an ordinary credit card you keep in your wallet. The challenge was to create an emotional bond between consumers and MasterCard without losing the brand's functional appeal. McCann-Erickson developed a sentimental campaign that uses ads that take the sum total of an experience and declare that it has no price tag. Each commercial and print ad ends with the theme "There are some things money can't buy. For everything else there's MasterCard" (Exhibit 6–13).

FIGURE 6–6
Levels of relationships with brands

Exhibit 6–13
MasterCard's "Priceless" campaign creates
an emotional bond with consumers

Exhibit 6–14
Porsche used teaser ads to create interest
in the new Cayenne SUV

A unique example of combining rational and emotional appeals is the use of
teaser advertising. Advertisers introducing a new product often use teaser advertising, which is designed to build curiosity, interest, and/or excitement about a
product or brand by talking about it but not actually showing it. Teasers, or *mystery
ads* as they are sometimes called, are also used by marketers to draw attention to
upcoming advertising campaigns and generate interest and publicity for them. For
example, Porsche used teaser ads to generate interest and excitement in the Cayenne
SUV (Exhibit 6–14).

Nike also used teaser ads to start its campaign for its successful "RunTO 10K"
running event in Toronto in 2003. Looking to generate awareness of the race,
establish a stronger link between Nike products and running, and encourage
average or non-runners to participate (register on-line or in-store, and actually
run), the creative featured "Running Guy" who represented all novice runners
determined to complete the challenge, despite not being in the best of shape.
Messages at various out-of-home locations and in newspapers such as "10 km to
a collapsed lung" and "10 km to the fetal position" preceded "Running Guy" thus
provoking curiosity and introducing his persona. The campaign garnered significant media publicity, especially with "Running Guy" participating in the
morning show of a radio station consistent with the target audience. In total,
7,500 runners finished the challenge that easily surpassed the per capita participation rate of other major international cities.[46]

SOURCE CHARACTERISTICS

The third creative strategy decision is the source of the
message appeal. We use the term **source** to mean the person involved in communicating a marketing message,
either directly or indirectly. A *direct source* is a spokesperson who delivers a
message and/or demonstrates a product or service, like tennis star Andre Agassi

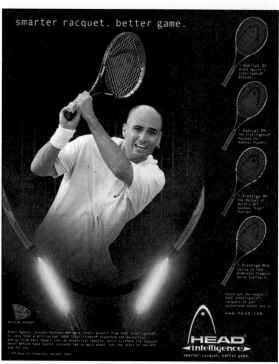

smarter racquet. better game.

Exhibit 6–15
Tennis star Andre Agassi serves as a spokesperson for Head

who endorses Head tennis rackets in Exhibit 6–15. An *indirect source*, say, a model, doesn't actually deliver a message but draws attention to and/or enhances the appearance of the ad. Some ads use neither a direct nor an indirect source; the source is the organization with the message to communicate. Since most research focuses on individuals as a message source, our examination of source factors follows this approach.

Companies are very careful when selecting individuals to deliver their selling messages. Many firms spend huge sums of money for a specific person to endorse their product or company. They recognize that the characteristics of the source affect the sales and advertising message. Marketers try to select individuals whose traits will maximize message influence. The source may be knowledgeable, popular, and/or physically attractive; typify the target audience; or have the power to reward or punish the receiver in some manner. Herbert Kelman developed three basic categories of source attributes: credibility, attractiveness, and power.[47] Each influences the recipient's attitude or behaviour through a different process (see Figure 6–7).

SOURCE CREDIBILITY

Credibility is the extent to which the recipient sees the source as having relevant knowledge, skill, or experience and trusts the source to give unbiased, objective information. There are two important dimensions to credibility, expertise and trustworthiness.

A communicator seen as knowledgeable—someone with expertise—is more persuasive than one with less expertise. But the source also has to be trustworthy—honest, ethical, and believable. The influence of a knowledgeable source will be lessened if audience members think he or she is biased or has underlying personal motives for advocating a position (such as being paid to endorse a product).

One of the most reliable effects found in communications research is that expert and/or trustworthy sources are more persuasive than sources who are less expert or trustworthy.[48] Information from a credible source influences beliefs, opinions, attitudes, and/or behaviour through a process known as **internalization**, which occurs when the receiver adopts the opinion of the credible communicator since he or she believes information from this source is accurate. Once the receiver internalizes an

FIGURE 6–7
Source attributes and receiver processing modes

Source attribute	Process
Credibility	Internalization
Attractiveness	Identification
Power	Compliance

opinion or attitude, it becomes integrated into his or her belief system and may be maintained even after the source of the message is forgotten.

A highly credible communicator is particularly important when message recipients have a negative position toward the product, service, company, or issue being promoted, because the credible source is likely to inhibit counterarguments. As discussed in Chapter 3, reduced counterarguing should result in greater message acceptance and persuasion.

Applying Expertise Because attitudes and opinions developed through an internalization process become part of the individual's belief system, marketers want to use communicators with high credibility. Spokespeople are often chosen because of their knowledge, experience, and expertise in a particular product or service area. Endorsements from individuals or groups recognized as experts, such as doctors or dentists, are also common in advertising (Exhibit 6–16). The importance of using expert sources was shown in a study by Roobina Ohanian, who found that the perceived expertise of celebrity endorsers was more important in explaining purchase intentions than their attractiveness or trustworthiness. She suggests that celebrity spokespeople are most effective when they are knowledgeable, experienced, and qualified to talk about the product they are endorsing.[49]

Exhibit 6–16
Dove promotes the fact that it is recommended by experts in skin care

Applying Trustworthiness While expertise is important, the target audience must also find the source believable. Finding celebrities or other figures with a trustworthy image is often difficult. Many trustworthy public figures hesitate to endorse products because of the potential impact on their reputation and image. Advertisers use various techniques to increase the perception that their sources are trustworthy. Hidden cameras are used to show that the consumer is not a paid spokesperson and is making an objective evaluation of the product. Disguised brands are compared. (Of course, the sponsor's brand always performs better than the consumer's regular brand, and he or she is always surprised.) Most consumers are skeptical of these techniques, so they may have limited value in enhancing perceptions of credibility.

Using Corporate Leaders as Spokespeople Another way of enhancing source credibility is to use the company president or chief executive officer as a spokesperson in the firm's advertising. Many companies believe the use of their president or CEO is the ultimate expression of the company's commitment to quality and customer service.

Some research suggests the use of a company president or CEO can improve attitudes and increase the likelihood that consumers will inquire about the company's product or service.[50] It is becoming common for local retailers to use the owner or president in their ads. Companies are likely to continue using their top executives in their advertising, particularly when they have celebrity value that helps enhance the firms' image. However, there can be problems with this strategy. CEO spokespeople who become very popular may get more attention than their company's product/service or advertising message. And if a firm's image becomes too closely tied to a popular leader, there can be problems if that person leaves the company.

Limitations of Credible Sources Several studies have shown that a high-credibility source is not always an asset, nor is a low-credibility source always a liability. High- and low-credibility sources are equally effective when they are arguing for a position opposing their own best interest.[51] A very credible source is more effective when message recipients are not in favour of the position advocated in the message.[52] However, a very credible source is less important when the audience has a

171

neutral position, and such a source may even be less effective than a moderately credible source when the receiver's initial attitude is favourable.[53]

Another reason a low-credibility source may be as effective as a high-credibility source is the **sleeper effect**, whereby the persuasiveness of a message increases with the passage of time. The immediate impact of a persuasive message may be inhibited because of its association with a low-credibility source. But with time, the association of the message with the source diminishes and the receiver's attention focuses more on favourable information in the message, resulting in more support arguing. However, many studies have failed to demonstrate the presence of a sleeper effect.[54] Many advertisers hesitate to count on the sleeper effect, since exposure to a credible source is a more reliable strategy.[55]

SOURCE ATTRACTIVENESS

A source characteristic frequently used by advertisers is **attractiveness**, which encompasses similarity, familiarity, and likability.[56] *Similarity* is a supposed resemblance between the source and the receiver of the message. *Familiarity* refers to knowledge of the source through exposure. *Likability* is an affection for the source as a result of physical appearance, behaviour, or other personal traits. Even when the sources are not famous, consumers often admire their physical appearance, talent, and/or personality.

Source attractiveness leads to persuasion through a process of **identification**, whereby the receiver is motivated to seek some type of relationship with the source and thus adopts similar beliefs, attitudes, preferences, or behaviour. Maintaining this position depends on the source's continued support for the position as well as the receiver's continued identification with the source. If the source changes position, the receiver may also change. Unlike internalization, identification does not usually integrate information from an attractive source into the receiver's belief system. The receiver may maintain the attitudinal position or behaviour only as long as it is supported by the source or the source remains attractive.

One requirement for a national campaign with an identifiable and likeable spokesperson who actually speaks in the ads is the fact that the person has to be fluent in both official languages. Danone did this with actress Sophie Lorain, who convincingly played a strong central character in all of their commercials. She demonstrated that Danone was for women who wanted yogurt as a healthy part of their busy everyday lives. Lorain had previously been the spokesperson in the Quebec ads for two years when Danone tested her in an English ad. The results were encouraging and the rest is history. While the language was a necessary requirement for success, Danone executives believed that Lorain's character (i.e., likability, similarity) communicated the benefits of the brand effectively, which was the primary concern.[57]

Applying Similarity   Marketers recognize that people are more likely to be influenced by a message coming from someone with whom they feel a sense of similarity.[58] If the communicator and receiver have similar needs, goals, interests, and lifestyles, the position advocated by the source is better understood and received. Similarity can be used to create a situation where the consumer feels empathy for the person shown in the commercial. In a slice-of-life commercial, the advertiser usually starts by presenting a predicament with the hope of getting the consumer to think, "I can see myself in that situation." This can help establish a bond of similarity between the communicator and the receiver, increasing the source's level of persuasiveness. Many companies feel that the best way to connect with consumers is by using regular-looking, everyday people with whom the average person can easily identify.

Applying Familiarity Familiarity through exposure from some other context can provide a strong source. In fact the connection can be quite surprising and very effective is some circumstances, especially for the British Columbia Automobile Association (BCAA). Three television commercials advertised its new Premier Membership with three former B.C. premiers, Dave Barrett, Bill Vander Zalm, and Glen Clark, each who faced varying political fortunes while leading Canada's western most province. Seeking to stay ahead of new competitive entrants in the roadside assistance market, BCAA sought to retain it market leadership position through higher sales growth while maintaining its reputation for strong products and excellent customer service. The answer of a risky creative that captured former premieres in humourous, self-depreciating situations that poked fun at themselves seemed the best bet to break through clutter and clearly identify the brand name Premiere. Each "actor" agreed to waive the fee in lieu of a donation to his favourite charity. Initial sales in the spring topped 2,000 and BCAA looked to up that to 10,000 by the end of 2004.[59]

Applying Likability: Using Celebrities Advertisers recognize the value of using spokespeople who are admired: TV and movie stars, athletes, musicians, and other popular public figures. A top celebrity endorser is golf phenom Tiger Woods, who has signed endorsement contracts worth more than $60 million with Nike, American Express, General Mills, and Buick (Exhibit 6–17). Most people would probably agree that P&G scored a winner when they signed Jamie Sale and David Pelletier to an endorsement contract for Crest Whitestrips right after the pair won the gold medal at the 2002 Olympic Games for figure-skating. Both have a natural and bright smile that reinforces the key brand benefit. And their victory and the excellent handling of the judging controversy will certainly add to the brand experience for consumers.[60]

Exhibit 6–17
Tiger Woods has endorsement contracts with a number of companies, including Buick

Why do companies spend huge sums to have celebrities appear in their ads and endorse their products? They think celebrities have stopping power. That is, they draw attention to advertising messages in a very cluttered media environment. Marketers think a popular celebrity will favourably influence consumers' feelings, attitudes, and purchase behaviour. And they believe celebrities can enhance the target audience's perceptions of the product in terms of image and/or performance. For example, a well-known athlete may convince potential buyers that the product will enhance their own performance.

A number of factors must be considered when a company decides to use a celebrity spokesperson, including the dangers of overshadowing the product and being overexposed, and the target audience's receptivity.

Overshadowing the Product How will the celebrity affect the target audience's processing of the advertising message? Consumers may focus their attention on the celebrity and fail to notice the brand. Advertisers should select a celebrity spokesperson who will attract attention and enhance the sales message, yet not overshadow the brand.

Overexposure Consumers are often skeptical of endorsements because they know the celebrities are being paid.[61] This problem is particularly pronounced when a celebrity endorses too many products or companies and becomes overexposed. Advertisers can protect themselves against overexposure with an exclusivity clause limiting the number of products a celebrity can endorse. However, such clauses are usually expensive, and most celebrities agree not to endorse similar products anyway. Many celebrities try to earn as much endorsement money as

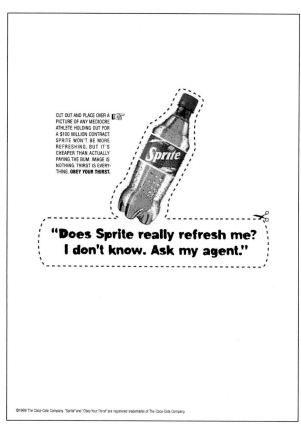

Exhibit 6–18
Sprite parodies the use of celebrity endorsers in this ad

possible, yet they must be careful not to damage their credibility by endorsing too many products. For example, Wayne Gretzky received some criticism for being a spokesperson for too many brands shortly after he retired from the NHL.

Target Audiences' Receptivity One of the most important considerations in choosing a celebrity endorser is how well the individual matches with and is received by the advertiser's target audience. Consumers who are particularly knowledgeable about a product or service or have strongly established attitudes may be less influenced by a celebrity than those with little knowledge or neutral attitudes. One study found that college-age students were more likely to have a positive attitude toward a product endorsed by a celebrity than were older consumers.[62] The teenage market has generally been very receptive to celebrity endorsers, as evidenced by the frequent use of entertainers and athletes in ads targeted to this group for products such as apparel, cosmetics, and beverages. However, many marketers are finding that teenage consumers are more skeptical and cynical toward the use of celebrity endorsers and respond better to ads using humour, irony, and unvarnished truth. Some marketers targeting teenagers have responded to this by no longer using celebrities in their campaigns or by poking fun at their use. For example, Sprite has developed a very effective campaign using ads that parody celebrity endorsers and carry the tagline "Image is nothing. Obey your thirst" (Exhibit 6–18).[63]

Understanding the Meaning of Celebrity Endorsers Advertisers must try to match the product or company's image, the characteristics of the target audience, and the personality of the celebrity.[64] The image that celebrities project to consumers can be just as important as their ability to attract attention. An interesting perspective on celebrity endorsement was developed by Grant McCracken.[65] He argues that credibility and attractiveness don't sufficiently explain how and why celebrity endorsements work and offers a model based on meaning transfer (Figure 6–8).

According to this model, a celebrity's effectiveness as an endorser depends on the culturally acquired meanings he or she brings to the endorsement process. Each celebrity contains many meanings, including status, class, gender, and age as well as personality and lifestyle. In explaining stage 1 of the meaning transfer process, McCracken notes:

> Celebrities draw these powerful meanings from the roles they assume in their television, movie, military, athletic, and other careers. Each new dramatic role brings the celebrity into contact with a range of objects, persons, and contexts. Out of these objects, persons, and contexts are transferred meanings that then reside in the celebrity.[66]

For example, cyclist Lance Armstrong has developed a very favourable image as a fierce competitor and an All-American superhero by winning the grueling Tour de France cycling race four times after overcoming a life-threatening form of testicular cancer.

McCracken suggests celebrity endorsers bring their meanings and image into the ad and transfer them to the product they are endorsing (stage 2 of the model in Figure 6–8). For example, PowerBar, the leading brand of energy performance bars, takes advantage of Armstrong's image as a competitor and champion with great determination in ads such as the one shown in Exhibit 6–19. He is also an effective

FIGURE 6–8 ☐☐☐☐ Meaning movement and the endorsement process

Key: ——▶ = Path of meaning movement

☐ = Stage of meaning movement

endorser for the product since he competes in a very gruelling and demanding sport where the benefits of sustained energy are very important.

In the final stage of McCracken's model, the meanings the celebrity has given to the product are transferred to the consumer. By using Armstrong in its ads, PowerBar hopes to enhance its image as a product that can provide extra energy to athletes and enhance their performance. McCracken notes that this final stage is complicated and difficult to achieve. The way consumers take possession of the meaning the celebrity has transferred to a product is probably the least understood part of the process.

The meaning transfer model has some important implications for companies using celebrity endorsers. Marketers must first decide on the image or symbolic meanings important to the target audience for the particular product, service, or company. They must then determine which celebrity best represents the meaning or image to be projected. An advertising campaign must be designed that captures that meaning in the product and moves it to the consumer. Marketing and advertising personnel often rely on intuition in choosing celebrity endorsers for their companies or products, but some companies conduct research studies to determine consumers' perceptions of celebrities' meaning.

Marketers may also pretest ads to determine whether they transfer the proper meaning to the product. When celebrity endorsers are used, the marketer should track the campaign's effectiveness. Does the celebrity continue to be effective in communicating the proper meaning to the target audience? Celebrities who are no longer in the limelight may lose their ability to transfer any significant meanings to the product.

As we have seen, marketers must consider many factors when choosing a celebrity to serve as an advertising spokesperson for the company or a particular brand. Studies have shown that advertising and marketing managers take these various factors into account when choosing a celebrity endorser.[67] Among the most important factors are the celebrity's match with the target audience and the product/service or brand, the overall image of the celebrity,

175

Exhibit 6–19
Cyclist Lance Armstrong helps position PowerBar as a product that provides energy to athletes

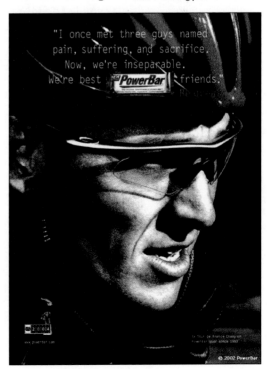

Exhibit 6–20
Revlon makes effective use of supermodel Cindy Crawford in this ad

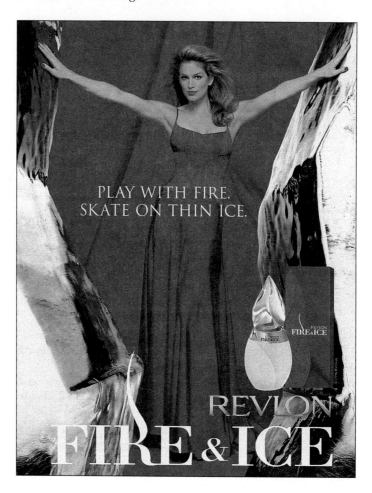

the cost of acquiring the celebrity, trustworthiness, the risk of controversy, and the celebrity's familiarity and likability among the target audience.

Applying Likability: Decorative Models   Advertisers often draw attention to their ads by featuring a physically attractive person who serves as a passive or decorative model rather than as an active communicator. Research suggests that physically attractive communicators generally have a positive impact and generate more favourable evaluations of both ads and products than less attractive models.[68] The gender appropriateness of the model for the product being advertised and his or her relevance to the product are also important considerations.[69] Products such as cosmetics or fashionable clothing are likely to benefit from the use of an attractive model, since physical appearance is very relevant in marketing these items. For example, Revlon uses supermodel Cindy Crawford in advertising for various cosmetics products such as its Fire & Ice fragrance (Exhibit 6–20).

Some models draw attention to the ad but not to the product or message. Studies show that an attractive model facilitates recognition of the ad but does not enhance copy readership or message recall. Thus, advertisers must ensure that the consumer's attention will go beyond the model to the product and advertising message.[70]

Marketers must also consider whether the use of highly attractive models might negatively impact advertising effectiveness. Some recent studies have shown that some women experience negative feelings when comparing themselves with beautiful models used in ads and the images of physical perfection they represent.[71]

SOURCE POWER

The final characteristic in Kelman's classification scheme is **source power**. A source has power when he or she can actually administer rewards and punishments to the receiver. As a result of this power, the source may be able to induce another person(s) to respond to the request or position he or she is advocating. The power of the source depends on several factors. The source must be perceived as being able to administer positive or negative sanctions to the receiver (*perceived control*) and the receiver must think the source cares about whether or not the receiver conforms (*perceived concern*). The receiver's estimate of the source's ability to observe conformity is also important (*perceived scrutiny*).

When a receiver perceives a source as having power, the influence process occurs through a process known as **compliance**. The receiver accepts the persuasive influence of the source and acquiesces to his or her position in hopes of obtaining a favourable reaction or avoiding punishment. The receiver may show public agreement with the source's position but not have an internal or private commitment to this position. Persuasion induced through compliance may be superficial and last only as long as the receiver perceives that the source can administer some reward or punishment.

Power as a source characteristic is very difficult to apply in a nonpersonal influence situation such as advertising. A communicator in an ad generally cannot apply any sanctions to the receiver or determine whether compliance actually occurs. An indirect way of using power is by using an individual with an authoritative personality as a spokesperson.

SUMMARY

The creative strategy often contains three key decisions. An important part of creative strategy is determining the creative theme of the campaign. There are several approaches to doing this, including using a unique selling proposition, creating a brand image, looking for inherent drama in the brand, and positioning. In general, the creative theme guides much of the advertising campaign or IMC program. Consistency and originality and its ability to effectively communicate are three key strengths of a good creative.

A message appeal, the second decision of the creative strategy is the central message used in the

ad to elicit cognitive and emotional processing responses and communication effects from the target audience. Appeals can be broken into two broad categories, rational and emotional. Rational appeals focus on consumers' practical, functional, or utilitarian need for the product or service; emotional appeals relate to social and/or psychological reasons for purchasing a product or service. Numerous types of appeals are available to advertisers within each category.

Selection of the appropriate source or communicator to deliver a message is the third creative strategy decision. Three important attributes are source

credibility, attractiveness, and power. Marketers enhance message effectiveness by hiring communicators who are experts in a particular area and/or have a trustworthy image. The use of celebrities to deliver advertising messages has become very popular; advertisers hope they will catch the receivers' attention and influence their attitudes or behaviour through an identification process. The chapter discusses the meaning a celebrity brings to the endorsement process and the importance of matching the image of the celebrity with that of the company or brand.

178

KEY TERMS

DISCUSSION QUESTIONS

1. How important was creativity for the Telus (previously Clearnet) campaign?

2. What are the differences between creative strategy and creative tactics? Why is it important to make a distinction between these two concepts?

3. Review the various advertising campaign themes used by Burger King that are shown in Figure 6–1. Why do you think Burger King has had such a difficult time finding an effective campaign theme?

4. What is your opinion of advertising awards, such as the Cannes Lions, that are based solely on creativity? If you were a marketer looking for an agency, would you take these creative awards into consideration in your agency evaluation process? Why or why not?

5. Find an example of a print ad that you think is very creative and an ad you feel is dull and boring. Evaluate each ad from a creative perspective. What makes one ad creative and the other bland?

6. Canadian Tire maintained similar creative themes for many years. Why do you think they did this for so long? Canadian Tire started a new theme in 2002. Can you describe it? Why did they change it?

7. Find an example of an ad or campaign that you think reflects one of the approaches used to develop a creative theme such as unique selling proposition, brand image, inherent drama, or positioning. Discuss how the creative theme is used in this ad or campaign.

8. Discuss the pros and cons of using a comparative advertising appeal for the following products: beer, cellphones, furniture, airlines.

9. Assume that you have been asked to consult for a government agency that wants to use a fear appeal message to encourage college and university students not to drink and drive. Explain how fear appeals might affect persuasion and what factors should be considered in developing the ads.

10. It has been observed that Canadian advertisers use fewer celebrity endorsers compared to American advertisers. Do you agree with this? If it is true, what is the explanation?

11. Find a celebrity who is currently appearing in ads for a particular company or brand and analyze and use McCracken's meaning transfer model (shown in Figure 6–8) to analyze the use of the celebrity as a spokesperson.

179

7

Creative Tactics Decisions

CHAPTER OBJECTIVES

- To identify three key decisions for creative tactics: execution style, message structure, and design elements.

- To analyze the various creative execution styles that advertisers can use and the advertising situations where they are most appropriate.

- To examine different types of message structures that can be used to develop a promotional message.

- To analyze various design elements involved in the creation of print advertising and TV commercials.

- To understand a planning model for making creative tactics decisions.

- To consider how clients evaluate the creative work of their agencies and discuss guidelines for the evaluation and approval process.

An Aha! Moment from Familiprix

How does Quebec's fourth largest pharmacy with 247 outlets in Quebec City and other provincial regions get noticed in the Montreal area as it tries to expand its presence? Faced with only a $2-million budget, about one-third the size of its major competitors, Familiprix knew that to get noticed it needed a very unusual creative execution and design for its television ads.

In a series of simple 15-second ads, a pharmacist wearing a standard white lab coat raises his hands and exclaims, "Aha! Familiprix!" when another character in the ad inevitably needs a pharmacy. With the song, "Don't You Just Know It" played in the background, the pharmacist witnesses a number of characters in familiar and obvious situations where we all know what will eventually occur.

A man using a hammer in his home eventually hits his thumb and the pharmacist exclaims, "Aha! Familiprix!" A woman in bed eventually replies to her partner that she has a headache and the pharmacist exclaims, "Aha! Familiprix!" A man sitting on the toilet has his wife eventually wondering what is taking him so long and the pharmacist explains, "Aha! Familiprix!"

All the situations shown in the ads are normal day-to-day occurrences. And the format of the ad never changes. The pharmacist sternly watches the scene and reacts the same way every time. The camera is completely stationary and there is only one scene shown for the entire length of the commercial.

The success of the campaign was phenomenal. Initial recall for Familiprix stood at 19 percent and grew to 46 percent in the first few months with expectations that it would go even higher by the end of the year. In fact the campaign generated substantial publicity as radio stations parodied the ads, clubs played the music from the ads, and Familiprix stores sold 4,000 CDs of the music. With such obvious acclaim, Familipix immediately produced two additional ads for the Christmas season and two more for the spring after the October 2003 launch of six initial spots.

Source: Danny Kucharsky, "Shot by Shot," *Marketing Magazine*, March 24, 2003.

In the previous chapter, we identified and described the three creative strategy decisions. This chapter focuses on the key creative tactics decisions. It examines various execution styles that can be used to develop the ad, the important message structure choices available, and the tactical issues involved in the design and production of effective advertising messages. We also present a framework for guiding the creative tactics decisions. We conclude by presenting some guidelines marketers can use to evaluate the creative recommendations they need to approve to effectively communicate their brand positioning strategy.

CREATIVE EXECUTION STYLE

Once the specific advertising appeal that will be used as the basis for the advertising message has been determined, the creative specialist or team decides the creative tactics. One critical creative tactic is the **creative execution style**, which is the way an advertising appeal is presented. While it is obviously important for an ad to have a meaningful appeal or message to communicate to the consumer, the manner in which the ad is executed is also important.

One of the best-known advocates of the importance of creative tactics in advertising was William Bernbach, founder of the Doyle Dane Bernbach agency. In his famous book on the advertising industry, *Madison Avenue*, Martin Mayer notes Bernbach's reply to David Ogilvy's rule for copywriters that "what you say in advertising is more important than how you say it." Bernbach replied, "Execution can become content, it can be just as important as what you say. A sick guy can utter some words and nothing happens; a healthy vital guy says them and they rock the world."[1] Bernbach was one of the revolutionaries of his time who changed advertising creativity on a fundamental level by redefining how headlines and visuals were used, how art directors and copywriters worked together, and how advertising could be used to arouse feelings and emotions.

An advertising message can be presented or executed in numerous ways:

- Straight sell or factual message
- Scientific/technical evidence
- Demonstration
- Comparison
- Testimonial
- Slice of life
- Animation
- Personality symbol
- Fantasy
- Dramatization
- Humour
- Combinations

Exhibit 7–1

Castrol uses a straight-sell execution style in this ad

We now examine these formats and considerations involved in their use. Many of these techniques can be combined to present the advertising message.

STRAIGHT SELL OR FACTUAL MESSAGE

One of the most basic types of creative executions is the straight sell or factual message. This type of ad relies on a straightforward presentation of information concerning the product or service. This execution is often used with rational appeals, where the focus of the message is the product or service and its specific attributes and/or benefits.

Straight-sell executions are commonly used in print ads. A picture of the product or service occupies part of the ad, and the factual copy takes up the rest of the space. (See the ad for Castrol Syntec motor oil in Exhibit 7–1.) They are also used in TV advertising, with an announcer generally delivering the sales message while the product/service is shown on the screen. Ads for high-involvement consumer products as well as industrial and other business-to-business products generally use this format.

182

SCIENTIFIC/TECHNICAL EVIDENCE

In a variation of the straight sell, scientific or technical evidence is presented in the ad. Advertisers often cite technical information, results of scientific or laboratory studies, or endorsements by scientific bodies or agencies to support their advertising claims. The ad for Dermasil Pharmaceutical Dry Skin Treatment shown in Exhibit 7–2 uses this execution style to emphasize the breakthrough from Vaseline Research.

DEMONSTRATION

Demonstration advertising is designed to illustrate the key advantages of the product/service by showing it in actual use or in some staged situation. Demonstration executions can be very effective in convincing consumers of a product's utility or quality and of the benefits of owning or using the brand. TV is particularly well suited for demonstration executions, since the benefits or advantages of the product can be shown right on the screen. Although perhaps a little less dramatic than TV, demonstration ads can also work in print, as shown in the ad for DuPont's Teflon® Bakeware Liners (Exhibit 7–3). Dove soap provides a neat example of demonstration presentation tactic. The magazines ads, TV ad, direct mail, and in-store demonstrations encouraged consumers to use litmus paper to test the alkalinity of various soaps. The key attribute of mildness of Dove was naturally communicated, albeit in a subtle manner, and the brand name was not highlighted in an obvious manner in the print and TV ads.[2] IMC Perspective 7–1 shows how Home Hardware and other retailers currently use a demonstration execution style in their advertising.

COMPARISON

Brand comparisons can also be the basis for the advertising execution. The comparison execution approach is increasingly popular among advertisers, since it offers a direct way of communicating a brand's particular advantage over its competitors or positioning a new or lesser-known brand with industry leaders. Comparison executions are often used to execute comparative appeals, as discussed earlier.

TESTIMONIAL

Many advertisers prefer to have their messages presented by way of a testimonial, where a person praises the product or service on the basis of his or her personal experience with it. Testimonial executions can have ordinary satisfied customers discuss their own experiences with the brand and the benefits of using it. This approach can be very effective when the person delivering the testimonial is someone with whom the target audience can identify or who has an interesting story to tell. The testimonial must be based on actual use of the product or service to avoid legal problems, and the spokesperson must be credible. Testimonials can be particularly effective when they come from a recognizable or popular source.

Exhibit 7–2
This Dermasil ad cites a scientific study

Exhibit 7–3
This ad demonstrates the benefits of Du Pont's Teflon® Bakeware Liners

183

Home Hardware Shows Us How

Home Hardware, a 1,000-plus chain that has 12 percent of the Canadian home improvement market, recently discovered that a demonstration execution style communicates its unique line of private label products very

effectively. Launched in the fall of 2002, each ad identifies a problem of a current product on the market and offers a Home Hardware product as a solution. For example, the Retract-A-Bit screwdriver is the solution to the problem of all the bits from a similar screwdriver falling to the floor while trying to use it. Or, the Flip-Grip dual-purpose pliers (i.e., needle-nose and flat-nose) minimize the inconvenience of finding two tools. And, each ad concludes with the message that the product can only be found at Home Hardware.

Used as a traffic builder, the ads entice gadget-type consumers to the outlets with the belief that most people will make other purchases. Furthermore, the ads indicate something unique about the retail location so that it becomes an important destination for consumers. But not only that, the products themselves are selling very well. For instance, Home Hardware sold 360,000 Retract-A-Bit screwdrivers in the first 10 months after running the ads for it. So, not only do the ads build awareness for Home Hardware, but managers also can assess their full impact through actual sales.

Such results give Home Hardware key information on which of its many hundreds of such products to feature in upcoming ads.

Home Hardware is not the only retailer using a demonstration execution style. Canadian Tire ran similar types of commercials with the same husband and wife couple using a variety of products. It began with eight in 2000 and reached 16 by 2002 when it placed them within their "Let's get started" campaign. The demonstration ads are also shown on in-store monitors along with display material and featured in the weekly flyer.

And another retailer that sells competing products is getting into the act too. Sears recently announced a significant change in its media mix moving from a print-broadcast ratio of 85–15 to 30–70 so that it could focus on its 12 private label brands like Kenmore appliances or Craftsman tools. The latter feature Bob Vila as a spokesperson who demonstrates how the Craftsman product solves a particular problem. Sears estimated that it would run approximately 20 private labels ads per year to compete with private label brands, and likely to compete with Canadian Tire and Home Hardware.

Source: Chris Powell, "Show & Tell," *Marketing Magazine*, February 24, 2003.

Toyota dealers in western Canada used actual customers to communicate their product's quality and dependability. Among four initially produced, a country veterinarian drove his 13-year-old Toyota 4Runner with 742,000 km in one spot and a travelling salesperson complained that the odometer of his Corolla only had six digits in another spot. All ads were based on actual customer experiences and although the campaign was a risky departure, the initial results appeared promising for a regional launch prior to the spring buying season in 2003.[3]

Apple Computer made effective use of testimonials as part of its "Switch" campaign, which features computer users from various walks of life discussing why they switched from Windows-based machines to Macintoshes (Exhibit 7–4). The people giving the testimonials in the ads are from various walks of life, including a writer, publisher, programmer, and Windows network administrator, and were chosen from a group of some 10,000 former PC users who wrote the company to proclaim their love for Apple. As part of the campaign Apple created a website that includes testimonials from PC users who switched to Macs and provides more detailed information for those considering switching.

Endorsements can also be from professional associations. Recall that the unique selling proposition for Trident was supported with an endorsement from the Canadian Dental Association as shown in Exhibit 6–2 in the previous chapter.

SLICE OF LIFE

A widely used advertising format, particularly for package-goods products, is the slice-of-life execution. This type of ad portrays a situation that consumers might face in their daily lives. The ad then shows how the advertiser's product or service can resolve the problem.

Exhibit 7–4
Apple's "Switch" campaign makes effective use of testimonials

Slice-of-life executions are often criticized for being unrealistic and irritating to watch because they are often used to remind consumers of problems of a personal nature, such as dandruff, bad breath, body odour, and laundry or cleaning problems. Often these ads come across as contrived, silly, phony, or even offensive to consumers. However, many advertisers still prefer this style because they believe it is effective at presenting a situation to which most consumers can relate and at registering the product feature or benefit.

Slice-of-life execution has also been used in ads for financial institutions that try to show how their products and services can help a consumer to improve their life or allow a customer to reach their future aspirations. We often see people moving into their first or dream home, finding ways to pay for life experiences such as post-secondary tuition or weddings, and planning for or enjoying their retirement. We've observed these types of executions from the major banks of Canada and recently from the Desjardins Group, an integrated financial co-operative similar to a credit union. The message of the ads reinforced the importance of balancing personal and financial aspects of people's lives with the repeated line "Money must always be at the service of people. Never the other way around."[4]

For many years, Procter & Gamble was known for its reliance on slice-of-life advertising executions. In 1980, two-thirds of the company's commercials used either the slice-of-life or testimonial format. However, P&G has begun using humour, animation, and other less traditional execution styles. Now only one in four of the company's ads relies on slice-of-life or testimonials.[5]

ANIMATION

An advertising execution approach that has become popular in recent years is animation. With this technique, animated scenes are drawn by artists or created on the computer, and cartoons, puppets, or other types of fictional characters may be used. Cartoon animation is especially popular for commercials targeted at children for products like toys and cereal.

Animation is a key element of a long-standing television commercial for Bits & Bites, a snack food directed to adults. The ad featured a man standing behind a fence as a friendly neighbour with his dog. First conceived in the 1970s, the light-hearted commercial continued to run into the 1980s and 1990s due to its significant appeal to consumers as indicated by market research. Faced with increased competition from a variety of snack foods, Kraft refreshed the graphics by brightening the colour of the scenes and adding more detail to the drawings. And for the first time ever, Kraft developed new versions of the ad by having three different "blooper out-takes" (i.e., line flubs, staging collapses, and character mishaps).[6]

PERSONALITY SYMBOL

Another type of advertising execution involves developing a central character or personality symbol that can deliver the advertising message and with which the product or service can be identified. This character can be a person, like the Maytag repairman, who sits anxiously by the phone but is never needed because the company's appliances are so reliable.

Canadian brands have been at the forefront in developing and nurturing a personality. Kool-Aid's "Face" icon and three-dimensional Kool-Aid pitcher provide an instantly recognizable character. In fact, established in Canada, the personality has been used in campaigns in the U.S. and Mexico. The American headquarters for Clorox invented The Man From Glad personality about 40 years ago, although he has not been seen in ads south of the border for 20 years, while continuously appearing in Canadian ads. Captain High Liner has been extolling the virtues of his brand of frozen fish products for over 25 years in Canada. A&W has used two types of personalities over the years, a person dressed as a bear and many family members to represent the different names of their burger products. Over time however, some personalities are changed or possibly retired. The St-Hubert chicken has been updated many times over the last 50 years, but executives are uncertain of its future since research indicates that it does not quite fit its new restaurant format and decor.[7]

FANTASY

An execution technique that is popular for emotional types of appeals such as image advertising is fantasy. Fantasy executions are particularly well suited for television, as the commercial can become a 30-second escape for the viewer into another lifestyle. The product or service becomes a central part of the situation created by the advertiser. Cosmetics ads often use fantasy executions to create images and symbols that become associated with the brand.

A certain amount of fantasy is accepted in advertising, however, at times the fantasy is too close to reality. Mega Bloks, a lower-priced building blocks toy similar to Lego, used a fantasy sequence in three ads to show how young boys used their imagination while playing with the blocks. An ad showed a boy using a plug and plugging it into his imagination with the ad ending, "Mega Bloks. Join the revolution." The association implied that boys had to join a club to purchase the product and that was not true. In all, only one of the three ads was run.[8]

DRAMATIZATION

Another execution technique particularly well suited to television is dramatization, where the focus is on telling a short story with the product or service as the star. Dramatization is somewhat akin to slice-of-life execution, but it uses more excitement and suspense in telling the story. The purpose of using drama is to draw the viewer into the action it portrays. Advocates of drama note that when it is successful, the audience becomes lost in the story and experiences the concerns and feelings of the characters.[9]

Although we typically see dramatization used in television or radio ads since they have audio capabilities it is possible to use this execution style in print. Good Year Tires conveyed the drama of driving in bad winter snow conditions with an effective newspaper ad that showed a car skidding through the weather page! Designed to look like the worst type of January weather, the fall campaign reminded consumers the importance of purchasing new snow tires before it was too late.[10]

The real challenge facing the creative team is how to encompass all these elements in a 30-second commercial. A good example of the dramatization execution technique is the ad for Zerex antifreeze in Exhibit 7–5, which shows a woman's sense of relief when her car starts at the airport on a cold winter night. The ad concludes with a strong identification slogan, "The temperature never drops below Zerex," which connects the brand name to its product benefit.

HUMOUR

Like comparisons, humour was discussed in Chapter 6 as a type of advertising appeal, but this technique can also be used as a way of presenting other advertising appeals. Humourous executions are particularly well suited to television or radio, although some print ads attempt to use this style. The pros and cons of using humour as an executional technique are similar to those associated with its use as an advertising appeal.

MESSAGE STRUCTURE

The way marketing communications are presented is very important in determining their effectiveness. Promotional managers must consider not only the content of their persuasive messages but also how this information will be structured for presentation. Advertising, in all media except radio, relies heavily on visual as well as verbal information. Many options are available with respect to the design and presentation of a message. This section examines the structure of messages, which is the second key creative tactic decision.

Marketing communications usually consist of a number of message points that the communicator wants to get across. It is important to communicate these points to overcome any opposing viewpoints audience members may hold. Extensive research has been conducted on how the structure of a persuasive message can influence its effectiveness, including order of presentation, conclusion drawing, message sidedness, and verbal versus visual message characteristics.

ORDER OF PRESENTATION

A basic consideration in the design of a persuasive message is the arguments' order of presentation. Should the most important message points be placed at the beginning of the message, in the middle, or at the end? Research on learning and memory generally indicates that items presented first and last are remembered better than those presented in the middle (see Figure 7–1).[11] This suggests that a communicator's strongest arguments should be presented early or late in the message but never in the middle.

Presenting the strongest arguments at the beginning of the message assumes a **primacy effect** is operating, whereby information presented first is most effective. Putting the strong points at the end assumes a **recency effect**, whereby the last arguments presented are most persuasive.

Whether to place the strongest selling points at the beginning or the end of the message depends on several factors. If the target audience is opposed to the communicator's position, presenting strong points first can reduce the level of counterarguing. Putting weak arguments first might lead to such a high level of counterarguing that strong arguments that followed would not be believed. Strong arguments work best at the beginning of the message if the audience is not interested in the topic, so they can arouse interest in

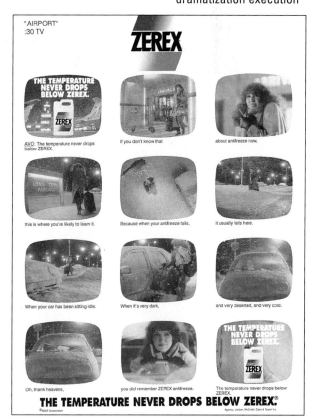

Exhibit 7–5
This Zerex ad uses a dramatization execution

187

FIGURE 7–1

Ad message recall as a function of order of presentation

□ □ □ □ □

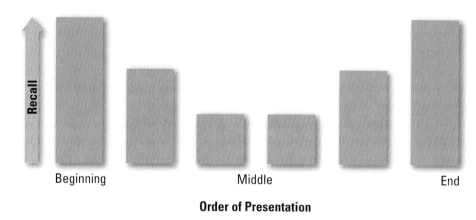

Recall

Beginning   Middle   End

Order of Presentation

the message. When the target audience is predisposed toward the communicator's position or is highly interested in the issue or product, strong arguments can be saved for the end of the message. This may result in a more favourable opinion as well as better retention of the information.

The order of presentation can be critical when a long, detailed message with many arguments is being presented. For short communications, such as a 15- or 30-second TV or radio commercial, the order may be less critical. However, many product and service messages are received by consumers with low involvement and minimal interest. Thus, an advertiser may want to present the brand name and key selling points early in the message and repeat them at the end to enhance recall and retention.

CONCLUSION DRAWING

Marketing communicators must decide whether their messages should explicitly draw a firm conclusion or allow receivers to draw their own conclusions. Research suggests that, in general, messages with explicit conclusions are more easily understood and effective in influencing attitudes. However, other studies have shown that the effectiveness of conclusion drawing may depend on the target audience, the type of issue or topic, and the nature of the situation.[12]

More highly educated people prefer to draw their own conclusions and may be annoyed at an attempt to explain the obvious or to draw an inference for them. But stating the conclusion may be necessary for a less educated audience, who may not draw any conclusion or may make an incorrect inference from the message. Marketers must also consider the audience's level of involvement in the topic. For highly personal or ego-involving issues, message recipients may want to make up their own minds and resent any attempts by the communicator to draw a conclusion. One study found that open-ended ads (without explicit conclusions) were more effective than closed-ended arguments that did include a specific conclusion—but only for involved audiences.[13]

Whether to draw a conclusion for the audience also depends on the complexity of the topic. Even a highly educated audience may need assistance if its knowledge level in a particular area is low. Does the marketer want the message to trigger immediate action or a more long-term effect? If immediate action is an objective, the message should draw a definite conclusion. When immediate impact is not the objective and repeated exposure will give the audience members opportunities to draw their own conclusions, an open-ended message may be used. Drawing a conclusion in a message may make sure the target audience gets the point the marketer intended. But many advertisers believe that letting customers draw their own conclusions reinforces the points being made in the message. The ad for Silk Soymilk in Exhibit 7–6 is a very good example of an open-ended message. The question in the headline encourages consumers to be open to the idea of drinking soymilk.

MESSAGE SIDEDNESS

Another message structure decision facing the marketer involves message sidedness. A **one-sided message** mentions only positive attributes or benefits. A **two-sided message** presents both good and bad points. One-sided messages are most effective when the target audience already holds a favourable opinion about the topic. They also work better with a less educated audience.[14]

Two-sided messages are more effective when the target audience holds an opposing opinion or is highly educated. Two-sided messages may enhance the credibility of the source.[15] A better-educated audience usually knows there are opposing arguments, so a communicator who presents both sides of an issue is likely to be seen as less biased and more objective.

Most advertisers use one-sided messages. They are concerned about the negative effects of acknowledging a weakness in their brand or don't want to say anything positive about their competitors. There are exceptions, however. Sometimes advertisers compare brands on several attributes and do not show their product as being the best on every one.

In some situations, marketers may focus on a negative attribute as a way of enhancing overall perceptions of the product. For example, W. K. Buckley Limited has become one of the leading brands of cough syrup by using a blunt two-sided slogan, "Buckley's Mixture. It tastes awful. And it works." Ads for the brand poke fun at the cough syrup's terrible taste but also suggest that the taste is a reason why the product is effective (Exhibit 7–7). They have used this slogan for many years and have built the brand from 2 percent to now 16 percent market share. It helps that this slogan is a bit of truth in advertising that consumers certainly appreciate.[16]

A special type of two-sided message is known as a **refutation**. The communicator presents both sides of an issue and then refutes the opposing viewpoint. Since this tends to "inoculate" the target audience against a competitor's counterclaims, they are more effective than one-sided messages in making consumers resistant to an opposing message.[17] Refutational messages may be useful when marketers wish to build attitudes that resist change and must defend against attacks or criticism of their products or the company. Market leaders, who are often the target of comparative messages, may find that acknowledging competitors' claims and then refuting them can help build resistant attitudes and customer loyalty.

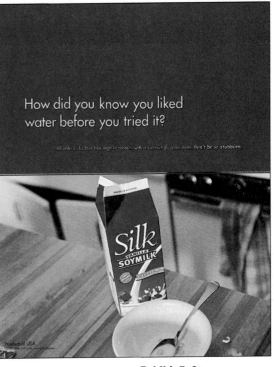

How did you know you liked water before you tried it?

Exhibit 7–6
This ad makes effective use of an open-ended approach

VERBAL VERSUS VISUAL MESSAGES

Thus far our discussion has focused on the information, or verbal, portion of the message. However, the nonverbal, visual elements of an ad are also very important. Many ads provide minimal amounts of information and rely on visual elements to communicate. Pictures are commonly used in advertising to convey information or reinforce copy or message claims.

Both the verbal and visual portions of an ad influence the way the advertising message is processed.[18] Consumers may develop images or impressions based on visual elements such as an illustration in an ad or the scenes in a TV commercial. In some cases, the visual portion of an ad may reduce its persuasiveness, since the processing stimulated by the picture may be less controlled and consequently less favourable than that stimulated by words.[19]

189

Exhibit 7–7
Buckley's Cough Syrup uses a two-sided message to promote the product's effectiveness

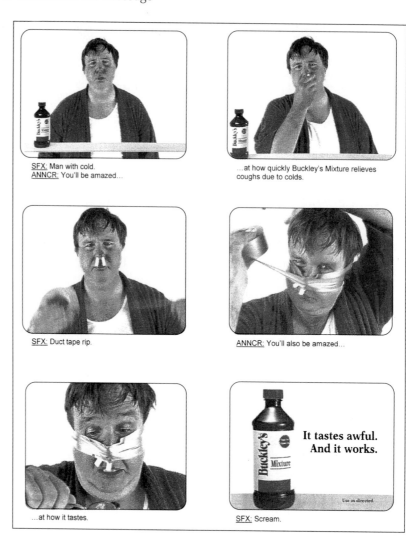

Exhibit 7–8
Visual images are often designed to support verbal appeals

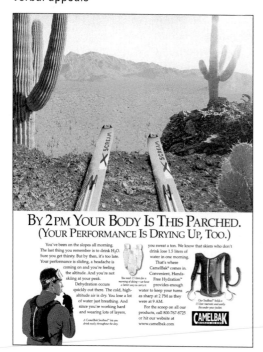

BY 2 PM YOUR BODY IS THIS PARCHED.
(YOUR PERFORMANCE IS DRYING UP, TOO.)

Pictures affect the way consumers process accompanying copy. A recent study showed that when verbal information was low in imagery value, the use of pictures providing examples increased both immediate and delayed recall of product attributes.[20] However, when the verbal information was already high in imagery value, the addition of pictures did not increase recall. Advertisers often design ads where the visual image supports the verbal appeal to create a compelling impression in the consumer's mind. Notice how the ad for the CamelBak SnoBowl uses visual elements to support the claims made in the copy regarding the importance of being hydrated when skiing (Exhibit 7–8).

Sometimes advertisers use a different strategy; they design ads in which the visual portion is incongruent with or contradicts the verbal information presented. The logic behind this strategy is that the use of an unexpected picture or visual image will grab consumers' attention and get them to engage in more effortful or elaborative processing.[21] A number of studies have shown that the use of a visual that is inconsistent with the verbal content leads to more recall and greater processing of the information presented.[22]

DESIGN ELEMENTS FOR IMC TOOLS

Once the creative strategy and initial two tactics decisions have been determined, attention turns to creating the actual advertisement. The design and production of advertising messages involve a number of activities, among them writing copy, developing illustrations and other visual elements of the ad, and bringing all of the pieces together to create an effective message. In this section, we examine the verbal and visual elements of an ad and discuss tactical considerations in creating print ads and TV commercials. Most of the points here can be applied to out-of-home print ads and radio ads.

CREATIVE TACTICS FOR PRINT ADVERTISING

The basic components of a print ad are the headline, the body copy, the visual or illustrations, and the layout (the way they all fit together). The headline and body copy portions of the ad are the responsibility of the copywriters; artists, often working under the direction of an art director, are responsible for the visual presentation. Art directors also work with the copywriters to develop a layout, or arrangement of the various components of the ad: headlines, subheads, body copy, illustrations, captions, logos, and the like. We briefly examine the three components of a print ad and how they are coordinated.

Headlines   The **headline** is the words in the leading position of the ad—the words that will be read first or are positioned to draw the most attention.[23] Headlines are usually set in larger, darker type and are often set apart from the body copy or text portion of the ad to give them prominence. Most advertising people consider the headline the most important part of a print ad.

The most important function of a headline is attracting readers' attention and interesting them in the rest of the message. While the visual portion of an ad is obviously important, the headline often shoulders most of the responsibility of attracting readers' attention. Research has shown the headline is generally the first thing people look at in a print ad, followed by the illustration. Only 20 percent of readers go beyond the headline and read the body copy.[24] So in addition to attracting attention, the headline must give the reader good reason to read the copy portion of the ad, which contains more detailed and persuasive information about the product or service. To do this, the headline must put forth the main theme, appeal, or proposition of the ad in a few words. Some print ads contain little if any body copy, so the headline must work with the illustration to communicate the entire advertising message.

Headlines also perform a segmentation function by engaging the attention and interest of consumers who are most likely to buy a particular product or service. Advertisers begin the segmentation process by choosing to advertise in certain types of publications (e.g., a travel, general interest, or fashion magazine). An effective headline goes even further in selecting good prospects for the product by addressing their specific needs, wants, or interests. For example, the headline in the ad for RCA's LYRA personal digital player shown in Exhibit 7–9 catches the attention of consumers who want the latest technology in audio products.

Types of Headlines   There are numerous headline possibilities. The type used depends on several factors, including the creative strategy, the particular advertising situation (e.g., product type, media vehicle(s) being used, timeliness), and its relation-

191

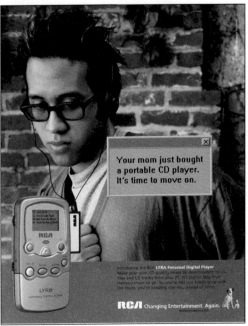

Exhibit 7–9
The headline of this ad catches the attention of young consumers

ship to other components of the ad, such as the illustration or body copy. Headlines can be categorized as direct and indirect. **Direct headlines** are straightforward and informative in terms of the message they are presenting and the target audience they are directed toward. Common types of direct headlines include those offering a specific benefit, making a promise, or announcing a reason the reader should be interested in the product or service.

Indirect headlines are not straightforward about identifying the product or service or getting to the point. But they are often more effective at attracting readers' attention and interest because they provoke curiosity and lure readers into the body copy to learn an answer or get an explanation. Techniques for writing indirect headlines include using questions, provocations, how-to statements, and challenges.

Indirect headlines rely on their ability to generate curiosity or intrigue so as to motivate readers to become involved with the ad and read the body copy to find out the point of the message. This can be risky if the headline is not provocative enough to get the readers' interest. Advertisers deal with this problem by using a visual appeal that helps attract attention and offers another reason for reading more of the message. For example, the ad for the Lexus GS sports sedan shown in Exhibit 7–10 uses a question as the headline that invites consumers to read the copy to learn more about the features of the car and decide how to categorize it. The visual portion of the ad supports the positioning theme by showing the GS 430 being driven on a windy road.

While many ads have only one headline, it is also common to see print ads containing the main head and one or more secondary heads, or **subheads**. Subheads are usually smaller than the main headline but larger than the body copy. They may appear above or below the main headline or within the body copy. The Cambridge SoundWorks ad shown in Exhibit 7–11 uses subheads within the body copy.

Exhibit 7–10

This ad uses a question-style headline and strong visual image that motivate consumers to read the copy

Exhibit 7–11

This ad uses subheads to make the copy easier to read

Subheads are often used to enhance the readability of the message by breaking up large amounts of body copy and highlighting key sales points. Their content reinforces the headline and advertising slogan or theme.

Body Copy   The main text portion of a print ad is referred to as the **body copy** (or sometimes just *copy*). While the body copy is usually the heart of the advertising message, getting the target audience to read it is often difficult. The copywriter faces a dilemma: The body copy must be long enough to communicate the advertiser's message yet short enough to hold readers' interest.

Body copy content often flows from the points made in the headline or various subheads, but the specific content depends on the type of advertising appeal and/or execution style being used. For example, straight-sell copy that presents relevant information, product features and benefits, or competitive advantages is often used with the various types of rational appeals discussed earlier in the chapter. Emotional appeals often use narrative copy that tells a story or provides an interesting account of a problem or situation involving the product.

Advertising body copy can be written to go along with various types of creative appeals and executions—comparisons, price appeals, demonstrations, humour, dramatizations, and the like. Copywriters choose a copy style that is appropriate for the type of appeal being used and effective for executing the creative strategy and communicating the advertiser's message to the target audience.

An interesting example of the use of a long copy occurred with Rogers (AT&T) Wireless. Borrowing from the idea that a picture is worth a thousand words, the poster ads extolled upon the attributes and benefits of picture messaging with a small photo of the product and exactly one thousand words! To garner attention and full processing of the copy, the ads involved the reader in personally relevant conversations that the target audience would be familiar with such as a woman talking to her man-friend about which shoes to wear to her high-school reunion, and a man talking to his buddy about his golfing triumphs. The entertaining dialogue provided a quick and enjoyable read, giving the feeling that one was actually experiencing the conversation.[25]

Visual Elements   The third major component of a print ad is the visual element. The illustration is often a dominant part of a print ad and plays an important role in determining its effectiveness. The visual portion of an ad must attract attention, communicate an idea or image, and work in a synergistic fashion with the headline and body copy to produce an effective message. In some print ads, the visual portion of the ad is essentially the message and thus must convey a strong and meaningful image. For example, the award-winning ad for Sims Snowboards shown in Exhibit 7–12 uses a powerful visual image. In a scene reminiscent of the protestor blocking military vehicles in Beijing's Tiananmen Square during the 1989 student uprising, a snowboarder stands in the path of snow-grooming machines (which pack the snow, to the distress of snowboarders). The single line of copy, "In a courageous act of solidarity, a lone snowboarder stands up for freedom," reinforces the message presented by the visual image.

Many decisions have to be made regarding the visual portion of the ad: what identification marks should be included

Exhibit 7–12
This ad for Sims Snowboards uses a strong visual image and a layout that resembles a newspaper page

In a courageous act of solidarity, a lone snowboarder stands up for freedom Store on 2C

Sims Snowboards

(brand name, company or trade name, trademarks, logos); whether to use photos or hand-drawn or painted illustrations; what colours to use (or even perhaps black and white or just a splash of colour); and what the focus of the visual should be.

Layout While each individual component of a print ad is important, the key factor is how these elements are blended into a finished advertisement. A **layout** is the physical arrangement of the various parts of the ad, including the headline, sub-heads, body copy, illustrations, and any identifying marks. The layout shows where each part of the ad will be placed and gives guidelines to the people working on the ad. For example, the layout helps the copywriter determine how much space he or she has to work with and how much copy should be written. The layout can also guide the art director in determining the size and type of photos. In the ad for Sims Snowboards shown in Exhibit 7–12, the layout is designed to make the ad look like it was reprinted from a newspaper page. Notice how this theme is carried through in the copy, which reads like a newspaper photo caption and ends with "Story on 2C." Layouts are often done in rough form to visualize what the ad will look like before moving on to the more costly stages of print production.

CREATIVE TACTICS FOR TELEVISION

As consumers, we see so many TV commercials that it's easy to take for granted the time, effort, and money that go into making them. Creating and producing commercials that break through the clutter on TV and communicate effectively is a detailed, expensive process. On a cost-per-minute basis, commercials are the most expensive productions seen on television.

TV is a unique and powerful advertising medium because it contains the elements of sight, sound, and motion, which can be combined to create a variety of advertising appeals and executions. In fact, the power of TV commercials is so pervasive, new forms are emerging as shown by BMW's example in IMC Perspective 7–2. However, for regular TV commercials, the viewer does not control the rate at which the message is presented, so there is no opportunity to review points of interest or reread things that are not communicated clearly. As with any form of advertising, one of the first goals in creating TV commercials is to get the viewers' attention and then maintain it. This can be particularly challenging because of the clutter and because people often view TV commercials while doing other things.

As you know, TV commercials have video and audio components that must work together to create the right impact and communicate the advertiser's message.

Video The video elements of a commercial are what the consumer sees on the TV screen. The visual portion generally dominates the commercial, so it must attract viewers' attention and communicate an idea, message, and/or image. A number of visual elements may have to be coordinated to produce a successful ad. Decisions have to be made regarding the product, the presenter, action sequences, demonstrations, and the like, as well as the setting(s), the talent or characters who will appear in the commercial, and such other factors as lighting, graphics, colour, and identifying symbols. Many TV commercials cost a small fortune in production costs to get the product and actors looking just right.

In attempting to attract new users who were of a younger demographic, Becel margarine used a new filming technique called Dogme that is very inexpensive but highly interesting, and as it turns out, highly effective. The filming is predicated on 35-mm film, no lighting, no sets, all shooting on location, natural sounds, and natural actors (no wardrobe or make-up). Becel was placed in several places to remind customers of the alternative, which was both a healthier way to live and a key reinforcement of Becel's positioning. For example, Becel was placed between elevator

BMW Canada's *drive*

The standard 30-second television commercial continues to evolve as seen by BMW Canada's *drive* execution. Making longer commercials and placing them in theatres or on the Internet has given advertisers the opportunity to enhance their target audience's experience with the brand. In fact, some believe these "short films" to be a new communication tool

entitled "brand entertainment" or "advertainment" and others claim that they are movies, not commercials. While one of these new names may stand the test of time, the underlying purpose of these executions is to combine video and audio in an exciting manner to capture the attention, initiate favourable responses, and achieve specific communication effects, just like television ads.

BMW Canada's *drive* featured its 5 Series positioned as a joyful, sophisticated, and very intelligent vehicle. The story of the short film presented a woman coming to terms with her life and ultimate demise. With the assistance of another character, Mr. Jones, the car is used to illustrate the woman's emotional journey. This approach was much more subtle than the U.S. execution entitled *The Hire*. These five to seven-minute films, directed by famous directors, showed all BMW vehicles performing in extreme conditions and situations.

The BMW execution is one example of an emerging trend that started in the U.S. a few years ago. For example, Reebok successfully used a film of an NFL football player, Buick featured Tiger Woods who challenged golfers to win a new Ranier SUV, and Pepsi posted short films, TV ads, and out-takes on its website. Some in the industry believe that BMW Canada's initial use of these tactics will spark other Canadian advertisers to jump at the opportunity.

However, before rushing in, a key part of BMW Canada's success was careful research that showed BMW Canada consumers were well informed of its products due to previous Internet research. Furthermore, BMW Canada felt the need to launch the 5 Series with a unique approach that connected rationally and emotionally to its customers since it is a premium brand. This was especially critical, as executives believed that its main competitors were copying the internationally famous BMW driving experience ads. And, like some things in marketing, the circumstances presented a good fit, as BMW Canada was a sponsor of Holt Renfrew's film festival entitled "Flick."

Source: Michelle Warren, "Calling All Copycats," *Marketing Magazine*, January 26, 2004.

doors so that consumers would use the stairs. Executives at the head office in Amsterdam took notice of the technique and message to new younger consumers and considered running the ads internationally.[26]

Audio   The audio portion of a commercial includes voices, music, and sound effects. Voices are used in different ways in commercials. They may be heard through the direct presentation of a spokesperson or as a conversation among various people appearing in the commercial. IMC Perspective 7–3 illustrates how John Sleeman effectively spoke in its many beer ads. A common method for presenting the audio portion of a commercial is through a **voiceover**, where the message is delivered or action on the screen is narrated or described by an announcer who is not visible. A trend among major advertisers is to have celebrities with distinctive voices do the voiceovers for their commercials.[27]

Music is also an important part of many TV commercials and can play a variety of roles.[28] In many commercials, the music provides a pleasant background or helps create the appropriate mood. Advertisers often use **needledrop**, which Linda Scott describes as follows:

> Needledrop is an occupational term common to advertising agencies and the music industry. It refers to music that is prefabricated, multipurpose, and highly conventional. It is, in that sense, the musical equivalent of stock photos, clip art, or canned copy. Needledrop is an inexpensive substitute for original music; paid for on a one-time basis, it is dropped into a commercial or film when a particular normative effect is desired.[29]

In some commercials, music is much more central to the advertising message. It can be used to get attention, break through the advertising clutter, communicate a key selling point, help establish an image or position, or add feeling.[30] For example, music can work through a classical conditioning process to create positive emotions that become associated with the advertised product or service. Music can also create a positive mood that makes the consumer more receptive toward the advertising message.[31]

Because music can play such an important role in the creative strategy, many companies have used popular songs in their commercials that reflect the selling message so uniquely. For example, Mitsubishi has made music a key element of its commercials, which usually show a group of young, fun adults in the car bopping to the beat or singing to the tunes of songs such as "Start the Commotion" or "One Week" by the Barenaked Ladies. Nortel Networks licensed the rights to use the classic Beatles' song "Come Together" (although it is performed by a different group) as the central theme in the company's global advertising campaign for its Internet products and services.[32] Bud Light spoofed love songs of the 1970s for its Bud Light Institute campaign. One infamous title is "I Love You Dearly Because You Let Me Go Out With My Friends On A Weekly Basis." Unexpectedly, people requested the songs, and the company responded by selling a complete CD entitled "Ulterior Emotions." Consumers can download the music featured in recent commercials from Coca-Cola and Bell Canada's websites. The widespread diffusion of technology has clearly created opportunities for marketers to enhance awareness.[33]

Sometimes, marketers creatively use music that previously existed. PEI tourism organizations asked Stompin' Tom Connors to re-record his song "Dial an Island" in a television ad that encouraged Canadians to call the toll-free phone number for information. With visuals of old home movies, the lyrics to the song along with a bouncing ball made music an integral part of the message to suggest PEI as a holiday option for the summer of 2004.[34] The Dairy Farmers of Canada used Beethoven's "Ode to Joy" in their ads that reminded us to "Drink milk, love life."[35]

Often music is composed specifically for a commercial. Musicians and composers participate early on in the process of developing the ad; alternatively, the creative specialists produce the ad look for very specific types of music to support the visuals. For example, the original musical score for the Canadian launch of the Mini was written after filming the ad. The visuals and the musical request led to a very unique sound that contributed to the brand positioning strategy in such a way that people thought it was previously recorded. In fact some in the industry believe that custom-written music is the best since it almost always works.[36]

Another important musical element in both TV and radio commercials is **jingles**, catchy songs about a product or service that usually carry the advertising theme and a simple message. For example, "Black's is photography" and "You always have time for Tim Hortons" are two retail jingles that have stood the test of time.

Sleeman Speaks His Mind in Quebec

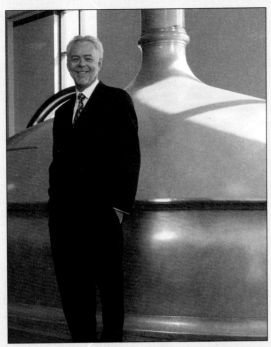

Parlez-vous Français, John? In an interesting turn of events, John Sleeman, chair and CEO of Sleeman Breweries, took to the radio airwaves speaking French in ads running in Quebec. John has been a spokesperson for the brewery in its home Ontario market, and when Sleeman entered the Quebec market, they continued with him. But in this case, French was not exactly his mother tongue. However, Sleeman speaking to French consumers in their language has won over their hearts!

John speaking in a relaxed manner on the radio to consumers who appreciate a craft beer from a micro-brewery was the strategy in Ontario for a few years. The plan was to use the same idea in Quebec for some of the same reasons. It was affordable for a low advertising budget, and the larger brewers were not in this media. However, as in Ontario, it meant that consumers would have to learn about the beer without seeing. Imagine, consumers having to purchase a beer by remembering the brand name and not recognizing its label or bottle on the shelves!

The Quebec agency recognized that they would have to use slightly different tactics since Quebecers might not be too receptive to a beer from Ontario in 1996, less than a year after the 1995 referendum. Furthermore, Quebec beer drinkers were accustomed to European craft beers that had relied on public relations and very little advertising. So an interesting radio tactic of not speaking the language perfectly correct was born and voilà, the Sleeman beer tactic

is "a typical case of turning a liability into an asset." The other key tactic was to use wittier dialogue so that consumers would overlook the language "liability." In fact, some of the earlier versions of the campaign poked fun at some cultural differences between French and English Canadians. Part of the success of the campaign can be seen by the fact that there have been over 30 creative executions, and one recent spot simply played the brand's jingle!

More recently, John Sleeman appeared on TV ads in Quebec after many radio ads, like he did in Ontario. Well, he sort of appeared on TV. Viewers heard his voice, like in the radio ads, but only saw his hands! Score another for Sleeman's using a unique tactic to effectively communicate. These ads continued a similar approach as the radio ads with witty dialogue, but each of three initial spots were curious comparisons to mainstream beers. One Sleeman executive attributes these new ads as a way of obtaining new customers from mainstream beers who are age 20 to 30 versus the usual target of age 30 to 40. And it appears to be working for Sleeman; it reached 25 percent of the premium beer market in Quebec and 2 percent of the overall market.

Sources: Danny Kucharsky, "Sex Doesn't Sell Sleeman in Quebec," *Marketing Magazine*, July 23, 2001; Eric Vincent, "Simplicity, Honesty, Authenticity . . . and No BS!" *Marketing Magazine*, December 17, 2001; Bertrand Cesvet, "The Universal Language of Beer," *Marketing Magazine*, October 23, 2000.

Jingles can be used by themselves as the basis for a musical commercial. Diet Coke brought back its old slogan "Just for the taste of it," set it to a luxurious musical score, and made it the basis of a multimillion-dollar ad campaign. In some commercials, jingles are used more as a form of product identification and appear at the end of the message. Jingles are often composed by companies that specialize in writing commercial music for advertising. These jingle houses work with the creative team to determine the role music will play in the commercial and the message that needs to be communicated.

Planning and Production of TV Commercials   Advertisers recognize that they need to do more than talk about, demonstrate, or compare their products or services. Their commercials have to break through the clutter and grab viewers' attention; they must often appeal to emotional, as well as rational, buying motives. Television is essentially an entertainment medium, and many advertisers recognize that their commercials are most successful when they entertain as well as inform. Many of the most popular advertising campaigns are characterized by commercials with strong entertainment value, like the Bud Light spots featuring many humourous situations, and the musical spots for the Gap. Some of the most popular commercials recently have been those created for Volkswagen's "Drivers wanted" campaign, which explores drivers' life experiences with their VWs[37] (Exhibit 7–13). Given the inherent entertainment value of television ads, it is no surprise that the planning and production resembles the making of a movie!

Planning the Commercial   The various elements of a TV commercial are brought together in a **script**, a written version of a commercial that provides a detailed description of its video and audio content. The script shows the various audio components of the commercial—the copy to be spoken by voices, the music, and sound effects. The video portion of the script provides the visual plan of the commercial—camera actions and angles, scenes, transitions, and other important descriptions. The script also shows how the video corresponds to the audio portion of the commercial.

Once the basic script has been conceived, the writer and art director get together to produce a storyboard, a series of drawings used to present the visual plan or layout of a proposed commercial. The storyboard contains still drawings of the video scenes and descriptions of the audio that accompanies each scene. Like layouts for print ads, storyboards provide those involved in the production and approval of the commercial with a good approximation of what the final commercial will look like. In some cases an aniamatic (a videotape of the storyboard along with the soundtrack) may be produced if a more finished form of the commercial is needed for client presentations or pretesting.

198

Exhibit 7–13
Volkswagen's award-winning commercials are some of the most popular in recent years

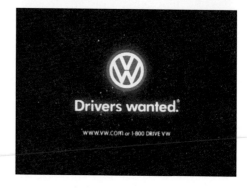

FIGURE 7–2 ☐☐☐☐ The three phases of production for commercials

Preproduction	Production	Postproduction

• Selecting a director
• Choosing a production company
• Bidding
• Cost estimation and timing
• Production timetable
   Set construction
   Location
   Agency and client approvals
   Casting
   Wardrobes
• Preproduction meeting
	• Location versus set shoots
	• Night/weekend shoots
	• Talent arrangements
		• Editing
		• Processing
		• Recording sound effects
		• Audio/video mixing
		• Opticals
		• Client/agency approval
		• Duplicating
		• Release/shipping

Production   Once the storyboard or aniamatic of the commercial is approved, it is ready to move to the production phase, which involves three stages:

1. *Preproduction*—all the work and activities that occur before the actual shooting/recording of the commercial.
2. *Production*—the period during which the commercial is filmed or videotaped and recorded.
3. *Postproduction*—activities and work that occur after the commercial has been filmed and recorded.

The various activities of each phase are shown in Figure 7–2. Before the final production process begins, the client must usually review and approve the creative strategy and the various tactics that will be used in creating the advertising message.

FRAMEWORKS FOR CREATIVE TACTICS

In this section, we present two models that guide the decision for selecting the most appropriate creative tactics. Each model builds on a perspective of the consumer response processes that we describe in Chapter 3. We discuss the models from a historical perspective to explain how the more recent model is an improvement over the initial model.

THE FCB PLANNING MODEL

An interesting approach to analyzing the communication situation comes from the work of Richard Vaughn of the Foote, Cone & Belding advertising agency. Vaughn and his associates developed an advertising planning model by building on traditional response theories such as the hierarchy of effects model and its variants and research on high and low involvement.[38] They added the dimension of thinking versus feeling processing at each involvement level by bringing in theories regarding brain specialization. The right/left brain theory suggests the left side of the brain is more capable of rational, cognitive thinking, while the right side is more visual and emotional and engages more in the affective (feeling) functions. Their model, which became known as the FCB grid, delineates four primary advertising planning strategies—informative, affective, habit formation, and satisfaction—along with the most appropriate variant of the alternative response hierarchies (Figure 7–3).

FIGURE 7–3

The Foote, Cone & Belding (FCB) grid

☐ ☐ ☐ ☐ ☐

	Thinking	Feeling
High involvement	**1. Informative (thinker)** Car–house–furnishings– new products model: Learn–feel–do (economic?) **Possible implications** Test: Recall Diagnosis Media: Long copy format Reflective vehicles Creative: Specific information Demonstration	**2. Affective (feeling)** Jewellery–cosmetics– fashion apparel– motorcycles model: Feel–learn–do (psychological?) **Possible implications** Test: Attitude change Emotional arousal Media: Large space Image specials Creative: Executional Impact
Low involvement	**1. Habit formation (doer)** Food–household items model: Do–learn–feel (responsive?) **Possible implications** Test: Sales Media: Small space ads 10-second I.D.s Radio; POS Creative: Reminder	**2. Self-satisfaction (reactor)** Cigarettes–liquor–candy model: Do–feel–learn (social?) **Possible implications** Test: Sales Media: Billboards Newspapers POS Creative: Attention

Vaughn suggests that the *informative strategy* is for highly involving products and services where rational thinking and economic considerations prevail and the standard learning hierarchy is the appropriate response model. The *affective strategy* is for highly involving/feeling purchases. For these types of products, advertising should stress psychological and emotional motives such as building self-esteem or enhancing one's ego or self-image.

The *habit formation strategy* is for low-involvement/thinking products with such routinized behaviour patterns that learning occurs most often after a trial purchase. The response process for these products is consistent with a behaviouristic learning-by-doing model known as operant conditioning. The *self-satisfaction strategy* is for low-involvement/feeling products where appeals to sensory pleasures and social motives are important. Again, the do → feel or do → learn hierarchy is operating, since product experience is an important part of the learning process. Vaughn acknowledges that some minimal level of awareness (passive learning) may precede purchase of both types of low-involvement products, but deeper, active learning is not necessary. This is consistent with the low-involvement hierarchy discussed earlier (learn → do → feel).

The FCB grid provides a useful way for those involved in the advertising planning process, such as creative specialists, to analyze consumer–product relationships and develop appropriate promotional strategies. Consumer research can be used to determine how consumers perceive products or brands on the involvement and thinking/feeling dimensions.[39] This information can then be used to develop effective creative options such as using rational versus emotional appeals, increasing involvement levels, or even getting consumers to evaluate a think-type product on the basis of feelings.

THE R&P PLANNING MODEL

We highlighted the R&P perspective in Chapter 4 when discussing objectives for the IMC plan. Another part of their framework concerns recommendations for creative tactics so that the appropriate communication effects will occur with the target audience while they are processing the message. On the surface, their planning model appears similar to the FCB planning model as both represent consumer attitudes and explain how marketers use creative tactics to influence attitudes. However, we will discuss four improvements as we explain the R&P model.

Brand Awareness Tactics   The first consideration is that the R&P model argues that brand awareness is a necessary precursor to brand attitude. According to R&P, both brand awareness and brand attitude are universal communication objectives for all circumstances (i.e., one ad, ad campaign, IMC plan). In this view, all communications should strive to achieve awareness to make brand attitude operational. R&P have three suggestions for awareness:

- Match the brand stimuli and the type of response behaviour of the target audience so that understanding of the brand in a category is unambiguous.
- Use a unique brand execution style to connect the brand to the category.
- Maximize brand contact time in the exposure to reinforce name and category connection.

In order for awareness to be fully established, the target audience needs to understand the context (brand, behaviour, category) as this is a clue as to how or why the brand exists. If the context is not clear, then the target audience has trouble remembering when it comes time to purchase. A unique execution style helps cut through the clutter. The connection to the category and sufficient enough exposure is required to make sure that the message is retained. For example, TV ads can sometimes show the package or brand name for too short a time for target audiences to fully grasp where the brand competes in the market.

We also noted that R&P suggest that awareness can be achieved via recognition and/or recall. R&P have two suggestions for recognition that require less media frequency as consumers need only to be familiar with the brand stimuli at the point of purchase:

- The brand package and name should have sufficient exposure in terms of time or size depending on the media.
- Category need should be mentioned or identified.

Since recall is a more difficult mental task, R&P have six suggestions for this aspect of awareness. Recall also requires high levels of frequency since the brand has to be remembered prior to being at the point of purchase:

- The brand and the category need should be connected in the primary benefit claim.
- The primary benefit claim should be short to be easily understood.
- Within an exposure, the primary benefit claim should be repeated often.
- The message should have or imply a clear personal reference.
- A bizarre or unusual execution style can be used if it is consistent with the brand attitude objective.
- A jingle or similar "memory" tactics should be included.

We have many more specific recommendations for recall since it is a much more difficult mental task for consumers. Advertisers have to help their target audience know their brand prior to purchasing. Thus, careful attention has to be put on all three creative tactics decisions to ensure the target audience can retrieve the brand name from long-term memory when the need to purchase a product category arises.

Brand Attitude Grid Tactics   The R&P view of consumer attitudes is also framed as a matrix with the dimensions of involvement and motivation. For each of these dimensions, R&P argue that their view is a more accurate representation of attitude for planning purposes than the FCB model, and the use of these two concepts represent the second and third improvements.

Low-involvement decision Informational motivation	Low-involvement decision Transformational motivation
High-involvement decision Informational motivation	High-involvement decision Transformational motivation

The involvement dimension is similar to the FCB model, from low involvement to high involvement. However, R&P argue that theirs is specific to the brand as the target audience makes a purchase decision. This point is consistent with an emerging view of involvement that we discussed in Chapter 3 where involvement was influenced by the target audience or the decision situation. Further, the high- and low-involvement levels are also consistent with the central and peripheral routes to persuasion. More precisely, R&P interpret involvement as the degree of risk perceived by the target audience (i.e., new category user or loyal customer) in choosing a particular brand for the next purchase occasion. One extension of this idea, not fully developed by R&P, is that the concept can extend to purchase-related behaviour that we discussed in Chapter 4. For example, how much risk does a person buying a car for the first time take in deciding to visit a particular dealer for a test drive?

The motivation dimension is a continuum from negative motive, or informational-based attitude, to positive motive, or transformational-based attitude. The historic interpretation of an informational-based attitude implies that it is based on careful reasoning that results from the cognitive responses that the target audience has while experiencing advertising messages. This purely cognitive orientation is also the foundation of the "think" dimension of the FCB model. However, R&P argue that this is too limiting as attitude is based on both cognition and affect. Accordingly, they suggest that creative tactics for this side of the matrix should account for the benefit claims (i.e., cognition) and the emotional portrayal of the motive (i.e., affect). Thus, in order for it to be an informational-based attitude, the emphasis of the benefit claim is stronger than the emotional portrayal of the negative motive. While this cognition and affect issue has been researched for many years, it is often the simplest observation that rings true as some very basic factual ads leave us with a smile on our faces.

The notion of transformational-based attitude is partly based on a recent idea. A transformational ad is defined as "one which associates the experience of using (consuming) the advertised brand with a unique set of psychological characteristics which would not typically be associated with the brand experience to the same degree without exposure to the advertisement."[40] Transformational ads create feelings, images, meanings, and beliefs about the product or service that may be activated when consumers use it, transforming their interpretation of the usage experience. Norwegian Cruise Lines used transformational advertising to create a unique image of the cruise experience and differentiate itself from competitors with its "As far from the everyday as a ship can take you. That's the Norwegian Way" campaign. The goal of the campaign was to demonstrate how Norwegian provides each guest with a unique reprieve from the mundane routines of everyday life. Both the dramatic visuals and ad copy depicted the vast array of experiences and activities to be enjoyed during one individual day on a Norwegian Cruise Line's voyage (Exhibit 7–14).

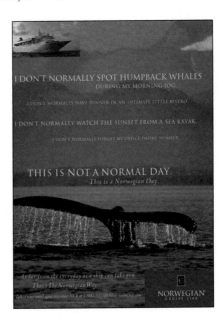

Exhibit 7–14
Norwegian Cruise Lines used transformational advertising to create a unique image of the cruise experience

Just like informational-based attitude is not purely cognitive, the transformational-based attitude is not purely based on emotion but includes some cognitive elements. Intuitively, this makes a lot of sense as some ads with a very strong fear appeal often leave us thinking. Overall, the emphasis of the emotional portrayal is stronger than the benefit claim for transformational-based attitude. Providing information in transformational ads is at the heart of two recent Saturn car ads. From a transformational perspective, both ads showed emotional elements of the purchase-and-consumption experience of owning a Saturn by demonstrating situations where the salesperson goes above and beyond "normal" service-level expectations to deliver a new Saturn. In both cases, however, key attribute information was conveyed. In one, online purchasing and its simplicity were communicated, while in the other, Saturn's 30-day/2,500-kilometre guarantee was explained.[41]

The fourth improvement of the R&P model is that its guidelines for creative tactics balance elements in the ad for both cognitive and emotional responses that contribute to both aspects of brand attitude. On the emotional side, we are concerned with how the motive is portrayed or conveyed in the ad. To consider this, we have three characteristics: its authenticity, or how real it appears to the target audience; whether the target audience likes the ad; and finally, the target audience's reaction to the execution style. On the informational side, we are concerned with the brand's message with respect to the benefit claims. We also have three characteristics to consider: the number, the intensity, and the repetition of the claims.

While the guidelines for all six characteristics may be a function of all three creative tactics decisions, we can make a stronger connection for some. The authenticity and whether the target audience likes the ad are typically associated with the design elements of the ad. Quite obviously, there is a direct connection between the execution style of the framework and that particular creative tactic decision discussed in this chapter. The benefit claims are mostly a function of the message structure since the latter concerns the details of explaining the product's benefits. It is also a function of the relative balance between a verbal and visual message. We now turn our attention to creative tactics recommendations for the four brand attitude cells.

Low Involvement—Informational Creative Tactics   Ads designed to influence target audiences' attitude based on low involvement—informational persuasion should have a very obvious benefit claim with an unusual execution style. Since the intention is to persuade the target audience so that they automatically learn the connection between the brand, its category, and the benefit, consumer acceptance or rejection of the message is not a factor. Further, the emotion demonstrated in the ad and whether the target audience likes the ad are not necessary as the message is intended to make a creative link among the brand, category, and benefit.

Low Involvement—Informational

Emotional portrayal of motive

Authenticity	Not necessary.
Like ad	Not necessary.
Execution style	Unusual, problem-solution format.

Benefit claim of brand message

Number of benefits	One or two, or one clear group.
Intensity of benefit claim	State extremely.
Repetition of benefit claim	Few required for reminder.

Low Involvement—Transformational Creative Tactics   Three emotional portrayal guidelines are critical for this type of attitude. These points are consistent with transformational ads described above. For example, the representation of the consumption of the brand in the drama or story of the ad must "ring true" with the target audience such that it is perceived as a very enjoyable ad. In a low-involvement situation, some benefit claims are still included but may be indirectly communicated through the story or emotion surrounding the story. Actual acceptance of the benefit claim is not a requirement; however, rejection of the overall message can lead to a reduction in the attitude of the target audience.

Low Involvement—Transformational

Emotional portrayal of motive

Authenticity	Key element and is the single benefit.
Like ad	Necessary.
Execution style	Unique to the brand.

Benefit claim of brand message

Number of benefits	One or two, or one clear group.
Intensity of benefit claim	Imply extremely by association.
Repetition of benefit claim	Many exposures to build-up before trial purchase and reinforce attitude after trial

High Involvement—Informational Creative Tactics   This side of the model illustrates the importance of information as high involvement implies the requirement of considerable and accurate benefit claims. Many benefits can be claimed here but they must be organized and presented in a manner that respects the current attitude of the target audience. Since this is an informational-based attitude, the emotional portrayal is important but not the primary consideration. Furthermore, the high-involvement characteristic means that the target audience has to accept the benefit claims. Rejection of the benefit claims may not result in any negative change in attitude if the copy respected the prior attitude of the target audience.

High Involvement—Informational

Emotional portrayal of motive

Authenticity	Key element early in product life cycle and declines as product reaches later stages.
Like ad	Not necessary.
Execution style	Unusual.

Benefit claim of brand message

Number of benefits	Overall claim to summarize multiple (no more than seven) benefits.
Intensity of benefit claim	Initial attitude is key reference point. Very accurate claim; cannot over-claim or under-claim. Comparative or refutation messages are strong options.
Repetition of benefit claim	Many claims within an exposure.

High Involvement—Transformational Creative Tactics Persuasion through this type of attitude formation requires strong emphasis of the emotion. A positive attitude towards the ad leads to a positive brand attitude. Likewise, the target audience must truly relate to the execution style and feel like the ad supports their lifestyle. The end result is that if the target audience rejects the message because the emotion is not accurate, then the persuasion will not work and may even cause significant attitude reduction. The remaining guidelines illustrate that considerable information is required similar to what is seen for the high involvement—informational attitude. Once again this implies that acceptance of the benefit claims are critical for the attitude to take hold with the target audience.

High Involvement—Transformational

Emotional portrayal of motive

Authenticity	Paramount; must reflect lifestyle of target audience.
Like ad	Necessary.
Execution style	Unique; target audience must identify with product, people, or consumption situation shown.

Benefit claim of brand message

Number of benefits	Acceptable number to provide key information.
Intensity of benefit claim	Very accurate claim; may over-claim but do not under-claim.
Repetition of benefit claim	Many are required to support informational message.

EVALUATING CREATIVE DESIGNS

While the creative specialists have much responsibility for determining the advertising appeal and execution style to be used in a campaign, the marketer must evaluate and approve the creative approach before any ads are produced. A number of people may be involved in evaluating the creative recommendation, including the advertising or communications manager, product or brand managers, marketing director or vice president, representatives from the legal department, and sometimes even the president or chief executive officer (CEO) of the company or the board of directors.

PROCESS OF EVALUATION

The amount of input each of these individuals has in the creative evaluation and approval process varies depending on the company's policies, the importance of the product to the company, the role of advertising in the marketing program, and the advertising approach being recommended. For example, the Chiat/Day agency had to convince Apple's board of directors to air the famous "1984" commercial used to introduce the Macintosh personal computer. Apple's board thought the commercial, which was based on the concept of Big Brother from George Orwell's classic novel *1984*, was too controversial and might be detrimental to its image, particularly in the business market. The spot used stark images of Orwell's dystopia, and a dramatic scene of a young woman throwing a mallet through a movie screen to destroy a controlling force, purportedly symbolizing its major competitor IBM (Exhibit 7–15). The agency convinced Apple's board to run the commercial during the 1984 Super Bowl, which is the only time it ever appeared as a commercial on TV, and the impact was tremendous. The spot was the focus of attention in the media and was the talk of the marketing and advertising industries. A few years ago, *TV Guide* named the "1984" spot the greatest television commercial of all time.

In situations where an advertising agency is used, top management is involved in selecting an ad agency and must approve the theme and creative strategy for the campaign. Evaluation and approval of the individual ads proposed by the agency often rest with the advertising and product managers who are primarily responsible for the brand. The account executive and a member of the creative team present the creative concept to the client's advertising and product and/or marketing managers for their approval before beginning production. A careful evaluation should be made before the ad actually enters production, since this stage requires considerable time and money as suppliers are hired to perform the various functions required to produce the actual ad. We review other elements of working with an advertising agency in Chapter 16.

The evaluation of the print layout or commercial storyboard can be difficult, since the advertising or brand manager is generally not a creative expert and must be careful not to reject viable creative approaches or accept ideas that will result in inferior advertising. However, the guidelines discussed next to judge the efficacy of creative approaches suggested by creative specialists can be used if needed.

GUIDELINES FOR EVALUATION

Advertisers use numerous criteria to evaluate the recommended creative approach. In some instances, the advertiser may want to have the rough layout or storyboard pretested to get quantitative information to assist in the evaluation. However, the evaluation process is usually more subjective; the advertising or brand manager relies on qualitative considerations. Basic criteria for evaluating creative approaches are discussed next:

- *Is the creative approach consistent with the brand's marketing and advertising objectives?* One of the most important factors the advertiser must consider is whether the creative strategy and tactics recommended by the agency are consistent with the marketing strategy for the brand and the role advertising and

Exhibit 7–15
Apple's famous "1984" commercial almost never made it to television

promotion have been assigned in the overall marketing program. This means the creative approach must be compatible with the image of the brand and the way it is positioned in the marketplace.

- *Is the creative approach consistent with the communication objectives?* The creative strategy and tactics must meet the established communication objectives. Creative specialists can lose sight of what the advertising message is supposed to be and come up with an approach that fails to execute the advertising strategy. Individuals responsible for approving the ad should ask the creative specialists to explain how the creative strategy and tactics achieve the creative and communications objectives.
- *Is the creative approach appropriate for the target audience?* Generally, much time has been spent defining, locating, and attempting to understand the target audience for the advertiser's product or service. Careful consideration should be given to whether the creative strategy and tactics recommended will appeal to, be understood by, and communicate effectively with the target audience. This involves studying all elements of the ad and how the audience will respond to them. Advertisers do not want to approve advertising that they believe will receive a negative reaction from the target audience.
- *Does the creative approach communicate a clear and convincing message to the customer?* Most ads are supposed to communicate a message that will help sell the brand. Many ads fail to communicate a clear and convincing message that motivates consumers to use a brand. While creativity is important in advertising, it is also important that the advertising communicate information attributes, features and benefits, and/or images that give consumers a reason to buy the brand.
- *Does the creative approach keep from overwhelming the message?* A common criticism of advertising, and TV commercials in particular, is that so much emphasis is placed on creative approach that the advertiser's message gets overshadowed. Many creative, entertaining commercials have failed to register the brand name and/or selling points effectively.

  With the increasing amount of clutter in most advertising media, it may be necessary to use a novel creative approach to gain the viewer's or reader's attention. However, the creative approach cannot overwhelm the message. Advertiser must walk a fine line: Make sure the sales message is not lost, but be careful not to stifle the efforts of the creative specialists and force them into producing dull, boring advertising.
- *Is the creative approach appropriate for the media environment in which it is likely to be seen?* Each media vehicle has its own specific climate that results from the nature of its editorial content, the type of reader or viewer it attracts, and the nature of the ads it contains. Consideration should be given to how well the ad fits into the media environment in which it will be shown.
- *Is the ad truthful and tasteful?* Marketers also have to consider whether an ad is truthful, as well as whether it might offend consumers. The ultimate responsibility for determining whether an ad deceives or offends the target audience lies with the client. It is the job of the advertising or brand manager to evaluate the approach suggested by the creative specialists against company standards. The firm's legal department may be asked to review the ad to determine whether the creative appeal, message content, or execution could cause any problems for the company. It is much better to catch any potential legal problems before the ad is shown to the public.

The advertising manager, brand manager, or other personnel on the client side can use these basic guidelines in reviewing, evaluating, and approving the ideas offered by the creative specialists. There may be other factors specific to the firm's advertising and marketing situation. Also, there may be situations where it is acceptable to deviate from the standards the firm usually uses in judging creative output. As we shall see in the next chapter, the client may want to move beyond these subjective criteria and use more sophisticated pretesting methods to determine the effectiveness of a particular approach suggested by the creative specialists.

SUMMARY

In this chapter, we examined how the advertising message is implemented and executed. Once the creative strategy that will guide the ad campaign has been determined, attention turns to the specific creative tactics that will enhance the cognitive and emotional processing of the message. This chapter summarizes three decisions that are critical when developing creative tactics: execution style, message structure, and design elements.

The creative execution style is the way the advertising appeal is presented in the message. A number of common execution techniques were examined in the chapter, along with considerations for their use. The most appropriate style is a matter of balancing uniqueness in the market versus effective communication to achieve the stated objectives.

The design of the advertising message is a critical part of the communication process and is the second creative tactic discussed. There are various options regarding the message structure, including order of presentation of message arguments, conclusion drawing, message sidedness, refutation, and verbal versus visual traits.

Attention was also given to tactical issues involved in creating print and TV advertising. The components of a print ad include headlines, body copy, illustrations, and layout. We also examined the video and audio components of TV commercials and various considerations involved in the planning and production of commercials. Together, these showed some of the important design decisions that have to be made to complete the creative approach.

We presented a framework for creative specialists and marketers to help them make the appropriate decisions for the creative tactics. The framework uses the target audience's attitude as the key factor when deciding upon the correct execution style, message structure, and design.

Creative specialists are responsible for determining the creative strategy and tactics from the marketer's input. However, the client must review, evaluate, and approve the creative approach before any ads are produced or run. A number of criteria can be used by advertising, product or brand managers, and others involved in the promotional process to evaluate the advertising messages before approving final production.

KEY TERMS

creative execution
    style, *182*
primacy effect, *187*
recency effect, *187*
one-sided message, *189*
two-sided message, *189*
refutation, *189*

headline, *191*
direct headlines, *192*
indirect headlines, *192*
subheads, *192*
body copy, *193*
layout, *194*
voiceover, *196*

needledrop, *196*
jingles, *196*
script, *198*
informational
    motive, *202*
transformational
    motive, *202*

low-involvement
    decision, *202*
high-involvement
    decision, *202*

DISCUSSION QUESTIONS

1. Discuss the difference between an advertising appeal and a creative execution style. Why is it important to make this distinction?

2. Explain how the dramatization advertising execution technique could be used for the following products: beer, cellphones, furniture, airlines.

3. Why do consumer packaged-goods advertisers such as Procter & Gamble often use slice-of-life executions? Can this advertising technique be used for business-to-business products?

4. Identify the various motives that can be used as the basis of rational advertising appeals and emotional advertising appeals. Are there any motives that can be addressed with both rational and emotional advertising appeals?

5. What emotions did "The Rant" commercial evoke from Canadian consumers? How did these emotional responses result in greater sales for Molson Canadian?

6. What is meant by one-sided versus two-sided message? Discuss some ofthe reasons marketers may or may not want to use a two-sided message.

7. Discuss the role of headlines and subheads in print advertisements. Would you say that headlines are more important for processing (i.e., gaining attention) or establishing a communication effect (i.e., awareness).

8. Discuss the role of music in advertising. Why might companies such as Microsoft and Nortel Networks pay large sums of money for the rights to use popular songs in their commercials?

9. What are the similarities and differences of creative tactics across the four cells of the planning matrix?

8

Measuring the Effectiveness of the Promotional Program

CHAPTER OBJECTIVES

- To understand reasons for measuring promotional program effectiveness.

- To know the various measures used in assessing promotional program effectiveness.

- To evaluate alternative methods for measuring promotional program effectiveness.

- To understand the requirements of proper effectiveness research.

Wacki Buns Produce Colourful Results

Wacki Buns from Weston Bakeries proved to be a winner of a product to encourage children to eat their barbecue meals in the summer. "Outrageous Orange" and "Punky Purple" hamburger and hot-dog buns provided children with a fun eating experience compared to the same old white bread alternative. With positive information from focus group research, executives quickly recognized that the campaign should target children and not their dubious mothers.

Weston's agency, Round Table Advertising, put together a 30-second television commercial that conveyed the wacky brand personality through a cartoon "spokesperson" named Moe who appeared in all communications. Weston also delivered its message in magazines and online.

Teletoon was the logical choice for reaching children and the partnership between this specialty channel and Weston produced the kinds of communication results that many advertisers look for when executing a campaign for a new product.

An enhanced part of the campaign suggested by Teletoon featured "Wacki Weekends" where programs were played based on the voting patterns of children during the previous week. Kids recognized the opportunity to vote online when the television screen turned to an orange or purple hue for 10 seconds after a Wacki Bun emerged from the corner. The online voting included other promotional activities (e.g., contests, games) to capture the imagination of the children and to reinforce continued communication of the brand.

These three enhancements, viewer influence of programming, custom animation, and changing the colour of the screen, were all firsts for Teletoon. It had never attempted to alter its presentation for an advertiser previously and this risk-taking venture was rewarded with a Media Innovation Award.

From a communications perspective, the campaign delivered many positive results for the station and the advertiser. Teletoon experienced one of its highest audiences—twenty percent higher than normal —during a relatively flat viewing time of the summer. The voting participation level achieved was higher than any other vote Teletoon had ever recorded. Children played the online game more than any other game previously as well.

Weston Bakeries received tremendous boosts in awareness and positive brand associations, as many children loved Moe at his many event appearances. And to top it all off, Weston sold an impressive number of buns. In fact its incremental sales, that is sales higher than the previous year, came in at 750,000 units. This contributed to growing the bun category by 1 percent when it had otherwise dropped 7 percent during the previous year.

Source: Fiona Gallagher, "Making Food More Fun," *Marketing Magazine*, March 15, 2004.

As marketers spend their communications dollars in diverse areas, the need to determine the effectiveness of these expenditures becomes increasingly important. Several methods for evaluating the effectiveness of these programs are used. Both clients and agencies are continually striving to determine whether their communications are working and how well they are working relative to other options. Measuring the effectiveness of the promotional program is a critical element in the promotional planning process. Research allows the marketing manager to evaluate the performance of specific program elements and provides input into the next period's situation analysis. It is a necessary ingredient to a continuing planning process, yet it is often not carried out.

In this chapter, we discuss some reasons firms should measure the effectiveness of their IMC programs, as well as why many decide not to. We also examine how, when, and where such measurements can be conducted. Most of our attention is devoted to measuring the effects of advertising because much more time and effort have been expended developing evaluation measures in advertising than in the other promotional areas. Furthermore, since most other promotional tools have an advertisement-like message, most of these research techniques can be applied. We will highlight methods of measuring effectiveness for these tools in their respective chapters later in the text.

It is important to understand that in this chapter we are concerned with research that is conducted in an evaluative role—that is, to measure the effectiveness of advertising and promotion and/or to assess various strategies before implementing them. This is not to be confused with research discussed earlier in the text to help develop the promotional program, although the two can (and should) be used together. While evaluative research may occur at various times throughout the promotional process (including the development stage), it is conducted specifically to assess the effects of various strategies. We begin our discussion with the reasons effectiveness should be measured as well as some of the reasons firms do not do so.

THE MEASURING ADVERTISING EFFECTIVENESS DEBATE

Almost any time one engages in a project or activity, whether for work or fun, some measure of performance occurs. In sports you may compare your golf score against par or your time on a ski course to other skiers' performance. In business, employees are generally given objectives to accomplish, and their job evaluations are based on their ability to achieve these objectives. Advertising and promotion should not be an exception. It is important to determine how well the communications program is working and to measure this performance against some standards.

REASONS FOR MEASURING ADVERTISING EFFECTIVENESS

Assessing the effectiveness of ads both before they are implemented and after the final versions have been completed and fielded offers a number of advantages:

Avoiding Costly Mistakes Total advertising topped $10 billion in 2004. This is a lot of money to be throwing around without some understanding of how well it is being spent. If the program is not achieving its objectives, the marketing manager needs to know so he or she can stop spending (wasting) money on it.

Just as important as the out-of-pocket costs is the opportunity loss due to poor communications. If the advertising and promotions program is not accomplishing its objectives, not only is the money spent lost but so too is the potential gain that could result from an effective program. Thus, measuring the effects of advertising does not just save money. It also helps the firm maximize its investment. For example, one mass merchant discovered that promoting Tide detergent generated more cross-selling opportunities than did promotions of nonpremium brands (Exhibit 8–1). At the same time, promotions of motor oil had no cross-selling impact.[1]

Evaluating Alternative Strategies Typically a firm has a number of strategies under consideration. For example, there may be some question as to which medium should be used or whether one message is more effective than another. Or the decision may be between two promotional program elements. For example, should research be spent on sponsorships or on advertising? One retailer found that advertising do-it-yourself products on the radio was effective in rural areas but not in urban locales.[2] Research may be designed to help the manager determine which strategy is most likely to be effective. Companies often test alternate versions of their advertising in different cities to determine which ad communicates most effectively.

Exhibit 8–1
Tide has been shown to be an effective promotional draw

Increasing Advertising Efficiency You may have heard the expression "can't see the forest for the trees." Sometimes advertisers get so close to the project they lose sight of what they are seeking, and because they know what they are trying to say, they expect their audience will also understand. They may use technical jargon that not everyone is familiar with. Or the creative department may get too creative or too sophisticated and lose the meaning that needs to be communicated. How many times have you seen an ad and asked yourself what it was trying to say, or how often have you seen an ad that you really like, but you can't remember the brand name? Conducting research helps companies develop more efficient and effective communications. An increasing number of clients are demanding accountability for their promotional programs and putting more pressure on the agencies to produce.

REASONS FOR NOT MEASURING ADVERTISING EFFECTIVENESS

Companies give a number of reasons for not measuring the effectiveness of advertising and promotions strategies:

Cost Perhaps the most commonly cited reason for not testing (particularly among smaller firms) is the expense. Good research can be expensive, in terms of both time and money. Many managers decide that time is critical and they must implement the program while the opportunity is available. Many believe the monies spent on research could be better spent on improved production of the ad, additional media buys, and the like.

While the first argument may have some merit, the second does not. Imagine what would happen if a poor campaign were developed or the incentive program did not motivate the target audience. Not only would you be spending money without the desired effects, but the effort could do more harm than good. Spending more money to buy media does not remedy a poor message or substitute for an improper promotional mix. For example, one firm watched its test-market sales for a new brand of beer fall short of expectations. The solution, it decided, was to buy all the TV time available that matched its target audience. After two months, sales had not improved, and the product was abandoned in the test market. Analysis showed the problem was not in the media but rather in the message, which communicated no reason to buy. Research would have identified the problem, and millions of dollars and a brand might have been saved. The moral: spending research monies to gain increased exposure to the wrong message is not a sound management decision.

213

Research Problems A second reason cited for not measuring effectiveness is that it is difficult to isolate the effects of promotional elements. Each variable in the marketing mix affects the success of a product or service. Because it is rarely possible to measure the contribution of each marketing element directly, some managers become frustrated and decide not to test at all. They say, "If I can't determine the specific effects, why spend the money?"

This argument also suffers from weak logic. While we agree that it is not always possible to determine the dollar amount of sales contributed by promotions, research can provide useful results. Communications effectiveness can be measured and may carry over to sales.

Disagreement On What to Test The objectives sought in the promotional program may differ by industry, by stage of the product life cycle, or even for different people within the firm. The sales manager may want to see the impact of promotions on sales, top management may wish to know the impact on corporate image, and those involved in the creative process may wish to assess recall and/or recognition of the ad. Lack of agreement on what to test often results in no testing.

Again, there is little rationale for this position. With the proper design, many or even all of the above might be measured. Since every promotional element is designed to accomplish its own objectives, research can be used to measure its effectiveness in doing so.

Objections of Creative Specialists It has been argued by many (and denied by others) that the creative department does not want its work to be tested and many agencies are reluctant to submit their work for testing. This is sometimes true. Ad agencies' creative departments argue that tests are not true measures of the creativity and effectiveness of ads; applying measures stifles their creativity; and the more creative the ad, the more likely it is to be successful. They want permission to be creative without the limiting guidelines marketing may impose.

At the same time, the marketing manager is ultimately responsible for the success of the product or brand. Given the substantial sums being allocated to advertising and promotion, it is the manager's right, and responsibility, to know how well a specific program—or a specific ad—will perform in the market.

DECISIONS FOR MEASURING ADVERTISING EFFECTIVENESS

We now identify some broad issues for measuring the communication effects of advertising. This section considers what elements to evaluate, as well as when and where such evaluations should occur. The issue of how to measure is covered in the next section.

WHAT TO TEST

The focus of the testing is mostly on the creative strategy and creative tactics decisions that the advertiser makes while putting a campaign together. In the beer example discussed earlier, the message never provided a reason for consumers to try the new product. In other instances, the message may not be strong enough to pull readers into the ad by attracting their attention, or it may not be clear enough to help them evaluate the product. Sometimes the message is memorable but doesn't achieve the other goals set by management. One study showed that 7 of the 25 products that scored highest on interest and memorability in Video Storyboard Tests' ad test had flat or declining sales.[3] As these few examples show, many of the creative strategy and creative tactics decisions regarding the message can be tested.

Creative Strategy Decisions The primary creative strategy decision—the creative theme—can be tested. When a company decides to change its theme or is planning to launch an unusual attention-getting approach, it may want to see the reactions of the target audience prior to investing in the media placement. Similarly, different message appeals can be tested (i.e., rational versus emotional), or different versions of one appeal can be tested. Finally, another important question is whether the spokesperson being used is effective and how the target audience will respond to him or her. A product spokesperson may be an excellent source initially but, owing to a variety of reasons, may lose impact over time in terms of attractiveness or likeability. Thus, all major creative strategy decisions can be tested.

Creative Tactics Decisions Different execution styles displayed on storyboards can be presented to members of the target audience in focus groups for their reaction. The message structure can be looked at such as reading the body-copy in an interview or some other method. Specific design elements, such as the music in a television ad or the headline of a print ad, can also be the focus or research. Overall, advertisers use a variety of research methods to test essentially any creative tactic that they are unsure about or that require confirmation.

Other Promotional Tools Many of the other tools we will discuss in this book have a creative or message associated with it. Many sales promotions have a visual as well as some advertising-like message that reinforces the brand position in the target audience's mind. Similarly, firms use many creative tactics to gain the attention of media personnel so that their story will get picked up by the media in order to get publicity exposure. Thus, while we have examined the creative in the context of advertising in the book, as we noted previously, all the decisions are relevant in the other promotional tools, and as expected, the same research is possible if the advertiser believes it necessary. We review a few specifics in each of the subsequent chapters to measure the effectiveness of other promotional tools.

WHEN TO TEST

Virtually all test measures can be classified according to when they are conducted. **Pretests** are measures taken before the campaign is implemented; **posttests** occur after the ad or commercial has been in the field. A variety of pretests and posttests are available to the marketer, each with its own methodology designed to measure some aspect of the advertising program. Figure 8–1 classifies these testing methods.

Pretesting Pretests may occur at a number of points, from as early on as idea generation to rough execution to testing the final version before implementing it. More than one type of pretest may be used. For example, concept testing (which is discussed later in this chapter) may take place at the earliest development of the ad or commercial, when little more than an idea, basic concept, or positioning statement is under consideration. GM used focus groups to derive the concepts to promote its new minivan. In other instances, layouts of the ad campaign that include headlines, some body copy, and rough illustrations are used. For TV commercials, storyboards and animatics may be tested. The GM minivan research also involved the evaluation of six animatics. In these tests specific shortcomings were identified, and the ads were changed to enhance certain executional elements.

The methodologies employed to conduct pretests vary. In focus groups, participants freely discuss the meanings they get from the ads, consider the relative advantages of alternatives, and even suggest improvements or additional themes. In addition to or instead of the focus groups, consumers are asked to evaluate the ad on a series of rating scales. (Different agencies use different measures.) In-home interviews, mall intercept, or laboratory methods may be used to gather the data.

FIGURE 8–1
Classification of testing methods
□ □ □ □ □

Pretests	Lab	Field
Concept	Concept tests	
Rough/copy/commercial	Rough tests	Comprehension and reaction tests
Finished print ads	Portfolio Readability	Dummy advertising vehicles
Finished TV ads	Theatre Physiological	On-air
Posttests		
Finished print ads in magazines		Inquiry tests Recognition tests Recall tests Tracking studies
Finished TV ads on-air		Recall tests Comprehensive measures Test marketing Single-source Tracking studies

The advantage of pretesting at this stage is that feedback is relatively inexpensive. Any problems with the concept or the way it is to be delivered are identified before large amounts of money are spent in development. Sometimes more than one version of the ad is evaluated to determine which is most likely to be effective.

A study of 4,637 on-air commercials designed to build normative intelligence conducted by McCollum Spielman Worldwide (MSW) found that only 19 percent were considered outstanding or really good. Nearly twice as many (34 percent) were failures. On the other hand, of those spots that were pretested before the final form was aired, the share of good to outstanding rose to 37 percent, while the failure rate fell to 9 percent.[4] This is certainly a testimonial to the value of pretesting.

The disadvantage is that mock-ups, storyboards, or animatics may not communicate nearly as effectively as the final product. The mood-enhancing and/or emotional aspects of the message are very difficult to communicate in this format. Another disadvantage is time delays. Many marketers believe being first in the market offers them a distinct advantage over competitors, so they forgo research to save time and ensure this position.

Posttesting Posttesting is also common among both advertisers and ad agencies (with the exception of testing commercials for wearout). Posttesting is designed to (1) determine if the campaign is accomplishing the objectives sought and (2) serve as input into the next period's situation analysis. An excellent example of using research to guide future advertising strategies is reflected in an experiment conducted by Lowes, a home improvement retailer in the U.S. In a study designed to test 36 different versions of covers for its catalogues (which are sent to between 30 and 40 million homes per year), the company determined that by putting more products on the covers, using real pictures rather than cartoons, and reducing the size of the catalogue, the catalogues were more effective. Other tests varying the number of TV spots, newspaper ads, and sports sponsorships led to increases in advertising spending and affirmation of the company's sponsorship of NASCAR auto racing.[5] A variety of posttest measures are available, most of which involve survey research methods.

WHERE TO TEST

In addition to when to test, decisions must be made as to *where*. These tests may take place in either laboratory or field settings.

Laboratory Tests In **laboratory tests**, people are brought to a particular location where they are shown ads and/or commercials. The testers either ask questions about them or measure participants' responses by other methods—for example, pupil dilation, eye tracking, or galvanic skin response.

The major advantage of the lab setting is the *control* it affords the researcher. Changes in copy, illustration, formats, colours, and the like can be manipulated inexpensively and the differential impact of each assessed. This makes it much easier for the researcher to isolate the contribution of each factor.

The major disadvantage is the lack of *realism*. Perhaps the greatest effect of this lack of realism is a **testing bias**. When people are brought into a lab (even if it has been designed to look like a living room), they may scrutinize the ads much more closely than they would at home. A second problem with this lack of realism is that it cannot duplicate the natural viewing situation, complete with the distractions or comforts of home. Looking at ads in a lab setting may not be the same as viewing at home on the couch, with the spouse, kids, dog, cat, and parakeet chirping in the background. (A bit later you will see that some testing techniques have made progress in correcting this deficiency. No, they did not bring in the dogs and the parakeets.) Overall, however, the control offered by this method probably outweighs the disadvantages, which accounts for the frequent use of lab methods.

Field Tests **Field tests** are tests of the ad or commercial under natural viewing situations, complete with the realism of noise, distractions, and the comforts of home. Field tests take into account the effects of repetition, program content, and even the presence of competitive messages.

The major disadvantage of field tests is the lack of control. It may be impossible to isolate causes of viewers' evaluations. If atypical events occur during the test, they may bias the results. Competitors may attempt to sabotage the research. And field tests usually take more time and money to conduct, so the results are not available to be acted on quickly. Thus, realism is gained at the expense of other important factors. It is up to the researcher to determine which trade-offs to make.

Our discussion of what should be tested, when, and where was general and designed to establish a basic understanding of the overall process as well as some key terms. In this section, we discuss more specifically some of the methods commonly used at each stage. First, however, it is important to establish some criteria by which to judge ads and commercials.

METHODS OF MEASURING ADVERTISING EFFECTIVENESS

Conducting evaluative research is not easy. In 1982, 21 of the largest U.S. ad agencies endorsed a set of principles aimed at "improving the research used in preparing and testing ads, providing a better creative product for clients, and controlling the cost of TV commercials."[6] This set of nine principles, called **PACT (Positioning Advertising Copy Testing)**, defines *copy testing* as research "which is undertaken when a decision is to be made about whether advertising should run in the marketplace. Whether this stage utilizes a single test or a combination of tests, its purpose is to aid in the judgment of specific advertising executions."[7] The nine principles of good copy testing are shown in Figure 8–2.

As you can see, advertisers and their clients are concerned about developing *appropriate* testing methods. Adherence to these principles may not make for perfect testing, but it goes a long way toward improving the state of the art and alleviates at least one of the testing problems cited earlier. Testing may occur at various points throughout the development of an ad or a campaign: (1) concept

FIGURE 8–2
Positioning Advertising
Copy Testing (PACT)

☐ ☐ ☐ ☐ ☐

1. Provide measurements that are relevant to the objectives of the advertising.
2. Require agreement about how the results will be used in advance of each specific test.
3. Provide multiple measurements (because single measurements are not adequate to assess ad performance).
4. Be based on a model of human response to communications—the reception of a stimulus, the comprehension of the stimulus, and the response to the stimulus.
5. Allow for consideration of whether the advertising stimulus should be exposed more than once.
6. Require that the more finished a piece of copy is, the more soundly it can be evaluated and require, as a minimum, that alternative executions be tested in the same degree of finish.
7. Provide controls to avoid the biasing effects of the exposure context.
8. Take into account basic considerations of sample definition.
9. Demonstrate reliability and validity.

generation research, (2) rough, prefinished art, copy, and/or commercial testing, (3) finished art or commercial pretesting, and (4) market testing of ads or commercials (posttesting).

CONCEPT GENERATION AND TESTING

Figure 8–3 describes the process involved in advertising **concept testing**, which is conducted very early in the campaign development process in order to explore the targeted consumer's response to a potential ad or campaign or have the consumer evaluate advertising alternatives. Positioning statements, copy, headlines, and/or illustrations may all be under scrutiny. The material to be evaluated may be just a headline or a rough sketch of the ad. The colours used, typeface, package designs, and even point-of-purchase materials may be evaluated.

One of the more commonly used methods for concept testing is focus groups, which usually consist of 8 to 10 people in the target market for the product. Companies have tested everything from product concepts to advertising concepts using focus groups. For most companies, the focus group is the first step in the research process. The number of focus groups used varies depending on group consensus, strength of response, and/or the degree to which participants like or dislike the concepts. In general, about 10 are usually needed to test a concept sufficiently. IMC Perspective 8–1 shows how one firm successfully used a concept test.

While focus groups continue to be a favourite of marketers, they are often overused. The methodology is attractive in that results are easily obtained, directly observable, and immediate. A variety of issues can be examined, and consumers are free to go into depth in areas they consider important. Also, focus groups don't

FIGURE 8–3
Concept testing

☐ ☐ ☐ ☐ ☐

Objective: Explores consumers' responses to various ad concepts as expressed in words, pictures, or symbols.

Method: Alternative concepts are exposed to consumers who match the characteristics of the target audience. Reactions and evaluations of each are sought through a variety of methods, including focus groups, direct questioning, and survey completion. Sample sizes vary depending on the number of concepts to be presented and the consensus of responses.

Output: Qualitative and/or quantitative data evaluating and comparing alternative concepts.

Hot French Fry Ad for Cavendish Farms

Running second place as a market follower in a category dominated by McCain and holding off the increased competitive pressure from private label products due to retail concentration, Cavendish Farms needed to rejuvenate its value-price brand position and go beyond its traditional communication strategy of newspaper inserts and in-store promotional activities.

Initial consumer focus group research conducted in three cities revealed that not only did consumers believe French fries to be a fast, simple, and appealing side dish, they felt a strong emotional connection to eating fries. Feelings of "nostalgia, joy, fun, contentment, comfort, being together as a family, and showing your family you care about them," all contributed to a much broader appeal than previously thought.

Current customers observed Cavendish Farms fries as having a golden appetizing colour and a consistent quality. Furthermore, for both customers and non-customers, the Cavendish Farms brand evoked associations of a potato specialist and a natural wholesome product. The participants in these focus groups also suggested that the brand name created images of "a farm where people are active and friendly and where potatoes are grown and harvested."

With an objective to spur trial from non-customers, Cavendish Farms looked to their agency to deliver a ground-breaking television commercial. After testing two separate creative concepts with more focus group research, the creative specialists and Cavendish Farms realized they had a successful idea with the "Sample Lady" who communicated a superior tasting message to non-customers.

The selected concept featured the extent to which a father and son would go to taste as many fries from the lady providing samples in the grocery store. The ad culminated with the father turning off the lights and a visual of both the father and son with there mouths stuffed with Cavendish Farms fries. Not only did the ad show non-customers desiring the product and trying the product, the ad reinforced the sampling program that Cavendish Farms implemented while running the ad.

Preliminary research indicated that the ad was recognized with very high levels and extremely well liked. Tracking research conducted after the first wave of the campaign demonstrated very high brand awareness levels and stronger usage and purchase intention results. Market share improved and sales exceeded the targeted objective.

Source: Steven Buckler, "Funny Farm," *Marketing Magazine*, February 16, 2004.

---

require quantitative analysis. Unfortunately, many managers are uncertain about research methods that require statistics, and focus groups, being qualitative in nature, don't demand much skill in interpretation. Weaknesses with focus groups are shown in Figure 8–4. Clearly, there are appropriate and inappropriate circumstances for employing this methodology.

Another way to gather consumers' opinions of concepts is mall intercepts, where consumers in shopping malls are approached and asked to evaluate rough ads and/or copy. Rather than participating in a group discussion, individuals assess the ads via questionnaires, rating scales, and/or rankings. New technologies allow for concept testing over the Internet, where advertisers can show concepts simultaneously to consumers throughout Canada, garnering feedback and analyzing the results almost instantaneously.

FIGURE 8–4

Weaknesses associated with focus group research

□□□□□

- The results are not quantifiable.
- Sample sizes are too small to generalize to larger populations.
- Group influences may bias participants' responses.
- One or two members of the group may steer the conversation or dominate the discussion.
- Consumers become instant "experts."
- Members may not represent the target market. (Are focus group participants a certain type of person?)
- Results may be taken to be more representative and/or definitive than they really are.

ROUGH ART, COPY, AND COMMERCIAL TESTING

Because of the high cost associated with the production of an ad or commercial (many network commercials cost hundreds of thousands of dollars to produce), advertisers are increasingly spending more monies testing a rendering of the final ad at early stages. Slides of the artwork posted on a screen or animatic and photomatic **rough tests** may be used at this stage. (See Figure 8–5 for an explanation of terminology.) Because such tests can be conducted for about $3,000 to $5,000, research at this stage is becoming ever more popular.

But cost is only one factor. The test is of little value if it does not provide relevant, accurate information. Rough tests must indicate how the finished commercial would perform. Some studies have demonstrated that these testing methods are reliable and the results typically correlate well with the finished ad.[8]

Most of the tests conducted at the rough stage involve lab settings, although some on-air field tests are also available. Popular tests include comprehension and reaction tests and consumer juries: Again, the Internet allows field settings to be employed.

Comprehension and Reaction Tests One key concern for the advertiser is whether the ad or commercial conveys the meaning intended. The second concern is the reaction the ad generates. Obviously, the advertiser does not want an ad that evokes a negative reaction or offends someone. **Comprehension and reaction tests** are designed to assess these responses (which makes you wonder why some ads are ever brought to the marketplace).

Tests of comprehension and reaction employ no one standard procedure. Personal interviews, group interviews, and focus groups have all been used for this purpose, and sample sizes vary according to the needs of the client; they typically range from 50 to 200 respondents.

FIGURE 8–5

Rough testing terminology

□□□□□

A rough commercial is an unfinished execution that may fall into three broad categories:

Animatic Rough	**Live-Action Rough**
Succession of drawings/cartoons	Live motion
Rendered artwork	Stand-in/nonunion talent
Still frames	Nonunion crew
Simulated movement: Panning/zooming of frame/rapid sequence	Limited props/minimal opticals
	Location settings
Photomatic Rough	**A Finished Commercial Uses**
Succession of photographs	Live motion/animation
Real people/scenery	Highly paid union talent
Still frames	Full union crew
Simulated movements: Panning/zooming of frame/rapid sequence	Exotic props/studio sets/special effects

Consumer Juries This method uses consumers representative of the target market to evaluate the probable success of an ad. **Consumer juries** may be asked to rate a selection of layouts or copy versions presented in pasteups on separate sheets. The objectives sought and methods employed in consumer juries are shown in Figure 8–6.[9] Sample questions asked of jurists are shown in Figure 8–7.

While the jury method offers the advantages of control and cost effectiveness, serious flaws in the methodology limit its usefulness:

- *The consumer may become a self-appointed expert.* One of the benefits sought from the jury method is the objectivity and involvement in the product or service that the targeted consumer can bring to the evaluation process. Sometimes, however, knowing they are being asked to critique ads, participants try to become more expert in their evaluations, paying more attention and being more critical than usual. The result may be a less than objective evaluation or an evaluation on elements other than those intended.

- *The number of ads that can be evaluated is limited.* Whether order of merit or paired comparison methods are used, the ranking procedure becomes tedious as the number of alternatives increases. Consider the ranking of 10 ads. While the top two and the bottom two may very well reveal differences, those ranked in the middle may not yield much useful information.

  In the paired comparison method, the number of evaluations required is calculated by the formula

$$\frac{n(n-1)}{2}$$

  If six alternatives are considered, 15 evaluations must be made. As the number of ads increases, the task becomes even more unmanageable.

- *A halo effect is possible.* Sometimes participants rate an ad good on all characteristics because they like a few and overlook specific weaknesses. This tendency, called the **halo effect**, distorts the ratings and defeats the ability to control for specific components. (Of course, the reverse may also occur—rating an ad bad overall due to only a few bad attributes.)

FIGURE 8–6

Consumer juries

Objective:	Potential viewers (consumers) are asked to evaluate ads and give their reactions to and evaluation of them. When two or more ads are tested, viewers are usually asked to rate or rank order the ads according to their preferences.
Method:	Respondents are asked to view ads and rate them according to either (1) the order of merit method or (2) the paired comparison method. In the former, the respondent is asked to view the ads, then rank them from one to *n* according to their perceived merit. In the latter, ads are compared only two at a time. Each ad is compared to every other ad in the group, and the winner is listed. The best ad is that which wins the most times. Consumer juries typically employ 50 to 100 participants.
Output:	An overall reaction to each ad under construction as well as a rank ordering of the ads based on the viewers' perceptions.

FIGURE 8–7

Questions asked in a consumer jury test

1. Which of these ads would you most likely read if you saw it in a magazine?
2. Which of these headlines would interest you the most in reading the ad further?
3. Which ad convinces you most of the quality or superiority of the product?
4. Which layout do you think would be most effective in causing you to buy?
5. Which ad did you like best?
6. Which ad did you find most interesting?

FIGURE 8–8
Diagnostic Research
Inc.'s print test

☐ ☐ ☐ ☐ ☐

Objective:	Tests recall and readers' impressions of print ads.
Method:	Mall intercepts in two or more cities are used to screen respondents and have them take home "test magazines" for reading. Participants are phoned the next day to determine opinions of the ads, recall of ad contents, and other questions of interest to the sponsor. Approximately 225 people constitute the sample.
Output:	Scores reported include related recall of copy and visual elements, sales messages, and other nonspecific elements. Both quantitative (table) scores and verbatim responses are reported.

• *Preferences for specific types of advertising may overshadow objectivity.* Ads that involve emotions or pictures may receive higher ratings or rankings than those employing copy, facts, and/or rational criteria. Even though the latter are often more effective in the marketplace, they may be judged less favourably by jurists who prefer emotional appeals.

Some of the problems noted here can be remedied by the use of ratings scales instead of rankings. But ratings are not always valid either. Thus, while consumer juries have been used for years, questions of bias have led researchers to doubt their validity. As a result, a variety of other methods (discussed later in this chapter) are more commonly employed.

PRETESTING OF FINISHED ADS

Pretesting finished ads is one of the more commonly employed studies among marketing researchers and their agencies. At this stage, a finished advertisement or commercial is used; since it has not been presented to the market, changes can still be made.

Many researchers believe testing the ad in final form provides better information. Several test procedures are available for print and broadcast ads, including both laboratory and field methodologies.

Print methods include portfolio tests, analyses of readability, and dummy advertising vehicles. Broadcast tests include theatre tests and on-air tests. Both print and broadcast may use physiological measures.

Pretesting Finished Print Messages   A number of methods for pretesting finished print ads are available. One is described in Figure 8–8. The most common of these methods are portfolio tests, readability tests, and dummy advertising vehicles.

Portfolio Tests   **Portfolio tests** are a laboratory methodology designed to expose a group of respondents to a portfolio consisting of both control and test ads. Respondents are then asked what information they recall from the ads. The assumption is that the ads that yield the *highest recall* are the most effective.

While portfolio tests offer the opportunity to compare alternative ads directly, a number of weaknesses limit their applicability:

1. Factors other than advertising creativity and/or presentation may affect recall. Interest in the product or product category, the fact that respondents know they are participating in a test, or interviewer instructions (among others) may account for more differences than the ad itself.
2. Recall may not be the best test. Some researchers argue that for certain types of products (those of low involvement) ability to recognize the ad when shown may be a better measure than recall.

One way to determine the validity of the portfolio method is to correlate its results with readership scores once the ad is placed in the field. Whether such validity tests are being conducted or not is not readily known, although the portfolio method remains popular in the industry.

Readability Tests   The communications efficiency of the copy in a print ad can be tested without reader interviews. This test uses the **Flesch formula**, named after its developer, Rudolph Flesch, to assess readability of the copy by determining the average number of syllables per 100 words. Human interest appeal of the material, length of sentences, and familiarity with certain words are also considered and correlated with the educational background of target audiences. Test results are compared to previously established norms for various target audiences. The test suggests that copy is best comprehended when sentences are short, words are concrete and familiar, and personal references are drawn.

This method eliminates many of the interviewee biases associated with other tests and avoids gross errors in understanding. The norms offer an attractive standard for comparison.

Disadvantages are also inherent, however. The copy may become too mechanical, and direct input from the receiver is not available. Without this input, contributing elements like creativity cannot be addressed. To be effective, this test should be used only in conjunction with other pretesting methods.

Dummy Advertising Vehicles   In an improvement on the portfolio test, ads are placed in "dummy" magazines developed by an agency or research firm. The magazines contain regular editorial features of interest to the reader, as well as the test ads, and are distributed to a *random sample* of homes in predetermined geographic areas. Readers are told the magazine publisher is interested in evaluations of editorial content and asked to read the magazines as they normally would. Then they are interviewed on their reactions to both editorial content and ads. Recall, readership, and interest-generating capabilities of the ad are assessed.

The advantage of this method is that it provides a more natural setting than the portfolio test. Readership occurs in the participant's own home, the test more closely approximates a natural reading situation, and the reader may go back to the magazine, as people typically do.

But the dummy magazine shares the other disadvantages associated with portfolio tests. The testing effect is not eliminated, and product interest may still bias the results. Thus, while this test offers some advantages over the portfolio method, it is not a guaranteed measure of the advertising's impact.

While all the previously described measures are available, the most popular form of pretesting of print ads now involves a series of measures that account for the shortcomings cited above. The tests can be used for rough and/or finished ads and are most commonly conducted in the respondents' homes enabling the researcher to collect multiple measures from many samples. One example is shown in Figure 8–9.

Pretesting Finished Broadcast Ads   A variety of methods for pretesting broadcast ads are available. The most popular are theatre tests, on-air tests, and physiological measures.

Theatre Tests   In the past, one of the most popular laboratory methods for pretesting finished commercials was **theatre testing**. In tests, participants are invited by telephone, mall intercepts, and/or tickets in the mail to view pilots of proposed TV

FIGURE 8–9
Ipsos-ASI's Next*Print

Objective:	To assist advertisers in copy testing of print advertisements to determine (1) main idea communication, (2) likes and dislikes, (3) believability, (4) ad attribute ratings, (5) overall likability, and (6) brand attribute ratings.
Method:	Tests are conducted in current issues of newsstand magazines. The recall measure consists of 150 responses. Diagnostic measures range from 105 to 150 responses. Highly targeted audiences are available through a version known as the Targeted Print Test.
Output:	Standard scores and specific diagnostics.

programs. In some instances, the show is actually being tested, but more commonly a standard program is used so that audience responses can be compared with normative responses established by previous viewers. Sample sizes range from 250 to 600 participants.

On entering the theatre, viewers are told a drawing will be held for gifts and asked to complete a product preference questionnaire asking which products they would prefer if they win. This form also requests demographic data. Participants may be seated in specific locations in the theatre to allow observation by age, sex, and so on. They view the program and commercials, and a form asking for evaluations is distributed. Participants are then asked to complete a second form for a drawing so that changes in product preference can be noted. In addition to product/brand preference, the form may request other information:

1. Interest in and reaction to the commercial.
2. Overall reaction to the commercial as measured by an adjective checklist.
3. Recall of various aspects of the commercial.
4. Interest in the brand under consideration.
5. Continuous (frame-by-frame) reactions throughout the commercial.

The methods of theatre testing operations vary, though all measure brand preference changes. For example, many of the services now use videotaped programs with the commercials embedded for viewing in one's office rather than in a theatre. Others establish viewing rooms in malls and/or hotel conference rooms. Some do not take all the measures listed here; others ask the consumers to turn dials or push buttons on a keypad to provide the continual responses. An example of one methodology is shown in Figure 8–10.

Those opposed to theatre tests cite a number of disadvantages. First, they say the environment is too artificial. The lab setting is bad enough, but asking respondents to turn dials or, as one service does, wiring people for physiological responses takes them too far from a natural viewing situation. Second, the contrived measure of brand preference change seems too phony to believe. Critics contend that participants will see through it and make changes just because they think they are supposed to. Finally, the group effect of having others present and overtly exhibiting their reactions may influence viewers who did not have any reactions themselves.

Proponents argue that theatre tests offer distinct advantages. In addition to control, the established norms (averages of commercials' performances) indicate how one's commercial will fare against others in the same product class that were already tested. Further, advocates say the brand preference measure is supported by actual sales results.

Despite the limitations of theatre testing, most major consumer product companies have used it to evaluate their commercials. This method may have shortcomings, but it allows them to identify strong or weak commercials and to compare them to other ads.

FIGURE 8–10
The AD*VANTAGE/ACT theatre methodology

☐ ☐ ☐ ☐ ☐

Advertising Control for Television (ACT), a lab procedure of The MSW Group, uses about 400 respondents representing four cities. It measures initial brand preference by asking participants which brands they most recently purchased. Respondents are then divided into groups of 25 to view a 30-minute program with seven commercials inserted in the middle. Four are test commercials; the other three are control commercials with established viewing norms. After viewing the program, respondents are given a recall test of the commercials. After the recall test, a second 30-minute program is shown, with each test commercial shown again. The second measure of brand preference is taken at this time, with persuasion measured by the percentage of viewers who switched preferences from their most recently purchased brand to one shown in the test commercials.

On-Air Tests Some of the firms conducting theatre tests also insert the commercials into actual TV programs in certain test markets. Typically, the commercials are in finished form, although the testing of ads earlier in the developmental process is becoming more common. This is referred to as an **on-air test** and often includes single-source ad research (discussed later in this chapter).

On-air testing techniques offer all the advantages of field methodologies, as well as all the disadvantages. Further, there are negative aspects to the specific measures taken through the on-air systems. One concern is associated with **day-after recall scores**, the primary measure used in these tests. Lyman Ostlund notes that measurement errors may result from the natural environment—the position of the ad in the series of commercials shown, the adjacent program content, and/or the number of commercials shown.[10] While the testing services believe their methods overcome many of these criticisms, each still uses recall as one of the primary measures of effectiveness. Since recall tests best reflect the degree of attention and interest in an ad, claims that the tests predict the ad's impact on sales may be going too far. (In 28 studies reviewed by Jack Haskins, only two demonstrated that factual recall could be related to sales.)[11] Joel Dubow's research indicates that recall is a necessary but not sufficient measure, while research by Jones and Blair was even more demonstrative, noting that "it is unwise to look to recall for an accurate assessment of a commercial's sales effect."[12]

On the plus side, most of the testing services have offered evidence of both validity and reliability for on-air pretesting of commercials. Some firms claim their pretest and posttest results yield the same recall scores 9 out of 10 times—a strong indication of reliability and a good predictor of the effect the ad is likely to have when shown to the population as a whole.

In summary, on-air pretesting of finished or rough commercials offers some distinct advantages over lab methods and some indications of the ad's likely success. Whether the measures used are as strong an indication as the providers say still remains in question.

Physiological Measures A less common method of pretesting finished commercials involves a laboratory setting in which physiological responses are measured. These measures indicate the receiver's *involuntary* response to the ad, theoretically eliminating biases associated with the voluntary measures reviewed to this point. (Involuntary responses are those over which the individual has no control, such as heartbeat and reflexes.) Physiological measures used to test both print and broadcast ads include pupil dilation, galvanic skin response, eye tracking, and brain waves:

1. *Pupil dilation.* Research in **pupillometrics** is designed to measure dilation and constriction of the pupils of the eyes in response to stimuli. Dilation is associated with action; constriction involves the body's conservation of energy.

   Advertisers have used pupillometrics to evaluate product and package design as well as to test ads. Pupil dilation suggests a stronger interest in (or preference for) an ad or implies arousal or attention-getting capabilities. Other attempts to determine the affective (liking or disliking) responses created by ads have met with less success.

   Because of high costs and some methodological problems, the use of pupillometrics has waned over the past decade. But it can be useful in evaluating certain aspects of advertising.

2. *Galvanic skin response.* Also known as **electrodermal response**, GSR measures the skin's resistance or conductance to a small amount of current passed between two electrodes. Response to a stimulus activates sweat glands, which in turn increases the conductance of the electrical current. Thus, GSR/EDR activity might reflect a reaction to advertising. In their review of the research in this area, Paul Watson and Robert Gatchel concluded that GSR/EDR (1) is sensitive to affective stimuli, (2) may present a picture of attention, (3) may be useful to measure long-term advertising recall, and (4) is useful in measuring ad effec-

tiveness.[13] In interviews with practitioners and reviews of case studies, Priscilla LaBarbera and Joel Tucciarone also concluded that GSR is an effective measure and is useful for measuring affect, or liking, for ads.[14] While a number of companies have offered skin response measures, this research methodology is not commonly used now, and LaBarbera and Tucciarone believe that it is underused, given its potential.

3. *Eye tracking.* A methodology that is more commonly employed is **eye tracking** (Figure 8–11), in which viewers are asked to view an ad while a sensor aims a beam of infrared light at the eye. The beam follows the movement of the eye and shows the exact spot on which the viewer is focusing. The continuous reading of responses demonstrates which elements of the ad are attracting attention, how long the viewer is focusing on them, and the sequence in which they are being viewed.

   Eye tracking can identify strengths and weaknesses in an ad. For example, attractive models or background action may distract the viewer's attention away from the brand or product being advertised. The advertiser can remedy this distraction before fielding the ad. In other instances, colours or illustrations may attract attention and create viewer interest in the ad.

4. *Brain waves.* **Electroencephalographic (EEG) measures** can be taken from the skull to determine electrical frequencies in the brain. These electrical impulses are used in two areas of research, alpha waves and hemispheric lateralization.

   - **Alpha activity** refers to the degree of brain activation. People are in an alpha state when they are inactive, resting, or sleeping. The theory is that a person in an alpha state is less likely to be processing information (recall correlates negatively with alpha levels) and that attention and processing require moving from this state. By measuring a subject's alpha level while viewing a commercial, researchers can assess the degree to which attention and processing are likely to occur.

   - **Hemispheric lateralization** distinguishes between alpha activity in the left and right sides of the brain. It has been hypothesized that the right side of the brain processes visual stimuli and the left processes verbal stimuli. The right hemisphere is thought to respond more to emotional stimuli, while the left responds to logic. The right determines recognition, while the left is responsible for recall.[15] If these hypotheses are correct, advertisers could design ads to increase learning and memory by creating stimuli to appeal to each hemisphere. However, some researchers believe the brain does not function laterally and an ad cannot be designed to appeal to one side or the other.

   While EEG research has engaged the attention of academic researchers, it has been much less successful in attracting the interest of practitioners.

MARKET TESTING OF ADS

The fact that the ad and/or campaign has been implemented does not mean there is no longer a need for testing. The pretests were conducted on smaller samples and may in some instances have questionable merit, so the marketer must find out how

FIGURE 8–11

Eye movement research

☐ ☐ ☐ ☐ ☐

Objective:	Tracks viewers' eye movements to determine what viewers read or view in print ads and where their attention is focused in TV commercials or billboards.
Method:	Fibre optics, digital data processing, and advanced electronics are used to follow eye movements of viewers and/or readers as they process an ad.
Output:	Relationship among what readers see, recall, and comprehend. Scan paths on print ads, billboards, commercials, and print materials. (Can also be used to evaluate package designs.)

the ad is doing in the field. In this section, we discuss methods for posttesting an ad. Some of the tests are similar to the pretests discussed in the previous section and are provided by the same companies.

Posttests of Print Ads   A variety of print posttests are available, including inquiry tests, recognition tests, and recall tests.

Inquiry Tests   Used in both consumer and business-to-business market testing, **inquiry tests** are designed to measure advertising effectiveness on the basis of inquiries generated from ads appearing in various print media, often referred to as "bingo cards." The inquiry may take the form of the number of coupons returned, phone calls generated, or direct inquiries through reader cards. Figure 8–12 shows that the reader response card is still the most commonly employed response to trade ads. For example, if you called in a response to an ad in a local medium recently, perhaps you were asked how you found out about the company or product or where you saw the ad. This is a very simple measure of the ad's or medium's effectiveness.

More complex methods of measuring effectiveness through inquiries may involve (1) running the ad in successive issues of the same medium, (2) running **split-run tests**, in which variations of the ad appear in different copies of the same newspaper or magazine, and/or (3) running the same ad in different media. Each of these methods yields information on different aspects of the strategy. The first measures the cumulative effects of the campaign; the second examines specific elements of the ad or variations on it. The final method measures the effectiveness of the medium rather than the ad itself.

While inquiry tests may yield useful information, weaknesses in this methodology limit its effectiveness. For example, inquiries may not be a true measure of the attention-getting or information-providing aspects of the ad. The reader may be attracted to

FIGURE 8–12
Ad response methods

Despite the rise in popularity of electronic response mechanisms, the traditional reader service, or "bingo card," remains the most common way to respond to trade publication advertising.

Ad Response Methods Used Frequently or Very Frequently*	
Indirect Methods	
Return reader service cards	41 %
Save ads for reference	35
Discuss advertised products with others	30
Pass ads on to others for possible action	26
Direct Methods	
Send back reply cards/coupons	31 %
Contact vendors' websites	28
Telephone manufacturers	23
Telephone local distributors/reps	22
Go to magazine websites	21
Stop at vendors' trade show exhibits	20
Discuss products with sales reps	20
Send faxes to vendors	17
Contact distributors' websites	15
Send e-mail messages	10
Mail notes to vendors	6

*The 2,705 respondents could name more than one method.

Exhibit 8–2

Example of a Starch-scored ad

an ad, read it, and even store the information but not be motivated to inquire at that particular time. Time constraints, lack of a need for the product or service at the time the ad is run, and other factors may limit the number of inquiries. But receiving a small number of inquiries doesn't mean the ad was not effective; attention, attitude change, awareness, and recall of copy points may all have been achieved. At the other extreme, a person with a particular need for the product may respond to any ad for it, regardless of specific qualities of the ad.

Major advantages of inquiry tests are that they are inexpensive to implement and they provide some feedback with respect to the general effectiveness of the ad or medium used. But they are usually not very effective for comparing different versions or specific creative aspects of an ad.

Recognition Tests Perhaps the most common posttest of print ads is the **recognition method**, most closely associated with Roper ASW. The *Starch Ad Readership Report* lets the advertiser assess the impact of an ad in a single issue of a magazine, over time, and/or across different magazines (see Figure 8–13). Starch measures over 75,000 ads in more than 1,000 issues representing more than 100 consumer, farm, and business magazines and newspapers per year and provides a number of measures of the ad's effectiveness. An example of a Starch-scored ad is shown in Exhibit 8–2.

Starch also offers the *Starch Impression Study* and the *Starch Ballot Readership Study*. The impression study provides consumers' qualitative impressions of ads (for example, company image and important features); the readership study measures readership in business magazines.

Starch claims that (1) the pulling power of various aspects of the ad can be assessed through the control offered, (2) the effectiveness of competitors' ads can be compared through the norms provided, (3) alternative ad executions can be tested, and (4) readership scores are a useful indication of consumers' involvement in the ad or campaign. (The theory is that a reader must read and become involved in the ad before the ad can communicate. To the degree that this readership can be shown, it is a direct indication of effectiveness.)

Of these claims, perhaps the most valid is the ability to judge specific aspects of the ad. Many researchers have criticized other aspects of the Starch recognition method (as well as other recognition measures) on the basis of problems of false claiming, interviewer sensitivities, and unreliable scores:

1. *False claiming.* Research shows that in recognition tests, respondents may claim to have seen an ad when they did not. False claims may be a result of having

FIGURE 8–13

The *Starch Ad Readership Report*

Objective:	Determining recognition of print ads and comparing them to other ads of the same variety or in the same magazine.
Method:	Samples are drawn from 20 to 30 urban areas reflecting the geographic circulation of the magazine. Personal interviewers screen readers for qualifications and determine exposure and readership. Samples include a minimum of 200 males and females, as well as specific audiences where required. Participants are asked to go through the magazines, looking at the ads, and provide specific responses.
Output:	*Starch Ad Readership Reports* generate three recognition scores:

- Noted score—the percentage of readers who remember seeing the ad.
- Seen-associated score—the percentage of readers who recall seeing or reading any part of the ad identifying the product or brand.
- Read-most score—the percentage of readers who report reading at least half of the copy portion of the ad.

seen similar ads elsewhere, expecting that such an ad would appear in the medium, or wanting to please the questioner. Interest in the product category also increases reporting of ad readership. Whether this false claiming is deliberate or not, it leads to an overreporting of effectiveness. On the flip side, factors such as interview fatigue may lead to an underreporting bias—that is, respondents not reporting an ad they did see.

2. *Interviewer sensitivities.* Any time research involves interviewers, there is a potential for bias. Respondents may want to impress the interviewer or fear looking unknowledgeable if they continually claim not to recognize an ad. There may also be variances associated with interviewer instructions, recordings, and so on, regardless of the amount of training and sophistication involved.

3. *Reliability of recognition scores.* Starch admits that the reliability and validity of its readership scores increase with the number of insertions tested, which essentially means that to test just one ad on a single exposure may not produce valid or reliable results.

In sum, despite critics, the Starch readership studies continue to dominate the posttesting of print ads. The value provided by norms and the fact that multiple exposures can improve reliability and validity may underlie the decisions to employ this methodology.

Recall Tests   There are several tests to measure recall of print ads. Perhaps the best known of these are the Ipsos-ASI Next*Print test and the Gallup & Robinson Magazine Impact Research Service (MIRS) (described in Figure 8–14). These **recall tests** are similar to those discussed in the section on pretesting broadcast ads in that they attempt to measure recall of specific ads.

In addition to having the same interviewer problems as recognition tests, recall tests have other disadvantages. The reader's degree of involvement with the product and/or the distinctiveness of the appeals and visuals may lead to higher-than-accurate recall scores, although in general the method may lead to lower levels of recall than actually exist (an error the advertiser would be happy with). Critics contend the test is not strong enough to reflect recall accurately, so many ads may score as less effective than they really are, and advertisers may abandon or modify them needlessly.

On the plus side, it is thought that recall tests can assess the ad's impact on memory. Proponents of recall tests say the major concern is not the results themselves but how they are interpreted. In one very interesting study of the effects of brand name suggestiveness on recall, Kevin Keller, Susan Heckler, and Michael Houston found that suggestive brand names (those that convey relevant attribute or benefit information about the product) facilitate the initial recall of the brand's benefits but inhibit recall of subsequently advertised claims. These results would seem to indicate that a suggestive brand name could facilitate initial positioning of the brand but

FIGURE 8–14
Gallup & Robinson Magazine Impact Research Service

Objective:	Tracking recall of advertising (and client's ads) appearing in magazines to assess performance and effectiveness.
Method:	Test magazines are placed in participants' homes and respondents are asked to read the magazine that day. A telephone interview is conducted the second day to assess recall of ads, recall of copy points, and consumers' impressions of the ads. Sample size is 150 people.
Output:	Three measurement scores are provided: • Proven name registration—the percentage of respondents who can accurately recall the ad. • Idea communication—the number of sales points the respondents can recall. • Favourable buying attitude—the extent of favourable purchase reaction to the brand or corporation.

make it more difficult to introduce new attributes at a later time. The authors suggest that these results might be useful in explaining why Jack in the Box has had trouble developing a more adult image and why Old Spice and Oldsmobile have had difficulty with younger audiences.[16]

A very extensive longitudinal study was conducted by the Netherlands Institute of Public Opinion (NIPO) to assess the relationship between recall and recognition. The results indicated that the average correlation between recall and recognition in both newspapers and magazines was very high ($r = .96$ and $.95$, respectively). The study concluded that recall actually stems from recognition, in that 99 percent of 3,632 cases of recall also had recorded recognition. In addition, likable and interesting ads doubled the recall scores and increased the recall share of recognition. Creative advertising was much more effective for creating perceptions and recall than was the size of the ad.[17]

Posttests of Broadcast Commercials   A variety of methods exist for posttesting broadcast commercials. The most common provide a combination of day-after recall tests, persuasion measures, and diagnostics. Test marketing and tracking studies, including single-source methods, are also employed.

Day-After Recall Tests   The most popular method of posttesting employed in the broadcasting industry for decades was the *Burke Day-After Recall test*. While a number of companies offered day-after recall methodologies, the "Burke test" for all intents and purposes became the generic name attached to these tests. While popular, day-after recall tests also had problems, including limited samples, high costs, and security issues (ads shown in test markets could be seen by competitors). In addition, the following disadvantages with recall tests were also suggested:

1. *DAR tests may favour unemotional appeals because respondents are asked to verbalize the message.* Thinking messages may be easier to recall than emotional communications, so recall scores for emotional ads may be lower.[18] A number of other studies have also indicated that emotional ads may be processed differently from thinking ones; some ad agencies, for example, Leo Burnett and BBDO Worldwide, have gone so far as to develop their own methods of determining emotional response to ads.[19]
2. *Program content may influence recall.* The programs in which the ad appears may lead to different recall scores for the same brand. The net result is a potential inaccuracy in the recall score and in the norms used to establish comparisons.[20]
3. *A prerecruited sample may pay increased attention to the program and the ads contained therein because the respondents know they will be tested the next day.* This effect would lead to a higher level of recall than really exists.

The major advantage of day-after recall tests is that they are field tests. The natural setting is supposed to provide a more realistic response profile. These tests are also popular because they provide norms that give advertisers a standard for comparing how well their ads are performing. In addition to recall, a number of different measures of the commercial's effectiveness are now offered, including persuasive measures and diagnostics. (The Burke test itself no longer exists.)

Comprehensive Measures   As noted earlier in our discussion of pretesting broadcast commercials, a measure of a commercial's persuasive effectiveness is gathered by asking consumers to choose a brand that they would want to win in a drawing and then—after exposure to the ad—ask the question again. In theatre settings, this is accomplished by announcing a series of prize drawings, with viewers indicating which of the brands they would choose if they won. In field settings, it is accomplished by taking a brand preference measure when the video is delivered and then again the next day. Some of the services offer additional persuasion measures, including purchase-intent and frequency-of-purchase criteria.

Objective:	To assist advertisers in copy testing of their commercials through multiple measures to determine (1) the potential of the commercial for impacting sales, (2) how the ad contributes to brand equity, (3) how well it is in line with existing advertising strategies and objectives, and (4) how to optimize effectiveness.
Method:	Consumers are recruited to evaluate a TV program, with ads embedded into the program as they would be on local prime-time television. Consumers view the program on a videotape in their homes to simulate actual field conditions. (The option to use local cable television programs with commercial inserts is also provided.)
Output:	Related recall (day-after recall) scores; persuasion scores, including brand preference shifts, purchase intent and frequency, brand equity differentiation, and relevance and communication; and reaction diagnostics to determine what viewers take away from the ad and how creative elements contribute to or distract from advertising effectiveness.

FIGURE 8–15
Ipsos-ASI's Next*TV

☐ ☐ ☐ ☐ ☐

Copy testing firms also provide diagnostic measures. These measures are designed to garner viewers' evaluations of the ads, as well as how clearly the creative idea is understood and how well the proposition is communicated. Rational and emotional reactions to the ads are also examined. While each of the measures just described provides specific input into the effectiveness of a commercial, many advertisers are interested in more than just one specific input. Thus, some companies provide comprehensive approaches in which each of the three measures just described (i.e., recall, persuasion, diagnostics) can be obtained through one testing program. Figure 8–15 describes one such comprehensive program, Ipsos-ASI's Next*TV test (Exhibit 8–3).

Test Marketing   Many companies conduct tests designed to measure their advertising effects in specific test markets before releasing them nationally. The markets chosen are representative of the target market. For example, a company may test its ads in London, Ontario; Peterborough, Ontario; or Winnipeg, Manitoba, if the demographic and socioeconomic profiles of these cities match the product's market. A variety of factors may be tested, including reactions to the ads (for example, alternative copy points), the effects of various budget sizes, or special offers. The ads run in finished form in the media where they might normally appear, and effectiveness is measured after the ads run.

Exhibit 8–3
Ipsos-ASI offers a comprehensive testing measure

231

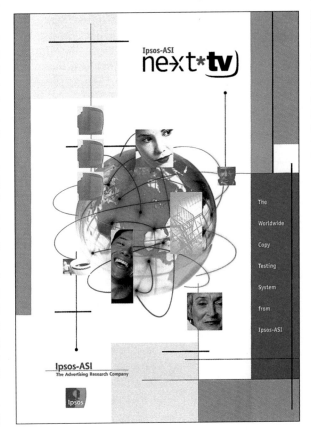

The advantage of test marketing of ads is realism. Regular viewing environments are used and the testing effects are minimized. A high degree of control can be attained if the test is designed successfully. For example, an extensive test market study was designed and conducted by Seagram and Time, Inc., over three years to measure the effects of advertising frequency on consumers' buying habits. This study demonstrated just how much could be learned from research conducted in a field setting but with some experimental controls. It also showed that proper research can provide strong insights into the impact of ad campaigns. (Many advertising researchers consider this study one of the most conclusive ever conducted in the attempt to demonstrate the effects of advertising on sales.)

The Seagram study also reveals some of the disadvantages associated with test market measures, not the least of which are cost and time. Few firms have the luxury to spend three years and hundreds of thousands of dollars on such a test. In addition, there is always the fear that competitors may discover and intervene in the research process. Test marketing can provide substantial insight into the effectiveness of advertising if care is taken to minimize the negative aspects of such tests.

Single-Source Tracking Studies   Since the 1980s, the focus of many research efforts has been on single-source tracking methods. **Single-source tracking methods** track the behaviours of consumers from the television set to the supermarket checkout counter. Participants in a designated area who have cable TV and agree to participate in the studies are given a card (similar to a credit card) that identifies their household and gives the research company their demographics. The households are split into matched groups; one group receives an ad while the other does not, or alternate ads are sent to each. Their purchases are recorded from the bar codes of the products bought. Commercial exposures are then correlated with purchase behaviours.

Earlier we mentioned the use of single-source ad research in pretesting commercials. One study demonstrated that the single-source method can also be used effectively to posttest ads, allowing for a variety of dependent measures and tracking the effects of increased ad budgets and different versions of ad copy—and even ad effects on sales.[21]

A 10-year study conducted by Information Resources' BehaviorScan service demonstrated long-term effects of advertising on sales. The study examined copy, media schedules, ad budgets, and the impact of trade promotions on sales in 10 markets throughout the United States and concluded that advertising can produce sales growth as long as two years after a campaign ends.[22] (The study also concluded that results of copy recall and persuasion tests were unlikely to predict sales reliably.) A number of single-source methods have been used, among them BehaviorScan (Information Resources) and MarketSource. The A.C. Nielsen company's Scantrack is another commonly employed single-source tracking system.

Many advertisers believe these single-source measures will change the way research is conducted due to the advantages of control and the ability to measure directly the ads' effects on sales. A number of major corporations and ad agencies are now employing this method, including Campbell Soup, Colgate-Palmolive, Nestlé, General Foods, P&G, Pepsi-Cola, Leo Burnett, and J. Walter Thompson. After using scanner data to review the advertising/sales relationship for 78 brands, John Jones concluded that single-source data are beginning to fulfill their promise now that more measurements are available.[23]

While single-source testing is a valuable tool, it still has some problems. One researcher says, "Scanner data focus on short-term sales effects, and as a result capture only 10 to 30 percent of what advertising does."[24] Others complain that the data are too complicated to deal with, as an overabundance of information is available. Still another disadvantage is the high cost of collecting single-source data. While the complexity of single-source data resulted in a slow adoption rate, this method of tracking advertising effectiveness became widely adopted in the 1990s.

Tracking Print/Broadcast Ads   One of the more useful and adaptable forms of posttesting involves tracking the effects of the ad campaign by taking measurements at regular intervals. **Tracking studies** have been used to measure the effects of advertising on awareness, recall, interest, and attitudes toward the ad and/or brand as well as purchase intentions. (Ad tracking may be applied to both print and broadcast ads but is much more common with the latter.) Personal interviews, phone surveys, mall intercepts, and even mail surveys have been used. Sample sizes typically range from 250 to 500 cases per period (usually quarterly or semiannually). Tracking studies yield perhaps the most valuable information available to the marketing manager for assessing current programs and planning for the future. (See Exhibit 8–4.) IMC Perspective 8–2 shows some tracking results of a very famous campaign.

The major advantage of tracking studies is that they can be tailored to each specific campaign and/or situation. A standard set of questions can track effects of the campaign over time. The effects of various media can also be determined, although with much less effectiveness. Tracking studies have also been used to measure the differential impact of different budget sizes, the effects of flighting, brand or corporate image, and recall of specific copy points. Finally, when designed properly, as shown in Figure 8–16, tracking studies offer a high degree of reliability and validity.[25]

Some of the problems of recall and recognition measures are inherent in tracking studies, since many other factors may affect both brand and advertising recall. Despite these limitations, however, tracking studies are a very effective way to assess the effects of advertising campaigns.

In summary, you can see that each of the testing methods considered in this chapter has its strengths and its limitations. You may wonder: Can we actually test advertising effectiveness? What can be done to ensure a valid, reliable test? The next section of this chapter suggests some answers.

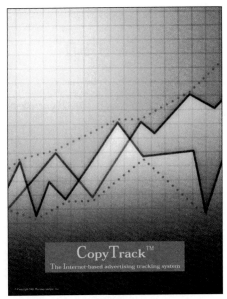

Exhibit 8–4
Tracking studies provide useful measures

ESTABLISHING A PROGRAM FOR MEASURING ADVERTISING EFFECTIVENESS

There is no surefire way to test advertising effectiveness. However, in reponse to pressures to determine the contribution of ads to the overall marketing effort, steps are being taken to improve this measurement task. Let's begin by reviewing the major problems with some existing methods and then examine possible improvements.

PROBLEMS WITH CURRENT RESEARCH METHODS

When current testing methods are compared to the criteria established by PACT (see Figure 8–2), it is clear that some of the principles important to good copy testing can

FIGURE 8–16
Factors that make or break tracking studies

1. Properly defined objectives
2. Alignment with sales objectives
3. Properly designed measures (e.g., adequate sample size, maximum control over interviewing process, adequate time between tracking periods)
4. Consistency through replication of the sampling plan
5. Random samples
6. Continuous interviewing (that is, not seasonal)
7. Evaluate measures related to behaviour (attitudes meet this criterion; recall of ads does not)
8. Critical evaluative questions asked early to eliminate bias
9. Measurement of competitors' performance
10. Skepticism about questions that ask where the advertising was seen or heard (TV always wins)
11. Building of news value into the study
12. "Moving averages" used to spot long-term trends and avoid seasonality
13. Data reported in terms of relationships rather than as isolated facts
14. Integration of key marketplace events with tracking results (e.g., advertising expenditures of self and competitors, promotional activities associated with price changes in ad campaigns, introductions of new brands, government announcements, changes in economic conditions)

I Am Canadian!

"My name is Joe, and I am Canadian!" So ends one of the most successful Canadian commercials of all time for Molson Breweries' brand Canadian. In March 2000, unsuspecting viewers in movie theatres were surprised with "The Rant," a tribute to Canadian culture and nationalistic pride. Later, the ad received extensive air time on television that has been the forefront of a successful IMC campaign.

Shortly before and during the campaign, Molson had been regaining its corporate focus on beer with divestment of non-related businesses and purchases of other beer brands internationally. Despite this, Molson needed a winner in 2000 as it had experienced weak sales in its traditionally strong brands of Canadian and Export and a roughly $100-million gap in profitability compared to its rival Labatt Breweries.

Molson began by replacing its agency of 42 years and hiring new agencies for key brands including Canadian. Curiously, the new agency found success with the already established theme "I AM," created in 1994 but since dropped. The link of "I AM" to Canadian was indirect in the initial campaign as the focus was more on an individual identity or independent attitude.

Does the message of nationalism play? Some argued that globalization of the past 10 years has given rise to a new view of Canada that is reflected in everyday life rather than our institutions or moral principles, which can now be leveraged in marketing programs. In contrast, others were concerned that the meaning of a brand gets lost with such extreme emotions. Luckily for Molson Canadian, the pride and brand go hand-in-hand, which makes it a powerful combination.

The campaign has garnered extensive publicity. The front page of the *National Post* reproduced a large and colourful image from the ad on April 12, 2000. The campaign was featured in many Canadian and American news publications and news shows. And to top it off, Jeff Douglas, The Rant's actor, re-enacted his performance prior to NHL games and other venues that tied in with Canadian's rock concert promotions. Perhaps the most flattering example of the campaign's success is that it was adapted for Foster's Beer in Australia with the theme "I Believe."

Sales promotions were a key part of the mix. In the spring of 2001, Canadian was inserting caps and T-shirts in its cases, and offering its "Best Seats in the House" contest and a ticket giveaway contest for the hockey playoffs. It was also the closed captioning sponsor on *Survivor*. The website www.iam.ca carried the promotions and featured other elements to support the nationalistic theme. And the ultimate sponsorship program emerged as Canadian organized a swearing-in ceremony of new Canadians prior to the hockey playoffs in Toronto and Ottawa.

A number of spots added momentum to the campaign. One included scenes that poked fun at many Canadian attributes (e.g., polite, nice, humble, passive). For Canada Day, viewers received birthday wishes from Joe and other friendly Molson Canadian beer drinkers. Molson also tweaked and ran a spot that followed a red maple leaf gliding along a small river. In 2001, Canada received a "toast" from a half-Scottish, half-Irish beer drinker who poetically describes many unique Canadian attributes (i.e., hockey hair, long underwear, and multi-coloured money), sang a new "anthem" that highlighted many historical Canadian images, and watched a Myles walk "500 miles" for a case of Canadian.

The campaign is a success based on a couple of factors. Unaided brand awareness rose from 55 percent to 61 percent among English Canadians for those in the legal drinking age (LDA) to 55 years category. The number of English Canadians claiming the brand as their regular beer rose from 16 to 17 percent in the same age bracket. Market share for Canadian increased by 1.8 percent in 2000 and 2.5 percent in 2001. Labatt's Blue market share experienced a similar decline each year. "The Rant" won a bronze at the

Cannes festival and a Gold in two categories for the Cassies. The entire campaign also earned Molson the Grand Prix at the Cassies.

Sources: "Post Goes Big with Molson Image," *Marketing Magazine*, April 12, 2000; Chris Daniels, "Cashing In on The New Nationalism," *Marketing Magazine*, May 22, 2000; Astrid Van Den Broek, "Molson Pours on More Stereotypes," *Marketing Magazine*, June 26, 2000; "A Down Under Twist on Molson's Rant," *Marketing Magazine*, September 18, 2000; Astrid Van Den Broek, "I AM Marketer of the Year," *Marketing Magazine*, December 18/25, 2000; "Molson Readies Canadian Hockey Promos," *Marketing Magazine*, March 15, 2001; Astrid Van Den Broek, "Molson Canadian Toasts Canadiana," *Marketing Magazine*, April 9, 2001; "Molson Sponsors' New Citizens," *Marketing Magazine*, April 23, 2001; "Molson's Anthem Tugs at History," *Marketing Magazine*, June 18, 2001; "Myles the Latest Molson Canadian Spot," *Marketing Magazine*, October 22, 2001; "Molson Canadian," *Marketing Magazine*, November 19, 2001; Lesley Young, "The Rant Dominates the Cassie Awards," *Marketing Magazine*, November 19, 2001; "Molson Canadian–Cassies Grand Prix Winner," *Marketing Magazine*, November 19, 2001.

be accomplished readily, whereas others require substantially more effort. For example, principle 6 (providing equivalent test ads) should require a minimum of effort. The researcher can easily control the state of completion of the test communications. Also fairly easy are principles 1 and 2 (providing measurements relative to the objectives sought and determining a priori how the results will be used).

We have seen throughout this text that each promotional medium, the message, and the budget all consider the marketing and communications objectives sought. The integrated marketing communications planning model establishes the roles of these elements. So by the time one gets to the measurement phase, the criteria by which these programs will be evaluated should simply fall into place.

Slightly more difficult are principles 3, 5, and 8, although again these factors are largely in the control of the researcher. Principle 3 (providing multiple measurements) may require little more than budgeting to make sure more than one test is conducted. At the most, it may require considering two similar measures to ensure reliability. Likewise, principle 5 (exposing the test ad more than once) can be accomplished with a proper research design. Finally, principle 8 (sample definition) requires little more than sound research methodology; any test should use the target audience to assess an ad's effectiveness. You would not use a sample of nondrinkers to evaluate new liquor commercials.

The most difficult factors to control—and the principles that may best differentiate between good and bad testing procedures—are PACT requirements 4, 7, and 9. Fortunately, however, addressing each of these contributes to the attainment of the others.

The best starting point is principle 4, which states the research should be guided by a model of human response to communications that encompasses reception, comprehension, and behavioural response. It is the best starting point, in our opinion, because it is the principle least addressed by practicing researchers. If you recall, Chapter 3 proposed a number of models that could fulfill this principle's requirements. Yet even though these models have existed for quite some time, few if any common research methods attempt to integrate them into their methodologies. Most current methods do little more than provide recall scores, despite the fact many researchers have shown that recall is a poor measure of effectiveness. Models that do claim to measure such factors as attitude change or brand preference change are often fraught with problems that severely limit their reliability. An effective measure must include some relationship to the communications process.

It might seem at first glance that principle 7 (providing a nonbiasing exposure) would be easy to accomplish. But lab measures, while offering control, are artificial and vulnerable to testing effects. And field measures, while more realistic, often lose control. The Seagram and Time study may have the best of both worlds, but it is too large a task for most firms to undertake. Some of the improvements associated with the single-source systems help to solve this problem. In addition, properly designed ad tracking studies provide truer measures of the impact of the communication. As technology develops and more attention is paid to this principle, we expect to see improvements in methodologies soon.

Last but not least is principle 9, the concern for reliability and validity. Most of the measures discussed are lacking in at least one of these criteria, yet these are two of the most critical distinctions between good and bad research. If a study is properly designed, and by that we mean it addresses principles 1 through 8, it should be both reliable and valid.

ESSENTIALS OF EFFECTIVE TESTING

Simply put, good tests of advertising effectiveness must address the nine principles established by PACT. One of the easiest ways to accomplish this is by following the decision sequence model in formulating promotional plans.

- *Establish communications objectives.* It is nearly impossible to show the direct impact of advertising on sales. The marketing objectives established for the promotional program are not good measures of communication effectiveness. On the other hand, attainment of communications objectives can be measured and leads to the accomplishment of marketing objectives.
- *Use a consumer response model.* Early in this text we reviewed hierarchy of effects models and cognitive response models, which provide an understanding of the effects of communications and lend themselves to achieving communications goals. We also presented Rossiter and Percy's model for stating communication objectives which could also be a basis for measurement.

- *Use both pretests and posttests.* From a cost standpoint—both actual cost outlays and opportunity costs—pretesting makes sense. It may mean the difference between success or failure of the campaign or the product. But it should work in conjunction with posttests, which avoid the limitations of pretests, use much larger samples, and take place in more natural settings. Posttesting may be required to determine the true effectiveness of the ad or campaign.
- *Use multiple measures.* Many attempts to measure the effectiveness of advertising focus on one major dependent variable—perhaps sales, recall, or recognition. As noted earlier in this chapter, advertising may have a variety of effects on the consumer, some of which can be measured through traditional methods, others that require updated thinking (recall the discussion on physiological responses). For a true assessment of advertising effectiveness, a number of measures may be required.
- *Understand and implement proper research.* It is critical to understand research methodology. What constitutes a good design? Is it valid and reliable? Does it measure what we need it to? There is no shortcut to this criterion, and there is no way to avoid it if you truly want to measure the effects of advertising.

A major study sponsored by the Advertising Research Foundation (ARF), involving interviews with 12,000 to 15,000 people, addressed some of these issues.[26] While we do not have the space to analyze this study here, note that the research was designed to evaluate measures of copy tests, compare copy testing procedures, and examine some of the PACT principles. Information on this study has been published in a number of academic and trade journals and by the ARF.

SUMMARY

This chapter introduced you to issues involved in measuring the effects of advertising and promotions. These issues include reasons for testing, reasons companies do not test, and the review and evaluation of various research methodologies. We arrived at a number of conclusions: (1) advertising research to measure effectiveness is important to the promotional program, (2) not enough companies test their ads, and (3) problems exist with current research methodologies. In addition, we reviewed the criteria for sound research and suggested some ways to accomplish effective studies.

All marketing managers want to know how well their promotional programs are working. This information is critical to planning for the next period, since program adjustments and/or maintenance are based on evaluation of current strategies. Problems often result when the measures taken to determine such effects are inaccurate or improperly used.

This chapter demonstrated that testing must meet a number of criteria (defined by PACT) to be successful. These evaluations should occur both before and after the campaigns are implemented.

A variety of research methods were discussed, many provided by syndicated research firms. Many companies have developed their own testing systems. Single-source research data such as BehaviorScan, Scantrack, and Market Source were discussed for measuring the effects of advertising. These single-source systems offer strong potential for improving the effectiveness of ad measures in the future, since commercial exposures and reactions may be correlated to actual purchase behaviours.

It is important to recognize that different measures of effectiveness may lead to different results. Depending on the criteria used, one measure may show that an ad or promotion is effective while another states that it is not. This is why clearly defined objectives and the use of multiple measures are critical to determining the true effects of an IMC program.

238

KEY TERMS

pretests, *215*
posttests, *215*
laboratory tests, *217*
testing bias, *217*
field tests, *217*
PACT (Positioning
    Advertising Copy
    Testing), *217*
concept testing, *218*
rough tests, *220*

comprehension and
    reaction tests, *220*
consumer juries, *221*
halo effect, *221*
portfolio tests, *222*
Flesch formula, *223*
theatre testing, *223*
on-air test, *225*
day-after recall scores, *225*
pupillometrics, *225*

electrodermal
    response, *225*
eye tracking, *226*
electroencephalographic
    (EEG) measures, *226*
alpha activity, *226*
hemispheric
    lateralization, *226*
inquiry tests, *227*
split-run tests, *227*

recognition method, *228*
recall tests, *229*
single-source tracking
    methods, *232*
tracking studies, *232*

DISCUSSION QUESTIONS

1. Discuss some of the reasons why some companies decide not to measure the effectiveness of their promotional programs. Explain why this may or may not be a good strategy.

2. Discuss the differences between pretesting and posttesting. Give examples of each.

3. What is the difference between a lab test and a field test? When should each be employed?

4. Give examples of the various types of rough testing methodologies. Describe why a company might wish to test at this phase of the process. When might they wish to test only completed ads?

5. Major changes have taken place in the way that theatre tests are conducted. Describe some of these changes and the changes in measures that have also occurred in this testing method.

6. Discuss some of the aspects of the communication program that advertisers may wish to test. Provide some examples.

7. The bottom line for advertisers is to evoke some behaviour—for example, sales. Explain why it may be difficult to use sales to measure advertising effectiveness.

8. Describe some of the effectiveness measures that might be used to get at nonquantifiable aspects of advertising and promotions.

Media Strategy, Tactics, and Budget Decisions

CHAPTER OBJECTIVES

- To understand the key terminology used in media planning.

- To know how a media plan is developed.

- To know the process of deciding and implementing media strategies and tactics.

- To understand the theoretical and managerial approaches for media budget setting.

Chevrolet Travels Quebec in a Day

In the fall of 2003, GM planned to launch six new Chevrolet vehicles. GM followed the customary approach of introducing each brand successively across the rest of Canada. However, with the advice of its agency, Cossette Communication, GM launched all six brands in one day on November 12 in Quebec to guarantee virtually 100-percent awareness throughout the province. The impetus for such an innovative approach lay in GM's desire to improve its overall marketing performance in Quebec. For example, GM had a 28-percent market share in Canada but only a 21-percent market share in Quebec for all vehicles sold. Furthermore, GM faced an even worse situation for cars with over a 30-percent market share in all provinces except B.C. and only an 18-percent share for Quebec. Moreover, if that was not motivation enough, sub-compact, compact, and small- to mid-size cars represented 80 percent of all cars sold by GM in Quebec compared to 50 percent for the rest of Canada and just 28 percent in the U.S. Without question, as part of the solution for reversing its fortunes in this market, GM saw the need to change its image from "my uncle's car" to "a cool car for me" with younger consumers in their 30s.

The campaign featured television, radio, print, billboards, Internet, sales promotion, and publicity, and represented 20 percent of Chevrolet's annual marketing budget for Quebec. For television, seven ads appeared just before 10:00 p.m. on seven networks and also at 5:00, 7:00, and 9:00 p.m. on Astral specialty channels. About 340 radio spots hit the airwaves and the Energie radio network sponsored a contest offering clues to listeners to help them in their search for Chevrolets hidden in Quebec's five major cities. The vehicles were hidden in actual car-size Hot Wheels style boxes. Print advertising included 1.5 million four-page inserts in every daily newspaper in the province. Approximately 700 billboards showed the new collection of cars, and 525 of these outdoor ads stayed until the end of the year. Ads on websites like canoe.qc.ca and msn.ca reached almost 1 million people and up to 58,000 interested consumers clicked on the ad banners. Finally, all major news media covered the pervasive launch and Cossette estimated the exposure value at about $150,000.

Overall, the campaign appeared successful. In follow-up research measured three days later, perceptions of the Chevrolet vehicles improved 23 percent. Awareness achieved 70-percent penetration and traffic at GMCanada.com was over 300 percent higher versus other days in the month. The campaign received a Gold Media Innovation Award from *Marketing Magazine* for campaigns under $1 million.

Sources: Danny Kucharsky, "One Day Wonder," *Marketing Magazine*, February 2, 2004; Media Innovation Awards, *Marketing Magazine*, November 4, 2004.

Since integrated marketing communications programs are a necessity, the marketer has many media opportunities available that require in-depth knowledge of all the alternatives. Media planners must now consider new options as well as recognize the changes that are occurring in traditional sources. New and evolving media contribute to the already difficult task of media planning. Planning when, where, and how the advertising message will be delivered is a complex and involved process. The purpose of the media plan is to develop a framework that will deliver the message to the target audience in the most efficient, cost-effective manner possible—that will communicate what the product, brand, and/or service can do.

This chapter illustrates the media planning process, discusses the development of decisions for media strategy and tactics, and presents issues related to setting a media budget. Later chapters will explore the relative strengths and limitations of the various media and examine each in more detail.

MEDIA PLANNING

Media planning is the series of decisions involved in delivering the promotional message to the prospective purchasers and/or users of the product or brand. Media planning is a process, which means a number of decisions are made, each of which may be altered or abandoned as the plan develops. Options include mass media such as television, newspapers, radio, and magazines (and the choices available within each of these categories) as well as out-of-the-home media such as outdoor advertising, transit advertising, and electronic billboards (Figure 9–1). A variety of support media such as direct marketing, interactive media, promotional products advertising, and in-store point-of-purchase options must also be considered.

While at first glance the choices among these alternatives might seem relatively straightforward, this is rarely the case. Part of the reason media selection becomes so involved is the nature of the media themselves. TV combines both sight and sound, an advantage not offered by other media. Magazines can convey more information and may keep the message available to the potential buyer for a much longer time. As you will soon appreciate, each media has its own particular strengths and limitations that must be considered in light of the communication problem or opportunity with which the marketer is faced. The media planning process becomes even more complicated when the manager has to choose between alternatives within the same medium. In this section, we review the media plan content and highlight key media planning challenges.

MEDIA PLAN

The media plan determines the best way to get the advertiser's message to the market. In a basic sense, the goal of the media plan is to find that combination of media that enables the marketer to communicate the message in the most effective manner to the largest number of potential customers at the lowest cost. Most media plans have a prescribed budget that the media planner must respect. Often, media planners face the challenge of developing a plan with limited financial resources. The activities involved in developing the media plan and the purposes of each are presented in Figure 9–2.

As you can see, a number of decisions must be made throughout this process. The promotional planning model in Chapter 1 discussed the process of identifying target audiences, establishing objectives, and formulating strategies for attaining them. The development of the media plan and strategies follows a similar path, except that the focus is to determine the best way to deliver the message. Thus, the media plan is generally comprised of a short section containing **media objectives**, an explanation of the **media strategy** decisions, and fine-tuning details that are known as media execution or **media tactics**. IMC Perspective 9–1 shows how the advertising industry recognizes good media plans.

242

FIGURE 9–1 ☐☐☐☐ Canadian market data: net advertising revenues

Components of Net Advertising Revenue by Medium (in millions of dollars)													
Medium		1996	%	1997	%	1998	%	1999	%	2000	%	2001	%
Television	Total	$1,982	26%	$2,103	26%	$2,312	26%	$2,387	26%	$2,456	26%	$2,561	26%
	Network	$440	6%	$423	5%	$452	5%	$449	5%	$444	5%	$482	5%
	Selective	$1,373	18%	$1,485	18%	$1,607	18%	$1,618	18%	$1,615	17%	$1,621	16%
	Specialty	$155	2%	$184	2%	$241	3%	$304	3%	$381	4%	$438	4%
	Infomercial	$14	0%	$12	0%	$12	0%	$15	0%	$17	0%	$20	0%
Radio	Total	$792	11%	$856	11%	$930	11%	$965	11%	$1,015	11%	$1,063	11%
Daily Newspapers (ex. classified)	Total	$1,315	18%	$1,546	19%	$1,596	18%	$1,629	18%	$1,732	18%	$1,678	17%
Consumer Magazines	Total	$318	4%	$347	4%	$451	5%	$460	5%	$514	5%	$541	5%
Outdoor & Transit	Total	$200	3%	$220	3%	$250	3%	$269	3%	$293	3%	$310	3%
Internet	Total	$10	0%	$25	0%	$56	1%	$110	1%	$116	1%		
Other	Total	$2,880	38%	$3,001	37%	$3,276	37%	$3,284	36%	$3,365	35%	$3,706	37%
	Yellow Pages	$892	12%	$899	11%	$935	11%	$975	11%	$1,000	11%	$1,040	10%
	Direct Mail	$1,110	15%	$1,168	14%	$1,251	14%	$1,190	13%	$1,200	13%	$1,489	15%
	Other Print (religious, school, farm, trade publication, community newspaper, weekend supp.)	$878	12%	$934	12%	$1,090	12%	$1,119	12%	$1,165	12%	$1,177	12%
Total, all media		**$7,487**		**$8,083**		**$8,840**		**$9,050**		**$9,485**		**$9,975**	

As compiled by the TVB from Statistics Canada, CRTC, CNA, CCNA/Les Hebdos du Quebec, Magazines Canada, CARD, CAN, TeleDirect, Canada Post, IAB, and Industry Estimates.
Note: Revisions from the last CMDC Digest have been made to previous years' estimates. Broadcast revenue is based on the broadcast calendar year ending Aug. of the year indicated.

Media Objectives Just as the situation analysis leads to establishment of marketing and communications objectives, it should also lead to specific media objectives. The media objectives are not ends in themselves. Rather, they are derived from and are designed to lead to the attainment of communication and marketing objectives. Media objectives are the goals for the media program and should be limited to those that can be accomplished through media strategies, as in the following example:

Create awareness in the target audience through the following:

- Use broadcast media to provide coverage of 80 percent of the target audience over a six-month period.
- Reach 60 percent of the target audience at least three times over the same six-month period.
- Concentrate heaviest advertising in winter and spring, with lighter emphasis in summer and fall.

The media objectives give direction for the media strategy and tactics decisions. Upon implementation, marketers need to know whether or not they were successful. Measures of effectiveness must consider two factors: (1) How well did these strategies achieve the media objectives? (2) How well did this media plan contribute to attaining the overall marketing and communications objectives? If the strategies were successful, they should be used in future plans. If not, their flaws should be analyzed.

FIGURE 9–2 ☐☐☐☐ Activities involved in developing the media plan

The situation analysis

Purpose: To understand the marketing problem. An analysis is made of a company and its competitors on the basis of:
1. Size and share of the total market.
2. Sales and history, costs, and profits.
3. Distribution practices.
4. Methods of selling.
5. Use of advertising.
6. Identification of prospects.
7. Nature of the product.

The marketing strategy plan

Purpose: To plan activities that will solve one or more of the marketing problems. Includes the determination of:
1. Marketing objectives.
2. Product and spending strategy.
3. Distribution strategy.
4. Which elements of the marketing mix are to be used.
5. Identification of the "best" market segments.

The creative strategy plan

Purpose: To determine what to communicate through advertisements. Includes the determination of:
1. How product can meet consumer needs.
2. How product will be positioned in advertisements.
3. Copy themes.
4. Specific objectives of each advertisement.
5. Number and sizes of advertisements.

Setting media objectives

Purpose: To translate marketing objectives and strategies into goals that media can accomplish.

Determining media strategy

Purpose: To translate media goals into general guidelines that will control the planner's selection and use of media. The best strategy alternatives should be selected.

Selecting broad media classes

Purpose: To determine which broad class of media best fulfills the criteria. Involves comparison and selection of broad media classes such as newspapers, magazines, radio, television, and others. The analysis is called intermedia comparisons. Audience size is one of the major factors used in comparing the various media classes.

Selecting media within classes

Purpose: To compare and select the best media within broad classes, again using predetermined criteria. Involves making decisions about the following:
1. If magazines were recommended, then which magazines?
2. If television was recommended, then
   a. Broadcast or cable television   c. If network, which program(s)?
   b. Network or spot television   d. If spot, which markets?
3. If radio or newspapers were recommended, then
   a. Which markets shall be used?   b. What criteria shall buyers use in making purchases of local media?

Media use decision— broadcast

1. What kind of sponsorship (sole, shared, participating, or other)?
2. What levels of reach and frequency will be required?
3. Scheduling: On which days and months are commercials to appear?
4. Placement of spots in programs or between programs?

Media use decision— print

1. Number of ads to appear and on which days and months.
2. Placements of ads: Any preferred position within media?
3. Special treatment: Gatefolds, bleeds, colour, etc.
4. Desired reach or frequency levels.

Media use decision— other media

1. Billboards
   a. Location of markets and plan of distribution.
   b. Kinds of outdoor boards to be used.
2. Direct mail or other media: Decisions peculiar to those media.

244

Media Innovation Awards I

Media Innovation Awards selected by a committee designated by *Marketing Magazine* recognized the important contribution of media in marketing communication. For 2004, the evaluation committee examined 108 entries and granted 34 medal winners—five gold, six silver, nine bronze, and fourteen certificates. The criteria for the awards are the following:

- The strategic media insight: What was the big idea that significantly improved the targeting precision of the delivery of the advertising message? Was there a bold new understanding of the message from the recipients' interaction with the selected medium or media?
- Tactical media creativity: What was the big idea that made the receptivity of the advertising message significantly greater? How did the tactics enhance the creative message carried and/or how did the tactics capitalize on a given medium's intrinsic attributes?
- Executional skill: What kind of "degree of difficulty" was involved in the implementation in terms of size and scope, budgetary limitations, and regulatory or media convention hurdles overcome?
- Results: Would results data substantiate exceptional achievement? What tangible evidence was there of the specific effect of the media contribution?

As noted in the opening vignette, Chevrolet received a gold for a mixed media campaign under $1 million. Nike's "You're Faster Than You Think" campaign received a gold for a mixed media campaign over $1 million. Nike wanted to associate sports innovation with its brand name and used the word "speed" as the key message for all contact points so that consumers would equate speed with Nike.

Nike delivered its media plan with a red line—a graphic illustration of speed found at every contact point. For example, magazine ads used a banner wrap to draw attention, floor decals appeared as a track, and specialized posters gave the illusion of athletes like Perdita Félicien racing with subway passengers. Nike also constructed unique and innovative billboards on consecutive walls of two downtown Toronto apartment buildings that demonstrated a man wearing Nike SPEED clothing running through the wall.

Nike also received a gold for the banner wrap of its double-page spread ad in *ELLE* Canada and *éclat*, a customer publication for Pharmaprix drug stores in Quebec. The wrap's intrusiveness essentially forced readers to see the ad since they had to remove it to read the magazine. Implementing the idea proved challenging since the banners had to be manually added. The advertising industry has taken notice of this clever tactic. The magazines received numerous telephone calls and Nike headquarters believed it to be the best idea from all Speed campaigns from around the world and considered its use elsewhere.

Source: Media Innovation Awards, *Marketing Magazine*, November 4, 2004.

Media Strategy As Figure 9–2 indicates, the primary media strategy decision concerns the use of media, moving from a broad perspective to a more specific one. The **medium** is the general category of available delivery systems, which includes broadcast media (like TV and radio), print media (like newspapers and magazines), direct marketing, out-of-home advertising, and other support media. After or during this evaluation, the media planner will consider the relative strengths and limitations of broad **media class** options.

In making the media strategy decisions, a media planner will consider the strategic implications of three concepts. **Reach** is a measure of the number of different audience members exposed at least once to a media vehicle in a given period of time. **Coverage** refers to the potential audience that might receive the message through a vehicle. Coverage relates to potential audience; reach refers to the actual audience delivered. (The importance of this distinction will become clearer later in this chapter.) Finally, **frequency** refers to the number of times the receiver is exposed to the media vehicle in a specified period.

Media Tactics After the general strategic direction of the media plan has been established, the media planner looks to more specific media decisions like the media vehicle. The **media vehicle** is the specific carrier within a media class. For example, *Maclean's* is a print vehicle; *Hockey Night in Canada* is a television vehicle. As you will see in later chapters, each vehicle has its own characteristics as well as its own relative strengths and limitations. Specific decisions must be made as to the value of each in delivering the message.

While making the media vehicle decision, the media planner evaluates the options carefully to maximize coverage, reach, frequency, and minimize costs. For example, according to Figure 9–2, once print has been established, the media planner has to decide which specific magazine(s) to select. In addition, there are certain placement factors that need to be carefully evaluated. These final considerations can lead to budget adjustments that translate into refinements in the allocation of the media dollars. Finally, the complete plan is summarized in a blocking chart. The chart may indicate gaps in media coverage or some other concern that would lead the media planner to perform additional evaluation prior to completing the media plan.

Flexibility While most media plans are written annually, advertisers find it necessary to alter their objectives and strategies because of the rapidly changing marketing environment. An effective media plan requires a degree of flexibility. If the plan has not built in some flexibility, opportunities may be lost and/or the company may not be able to address new threats. Flexibility may be needed to address the following:

1. *Market opportunities.* Sometimes a market opportunity arises that the advertiser wishes to take advantage of. For example, a special television show may prompt an advertiser to shift their expenditures from another media.
2. *Market threats.* External factors may pose a threat to the firm, and a change in media strategy is dictated. For example, a competitor may alter its media strategy to gain an edge. Failure to respond to this challenge could create problems for the firm.
3. *Availability of media.* Sometimes a desired medium (or vehicle) is not available to the marketer. Perhaps the medium does not reach a particular target audience or has no time or space available. There are still some geographic areas that certain media do not reach. Alternative vehicles or media must then be considered.
4. *Changes in media vehicles.* A change in a particular media vehicle may require a change in the media strategy. A drop in ratings or a change in editorial format may lead the advertiser to use different programs or print alternatives.

MEDIA PLANNING CHALLENGES

Unfortunately, media planning has not become a standardized task. A number of problems contribute to the difficulty of establishing the plan and reduce its effectiveness. These problems include insufficient information, inconsistent terminologies, and difficulty measuring effectiveness.

Insufficient Information While a great deal of information about markets and the media exists, media planners often require more than is available. Some data are just not measured, either because they cannot be or because measuring them would be too expensive. For example, continuous measures of radio listenership exist, but only periodic listenership studies are reported due to sample size and cost constraints.

The timing of measurements is also a problem; some audience measures are taken only at specific times of the year. (For example, **sweeps periods** in February, May, July, and November are used for measuring TV audiences and setting advertising rates.) This information is then generalized to succeeding months, so future planning decisions must be made on past data that may not reflect current behaviours. Think about planning for TV advertising for the fall season. There are no data on the audiences of new shows, and audience information taken on existing programs during the summer may not indicate how these programs will do in the fall because summer viewership is generally much lower. While the advertisers can review these programs before they air, they do not have actual audience figures.

The lack of information is even more of a problem for small advertisers, who may not be able to afford to purchase the information they require. As a result, their decisions are based on limited or out-of-date data that was provided by the media themselves, or no data at all.

Compared to media planners in the United States, Canadian media planners face additional pressures of insufficient information. The size of the American population permits extensive economies of scale, so it is not unexpected that larger U.S.-based media buying organizations would have valuable resources. Combined with similar media consumption (e.g., popular television shows) between American and English-Canadians, there is a movement to coordinate media purchasing across North America. The end result may be improved efficiency and effectiveness of the media purchase with the sharing of information.[1]

Inconsistent Terminologies   Problems arise because the cost bases used by different media often vary and the standards of measurement used to establish these costs are not always consistent. For example, print media may present cost efficiency data in terms of the cost to reach a thousand people (cost per thousand, or CPM), while broadcast and outdoor media use the cost per ratings point (CPRP). Audience information that is used as a basis for these costs has also been collected by different methods. Finally, terms that actually mean something different (such as *reach* and *coverage*) may be used synonymously, adding to the confusion.

Difficulty Measuring Effectiveness   Because it is so hard to measure the effectiveness of advertising and promotions in general, it is also difficult to determine the relative effectiveness of various media or media vehicles. While progress is being made in this regard (particularly in the area of direct-response advertising), the media planner must usually guess at the impact of these alternatives.

Because of these problems, not all media decisions are quantitatively determined. Sometimes managers have to assume the image of a medium in a market with which they are not familiar, anticipate the impact of recent events, or make judgments without full knowledge of all the available alternatives.

While these problems complicate the media planning process, they do not render it an entirely subjective exercise. The next section of this chapter explores in more detail how media strategies are developed and ways to increase their effectiveness.

MEDIA STRATEGY DECISIONS

Having determined what is to be accomplished, media planners consider how to achieve the media objectives. They develop and implement media strategies that consist of five main topics for decision:

- media mix
- target audience coverage
- geographic coverage
- scheduling
- reach vs frequency

FIGURE 9–3 ☐ ☐ ☐ ☐   Ad techniques—What's acceptable for Canadians?

	Acceptable 2002	Acceptable 2003	% change
Print advertising in newspapers	73%	81%	+8%
Radio advertising	68%	77%	+9%
Posters on buses or subways	71%	75%	+4%
Television advertising	65%	72%	+7%
Billboards along the roads	57%	63%	+6%
Product placement in television shows	50%	56%	+6%
Ads in washrooms	45%	46%	+1%
Banner advertising on the Internet	30%	34%	+4%
Ads placed on personal property, like baby carriages	23%	32%	+9%
Ads on cellphone displays	30%	25%	-5%
Famous people appearing on talk shows praising prescription drugs without mentioning they are paid	16%	20%	+4%
Pop up windows with advertising on the Internet	14%	17%	+3%

Source: Jean-Marc Leger and Dave Scholz, "Back From the Saturation Brink," *Marketing Magazine*, December 1, 2003.

THE MEDIA MIX

A wide variety of media are available to advertisers. While it is possible that only one might be employed, it is much more likely that a number of alternatives will be used. The objectives sought, the characteristics of the product or service, the size of the budget, and individual preferences are just some of the factors that determine what combination of media will be used.

As an example, consider a promotional situation in which a product requires a visual demonstration to be communicated effectively. In this case, TV may be the most effective medium. If the promotional strategy calls for coupons to stimulate trial, print media may be necessary. For in-depth information, the Internet may be best. IMC Perspective 9–2 shows some more innovative media choices.

While an evaluation of each media occurs within the perspective of the communication situation a media planner faces, each media has certain degrees of acceptability with Canadians as shown in Figure 9–3.

The context of the medium in which the ad is placed may also affect viewers' perceptions. A specific creative strategy may require certain media. Because TV provides both sight and sound, it may be more effective in generating emotions than other media; magazines may create different perceptions from newspapers. It is possible to increase the success of a product significantly through a strong creative campaign. But to implement this creativity, you must employ a medium that will support such a strategy. Kodak and McDonald's, among many others, have effectively used TV to create emotional appeals. In some situations, the media strategy to be pursued may be the driving force behind the creative strategy, as the media and creative departments work closely together to achieve the greatest impact with the audience of the specific media.

By employing a media mix, advertisers can add more versatility to their media strategies, since each medium contributes its own distinct advantages. By combining media, marketers can increase coverage, reach, and frequency levels while improving the likelihood of achieving overall communications and marketing goals.

Media Innovation Awards II

The Best of Show and gold award for television went to B.C. Hydro. Attempting to reduce energy consumption in the province, B.C. Hydro planned to give residents a voucher for two free compact fluorescent light bulbs that last up to eight times longer than regular incandescent bulbs. To encourage voucher redemption at retail locations, the utility needed to demonstrate the product and its benefits and found the perfect solution on television.

B.C. Hydro found an ingenious idea that captured the attention of the target audience and actually showed how the bulb lasted longer. It used traditional closed captioning sponsorship and extended the sponsorship by having the light bulb remain on the screen longer while superimposed onto the regular station program, right where the station logo would normally appear, and then added its closing message about redeeming the voucher.

The implementation of the idea met with some obstacles due to the reluctance of stations to disrupt the regular programming, however four Vancouver stations agreed and assisted with the production. Overall the campaign exposed the 16 different executions a total of 300 times to ensure optimal reach and frequency. Although no communication tracking occurred, the media plan appeared a success

since B.C. Hydro gave away more than 1.25 million bulbs, 74 percent higher than expected. It also concluded that tactics designed to surprise viewers and change their regular processing of a message could generate additional attention.

The final gold award for 2004 went to Nike, once again, for its almost illegal lawn signs. Nike had only three weeks and a limited budget to attract runners to its half-marathon race and recognized that it had to reach more serious runners who would be prepared for such a race. The innovative idea focused on placing the message exactly where the runners would be taking their usual run, along the 350-km bicycle paths in Montreal. The ads were sequenced so that runners could experience the complete message while they ran. Since ad placement on public property was illegal, NewAd placed the lawn signs on various routes on a Friday evening and returned 48 hours later and retrieved them before any city employee noticed. Fortunately for Nike, no fines ensued and it received 19,000 unique visits to the race's website and attracted 1,000 runners.

Source: Media Innovation Awards, *Marketing Magazine*, November 4, 2004.

In Chapters 10, 11, and 12, you will see that each medium has its own characteristics that make it better or worse for attaining specific communication objectives. We have organized these as media and media-usage characteristics.

Media Characteristics
- target audience selectivity
- target audience coverage
- geographic coverage
- scheduling flexibility
- reach
- frequency
- cost efficiency
- absolute costs for placement and production

Media-Usage Characteristics
- control for selective exposure
- attention
- creativity for cognitive responses
- creativity for emotional responses
- amount of processing time
- involvement
- clutter
- media image

Figure 9-4 provides a summary of the strengths and limitations of each media reviewed in the next three chapters using the above characteristics. We continue with these characteristics for direct marketing and Internet marketing in their respective chapters. With so many competing variables, it becomes clear why media planners spend considerable efforts getting the media mix decision right. Finally, keep in mind that these are general characteristics that give guidance to the media mix decision. Citing these to make a media mix decision is not sufficient. Each strength and limitation needs to be related to the communication situation a specific brand faces and how the media characteristics will help the brand reach its relevant objectives.

FIGURE 9–4 ☐ ☐ ☐ ☐   Strengths and limitations of media characteristics

	Strengths	Limitations
Television	Target audience coverage Geographic coverage Creativity for emotional responses Creativity for cognitive responses Reach Frequency Scheduling flexibility Cost efficiency Attention Media image	Selective exposure Target audience selectivity Absolute cost Amount of processing time Involvement Clutter Media image
Radio	Cost efficiency Absolute cost Target audience selectivity Geographic coverage Scheduling flexibility Creativity for cognitive responses Reach Frequency Media image	Amount of processing time Selective exposure Attention Clutter Creativity for emotional responses without visual Involvement Target audience coverage
Magazines	Target audience selectivity Geographic coverage Selective exposure Attention Involvement Amount of processing time Creativity for cognitive responses Creativity for emotional responses Media image	Target audience coverage Reach Frequency Scheduling flexibility Cost efficiency Absolute cost Clutter
Newspapers	Scheduling flexibility Reach Frequency Geographic coverage Cost efficiency Absolute cost Target audience coverage Media image Involvement Processing time Creativity for cognitive responses	Target audience selectivity Clutter Selective exposure Attention Creativity for emotional responses

	Strengths	Limitations
Outdoor	Frequency Attention Geographic coverage Reach Cost efficiency Selective exposure Creativity for emotional responses	Amount of processing time Media image Target audience selectivity Target audience coverage Scheduling flexibility Absolute cost Clutter Low involvement Creativity for cognitive responses
Transit	Target audience coverage Geographic coverage Reach Frequency Amount of processing time Creativity for emotional responses Selective exposure Attention	Target audience selectivity Scheduling flexibility Cost efficiency Absolute cost Creativity for cognitive responses Involvement

For example, it appears that Toyota got its media mix right for its launch of the Echo hatchback in Quebec in the fall of 2003. Using television, radio, and outdoor events, Toyota successfully attracted 1,500 test drives within a three-week campaign targeted to young men, aged 18–29. An Echo, covered with the radio station's identity and driven by their DJs, gave consumers the opportunity to get in the car for a test drive. Periodically the DJs would announce that the current driver was the winner and the lucky driver would receive the contents of the hatchback (e.g., DVD players, CDs, cellphones, Walkmans, and tickets to shows and movies).[2]

TARGET AUDIENCE COVERAGE

The media planner determines which target audiences should receive the most media emphasis. Developing media strategies involves matching the most appropriate media to this audience by asking, "Through which media and media vehicles can I best get my message to prospective buyers?" The issue here is to get coverage of the audience, as shown in Figure 9–5. The optimal goal is full audience coverage, shown in the second pie chart. But this is a very optimistic scenario. More realistically, conditions shown in the third and fourth charts are most likely to occur. In the

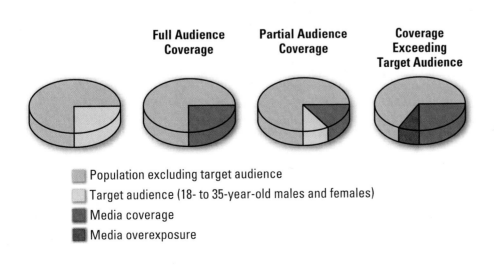

Full Audience Coverage **Partial Audience Coverage** **Coverage Exceeding Target Audience**

Population excluding target audience
Target audience (18- to 35-year-old males and females)
Media coverage
Media overexposure

FIGURE 9–5
Marketing coverage possibilities

251

third chart, the coverage of the media does not allow for coverage of the entire audience, leaving some potential customers without exposure to the message. In the fourth chart, the marketer is faced with a problem of overexposure (also called **waste coverage**), in which the media coverage exceeds the targeted audience. If media coverage reaches people who are not sought as buyers and are not potential users, then it is wasted. (This term is used for coverage that reaches people who are not potential buyers and/or users. Consumers may not be part of the intended target audience but may still be considered as potential—for example, those who buy the product as a gift for someone else.)

The goal of the media planner is to extend media coverage to as many of the members of the target audience as possible while minimizing the amount of waste coverage. The situation usually involves trade-offs. Sometimes one has to live with less coverage than desired; other times, the most effective media expose people not sought. In this instance, waste coverage is justified because the media employed are likely to be the most effective means of delivery available and the cost of the waste coverage is exceeded by the value gained from their use.

A variety of factors can assist media planners in making the target audience coverage decision. Some will require primary research, whereas others will be available from published (secondary) sources. This research can show the number of consumers for a particular product category across many demographic variables. We review audience information in Chapters 10, 11, and 12 as each media has its own method.

When examining this data, media planners are often more concerned with the percentage figures and index numbers than with the raw numbers. This is largely due to the fact that the numbers provided may not be specific enough for their needs, or they question the numbers provided because of the methods by which they were collected. Another key reason is that index numbers and percentages provide a comparative view of the market.

Overall, the **index number** is considered a good indicator of the potential of the market. This number is derived from the formula

$$\text{Index} = \frac{\text{Percentage of users in a demographic segment}}{\text{Percentage of population in the same segment}} \times 100$$

An index number over 100 means use of the product is proportionately greater in that segment than in one that is average (100) or less than 100. Depending on their overall strategy, marketers may wish to use this information to determine which groups are now using the product and target them or to identify a group that is currently using the product less and attempt to develop that segment. While the index is helpful, it should not be used alone. Percentages and product usage figures are also needed to get an accurate picture of the market. Just because the index for a particular segment of the population is very high, that doesn't always mean it is the only attractive segment to target. The high index may be a result of a low denominator (a very small proportion of the population in this segment).

Understanding coverage in a multimedia environment is proving difficult for media planners. Recent research suggests that younger consumers frequently engage in the consumption of more than one media at a time. It suggests that up to 34 percent of young people aged 12–17 use the Internet while watching television.[3] This is a significant trend since coverage historically implied a reasonably close association with exposure and processing of the advertising message. Clearly, the communication is limited even further if other media are competing for the young people's attention.

GEOGRAPHIC COVERAGE

The question of where to promote relates to geographic considerations. The question is, where will the ad dollars be more wisely spent? Should we allocate additional promotional monies to those markets where the brand is already the leader to maintain market share, or does more potential exist in those markets where the firm is

$$BDI = \frac{\text{Percentage of brand sales in Ontario}}{\text{Percentage of Canadian population in Ontario}} \times 100$$

$$= \frac{50\%}{38\%} \times 100$$

$$= 132$$

FIGURE 9–6

Calculating BDI

□□□□□

not doing as well and there is more room to grow? Perhaps the best answer is that the firm should spend advertising and promotion dollars where they will be the most effective—that is, in those markets where they will achieve the desired objectives. Two useful calculations that marketers examine to make this decision are the Brand Development Index and the Category Development Index.

The **Brand Development Index (BDI)** helps marketers factor the rate of product usage by geographic area into the decision process.

$$BDI = \frac{\text{Percentage of brand to total Canadian sales in the market}}{\text{Percentage of total Canadian population in the market}} \times 100$$

The BDI compares the percentage of the brand's total sales in a given market area with the percentage of the total population in the market to determine the sales potential for that brand in that market area. An example of this calculation is shown in Figure 9–6. The higher the index number, the more market potential exists. In this case, the index number indicates this market has high potential for brand development.

The **Category Development Index (CDI)** is computed in the same manner as the BDI, except it uses information regarding the product category (as opposed to the brand) in the numerator:

$$CDI = \frac{\text{Percentage of product category total sales in market}}{\text{Percentage of total Canadian population in market}} \times 100$$

The CDI provides information on the potential for development of the total product category rather than specific brands. When this information is combined with the BDI, a much more insightful promotional strategy may be developed. One might first look at how well the product category does in a specific market area. In Alberta, for example, the category potential is low (see Figure 9–7). The marketer analyzes the BDI to find how the brand is doing relative to other brands in this area. This information can then be used in determining how well a particular product category and a particular brand are performing and figuring what media weight (or quantity of advertising) would be required to gain additional market share, as shown in Figure 9–8.

In addition to the BDI and CDI considerations, some geographic decisions are based on the availability of the product. For example, Primus launched the first national Web telephone service in North America using voice-over Internet protocol

$$CDI = \frac{\text{Percentage of product category sales in Alberta}}{\text{Percentage of total Canadian population in Alberta}} \times 100$$

$$= \frac{8\%}{10\%} \times 100$$

$$= 80$$

$$BDI = \frac{\text{Percentage of total brand sales in Alberta}}{\text{Percentage of total Canadian population in Alberta}} \times 100$$

$$= \frac{15\%}{10\%} \times 100$$

$$= 150$$

FIGURE 9–7

Using CDI and BDI to determine market potential

FIGURE 9–8
Using BDI and CDI
indexes
□ □ □ □ □

	High BDI	Low BDI
High CDI	High market share Good market potential	Low market share Good market potential
Low CDI	High market share Monitor for sales decline	Low market share Poor market potential

High BDI and high CDI	This market usually represents good sales potential for both the product category and the brand.
High BDI and low CDI	The category is not selling well, but the brand is; probably a good market to advertise in but should be monitored for declining sales.
Low BDI and high CDI	The product category shows high potential but the brand is not doing well; the reasons should be determined.
Low BDI and low CDI	Both the product category and the brand are doing poorly; not likely to be a good place for advertising.

(VOIP) technology. The TalkBroadband offering promises long distance savings of 15 percent and attempts to pre-empt cable companies in the long-distance phone market and sway current telephone users. While national in scope for the long-term, the radio, print, and transit ads are shown in Toronto, Montreal, Vancouver, Halifax, Calgary, Ottawa, and Edmonton, cities where the product is initially sold.[4]

SCHEDULING

Obviously, companies would like to keep their advertising in front of consumers at all times as a constant reminder of the product and/or brand name. In reality, this is not possible for a variety of reasons (not the least of which is the budget). Nor is it necessary. The primary objective of scheduling is to time promotional efforts so that they will coincide with the highest potential buying times. For some products these times are not easy to identify; for others they are very obvious. Three scheduling methods available to the media planner—continuity, flighting, and pulsing—are shown in Figure 9–9.

Continuity refers to a continuous pattern of advertising, which may mean every day, every week, or every month. The key is that a regular (continuous) pattern is developed without gaps or nonadvertising periods. Such strategies might be used for advertising for food products, laundry detergents, or other products consumed on an ongoing basis without regard for seasonality.

A second method, **flighting**, employs a less regular schedule, with intermittent periods of advertising and nonadvertising. At some time periods there are heavier

FIGURE 9–9
Three methods of
promotional scheduling
□ □ □ □ □

promotional expenditures, and at others there may be no advertising. Many banks, for example, spend no money on advertising in the summer but maintain advertising throughout the rest of the year. Snow skis are advertised heavily between October and April; less in May, August, and September; and not at all in June and July.

Pulsing is actually a combination of the first two methods. In a pulsing strategy, continuity is maintained, but at certain times promotional efforts are stepped up. In the automobile industry, advertising continues throughout the year but may increase in April (income-tax refund time), September (when new models are brought out), and the end of the model year. The scheduling strategy depends on the objectives, buying cycles, and the budget, among other factors. There are certain advantages and disadvantages to each scheduling method, as shown in Figure 9–10. One very recent and comprehensive study (acclaimed by many in the TV research community as "the most comprehensive study ever to shed light on scheduling") indicates that continuity is more effective than flighting. On the basis of the idea that it is important to get exposure to the message as close as possible to when the consumer is going to make the purchase, the study concludes that advertisers should continue weekly schedules as long as possible.[5] The key here may be the "as long as possible" qualification. Given a significant budget, continuity may be more of an option than it is for those with more limited budgets.

An interesting twist on scheduling is with Campbell's soup where ads are run when the temperature drops below -5 degrees. A 10-second ad appearing on The Weather Network demonstrates the falling temperature of a thermometer turning into a Campbell's soup can. The voice-over concludes with, "When it's cold outside … warm up with Campbell's," while the visual shows a bowl of soup and the Campbell's slogan "M'm! M'm! Good!" The campaign also features a Web banner in ads in daily e-mails sent by The Weather Network and in newspaper ads adjacent to the weather information in some Toronto newspapers.[6]

255

FIGURE 9–10
Characteristics of scheduling methods

Continuity	
Advantages	Serves as a constant reminder to the consumer Covers the entire buying cycle Allows for media priorities (quantity discounts, preferred locations, etc.)
Disadvantages	Higher costs Potential for overexposure Limited media allocation possible

Flighting	
Advantages	Cost efficiency of advertising only during purchase cycles May allow for inclusion of more than one medium or vehicle with limited budgets
Disadvantages	Weighting may offer more exposure and advantage over competitors Increased likelihood of wearout Lack of awareness, interest, retention or promotional message during nonscheduled times Vulnerability to competitive efforts during nonscheduled periods

Pulsing	
Advantages	All of the same as the previous two methods
Disadvantages	Not required for seasonal products (or other cyclical products)

REACH VERSUS FREQUENCY

Since advertisers have a variety of objectives and face budget constraints, they usually must trade off reach and frequency. They must decide whether to have the message be seen or heard by more people (reach) or by fewer people more often (frequency).

How Much Reach Is Necessary? A universal communication objective is awareness of the product and/or brand. The more consumers are aware, the more they are likely to consider the brand throughout the decision-making process. Achieving awareness requires reach—that is, exposing potential buyers to the message. New brands or products need a very high level of reach, since the objective is to make all potential buyers aware of the new entry. High reach is also desired at later purchase-decision stages. For example, a promotional strategy might use cents-off coupons or free samples to encourage brand trial. An objective of the marketer is to reach a larger number of people with these samples, in an attempt to make them learn of the product, try it, and develop favourable attitudes toward it. (In turn, these attitudes may lead to purchase.)

The problem arises because there is no known way of determining how much reach is required to achieve levels of awareness, attitude change, or buying intentions, nor can we be sure an ad placed in a vehicle will actually reach the intended audience. (There has been some research on the first problem, which will be discussed in the section below on effective reach.)

If you buy advertising time on a popular news program, will everyone who is tuned to the program see the ad? No. Many viewers will leave the room, be distracted during the commercial, and so on, as shown in Figure 9–11 (which also provides a good example of the difference between reach and coverage). If I expose everyone in my target audience to the message once, will this be sufficient to create a 100 percent level of awareness? The answer again is no. This leads to the next question: What frequency of exposure is necessary for the ad to be seen and to have a communication effect?

What Frequency Level Is Needed? With respect to media planning, *frequency* carries a slightly different meaning. (Remember when we said one of the problems in

FIGURE 9–11 ◻ ◻ ◻ ◻   Who's still there to watch the ads?

How many viewers actually watch a commercial? R.D. Percy & Co. reports that its advanced people meters, equipped with heat sensors that detect viewers present, indicate that spots retain, on average, 82 percent of the average-minute ratings for the quarter hour. During early morning news programs, "commercial efficiency" (as Percy calls it), is lower because so many people are bustling about, out of the room (green), but the rate rises at night.

A. Efficiency of Spots during News Programming

6–9 A.M. Mon.–Fri.

| 60 | 35 | 5 |

5–7 P.M. Mon.–Fri.

| 86 | 9 | 5 |

7–8 P.M. Mon.–Fri.

| 84 | 9 | 7 |

11–11:30 P.M. Mon.–Fri.

| 88 | 10 | 2 |

B. Efficiency of Spots during Sports Programming

Noon–3 P.M. Sat.–Sun

| 80 | 6 | 14 |

3–5 P.M. Sat.–Sun

| 79 | 10 | 11 |

5–7 P.M. Sat.–Sun

| 84 | 6 | 10 |

8–11 P.M. Sat.–Sun

| 88 | 1 | 11 |

Percent of program audience retained by spot (commercial efficiency)   Percent of audience lost: out of the room   Percent of audience lost: changing channels media planning is that terms often take on different meanings?) Here frequency is the number of times one is exposed to the media vehicle, not necessarily to the ad itself. While one study has estimated the actual audience for a commercial may be as much as 30 percent lower than that for the program, not all researchers agree.[7] Figure 9–11 demonstrates that depending on the program, this number may range from 12 percent to 40 percent.

Most advertisers do agree that a 1:1 exposure ratio does not exist. So while your ad may be placed in a certain vehicle, the fact that a consumer has been exposed to that vehicle does not ensure that your ad has been seen. As a result, the frequency level expressed in the media plan overstates the actual level of exposure to the ad. This overstatement has led some media buyers to refer to the reach of the media vehicle as "opportunities to see" an ad rather than actual exposure to it.

Because the advertiser has no sure way of knowing whether exposure to a vehicle results in exposure to the ad, the media and advertisers have adopted a compromise: One exposure to the vehicle constitutes reach, given that this exposure must occur for the viewer even to have an opportunity to see the ad. Thus, the exposure figure is used to calculate reach and frequency levels. But this compromise does not help determine the frequency required to make an impact. The creativity of the ad, the involvement of the receiver, noise, and many other intervening factors confound any attempts to make a precise determination.

At this point, you may be thinking, "If nobody knows this stuff, how do they make these decisions?" That's a good question, and the truth is that the decisions are not always made on hard data. Says Joseph Ostrow, executive vice president/director of communications services with Young and Rubicam, "Establishing frequency goals for an advertising campaign is a mix of art and science but with a definite bias toward art."[8] Let us first examine the process involved in setting reach and frequency objectives and then discuss the logic of each.

Establishing Reach and Frequency Levels   It is possible to be exposed to more than one media vehicle with an ad, resulting in repetition (frequency). If one ad is placed on one TV show one time, the number of people exposed is the reach. If the ad is placed on two shows, the total number exposed once is **unduplicated reach**. Some people will see the ad twice. The reach of the two shows, as depicted in Figure 9–12, includes a number of people who were reached by both shows (C). This overlap is referred to as **duplicated reach**.

A. Reach of One TV Program

Total market audience reached

B. Reach of Two Programs

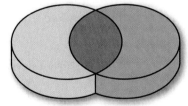

Total market audience reached

C. Duplicate Reach

Total market reached
with both shows

D. Unduplicated Reach

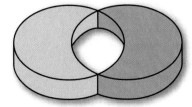

Total reach less
duplicated reach

FIGURE 9–12

Representation of reach
and frequency

257

Both unduplicated and duplicated reach figures are important. Unduplicated reach indicates potential new exposures, while duplicated reach provides an estimate of frequency. Most media buys include both forms of reach. Let us consider an example.

A measure of potential reach in the broadcast industry is the TV (or radio) **program rating**. This number is expressed as a percentage. For an estimate of the total number of homes reached, multiply this percentage times the number of homes with TV sets. For example, if there are 12 million homes with TV sets in Canada and the program has a rating of 30, then the calculation is 0.30 times 12, or 3.6 million homes. (We go into much more detail on ratings and other broadcast terms in Chapter 10.)

Using Gross Ratings Points The media buyer typically uses a numerical indicator to know how many potential audience members may be exposed to a series of commercials. A summary measure that combines the program rating and the average number of times the home is reached during this period (frequency of exposure) is a commonly used reference point known as **gross ratings points (GRP)**:

$$\text{GRP} = \text{Reach} \times \text{Frequency}$$

GRPs are based on the total audience the media schedule may reach; they use a duplicated reach estimate. GRPs can be calculated for the total population aged 2+, Adults 18+, Adults 18–34, Adults 18–49, or several other measured demographic groups.

The advertiser must ask: How many GRPs are needed to attain a certain reach? How do these GRPs translate into effective reach? For example, how many GRPs must one purchase to attain an unduplicated reach of 50 percent, and what frequency of exposure will this schedule deliver? The following example may help you to understand how this process works.

First you must know what these ratings points represent. A purchase of 100 GRPs could mean 100 percent of the market is exposed once or 50 percent of the market is exposed twice or 25 percent of the market is exposed four times, and so on. As you can see, this information must be more specific for the marketer to use it effectively. To know how many GRPs are necessary, the manager needs to know how many members of the intended audience the schedule actually reaches. The chart in Figure 9–13 helps make this determination.

In Figure 9–13, a purchase of 100 GRPs on one network would yield an estimated reach of 32 percent of the total households in the target audience. This figure would climb to 37.2 percent if two networks were used and 44.5 percent with three. Working backward through the formula for GRPs, the estimate of frequency of exposure—3.125, 2.688, and 2.247, respectively—demonstrates the trade-off between reach and frequency. This naturally leads to the question of how much frequency is required.

Figure 9–14 summarizes the effects that can be expected at different levels of exposure, on the basis of research in this area. A number of factors may be operating,

FIGURE 9–13

Estimates of reach for network GRPs

☐☐☐☐☐

A = 1 network   B = 2 networks   C = 3 networks

FIGURE 9–14
The effects of reach and frequency
☐ ☐ ☐ ☐ ☐

1. One exposure of an ad to a target group within a purchase cycle has little or no effect in most circumstances.

2. Since one exposure is usually ineffective, the central goal of productive media planning should be to enhance frequency rather than reach.

3. The evidence suggests strongly that an exposure frequency of two within a purchase cycle is an effective level.

4. Beyond three exposures within a brand purchase cycle or over a period of four or even eight weeks, increasing frequency continues to build advertising effectiveness at a decreasing rate but with no evidence of decline.

5. Although there are general principles with respect to frequency of exposure and its relationship to advertising effectiveness, differential effects by brand are equally important.

6. Nothing we have seen suggests that frequency response principles or generalizations vary by medium.

7. The data strongly suggest that wearout is not a function of too much frequency; it is more of a creative or copy problem.

and direct relationships may be difficult to establish.[9] In addition to the results shown in Figure 9–14, Joseph Ostrow has shown that while the number of repetitions increases awareness rapidly, it has much less impact on attitudinal and behavioural responses.[10]

Determining Effective Reach   Since marketers have budget constraints, they must decide whether to increase reach at the expense of frequency or increase the frequency of exposure but to a smaller audience. A number of factors influence this decision. For example, a new product or brand introduction will attempt to maximize reach, particularly unduplicated reach, to create awareness in as many people as possible as quickly as possible. At the same time, for a high-involvement product or one whose benefits are not obvious, a certain level of frequency is needed to achieve effective reach.

   Effective reach represents the percentage of a vehicle's audience reached at each effective frequency increment. This concept is based on the assumption that one exposure to an ad may not be enough to convey the desired message. As we saw earlier, no one knows the exact number of exposures necessary for an ad to make an impact, although advertisers have settled on three as the minimum. Effective reach (exposure) is shown in the shaded area in Figure 9–15 in the range of 3 to 10 exposures. Fewer

FIGURE 9–15 ☐ ☐ ☐ ☐   Graph of effective reach

Total Exposure versus Effective Exposure of a Prime-Time Television Schedule

Total exposure = 400 GRPs
Effective exposure = 221 ERPs

GRPs = Gross rating points
ERPs = Effective rating points

No exposure
Ineffective exposure
Threshold of effectiveness
Reinforcement of effectiveness
Effective exposure
Excessive exposure
Negative exposure

Percent reach

Number of exposures

than 3 exposures is considered insufficient reach, while more than 10 is considered overexposure and thus ineffective reach. This exposure level is no guarantee of effective communication; different messages may require more or fewer exposures. For example, Jack Myers, president of Myers Reports, argues that the three-exposure theory was valid in the 1970s when consumers were exposed to approximately 1,000 ads per day. Now that they are exposed to 3,000 to 5,000 per day, three exposures may not be enough. Adding in the fragmentation of television, the proliferation of magazines, and the advent of a variety of alternative media leads Myers to believe that 12 exposures may be the minimum level of frequency required. Also, Jim Surmanek, vice president of International Communications Group, contends that the complexity of the message, message length, and recency of exposure also impact this figure.[11]

Since they do not know how many times the viewer will actually be exposed, advertisers typically purchase GRPs that lead to more than three exposures to increase the likelihood of effective reach and frequency.

Determining effective reach is further complicated by the fact that when calculating GRPs, advertisers use a figure that they call **average frequency**, or the average number of times the target audience reached by a media schedule is exposed to the vehicle over a specified period. The problem with this figure is revealed in the following scenario:

Consider a media buy in which:

50 percent of audience is reached 1 time.
30 percent of audience is reached 5 times.
20 percent of audience is reached 10 times.
Average frequency = 4

In this media buy, the average frequency is 4, which is slightly more than the number established as effective. Yet a full 50 percent of the audience receives only one exposure. Thus, the average frequency number can be misleading, and using it to calculate GRPs might result in underexposing the audience.

Although GRPs have their problems, they can provide useful information to the marketer. A certain level of GRPs is necessary to achieve awareness, and increases in GRPs are likely to lead to more exposures and/or more repetitions—both of which are necessary to have an effect on higher-order objectives. Perhaps the best advice for purchasing GRPs is offered by Ostrow, who recommends the following strategies:[12]

1. Instead of using average frequency, the marketer should decide what minimum frequency goal is needed to reach the advertising objectives effectively and then maximize reach at that frequency level.
2. To determine effective frequency, one must consider marketing factors, message factors, and media factors. (See Figure 9–16.)

In summary, the reach-versus-frequency decision, while critical, is very difficult to make. A number of factors must be considered, and concrete rules do not always apply. The decision is often more of an art than a science.

MEDIA TACTICS DECISIONS

Once the initial media strategy has been determined, the marketer addresses three media tactics decisions: media vehicle, budget adjustments, and blocking chart.

MEDIA VEHICLE

Once the medium or media has been determined, the media planner must consider the most suitable media vehicle. Certain media vehicles enhance the creativity of a message because they create a mood that carries over to the communication. For example, think about the moods created by the following magazines: *Gourmet,*

Marketing Factors

- *Brand history.* Is the brand new or established? New brands generally require higher frequency levels.
- *Brand share.* An inverse relationship exists between brand share and frequency. The higher the brand share, the lower the frequency level required.
- *Brand loyalty.* An inverse relationship exists between loyalty and frequency. The higher the loyalty, the lower the frequency level required.
- *Purchase cycles.* Shorter purchasing cycles require higher frequency levels to maintain top-of-mind awareness.
- *Usage cycle.* Products used daily or more often need to be replaced quickly, so a higher level of frequency is desired.
- *Competitive share of voice.* Higher frequency levels are required when a lot of competitive noise exists and when the goal is to meet or beat competitors.
- *Target group.* The ability of the target group to learn and to retain messages has a direct effect on frequency.

Message or Creative Factors

- *Message complexity.* The simpler the message, the less frequency required.
- *Message uniqueness.* The more unique the message, the lower the frequency level required.
- *New versus continuing campaigns.* New campaigns require higher levels of frequency to register the message.
- *Image versus product sell.* Creating an image requires higher levels of frequency than does a specific product sell.
- *Message variation.* A single message requires less frequency; a variety of messages requires more.
- *Wearout.* Higher frequency may lead to wearout. This effect must be tracked and used to evaluate frequency levels.
- *Advertising units.* Larger units of advertising require less frequency than smaller ones to get the message across.

Media Factors

- *Clutter.* The more advertising that appears in the media used, the more frequency is needed to break through the clutter.
- *Editorial environment.* The more consistent the ad is with the editorial environment, the less frequency is needed.
- *Attentiveness.* The higher the level of attention achieved by the media vehicle, the less frequency is required. Low-attention-getting media require more repetitions.
- *Scheduling.* Continuous scheduling requires less frequency than does flighting or pulsing.
- *Number of media used.* The fewer media used, the lower the level of frequency required.
- *Repeat exposures.* Media that allow for more repeat exposures (for example, monthly magazines) require less frequency.

FIGURE 9–16

Factors important in determining frequency levels

261

Skiing, Travel, and *House Beautiful.* Each of these special-interest vehicles puts the reader in a particular mood. The promotion of fine wines, ski boots, luggage, and home products is enhanced by this mood. What different images might be created for your product if you advertised it in the following media?

The National Post versus the *Toronto Star*
Architectural Digest versus *Reader's Digest*
A highly rated prime-time TV show versus an old rerun

The message may require a specific medium and a certain media vehicle to achieve its objectives. Likewise, certain media and vehicles have images that may carry over to the perceptions of messages placed within them. The explanation of these considerations is the **vehicle option source effect**, "the differential impact that the advertising exposure will have on the same audience member if the exposure occurs in one media option rather than another."[13] People perceive ads differently depending on their context.[14]

Once the media vehicle consideration is resolved, the media planner considers some other fine-tuning. The location within a particular medium (front page versus back page) and size of ad or length of commercial also merit examination. For example, research has demonstrated that readers pay more attention to larger ads.[15]

BUDGET ADJUSTMENTS

One of the more important decisions in the development of media strategy is cost estimating. The value of any strategy can be determined by how well it delivers the message to the audience with the lowest cost and the least waste. We have already explored a number of factors, such as reach, frequency, and availability, that affect this decision. The marketer tries to arrive at the optimal delivery by balancing cost with each of these. As the following discussion shows, understanding cost figures may not be as easy as it seems and knowledge of them can improve a media plan as it reaches the tactical stage.

Advertising and promotional costs can be categorized in two ways. The **absolute cost** of the medium or vehicle is the actual total cost required to place the message. For example, a full-page four-colour ad in Chatelaine magazine costs about $42,000. **Relative cost** refers to the relationship between the price paid for advertising time or space and the size of the audience delivered; it is used to compare media vehicles. Relative costs are important because the manager must try to optimize audience delivery within budget constraints. Since a number of alternatives are available for delivering the message, the advertiser must evaluate the relative costs associated with these choices. The way media costs are provided and problems in comparing these costs across media often make such evaluations difficult.

Determining Relative Costs of Media To evaluate alternatives, advertisers must compare the relative costs of media as well as vehicles within these media. Unfortunately, the broadcast, print, and out-of-home media do not always provide the same cost breakdowns, nor necessarily do vehicles within the print media. Following are the cost bases used:

1. **Cost per thousand (CPM).** For years the magazine industry has provided cost breakdowns on the basis of cost per thousand people reached. The formula for this computation is

$$\text{CPM} = \frac{\text{Cost of ad space (absolute cost)}}{\text{Circulation}} \times 1,000$$

Figure 9–17 provides an example of this computation for two vehicles in the same medium—*Canadian Living* and *Chatelaine*—and shows that (all other things being equal) *Canadian Living* is a more cost-effective buy. (We will come back to "all other things being equal" in a moment.)

FIGURE 9–17
Cost per thousand computations: *Canadian Living* versus *Chatelaine*

□□□□□

	Canadian Living	*Chatelaine*
Per-page cost	$30,935	$41,750
Circulation	542,815	717,249
Calculation of CPM	$\dfrac{\$30,935 \times 1,000}{542,815}$	$\dfrac{\$41,750 \times 1,000}{717,249}$
CPM	$56.99	$58.21

	CSI	Survivor
Cost per spot ad	$9,000	$8,000
Rating	20	19
Reach (households)	195,140	185,383
Calculation	$9,000/20	$8,000/19
CPRP (CPP)	$450	$421

FIGURE 9–18
Comparison of cost per ratings point: *CSI* versus *Survivor* in a local TV market
☐ ☐ ☐ ☐ ☐

2. **Cost per ratings point (CPRP).** The broadcast media provide a different comparative cost figure, referred to as cost per ratings point or *cost per point (CPP)*, based on the following formula:

$$CPRP = \frac{\text{Cost of commercial time}}{\text{Program rating}}$$

An example of this calculation for a spot ad in a local TV market is shown in Figure 9–18. It indicates that *Survivor* would be more cost-effective than *CSI*.

3. **Daily inch rate.** Like magazines, newspapers now use the cost-per-thousand formula discussed earlier to determine relative costs. As shown in Figure 9–19, the *National Post* costs significantly more to advertise in than does the *Globe and Mail* (again, all other things being equal).

As you can see, it is difficult to make comparisons across various media. What is the broadcast equivalent of cost per thousand? In an attempt to standardize relative costing procedures, the broadcast and newspaper media have begun to provide costs per thousand, using the following formulas:

Television: $\dfrac{\text{Cost of 1 unit of time} \times 1,000}{\text{Program rating}}$ Newspapers: $\dfrac{\text{Cost of ad space} \times 1,000}{\text{Circulation}}$

While the comparison of media on a cost-per-thousand basis is important, inter-media comparisons can be misleading. The ability of TV to provide both sight and sound, the longevity of magazines, and other characteristics of each medium make direct comparisons difficult. The media planner should use the cost-per-thousand numbers but must also consider the specific characteristics of each medium and each media vehicle in the decision.

The cost per thousand may overestimate or underestimate the actual cost effectiveness. Consider a situation where some waste coverage is inevitable because the circulation exceeds the target audience. If the people reached by this message are not potential buyers of the product, then having to pay to reach them results in too low a cost per thousand, as shown in scenario A of Figure 9–20. We must use the potential reach to the target audience—the destination sought—rather than the overall circulation figure. A medium with a much higher cost per thousand may be

263

	Globe and Mail	National Post
Cost per page	$50,850	$45,993
Circulation	363,058	311,343
Calculation	$CPM = \dfrac{\text{Page cost} \times 1,000}{\text{Circulation}}$	
	$= \dfrac{\$50,850 \times 1,000}{363,058}$	$\dfrac{\$45,993 \times 1,000}{311,343}$
	$140.06	$147.72

FIGURE 9–19
Comparative costs in newspaper advertising
☐ ☐ ☐ ☐ ☐

FIGURE 9–20
Cost per thousand
estimates
☐☐☐☐☐

Scenario A: Overestimation of Efficiency

Target audience	18–49
Magazine circulation	400,000
Circulation to target audience	65% (260,000)
Cost per page	$15,600

$$\text{CPM} = \frac{\$15,600 \times 1,000}{400,000} = \$39$$

$$\text{CPM (actual target audience)} = \frac{\$15,600 \times 1,000}{260,000} = \$60$$

Scenario B: Underestimation of Efficiency

Target audience	All age groups, male and female
Magazine circulation	400,000
Cost per page	$15,600
Pass-along rate	3

$$\text{CPM (based on readers per copy)} = \frac{\text{Page cost} \times 1,000}{260,000 + 3(260,000)} = \frac{\$15,600 \times 1,000}{1,040,000}$$

$$= \$15.00$$

*Assuming pass-along was valid.

a wiser buy if it is reaching more potential receivers. (Most media buyers rely on **target CPM (TCPM)**, which calculates CPMs based on the target audience, not the overall audience.)

CPM may also underestimate cost efficiency. Magazine advertising space sellers have argued for years that because more than one person may read an issue, the actual reach is underestimated. They want to use the number of **readers per copy** as the true circulation. This would include a **pass-along rate**, estimating the number of people who read the magazine without buying it. Scenario B in Figure 9–20 shows how this underestimates cost efficiency. Consider a family in which a father, mother, and two teenagers read each issue of *Maclean's*. While the circulation figure includes only one magazine, in reality there are four potential exposures in these households, increasing the total reach.

While the number of readers per copy makes intuitive sense, it has the potential to be extremely inaccurate. The actual number of times the magazine changes hands is difficult to determine. While research is conducted, pass-along estimates are very subjective and using them to estimate reach is speculative. These figures are regularly provided by the media, but managers are selective about using them. At the same time, the art of media buying enters, for many magazines' managers have a good idea how much greater the reach is than their circulation figures provided.

In addition to the potential for over- or underestimation of cost efficiencies, CPMs are limited in that they make only quantitative estimates of the value of media. While they may be good for comparing very similar vehicles, they are less valuable in making intermedia comparisons. We have already noted some differences among media that preclude direct comparisons.

BLOCKING CHART

The media planning process typically concludes with a blocking chart. The **blocking chart** summarizes many of the media strategy and media tactics decisions made thus far, and includes extensive implementation details that guide the media buyers as they attempt to achieve the media objectives.

A blocking chart is typically formatted according to some type of calendar. While it is often done on a weekly basis, a firm with limited communications may organize it monthly. On the other hand, a firm with extensive communications may produce a blocking chart on a daily basis for all or critical parts of its annual media plan. For example, if a firm launches a new product, daily communications during the first few weeks can be critical and specific media exposure is planned in minute detail.

A synopsis of the media choice decisions with respect to television, print, and out-of-home media may also be contained in the blocking chart. In this age of IMC, the blocking chart can also contain elements of other communication tools such as marketing events, public relations, or direct response tools. In all likelihood, the blocking chart will break these media choices down by different vehicles and different geographic markets.

Another key detail of the blocking chart is showing the relative weight of media expenditures. For example, it could illustrate the number of GRPs per week for each city. Related to this is a clear indication of the reach and frequency of each media decision.

Because the blocking chart concludes the media planning process, the media expenditures have to be included either in summary form or accompanying the blocking chart. This information allows managers to assess the quality of the media plan and to determine if any adjustments need to be made during the planning time frame.

While we have briefly highlighted the nature of a blocking chart, it may in fact be more than one chart. If a firm is using multiple media across many months and geographic markets, it may have one summary chart and other supporting charts that break the information down into more readable and action-oriented subsections. Remember that a blocking chart is also a communication tool that has to be organized and presented so that all participants are familiar with all decisions.

MEDIA BUDGET

We noted earlier in this chapter that the media plan has to contribute its part in achieving communication objectives such as brand awareness and brand attitude. While establishing media and communication objectives are an important part of the planning process, the degree to which these objectives can be obtained is a function of the media budget or how much the firm wishes to invest in advertising. No organization has an unlimited budget, so objectives must be set with the budget in mind and the budget has to be realistic to achieve any media and communication objectives.

We include the media budget issues in this chapter because of this inherent trade-off between objectives and financial resources. We do not discuss budget issues for other IMC tools extensively in this book for two reasons. First, the remaining IMC tools are often dependent on media expenditures. For example, aspects of public relations campaigns use media. Advertisers use media advertising to direct visitors to their websites. Second, as we noted earlier in this book, the planning process for all marketing communications follows or is consistent with established planning processes of advertising. Thus, the budgeting concepts here directly transfer to other IMC tools.

The size of a firm's advertising and promotions budget can vary from a few thousand dollars to millions. When companies such as Procter & Gamble and General Motors spend millions of dollars per year to promote their products, they expect such expenditures to accomplish their stated objectives. The budget decision is no less critical to a firm spending only a few thousand dollars; its ultimate success or failure may depend on the monies spent. One of the most critical decisions facing the marketing manager is how much to spend on the promotional effort.

Unfortunately, many managers fail to realize the value of advertising and promotion. They treat the communications budget as an expense rather than an investment. Instead of viewing the dollars spent as contributing to additional sales and market share, they see budget expenses as cutting into profits. As a result, when times get tough, the advertising and promotional budget is the first to be cut—even though there is strong evidence that exactly the opposite should occur. Moreover, the decision is not a one-time responsibility. A new budget is formulated every year, each time a new product is introduced, or when either internal or external factors necessitate a change to maintain competitiveness.

The remainder of this section provides insight into some underlying theory with respect to budget setting, discusses how companies budget for promotional efforts, and demonstrates the inherent strengths and weaknesses associated with these theoretical and managerial approaches.

THEORETICAL APPROACHES IN BUDGET SETTING

Most of the approaches used to establish advertising budgets are based on marginal analysis or sales response models.

Marginal Analysis Figure 9–21 graphically represents the concept of **marginal analysis**. As advertising/promotional expenditures increase, sales and gross margins also increase to a point, but then they level off. Profits are shown to be a result of the gross margin minus advertising expenditures. Using this theory to establish its budget, a firm would continue to spend advertising/promotional dollars as long as the marginal revenues created by these expenditures exceeded the incremental advertising/promotional costs. As shown on the graph, the optimal expenditure level is the point where marginal costs equal the marginal revenues they generate (point A). If the sum of the advertising/promotional expenditures exceeded the revenues they generated, one would conclude the appropriations were too high and scale down the budget. If revenues were higher, a higher budget might be in order.

While marginal analysis seems logical intuitively, certain weaknesses limit its usefulness. These weaknesses include the assumptions that (1) sales are a direct result of advertising and promotional expenditures and this effect can be measured and (2) advertising and promotion are solely responsible for sales. Let us examine each of these assumptions in more detail.

1. *Assumption that sales are a direct measure of advertising and promotions efforts.* Previously, we discussed the fact that the advertiser needs to set communications objectives that contribute to accomplishing overall marketing objectives but at the same time are separate. One reason for this strategy is that it is often difficult, if not impossible, to demonstrate the effects of advertising and promotions on sales. In studies using sales as a direct measure, it has been almost impossible to establish the contribution of advertising and promotion.[16] Thus, to try to show that the size of the budget will directly affect sales of the product is misleading. A more logical approach would be to examine the impact of specific budgets for each communication tool on the attainment of specific communications objectives for each tool.

FIGURE 9–21
Marginal analysis
□ □ □ □ □

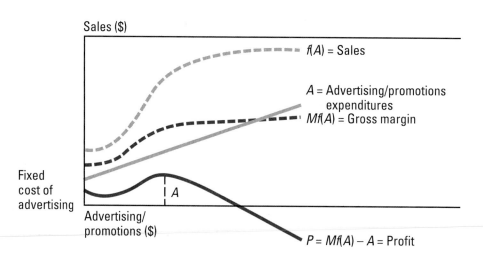

Sales ($)

$f(A)$ = Sales

A = Advertising/promotions expenditures
$Mf(A)$ = Gross margin

Fixed cost of advertising

A

Advertising/promotions ($)

$P = Mf(A) - A$ = Profit

2. *Assumption that sales are determined solely by advertising and promotion.* This assumption ignores the remaining elements of the marketing mix—price, product, and distribution—which do contribute to a company's success. Environmental factors may also affect the promotional program, leading the marketing manager to assume the advertising was or was not effective when some other factor may have helped or hindered the accomplishment of the desired objectives.

Sales Response Models You may have wondered why the sales curve in Figure 9–21 shows sales levelling off even though advertising and promotions efforts continue to increase. The relationship between advertising and sales has been the topic of much research and discussion designed to determine the shape of the response curve.

Almost all advertisers subscribe to one of two models of the advertising/sales response function: the concave-downward function or the S-shaped response curve.

- *The concave-downward function.* After reviewing more than 100 studies of the effects of advertising on sales, Julian Simon and Johan Arndt concluded that the effects of advertising budgets follow the microeconomic law of diminishing returns.[17] That is, as the amount of advertising increases, its incremental value decreases. The logic is that those with the greatest potential to buy will likely act on the first (or earliest) exposures, while those less likely to buy are not likely to change as a result of the advertising. For those who may be potential buyers, each additional ad will supply little or no new information that will affect their decision. Thus, according to the **concave-downward function model**, the effects of advertising quickly begin to diminish, as shown in Figure 9–22A. Budgeting under this model suggests that fewer advertising dollars may be needed to create the optimal influence on sales.
- *The S-shaped response function.* Many advertising managers assume the **S-shaped response curve** (Figure 9–22B), which projects an S-shaped response function to the budget outlay (again measured in sales). Initial outlays of the advertising budget have little impact (as indicated by the essentially flat sales curve in range A). After a certain budget level has been reached (the beginning of range B), advertising and promotional efforts begin to have an effect, as additional increments of expenditures result in increased sales. This incremental gain continues only to a point, however, because at the

FIGURE 9–22 □ □ □ □ Advertising sales/response functions

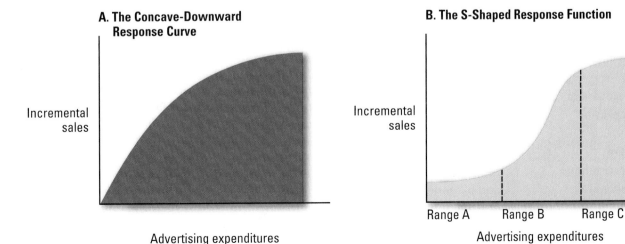

A. The Concave-Downward Response Curve

Incremental sales

Advertising expenditures

B. The S-Shaped Response Function

Incremental sales

Range A   Range B   Range C

Advertising expenditures

beginning of range C additional expenditures begin to return little or nothing in the way of sales. This model suggests a small advertising budget is likely to have no impact beyond the sales that may have been generated through other means (for example, word of mouth). At the other extreme, more does not necessarily mean better: Additional dollars spent beyond range B have no additional impact on sales and for the most part can be considered wasted. As with marginal analysis, one would attempt to operate at that point on the curve in area B where the maximum return for the money is attained.

Even though marginal analysis and the sales response curves may not apply directly, they give managers some insight into a theoretical basis of how the budgeting process should work. Some empirical evidence indicates the models may have validity. One study, based on industry experience, has provided support for the S-shaped response curve; the results indicate that a minimum amount of advertising dollars must be spent before there is a noticeable effect on sales.[18] Despite this, it is important to consider other issues.

A weakness in attempting to use sales as a direct measure of response to advertising is that various situational factors may have an effect. In one comprehensive study, 20 variables were shown to affect the advertising/sales ratio. Figure 9–23 lists these factors and their relationships.[19] For a product characterized by emotional buying motives, hidden product qualities, and/or a strong basis for differentiation, advertising would have a noticeable impact on sales. Products characterized as large dollar purchases and those in the maturity or decline stages of the product would be less likely to benefit. The study showed that other factors involving the market, customer, costs, and strategies employed have different effects.

FIGURE 9–23 ☐ ☐ ☐ ☐   Factors influencing advertising budgets

Factor	Relationship of Advertising/Sales	Factor	Relationship of Advertising/Sales
Product Factors		**Customer Factors**	
Basis for differentiation	+	Industrial products users	—
Hidden product qualities	+	Concentration of users	+
Emotional buying motives	+	**Strategy Factors**	
Durability	—	Regional markets	—
Large dollar purchase	—	Early stage of brand life cycle	+
Purchase frequency	Curvilinear	High margins in channels	—
Market Factors		Long channels of distribution	+
Stage of product life cycle		High prices	+
Introductory	+	High quality	+
Growth	+	**Cost Factors**	
Maturity	—	High profit margins	+
Decline	—		
Inelastic demand	+		
Market share	—		
Competition			
Active	+		
Concentrated	+		
Pioneer in market	—		

Note: + relationship means the factor leads to a positive effect of advertising on sales; — relationship indicates little or no effect of advertising on sales.

The results of this study are interesting but limited, since they relate primarily to the percentage of sales dollars allocated to advertising and the factors influencing these ratios. As we will see later in this chapter, the percentage-of-sales method of budgeting has inherent weaknesses in that the advertising and sales effects may be reversed. So we cannot be sure whether the situation actually led to the advertising/sales relationship or vice versa. Thus, while these factors should be considered in the budget appropriation decision, they should not be the sole determinants of where and when to increase or decrease expenditures.

MANAGERIAL APPROACHES IN BUDGET SETTING

The theoretical approaches to establishing the promotional budget are seldom employed. In smaller firms, they may never be used. Instead, a number of methods developed through practice and experience are implemented. This section reviews some of the more traditional methods of setting budgets and the relative advantages and disadvantages of each. First, you must understand two things: (1) Many firms employ more than one method, and (2) budgeting approaches vary according to the size and sophistication of the firm. Prior to discussing these approaches, we review a few factors that managers consider as they set the budget.

Factors Influencing the Budget Decision

Market Size   The size of the market affects the amount of money invested in promotion. In smaller markets, it is often easier and less expensive to reach the target audience. Too much of an expenditure in these markets will lead to saturation and a lack of effective spending. In larger markets, the target audience may be more dispersed and thus more expensive to reach. These cost issues are explored further in the media tactics section.

Market Potential   For a variety of reasons, some markets hold more potential than others. When particular markets hold higher potential, the marketing manager may decide to allocate additional monies to them. Keep in mind that just because a market does not have high sales does not mean it should be ignored. The key is potential—and a market with low sales but high potential may be a candidate for additional appropriations.

Market Share Goals   Two recent studies in the *Harvard Business Review* discussed advertising spending with the goal of maintaining and increasing market share.[20] John Jones compared the brand's share of market with its share of advertising voice (the total value of the main media exposure in the product category). Jones classified the brands as "profit taking brands, or underspenders" and "investment brands, those whose share of voice is clearly above their share of market." His study indicated that for those brands with small market shares, profit takers are in the minority; however, as the brands increase their market share, nearly three out of five have a proportionately smaller share of voice.

Jones noted that three factors can be cited to explain this change. First, new brands generally receive higher-than-average advertising support. Second, older, more mature brands are often "milked"—that is, when they reach the maturity stage, advertising support is reduced. Third, there's an advertising economy of scale whereby advertising works harder for well-established brands, so a lower expenditure is required. Jones concluded that for larger brands, it may be possible to reduce advertising expenditures and still maintain market share. Smaller brands, on the other hand, have to continue to maintain a large share of voice.

James Schroer addressed the advertising budget in a situation where the marketer wishes to increase market share. His analysis suggests that marketers should:

- Segment markets, focusing on those markets where competition is weak and/or underspending instead of on a national advertising effort.

- Determine their competitors' cost positions (how long the competition can continue to spend at the current or increased rate).
- Resist the lure of short-term profits that result from ad budget cuts.
- Consider niching strategies as opposed to long-term wars.

Figure 9–24 shows Schroer's suggestions for spending priorities in various markets.

Economies of Scale in Advertising   Some studies have presented evidence that firms and/or brands maintaining a large share of the market have an advantage over smaller competitors and thus can spend less money on advertising and realize a better return.[21] Larger advertisers can maintain advertising shares that are smaller than their market shares because they get better advertising rates, have declining average costs of production, and accrue the advantages of advertising several products jointly. In addition, they are likely to enjoy more favourable time and space positions, cooperation of middlepeople, and favourable publicity. These advantages are known as **economies of scale**.

Reviewing the studies in support of this position and then conducting research over a variety of small package products, Kent Lancaster found that this situation did not hold true and that in fact larger brand share products might actually be at a disadvantage.[22] His results indicated that leading brands spend an average of 2.5 percentage points more than their brand share on advertising. The results of this and other studies suggest there really are no economies of scale to be accrued from the size of the firm or the market share of the brand.[23]

IMC Tools   Direct marketing, the Internet, and other promotional tools are also receiving increased attention and requiring additional budget for marketing communications. The degree to which a firm engages in more tools to achieve its communication objectives also has an impact on a firm's investment in marketing communications. This strategic decision among IMC tools has organization implications that guide the marketing communications investment.

In a review of the literature on how allocation decisions are made between advertising and sales promotion, George Low and Jakki Mohr concluded that organizational factors play an important role in determining how communications dollars are spent.[24] The authors note that the following factors influence the allocation decision. These factors vary from one organization to another, and each influences the relative amounts assigned to advertising and promotion:

- The organization's structure—centralized versus decentralized, formalization, and complexity.
- Power and politics in the organizational hierarchy.
- The use of expert opinions (e.g., consultants).
- Characteristics of the decision maker (preferences and experience).
- Approval and negotiation channels.
- Pressure on senior managers to arrive at the optimal budget.

One example of how these factors might influence allocations relates to the level of interaction between marketing and other functional departments, such as

FIGURE 9–24

The share of voice (SOV) effect and ad spending: priorities in individual markets accounting and operations. The authors note that the relative importance of advertising versus sales promotion might vary from department to department. Accountants, being dollars-and-cents minded, would argue for the sales impact of promotions, while operations would argue against sales promotions because the sudden surges in demand that might result would throw off production schedules. The marketing department might be influenced by the thinking of either of these groups in making its decision.

Top-Down Approaches   The approaches discussed in this section may be referred to as **top-down approaches** because a budgetary amount is established (usually at an executive level) and then the monies are passed down to the various departments (as shown in Figure 9–25). These budgets are essentially predetermined and have no true theoretical basis. Top-down methods include the affordable method, arbitrary allocation, percentage of sales, competitive parity, and return on investment (ROI).

The Affordable Method   In the **affordable method** (often referred to as the "all-you-can-afford method"), the firm determines the amount to be spent in various areas such as production and operations. Then it allocates what's left to advertising and promotion, considering this to be the amount it can afford. The task to be performed by the advertising/promotions function is not considered, and the likelihood of under- or overspending is high, as no guidelines for measuring the effects of various budgets are established.

Strange as it may seem, this approach is common among small firms. Unfortunately, it is also used in large firms, particularly those that are not marketing-driven and do not understand the role of advertising and promotion. For example, many high-tech firms focus on new product development and engineering and assume that the product, if good enough, will sell itself. In these companies, little money may be left for performing the advertising and promotions tasks.

The logic for this approach stems from "We can't be hurt with this method" thinking. That is, if we know what we can afford and we do not exceed it, we will not get into financial problems. While this may be true in a strictly accounting sense, it does not reflect sound managerial decision making from a marketing perspective. Often this method does not allocate enough money to get the product off the ground and into the market. In terms of the S-shaped sales response model, the firm is operat-

271

Top-Down Budgeting

Top management sets the spending limit

↓

Promotion budget set to stay within spending limit

Bottom-Up Budgeting

Promotion objectives are set

↓

Activities needed to achieve objectives are planned

↓

Costs of promotion activities are budgeted

↓

Total promotion budget is approved by top management

FIGURE 9–25
Top-down versus bottom-up approaches to budget setting

ing in range A. Or the firm may be spending more than necessary, operating in range C. When the market gets tough and sales and/or profits begin to fall, this method is likely to lead to budget cuts at a time when the budget should be increased.

Arbitrary Allocation   Perhaps an even weaker method than the affordable method for establishing a budget is **arbitrary allocation**, in which virtually no theoretical basis is considered and the budgetary amount is often set by fiat. That is, the budget is determined by management solely on the basis of what is felt to be necessary. In a discussion of how managers set advertising budgets, Melvin Salveson reported that these decisions may reflect "as much upon the managers' psychological profile as they do economic criteria."[25] While Salveson was referring to larger corporations, the approach is no less common in small firms and nonprofit organizations.

The arbitrary allocation approach has no obvious advantages. No systematic thinking has occurred, no objectives have been budgeted for, and the concept and purpose of advertising and promotion have been largely ignored. Other than the fact that the manager believes some monies must be spent on advertising and promotion and then picks a number, there is no good explanation why this approach continues to be used. Yet budgets continue to be set this way, and our purpose in discussing this method is to point out only that it is used—not recommended.

Percentage of Sales   Perhaps the most commonly used method for budget setting (particularly in large firms) is the **percentage-of-sales method**, in which the advertising and promotions budget is based on sales of the product. Management determines the amount by either (1) taking a percentage of the sales dollars or (2) assigning a fixed amount of the unit product cost to promotion and multiplying this amount by the number of units sold. These two methods are shown in Figure 9–26.

Proponents of the percentage-of-sales method cite a number of advantages. It is financially safe and keeps ad spending within reasonable limits, as it bases spending on the past year's sales or what the firm expects to sell in the upcoming year. Thus, there will be sufficient monies to cover this budget, with increases in sales leading to budget increases and sales decreases resulting in advertising decreases. The percentage-of-sales method is simple, straightforward, and easy to implement. Regardless of which basis—past or future sales—is employed, the calculations used to arrive at a budget are not difficult. Finally, this budgeting approach is generally stable. While the budget may vary with increases and decreases in sales, as long as these changes are not drastic the manager will have a reasonable idea of the parameters of the budget.

At the same time, the percentage-of-sales method has some serious disadvantages, including the basic premise on which the budget is established: sales. Letting the level of sales determine the amount of advertising and promotions dollars to be spent

FIGURE 9–26

Alternative methods for computing percentage of sales for Eve Cologne

☐ ☐ ☐ ☐ ☐

Method 1: Straight Percentage of Sales		
2000	Total dollar sales	$1,000,000
	Straight % of sales at 10%	$100,000
2001	Advertising budget	$100,000

Method 2: Percentage of Unit Cost		
2000	Cost per bottle to manufacturer	$4.00
	Unit cost allocated to advertising	$1.00
2001	Forecasted sales, 100,000 units	
2001	Advertising budget (100,000 × $1)	$100,000

reverses the cause-and-effect relationship between advertising and sales. It treats advertising as an expense associated with making a sale rather than an investment.

Another problem with this approach was actually cited as an advantage earlier: stability. Proponents say that if all firms use a similar percentage, that will bring stability to the marketplace. But what happens if someone varies from this standard percentage? The problem is that this method does not allow for changes in strategy either internally or from competitors. An aggressive firm may wish to allocate more monies to the advertising and promotions budget, a strategy that is not possible with a per-centage-of-sales method unless the manager is willing to deviate from industry standards.

The percentage-of-sales method of budgeting may result in severe misappropriation of funds. If advertising and promotion have a role to perform in marketing a product, then allocating more monies to advertising will, as shown in the S-shaped curve, generate incremental sales (to a point). If products with low sales have smaller pro-motion budgets, this will hinder sales progress. At the other extreme, very successful products may have excess budgets, some of which may be better appropriated elsewhere.

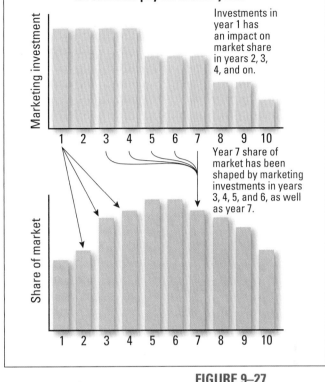

FIGURE 9–27
Investments pay off in later years

□ □ □ □ □

The percentage-of-sales method is also difficult to employ for new product intro-ductions. If no sales histories are available, there is no basis for establishing the budget. Projections of future sales may be difficult, particularly if the product is highly innovative and/or has fluctuating sales patterns.

Finally, if the budget is contingent on sales, decreases in sales will lead to decreases in budgets when they most need to be increased. Continuing to cut the advertising and promotion budgets may just add impetus to the downward sales trend (Figure 9–27). On the other hand, some of the more successful companies have allocated additional funds during hard times or downturns in the cycle of sales. Companies that maintain or increase their ad expenditures during recessions achieve increased visibility and higher growth in both sales and market share (compared to those that reduce advertis-ing outlays). For example, Sunkist can attribute at least some of its success in maintaining its strong image to the fact that it has maintained consistent levels of adver-tising expenditures over 80 years, despite recessions.[26]

A variation on the percentage-of-sales method uses a percentage of projected future sales as a base. This method also uses either a straight percentage of projected sales or a unit cost projection. One advantage of using future sales as a base is that the budget is not based on last year's sales. As the market changes, management must factor the effect of these changes on sales into next year's forecast rather than relying on past data. The resulting budget is more likely to reflect current conditions and be more appropriate. While this appears to be a remedy for some of the prob-lems discussed here, the reality is that problems with forecasting, cyclical growth, and uncontrollable factors limit its effectiveness.

Competitive Parity   If you asked marketing managers if they ever set their advertis-ing and promotions budgets on the basis of what their competitors allocate, they would probably deny it. Yet if you examined the advertising expenditures of these companies, both as a percentage of sales and in respect to the media where they are allocated, you would see little variation in the percentage-of-sales figures for firms within a given industry. Such results do not happen by chance alone. Companies that provide competitive advertising information, trade associations, and other advertising industry periodicals are sources for competitors' expenditures. Larger corporations often subscribe to services that track media and other communication expenditures. For example, videotape services provide competitors with information, and Nielsen's new technology (discussed in Chapter 10) allows full reporting of all commercials. Smaller companies often use a **clipping service**, which clips competitors' ads from local print media, allowing the company to work backward to determine the cumulative costs of the ads placed.

In the **competitive parity method**, managers establish budget amounts by matching the competition's percentage-of-sales expenditures. The argument is that setting budgets in this fashion takes advantage of the collective wisdom of the industry. It also takes the competition into consideration, which leads to stability in the marketplace by minimizing marketing warfare. If companies know that competitors are unlikely to match their increases in promotional spending, they are less likely to take an aggressive posture to attempt to gain market share. This minimizes unusual or unrealistic ad expenditures.

The competitive parity method has a number of disadvantages, however. For one, it ignores the fact that advertising and promotions are designed to accomplish specific objectives by addressing certain problems and opportunities. Second, it assumes that because firms have similar expenditures, their programs will be equally effective. This assumption ignores the contributions of creative executions and/or media allocations, as well as the success or failure of various promotions. Further, it ignores possible advantages of the firm itself; some companies simply make better products than others.

Also, there is no guarantee that competitors will continue to pursue their existing strategies. Since competitive parity figures are determined by examination of competitors' previous years' promotional expenditures (short of corporate espionage), changes in market emphasis and/or spending may not be recognized until the competition has already established an advantage. Further, there is no guarantee that a competitor will not increase or decrease its own expenditures, regardless of what other companies do. Finally, competitive parity may not avoid promotional wars.

In summary, few firms employ the competitive parity method as a sole means of establishing the promotional budget. This method is typically used in conjunction with the percentage-of-sales or other methods. It is never wise to ignore the competition; managers must always be aware of what competitors are doing. But they should not just emulate them in setting goals and developing strategies.

Return on Investment (ROI) In the percentage-of-sales method, sales dictate the level of advertising appropriations. But advertising causes sales. In the marginal analysis and S-shaped curve approaches, incremental investments in advertising and promotions lead to increases in sales. The key word here is *investment*. In the **ROI budgeting method**, advertising and promotions are considered investments, like plant and equipment. Thus, the budgetary appropriation (investment) leads to certain returns. Like other aspects of the firm's efforts, advertising and promotion are expected to earn a certain return.

While the ROI method looks good on paper, the reality is that it is rarely possible to assess the returns provided by the promotional effort—at least as long as sales continue to be the basis for evaluation. Thus, while managers are certain to ask how much return they are getting for such expenditures, the question remains unanswered, and ROI remains a virtually unused method of budgeting.

Summary of Top-Down Budgeting Methods You are probably asking yourself why we even discussed these budgeting methods if they are not recommended for use or have severe disadvantages that limit their effectiveness. But you must understand the various methods used in order to recognize their limitations, especially since these flawed methods are commonly employed by marketers throughout the United States, Europe, and Canada, as demonstrated in the results of a number of research studies shown in Figure 9–28. Tradition and top management's desire for control are probably the major reasons why top-down methods continue to be popular. As shown in Figure 9–28, the use of percentage-of-sales methods and competitive parity remains high. Unfortunately, the affordable method appears to be on the increase. We now turn our attention to two methods in the figure that are considered to be **bottom-up approaches**.

Bottom-Up Approaches   The major flaw associated with the top-down methods is that these judgmental approaches lead to predetermined budget appropriations often not linked to objectives and the strategies designed to accomplish them. A more effective budgeting strategy would be to consider the firm's communications objectives and budget what is deemed necessary to attain these goals. As noted earlier, the promotional planning model shows the budget decision as an interactive process, with the communications objectives on one hand and the promotional mix alternatives on the other. The idea is to budget so these promotional mix strategies can be implemented to achieve the stated objectives.

Objective and Task Method   It is important that objective setting and budgeting go hand in hand rather than sequentially. It is difficult to establish a budget without specific objectives in mind, and setting objectives without regard to how much money is available makes no sense. For example, a company may wish to create awareness among X percent of its target market. A minimal budget amount will be required to accomplish this goal, and the firm must be willing to spend this amount.

The **objective and task method** of budget setting consists of three steps: (1) defining the communications objectives to be accomplished, (2) determining the specific

FIGURE 9–28 □□□□   Comparison of methods for budgeting

Study	San Augustine and Foley (1975)	Patti and Blasko (1981)	Lancaster and Stern (1983)	Blasko and Patti (1984)	Hung and West (1991)
Population	Large Consumer/ Industrial Advertisers	Large Consumer/ Services Advertisers	Large Consumer Advertisers	Large Industrial Advertisers	Large & Medium Advertisers in U.K., U.S., & Canada
Sample	50/50	54	60	64	100
Methods					
Quantitative models	2/4	51	20	3	NA
Objective and task	6/10	63	80	74	61
Percent anticipated sales	50/28	53	53	16	32
Unit anticipated sales	8/10	22	28	NA	9
Percent past year's sales	14/16	20	20	23	10
Unit past year's sales	6/4	NA	15	2	NA
Affordable	30/26	20	13	33	41
Arbitrary	12/34	4	NA	13	NA
Competitive parity	NA	24	33	21	25
Previous budget	NA	NA	3	NA	NA
Share of voice	NA	NA	5	NA	NA
Others	26/10	NA	12	NA	NA

Note: Figures exceed 100% due to multiple responses. NA = No answer.

strategies and tasks needed to attain them, and (3) estimating the costs associated with performance of these strategies and tasks. The total budget is based on the accumulation of these costs.

Implementing the objective and task approach is somewhat more involved. The manager must monitor this process throughout and change strategies depending on how well objectives are attained. As shown in Figure 9–29, this process involves several steps:

1. *Isolate objectives.* When the promotional planning model is presented, a company will have two sets of objectives to accomplish—the marketing objectives for the product and the communications objectives. After the former are established, the task involves determining what specific communications objectives will be designed to accomplish these goals. Communications objectives must be specific, attainable, and measurable, as well as time limited.

2. *Determine tasks required.* A number of elements are involved in the strategic plan designed to attain the objectives established. (These strategies constitute the remaining chapters in this text.) These tasks may include advertising in various media, sales promotions, and/or other elements of the promotional mix, each with its own role to perform.

3. *Estimate required expenditures.* Buildup analysis requires determining the estimated costs associated with the tasks developed in the previous step. For example, it involves costs for developing awareness through advertising, trial through sampling, and so forth.

4. *Monitor.* As we saw in Chapter 8 on measuring effectiveness, there are ways to determine how well one is attaining established objectives. Performance should be monitored and evaluated in light of the budget appropriated.

5. *Reevaluate objectives.* Once specific objectives have been attained, monies may be better spent on new goals. Thus, if one has achieved the level of consumer awareness sought, the budget should be altered to stress a higher-order objective such as evaluation or trial.

The major advantage of the objective and task method is that the budget is driven by the objectives to be attained. The managers closest to the marketing effort will have specific strategies and input into the budget-setting process.

FIGURE 9–29

The objective and task method

□ □ □ □ □

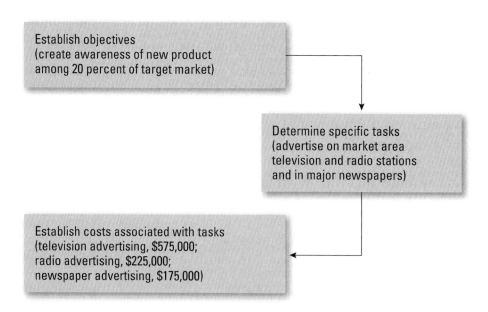

Establish objectives
(create awareness of new product among 20 percent of target market)

Determine specific tasks
(advertise on market area television and radio stations and in major newspapers)

Establish costs associated with tasks
(television advertising, $575,000; radio advertising, $225,000; newspaper advertising, $175,000)

The major disadvantage of this method is the difficulty of determining which tasks will be required and the costs associated with each. For example, specifically what tasks are needed to attain awareness among 50 percent of the target market? How much will it cost to perform these tasks? While these decisions are easier to determine for certain objectives—for example, estimating the costs of sampling required to stimulate trial in a defined market area—it is not always possible to know exactly what is required and/or how much it will cost to complete the job. This process is easier if there is past experience to use as a guide, with either the existing product or a similar one in the same product category. But it is especially difficult for new product introductions. As a result, budget setting using this method is not as easy to perform or as stable as some of the methods discussed earlier. Given this disadvantage, many marketing managers have stayed with those top-down approaches for setting the total expenditure amount.

The objective and task method offers advantages over methods discussed earlier but is more difficult to implement when there is no track record for the product. The following section addresses the problem of budgeting for new product introductions.

Payout Planning   The first months of a new product's introduction typically require heavier-than-normal advertising and promotion appropriations to stimulate higher levels of awareness and subsequent trial. After studying more than 40 years of Nielsen figures, James O. Peckham estimated that the average share of advertising to sales ratio necessary to launch a new product successfully is approximately 1.5:2.0.[27] This means that a new entry should be spending at approximately twice the desired market share, as shown in the two examples in Figure 9–30. For example, in the food industry, brand 101 gained a 12.6 percent market share by spending 34 percent of the total advertising dollars in this category. Likewise, brand 401 in the toiletry industry had a 30 percent share of advertising dollars to gain 19.5 percent of sales.

To determine how much to spend, marketers often develop a **payout plan** that determines the investment value of the advertising and promotion appropriation. The basic idea is to project the revenues the product will generate, as well as the costs it will incur, over two to three years. Based on an expected rate of return, the payout plan will assist in determining how much advertising and promotions expenditure will be necessary when the return might be expected. A three-year payout plan is shown in Figure 9–31. The product would lose money in year 1, almost break even in year 2, and finally begin to show substantial profits by the end of year 3.

The advertising and promotion figures are highest in year 1 and decline in years 2 and 3. This appropriation is consistent with Peckham's findings and reflects the additional outlays needed to make as rapid an impact as possible. (Keep in mind that shelf space is limited, and store owners are not likely to wait around for a product to become successful.) The budget also reflects the firm's guidelines for new product expenditures, since companies generally have established deadlines by which the product must begin to show a profit. Finally, keep in mind that building market share may be more difficult than maintaining it—thus the substantial dropoff in expenditures in later years.

While the payout plan is not always perfect, it does guide the manager in establishing the budget. When used in conjunction with the objective and task method, it provides a much more logical approach to budget setting than the top-down approaches previously discussed. Yet on the basis of the studies reported on in Figure 9–28, payout planning does not seem to be a widely employed method.

277

FIGURE 9–30
Share of advertising/
sales relationship (two-
year summary)

□ □ □ □ □

A. New Brands of Food Products

Brand	Average share of advertising	Attained share of sales	Ratio of share of advertising to share of sales
101	34%	12.6%	2.7
102	16	10.0	1.6
103	8	7.6	1.1
104	4	2.6	1.5
105	3	2.1	1.4

B. New Brands of Toiletry Products

Brand	Average share of advertising	Attained share of sales	Ratio of share of advertising to share of sales
401	30%	19.5%	1.5
402	25	16.5	1.5
403	20	16.2	1.2
404	12	9.4	1.3
405	16	8.7	1.8
406	19	7.3	2.6
407	14	7.2	1.9
408	10	6.0	1.7
409	7	6.0	1.2
410	6	5.9	1.0
411	10	5.9	1.7
412	6	5.2	1.2

	Year 1	Year 2	Year 3
Product sales	15.0	35.50	60.75
Profit contribution (@ $0.50/case)	7.5	17.75	30.38
Advertising/promotions	15.0	10.50	8.50
Profit (loss)	(7.5)	7.25	21.88
Cumulative profit (loss)	(7.5)	(0.25)	21.63

FIGURE 9–31
Example of three-year payout plan ($ millions)
□ □ □ □ □

Summary of Budgeting Methods   There is no universally accepted method of setting a budget figure. Weaknesses in each method may make it unfeasible or inappropriate. As Figure 9–28 shows, the use of the objective and task method continues to increase, whereas less sophisticated methods are declining in favour. More advertisers are also employing the payout planning approach.

In a more recent study of how managers make decisions regarding advertising and promotion budgeting decisions, George Low and Jakki Mohr interviewed 21 managers in eight consumer-product firms. Their research focused on the decision processes and procedures used to set spending levels on the factors that influence the allocation of advertising and promotion dollars.

On the basis of their results, the authors concluded that the budget-setting process is still a perplexing issue to many managers and that institutional pressures led to a greater proportion of dollars being spent on sales promotions than managers would have preferred. In addition, the authors concluded that to successfully develop and implement the budget, managers must (1) employ a comprehensive strategy to guide the process, avoiding the piecemeal approach often employed, (2) develop a strategic planning framework that employs an integrated marketing communications philosophy, (3) build in contingency plans, (4) focus on long-term objectives, and (5) consistently evaluate the effectiveness of programs.[28]

279

SUMMARY

The media strategy must be designed to supplement and support the overall marketing and communications objectives. The objectives of this plan are designed to deliver the message the program has developed.

The basic task involved in the development of media strategy is to determine the best matching of media to the target audience, given the constraints of the budget. The media planner attempts to balance reach and frequency and to deliver the message to the intended audience with a minimum of waste coverage. At the same time, a number of additional factors affect the media decision. Media strategy development has been called more of an art than a science because while many quantitative data are available, the planner also relies on creativity and nonquantifiable factors.

This chapter discussed many media strategy decisions, including developing a proper media mix, determining target audience, geographic coverage, scheduling, and balancing reach and frequency. A summary chart of strengths and limitations of various media was provided. The chapter also looked at key media tactics decisions that fine-tune the media strategy.

This chapter summarized various perspectives for determining the media budget. Theoretical methods for determining the media budget have some major problems. Economic models are limited, often try to demonstrate the effects on sales directly, and ignore other elements of the marketing mix. Some of the methods discussed have no theoretical basis and ignore the roles advertising and promotion are meant to perform.

One possible way to improve the budget appropriation is to tie the measures of effectiveness to communications objectives rather than to the broader-based marketing objectives. Using the objective and task approach with communications objectives may not be the ultimate solution to the budgeting problem, but it is an improvement over the top-down methods. Marketers often find it advantageous to employ a combination of methods.

280

KEY TERMS

media planning, 242
media objectives, 242
media strategy, 242
media tactics, 242
medium, 245
media class, 245
reach, 245
coverage, 246
frequency, 246
media vehicle, 246
sweeps periods, 247
waste coverage, 252
index number, 252
Brand Development
  Index (BDI), 253

Category Development
  Index (CDI), 253
continuity, 254
flighting, 254
pulsing, 255
unduplicated reach, 257
duplicated reach, 257
program rating, 258
gross ratings points
  (GRP), 258
effective reach, 259
average frequency, 260
vehicle option source
  effect, 262
absolute cost, 262

relative cost, 262
cost per thousand
  (CPM), 262
cost per ratings point
  (CPRP), 263
daily inch rate, 263
target CPM (TCPM), 264
readers per copy, 264
pass-along rate, 264
blocking chart, 264
marginal analysis, 266
concave-downward
  function model, 267
S-shaped response
  curve, 267

economies of scale, 270
top-down approaches, 271
affordable method, 271
arbitrary allocation, 272
percentage-of-sales
  method, 272
clipping service, 274
competitive parity
  method, 274
ROI budgeting method, 274
bottom-up approach, 275
objective and task
  method, 275
payout plan, 277

DISCUSSION QUESTIONS

1. Using the BDI and CDI indices, explain the least desirable market situation for marketers. Provide an example. Then do the same for the most desirable situation.

2. Media planning involves a tradeoff between reach and frequency. Explain what this means and give examples of when reach should be emphasized over frequency and vice versa.

3. What is meant by readers per copy? Explain the advantages and disadvantages associated with the use of this figure.

4. One long-time advertising agency executive noted that buying media is both an art and a science, with a leaning toward art. Explain what this means and provide examples.

5. Discuss some of the factors that are important in determining frequency levels. Give examples of each factor.

6. What are the advantages and disadvantages of CPM?

7. Describe what is meant by waste coverage. The decision must often be made between waste coverage and under coverage. Give examples when the marketer might have to choose between the two, and when it may be acceptable to live with waste coverage.

8. Discuss some of the reasons managers continue to set budgets using "top-down" budgeting methods.

9. Explain the difference between investing in advertising and spending. Cite examples of companies that have successfully invested.

10. Discuss how you would explain to a small-business owner why he or she needs to budget a larger amount to advertising and promotion. Base your argument on the S-shaped response function.

11. Some advertisers believe economies of scale are accrued in the advertising process. Discuss their reasons for taking this position. Does research evidence support it?

Broadcast Media

CHAPTER OBJECTIVES

- To examine the structure of the television and radio industries and the role of each medium in the advertising program.

- To consider the strengths and limitations of TV and radio as advertising media.

- To explain how advertising time is purchased for television and radio media, how audiences are measured, and how rates are determined.

A Live Ad for Nicoderm

To commemorate the 50th anniversary of CBC television, the national network envisioned a program entitled *Live to Air* that would be broadcast live—just like television when it first aired in Canada so many years ago. Jumping on the opportunity, Pharmacia Consumer Healthcare's [now Pfizer] smoking cessation product, Nicoderm, along with their agency Le Groupe TMC, visualized a live television commercial associated with a live television show. Despite the CBC changing their plans for a live show, Pharmacia pursued the idea to a successful completion as it executed the first Canadian live television commercial since the 1950s.

The original idea called for two 60-second spots during the live show, however, that all changed when the television show moved to a pre-recorded format. Instead, Pharmacia and its agency saw an opportunity to develop the media opportunity further by running a full two-minute live commercial for a more resounding impact that they hoped would lead to stronger brand recall.

A creative theme of a journey back in time to the dawn of television exactly 50 years ago captured the essence of the product's benefits and fit the theme of the television show like a glove. A 1952 couple, visited by a Nicoderm doctor from the future, learned about the dangers of smoking. Although a serious message, the ad contained music, dancing, and laughter to keep the tone light-hearted.

Pharmacia supported the live ad with additional communication to maximize exposure. Feature articles ran in various newspaper publications. Advanced notice of the ad occurred on a TV spot and an ad in *TV Guide*. A contest also sparked interest and garnered stronger participation in the campaign. Although specific success measures never materialized publicly, Pharmacia claimed success and received an award for outstanding creativity in media usage for their risky adventure.

Source: Tiffany St-Germain, "Five, Four, Three, Two—You're Live!" *Marketing Magazine*, February 24, 2003.

TV has virtually saturated households throughout Canada and most other countries and has become a mainstay in the lives of most people. The average Canadian household watches almost six hours of TV a day, and the average person (age 2+) watches about 3.5 hours of TV per day.[1] The large numbers of people who watch television are important to the TV networks and stations because they can sell time on these programs to marketers who want to reach that audience with their advertising messages. Moreover, the qualities that make TV a great medium for news and entertainment also encourage creative ads that can have a strong impact on customers.

Radio is also an integral part of our lives. Many of us wake up to clock radios in the morning and rely on radio to inform and/or entertain us while we drive to work or school. For many people, radio is a constant companion in their cars, at home, even at work. The average Canadian listens to the radio about three hours each day.[2] Like TV viewers, radio listeners are an important audience for marketers.

In this chapter, we examine TV and radio media, including the general characteristics of each as well as their specific strengths and limitations. We examine how advertisers use TV and radio as part of their advertising and media strategies, how they buy TV and radio time, and how audiences are measured and evaluated for each medium. We also examine the factors that are changing the role of TV and radio as advertising media.

TELEVISION

It has often been said that television is the ideal advertising medium. Its ability to combine visual images, sound, motion, and colour presents the advertiser with the opportunity to develop the most creative and imaginative appeals of any medium. However, TV does have certain characteristics that limit or even prevent its use by many advertisers.

STRENGTHS OF TELEVISION

TV has numerous strengths compared to other media, including creativity, target audience coverage, cost efficiency, attention, scheduling flexibility, geographic coverage, reach, frequency, and acceptable image.

Creativity for Cognitive and Emotional Responses   Perhaps the greatest advantage of TV is the opportunity it provides for presenting the advertising message. The interaction of sight, sound, and motion offers tremendous creative flexibility and makes possible dramatic, lifelike representations of products and services. TV commercials can be used to convey a mood or image for a brand as well as to develop emotional or entertaining appeals that help make a dull product appear interesting. The overall impact of TV's characteristics provides unlimited options for generating optimal cognitive and emotional responses to highly imaginative ads.

Television is also an excellent medium for demonstrating a product or service. For example, print ads are effective for showing a car and communicating information regarding its features, but only a TV commercial can put you in the driver's seat and give you the sense of actually driving, as shown by the Porsche commercial in Exhibit 10–1.

Target Audience Coverage   Television advertising makes it possible to reach large audiences. Nearly everyone, regardless of age, sex, income, or educational level, watches at least some TV. During prime time (7:00 p.m. to 11:00 p.m.), an average of 40 percent of adults will tune in (see Figure 10–1). Most people do so on a regular basis since 99 percent of all Canadian households own a TV, and 57 percent have more than one. Marketers selling products and services that appeal to broad target audiences find that TV lets them reach mass markets.

Exhibit 10–1 This TV commercial helps viewers feel the sensation of driving a sports car

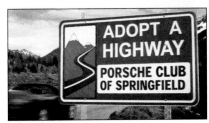

Cost Efficiency Compared to many other media, the cost to reach individuals by television is reasonably affordable. For example, one estimate is that the average cost per thousand (cpm) to reach English-speaking women 18 to 49 is about $18.[3] Because of its ability to reach large audiences in a cost-efficient manner, TV is a popular medium among companies selling mass-consumption products. Companies with widespread distribution and availability of their products and services use TV to reach the mass market and deliver their advertising messages at a very low cost per thousand. Television has become indispensable to large consumer package-goods companies, carmakers, and major retailers. Companies like Procter & Gamble and Coca-Cola spend a high percentage of their media advertising budget on television.

Attention Television is basically intrusive in that commercials impose themselves on viewers as they watch their favourite programs. Unless we make a special effort to avoid commercials, most of us are exposed to thousands of them each year. This seemingly continuous exposure implies that viewers devote some attention (i.e., selective attention) to many advertising messages. As discussed in Chapter 3, the low-involvement nature of consumer learning and response processes may mean TV ads have an effect on consumers simply through heavy repetition and exposure to catchy slogans and jingles.

285

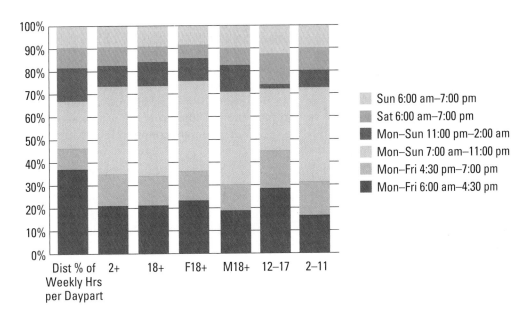

FIGURE 10–1

Percent distribution of weekly per-capita hours by daypart: total Canada

Scheduling Flexibility   Television has often been criticized for being a nonselective medium, since it is difficult to reach a precisely defined target audience through the use of TV advertising. But some selectivity is possible due to variations in the composition of audiences as a result of broadcast time and program content. For example, Saturday morning TV caters to children; Saturday and Sunday afternoon programs are geared to the sports-oriented male; and weekday daytime shows appeal heavily to homemakers. With the growth of specialty channels, advertisers refine their coverage further by appealing to groups with specific interests such as sports, news, history, the arts, or music.

Geographic Coverage   Advertisers can also adjust their media strategies to take advantage of different geographic markets through spot ads in specific market areas. Ads can be scheduled to run repeatedly in more favourable markets. Alternatively, advertisers can obtain national coverage or regional coverage depending upon their marketing objectives.

Reach   Television viewing is a closely monitored activity such that the size of the audience for a television program is known fairly quickly. Placement of TV ads on certain combinations of shows allows an advertiser to reach as many in their target audience as they feel necessary. Availability of airtime and amount of budget are the main constraints from allowing an advertiser to reach as large an audience as possible.

Frequency   Scheduling television permits frequency in concentrated blocks throughout a program, evening, week, month, or season. Heightened frequency may be necessary for a new product launch or an effort to obtain switching while lower levels of frequency may be feasible for advertisers desiring more continuous exposure.

Media Image   Given the prominence television has with its mass-market characteristic, TV advertising often carries a high degree of acceptability. Television is usually viewed favourably due to the higher costs of placement and production that demonstrates a level of acceptance or establishment for those who advertise with this medium. In fact, Figure 9–4 of the previous chapter shows that the degree of acceptability of advertising on television is at a remarkable 72-percent acceptance level.

LIMITATIONS OF TELEVISION

Although television is unsurpassed from a creative perspective, the medium has several limitations that preclude its use by many advertisers. These problems include high absolute costs, low target audience selectivity, short processing time, extensive clutter, high selective exposure, low involvement, and distrustful image.

Absolute Cost   Despite the efficiency of TV in reaching large audiences, it is an expensive medium in which to advertise. The high cost of TV stems not only from the expense of buying airtime but also from the costs of producing a quality commercial. Production costs for a national brand 30-second spot average nearly $300,000 and can reach over a million for more elaborate commercials.[4] More advertisers are using media-driven creative strategies that require production of a variety of commercials, which drive up their costs. Even local ads can be expensive to produce and often are not of high quality. The high costs of producing and airing commercials often price small- and medium-size advertisers out of the market.

Target Audience Selectivity   Some selectivity is available in television through scheduling, but advertisers who are seeking a very specific, often small, target audience find the coverage of TV often extends beyond their market, reducing its cost effectiveness (as discussed in Chapter 9). Geographic selectivity can be a problem for local advertisers such as retailers, since a station bases its rates on the total market area it reaches. For example, stations in Ottawa reach viewers in western Quebec and eastern Ontario. The small company whose market is limited to the immediate Ottawa area may find TV an inefficient media buy, since the stations cover a larger geographic area than the merchant's trade area.

Audience selectivity is improving as advertisers target certain groups of consumers through the type of program or day and/or time when they choose to advertise. However, TV still does not offer as much audience selectivity as radio, magazines, newspapers, or direct mail for reaching precise segments of the market.

Amount of Processing Time TV commercials usually last only 30 or 15 seconds and leave nothing tangible for the viewer to examine or consider. Commercials have become shorter and shorter as the demand for a limited amount of broadcast time has intensified and advertisers try to get more impressions from their media budgets.

An important factor in the decline in commercial length has been the spiraling inflation in media costs over the past two decades. Many advertisers see shorter commercials as the only way to keep their media costs in line. A 15-second spot typically sells for about two-thirds the price of a 30-second spot. By using 15-second commercials, advertisers think they can run additional spots to reinforce the message or reach a larger audience. Some advertisers believe shorter commercials can deliver a message just as effectively as longer spots for much less money.

Clutter The problems of short messages are compounded by the fact that the advertiser's message is only one of many spots and other nonprogramming material seen during a commercial break, so it may have trouble being noticed. One of advertisers' greatest concerns with TV advertising is the potential decline in effectiveness because of such *clutter*.

The next time you watch TV, count the number of commercials, promotions for the news or upcoming programs, or public service announcements that appear during a station break and you will appreciate why clutter is a major concern. In the USA, a recent study sponsored by the advertising industry found a record level of clutter during prime-time television broadcasts on the major networks. The study analyzed one week of broadcasts during May and November of 1999 and found that the four major networks averaged 16 minutes and 43 seconds of nonprogramming content. The hour-long police drama *NYPD Blue* had the most clutter of any prime-time show with one episode having nearly 18 minutes of clutter.[5] With all of these messages competing for our attention, it is easy to understand why the viewer comes away confused or even annoyed and unable to remember or properly identify the product or service advertised.

One cause of clutter is the use of shorter commercials and **split-30s**, 30-second spots in which the advertiser promotes two different products with separate messages. Clutter also results when the networks and individual stations run promotional announcements for their shows, make more time available for commercials, and redistribute time to popular programs. The Canadian Radio-television and Telecommunications Commission (CRTC), which regulates television only permits 12 minutes of commercials per hour. However, when simulcast Canadian commercials are run, there is extra "time" since U.S. TV stations often show more than 12 minutes of commercials. To fill this "time," Canadian stations run "ads" for other shows, public service announcements, or news/entertainment vignettes. Thus, Canadian viewers experience a different kind of clutter than their American counterparts.

Selective Exposure When advertisers buy time on a TV program, they are not purchasing guaranteed exposure but rather the opportunity to communicate a message to large numbers of consumers. But there is increasing evidence that the size of the viewing audience shrinks during a commercial break. People leave the room to go to the bathroom or to get something to eat or drink, or they are distracted in some other way during commercials, or they decide to change the channel. Studies of consumers' viewing habits found that as much as a third of program audiences may be lost during commercial breaks.[6] Thus, for a variety of reasons viewers engage in selective exposure to television commercials. Advertisers are very concerned with zapping and zipping.

Zapping refers to changing channels to avoid commercials. An observational study conducted by John Cronin found as much as a third of program audiences may be lost to electronic zapping when commercials appear.[7] The Nielsen study found that most commercial zapping occurs at the beginning and, to a lesser extent, the end of a program. Zapping at these points is likely to occur because commercial breaks are so long and predictable. Zapping has also been fueled by the emergence of 24-hour continuous-format programming on cable channels. Viewers can switch over for a few news headlines, sports scores, or a music video and then switch back to the program. Research shows that young adults zap more than older adults, and men are more likely to zap than women.[8]

How to inhibit zapping? The networks use certain tactics to hold viewers' attention, such as previews of the next week's show or short closing scenes at the end of a program. Some programs start with action sequences before the opening credits and commercials. Some advertisers believe that producing different executions of a campaign theme is one way to maintain viewers' attention. Others think the ultimate way to zap-proof commercials is to produce creative advertising messages that will attract and hold viewers' attention. However, this is easier said than done, as many consumers just do not want to watch commercials. As more viewers gain access to remote controls and the number of channels increases, the zapping problem is likely to continue.

A recent study on zapping among viewers of the five major commercial channels in the Netherlands was conducted by Lex van Meurs.[9] He found that during commercial breaks, 29 percent of the audience stopped watching television or switched away to another channel. This loss of viewers was partially compensated for by an average increase of 7 percent of new viewers who zapped in from another channel. The study also found that people stop viewing TV during a commercial break because they have a reason to stop watching television altogether or they want to find out what is being shown on other channels. The number of people zapping in and out during breaks was not caused by the type of products being advertised or by specific characteristics of the commercials. IMC Perspective 10–1 shows how new technology may change how we view television in the future.

Based on your own behaviour, you can surmise that there are other ways we can try to minimize our contact with persuasive messages. In a representative sample of Canadians on what they do to limit their exposure to television, radio, and online advertising it shows a number of alternatives. Figure 10–2 illustrates the frequencies of those efforts that most pertain to television. Canadians engage in considerable zapping—at 61 percent or about double the amount of zapping cited in previous studies. Actual amount of zapping versus perceived amount of zapping may account for this difference. This would suggest that people's attitude towards an ad and their actual behaviour towards it are dramatically at odds. Alternatively, the different statistics may indicate a trend to increased zapping or more technological usage on the part of Canadians to avoid ads.[10]

The increased penetration of VCRs, remote controls, and other automatic devices have made it easier for TV viewers to avoid commercial messages. **Zipping** occurs when customers fast-forward through commercials as they play back a previously recorded program. A study by Nielsen Media Research found that while 80 percent of recorded shows are actually played back, viewers zip past more than half of the commercials.[11] Another study found that most viewers fully or partially zipped commercials when watching a prerecorded program.[12]

	Age					
	Total#8224 (n=1285)	15–19 (n=120)*	20–29 (n=204)*	30–39 (n=246)*	40–49 (n=270)*	50+ (n=445)*
Change TV channels	61	83	79	66	64	43
Use mute button	18	7	7	14	14	29
Leave room/walk away	14	8	9	13	17	18
Do something else	12	7	7	11	13	15
Turn it off	7	10	8	6	6	7
Fast forward through ads	6	1	4	5	8	9
Get food/drink	6	3	2	5	7	10
Do household task	4	2	3	3	4	5
Ignore it	4	2	4	2	3	6
Read something	3	1	1	1	2	7
Watch TV channels that don't have ads	2	–	3	2	2	2
Turn down volume	2	1	–	2	2	3
Other/don't know	4	4	4	5	3	3

Source: The Strategic Counsel, Toronto.
*n = the number of respondents.
Note: Total does not equal 100 percent because more than one response was accepted.

FIGURE 10–2

How Canadians avoid television advertising

☐☐☐☐☐

Involvement The cumulative effect of the varied television characteristics generally implies that it is a low-involvement medium. While its invasiveness can expose the message to us readily and perhaps hold our attention with significant creative strategies and tactics, the relative short processing time and clutter makes for less effective media for an advertiser to significantly persuade a target audience.

Media Image To many critics of advertising, TV commercials personify everything that is wrong with the industry. Critics often single out TV commercials because of their pervasiveness and the intrusive nature of the medium. Consumers are seen as defenseless against the barrage of TV ads, since they cannot control the transmission of the message and what appears on their screens. Viewers dislike TV advertising when they believe it is offensive, uninformative, or shown too frequently or when they do not like its content.[13] Studies have shown that of the various forms of advertising, distrust is generally the highest for TV commercials.[14] Also, concern has been raised about the effects of TV advertising on specific groups, such as children or the elderly.[15]

BUYING TELEVISION ADVERTISING TIME

A number of options are available to advertisers that choose to use TV as part of their media mix. They can purchase ads on shows that are shown across the national or regional network versus a local spot announcement in a few cities. They can sponsor an entire program. They can purchase time in a variety of program formats that appeal to various types and sizes of audiences. With the growth of new television services, advertisers decide the degree to which they want to advertise on specialty channels. We explore these four decisions in this section.

The purchase of TV advertising time is a highly specialized phase of the advertising business, particularly for large companies spending huge sums of money. Large advertisers that do a lot of TV advertising generally use agency media specialists or specialized media buying services to arrange the media schedule and purchase TV time. Consequently, we conclude this section with a discussion on

289

The Future of Television Viewing

How much would you be willing to pay to never have to watch another TV commercial, be able to automatically record shows with your favourite actor, or record more than one show at a time? How about being able to leave the room in the middle of an exciting hockey game and, when you return, being able to resume watching the game from the point where you left off? These capabilities are no longer the dreams of TV viewers. They are now the reality thanks to a new consumer electronic device called personal video recorders (PVR). And while it may be the answer to TV viewers' dreams many argue that PVRs may be the television and advertising industries' worst nightmare.

PVRs digitally record television shows and save them on a massive multi-gigabyte internal hard drive that can hold up to 55 hours of programming. Consumers can also download program schedules that pop up on the screen, and, with some simple programming through a remote control, consumers can click on shows they want to watch. PVRs also allow users to rewind or pause in the middle of a live broadcast while it keeps recording, resume watching from the point where they stopped, and then skip ahead to catch up on the live broadcast. Anticipated future versions of the technology will automatically skip past commercials.

According to Bell ExpressVu's director of communications, "It really does change the way you watch TV." The technology emerged in Canada in 2001 and although demand for PVR is at a relatively low 1 percent of all Canadian households, many believe the penetration is set to take off once prices become more affordable for the average consumer in the next three to five years. In the U.S., similar penetration of 1 percent of households occurred over the past few years with two main brands, TiVo and Sonicblue, dominating.

Naturally, broadcasters are concerned as advertisers may question the effectiveness of placing commercials in established prime-time slots. However, others suggest that the technology permits an opportunity for advertisers to innovate beyond the limitations of older technology. For example, for an episode of the show *24*, Ford in the U.S. placed new vehicles in the first episode, sponsored the episode so it was commercial-free, and added a two-minute "Ford film" that had a *24*-like storyline. North of the border, Canadian actor and star of *24*, Kiefer Sutherland, performed the voice-over for the new Ford F-Series commercials. Additional exclusive sponsorship arrangements heightened Ford's exposure associated with the show. While the future of television viewing is open to prediction at this point in time, one expert believes that the typical 30-second commercial and conventional TV will be a key part of most TV campaigns, but they will be augmented with additional ad-like entertainment, product placement, and customized content.

Source: Bruce Neve, "Better, Smarter, Stronger," *Marketing Magazine*, February 16, 2004; Paul-Mark Rendon, "Zapping Power," *Marketing Magazine*, May 5, 2003.

measuring TV audiences since it is a critical input for TV decisions. Figure 10–3 illustrates how the percentage of hours tuned to various types of television stations has changed over time.

NETWORK, SPOT, SPONSORSHIP

A basic decision for all advertisers is allocating their TV media budget to network versus local or spot announcements. Most national advertisers use network schedules to provide national coverage and supplement this with regional or local spot purchases to reach markets where additional coverage is desired.

FIGURE 10–3

TVBasics 2003–2004:
Share of hours tuned by
station group

□ □ □ □ □

Station	FALL				
	1999	2000	2001	2002	2003
Conventional Station					
CBC	4.6	4.8	4.4	4.5	4.7
CBC affiliates	1.1	1	0.9	0.7	0.7
CBC TOTAL	**5.7**	**5.8**	**5.4**	**5.3**	**5.6**
CTV	14.8	14.5	11.3	12.2	11.9
Independent English	9.1	7.7	7.6	8	9.4
Global	5.8	6.4	7.7	7.9	7.5
Radio Canada	4.6	4.0	4.1	3.4	2.7
Radio Canada affiliates	1.3	1.1	0.9	0.8	0.6
RADIO CANADA TOTAL	**5.9**	**5.1**	**5.1**	**4.2**	**3.3**
TVA	9.7	9.3	8.7	8.7	8.2
Télé-Québec	0.6	0.5	0.6	0.7	0.7
Quatre Saisons	3.1	3.5	3.4	3.5	4.1
Total Cdn. Convent	**54.7**	**52.8**	**49.8**	**50.4**	**50.7**
U.S. Conventional TV					
ABC affiliates	2.4	2.4	2.4	2.1	1.9
NBC affiliates	2.4	2.2	2.3	2.0	2.1
CBS affiliates	2.8	2.4	2.1	2.1	2.2
FOX affiliates	2.3	2.4	2.5	2.0	2.0
PBS	1.4	1.6	1.4	1.1	1.1
Independent/UPN/WB	0.9	0.8	1.5	1.6	1.4
Total U.S. Convent	**12.2**	**11.8**	**12.2**	**10.9**	**10.7**
Cable	0.3	0.3	0.3	0.4	0.3
International	0.1	0.1	0.1		
Provincial	1.2	1.2	1.2	1.4	1.2
VCR	5.2	4.6	4.2	4.5	4.5
CDN. Specialty/Pay	16.7	19.2	21.4	22.8	23.8
U.S. Specialty/Pay	7.7	9	9.2	8	7.2
Others	2.1	1	1.4	1.4	1.6
Total Hours (Millions)	**659.6**	**644.3**	**642.9**	**659.4**	**667.4**

Network Advertising A common way advertisers disseminate their messages is by purchasing airtime from a **television network**. A network assembles a series of affiliated local TV stations, or **affiliates**, to which it supplies programming and services. These affiliates, most of which are independently owned, contractually agree to preempt time during specified hours for programming provided by the networks and to carry the national advertising within the program. The networks share the advertising revenue they receive during these time periods with the affiliates. The affiliates are also free to sell commercial time in non-network periods and during station breaks in the pre-empted periods to both national and local advertisers.

Canada's television industry features three national networks. The Canadian Broadcasting Corporation (CBC) is a Crown corporation of the federal government of Canada. Its full network includes 34 stations, including 19 private affiliates that reach 99 percent of English-language homes. Radio-Canada is the CBC cousin for the French-language network consisting of 13 stations (7 in Quebec, 6 outside of Quebec). The Canadian Television Network (CTV) operates as a national English-language service and owns 22 stations in most Canadian provinces.

Canada has a number of regional networks. The CBC also consists of five regional networks; Atlantic, Central (Ontario and English Montreal), Pacific (B.C.), Western, and North (NWT). CTV has three regional networks: Ontario, Atlantic, and Saskatchewan. Global Television Network sends its signal from Toronto to 14 transmitters to reach 97 percent of the Ontario population. Global Atlantic operates in a similar manner to reach the majority of people in New Brunswick, PEI, and Nova Scotia. NewNet is an amalgamation of five Ontario stations reaching over 4 million people. Citytv, based in Toronto, reaches an audience of 4 million households from Windsor to Ottawa. CHTV operates similarly out of Toronto/Hamilton and covers 90 percent of Ontario through its seven transmitters. There are three regional networks in Quebec. TVA has 10 stations and reaches 99 percent of the province. Television Quatre Saisons has nine stations and reaches 94 percent of the province. Finally, sports programming has reached the regional network status as Sportsnet operates in four regions: Pacific, West, Ontario, and East.

The networks have affiliates throughout the nation for almost complete national coverage. When an advertiser purchases airtime from one of the national networks, the commercial is transmitted across the nation through the affiliate station network. Network advertising truly represents a mass medium, as the advertiser can broadcast its message simultaneously throughout the country.

A major advantage of network advertising is the simplification of the purchase process. The advertiser has to deal with only one party or media representative to air a commercial nationwide. The networks also offer the most popular programs and generally control prime-time programming. Advertisers interested in reaching huge nationwide audiences generally buy network time during the prime viewing hours of 8 to 11 p.m. eastern time.

The major drawback is the high cost of network time. Figure 10–4 shows cost estimates for a 30-second spot on many national and regional networks for the 2002–2003 television season. The cost for a most watched show or special on the CTV network would be $80,000. As an absolute cost, this is quite prohibitive for many marketers. As a result, only about 20 percent of all TV advertising is done in this manner.

Availability of time can also be a problem as more advertisers turn to network advertising to reach mass markets. Traditionally, most prime-time commercial spots, particularly on the popular shows, are sold during the buying period in May/June/July that occurs before the TV season begins. Advertisers hoping to use prime-time network advertising must plan their media schedules and often purchase TV time as much as a year in advance. Demands from large clients who are heavy TV advertisers force the biggest agencies to participate in the up-front market. However, TV time is also purchased during the **scatter market** that runs through the TV season. Some key incentives for buying up front, such as cancellation options and lower prices, are becoming more available in the quarterly scatter market. Network TV can also be purchased on a regional basis, so an advertiser's message can be aired in certain sections of the country with one media purchase.

Buying Television The marketing and selling of advertising space by the network producers of television shows to buyers of advertising can be less challenging with an established brand like the television series *Canadian Idol*. However, the challenge can be enormous for new television shows with a low profile. The producers of the hit show, *Corner Gas*, marketed to television viewers directly to build the audience, thus making the show very attractive to advertisers. CTV used publicity, on-air ads, website promotions, and a cross-country tour of Brent Butt (a comedian and star of the show) to appeal to a core group who would like a show that was described as original, familiar, and fun. At its peak, *Corner Gas* is in the top 15 shows watched in Canada with an audience of 1.5 million, topping many American situation comedies.[16]

Similarly, Alliance Atlantis Broadcasting takes a packaged-goods marketing approach in its planning and organizing to develop the market for its imported

Network	# of Stations	Basic Range $	Network	# of Stations	Basic Range $
National			**Specialty**		
CBC Full	34	100–52,000	Bravo!	1	150–5,500
CBC Metronet	17	100–25,000	Canal D	1	75–1,365
CTV	22	2,500–80,000	Canal Vie	1	50–1,785
Radio Canada	13	200–25,000	Canal Z	1	40–960
TVA	10	Various	CBC Newsworld	1	250–1,000
			CMT	1	30–1,000
Regional			Comedy	1	40–1,600
ASN	1	30–640	Discovery	1	500–5,000
ATV	3	450–3,300	Food Network	1	100–3,500
			HGTV Canada	1	100–3,500
CBC Regional			Historia	1	40–310
Atlantic	6	100–2,800	History	1	100–2,800
Central	12	100–21,000	Life Network	1	100–3,700
Western	12	100–7,500	MuchMusic	1	1,050–3,000
Pacific	6	100–4,200	Musique Plus	1	480–600
Global	1	150–48,000	OLN	1	15–1,300
MITV	2	55–33,400	Prime	1	10–1,500
CTV Ontario	5	1,700–33,000	RDI	1	50–550
TQS	10	315–12,000	RDS	1	250–18,000
Tele-Quebec	10	200–2,500	Score, The	1	60–5,000
CTV Saskatchewan	4	120–2,500	Series+	1	40–1,140
			Showcase	1	100–4,700
			Space	1	50–3,200
			Sportsnet	4	100–7,500
			Teletoon (English)	1	75–1,400
			TSN	1	500–20,000
			Vision TV	1	400–1,000
			Weather Network	1	90–300
			W Network	1	25–1,475
			YTV	1	150–4,500

FIGURE 10–4
Estimated cost of network commercials 2002–2003 (30-second rates)

☐ ☐ ☐ ☐ ☐

specialty channels like HGTV, National Geographic Channel, and BBC Canada or domestic specialty channels like Showcase and History Television. In addition, it uses innovative creative tactics to ensure large audiences for its advertisers. For example, during the *Six Feet Under* launch, it used an unusual mobile display to a record-breaking 735,000 viewers, establishing it as the most watched specialty channel program.[17]

Spot Advertising   **Spot advertising** refers to commercials shown on local TV stations, with time negotiated and purchased directly from the individual stations or their national station representatives. **Station reps** act as sales agents for a number of local stations in dealing with national advertisers.

Spot advertising offers the national advertiser flexibility in adjusting to local market conditions. The advertiser can concentrate commercials in areas where market potential is greatest or where additional support is needed. This appeals to advertisers with uneven distribution or limited advertising budgets, as well as those interested in test marketing or introducing a product in limited market areas. National advertisers sometimes use spot television advertising through local retailers or dealers as part of their cooperative advertising programs and to provide local dealer support. This attractive option is most prevalent in Canada with about 60 percent of all TV ads.

Sponsorship Advertising   Under a **sponsorship** arrangement, an advertiser assumes responsibility for the production and usually the content of the program as well as the advertising that appears within it. In the early days of TV, most programs were produced and sponsored by corporations and were identified by their name. Today most shows are produced by either the networks or independent production companies that sell them to a network, however, sponsorship is a good option in some situations.

Several major companies have been sponsoring special programs for many years, such as the Kraft Masterpiece Theater and Hallmark Hall of Fame dramatic series. In 1994 Hallmark acquired RHI Entertainment Inc., the company that produces its wholesome Hall of Fame productions as well as TV miniseries and movies. Sole sponsorship of programs is usually limited to specials and has been declining. However, some companies do still use program sponsorships occasionally.

A company might choose to sponsor a program for several reasons. Sponsorship allows the firm to capitalize on the prestige of a high-quality program, enhancing the image of the company and its products. For example, the Ford Motor Company received a great deal of favourable publicity when it sponsored the commercial-free television debut of the Holocaust movie *Schindler's List*. Companies also sponsor programs to gain more control over the shows carrying their commercials. For example, Wendy's International has been involved in sponsorship of family-oriented programs.

Another reason is that the sponsor has control over the number, placement, and content of its commercials. Commercials can be of any length as long as the total amount of commercial time does not exceed network or station regulations. Advertisers introducing a new product line often sponsor a program and run commercials that are several minutes long to introduce and explain the product. While these factors make sponsorship attractive to some companies, the high costs of sole sponsorship limit this option to large firms.

Scotiabank provides an excellent example of innovative sponsorship. Historically, Scotiabank was successful with its sponsorship of CTV's "Business Report," shown during its *Canada AM* morning show. Looking for a consistent message across many of CTV's banners, Scotiabank hit on the solution of using the Report on Business Television's financial news show, *Dollars & Sense*, as shown in Figure 10–5.[18]

FIGURE 10–5
The *Dollars & Sense* breakout
☐ ☐ ☐ ☐ ☐

Participants: Report on Business Television, CTV Newsnet, *Canada AM*, *CTV News*, CTV.ca, ROBTV.com and other Bell Globemedia relevant websites.

Run: For 10 weeks starting Oct. 6, 2003 and for 20 weeks starting Jan. 5, 2004.

Production: 150 original two-minute *Dollars & Sense* segments airing on Report on Business Television; 30 original 30-second *Dollars & Sense* interstitial vignettes airing on CTV Newsnet and *Canada AM*.

Online: Digitized content so interstitials and long-version *Dollars & Sense* segments are available online supporting the advertising.

Component breakdown:

Report on Business Television runs two-minute editorial segments titled *Dollars & Sense*; airing four times per day, with unique content, Monday to Friday. Editorial segments are sponsored by Scotiabank and packaged with a 10-second opening and closing billboard and a 30-second adjacent Scotiabank commercial. Scotiabank-branded stock ticker appears on screen during the editorial content.

CTV Newsnet runs 30-second *Dollars & Sense* interstitial vignettes (similar content to longer version but more compact and focused in-content delivery), airing two times per day, Monday to Friday; 30-second commercial adjacency following interstitial; 10-second customized closed captioning campaign promoting "*Dollars & Sense* brought to you by Scotiabank," Monday to Saturday.

Canada AM runs 30-second *Dollars & Sense* interstitial in fixed position on Wednesdays and Fridays with 30-second commercial adjacency.

CTV News runs 10-second customized closed-captioning campaign promoting "*Dollars & Sense* brought to you by Scotiabank," Monday to Friday.

TIME PERIODS AND PROGRAMS

Another decision in buying TV time is selecting the right period and program for the advertiser's commercial messages. The cost of TV advertising time varies depending on the time of day and the particular program, since audience size varies as a function of these two factors. TV time periods are divided into **dayparts**, which are specific segments of a broadcast day.

The time segments that make up the programming day vary from station to station. However, a typical classification of dayparts for a weekday is shown in Figure 10–6. The various daypart segments attract different audiences in both size and nature, so advertising rates vary accordingly. Prime-time draws the largest audiences, with 8:30 to 9:00 P.M. being the most watched half-hour time period and Sunday the most popular night for television. Since firms that advertise during prime time must pay premium rates, this daypart is dominated by the large national advertisers.

The various dayparts are important to advertisers since they attract different demographic groups. For example, daytime TV generally attracts women; early morning attracts women and children. The late-fringe (late-night) daypart period has become popular among advertisers trying to reach young adults. Audience size and demographic composition also vary depending on the type of program. Situation comedies attract the largest prime-time audiences, with women 18 to 34 comprising the greatest segment of the audience. Feature films rank second, followed by general drama shows. Women 55 and older are the largest audience segment for these programs. Another factor to consider is the time of year. Figure 10–7 shows that TV viewership drops significantly in the summer.

SPECIALTY TELEVISION ADVERTISING

Canada has an extensive variety of specialty networks and digital specialty networks that advertisers run commercials on to reach specific target audiences. These specialty networks require either cable or satellite technology on the part of consumers

Morning	7:00 a.m.–9:00 a.m., Monday through Friday
Daytime	9:00 a.m.–4:30 p.m., Monday through Friday
Early fringe	4:30 p.m.–7:30 p.m., Monday through Friday
Prime-time access	7:30 p.m.–8:00 p.m., Sunday through Saturday
Prime time	8:00 p.m.–11:00 p.m., Monday through Saturday, and 7:00 p.m.–11:00 p.m., Sunday
Late news	11:00–11:30 p.m., Monday through Friday
Late fringe	11:30–1:00 a.m., Monday through Friday

FIGURE 10–6
Common television dayparts
☐ ☐ ☐ ☐ ☐

FIGURE 10–7 ☐ ☐ ☐ ☐ Television summer dropoff

	Total hours tuned: % difference					
	Daytime: M–F 6 a.m.–4:30 p.m.	Fringe: M–F 4:30 p.m.–7 p.m.	Prime time: M–Sun 7 p.m.–11 p.m.	Late night: M–Sun 11 p.m.–2 a.m.	Weekend: Sat/Sun 6 a.m.–7 p.m.	Total
All 2+	-10	-27	-31	1	-33	-25
Adults 18+	2	-38	-26	57	-33	-20
Women 18+	69	-23	-26	56	-29	-8
Men 18+	-14	-24	-31	-2	-31	-29
Teens 12–17	-19	-30	-33	-3	-37	-24

Total=% drop-off from Fall and Spring averages for 9 EMs (Halifax, Quebec, Montreal, Ottawa-Hull, Kitchener-Waterloo, London, Winnipeg, Calgary, Edmonton)
Source: BBM Summer, Fall, Spring 2002

to access this entertainment. We will briefly review these two technologies and then discuss the advertising on these specialty channels.

Cable and Satellite Technology Perhaps the most significant development in the broadcast media has been the expansion of **cable television**. Cable, or CATV (community antenna television), which delivers TV signals through fibre or coaxial wire rather than the airways, was developed to provide reception to remote areas that couldn't receive broadcast signals. Canadians readily accepted cable in the 1970s since it was the easiest or only method of receiving the feed of American channels. Today, cable penetration stands at about 67 percent.

Direct broadcast satellite (DBS) services emerged in the 1990s. TV and radio programs are sent digitally from a satellite to homes equipped with a small dish. DBS penetration reached 22 percent in 2003, mostly at the expense of cable companies. DBS companies have been aggressively marketing their service, superior picture quality, and greater channel choice as subscribers receive as many as 200 channels that include news, music, and sports in crisp, digital video and CD-quality sound. However, the pendulum can swing back the other way as more cable operators offer digital cable that allows them to match the number of channels received on satellites. Note that the combined penetration of these technologies is 89 percent indicating that a sizable number of Canadians cannot be reached through specialty television advertising.

Cable and satellite subscribers pay a monthly fee for which they receive many channels, including the local Canadian and American network affiliates and independent stations, various specialty networks, American **superstations**, and local cable system channels. Both operators also offer programming that is not supported by commercial sponsorship and is available only to households willing to pay a fee beyond the monthly subscription charge (e.g., The Movie Channel). Cable and satellite broadens the program options available to the viewer as well as the advertiser by offering specialty channels, including all-news, pop music, country music, sports, weather, educational, and cultural channels as well as children's programming. Many cable systems also carry American superstations, independent local stations that send their signals via satellite to operators to make their programs available to subscribers. Programming on superstations such as TBS and WGN generally consists of sports, movies, and reruns of network shows.

Specialty Networks The proliferation of channels in both technologies has influenced the nature of television as an advertising medium. Expanded viewing options have led to considerable audience fragmentation. Much of the audience growth of specialty networks has come at the expense of national and regional networks. Specialty networks now have about 28 percent of the viewing audience. Many specialty networks have become very popular among consumers, leading advertisers to re-evaluate their media plans and the prices they are willing to pay for network and spot commercials on network affiliate stations. Advertising on specialty networks reached $438 million in 2001 up from $109 million in 1994. In comparison, all other television ad revenue increased from $1.663 billion in 1994 to $2.123 billion.

This change in advertising revenue indicates that advertisers are using specialty networks to reach specific target audiences. Advertisers are also interested in specialty networks because of their low cost and flexibility. Advertising rates on cable programs are much lower than those for the shows on the major networks (see Figure 10–4). This makes TV a much more viable media option for smaller advertisers with limited budgets and those interested in targeting their commercials to a well-defined target audience. Also, specialty network advertisers generally do not have to make the large up-front commitments, which may be as much as a year in advance, the networks require.

In addition to costing less, specialty networks give advertisers much greater flexibility in the type of commercials that can be used. While most network commercials are 30- or 15-second spots, commercials on specialty networks can be longer (i.e., **infomercials** ranging from 3 to 30 minutes in length). Direct-response advertisers often use these longer ads to describe their products or services and encourage consumers to call in their orders during the commercial. The use of infomercials by direct-response advertisers is discussed in Chapter 15. Finally, specialty network advertising can be purchased on a national or a regional basis. Many large marketers advertise on specialty networks to reach large numbers of viewers across the country with a single media buy. Regional advertising on specialty networks is available but limited.

While specialty networks have become increasingly popular among national, regional, and local advertisers, they still have limitations. One concern is that specialty networks are overshadowed by the networks. The average person will watch more hours per week of a CBC or CTV affiliate than a single specialty network, although this is changing. Figure 10–8 shows a summary of the more highly viewed specialty channels. The average Canadian watches TSN an average of 1.5 hours per

FIGURE 10–8
Average hours watched per week for selected specialty channels

TVBasics 2003-2004						
	Fall 2002			Fall 2003		
SPECIALTY	Hours (000)	Reach (000)	Avg Hrs	Hours (000)	Reach (000)	Avg Hrs
Bravo	5,488	6,073	0.9	5,936	6,026	1.0
Canal D	5,040	2,546	2.0	3,920	2,547	1.5
Canal Vie	3,136	2,232	1.4	3,584	2,191	1.6
Canal Z	2,128	1,225	1.7	1,904	1,249	1.5
CBC Newsworld	5,264	5,490	1.0	5,600	5,334	1.0
Country Music Television	3,080	4,783	0.8	3,472	4,325	0.8
Discovery	6,832	7,341	0.9	7,616	7,134	1.1
Food Network Canada	2,688	2,799	1.0	2,912	2,753	1.1
HGTV Canada	4,480	4,432	1.0	4,256	4,268	1.0
Historia	1,456	1,082	1.3	1,568	1,077	1.5
History Television	6,048	4,655	1.3	5,600	4,440	1.3
Life Network	3,024	5,568	0.5	3,136	5,652	0.6
MuchMusic	4,592	6,071	0.8	4,256	5,980	0.7
Musique Plus	1,232	2,059	0.6	1,008	1,835	0.5
Outdoor Life	1,568	3,325	0.5	1,344	3,124	0.4
Prime TV	7,056	4,824	1.5	6,944	4,751	1.5
RDS - Le Reseau des Sports	6,944	2,766	2.5	5,936	2,598	2.3
RDI - Le Reseau de L'information	3,472	2,436	1.4	3,696	2,662	1.4
Score Television Network	N/A	N/A	N/A	2,352	3,411	0.7
Series +	4,256	1,330	3.2	5,040	1,227	4.1
Showcase	5,488	5,937	0.9	6,496	6,032	1.1
Space	7,168	4,838	1.5	6,272	4,422	1.4
Sports Net	7,280	6,816	1.1	10,864	6,815	1.6
Teletoon English	7,840	4,978	1.6	8,736	5,483	1.6
Teletoon French	4,704	1,978	2.4	5,040	1,966	2.6
The Comedy Network	3,920	5,301	0.7	3,472	4,969	0.7
The Family Channel	9,520	6,120	1.6	10,304	6,189	1.7
The Weather Network	2,688	4,594	0.6	2,576	4,882	0.5
TSN	14,112	9,155	1.5	12,544	8,386	1.5
W Network	4,480	5,473	0.8	5,040	5,158	1.0
TOTAL DIGITAL NETWORKS	13,328	3,888	3.4	13,776	4,624	3.0

*Numbers represent an average of eight weeks: Sep 30-Oct 6, 02 to Nov 18-Nov 24, 02; Sep 29-Oct 5, 03 to Nov 17-Nov 23, 03

Source: Nielsen Media Research, People Meter Data

297

week while the average person in Ottawa watches the CBC affiliate 2.6 hours per week. Although specialty networks' share of the TV viewing audience has increased significantly, the viewers are spread out among the large number of channels available. Collectively, the specialty channels contribute to greater audience fragmentation as the number of viewers who watch any one cable channel is generally quite low. Figure 10–9 shows a breakout of television viewership across all formats.

The emergence of dozens of digital specialty channels a few years ago raises the question as to how well they are performing in attracting audiences in sufficient numbers for advertisers to consider them as a viable television vehicle. While their share of 1 or 2 percent of the television market may be considered disappointing, another perspective suggests that a more realistic benchmark should be used. Since access to a specific digital specialty channel requires a subscription similar to that of magazines, a more important comparison is to look at the leaders for each media. In fact, about three-quarters of the digital specialty channels have more than half a million subscribers, something only three subscription magazines can claim.[19]

Recent research suggests that over the past few years, 45 percent of all viewers watch more programs on specialty channels with 41 percent indicating their perception that these channels have more interesting/entertaining programming versus conventional channels. Furthermore, 37 percent devote more than half of their viewing time to specialty channels and a similar number will consider a specialty channel first when they do not have a planned program to watch. With cost per rating point being about 50 percent lower and a greater ability to target an audience, it is not surprising to see that advertising revenues for specialty channels is growing significantly faster compared to conventional channels.[20]

MEASURING THE TV AUDIENCE

One of the most important considerations in TV advertising is the size and composition of the viewing audience. Audience measurement is critical to advertisers as well as to the networks and stations. Advertisers want to know the size and characteristics of the audience they are reaching when they purchase time on a particular program. And since the rates they pay are a function of audience size, advertisers want to be sure audience measurements are accurate.

Audience size and composition are also important to the network or station, since they determine the amount it can charge for commercial time. Shows are frequently cancelled because they fail to attract enough viewers to make their commercial time attractive to potential advertisers. Determining audience size is not an exact science

FIGURE 10–9
Viewing habits of Canadians 2+ by station groups (NMR 2002 weeks 5–13)
□ □ □ □ □

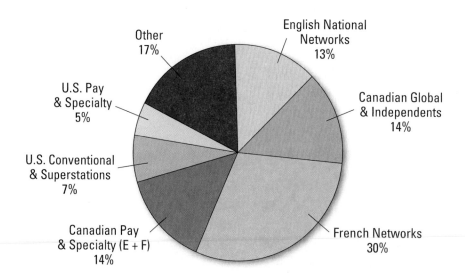

and has been the subject of considerable controversy through the years. In this section, we examine how audiences are measured and how advertisers use this information in planning their media schedules.

Audience Measurement Resources   The size and composition of television audiences are important to media planners as they weigh the value of buying commercial time on a program. In Canada, television audiences are measured and communicated by BBM Bureau of Measurement of Canada (BBM Canada) and Nielsen Media Research. A third organization, the Television Bureau of Canada, offers additional information related to television audiences.

BBM Canada   BBM Canada is a not-for-profit broadcast research company based on cooperative between the Canadian Association of Broadcasters, the Association of Canadian Advertisers, and Canadian advertising agencies. BBM Canada produces audience measurement data for its TV and radio members. This member relationship gives BBM Canada the reputation as the industry's rating service.

BBM Canada uses the diary research method for collecting television audience information in 35 smaller local markets during the fall and spring, and 12 larger local markets during the fall, spring, and summer. A booklet for each television owned in the household is sent to a representative sample of households. BBM gathers viewership information from this sample and then projects this information to the total viewing area.

The diary method work as follows. Each person aged two years or older records his or her viewing for one week in the booklet. The recordings are based on 15-minute increments from 6:00 A.M. until 2:00 A.M. Viewers write down station call letters, channel numbers, programs, and who is watching. The booklet also contains a number of based demographic questions to be completed by each individual. All participants receive a small incentive to encourage their responses. BBM receives completed diaries from about 40 percent of those that are mailed, although the rates vary by region and other factors. These and other aspects of the research process are done according to standard market research practices to ensure valid and reliable information; however, one drawback is that some diaries are not filled out correctly.

Due to this methodological concern and the pace of technology, BBM Canada is currently implementing the people-meter technology for local audience measurement. BBM Canada has begun to use meters to continuously record television audiences for local and regional markets. It started with Vancouver in 1998 and has now reached the Toronto local market and the Ontario and Quebec regional markets. As of June 2002, BBM Canada had tested preliminary data from a national panel of 2,100 households and plans a commercial launch of the service in the near future.

To help its customers understand the data, BBM Canada provides an extensive array of products. Market reports are a summary of the audience sizes across all markets by time block, program listings, and time period. Their reach book summarizes the demographic information across each province, data area, and station. BBM Canada also offers guidelines on population estimates and booklets that assist its members in understanding the geographic boundaries studied and the research methodology. BBM Canada's television data book breaks down the viewing habits across different markets with user-friendly graphs and charts. The EM Stats Card provides detailed information for each extended market in terms of cable, satellite, and VCR penetration in addition to other similar macro-level data. Finally, two different documents tabulate the audiences for the different televisions shows. As a complement, BBM Canada also offers four different software packages that allow its members to analyze the data in a variety of ways.

Nielsen Media Research   Nielsen is a Canadian subsidiary of an American firm with the same name. Nielsen gathers viewership information from a panel of TV homes that is a representative sample. It then projects this information to the total viewing area. The resulting data is presented as the Nielsen Television Index (NTI).

In Canada, the only technique used to gather audience measurement information is the electronic meter. Nielsen had previously used both the diary and electronic meter in Canada, like the practice done in the United States. In 2002, Nielsen's had the technology to measure audiences for the national market and for the Vancouver, Calgary, Toronto/Hamilton, and Montreal (French only) markets. Nielsen has recently launched a similar service to measure the audiences for the new digital channels offered on both cable and satellite.

Nielsen provides audience viewing information by household across a number of variables including income, language, cable status, pay TV, children residing, household size, age of head of household, number of TVs, rent or own home, kind of dwelling, ownership of VCRs and other durables, principal shopper, and restaurant and movie usage. The data is also presented by age, gender, education, and occupation. Like BBM Canada, Nielsen also provides various data management tools and services to help its clients understand the data. IMC Perspective 10–2 describes another service offered by Nielsen.

With BBM Canada and Nielsen offering very similar services, Canada is in a unique position of being the only country in the world that has two firms measuring TV audiences. The U.S. has only Nielsen; historically, there has been significant concern as to whether the advertisers are getting their money's worth and whether the data is sufficiently accurate as Nielsen uses two different methods (i.e., diary and meter). In Canada, the debate has centred on a couple of other facets. Some argue that Canada should return to a single firm measuring TV audiences as this would reduce overall costs; however, others contend that a dual system gives advertisers and agencies greater choice in making their TV media purchases.[21]

Television Bureau of Canada (TVB)   The TVB is an industry association for television networks, television stations, and sales firms that sell television advertising time. It offers resources to those in the television industry to demonstrate the value and importance of television as a media versus competing media (i.e., magazines). It publishes basic facts garnered from various sources and conducts primary research through independent market research firms.

Most of the information is from BBM Canada or Nielsen Media Research. Based on this research, television consistently outperforms the other media on a number of variables. Television reaches 85 percent of the country on a daily basis, with the average Canadian watching about 3.5 hours per day. Furthermore, television is perceived as being the most authoritative (43 percent) and most influential (71 percent) compared to radio, the Internet, daily newspapers, and magazines.

Audience Measures   We now review some of the concepts associated with television audience measurement that are the basis for the reports published by these three organizations.

Television Households   The number of households in the market that own a TV is sometimes referred to as the *universe estimate* (UE). Since over 98 percent of Canadian households own a TV set, **television households** generally correspond to the number of households in a given market.

Program Rating   Probably the best known of all audience measurement figures is the **program rating**, the percentage of TV households in an area that are tuned to a specific program during a specific time period. The program rating is calculated by dividing the number of households tuned to a particular show by the total number of households in the area. For example, if 1.2 million households (HH) watched a show, the national rating would be 10.9, calculated as follows:

$$\text{Rating} = \frac{\text{HH tuned to show}}{\text{Total HH}} = \frac{1{,}200{,}000}{11{,}000{,}000} = 10.9$$

Tracking Your Competitors

You're ready to launch a huge multi-million dollar advertising campaign with the majority of your budget dedicated to television spots on numerous networks. You've analyzed everything, from your target audience and their viewing patterns to which local TV stations are best suited to run your commercials. You're now ready to execute the planning and strategy of your media plan. But there is one important factor you overlooked, one that could either increase or reduce the effectiveness of your entire television campaign. That factor is the past and present success of your competitor's media strategies.

In the past, big marketing players in Canada's television world had a tough time reading what their competitors were doing in their media plans. The only way one could get a sense of their competitor's media plans was by wading through loads of numbers or watching a heck of a lot of TV!

Enter SpotWatch, a new service available through Nielsen Media Research of Markham, Ont. Nielsen bills SpotWatch as "the highest-quality competitive advertising intelligence and spot verification service available for television in Canada." The system automatically identifies when programs and commercials are aired through "passive pattern recognition" technology. Each ad has a video and audio signature that signals to the system so that key information is stored (i.e., when and where it has aired). This data is also linked to Nielsen's TV viewing data to determine who has received the messages.

The most obvious benefit is that the service offers accuracy in determining audience delivery for particular commercials and campaigns. But more importantly, the reports are especially detailed since SpotWatch can provide charts for each brand's TV spot, or for a whole category, that include the distributor, creative theme, day of the week and time it aired, position of the ad in a pod (commercial break), length, flighting patterns (periods of activity and inactivity for a campaign), and share of voice (the percentage of a brand's advertising in relation to the total advertising in its category). Another key benefit is the fact that Nielsen is providing the reports in 15 days so that planners have the opportunity to make quick appropriate changes depending upon what the data indicates. And finally, there is a user-friendly decision support system to let planners work with the data.

It all sounds pretty good but there are a few potential drawbacks. The cost ranges from $200 to $1,500 per month, depending on the category. And while the service boasts a correct identification for commercials about 95 percent of the time, which many people are happy with, it is still not 100 percent accurate. Finally, the distribution was still limited to Toronto and Vancouver in 2001. In all, however, you can be sure that Nielsen's SpotWatch service will level the competitive media planning and strategy playing field.

Source: Sarah Smith, "The Spying Game," *Marketing Magazine*, May 7, 2001.

A **ratings point** represents 1 percent of all the television households in a particular area tuned to a specific program. On a national level, 1 ratings point represents 110,000 households. Thus, a top-rated program with an average rating of 19 reaches 2.1 million households each week (19 × 110,000).

The program rating is the key number to the stations, since the amount of money they can charge for commercial time is based on it. Ratings points are very important to the networks as well as to individual stations. A 1 percent change in a program's ratings over the course of a viewing season can gain or lose millions of dollars in advertising revenue. Advertisers also follow ratings closely, since they are the key measure for audience size and commercial rates.

Households Using Television The percentage of homes in a given area where TV is being watched during a specific time period is called **households using television (HUT)**. This figure, sometimes referred to as sets in use, is always expressed as a percentage. For example, if 5.5 million of Canadian TV households have their sets turned on at 10 p.m. on a Thursday night, the HUT figure is 50 percent (5.5 million out of 11 million). Television usage varies widely depending on the time of day and season of the year.

Share of Audience Another important audience measurement figure is the **share of audience**, which is the percentage of households using TV in a specified time period that are tuned to a specific program. This figure considers variations in the number of sets in use and the total size of the potential audience, since it is based only on those households that have their sets turned on. Audience share is calculated by dividing the number of households (HH) tuned to a show by the number of households using television (HUT). Thus, if 5.5 million Canadian households had their sets turned on during the 10 p.m. time slot, the share of audience would be 20, calculated as follows:

$$\text{Share} = \frac{\text{HH tuned to show}}{\text{Households using TV}} = \frac{1.1}{5.5} = 20$$

Audience share is always higher than the program rating unless all the households have their sets turned on (in which case they would be equal). Share figures are important since they reveal how well a program does with the available viewing audience. For example, late at night the size of the viewing audience drops substantially, so the best way to assess the popularity of a late-night program is to examine the share of the available audience it attracts relative to competing programs.

Ratings services also provide an audience statistic known as **total audience**, the total number of homes viewing any five-minute part of a telecast. This number can be broken down to provide audience composition figures that are based on the distribution of the audience into demographic categories.

Audience Measurement Technology

Nielsen Television Index The source of national and network TV audience information is the Nielsen Television Index (NTI), which provides daily and weekly estimates of TV viewing and national sponsored network and major cable program audiences. Currently, BBM Canada is planning a national service to be launched in the spring of 2002. Historically, Nielsen provided this information using a two-pronged system consisting of a national sample of metered households along with a separate sample of diary households. In the metered households, an electronic measurement device known as the **audimeter** (audience meter) was hooked up to the TV set to continuously measure the channels to which the set was tuned. Network viewing for the country (the famous Nielsen ratings) was based on the results provided by audimeters placed in a national sample of homes carefully selected to represent the population of households. The metered households were supported by a separate panel of households that recorded viewing information in diaries. Since the audimeter could measure only the channel to which the set was tuned, the diary panel was used to gather demographic data on the viewing audience.

For many years, the television and advertising industries expressed concern over the audimeter/diary system. The information from diaries was not available to the network and advertising analysts for several weeks, and studies indicated the method was overstating the size of some key demographic audiences. Cooperation rates among diary keepers declined, and often the person who kept a household's diary did not note what other family members watched when he or she wasn't home. The complex new video environment and explosion in viewing options also made it difficult for diary keepers to maintain accurate viewing records.

As a result of these problems, and in response to competitive pressure from an audience measurement company from England, AGB, in 1987 Nielsen made the people meter the sole basis of its national rating system and eliminated the use of the diary panel.

The People Meter The **People Meter** is an electronic measuring device that incorporates the technology of the audimeter in a system that records not only what is being watched but also by whom in 3350 homes. The actual device is a small box with eight buttons—six for the family and two for visitors—that can be placed on the top of the TV set (Exhibit 10–2). A remote control unit permits electronic entries from anywhere in the room. Each member of the sample household is assigned a button that indicates his or her presence as a viewer. The People Meter collects what station is being tuned and, through interaction with the meter, who is sitting down and watching the programs.

The viewership information the People Meter collects from the household is stored in the Home Unit which in turn reports television use over a telephone line to a central computer at Nielsen Media Research head office. Data collected include when the set is turned on, which channel is viewed, when the channel is changed, and when the set is off, in addition to who is viewing. The demographic characteristics of the viewers are also in the system, and viewership can be matched to these traits. Nielsen's operation centre processes all this information each night for release to the TV and advertising industries. Nielsen uses a sample of metered households to provide overnight viewing results.

Many people believe People Meters are only the first step in improving the way audiences are measured. While the People Meter is seen as an improvement over the diary method, it still requires cooperation on an ongoing basis from people in the metered homes. Viewers in the Nielsen households, including young children, must punch a preassigned number on the remote control device each time they start or stop watching.

Exhibit 10–2
Nielsen Media Research uses the People Meter to measure national TV audiences

RADIO

Television has often been referred to as the ideal advertising medium, and to many people it personifies the glamour and excitement of the industry. Radio, on the other hand, has been called the Rodney Dangerfield of media because it gets no respect from many advertisers. Dominated by network programming and national advertisers before the growth of TV, radio has evolved into a primarily local advertising medium. Radio has also become a medium characterized by highly specialized programming appealing to very narrow segments of the population.

The importance of radio is best demonstrated by the numbers. There are 941 radio stations in Canada, including 274 AM stations and 667 FM stations. Radio reaches 93 percent of all Canadians over the age of 12 each week and has grown into a ubiquitous background to many activities, among them reading, driving, running, working, and socializing. The average Canadian listens to radio three hours per day or 21 hours per week. The pervasiveness of this medium has not gone unnoticed by advertisers; radio advertising revenue grew from $741 million in 1994 to $1.1 billion in 2001.

Radio has survived and flourished as an advertising medium because it offers advertisers certain strengths for communicating messages to their potential customers. However, radio has inherent limitations that affect its role in the advertiser's media strategy. IMC Perspective 10–3 highlights radio's recent attractiveness.

STRENGTHS OF RADIO

Radio has many strengths compared to other media, including cost efficiency and low absolute costs, reach and frequency, target audience selectivity, geographic coverage, scheduling flexibility, creativity, and image.

303

Radio's Resurgence

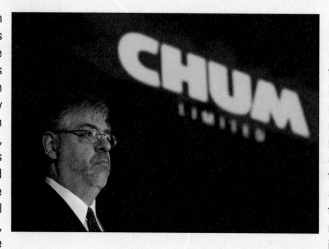

With the great blackout in Eastern Canada and various natural disasters across the country, 2003 will go down as the year of the radio. Although listenership peaked to satisfy people's need for information during those trying times, advertisers for national brands discovered or rediscovered the power of radio. With the coming technology of digital audio broadcasting (DAB), consumer interaction with the media, and the cost of media placement, radio is a strong option for a comprehensive IMC plan.

Brand development through radio appeared as a strong possibility and Goodyear Canada made this traditional media work. Building on the successful image from its TV ads, the radio ads used the highly recognizable spokesperson Tom Sharp with his distinctive and recognizable voice. The campaign focused on safety by informing consumers that various safety vehicles (e.g., ambulance, police car, or school bus) used Goodyear tires.

Technologically, radio is going digital like television. Compared to traditional analogue-based AM and FM stations, DAB offers CD-quality sound and a screen display that can communicate song credits, traffic, and emergency information, and possibly marketing messages. A consortium of major radio broadcasters (e.g., Chum, Rogers) launched a radio campaign describing these benefits of DAB with a suggestion to visit its website digitalradio.ca for more information. Many stations already offer DAB, however, consumers need to purchase a relatively inexpensive receiver. Some media planners remained skeptical, as consumers' perceptions of the benefits of DAB may not arise if they focus solely on the additional cost of the receiver. Moreover, the importance of the visual display was unclear and the availability in all markets limited the overall penetration.

Overall, radio's numbers speak for themselves. Its daily share of media time (i.e., three hours) is equal to television at 37 percent with daily newspapers trailing in third with 10 percent. Radio advertising revenues increased 6 percent for a total of $1.1 billion, easily surpassing all other media beyond television and daily newspapers. Although some believe radio's resurgence is a backlash against the higher costs of TV production and placement, others note that advertisers are tracking positive results and buy radio for 52 weeks a year. Moreover, with such an extensive investment, these kinds of advertisers look for ways to integrate radio with their other media.

Source: Andrea Zoe Aster, "Radio's New Wavelength," *Marketing Magazine*, February 2, 2004.

Cost Efficiency and Absolute Cost   One of the main strengths of radio as an advertising medium is its low cost. Radio commercials are very inexpensive to produce. They require only a script of the commercial to be read by the radio announcer or a copy of a prerecorded message that can be broadcast by the station. The cost for radio time is also low. The low relative costs of radio make it one of the most efficient of all advertising media, and the low absolute cost means the budget needed for an effective radio campaign is often lower than that for other media.

Reach and Frequency   The low cost of radio means advertisers can build more reach and frequency into their media schedule within a certain budget. They can use different stations to broaden the reach of their messages and multiple spots to ensure adequate frequency. Radio commercials can be produced more quickly than TV spots, and the companies can afford to run them more often.[22] Many national advertisers also recognize the cost efficiency of radio and use it as part of their media strategy.

Target Audience Selectivity   Another major advantage of radio is the high degree of audience selectivity available through the various program formats and geographic coverage of the numerous stations. Radio lets companies focus their advertising on specialized audiences such as certain demographic and lifestyle groups. Most areas have radio stations with formats such as adult contemporary, easy listening, classical music, country, news/talk shows, jazz, and all news, to name a few. For example, among 18- to 24-year olds, the most popular radio format is top 40, while those between the ages of 45 and 54 prefer news/talk. Elusive consumers like teenagers, college students, and working adults can be reached more easily through radio than most other media.

Radio can reach consumers other media can't. Light television viewers spend considerably more time with radio than with TV and are generally an upscale market in terms of income and education level. Light readers of magazines and newspapers also spend more time listening to radio. As mass marketing gives way to market segmentation and regional marketing, radio will continue to grow in importance.

Geographic Coverage   Radio is essentially a local media. In this respect, since all listeners can tune in, it offers excellent coverage within its geographic scope. Radio stations become an integral part of many communities, and the deejays and program hosts may become popular figures. Advertisers often use radio stations and personalities to enhance their involvement with a local market and to gain influence with local retailers. Radio also works very effectively in conjunction with place-based/point-of-purchase promotions. Retailers often use on-site radio broadcasts combined with special sales or promotions to attract consumers to their stores and get them to make a purchase (Exhibit 10–3). Live radio broadcasts are also used in conjunction with event marketing.

Scheduling Flexibility   Radio is probably the most flexible of all the advertising media because it has a very short closing period, which means advertisers can change their message almost up to the time it goes on the air. Radio commercials can usually be produced and scheduled on very short notice. Radio advertisers can easily adjust their messages to local market conditions and marketing situations.

Creativity for Cognitive Responses   The verbal nature of radio ads make them ideal for long copy to select target audiences who may appreciate greater detailed information for some products. Alternatively, radio ads can also provide more concise brand information in a timely manner. Moreover, both of these factors are highly relevant for those listening in their car, which is a significant percent of radio listenership. In either case, the informative nature of radio advertising makes it an opportunistic media to connect with a target audience on a more rational level.

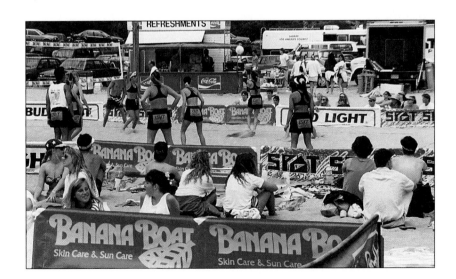

Exhibit 10–3
Banana Boat uses live radio broadcasts to promote its sun-care products

Media Image Radio advertising in general has a good media image. Consumers rely on radio for news, weather, and traffic information, not to mention the obvious program content. Thus, radio is well appreciated and this spills over to the ads as 77 percent of Canadians feel that radio advertising is acceptable.

LIMITATIONS OF RADIO

Several factors limit the effectiveness of radio as an advertising medium, among them weak creativity, short processing time, target audience coverage, limited listener attention, potential selective exposure, clutter, and low involvement. The media planner must consider them in determining the role the medium will play in the advertising program.

Creativity for Emotional Responses A major drawback of radio as an advertising medium is the absence of a visual image. The radio advertiser cannot show the product, demonstrate it, or use any type of visual appeal or information. While the creative options of radio are limited, many advertisers take advantage of the absence of a visual element to let consumers create their own picture of what is happening in a radio message. Some ads encourage listeners to use their imagination when processing a commercial message.

Radio may also reinforce television messages through a technique called **image transfer**, where the images of a TV commercial are implanted into a radio spot.[23] First the marketer establishes the video image of a TV commercial. Then it uses a similar, or even the same, audio portion (spoken words and/or jingle) as the basis for the radio counterpart. The idea is that when consumers hear the radio message, they will make the connection to the TV commercial, reinforcing its video images. Image transfer offers advertisers a way to make radio and TV ads work together. This promotional piece put out by the Radio Advertising Bureau of the U.S. shows how the image transfer process works (Exhibit 10–4).

Exhibit 10–4
The Radio Advertising Bureau promotes the concept of imagery transfer

306

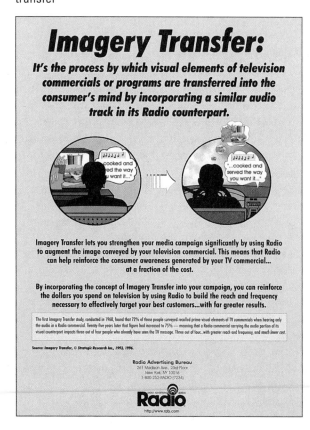

Amount of Processing Time A radio commercial is, like a TV ad, a short-lived and fleeting message that is externally paced and does not allow the receiver to control the rate at which it is processed.

Target Audience Coverage Another problem with radio is the high level of audience fragmentation due to the large number of stations. The percentage of the market tuned to any particular station is usually very small. The top-rated radio station in many major metropolitan areas with a number of AM and FM stations may attract less than 10 percent of the total listening audience. Advertisers that want a broad reach in their radio advertising media schedule have to buy time on a number of stations to cover even a local market.

Attention Another problem that plagues radio is that it is difficult to retain listener attention to commercials. Radio programming, particularly music, is often the background to some other activity and may not receive the listeners' full attention. Thus they may miss all or some of the commercials.

Selective Exposure One environment where radio has a more captive audience is in cars. But getting listeners to expose themselves to commercials can still be difficult.

Most people preprogram their car radio and change stations during commercial breaks. A study by Avery Abernethy found large differences between exposure to radio programs versus advertising for listeners in cars. They were exposed to only half of the advertising broadcast and changed stations frequently to avoid commercials.[24] Another factor that is detracting from radio listening in motor vehicles is the rapid growth of cellular phones. A recent study found that half of commuters surveyed who own a cellphone reported listening to less radio than they did a year earlier.[25]

Clutter Clutter is just as much a problem with radio as with other advertising media. Radio stations can play as many minutes of advertising as they like. Most radio stations carry an average of nearly 10 minutes of commercials every hour. During the popular morning and evening rush hours, the amount of commercial time may exceed 12 minutes. Advertisers must create commercials that break through the clutter or use heavy repetition to make sure their messages reach consumers. In a study of radio listeners conducted by Edison Research, perceptions of increased ad clutter were cited by participants as a reason for spending less time listening to radio.[26]

Low Involvement Similar to television, radio is generally considered a low-involvement media since it is faced with the same characteristics of short processing time and clutter. In fact, it may be seen as being less involving since it has the additional limitation of no visual.

BUYING RADIO TIME

The purchase of radio time is similar to that of television, as advertisers can make either network, or spot buys. Since these options were reviewed in the section on buying TV time, they are discussed here only briefly.

Network Radio Advertising time on radio can be purchased on a network basis. This is a relatively new option for advertisers who can now run ads on the CHUM radio network, The Team Sports Radio Network, and a few others. Using networks minimizes the amount of negotiation and administrative work needed to get national or regional coverage, and the costs are lower than those for individual stations. However, the number of affiliated stations on the network roster and the types of audiences they reach may vary, so the use of network radio reduces advertisers' flexibility in selecting stations.

Spot Radio National advertisers can also use spot radio to purchase airtime on individual stations in various markets. The purchase of spot radio provides greater flexibility in selecting markets, individual stations, and airtime and adjusting the message for local market conditions. By far the heaviest users of radio are local advertisers; the majority of radio advertising time is purchased from individual stations by local companies. Auto dealers, retailers, restaurants, and financial institutions are among the heaviest users of local radio advertising.

TIME CLASSIFICATIONS

As with television, the broadcast day for radio is divided into various time periods or dayparts, as shown in Figure 10–10. The size of the radio listening audience varies widely across the dayparts, and advertising rates follow accordingly. The largest radio audiences (and thus the highest rates) occur during the early morning and late afternoon drive times. Radio rates also vary according to the number of spots or type of audience plan purchased, the supply and demand of time available in the local market, and the ratings of the individual station. Rate information is available directly from the stations and is summarized in CARD. Some stations issue grid rate cards. But many

FIGURE 10–10
Dayparts for radio
☐ ☐ ☐ ☐ ☐

Morning drive time	6:00–10:00 A.M.
Daytime	10:00 A.M.–3:00 P.M.
Afternoon/evening drive time	3:00–7:00 P.M.
Nighttime	7:00 P.M.–12:00 A.M.
All night	12:00–6:00 A.M.

stations do not adhere strictly to rate cards. Their rates are negotiable and depend on factors such as availability, time period, and number of spots purchased.

MEASURING THE RADIO AUDIENCE

As noted earlier, BBM Canada also provides information on radio listenership using a diary method similar to television. Surveys are done up to three times per year in over 130 radio markets. BBM Canada publishes many reports associated with these surveys. Market reports summarize each radio station's audience by occupation, language, and other important characteristics. Other similar reports with greater aggregation across regions are also published. As for television, BBM Canada provides its members with many supporting documents to understand how to use radio as a communication tool. It also offers many software applications so that advertisers can purchase radio media effectively and efficiently. The three basic elements in the BBM Canada reports are:

- Person estimates—the estimated number of people listening.
- Rating—the percentage of listeners in the survey area population.
- Share—the percentage of the total estimated listening audience.

These three estimates are further defined by using quarter-hour and cume figures. The **average quarter-hour (AQH) figure** expresses the average number of people estimated to have listened to a station for a minimum of five minutes during any quarter-hour in a time period. This figure helps to determine the audience and cost of a spot schedule within a particular time period.

Cume stands for cumulative audience, the estimated total number of different people who listened to a station for at least five minutes in a quarter-hour period within a reported daypart. Cume estimates the reach potential of a radio station.

FIGURE 10–11
Weekly reach and share of total hours tuned by demographics
☐ ☐ ☐ ☐ ☐

Canada		Reach AM (%)	Reach FM (%)	Share AM (%)	Share FM (%)
12+		38.5	80.4	26.3	73.7
Women 18+		39.1	80.2	27.3	72.7
Men 18+		43.0	80.2	27.1	72.9
Teens 12–17		14.7	82.6	6.0	94.0

Source: BBM, Fall '02

Quebec	Language	Reach AM (%)	Reach FM (%)	Share AM (%)	Share FM (%)
12+	(Fr.)	21.1	88.8	12.3	87.7
	(Eng.)	40.5	83.0	26.1	73.9
Women 18+	(Fr.)	20.6	90.4	12.9	87.1
	(Eng.)	40.3	83.0	26.7	73.3
Men 18+	(Fr.)	24.8	88.8	12.3	87.7
	(Eng.)	45.3	83.2	26.9	73.1
Teens 12–17	(Fr.)	5.0	79.6	2.3	97.7
	(Eng.)	15.8	81.8	5.9	94.1

Source: BBM, Fall '02 *Home Language

Time Block			Women 18+ (%)	Men 18+ (%)	Teens 12–17 (%)
Breakfast	Mon–Fri	6–10a	49	47	4
Midday	Mon–Fri	10–4p	51	47	2
Drive	Mon–Fri	4–7p	46	49	5
Evening	Mon–Fri	7p–12a	43	47	10

Source: BBM, Fall '02

FIGURE 10–12
Audience composition by time block
☐ ☐ ☐ ☐ ☐

The **average quarter-hour rating (AQH RTG)** expresses the estimated number of listeners as a percentage of the survey area population. The **average quarter-hour share (AQH SHR)** is the percentage of the total listening audience tuned to each station. It shows the share of listeners each station captures out of the total listening audience in the survey area. Figures 10–11 to 10–15 provide a summary of Canadian radio listening habits.

Audience research data on radio are often limited, particularly compared with TV, magazines, or newspapers. The BBM audience research measurement mostly focuses on demographics and a handful of lifestyle factors. Most users of radio are local companies that cannot support research on radio listenership in their markets. Thus, media planners do not have as much audience information available to guide them in their purchase of radio time as they do with other media.

The Radio Marketing Bureau (RMB) is an organization that plays a similar role for radio as the Television Bureau of Canada, discussed earlier in this chapter. It acts as a resource for radio stations and those involved with selling airtime for radios. Its mission is to educate advertisers on the effective use of the radio medium and to assist advertisers in meeting their communication objectives. The Radio Marketing Bureau offers professional services to advertisers if needed. It also offers a training and certificate program for those working in the radio industry. Finally, this organization does some research to help support radio as a viable communication medium.

FIGURE 10–13
Percent weekly reach and hours tuned by major demographic
☐ ☐ ☐ ☐ ☐

FIGURE 10–14
Percentage of listening by location
☐ ☐ ☐ ☐

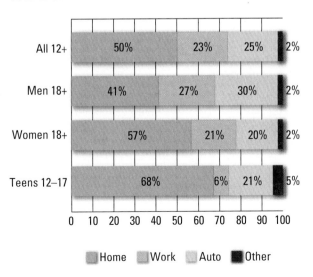

FIGURE 10–15
Percent weekly reach by major demographic, by location
☐ ☐ ☐ ☐

309

SUMMARY

Television and radio media are the most pervasive media in most consumers' daily lives and offer advertisers the opportunity to reach vast audiences. Both media are time rather than space oriented and organized similarly in that they use a system of affiliated stations belonging to a network, as well as individual stations, to broadcast their programs and commercial messages. Advertising on radio or TV can be done on national or regional network programs or purchased in spots from local stations.

TV has grown faster than any other advertising medium in history and has become the leading medium for national advertisers. No other medium offers its creative capabilities; the combination of sight, sound, and movement give the advertiser a vast number of options for presenting a commercial message with high impact. Television also offers advertisers mass coverage at a low relative cost. Variations in programming and audience composition, along with the growth of cable, are helping TV offer more audience selectivity to advertisers. While television is often viewed as the ultimate advertising medium, it has several limitations, including the high absolute cost of producing and airing commercials, low target audience selectivity, short processing time, extensive clutter, high selective exposure, and distrustful image.

Information regarding the size and composition of national and local TV audiences is provided by BBM Canada and Nielsen. The amount of money networks or stations can charge for commercial time on their programs is based on its audience measurement figures. This information is also important to media planners, as it is used to determine the combination of shows needed to attain specific levels of reach and frequency with the advertiser's target audience.

The role of radio as an entertainment and advertising medium has changed with the rapid growth of television. Radio has evolved into a primarily local advertising medium that offers highly specialized programming appealing to narrow segments of the market. Radio offers advertisers cost efficiency and low absolute costs, reach and frequency, target audience selectivity, geographic coveage, scheduling flexibility, creativity, and image.

The major drawback of radio is its weak creativity owing to the absence of a visual image. The short and fleeting nature of the radio commercial, the highly fragmented nature of the radio audience, low involvement, and clutter are also problems.

As with TV, the rate structure for radio advertising time varies with the size of the audience delivered. The primary sources of listener information are BBM and RMB.

310

KEY TERMS

split-30s, *287*
zapping, *288*
zipping, *288*
television network, *291*
affiliates, *291*
scatter market, *292*
spot advertising, *293*
station reps, *293*

sponsorship, *293*
dayparts, *295*
cable television, *296*
direct broadcast satellite (DBS) services, *296*
superstations, *296*
infomercials, *297*
television households, *300*

program rating, *300*
ratings point, *301*
households using television (HUT), *302*
share of audience, *302*
total audience, *302*
audimeter, *302*
People Meter, *303*

image transfer, *306*
average quarter-hour (AQH) figure, *308*
cume, *308*
average quarter-hour rating (AQH RTG), *309*
average quarter-hour share (AQH SHR), *309*

DISCUSSION QUESTIONS

1. Discuss the advantages of television as an advertising medium and the importance of these factors to major advertisers such as automobile companies or packaged goods marketers.

2. Television is often described as a mass medium that offers little selectivity to advertisers. Do you agree with this statement? What are some of the ways selectivity can be achieved through TV advertising?

3. Choose a particular television daypart other than prime time and analyze the products and services advertised during this period. Why do you think these companies have chosen to advertise during this daypart?

4. Explain what is meant by zapping and zipping and how they affect television viewing behaviour. Discuss some of the ways that advertisers can deal with these problems.

5. Discuss the advantages and limitation of advertising on specialty channels. Discuss how both large national advertisers and small local companies might use cable TV effectively in their media plans.

6. Discuss the methods used to measure network and local TV viewing audiences. Do you think the measurement methods used for each are producing reliable and valid estimates of the viewing audiences? How might they be improved?

7. What are the advantages and disadvantages of advertising on radio? What types of advertisers are most likely to use radio?

8. What is meant by image transfer in radio advertising? Find an example of a radio campaign that is using this concept and evaluate it.

9. Discuss some of the factors that media buyers should take into consideration when buying advertising time on radio.

311

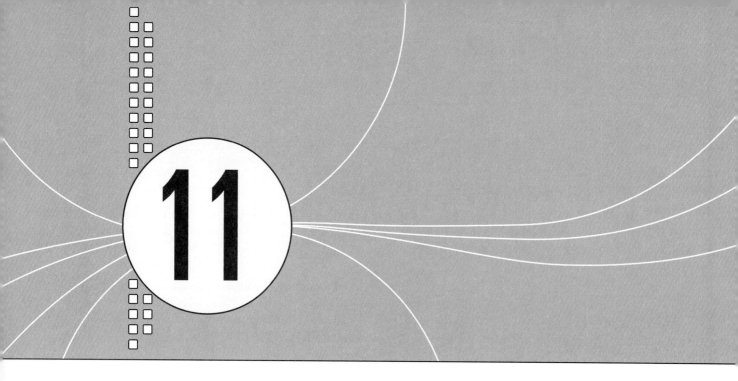

11

Print Media

CHAPTER OBJECTIVES

- To examine the structure of the magazine and newspaper industries and the role of each medium in the advertising program.

- To analyze the strengths and limitations of magazines and newspapers as advertising media.

- To examine the various types of magazines and newspapers and the value of each as an advertising medium.

- To discuss how advertising space is purchased in magazines and newspapers, how readership is measured, and how rates are determined.

- To consider future developments in magazines and newspapers and how these trends will influence their use as advertising media.

Growth of Men's Magazines

Just a few years ago, advertisers faced a print environment nearly void of any magazines directed towards Canadian men, however that has all changed with the advent of *UMM, Toro, Menz,* and *Rev*. Historically, publications directed towards men were not financially viable although many in the industry admit that men have perceived the need for this type of reading material for quite some time.

Seen as bit of a *Maxim*-copycat, *UMM,* or *Urban Male Magazine,* showed advertisers and agencies that a category of Canadian men's magazines was possible. *UMM* started the trend about five years ago, progressed at a steady pace, and has now moved to eight issues in 2004, up from a previous six issues. With a paid circulation of 75,000, some agencies view *UMM* as the undisputed leader, especially considering that half of this is based on subscriptions.

Toro is a high quality, general interest magazine targeting men between the ages of 25 and 54 with an income greater than $75,000. With a circulation of 220,000 through its *Globe and Mail* distribution, *Toro* did not rely on newsstand or subscription sales when launched in 2003. Its

debut issue attracted 27 pages of ads from major advertisers such as Absolut, CIBC, and Toyota. The most represented product categories included fashion and beauty, alcohol, and automotive. For 2004, it appeared to be on track for eight issues per year up from an initial five issues in 2003.

Rev, a custom-published venture from Imperial Tobacco, distributed its new quarterly magazine to 150,000 male smokers listed in its database in 2003. Looking to communicate more directly to consumers because of anti-smoking legislation, Imperial planned to expand to newsstand sales in 2004 in order to reach a larger readership.

Menz started purely as a men's magazine, but had recently changed to more of an adventure travel magazine that still provides similar content to the other competitors (e.g., health, sex, careers, relationships). The Montreal-based publication developed a solid circulation of 30,000 by the end of 2003.

Source: Chris Daniels, "The RISE of Men's Mags," *Marketing Magazine,* September 22, 2003.

Magazines and newspapers have been advertising media for more than two centuries; for many years, they were the only major media available to advertisers. With the growth of the broadcast media, particularly television, reading habits declined. More consumers turned to TV viewing not only as their primary source of entertainment but also for news and information. But despite the competition from the broadcast media, newspapers and magazines have remained important media classes to both consumers and advertisers.

Thousands of magazines are published in Canada and throughout the world. They appeal to nearly every specific consumer interest and lifestyle, as well as to thousands of businesses and occupations. By becoming a highly specialized medium that reaches specific target audiences, the magazine industry has prospered. Newspapers are still the primary advertising medium in terms of both ad revenue and number of advertisers. Newspapers are particularly important as a local advertising medium for hundreds of thousands of retail businesses and are often used by large national advertisers as well.

Magazines and newspapers are an important part of our lives. For many consumers, newspapers are their primary source of product information. They would not think of going shopping without checking to see who is having a sale or clipping coupons from the weekly food section or Saturday inserts. Many people read a number of different magazines each week or month to become better informed or simply entertained. Individuals employed in various occupations rely on business magazines to keep them current about trends and developments in their industries as well as in business in general.

The role of magazines and newspapers in the advertiser's media plan differs from that of the broadcast media because they allow the presentation of detailed information that can be processed at the reader's own pace. The print media are not intrusive like radio and TV, and they generally require some effort on the part of the reader for the advertising message to have an impact. For this reason, newspapers and magazines are often referred to as *high-involvement media*.[1] While both magazines and newspapers are print media, the strengths and limitations of the two are quite different, as are the types of advertising each attracts. This chapter focuses on these two major forms of print media. It examines the specific strengths and limitations of each, along with factors that are important in determining when and how to use newspapers and magazines in the media plan.

EVALUATION OF MAGAZINES

Over the past several decades, magazines have grown rapidly to serve the educational, informational, and entertainment needs of a wide range of readers in both the consumer and business markets. Magazines are the most specialized of all advertising media. While some magazines—such as *Reader's Digest*, *Time*, and *TV Guide*—are general mass-appeal publications, most are targeted to a very specific audience. There is a magazine designed to appeal to nearly every type of consumer in terms of demographics, lifestyle, activities, interests, or fascination. Numerous magazines are targeted toward specific businesses and industries as well as toward individuals engaged in various professions.

The wide variety makes magazines an appealing medium to a vast number of advertisers. Users of magazines range from large consumer products companies such as Procter & Gamble and General Motors to a small company advertising gardening equipment in *Canadian Gardening* magazine.

CLASSIFICATIONS OF MAGAZINES

To gain some perspective on the various types of magazines available and the advertisers that use them, consider the way magazines are generally classified. Canadian Advertising Rates and Data (CARD), the primary reference source on periodicals for

314

media planners, divides magazines into three broad categories based on the audience to which they are directed: consumer, farm, and business publications. Each category is then further classified according to the magazine's editorial content and audience appeal.

Consumer Magazines   Consumer magazines are bought by the general public for information and/or entertainment. CARD divides 550 domestic consumer magazines into 44 classifications, among them general interest, sports, travel and tourism, and women's. Another way of classifying consumer magazines is by distribution: They can be sold through subscription, store distribution, or controlled distribution (free) to selected individuals. Figures 11–1 and 11–2 show the top Canadian magazines in terms of circulation. Magazines can also be classified by frequency; weekly, monthly, and bimonthly are the most common. Figure 11–3 shows the top U.S. magazines with paid Canadian circulation.

Consumer magazines represent the major portion of the magazine industry, accounting for nearly two-thirds of all advertising dollars spent in magazines. The distribution of advertising revenue in consumer magazines is highly concentrated; the top 10 magazines receive more than 60 percent of total consumer magazine advertising. Consumer magazines are best suited to marketers interested in reaching general consumers of products and services as well as to companies trying to reach a specific target market. The most frequently advertised categories in consumer magazines are automotive, direct response, toiletries and cosmetics, computers, office equipment and stationery, and business and consumer services.

While large national advertisers tend to dominate consumer magazine advertising in terms of expenditures, consumer magazines are also important to smaller companies selling products that appeal to specialized markets. Special-interest magazines assemble consumers with similar lifestyles or interests and offer marketers an efficient way to reach these people with little wasted coverage or circulation. For example, a manufacturer of ski equipment such as Nordica, Rossignol, or Salomon might find *Ski Canada* magazine the best vehicle for advertising to serious skiers. Not only are these specialty magazines of value to firms

315

Publication	Average Total Circulation	IP 4CB Rate ($)	Readers Per Copy	(000s) Total
LeisureWays/ Journey/Going Places	1,393,554	28,460	1.0	1,327
Westworld	1,118,962	25,460	1.3	1,288
Reader's Digest	1,037,304	34,140	6.8	7,029
Feature	803,989	11,375	N/A	754
Chatelaine	704,779	41,750	6.0	3,993
Journey/Going Places	702,432	16,170	N/A	N/A
LeisureWays	691,122	16,170	N/A	1,327
Ski Press (bilingual)	623,643	15,615	N/A	N/A
Canadian Living	543,826	31,865	8.4	4,287
Touring (bilingual)	540,679	11,730	1.6	826
Food & Drink	515,115	14,255	3.2	1,534
Click: Smart Living	517,112	17,100	N/A	N/A
Homemaker's	501,402	21,260	3.9	1,886
Tribute	500,050	17,500	3.3	1,211
Maclean's	450,615	32,600	6.3	2,830
Economist	403,131	28,555	N/A	N/A

Source: PMB 2003 rates and circulation as of April 2003 CARD

FIGURE 11–1

Top English-language magazines by circulation and readership

☐ ☐ ☐ ☐ ☐

FIGURE 11–2

Top French-language magazines by circulation and readership

☐☐☐☐☐

Publication	Average Total Circulation	IP 4CB Rate ($)	Readers Per Copy	(000s) Total
Ski Presse	623,643	15,615	N/A	N/A
Touring (bilingual)	540,679	11,730	1.6	826
Primeurs	399,374	7,125	1.7	567
Sélection du Reader's Digest	232,767	11,080	4.9	1,091
Coup de Pouce	217,068	11,230	6.6	1,144
Virage	214,589	4,730	N/A	N/A
Châtelaine	191,398	13,910	6.0	992
L'âctualité	187,700	16,785	5.4	954
Enroute	171,632	18,500	4.8	811
Voir (Montréal/Quebec City)	157,081	14,420	3.2	478
Le Bel Âge	151,731	6,445	5.6	817
Le Coureur des Neiges	145,105	5,880	N/A	N/A
Madame	109,880	6,715	4.1	435
7 Jours	108,767	11,710	10.9	1,091

Source: PMB 2003 rates and circulation as of April 2003 CARD

interested in reaching a specific market segment, but their editorial content often creates a very favourable advertising environment for relevant products and services (see Exhibit 11–1).

Farm Publications   The second major CARD category consists of all the magazines directed to farmers and their families. About 86 publications are tailored to nearly every possible type of farming or agricultural interest (e.g., *Ontario Milk Producer*, *Ontario Produce Farmer*). A number of farm publications are directed at farmers in specific provinces or regions, such as Alberta Beef (see Exhibit 11–2). Farm publications are not classified with business publications because historically farms were not perceived as businesses.

FIGURE 11–3

Top U.S. magazines with paid Canadian circulation

☐☐☐☐☐

Publication	Circulation
National Geographic	390,508
Cosmopolitan	225,651
Maxim	203,261
People	186,515
Prevention	186,444
Martha Stewart Living	170,479
National Enquirer	148,965
Star	147,312
In Style	145,350
YM	113,849
First For Women	111,770
Teen People	108,506

Source: SRDS 2003

Business Publications   Business publications are those magazines or trade journals published for specific businesses, industries, or occupations. CARD breaks down magazines and trade journals into 109 categories. The major categories include

1. Magazines directed at specific professional groups, such as *Canadian Lawyer* for lawyers and *Canadian Architect* for architects.
2. Industrial magazines directed at businesspeople in various manufacturing and production industries—for example, *Process Equipment and Control News* and *Heavy Construction*.
3. Trade magazines targeted to wholesalers, dealers, distributors, and retailers, among them *Canadian Grocer*.
4. General business magazines aimed at executives in all areas of business, such as *Canadian Grocer*.

The numerous business publications reach specific types of professional people with particular interests and give them important information relevant to their industry, occupation, and/or careers. Business publications are important to advertisers because they provide an efficient way of reaching the specific types of individuals who constitute their target market. Much marketing occurs at the trade and business-to-business level, where one company sells its products or services directly to another. IMC Perspective 11–1 describes a new magazine format that has arrived in Canada.

316

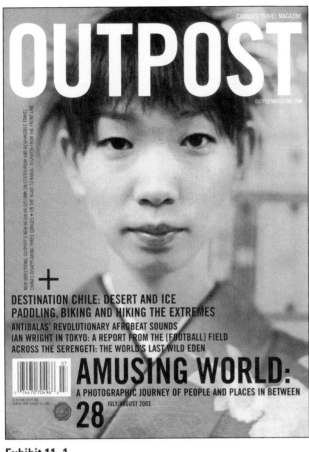

Exhibit 11–1
Outpost magazine is an excellent vehicle for reaching adventure travel tourists

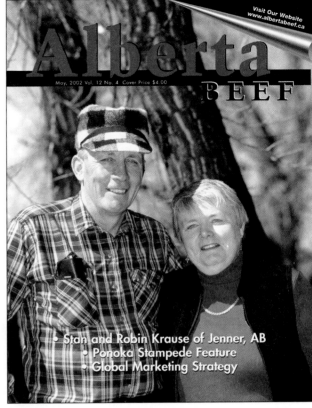

Exhibit 11–2
Alberta Beef is read by many cattle ranchers

317

STRENGTHS OF MAGAZINES

Magazines have a number of characteristics that make them attractive as an advertising medium. Strengths of magazines include their target audience selectivity, geographic coverage, creativity options, permanence, prestige image, and readers' acceptable selective exposure and attention levels.

Target Audience Selectivity   One of the main advantages of using magazines as an advertising medium is their **selectivity**, or ability to reach a specific target audience. Magazines are the most selective of all media except direct mail. Most magazines are published for readers with very specific interests. The thousands of magazines published in Canada reach all types of consumers and businesses and allow advertisers to target their advertising to segments of the population who buy their products. For example, *PhotoLife* is targeted toward camera buffs, *Exclaim!* reaches those with an avid interest in music, and *What!* claims to be "the voice and choice of Canadian youth." Many new magazines are introduced each year targeting new interests and trends.

One of the most recent and interesting titles to come about is *Vice*. This Canadian success story has an international circulation of 350,000 and has versions in the U.S., the U.K., and Japan with plans for versions in Scandinavia, Germany, Holland, and France. Designed for the hip, urban, young consumer, *Vice* has steadily built an "edgy" reputation making some advertisers critical of the magazine's content and wary about advertising in it. In contrast, Canada now has *Nuvo* magazine, a refined publication (non-paid circulation) catering to the very affluent who appreciate a refined lifestyle of luxury.[2]

Shopping Magazines for Women

Canadian publishers joined an international trend of shopping magazines in 2004 with the launch of three titles, *Shopping Clin d'Oeil, Fashion Shops,* and *Loulou.* Shopping magazines are fashion and beauty publications designed to show women the selection available and the prices for a variety of products. In contrast, typical fashion/beauty lifestyle magazines continue to offer editorial content on celebrities, fashion trends, and the like.

Lucky, the most acclaimed international shopping magazine racked up a circulation of 900,000 in just three years, turned a profit recently, and received the award for Magazine of the Year from *Advertising Age*. With a simple formula of a fashion magazine stripped of its thin models and editorial content, *Lucky* provided interested shoppers with detailed product information, prices, and store locations. In fact, it added stickers to allow consumers to mark items as "yes" or "maybe." Follow-up research supported the venture by showing that 80 percent of the readers bought something after seeing an ad for it in *Lucky*.

Shopping Clin d'Oeil, based on the women's magazine, *Clin d'Oeil*, offered the first Canadian shopping magazine in March of 2004. It planned three initial issues of 144 pages each to be distributed to existing readers representing 25- to 35-year-old women. Similarly, the anticipated *Fashion Shops*, an off-shoot of *Fashion*, is viewed by its publishers

as the 11th and 12th issues. Despite its brand extension status, *Fashion Shops* would contain planning tools and shopping lists to help facilitate consumer purchases. *Loulou* targeted urban professional women aged 18–35 and its publishers planned for 100,000 English and 60,000 French subscribers.

Naturally, this new publishing format attracted advertisers who jumped at the opportunity to build their brand one step closer to the purchase action or the actual purchase decision. Some advertising executives believed shopping magazines could replace some of their traditional advertising placements that have less reach or greater per reader costs. Another predicted that by the end of 2005, shopping magazines would be a normal placement on the part of advertisers even though audience characteristics and sizes would not be ascertained until 2007 by the Print Measurement Bureau. However, advertisers look to existing PMB research that indicates over 40 percent of the 7.5 million Canadian women aged 18–49 really enjoy shopping for clothes and try to stay informed of style and fashion trends.

Sources: Orville Manangan, "Pick and Choose," *Marketing Magazine*, April 19, 2004; Chris Powell, "Mags Target Shopping Fashionistas," *Marketing Magazine*, November 24, 2003; Andrea Zoe, "Aster Shopping Basics," *Marketing Magazine*, April 19, 2004.

In addition to providing selectivity based on interests, magazines can provide advertisers with high demographic selectivity. *Demographic selectivity*, or the ability to reach specific demographic groups, is available in two ways. First, most magazines are, as a result of editorial content, aimed at fairly well-defined demographic segments. *Canadian Living* and *Chatelaine* are read predominantly by women; *The Hockey News* is read mostly by men. Older consumers can be reached through publications like *FiftyPlus*.

Selectivity through demographics is an approach used to reach different target audiences that participate in group purchase decisions. Sun-Rype's Fruit to Go used magazines to deliver specific appeals to mothers and their children in a recent campaign. Ads in *Canadian Living, Canadian House & Home* and *Today's Parent*, communicated the health benefits of the 100-percent fruit bars. Ads in YTV's *Whoa!, Kidsworld, Pop!* and *News for Kids* delivered fun consumption and lifestyle benefits. Overall response has been positive according to a Sun-Rype executive who claims that both mothers and children have positive views of the brand and that sales have increased dramatically.[3]

Selectivity can be applied effectively by tailoring the message by language. As you might expect, Canada has magazines written in both English and French. In fact the latter has seen tremendous change recently with the relaunching of several titles prompting significant readership and ad revenue growth.[4]

Geographic Coverage One way to achieve specific geographic coverage is by using a magazine that is targeted toward a particular area. One of the more successful media developments of recent years has been the growth of city magazines in some Canadian cities. *Toronto Life, Vancouver Magazine,* and *Montréal Scope*, to name a few, provide residents of these areas with articles concerning lifestyle, events, and the like, in these cities and their surrounding metropolitan areas (Exhibit 11–3).

Another way to achieve selective geographic coverage in magazines is through purchasing ad space in specific geographic editions of national or regional magazines. A number of publications (e.g., *Maclean's, Chatelaine*) divide their circulation into groupings based on regions or major metropolitan areas and offer advertisers the option of concentrating their ads in these editions.

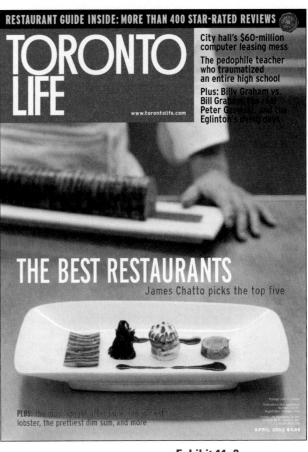

Exhibit 11–3
City magazines such as Toronto Life offer advertisers high geographic selectivity

CARD lists the consumer magazines offering geographic editions. Regional advertisers can purchase space in editions that reach only areas where they have distribution, yet still enjoy the prestige of advertising in a major national magazine. National advertisers can use the geographic editions to focus their advertising on areas with the greatest potential or those needing more promotional support. They can also use regional editions to test-market products or alternative promotional campaigns in various regions of the country.

Ads in regional editions can also list the names of retailers or distributors in various markets, thus encouraging greater local support from the trade. The trend toward regional marketing is increasing the importance of having regional media available to marketers. The availability of regional and demographic editions can also reduce the cost per thousand for reaching desired audiences.

Creativity for Cognitive and Emotional Responses One of the most valued attributes of magazine advertising is the reproduction quality of the ads. Magazines are generally printed on high-quality paper stock and use printing processes that provide excellent reproduction in black and white or colour. Since magazines are a visual medium where illustrations are often a dominant part of an ad, this is a very important property. The reproduction quality of most magazines is far superior to that offered by the other major print medium of newspapers, particularly when colour is needed. The use of colour has become a virtual necessity in most product categories, and more than two-thirds of all magazine ads now use colour.

In addition to their excellent reproduction capabilities, magazines also offer advertisers a great deal of flexibility in terms of the type, size, and placement of the advertising material. Some magazines offer (often at extra charge) a variety of special options that can enhance the creative appeal of the ad and increase attention and readership. Examples include gatefolds, bleed pages, inserts, and creative space buys.

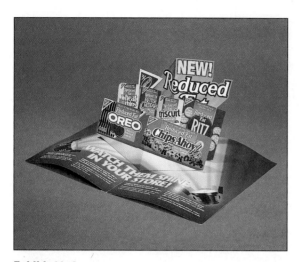

Exhibit 11–4
Nabisco used a pop-up ad to get the attention of trade magazine readers

Gatefolds enable an advertiser to make a striking presentation by using a third page that folds out and gives the ad an extra-large spread. Gatefolds are often found at the inside cover of large consumer magazines or on some inside pages. Advertisers use gatefolds to make a very strong impression, especially on special occasions such as the introduction of a new product or brand. For example, automobile advertisers often use gatefolds to introduce new versions of their cars each model year. Not all magazines offer gatefolds, however, and they must be reserved well in advance and are sold at a premium.

Bleed pages are those where the advertisement extends all the way to the end of the page, with no margin of white space around the ad. Bleeds give the ad an impression of being larger and make a more dramatic impact. Many magazines charge an extra 10 to 20 percent for bleeds.

In addition to gatefolds and bleed pages, creative options available through magazines include unusual page sizes and shapes. Some advertisers have grabbed readers' attention by developing three-dimensional pop-up ads that jump off the page. Exhibit 11–4 shows a pop-up ad that Nabisco used in several trade magazines to promote its Reduced Fat cracker and cookie products.

Various other *inserts* are used in many magazines. These include return cards, recipe booklets, coupons, and even product samples. Cosmetic companies use scratch-and-sniff inserts to introduce new fragrances, and some companies use them to promote deodorants, laundry detergents, or other products whose scent is important. Inserts are also used in conjunction with direct-response ads and as part of sales promotion strategies.

Scented ads, pop-ups, singing ads, and other techniques are ways to break through the clutter in magazines and capture consumers' attention. However, there recently has been some backlash against various types of *printaculars*. Critics argue that they alter the appearance and feel of a magazine and the reader's relationship to it. Advertisers do not want to run regular ads that have to compete against heavy inserts, pop-ups, talking ads, or other distractions. Some advertisers and agencies are even asking publishers to notify them when they plan to run any spectacular inserts so that they can decide whether to pull their regular ads from the issue.[5]

Creative space buys are another option of magazines. Some magazines let advertisers purchase space units in certain combinations to increase the impact of their media budget. For example, WD-40, an all-purpose lubrication product, uses half- or quarter-page ads on consecutive pages of several magazines, mentioning a different use for the product on each page, as shown in Exhibit 11–5. This strategy gives the company greater impact for its media dollars and is helpful in promoting the product's variety of uses.

Permanence A distinctive strength offered by magazines is their long life span. TV and radio are characterized by fleeting messages that have a very short life span; newspapers are generally discarded soon after being read. Magazines, however, are generally read over several days and are often kept for reference. They are retained in the home longer than any other medium and are generally referred to on several occasions. A study of magazine audiences found that readers devote nearly an hour over a period of two or three days to reading an average magazine.[6] Studies have also found that nearly 75 percent of consumers retain magazines for future reference.[7] One benefit of the longer life of magazines is that reading occurs at a less hurried pace and there is more opportunity to examine ads in considerable detail. This means ads can use longer and more detailed copy, which can be very important for high-involvement and complex products or services. The permanence of magazines also means readers can be exposed to ads on multiple occasions and can pass mag-

Exhibit 11–5
WD-40 uses quarter-page ads to get greater impact from its media budget

azines along to other readers. In conclusion, magazines feature very significant involvement levels with an extensive amount of processing time.

Media Image   Another positive feature of magazine advertising is the prestige the product or service may gain from advertising in publications with a favourable image. Companies whose products rely heavily on perceived quality, reputation, and/or image often buy space in prestigious publications with high-quality editorial content whose consumers have a high level of interest in the advertising pages. For example, *Flare* covers young women's fashions in a very favourable environment, and a clothing manufacturer may advertise its products in these magazines to enhance the prestige of its lines. *Canadian Geographic* provides an impressive editorial environment that includes high-quality photography. The magazine's upscale readers are likely to have a favourable image of the publication that may transfer to the products advertised on its pages.

While most media planners recognize that the environment created by a publication is important, it can be difficult to determine the image a magazine provides. Subjective estimates based on media planners' experience are often used to assess a magazine's prestige, as are objective measures such as reader opinion surveys.

Selective Exposure and Attention   With the exception of newspapers, consumers are more receptive to advertising in magazines than in any other medium. Magazines are generally purchased because the information they contain interests the reader, and ads provide additional information that may be of value in making a purchase decision.

In addition to their relevance, magazine ads are likely to be received favourably by consumers because, unlike broadcast ads, they are nonintrusive and can easily be ignored. Studies show that the majority of magazine readers welcome ads; only a

321

small percentage have negative attitudes toward magazine advertising.[8] Some magazines, such as bridal or fashion publications, are purchased as much for their advertising as for their editorial content. Some studies have shown that magazine readers are more likely to attend to and recall ads than are TV viewers.

LIMITATIONS OF MAGAZINES

Although the strengths offered by magazines are considerable, they have certain drawbacks too. These include the costs of advertising, their limited reach and frequency, the long lead time required in placing an ad, weak target audience coveage, and the problem of clutter.

Absolute Cost and Cost Efficiency The costs of advertising in magazines vary according to the size of the audience they reach and their selectivity. Advertising in large mass-circulation magazines like *Maclean's* can be very expensive. For example, a full-page, four-colour ad in *Maclean's* magazine's national edition (circulation 500,000) cost $25,000 as of June, 2000. Popular positions such as the back cover cost even more.

Like any medium, magazines must be considered not only from an absolute cost perspective but also in terms of relative costs. Most magazines emphasize their effectiveness in reaching specific target audiences at a low cost per thousand. Media planners generally focus on the relative costs of a publication in reaching their target audience. However, they may recommend a magazine with a high cost per thousand because of its ability to reach a small, specialized market segment. Of course, advertisers with limited budgets will be interested in the absolute costs of space in a magazine and the costs of producing quality ads for these publications.

Reach and Frequency Magazines are generally not as effective as other media in offering reach and frequency. While adults in Canada read one or more consumer magazines each month, the percentage of adults reading any individual publication tends to be much smaller, so magazines have a thin penetration of households. For example, *Maclean's* has a high circulation, but it represents only 4 percent of the 11.6 million households in Canada.

Thus, advertisers seeking broad reach must make media buys in a number of magazines, which means more negotiations and transactions. For a broad reach strategy, magazines are used in conjunction with other media. Since most magazines are monthly or at best weekly publications, the opportunity for building frequency through the use of the same publication is limited. Using multiple ads in the same issue of a publication is an inefficient way to build frequency. Most advertisers try to achieve frequency by adding other magazines with similar audiences to the media schedule.

Long Lead Time Another drawback of magazines is the long lead time needed to place an ad thus reducing scheduling flexibility. Most major publications have a 30- to 90-day lead time, which means space must be purchased and the ad must be prepared well in advance of the actual publication date. No changes in the art or copy of the ad can be made after the closing date. This long lead time means magazine ads cannot be as timely as other media, such as radio or newspapers, in responding to current events or changing market conditions.

Target Audience Coverage The flipside of the strength of target audience selectivity is the limitation of magazines in providing extensive target audience coverage. Even though a magazine may draw an audience with a particular interest, for example, hockey with *The Hockey News*, the number of people reading the publication versus the number of people who actually play hockey is substantially disproportionate.

Clutter While the problem of advertising clutter is generally discussed in reference to the broadcast media, magazines also have this drawback. Clutter is not as serious an issue for the print media as for radio or TV, since consumers tend to be more receptive and tolerant of print advertising. They can also control their exposure to a magazine ad simply by turning the page. The clutter problem for magazines is something of a paradox: The more successful a magazine becomes, the more advertising pages it attracts, and this leads to greater clutter. In fact, magazines generally gauge their success in terms of the number of advertising pages they sell.

Magazine publishers do attempt to control the clutter problem by maintaining a reasonable balance of editorial pages to advertising. However, many magazines contain ads on more than half of their pages. This clutter makes it difficult for an advertiser to gain readers' attention and draw them into the ad. Thus, many print ads use strong visual images, catchy headlines, or some of the creative techniques discussed earlier to grab the interest of magazine readers. Some advertisers create their own custom magazines to sidestep the advertising clutter problem as well as to have control over editorial content. A number of companies have also been publishing their own magazines to build relationships with their customers. Federal Express publishes *Via FedEx*, a free magazine full of career and office management tips for some of its most important customers, professional secretaries.

Fashion retailer Holt Renfrew custom-published its own shopping magazine, *Holt's*, to reach a sophisticated clientele who shop all around the world. This contributed to Holt Renfrew's established connections with the high profile publication, *Lucky*, where the fashion retailer consistently linked its brand with the world-renowned fashion and beauty brands through product placement and cooperative media opportunities. In the future, Holt Renfrew looks to establish more permanent advertising placements in Canada's newest fashion magazines *Loulou, Fashion Shops* and *Shopping Clin d'Oeil* and achieve an optimal balance between custom-published and regular magazines.[9]

A recent trend among some companies is to enter into joint agreement with traditional publishers to produce custom magazines that they sell to their customers. For example, Swedish retailer IKEA has partnered with John Brown Contract Publishing to custom-publish a magazine titled *space*.[10] *space* is both a showcase for IKEA merchandise and a magazine that contains informative articles about home furnishings, modern design, and lifestyle trends. *space* is sold at IKEA stores, and on newsstands, throughout North America. The custom-publishing division of Hachette Filapacchi publishes a magazine for Ray-Ban Sunglasses called *Sun* and one for Sony that doubles as a catalogue called *Sony Style*.

BUYING MAGAZINE ADVERTISING SPACE

The strengths and limitations of magazines are part of the decision to use this media. Another key factor is a complete understanding of the readers of magazines to assess whether there is a fit between them and the target audience of the promotion plan. In this section, we review a few issues related to this part of the decision: circulation and readership, audience measurement, and magazine advertising rates.

MAGAZINE CIRCULATION AND READERSHIP

Two of the most important considerations in deciding whether to use a magazine in the advertising media plan are the size and characteristics of the audience it reaches. Media buyers evaluate magazines on the basis of their ability to deliver the advertiser's message to as many people as possible in the target audience. To do this, they must consider the circulation of the publication as well as its total readership and match these figures against the audience they are attempting to reach.

Circulation   Circulation figures represent the number of individuals who receive a publication through either subscription or store purchase, or through controlled distribution (free). Given that circulation figures are the basis for a magazine's advertising rates and one of the primary considerations in selecting a publication for placement, the credibility of circulation figures is important. Most major publications are audited by the Audit Bureau of Circulations (ABC), which was organized in 1914 and is sponsored by advertisers, agencies, and publishers. The Canadian division of this U.S.-based organization is known as the Canadian Circulations Audit Board. ABC collects and evaluates information regarding the subscriptions and sales of magazines and newspapers to verify their circulation figures. Only publications with 70 percent or more paid circulation (which means the purchaser paid at least half the magazine's established base price) are eligible for verification audits by ABC. Certain business publications are audited by the Business Publications Audit (BPA) of Circulation. Many of these are published on a **controlled-circulation basis**, meaning copies are sent (usually free) to individuals who the publisher believes can influence the company's purchases.

ABC provides media planners with reliable figures regarding the size and distribution of a magazine's circulation, which helps them evaluate its worth as a media vehicle. The ABC statement also provides detailed circulation information that gives a media planner an indication of the quality of the target audience. For example, it shows how the subscription was sold, the percentage of circulation sold at less than full value, the percentage of circulation sold with some kind of incentive, and the percentage of subscriptions given away. Many advertisers believe that subscribers who pay for a magazine are more likely to read it than are those who get it at a discount or for free. Media buyers are generally skeptical about publications whose circulation figures are not audited and will not advertise in unaudited publications. Circulation data, along with the auditing source, are available from CARD or from the publication itself.

Readership   Advertisers are often interested in the number of people a publication reaches as a result of secondary, or pass-along, readership. **Pass-along readership** can occur when the primary subscriber or purchaser gives a magazine to another person or when the publication is read in doctors' waiting rooms or beauty salons, on airplanes, and so forth.

Advertisers generally attach greater value to the primary in-home reader than the pass-along reader or out-of-home reader, as the former generally spends more time with the publication, picks it up more often, and receives greater satisfaction from it. Thus, this reader is more likely to be attentive and responsive to ads. However, the value of pass-along readers should not be discounted. They can greatly expand a magazine's readership.

You can calculate the **total audience**, or **readership**, of a magazine by multiplying the readers per copy (the total number of primary and pass-along readers) by the circulation of an average issue. For example, a magazine that has a circulation of 1 million and 3.5 readers per copy has a total audience of 3.5 million. However, rate structures are generally based on the more verifiable primary circulation figures, and many media planners devalue pass-along readers by as much as 50 percent. Total readership estimates are reported by the Print Measurement Bureau (PMB), to which we now turn our attention.

MAGAZINE AUDIENCE MEASUREMENT—PMB

Print Measurement Bureau (PMB) is a non-profit Canadian industry association of nearly 500 members drawn from advertisers, print magazine publishers, and advertising agencies. Its primary mandate is to collect readership information for print magazines, which allows all three constituents to make more effective advertising decisions. Its foremost research is known simply as the **PMB study**.

The first national PMB study was conducted in 1973 and originally concerned print magazines only. It has grown since then and is now Canada's primary syndicated source for print and non-print media exposure, as well as responses to survey questions. The current study has resulted in a two-year database of 30,000 respondents, over 2,500 products, and over 3,500 brands.

The research method is an in-home interview conducted throughout the year. Respondents are screened by asking whether they have read any of the listed publications within the past 12 months; they are subsequently qualified if they have read the publications recently enough, depending upon the frequency of publication (e.g., weekly, monthly). A number of reading-related questions are asked, including frequency of reading, number of reading occasions, time spent reading, source of copy, where read, and interest.

Respondents are then asked many demographic, lifestyle, media consumption, product usage, retail shopping, and psychographic questions. The demographic questions are quite exhaustive and total over 20 in number. The lifestyle questions include life events, leisure activities, education, sporting activities, and attendance of sporting events. Media consumption questions are very extensive and include TV viewing, radio listening, community and daily newspaper reading, transit usage, distance traveled, shopping mall trips, and Yellow Pages usage. Product usage data is recorded for 17 broad product categories (e.g., personal care, groceries, financial, business, and so on). Questions pertaining to shopping at approximately 30 different retail environments are also asked. And finally, many questions are asked to determine psychographic clusters for nine broad product categories and one general societal category.

As you may imagine, the data available for analysis is a virtual gold mine of information for media planners. They can relate many of the variables together to accurately reach a specific target audience in terms of their behaviour (i.e., the primary target variable), demographics, lifestyle, and psychographics. And, as you also may expect, the database works with specialized software to allow media planners to make their effective decisions efficiently.

One final useful feature of the PMB study is "return to sample." Individual firms can confidentially re-contact respondents to ask them proprietary questions with respect to specific brand attitudes, purchase intentions, or purchase influences. An advertiser would then have the broad data tied in with some specific measures of their own brand.

MAGAZINE ADVERTISING RATES

Magazine rates are primarily a function of circulation: the greater the circulation, the higher cost of the ad. Other variables include the size of the ad, its position in the publication, the particular editions (geographic, demographic) chosen, any special mechanical or production requirements, the number and frequency of insertions, and whether the circulation is controlled (free) or paid.

Advertising space is generally sold on the basis of space units such as full page, half page, and quarter page, although some publications quote rates on the basis of column inches. The larger the ad, the greater the cost. However, many advertisers use full-page ads since they result in more attention and readership. Studies have found that full-page ads generated 36 percent more readership than half-page ads.[11]

Ads can be produced or run using black and white, black and white plus one colour, or four colours. The more colour used in the ad, the greater the expense because of the increased printing costs. On average, a four-colour ad costs 30 percent more than a black-and-white ad. Advertisers generally prefer colour ads because they have greater visual impact and are superior for attracting and holding attention.[12] Starch INRA Hooper, Inc., analyzed the effect of various factors on the readership of magazine ads. The "noted" scores (the percentage of readers who remember seeing the ad in a publication they read) are 45 percent higher for a four-

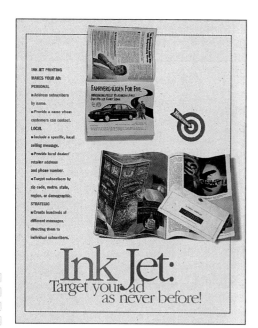

Exhibit 11–6
Newsweek promotes the value of ink-jet imaging

colour full-page ad than for a black-and-white ad. A four-colour spread (two facing pages) outperforms a black-and-white spread by 53 percent.[13] Ads requiring special mechanical production such as bleed pages or inserts may also cost extra.

Rates for magazine ad space can also vary according to the number of times an ad runs and the amount of money spent during a specific period. The more often an advertiser contracts to run an ad, the lower are the space charges. Volume discounts are based on the total space purchased within a contract year, measured in dollars or number of insertions.

THE FUTURE FOR MAGAZINES

Consumer magazine advertising revenue totalled $541 million in 2001, up from $318 million in 1996. This represents about a 10-percent growth per year. We identify four factors—advances in technology, online delivery methods, Canadian titles, and government support—that appear to be significant issues or trends in the magazine industry.

Advances in Technology Two important technological developments are making it possible for advertisers to deliver personalized messages to tightly targeted audiences: selective binding technology and ink-jet imaging. **Selective binding** is a computerized production process that allows the creation of hundreds of copies of a magazine in one continuous sequence. Selective binding enables magazines to target and address specific groups within a magazine's circulation base. They can then send different editorial or advertising messages to various groups of subscribers within the same issue of a publication. **Ink-jet imaging** reproduces a message by projecting ink onto paper rather than using mechanical plates. This process makes it possible to personalize an advertising message. Many publishers believe selective binding and ink-jet imaging will let advertisers target their messages more finely and let magazines compete more effectively with direct mail and other direct-marketing vehicles. Exhibit 11–6 shows how *Newsweek* promotes the capabilities of ink-jet imaging for targeting advertising messages.

Publishers are also developing new technologies that will enhance the creative opportunities available to magazine advertisers. Advertisers use a variety of techniques in print ads to capture readers' attention, including sound, scents, moving images, and pop-up ads. Current technologies are being refined and made more cost effective, and a number of new technologies will be incorporated into print ads soon. These include anaglyphic images (three-dimensional materials that are viewed with coloured glasses); lenticular (colour) images printed on finely corrugated plastic that seem to move when tilted; and pressure- or heat-sensitive inks that change colour on contact. These new technologies will give advertisers ways to break through the advertising clutter. However, these new print technologies can be very costly. Moreover, many advertisers and agencies are concerned that ads that use these new technologies may do so at the expense of other ads in the magazine, so they may pressure publishers to control their use. Some creative people have also expressed concern that these new technologies are gimmicks being substituted for creative advertising ideas.[14]

Online Delivery Methods Many magazines are keeping pace with the digital revolution and the continuing consumer interest in technology by making their publications available online (Exhibit 11–7). They provide advertisers with the opportunity for sponsorships as well as banner ads and promotions on the online versions of the magazines. However, it remains to be seen whether people will want their magazines delivered online or prefer to read them in more traditional

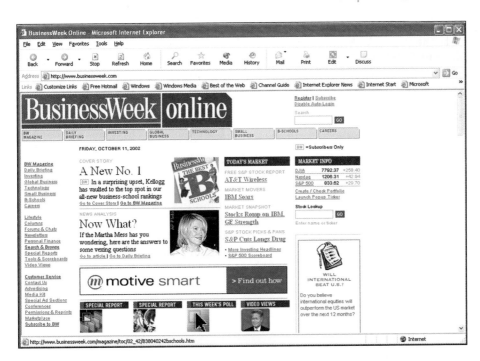

Exhibit 11–7
Magazines such as
Business Week are
now available online

form. As the presence of magazines online grows, the industry will also have to address important issues regarding audience measurement and how to determine consumers' exposure to and interactions with online advertising. Advertising on the Internet is discussed in Chapter 16.

Canadian Titles Canadian magazines account for approximately 50 percent of newsstand and subscription sales while U.S. publications account for about 90 percent of newsstand sales. Despite these numbers, according to research done by the Canadian Magazine Publishers Association (CMPA), Canadians have a preference for Canadian magazines. Unfortunately, many Canadians have difficulty distinguishing the difference despite having a specific preference. The recent campaigns in 2002 and 2003 that identify a publication as Canadian attempted to resolve this dilemma. And the initial result looks promising with 2002 newsstand sales up 6 percent. Building on this success, the $7-million 2003 campaign used a simple brand symbol—a red maple leaf on white magazine background—and continued with print, television, newsstand promotions, direct marketing, and public relations.[15]

In fact the preference for Canadian magazines can be seen in other ways. Many popular publications have been left for dead, only to return after being freshened up. *Canadian Living* survived a scare 20 years ago and is now one of the more popular women's magazines. *Saturday Night*, a 116 year-old legend, has lived and died a few times and is now a supplement for the *National Post*.[16] A similar story is told by *Homemaker's*, which was revived in the late 1980s and is now enlarged to be a super-sized digest. In addition, the success of *Canadian Living* allowed it to branch out to producing a Healthy Meal program to be shown on closed-circuit televisions in the waiting rooms of 800 health-care facilities.[17]

Government Support Due to the size of our population and the ease with which Canadians can read American publications, the success of the Canadian magazine industry has always been precarious. Over the years, the federal government has intervened with certain supportive measures. One such program, established in 1999, is the Canadian Magazine Fund (CMF) from the Department of Canadian Heritage. Under the current plan, it no longer supports free magazines, and offers less support for large consumer and trade magazines while increasing its support for small, aboriginal and ethnically diverse publications. Citing an overall 40-percent

327

decline in the CMF during 2003, the Canadian Magazine Publishers Association fears for the success of some magazines, however, historical support still exists to cushion the blow. The implication for advertisers could be a concentration of titles leading to more efficient magazine advertising buys.[18]

EVALUATION OF NEWSPAPERS

Newspapers, the second major form of print media, are the largest of all advertising media in terms of total dollar volume. In 1999 more than $1.6 billion was spent on daily newspaper advertising, or about 18 percent of the total advertising expenditures in Canada. Community newspapers accounted for almost $800 million, or 9 percent. Newspapers are an especially important advertising medium to local advertisers, particularly retailers. However, newspapers are also valuable to national advertisers. Many of the advertising dollars spent by local retailers are actually provided by national advertisers through cooperative advertising programs (discussed in Chapter 13). Newspapers vary in terms of their characteristics and their role as an advertising medium.

TYPES OF NEWSPAPERS

The traditional role of newspapers has been to deliver prompt, detailed coverage of news as well as to supply other information and features that appeal to readers. The vast majority of newspapers are daily publications serving a local community. However, weekly, national, and special-audience newspapers have special characteristics that can be valuable to advertisers.

Daily Newspapers Daily newspapers, which are published each weekday, are found in cities and larger towns across the country. Many areas have more than one daily paper. Daily newspapers are read by nearly 60 percent of adults each weekday. They provide detailed coverage of news, events, and issues concerning the local area as well as business, sports, and other relevant information and entertainment. Daily newspapers can further be classified as morning, evening, or Sunday publications. In 2003, there were 105 daily newspapers in Canada; of these, 93 were English-language papers and 12 were French-language papers. There were also 32 Sunday newspapers, most of which were published by daily newspapers.

Community Newspapers Most community newspapers publish weekly and originate in small towns or suburbs where the volume of news and advertising cannot support a daily newspaper. These papers focus primarily on news, sports, and events relevant to the local area and usually ignore national and world news, sports, and financial and business news. Community newspapers appeal primarily to local advertisers because of their geographic focus and lower absolute cost. Most national advertisers avoid community newspapers because of their duplicate circulation with daily papers in the large metropolitan areas.

While smaller daily and community newspapers have historically been a fragmented market and difficult for national or regional advertisers to use as an effective newspaper vehicle, their emerging force in Ontario promises to create an interesting opportunity. Recently, Osprey Media Group purchased many daily newspapers in small towns and cities (e.g., Kingston, Sarnia, Sudbury, etc.) with a total circulation of 622,000. When combined with weekly newspapers, the new media giant can reach nearly 1 million people in 45 markets. In total, Osprey owns 22 dailies and 24 weeklies. In comparison, two other similar companies own 60-plus newspapers, thus indicating the beginning of some concentration in the media option. The implication for advertisers is significant. In addition to providing advertisers with the ability to reach many local markets easily, these newspapers allow advertisers to reach a very attractive market since disposable income tends to be higher in those towns and cities with lower property/mortgage costs.[19]

National Newspapers Newspapers in Canada with national circulation include *The National Post* and *The Globe and Mail*. Both are daily publications and have editorial content with a national appeal. *The National Post* has a weekday circulation of about 246,000 and a Saturday circulation of almost 270,000. *The Globe and Mail* has a weekday circulation of about 314,000 and a Saturday circulation of approximately 395,000. National newspapers appeal primarily to large national advertisers and to regional advertisers that use specific geographic editions of these publications.

Special-Audience Newspapers A variety of papers offer specialized editorial content and are published for particular groups, including labour unions, professional organizations, industries, and hobbyists. Many people working in advertising and marketing read *Marketing Magazine*. Specialized newspapers are also published in areas with large foreign-language-speaking ethnic groups, among them Chinese. Newspapers targeted at various religious groups compose another large class of special-interest papers. Another type of special-audience newspaper is one most of you probably read regularly during the school year, the university newspaper. A recent trend has been the establishment of local business newspapers. In western Canada, *Business Edge* reaches 47,000 readers in Alberta and 30,000 in B.C. It receives advertising from regional and small firms, and also from large firms like Telus and Rogers Wireless.[20]

Newspaper Supplements Although not a category of newspapers per se, some papers include magazine-type supplements. For example, *The Globe and Mail* publishes a glossy *Report on Business* magazine at the end of each month.

TYPES OF NEWSPAPER ADVERTISING

The ads appearing in newspapers can also be divided into different categories. The major types of newspaper advertising are display and classified. Other special types of ads and preprinted inserts also appear in newspapers.

Display Advertising **Display advertising** is found throughout the newspaper and generally uses illustrations, headlines, white space, and other visual devices in addition to the copy text. Display ads account for approximately 70 percent of the advertising revenue of the average newspaper. The two types of display advertising in newspapers are local and national (general).

Local advertising refers to ads placed by local organizations, businesses, and individuals who want to communicate with consumers in the market area served by the newspaper. Supermarkets and department stores are among the leading local display advertisers, along with numerous other retailers and service operations such as banks and travel agents. Local advertising is sometimes referred to as retail advertising because retailers account for 85 percent of local display ads.

National or general advertising refers to newspaper display advertising done by marketers of branded products or services that are sold on a national or regional level. These ads are designed to create and maintain demand for a company's product or service and to complement the efforts of local retailers that stock and promote the advertiser's products. Major retail chains, automakers, and airlines are heavy users of newspaper advertising.

Classified Advertising **Classified advertising** also provides newspapers with a substantial amount of revenue. These ads are arranged under subheads according to the product, service, or offering being advertised. Employment, real estate, and automotive are the three major categories of classified advertising. While most classified ads are just text set in small type, some newspapers also accept classified display advertising. These ads are run in the classified section of the paper but use illustrations, larger type sizes, white space, borders, and even colour to stand out.

Special Ads and Inserts   Special advertisements in newspapers include a variety of government and financial reports and notices and public notices of changes in business and personal relationships. Other types of advertising in newspapers include political or special-interest ads promoting a particular candidate, issue, or cause. **Preprinted inserts** are another type of advertising distributed through newspapers. These ads do not appear in the paper itself; they are printed by the advertiser and then taken to the newspaper to be inserted before delivery. Many retailers use inserts such as circulars, catalogues, or brochures in specific circulation zones to reach shoppers in their particular trade areas.

STRENGTHS OF NEWSPAPERS

Newspapers have a number of characteristics that make them popular among both local and national advertisers. These include their reach and frequency, scheduling flexibility, geographic coverage, reader involvement, creative impact, absolute costs, and target audience coverage. IMC Perspective 11–2 discusses the newspaper placement of competing brands that see the value of this media.

Reach and Frequency   One of the primary strengths of newspapers is the high degree of market coverage, or penetration, they offer an advertiser. In most areas, 60 percent or more of households read a daily newspaper, and the reach figure may exceed 70 percent among households with higher incomes and education levels. Most areas are served by one or two daily newspapers.

The extensive penetration of newspapers makes them a truly mass medium and provides advertisers with an excellent opportunity for reaching all segments of the population with their message. Also, since many newspapers are published and read daily, the advertiser can build a high level of frequency into the media schedule.

Scheduling Flexibility   Another strength of newspapers is the flexibility they offer advertisers in terms of requirements for producing and running the ads. Newspaper ads can be written, laid out, and prepared in a matter of hours. For most dailies, the closing time by which the ad must be received is usually only 48 hours before publication (although closing dates for special ads, such as those using colour, and supplements are longer). The short production time and closing dates make newspapers an excellent medium for responding to current events or presenting timely information to consumers. For example, the Archdiocese of Montreal ran an ad a few days after the terrorist attacks of September 11, 2001 that showed the repeated text of the Lord's Prayer in the shape of the twin towers. The meanings of this message are numerous for many people, however, the most significant point is that the message would not have been as effective if it had been placed in a magazine a month later.[21] Finally, a variety of scheduling options are possible, depending on the advertiser's purpose.

Geographic Coverage   Newspapers generally offer advertisers targeted geographic or territorial coverage. Advertisers can vary their coverage by choosing a paper—or combination of papers—that reaches the areas with the greatest sales potential. National advertisers take advantage of the geographic coverage of newspapers to concentrate their advertising in specific areas they can't reach with other media or to take advantage of strong sales potential in a particular area. For example, more expensive automobile manufacturers advertise in Toronto newspapers that reach the greater Toronto area and beyond with their wide distribution.

Luxury Car Companies Use Similar Media Strategy

A car purchase is typically a drawn-out affair where consumers will engage in all steps of the buyer decision process and take up to six months to make a new car purchase (or lease). Print ads are an option for creating awareness and highlighting key attributes and benefits to consumers as they proceed through the information

search and evaluation stages. In fact, newspaper print ads played a key role in the recent launch of two luxury cars, the Infiniti G35 by Nissan and the Lexus ES 300 by Toyota.

As a new high-performance luxury sedan, the G35 was targeting European sports-sedan consumers, or those who were intending to purchase one. The plan was to develop a specific G35 brand image instead of riding on the coattails of Infiniti advertising and branding. Media research indicated that the luxury automotive buyer was a heavy newspaper reader. In fact, about half a billion dollars is spent on newspaper ads in Canada per year, and new car launches for the luxury market typically spend 71 percent of their budget in newspaper ads.

To attract the attention of consumers in the market for a European sports sedan, while they were reading the news, the G35 used compelling, full-page, four-colour ads in newspaper "A" sections. Supporting this initial exposure were black-and-white ads in automotive sections. The clear intention of the ad was to put the G35 in the target audience's evoked set such that they would visit the Infiniti dealer. And the message was clear at promising a

key attribute of power via the 260-horsepower engine, something that would definitely get the target audience to give it serious consideration. The result? Sales exceeded the target of 57 percent, and dealership traffic was very high.

The decision by Lexus to use newspaper print media as a key part of their media strategy had different reasons, but the end result of its usage was similar to Infiniti's. The agency for Lexus considered many innovative media alternatives to reach current Lexus buyers who would be interested in the new ES 300 model. However, it decided that while the Lexus brand was somewhat young, it still had a well-defined brand image with its current users who preferred to receive factual messages of the automobile's benefits.

Naturally, newspaper was a useful vehicle to communicate the comfort and tranquility of driving the new Lexus. And since the target audience of Lexus was known to routinely read certain parts of identifiable newspapers, it was a logical choice to show the creative with full-page ads that would truly capture their attention and achieve the intended communications objectives. In the end, the agency says that the plan is living up to expectations.

Sources: "How to get noticed ... fast," *Marketing Magazine*, May 6, 2002; "Driving the Message Home," *Marketing Magazine*, February 4, 2002.

A number of companies use newspapers in their regional marketing strategies. Newspaper advertising lets them feature products on a market-by-market basis, respond and adapt campaigns to local market conditions, and tie into more retailer promotions, fostering more support from the trade.

Local advertisers like retailers are interested in geographic coverage within a specific market or trade area. Their media goal is to concentrate their advertising on the areas where most of their customers are. Many newspapers now offer advertisers various geographic areas or zones for this purpose.

Reader Involvement and Amount of Processing Time   Another important feature of newspapers is consumers' level of acceptance and involvement with papers and the ads they contain. The typical newspaper reader spends considerable time each day reading. Most consumers rely heavily on newspapers not only for news, information, and entertainment but also for assistance with consumption decisions.

Many consumers actually purchase a newspaper *because* of the advertising it contains. Consumers use retail ads to determine product prices and availability and to see who is having a sale. One aspect of newspapers that is helpful to advertisers is readers' knowledge about particular sections of the paper. Most of us know that ads for automotive products and sporting goods are generally found in the sports section, while ads for financial services are found in the business section. The weekly food section in many newspapers is popular for recipe and menu ideas as well as for the grocery store ads and coupons offered by many stores and companies.

Media Image The value of newspaper advertising as a source of information has been shown in several studies. One study found that consumers look forward to ads in newspapers more than in other media. In another study, 80 percent of consumers said newspaper ads were most helpful to them in doing their weekly shopping. Newspaper advertising has also been rated the most believable form of advertising in numerous studies.

Creativity for Cognitive Responses Newspapers offer the opportunity for extremely long copy, perhaps a thousand words extolling the attributes and benefits of a product. The option of considerable explanation of a product could be quite important for marketers looking to persuade consumers who are at the information search stage of the decision-making process. Furthermore, newspapers offer numerous creative options as ads can be run in various sizes, shapes, and formats to persuade the reader.

Absolute Cost and Cost Efficiency Newspapers assist small companies through free copywriting and art services. Small advertisers without an agency or advertising department often rely on the newspaper to help them write and produce their ads. Production costs of ads are reasonable since many are comprised of simple copy with a standard image or photo-stock visual. The creative flexibility of newspapers in terms of size and format of the ad makes it difficult to exactly conclude the cost implications of this media. Small and local businesses can run a small ad with a reasonable CPM (cost per thousand) compared to magazines.

Target Audience Coverage Coverage of a specific target audience is argued to be a limitation for newspapers in comparison to its print cousin, magazines. However, placement of ads in certain sections of the newspaper that occur everyday (e.g., sports, business, entertainment) or once a week (e.g., food, cars, finances) can be advantageous for some marketers.

LIMITATIONS OF NEWSPAPERS

While newspapers have many strengths, like all media they also have limitations that media planners must consider. The limitations of newspapers include their weak creative impact, potential for selective exposure, lack of target audience selectivity, and clutter.

Creativity Impact for Emotional Responses One of the greatest limitations of newspapers as an advertising medium is their poor reproduction quality. The coarse paper stock used for newspapers and the absence of extensive colour limits the quality of most newspaper ads. Newspapers have improved their reproduction quality in recent years, and colour reproduction has become more available. Also, advertisers desiring high-quality colour in newspaper ads can turn to such alternatives as freestanding inserts or supplements. However, these are more costly and may not be desirable to many advertisers. As a general rule, if the visual appearance of the product is important, the advertiser will not rely on newspaper ads. Ads for food products and fashions generally use magazines to capitalize on their superior reproduction quality and colour.

Selective Exposure and Poor Attention   Unlike magazines, which may be retained around the house for several weeks, a daily newspaper is generally kept less than a day. So an ad is unlikely to have any impact beyond the day of publication, and repeat exposure is very unlikely. Compounding this problem are the short amount of time many consumers spend with the newspaper and the possibility they may not even open certain sections of the paper. Media planners can offset these problems somewhat by using high frequency in the newspaper schedule and advertising in a section where consumers who are in the market for a particular product or service are likely to look.

Target Audience Selectivity   While newspapers can offer advertisers geographic selectivity, they are not a selective medium in terms of demographics or lifestyle characteristics. Most newspapers reach broad and very diverse groups of consumers, which makes it difficult for marketers to focus on narrowly defined market segments. For example, manufacturers of fishing rods and reels will find newspapers very inefficient because of the wasted circulation that results from reaching all the newspaper readers who don't fish. Thus, they are more likely to use special-interest magazines. Any newspaper ads for their products will be done through cooperative plans whereby retailers share the costs or spread them over a number of sporting goods featured in the ad.

Clutter   Newspapers, like most other advertising media, suffer from clutter. Because a substantial amount of the average daily newspaper in Canada is devoted to advertising, the advertiser's message must compete with numerous other ads for consumers' attention and interest. Moreover, the creative options in newspapers are limited by the fact that most ads are black and white. Thus, it can be difficult for a newspaper advertiser to break through the clutter without using costly measures such as large space buys or colour. Some advertisers use creative techniques like island ads—ads surrounded by editorial material. Island ads are found in the middle of the stock market quotes on the financial pages of many newspapers. Exhibit 11–8 shows an island ad for Cathay Pacific Airways that targets business travellers to Hong Kong and other Asian destinations.

Exhibit 11–8
Island ads are a way to break through the clutter in newspaper advertising

BUYING NEWSPAPER ADVERTISING SPACE

The strengths and limitations of newspapers are part of the decision to use this media. Another key factor is a complete understanding of the readers of newspapers to assess whether there is a fit between them and the target audience of the promotion plan. In this section, we review a few issues related to this part of the decision: circulation and readership, audience measurement, and newspaper advertising rates.

NEWSPAPER CIRCULATION AND READERSHIP

As with any medium, the media planner must understand the nature and size of the audience reached by a newspaper in considering its value in the media plan. Since newspapers as a class of media do an excellent job of penetrating their market, the typical daily newspaper gives advertisers the opportunity to reach most of the households in a market. But, while local advertisers aim to cover a particular market or trade area, national advertisers want to reach broad regions or even the entire country. They must purchase space in a number of papers to achieve the desired level of coverage. IMC Perspective 11–3 looks at Toronto's competitive newspaper market.

Newspaper Wars in Toronto

Imagine a city with six daily newspapers, each with its own identity and target market, something few cities in the world can claim. The spring 2004 release of the Newspaper Audience Databank (NADbank) annual readership study had the publishers of all Toronto-based newspapers smiling. The *Toronto Star* maintained its position as a consistent leader. The *National Post* strengthened its position in key metro markets. *The Globe and Mail* held its position of reaching a strong, nation-wide demographic. Readership for the *Toronto Sun* remained relatively stable versus the previous year.

The most recent battle heating up concerns the free tabloid-like publications *Metro Toronto* and *24 hours*. *Metro Toronto* posted a 23-percent readership growth with an average of 382,000 Monday-to-Friday readers. In contrast, executives claimed it prints 240,000 copies per day with a pick-up in excess of 200,000. (Readership numbers for *24 hours* were not gathered due to the timing of its recent launch during the fall of 2003.)

Metro Toronto, printed on semi-gloss paper and distributed in key locations along TTC and GO transit routes, looked every bit the supermarket tabloid with its content featuring wire-copy "human interest" stories. However, with a three-year publishing record targeting females aged 18–34 and major advertisers like Rogers, Fido, and Expedica.ca, this formidable competitor appeared ready to battle the new up-start *24 hours*. With a track record of delivering strong readership and many advertising options (e.g., cover wraps and unusually shaped ads), *Metro Toronto* confidently raised its rates by 20 percent signalling a premium quality compared to *24 hours*.

Alternatively, *24 hours* targeted the outlying regions of Toronto and looked to find a content niche that would appeal to a broader target market of females aged 25–49. To entice advertisers, *24 hours* discounted its rates substantially to offer a $20 CPM, considerably less than other newspapers. And some media buyers began experimenting with short test runs to see if the new publication delivered results more efficiently than *Metro Toronto*. Finally, internal research for *24 hours* revealed that 27 percent of its readers indicated that they had not read any daily newspaper prior to its initial publication.

Sources: Chris Powell, "Second Time Around," *Marketing Magazine*, February 9, 2004; Chris Powell, "The Spin on NADbank," *Marketing Magazine*, April 19, 2004.

Circulation   The basic source of information concerning the audience size of newspapers comes from circulation figures available through CARD, discussed earlier in this chapter. The Audit Bureau of Circulation (ABC) verifies circulation figures for many newspapers, as illustrated in the media section. Advertisers using a number of papers in their media plan generally find CARD to be the most convenient source. The Canadian Community Newspapers Association (CCNA) verifies the circulation if an advertiser decides to use this vehicle.

The CCNA is a network of seven regional newspaper associations: Atlantic Community Newspapers Association, the Quebec Community Newspapers

Association, the Ontario Community Newspapers Association, the Manitoba Community Newspapers Association, the Saskatchewan Weekly Newspapers Association, the Alberta Weekly Newspapers Association, and the British Columbia & Yukon Community Newspapers Association. Membership of an individual community newspaper in a regional association includes membership in the national association. CCNA currently represents more than 670 English-language community newspapers with a total first-edition circulation of more than 6.8 million copies per week.

The CCNA gives an individual community newspaper a national voice in working with the public, business, and government, and its mission is to ensure a strong community newspaper industry. For advertisers, the CCNA plays a strong role in coordinating the placement of ads throughout the network. Its services include a one-order–one-bill system, ROP ads and pre-printed inserts, digital transmission of ads, Geographic Information System (GIS), and national or regional classified advertising. Presently, CCNA does not have audience information like NADbank; however, in June 2002, CCNA announced the implementation of a readership study. Despite this limitation, the CCNA claims community newspapers offer key benefits: precise coverage of specific markets with no wasted circulation, strong household penetration, state-of-the-art newspaper reproduction, and audited circulation figures.

CCNA has a self-administered audit program for all its members. The program includes a manual with detailed instructions and necessary forms. The member newspaper collects its own circulation data according to the VC rules and regulations. These data are reported to the CCNA and the CCNA Circulation Auditor or a Public (Chartered) Accountant audits the data thoroughly and a circulation report is published.

Newspaper circulation figures are generally broken down into three categories: the city zone, the retail trading zone, and all other areas. The **city zone** is a market area composed of the city where the paper is published and contiguous areas similar in character to the city. The **retail trading zone** is the market outside the city zone whose residents regularly trade with merchants within the city zone. The "all other" category covers all circulation not included in the city or retail trade zone.

Sometimes circulation figures are provided only for the primary market, which is the city and retail trade zones combined, and the other area. Both local and national advertisers consider the circulation patterns across the various categories in evaluating and selecting newspapers.

Readership Circulation figures provide the media planner with the basic data for assessing the value of newspapers and their ability to cover various market areas. However, the media planner also wants to match the characteristics of a newspaper's readers with those of the advertiser's target audience. Data on newspaper audience size and characteristics are available from NADbank. Figures 11–4 and 11–5 give you an overview of the Canadian newspaper reader

NEWSPAPER AUDIENCE MEASUREMENT

NADbank Newspaper Audience Databank Inc. (NADbank) is an organization comprised of newspaper, advertising agency, and advertiser members. Its primary mandate is to publish audience research information of Canadian daily newspapers. The purpose of this

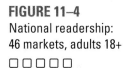

FIGURE 11–4

National readership: 46 markets, adults 18+

Source: NADBank 2003

335

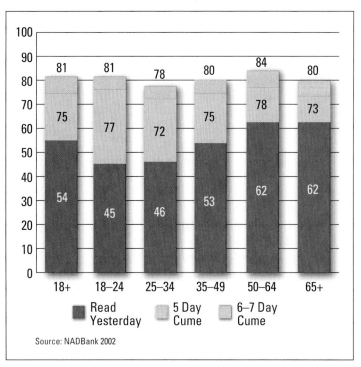

FIGURE 11–5
Newspaper readableship by age
☐☐☐☐☐

Source: NADBank 2002

research is to provide its members with valid readership information to facilitate the buying and selling of newspaper advertising space.

NADbank uses a phone interview of respondents that takes approximately 15 minutes. The interview asks questions pertaining to readership of local and non-local newspapers, time spent reading, frequency of reading, method of receipt of newspapers into the home or outside the home, readership of TV magazine publications, radio listening, TV viewing and magazine readership, Internet readership of online newspapers, demographics, and media reliance. Product usage data is collected by a self-completion questionnaire that is sent to respondents after the telephone interview. These questions focus on 28 product categories and 18 retail shopping categories.

The study is conducted in 46 Canadian urban markets covering 76 newspapers. Sixteen markets annually receive both the media and product usage surveys while 10 markets annually receive the media survey only. Another 20 smaller markets receive the media survey once every three years. NADbank recently updated the data collection process to minimize any seasonal effects. For 2002, data was collected for 17 weeks during January to June and 16 weeks during September to December. The schedule called for publication of results in the spring of 2003 when media planners need data updated to finalize their decisions for the fall.

The readership study indicates that adults read the newspaper an average of 48 minutes per weekday and over 90 minutes on the weekend. The reach of newspaper is quite pervasive even though there are many media choices and reading is more time-consuming and involving than other media. For example, 57 percent of adults 18 and older across all markets read a newspaper yesterday, 64 percent read a newspaper last weekend, and 83 percent have read a newspaper in the past week.

As we have seen in the audience measurement for other media, the NADbank data is available to use with specialized software that is available through two authorized suppliers (IMS and Harris/Telmar). It provides consultation services to assist its members who use the information. Proprietary questions may also be added to the survey if an advertiser or marketer wants to link brand specific data with the media and product usage data.

ComBase ComBase administers the audience measurement for CCNA. ComBase is also the name of the study. ComBase is an organization with a similar composition and mandate as NADbank. The independent board features newspapers, advertisers, and advertising agencies. Its mandate is to publish audience research information of the 700 community newspapers throughout Canada to allow them to sell their advertising space more effectively. In addition, ComBase accounts for listenership of 900 radio stations. The first bi-annual study surveyed 24,000 English-speaking Canadians in over 400 markets in 2003.

The "Recent Reading" methodology used by ComBase is as thorough as the Nadbank and PMB studies. In fact, an independent organization, the Canadian Advertising Research Foundation (CARF), appraised and endorsed the methodology. Of note, the survey determines all the publications read with an intensive investigation over a three-month time period. The survey also features excellent sample sizes and response rates and conducts the survey appropriately over time to ensure authenticity.

ComBase conducts 10-minute telephone interviews in English of adults selected at random. The interviewer asks questions pertaining to readership of community newspapers, local and non-resident; readership of daily newspapers, including nationals; readership of other print press including shoppers, agricultural press, alternative publications; amount of paper read; frequency of reading; newspaper preferred if more than one read; rating of newspapers read; radio listening, TV viewing; and demographic information about the respondent and household.

Results of the data can be compiled along a number of dimensions; Census Metropolitan Area (CMA) with population of 100,000 or more in an urbanized core; Census Agglomeration (CA) with population of 10,000 or more in an urbanized core; suburbs; newspaper distribution areas; Census Subdivisions (CSD) like towns, and villages; economic regions with areas of common economic interests as defined by Statistics Canada; and provinces. Data can be accessed and used with existing media software, a similar situation we saw with NADbank. The following results demonstrate the significance of community newspapers:

- 70 percent read last weekday's issue of their community newspaper
- 48 percent read yesterday's weekday daily
- 25 percent of readers are exclusive
- 40 percent of Canadians are light TV viewers
- 26 percent of Canadians did not listen to radio yesterday

NEWSPAPER ADVERTISING RATES

Advertisers are faced with a number of options and pricing structures when purchasing newspaper space. The cost of advertising space depends on the circulation, and whether the circulation is controlled (free) or paid. It also depends on factors such as premium charges for colour in a special section, as well as discounts available. National rates can be about 15 percent higher than local rates, to account for agency commission. Figures 11–6 and 11–7 provide a summary of newspaper advertising rates.

	Atlantic	Quebec	Ontario	Prairies	B.C. & Yukon	Total
Number of markets	13	6	38	15	16	88
Number of dailies	15	11	44	18	17	105
Circulation (000s)	500	743	2,424	929	352	4,948
Mon.–Thurs. B/W line rate ($)	22	44	157	46	35.04	306
Half-page* B/W cost ($)	27,453	49,052	179,208	50,377	46,979	353,070
Black + 1C premium ($)	7,605	15,485	38,434	9,849	10,310	81,683
Black + 2C premium ($)	11,325	13,753	45,954	14,123	14,658	99,813
Black + 3C premium ($)	14,831	23,974	62,349	19,723	18,912	139,789
Half-page* Full colour** cost ($)	42,284	73,026	241,557	70,100	65,892	492,860

FIGURE 11–6

2003 Daily newspaper circulation and cost by region

Source: April 2003 CARD (Mon–Friday Paid Circulation)

*Half Page sizes generally run 10 x 150 agate lines in most Broadsheets, 8 x 85 agate lines in most Tabloids. ** Full Colour is Black + 3 Colour premium.

FIGURE 11-7
2003 Daily newspaper circulations and costs by population groups
☐ ☐ ☐ ☐ ☐

	1MM+	500M -1MM	100M -500M	50M -100M	Under 50M	Total
Number of markets	5	4	23	15	41	88
Number of dailies	16	7	26	15	41	105
Circulation (000s)	2,581	825	1,061	240	240	4,948
Mon.–Thurs. B/W line rate ($)	144	43	66	14	36	306
Half-page* B/W cost ($)	157,495	43,038	85,244	21,796	45,496	353,070
Spot colour ($)	39,603	9,939	15,566	4,757	11,817	81,683
Process colour ($)	58,204	18,940	31,908	8,166	22,571	139,789
Half-page* Full colour** cost ($)	215,699	61,978	117,152	29,962	68,067	492,860

Source: April 2003 CARD

*Half Page sizes generally run 10 x 150 agate lines in most Broadsheets, 8 x 85 agate lines in most Tabloids. ** Full Colour is Black + 3 Colour premium.

Newspaper is sold by the **agate line** and **column width**. A line (or agate line) is a unit of space measuring one column wide and $\frac{1}{14}$-inch deep. One problem with this unit is that newspapers use columns of varying width, from 6 columns per page to 10 columns per page, which affects the size, shape, and costs of an ad. This results in a complicated production and buying process for national advertisers that purchase space in a number of newspapers.

Advertisers need to know the number of lines and number of columns on a newspaper page in order to calculate the cost of an ad. For example, the following calculation is for the weekday cost of a full-page ad in the national edition of *The National Post*. The paper has 301 lines and 10 columns per page, and the open cost per line is $15.28.

$$10 \text{ columns} \times 301 \text{ lines} \times \$15.28/\text{line per column} = \$45,993$$

This calculation could be done differently with the same result when you know the entire length of the paper (301 lines/14 agate lines per column inch).

$$10 \text{ columns} \times 21.5 \text{ inches} \times 14 \text{ agate lines per column inch} \times \$15.28 = \$45,993$$

You can use this principle to calculate the cost of ads of various sizes once you know the size of the ad in terms of columns and inches deep. For example, for an ad that is 5 columns wide and 6 inches deep, the calculation would then be the following:

$$5 \text{ columns} \times 6 \text{ inches} \times 14 \text{ agate lines per column inch}$$
$$\times \$15.28 \text{ per column inch} = \$6,418$$

Newspaper rates for local advertisers continue to be based on the column inch, which is 1 inch deep by 1 column wide. Advertising rates for local advertisers are quoted per column inch, and media planners calculate total space costs by multiplying the ad's number of column inches by the cost per inch.

Most newspapers have an **open-rate structure**, which means various discounts are available. These discounts are generally based on frequency or bulk purchases of space and depend on the number of column inches purchased in a year.

Newspaper space rates also vary with an advertiser's special requests, such as preferred position or colour. The basic rates quoted by a newspaper are **run of paper (ROP)**, which means the paper can place the ad on any page or in any position it desires. While most newspapers try to place an ad in a requested position, the advertiser can ensure a specific section and/or position on a page by paying a higher **preferred position rate**. Colour advertising is also available in many newspapers on an ROP basis or through preprinted inserts or supplements.

Recently, advertising rates have come under fire from media buyers with an equally contentious response from the media vendors. Historically, media buyers paid what newspapers set as their price without much criticism. However, newspaper rates have been questioned from larger advertising agencies and media buying organizations that have emerged with amalgamations in the industry. While media buyers usually investigate and evaluate the audience size and price for television advertising rates, this behaviour was not generally expected with newspapers. In particular, *The National Post*, and *The Globe and Mail*, reacted strongly to those buyers who have put increased pressure on lower rates as they represent very large advertisers who purchase millions of agate lines per year. To contribute to the discussion, *The Globe and Mail* worked with an independent data analysis firm that tracked the sales impact of newspaper ad placement.[22]

THE FUTURE FOR NEWSPAPERS

Newspapers' major strength lies in their role as a medium that can be used effectively by local advertisers on a continual basis. It is unlikely that newspapers' importance to local advertisers will change in the near future. However, there are a number of problems and issues newspapers must address to maintain their strong position as a dominant local advertising medium and to gain more national advertising. These include competition from other advertising media and declining readership.

The newspaper industry's battle to increase its share of national advertising volume has been difficult. In addition to the problems of reproduction quality and rate differentials, newspapers face competition from other media for both national and local advertisers' budgets. The newspaper industry is particularly concerned about the bypass, or loss of advertisers to direct marketing and telemarketing.

The intermedia battle that newspapers find themselves involved in is no longer limited to national advertising. Many companies are investigating the Internet as a marketing tool and a place to invest advertising dollars that might otherwise go to newspapers. Local radio and TV stations, as well as the Yellow Pages, are aggressively pursuing local advertisers. Newspapers will have to fight harder to retain those advertisers. Many newspapers have expanded their marketing capabilities and are making efforts to develop and sustain relationships with their advertisers.

The growth of the Internet and online services is another factor that may erode newspaper readership. As penetration of the Internet into households increases, newspapers and magazines are among the most threatened of the major media. A survey conducted for *Advertising Age* found that consumers with home Internet access are less likely to use magazines or newspapers as a primary information source when shopping for a car, financial services, travel, or fashion. The study also found that consumers from teens to seniors are comfortable with the idea of using the Internet in the future to read books, magazines, and newspapers.[23] Newspaper publishers are addressing this threat by making their papers available online. Nearly every major newspaper has established a website, and many publishers now make their papers available online.

SUMMARY

Magazines and newspapers, the two major forms of print media, play an important role in the media plans and strategy of many advertisers. Magazines are a very selective medium and are very valuable for reaching specific types of customers and market segments. The three broad categories of magazines are consumer, farm, and business publications. Each of these categories can be further classified according to the publication's editorial content and audience appeal.

In addition to their selectivity, the strengths of magazines include their target audience selectivity, geographic coverage, creativity options, permanence, prestige image, and readers' acceptable selective exposure and attention levels. Limitations of magazines include their high cost, limited reach and frequency, long lead time, weak target audience coverage, and the advertising clutter in most publications.

Advertising space rates in magazines vary according to a number of factors, among them the size of the ad, position in the publication, particular editions purchased, use of colour, and number and frequency of insertions. Rates for magazines are compared on the basis of the cost per thousand, although other factors such as the editorial content of the publication and its ability to reach specific target audiences must also be considered.

Newspapers represent the largest advertising medium in terms of total volume, receiving about a fourth of all advertising dollars. Newspapers are a very important medium to local advertisers, especially retailers.

Newspapers are a broad-based medium that reaches a large percentage of households in a particular area. Newspapers' other advantages include scheduling flexibility, geographic coverage, reader involvement and amount of processing time, creative impact, and costs. Drawbacks of newspapers include weak creative impact, selective exposure, lack of target audience selectivity, and clutter.

Trends toward market segmentation and regional marketing are prompting many advertisers to make more use of newspapers and magazines. However, both magazines and newspapers face increasing competition from such other media as direct marketing and the Internet, and both are working to improve the quality of their circulation bases.

KEY TERMS

selectivity, *317*
gatefolds, *320*
bleed pages, *320*
controlled-circulation
    basis, *324*
pass-along readership, *324*

total audience/
    readership, *324*
PMB study, *324*
selective binding, *326*
ink-jet imaging, *326*
display advertising, *329*

classified advertising, *329*
preprinted inserts, *330*
city zone, *335*
retail trading zone, *335*
agate line, *338*
column width, *338*

open-rate structure, *338*
run of paper (ROP), *339*
preferred position
    rate, *339*

DISCUSSION QUESTIONS

1. Discuss the strengths and limitations of magazines as an advertising medium. How do magazines differ from television and radio as advertising media?

2. Describe what is meant by selectivity with regard to the purchase of advertising media and discuss some of the ways magazines provide selectivity to advertisers.

3. Explain why advertisers of products such as cosmetics or women's clothing would choose to advertise in magazines such as *Flare*, *Elm Street*, or *Chatelaine*.

4. Discuss how circulation figures are used in evaluating magazines and newspapers as part of a media plan and setting advertising rates.

5. If you were purchasing magazine ad space for a manufacturer of snowboarding equipment, what factors would you consider? Would your selection of magazines be limited to snowboarding publications? Why or why not?

6. Discuss the strengths and limitations of newspapers as an advertising medium. How might the decision to use newspapers in a media plan differ for national versus local advertisers?

7. Discuss the challenges and opportunities magazines and newspapers are facing from the growth of the Internet.

8. Cereal advertizers would typically use magazines for advertising, but some have recently used newspapers. Why would they select this new option? Your answer should address how the media would help achieve the advertiser's communication objectives.

Out-of-Home and Support Media

CHAPTER OBJECTIVES

- To recognize the various out-of-home and support media available to the marketer in developing an IMC program.

- To develop an understanding of the strengths and limitations of out-of-home and support media.

- To know how audiences for out-of-home and support media are measured.

Street Word-of-Mouth

One day, Harry Potter look-alikes arrived at train stations in Toronto and Vancouver searching for "Platform 9 ¾." Another day, commuters on the Toronto subway system found folded paper between the seats. And perhaps on an even more surprising day, patrons of a Toronto train station discovered a living room with instructions to steal the furniture! What do all these unusual occurrences have in common? Simply put, a new trend of staging a unique form of "advertising" to an unsuspecting audience with the intention of encouraging positive word-of-mouth communication.

To launch *Harry Potter and the Order of the Phoenix*, the latest in a series featuring the well known wizard-in-training, its publisher desired communication that consumers would really notice. And notice they did, and even more, observers noted that the commuters could not help but smile at the spectacle and continue talking about it all the way home. And for a mere $20,000, or 5 percent of their overall budget, this new-found out-of-home "media" accomplished its task far easier than many other outdoor options.

On the folded pieces of paper, potential consumers viewed a picture of Adidas's new SLIV athletic shoe along with the "scrawled notes from an anonymous shoe fanatic." Looking like anything but an ad, the unusual format piqued the attention of those curious and naturally, they could not help but read the "ad" to its final conclusion. And with all probability, these interested receivers of the message quite likely talked about their interesting experience with their friends.

Picking up on its television ads where interior designers created living spaces in unusual locations, Ikea placed a real living room in a train station so passersby could visualize the essence of their product. And in fact, who would not want to brag about taking home a free lamp, or table, or couch?

As these three examples demonstrate, out-of-home media has evolved to some unusual options in an attempt to generate word-of-mouth communication. However, despite its apparent communication success, marketers are not moving towards this in droves due to a few factors. One concern is that no matter how innovative or attention-getting the "media" there are numerous logistical obstacles to overcome for implementation. Furthermore, it may be a challenge to find the right street experience that matches the strategy for the brand. And whatever option is selected, there is an inherent trade-off in not spending the money in more traditional out-of-home media. Related to this is the question of efficiency since it is difficult to gauge how many people are exposed to the media, and the question of effectiveness since it probably requires some kind of immediate market research to assess the communication effects.

Source: Paul-Mark Rendon, "Heard on the Streets," *Marketing Magazine*, September 15, 2003.

Every time we step out of the house, we encounter media directing an advertising message to us. Often we see ads while travelling. Most places we go have some form of advertising. And when we shop, we continue to see more ads! **Out-of-home media** is quite pervasive, and it delivers the advertising messages that we encounter while moving throughout our town or city, accomplishing our day-to-day activities. Some are new to the marketplace, and others have been around a while. In this chapter, we review four broad categories of out-of-home media: outdoor, transit, place-based, and point-of-purchase. We discuss the relative strengths and limitations, cost information, and audience measurement of each.

Exhibit 12–1
Outdoor advertising

We use the term out-of-home media because it is a general term that encompasses all media that goes beyond the traditional media—broadcast or print—that we consume typically at home. Often it is referred to as outdoor media; however, as we shall see, some of the media is, in fact, not outdoor. An example of this confusion is the fact that all of these media represent $310 million in advertising revenue that is often labelled outdoor media, but may never see the sun! To give you an idea of what out-of-home media involves, we refer you to Figure 12–1, which shows the main options for each of the four types covered in this chapter.

A major reason for the continued success of out-of-home media is its ability to remain innovative. As Exhibit 12–1 shows, billboards are no longer limited to standard sizes and two dimensions; 3-D forms and extensions are now used to attract attention. You probably have been exposed to either signboards or electronic billboards at sports stadiums, in supermarkets, in the campus bookstore and dining halls, in shopping malls, or on the highways, or from neon signs on the sides of buildings in major Canadian cities.

We also encounter ads from non-traditional media. **Support media** are used to reach those people in the target audience that the primary media may not have reached or to reinforce the message contained in primary media. We conclude this chapter by summarizing two broad categories of support media: promotional products and product placement.

Outdoor Media

Outdoor media is pervasive, and if you really tried to pay attention to the many exposures possible, you would find that we appear to be surrounded. However, the amount spent on this media is over $200 million, which is about 10 percent of TV or newspaper advertising revenue. Despite this, outdoor media have just about doubled recently, compared to the 25- to 35-percent growth for TV and newspaper media. The role of outdoor media in contributing to sales may be a key factor. In a study reported by BBDO advertising, 35 percent of consumers surveyed said they had called a phone number they saw on an out-of-home ad.[1] A study reported by Mukesh Bhargava and Naveen Donthu showed that outdoor advertising can have a significant effect on sales, particularly when combined with a promotion.[2] We now turn our attention to the many outdoor media options available for an advertiser.

OUTDOOR MEDIA OPTIONS

Posters describe the typical billboard, which can be horizontal (e.g., 3m by 6m) or vertical (e.g., 4m by 5m). These displays are front lit for visibility at night and are

FIGURE 12–1
Out-of-home media
☐ ☐ ☐ ☐ ☐

Outdoor	Transit	Place-Based	Point of Purchase
Horizantal/vertical poster	Exterior bus posters	Bar, restaurant, hotel	On-premise sign
Backlit poster	Interior overhead door card	Cinema	Window display
Superboard	Station poster	Mall	Modular display rack
Electronic	Transit shelter	Parking lot	Preassembled display
Street level	Super-bus, bus mural	Arena, stadium	Display shipper
Wall banner, mural	Subway online	Golf, ski, fitness centre	Wall display
Mobile mural/poster	Airport display	Washroom, floor	Display card
Aerial, bench, receptacle	In-flight	Elevator, escalator	TV display

located in high vehicle-traffic areas. They may be purchased on an individual basis or for a certain level of GRPs in cities such as Toronto or in smaller markets such as Timmins, Ontario. As the name implies, **backlit posters** are posters of generally the same size that have a light behind them so that they are more clearly illuminated. These units are located at major intersections or high traffic-volume areas in or near major cities in Canada.

Taking a cue from retail merchandising used by The Gap, Scotiabank recently added posters to its exterior windows and placed interior posters throughout each of its branches. The overall strategy called for significant visuals that emphasized the current customer service strategy and meshed with other communication materials. A guiding constraint included the task of making the posters fit with the decor of each bank location, much like Scotiabank managers had observed at The Gap. Each poster featured a horizontal split with a simple 10-word message on one side and a strong visual on the other. External window posters and those near personal banking offices communicated the Scotiabank brand of "human" while posters near customer service representatives and automatic banking machines communicated specific products. A dual messaging approach permitted specific brand experiences for unique target audiences. Scotiabank planned to expand the customized message for each brand depending upon customer mix for each local market.[3]

Larger billboards, known as **bulletins**, **superboards**, or **spectaculars**, are larger displays (two to three times larger) that have a variety of sizes depending upon the media company. These displays are sold on a per location basis due to their size and the low number of options available in major Canadian markets. Smaller backlit displays, known as **street-level posters** and measuring about 2m by 1m, are available across the country.

The aforementioned outdoor options are typically purchased for four weeks and provide anywhere from 25 GRPs to 150 GRPs per day, depending upon the number of displays or showings chosen within a local market. Recall from Chapter 9 that one GRP represents 1 percent of the market seeing the ad once. Thus, buying 50 GRPs implies that the marketer is reaching 50 percent of the market every day. (Figure 12–2 shows some outdoor rates broken down by three GRP levels.)

Most outdoor operators can present examples of past outdoor campaigns producing awareness and other communication effects. The examples can be for a product category or for individual campaigns. The operators can also provide maps to illustrate the posters' locations and other relevant data (e.g., demographics).

A number of innovative outdoor tools have emerged in Canada. Some firms are setting up large video-display units that have full animation and colour. For example, Dundas Square, near the Eaton Centre in downtown Toronto, features a 12 metre wide by 9 metre high full-colour video screen in addition to eight display faces and Canada's largest neon sign, at 18 metres in diameter. Many of Canada's largest advertisers secure

FIGURE 12–2 ☐☐☐☐   Outdoor rates–by daily GRP delivery

Type of Poster and Markets	25 GRPs Daily		50 GRPs Daily		75 GRPs Daily	
	# of panels	4-week rate Cost range (000s)	# of Panels	4-week rate Cost range (000s)	# of Panels	4-week rate Cost range (000s)
Horizantal Posters						
Top 3 markets	105–155	$185–229	211–308	$349–376	284–462	$512–558
Top 10 markets	171–286	$286–348	329–567	$548–603	508–798	$768–826
Vertical Posters						
*Top 3 markets	88–107	$125–160	*154–216	$283–300	*235–420	$424–452
*Top 10 markets	130–164	$190–220	232–294	$375–392	444–515	$538–775
Street Level/TSAs						
Top 3 markets	155–177	$113–130	314–353	$217–248	476–529	$316–372
Top 10 markets	188–300	$182–195	499–594	$347–371	754–893	$504–556
Mall						
Top 3 markets	84	$40	168	$72	252	$94
Top 10 markets	136	$63	267	$113	399	$148.5
Backlit						
Top 3 markets	13–15	$23–37	30–31	$53–74	44–47	$78–109
Top 10 markets	26–28	$50–57	48–51	$89–113	66–75	$129–157
Superboards						
*Top 3 markets						
Series 10		$8				
Series 14		$22–28				
*Top 10 markets						
Series 10		$19				
Series 14		$27–36				

Note: Data range reflects the expected minimum and maximum number of panels and cost generically by product, taking into account all major suppliers including Pattison and Astral Media. Buyers should check with sales reps for current inventory and pricing. Top 3 Markets: Toronto/Oshawa/Hamilton, Montreal, Vancouver. Top 10 Markets Toronto/Oshawa/Hamilton, Montreal, Vancouver, Ottawa, Calgary, Edmonton, Quebec City, Windsor, Kitchener, London.
Source: CARD, April 2003
* All Markets not available in this medium. All rates are net.

space in this very prominent location, which receives extensive pedestrian and vehicular traffic (see Exhibit 12–2).[4] Electronic message signs offer short ads (e.g., 10 seconds) on 2- or 3-minute rotation. As expected, both of these displays are located in high-traffic locations in a few large urban markets, with various sizes and packages available depending on the media firm. Murals and wall banners are sold in a few major markets in Canada (e.g., Toronto, Vancouver) with varying sizes. A number of firms offer **mobile signage** by placing displays on trucks or vehicles (see Exhibit 12–3). These are sold by the number of vehicles and the number of months.

Finally, we find outdoor media in some unusual outdoor locations. Signage is placed on benches, bicycle racks, garbage receptacles, and in the air through aerial advertising on airplanes or hot-air balloons. It seems that no matter where we turn outside, there will be some form of advertising message directed towards us (see Exhibit 12–3).

Despite the pervasiveness of outdoor advertising, there is some concern. In a Maritz AmeriPoll asking consumers about their opinions of billboards, 62 percent of the respondents said that they thought billboards should not be banned, while 52 percent said that they should be strictly regulated. When asked if billboards were entertaining, 80 percent of those surveyed said no; when asked if billboards could be beautiful, only 27 percent said yes.[5] Media buyers have not completely adopted outdoor media, partially because of image problems and the limited message that can be communicated.

Historically, advertisers considered outdoor ads as a support media to broadcast or print. However, current usage indicates it can be used successfully as a primary media as seen by Clover Leaf's recent strategic emphasis. Hoping to expand the overall tuna category to both men and women with their flavoured varieties (e.g., sun-dried tomato and basil), the only nationally distributed tuna producer showed interesting and innovative ways of thinking about tuna (e.g., salad or wrap) with its more exotic tastes sensations. Outdoor (e.g., posters, transit shelters, street columns) became the focal point to communicate the images and messages that easily transferred to other out-of-home media (e.g., in-store, health club posters) and sales promotions (e.g., coupons, samples).[6]

AUDIENCE MEASUREMENT FOR OUTDOOR MEDIA

Audience measurement to determine the amount of reach and frequency is done by the Canadian Outdoor Measurement Bureau (COMB), an independent organization comprised of members from advertisers, advertising agencies, and media firms known as outdoor operators. COMB maintains a national database of all products for outdoor operators in order to calculate daily or weekly audience averages for each media in all markets. COMB acts as an auditor to ensure an authentic media purchase and produces specific reports as documentation. COMB conducts 6,000 randomly selected field audits per year, calculates performance statistics for all operators, and disseminates these findings to all members.

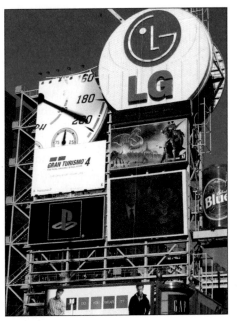

Exhibit 12–2
Outdoor media goes beyond two dimensions

You may wonder whether the GRPs are accurate. COMB's methodology to determine the reach and frequency is comprehensive. COMB obtains traffic circulation numbers from municipalities. This data is then analysed with respect to three key questions:

- What is the average number of people in the vehicle?
- What is the vehicle's origin within the CMA?
- Is the sign illuminated? If so, for how long?

This analysis is known as the total number of circulations. These circulations are applied to each poster along a certain part of the road that is known as a link. The numbers are adjusted to account for time-of-day variations throughout the week to arrive at an adjusted circulation, which is then divided by the target population so that the reach is expressed as 1 percent of the population.

This involved measurement process has resulted in a system that COMB claims as being the most accurate and reliable method in the world. In contrast, some media buyers are concerned that the measurement tracks opportunity for exposure and not actual exposure to the ads. While this discrepancy is an inherent problem with all media, it appears to be particularly strong with outdoor media. Furthermore, it is not clear how many people are in each vehicle that may be exposed to the ads. Despite this success and constructive criticism, COMB strives to

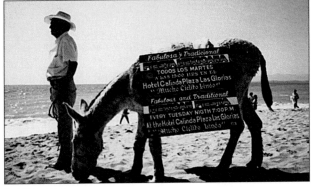

Exhibit 12–3
An interesting and unusual example of a mobile billboard

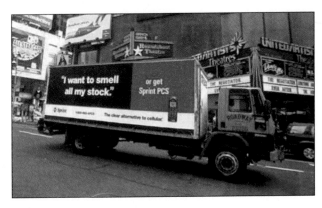

Trucks often serve as mobile billboards

find the best system possible to ensure a larger piece of the advertising industry beyond its usual 4-percent share compared to broadcast or print.

Recently, COMB tested the use of a global positioning system (GPS) to track driving behaviour more accurately in selected Canadian cities. The device was installed in cars to track driving patterns and to track which outdoor ads drviers had driven past. Pre- and posttest interviews obtained demographic and other information that was linked to other data sources to estimate reach and frequency. Preliminary results indicated that people were exposed to many ads but with less frequency to each ad, thus suggesting the usefulness of maximizing reach over frequency with outdoor ads.

The future of measurement in Canada may in found in the United Kingdom where an innovative technology that tracks a driver's eye movement while behind the wheel can assess which ads are actually seen. Taking into the account the size of the ad and the distance from the road, this new method is demonstrating more accurate numbers and some believe it has led to a growth of advertising revenue that now stands at 8 percent.[7]

STRENGTHS OF OUTDOOR MEDIA

Reach With proper placement, a broad base of exposure is possible in a given market, with both day and night presence. A 100 GRP **showing** (the percentage of duplicated audience exposed to an outdoor poster daily) could yield exposure to an equivalent of 100 percent of the marketplace daily! This level of coverage is likely to yield high levels of reach.

Frequency Because purchase cycles for outdoor media are typically for 30-day periods, consumers are usually exposed a number of times, resulting in high levels of frequency.

Geographic Coverage Outdoor media can be placed along highways, near stores, or on mobile billboards, almost anywhere that the law permits. Local, regional, or even national markets may be covered.

Creativity for Emotional Responses As shown in Exhibit 12–1, outdoor ads can be very creative. Large print, colours, and other elements attract attention and tend to generate short emotional responses that connect the target audience to the brand.

Cost Efficiency Outdoor ads usually have a very competitive CPM when compared to other media. The average CPM of outdoor ads is less than that of radio, TV, magazines, and newspapers.

Scheduling Flexibility Modern technologies have reduced production times for outdoor advertising to allow for rapid turnaround time. Placement can be done on a monthly basis assuming availability exists.

Selective Exposure On the one hand, outdoor ads are difficult for consumers to avoid since they are so pervasive. Moreover, a consumer has little control like television or radio to change the channel or station. On the other hand, consumers can deliberately ignore outdoor ads, however, the high profile of the ads makes this a difficult task at times.

Attention The sheer size, strategic placement, and the creative elements of colour make outdoor advertising an attractive media to draw the attention of the target audience.

LIMITATIONS OF OUTDOOR MEDIA

Target Audience Coverage With the broad base reach of outdoor advertising, it is difficult to ensure that the specific target audience coverage is sufficient. While it is possible to reach an audience with select location placement, in many cases the purchase of outdoor ads results in a high degree of waste coverage. It is not likely that everyone driving past a billboard is part of the target audience.

Amount of Processing Time Because of the speed with which most people pass by outdoor ads, exposure time is short, so messages are limited to a few words and/or an illustration.

Creativity for Cognitive Responses Lengthy appeals are not physically possible in many instances, and if they were, they have less likelihood of complete comprehension. Thus, it is expected that outdoor ads suffer from their inability to fully persuade consumers with an involved message.

Absolute Cost A basic level of 25 GRPs per day over four weeks in 10 or even three major cities can be quite prohibitive for many advertisers. For smaller businesses selecting a few strategic locations in a local market could overcome this limitation.

Media Image Outdoor advertising has suffered some image problems as well as some disregard among consumers. This may be in part due to fatigue of the high frequency of exposures that may lead to wearout—people are likely to get tired of seeing the same ad every day.

Target Audience Selectivity Reaching a specific target audience is challenging due to the broad exposure of outdoor media in general. However, strategic use can overcome this limitation, for example, by using reminder ads for a type of product near the retail outlets.

Clutter By its very nature, outdoor ads have competing messages. At any streetscape or location where outdoor ads are featured, it is very likely that other messages will be also vying for consumer attention.

Low Involvement The overall effect of the short repeated message is that outdoor ads tend to be considered as a low-involvement media.

TRANSIT MEDIA

Another form of out-of-home advertising is **transit advertising**. While similar to outdoor in the sense that it uses billboards and electronic messages, transit is targeted at the millions of people who are exposed to commercial transportation facilities, including buses, subways, light-rail trains, and airplanes. The first three we cover in the form of local transit options, and then we consider the airplane option. Transit advertising has been around for a long time, but recent years have seen a renewed interest in this medium due in part to the increased number of women in the work force (they can be reached on their way to work more easily than at home), audience segmentation, and the rising cost of TV advertising.

COMMUTER TRANSIT OPTIONS

If you have ever taken public transit, you have probably noticed the **interior transit cards** placed above the seating area that advertises restaurants, TV or radio stations, or a myriad of other products and services. Ads are positioned in backlit units above windows and along both sides of the bus, streetcar, subway, or light-rail transit cars. **Interior door cards** are available in major markets where there is subway-like transit. These cards are placed on both sides of the doors and are about 50 percent larger than the aforementioned cards.

While waiting for a taxicab, you cannot help but notice the ads on the side or back of the cab going in the opposite direction or on another street (see Exhibit 12–4). These **exterior posters** may appear on the sides, backs, and/or roofs of buses, taxis, trains, and subway and street cars.

Discovery Channel has always used out-of-home media to establish itself as a legitimate television alternative and to advertise its specific series, specials, or theme weeks. For example, during Shark week in 2002, they turned transit shelters into giant shark tanks. Following this, a summer transit shelter campaign in downtown Toronto

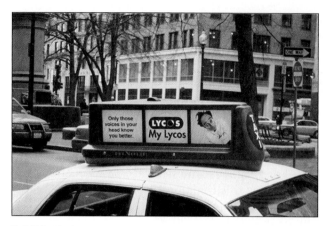

Exhibit 12–4
Electronic outside posters often appear on taxicabs

attempted to establish an audience for *Nefertiti Resurrected* and to increase awareness and viewership of Discovery Channel in general. The ads featured an air of glamour and mystery to attract new viewers. In addition, Nefertiti models passed by the transit ads during a two-week period and allowed people to ask questions and take photographs. Discovery Channel believes these transit ads and street-level events played an important supporting role with the on-air ads in setting a record audience, 10 percent higher than previously achieved.[8]

Station posters are of varying sizes and forms that attempt to attract the attention of those waiting for a subway-like ride. The most common size is 1 m by 2 m. As Exhibit 12–5 shows, station posters can be very attractive and attention-getting. Similar-sized posters are found at bus or street car **transit shelters** and often provide the advertiser with expanded coverage where other outdoor boards may be restricted.

Transit media is sold in select markets on a four-week basis with a certain desired level of GRPs. The range of GRPs is quite varied, going from a low of 5 GRPs to a high of 100 GRPs. Other purchases of transit media are based on the number of showings. For example, if an operator has the rights to 400 buses or subway cars, then an advertiser could typically buy displays in varying numbers (i.e., 25 percent, 50 percent, 75 percent, 100 percent) over a four-week time period. (Figure 12–3 shows some transit rates broken down by a number of GRP levels.)

Recent innovations in transit media include the super-bus where an advertiser "owns the bus" and places a vinyl ad on the entire surface of the bus. This is often done for a longer-term contract of a half- or full-year because of the application on the bus. On a less grand scale in a few select markets, smaller bus murals can be applied to the side or tail for a shorter period of time. Recently, the Toronto and Montreal subway systems have featured station domination where a single advertiser can be the sole sponsor of all points of communication within that station. **Subway online** is located in the 10 busiest subway stations in Toronto. It features digital news centres with video capabilities that delivers news, sports, and weather highlights with 20-second ads. IMC Perspective 12–1 indicates that the future of outdoor advertising may be more flexible.

STRENGTHS OF TRANSIT ADVERTISING

Amount of Processing Time Long length of exposure to an ad is a major strength of indoor forms. The audience is essentially a captive one, with nowhere else to go and nothing much to do. As a result, riders are likely to read the ads—more than once.

Exhibit 12–5
Station posters can be used to attract attention

Reach Transit advertising benefits from the absolute number of people exposed. Millions of people ride mass transit every week, providing a substantial number of potential viewers that can be reached.

Frequency Because our daily routines are standard, those who ride buses, subways, and the like are exposed to the ads repeatedly. If you rode the same subway to work and back every day, in one month you would have the opportunity to see the ad 20 to 40 times. The locations of station and shelter signs also afford high frequency of exposure.

Geographic Coverage For local advertisers in particular, transit advertising provides an opportunity to reach a very select segment of the population. A purchase of a location

FIGURE 12–3 □ □ □ □   Transit advertising rates for selected buys (all costs in $000s)

| Markets* | Fleet Size | Exterior 70s | | | | Exterior Kings | | | |
| | | 25 Daily GRPs | | 50 Daily GRPs | | 25 Daily GRPs | | 50 Daily GRPs | |
		Cost/4wks.	#Units	Cost/4wks.	#Units	Cost/4wks.	#Units	Cost/4wks.	#Units
Top 3 total	5,025	$96.4	320	$186.3	670	$112.3	267	$212.7	534
Top 10 total	8,664	$140.2	528	$270.0	1,085	$163.9	443	$311.3	884
Top 25 total	9,923	$173.6	659	$336.9	1,351	$201.6	690	$382.0	1,108

| Markets* | Fleet Size | Interior Singles | | | | Interior Doubles | | | |
| | | ½ Showing | | Full Showing | | ½ Showing | | Full Showing | |
		Cost/4wks.	#Units	Cost/4wks.	#Units	Cost/4wks.	#Units	Cost/4wks.	#Units
Top 3 total	5,025	$67.5	3,384	$125.0	6,766	$102.9	2,919	$199.0	5,992
Top 10 total	8,664	$91.1	5,248	$166.9	10,493	$143.0	4,783	$271.0	9,719
Top 25 total	9,952	$100.4	5,911	$185.4	11,828	$159.1	5,446	$302.2	11,054

* Top 3, 10, & 25: Based upon Top 25 markets by population. Check other available suppliers in CARD.

Source: April 2003, CARD

in a certain neighbourhood will lead to exposure to people of specific ethnic backgrounds, demographic characteristics, and so on.

Absolute Cost and Cost Efficiency   Transit advertising tends to be one of the least expensive media in terms of both absolute and relative costs. An ad on the side of a bus can be purchased for a very reasonable CPM.

Control for Selective Exposure   Similar to outdoor advertising, transit ads are quite pervasive for those using the service and consumers have little control over the use of the media.

Scheduling Flexibility   The capacity available for transit ads makes it fairly good for placement. Ads can be produced quickly and inserted internally or externally.

LIMITATIONS OF TRANSIT MEDIA

Media Image   To many advertisers, transit advertising does not carry the image they would like to represent for their products or services. Some advertisers may think having their name on the side of a bus or in a bus does not reflect well on the firm.

Target Audience Selectivity   While a strength of transit advertising is the ability to provide exposure to a large number of people, this audience may have certain lifestyles and/or behavioural characteristics that are not true of the target audience as a whole. For example, in rural or suburban areas, mass transit is limited or non-existent, so the medium is not very effective for reaching these people.

Target Audience Coverage   While geographic selectivity may be an advantage, not everyone who rides a transportation vehicle or is exposed to transit advertising is a potential customer. For products that do not have specific geographic segments, this form of advertising incurs a good deal of waste coverage. Another problem is that the same bus may not run the same route every day. To save wear and tear on the vehicles, some transit companies alternate city routes (with much stop and go) with longer suburban routes. Thus, a bus may go downtown one day and reach the desired target group but spend the next day in the suburbs, where there may be little market potential.

New Options in Out-of-Home Media

The only entertaining thing to do when waiting for a bus in a bus shelter is probably to meticulously stare at the bus shelter advertisement in all its glory from multiple perspectives. However, after the 15th day of staring at the same creative, the ad loses its punch, and can even become annoying. Thankfully for daily commuters, transit advertising is becoming almost as instantaneous as radio, as visual as television, and as responsive as newspapers. One-week shelter campaigns scrolling ads, and redesigned glass transit shelters that allow ads to be seen clearly by both pedestrians and passing motorists are coming to a bus stop near you.

up to 250 transit shelters and two-day postings/takedown for anything above 250 shelters.

Another development in transit-shelter advertising is the scrolling units that Viacom is placing in some downtown Toronto locations. The units allow the company to increase the number of ad faces it offers per location and allows advertisers to change their creative in as little as three seconds. The ads in the units are regular posters that scroll from one creative to the next. As Viacom suggests, this could be ideal for businesses such as restaurants. One could promote its breakfast menu until noon, then promote its lunch menu, and end the day with a dinner menu offer.

Viacom Outdoor Canada, previously known as Mediacom, is now selling seven-day transit-shelter campaigns in Toronto and Montreal that are targeted to advertisers like retailers and car dealerships who have short-term promotions. Furthermore, the idea is "good for someone who wants to change their creative a lot, for those who want to say more in a short period of time," says Viacom marketing director Kim Warburton. Alternatively, it is a wonderful tool to reach consumers as they near their purchase decision. Toronto-based Labatt Breweries of Canada, for example, used outdoor advertising to promote the Carlsberg brand in specific locations, close to beer stores or clubs, for example. To facilitate this, Viacom guarantees one-day posting and takedown for

Viacom's final innovation is new transit shelters that have a clear view of the ads, which are to be installed in Toronto and Mississauga over the next seven years. The roof of the shelter is slightly curved glass, giving the creative a more distinct look. "The new bus shelters are great. That'll be the bus shelter of the future," predicts Glenn McConnell, president of Viacom's main rival, Pattison Outdoor. It sure sounds like waiting for the bus won't be quite the same anymore!

Source: "Short and Sweet," *Marketing Magazine*, November 19, 2001.

Creativity for Emotional and Cognitive Responses It may be very difficult to place colourful and attractive ads on cards, thus limiting their emotional content. And while much copy can be provided on inside cards, the short copy on the outside of a bus provides less rational persuasion.

Clutter Inside ads suffer from clutter of competing ads and outside ads feel the pressure of other street level ads. Furthermore, the environment is cluttered in another sense as sitting or standing on a crowded subway may not be conducive to reading advertising, let alone experiencing the mood the advertiser would like to create.

Attention The smaller size and location of transit ads make it difficult to use the creative elements to attract attention.

Involvement Like outdoor advertising, with shorter copy and seemingly fleeting messages of short copy, transit ads are generally considered to be low-involvement media.

AIRLINE TRANSIT OPTIONS

Related to transit media while travelling *within* cities and towns is media while travelling *between* cities and towns. As the number of flying passengers increases so too does the attractiveness of four **in-flight advertising** options and many airport terminal options. In-flight magazines are free magazines published by the airlines and are offered on almost every plane in the air (see Exhibit 12–6). In-flight videos have been common on international flights for some time and are now being used on domestic flights. Commercials were not originally included in these videos. Now, Air Canada sells different packages depending on the type of show (e.g., news, movie). Some of these commercial messages are as long as three minutes. In-flight radio is a pleasant way to pass the time while flying, and it offers another opportunity for advertisers to deliver an audio message beyond standard radio. Ads can be placed on various collateral material such as boarding passes, ticket jackets, and meal trays. Finally, similar to transit and outdoor, **airport displays** are available ranging from smaller backlit posters in the terminal to superboards near the terminal and various other types of displays depending upon the media company and airport terminal. Since we have covered broadcast, print, and poster ads thus far in the text, the strengths and limitations of these media in an airline context are readily transferred. The following points are a few unique strengths and limitations of using media in this particular context that are consistent with the same terminology used previously.

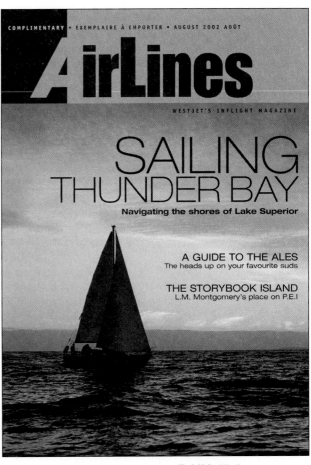

Exhibit 12–6
In-flight magazines are available on most carriers

STRENGTHS OF IN-FLIGHT ADVERTISING

Target Audience Selectivity In-flight allows the advertiser to reach specific demographic groups, as well as travellers to a specific destination. Both business and tourist travellers tend to be upscale, an attractive audience to companies targeting these groups. Many of these passengers hold top management positions in their firms.

Selective Exposure The audience in an airplane cannot leave the room. Particularly on long flights, many passengers are willing (and even happy) to have in-flight magazines to read, news to listen to, and even commercials to watch.

Absolute Cost The cost of in-flight commercials is lower than that of business print media. For example, $10,000 can get considerable exposure on Air Canada flights.

LIMITATIONS OF IN-FLIGHT ADVERTISING

Media Image Many consumers are not pleased with the idea of ads in general and believe they are already too intrusive. In-flight commercials are just one more place, they think, where advertisers are intruding.

353

Scheduling Flexibility Many airlines limit the amount of time they allow for in-flight commercials. Japan Air Lines, for example, allows a mere 220 seconds per flight.

Attention Many passengers may decide to tune out the ads, not purchase the head-sets required to get the volume, or simply ignore the commercials.

PLACE-BASED MEDIA

As noted earlier in this chapter, the variety of out-of-home media continues to increase, and discussing or even mentioning all of it is beyond the scope of this text. The idea of bringing the advertising medium to consumers wherever they may be underlies the strategy behind place-based media. However, the following are provided to illustrate a few of the many options.

PLACE-BASED MEDIA OPTIONS

An original example of place-based media is signage and displays in malls. The popular mall poster is often backlit like the transit shelter or transit-station poster and is located throughout a shopping mall. The key feature of the mall poster is that it is in the shopping environment and therefore one step closer to the actual purchase. These posters are sold in most markets across the country similarly to outdoor posters with individual spot buys and varying levels of GRPs. Firms also sell various sizes of mall banners for branding purposes.

A number of place-based media are outdoor media brought into a particular environment. Backlit posters, superboards, electronic message signs, and video displays are used in many other locations such as convention centres, movie theatres, hotels, sports stadiums or arenas, or wherever there is a sufficient number of people. The method of selling the time or space is similar to what was described above.

Continuing this idea of bringing a message to a target audience based on where they are illustrates two emerging place-based media outlets. Firms attempt to reach younger consumers on the campuses of many universities with various sizes of indoor posters that are standard and non-standard. Furthermore, with closed-circuit television, firms attempt to reach travellers or patients in designated hotel rooms or hospital or doctor waiting rooms, respectively. And to reach virtually anyone and everyone, it is possible to place small print ads inside elevators or washrooms and on floors or escalator handrails. IMC Perspective 12–2 covers a heated battle for washroom ad supremacy.

STRENGTHS OF PLACE-BASED MEDIA

Target Audience Selectivity The main purpose of place-based media is to reach a specific target audience or to reach the target audience while closer to the purchase decision.

Absolute Cost and Cost Efficiency The absolute cost and CPM are generally reasonable compared to other media options.

Creativity for Processing Responses Because the target and place are intertwined, the message may generate more in-depth cognitive responses or stronger emotional responses.

Selective Exposure and Attention Since many of these media options have or nearly have captive audiences, the opportunity for consumers to avoid the ads or direct their attention elsewhere is minimal compared to other media.

The NewAd–Zoom Battle

Chances are you've seen one or both of these company's logos with strategically placed ads in very private locations. What better place is there to capture the attention of the target audience than the washroom of a favourite bar, club, or restaurant? Welcome to one of Canada's most interesting and captive forms of out-of-home media where two firms, NewAd of Toronto and Zoom of Montreal continue to grow intensively after their humble beginnings a few years ago.

Part of the success of each company has been to focus in locations to reach a younger demographic aged 18–34 representing 6.2 million people, or about 20 percent of the total population of Canada. So it is no surprise to find that each company also targets university and college campuses, and gyms and fitness centres. All told, NewAd placed ads in 192 fitness clubs, 76 universities and colleges, 1,883 restaurants and bars while Zoom had corresponding numbers of 200, 71, and 1,600, respectively. Clearly both firms are locked in a heated battle for advertisers' dollars. However, the head-to-head competition between these two rivals started to put pressure on each firm to drop their rates to entice more advertisers.

With such a competitive environment, both firms looked to various forms of expansion for future growth. Zoom planned a continued focus on the younger demographic so that it could be known as the primary media option for this type of consumer. It also looked towards strategic acquisitions of other media that complemented its recent expansion into the U.S. NewAd appeared interested in expanding to other types of direct out-of-home contact with consumers to more fully ensure a complete presence for a brand during its campaign. This integrated approach appeared consistent with an increased emphasis of providing solid media research for its clients when they decide to purchase innovative forms of out-of-home media.

Source: David Chilton, "Head to Head Competition," *Marketing Magazine*, March 10, 2003.

Involvement   With the above strengths of many place-based media options, the collective conclusion suggests that the target audience may be more involved with the advertising message than some other similar media in different contexts.

LIMITATIONS OF PLACE-BASED MEDIA

Poor Media Image   Often, place-based media are exposed to consumers when they do not expect a selling message to occur, which may cause some amount of resentment.

Clutter   The clutter that consumers feel while watching television or reading a magazine may also be felt.

Reach and Frequency   Place-based media plays more of a supporting role to other media since it is very difficult to ensure high levels of either reach or frequency. Some exceptions to these can be considered, but in general media planners will look for other media to maximize these two factors.

Target Audience and Geographic Coverage   The logistical availability of these types of media make full coverage difficult or quite challenging to implement or nearly impossible to get complete geographic coverage.

Amount of Processing Time For the most part, place-based media suffer from very short messages to target audiences that are more likely preoccupied with some other task.

Scheduling Flexibility While not a complete or comprehensive limitation, the logistics of changing place-based media makes the scheduling, which is done on a monthly basis, put certain restrictions on an advertiser for a timely message.

PLACE-BASED MEDIA AT THE MOVIES

We now turn our attention to a specific form of place-based media: movie theatres. One of the first advertisers at the movies was Coca-Cola, which advertised Coke Classic and Fruitopia. Some of the original advertisers faced hostile crowds who would boo and throw popcorn at the screen. It is estimated that about $25 to $30 million in advertising is spent in theatres on commercials, slides, posters, and sales promotions, with about $15 million of that for the commercials. And with the commercials lasting 60 to 90 seconds, advertisers have a unique opportunity to communicate for a longer period of time than with a TV ad, which typically runs 30 seconds. In fact, 95 percent of the theatre ads are also shown on television, albeit in a shortened format. A wide variety of products have been advertised using the medium including cars, government, telcos, food, video games, and health and beauty products, representing main brand names such as Toyota, Nissan, Telus, Bell Mobility, Health Canada, Department of National Defence, and Pepsi-Cola.

As a media grows, so does its sophistication, and theatre media is no exception; it now reports audience measurement information. One study estimated that total recall (aided plus unaided) reached 74 percent compared to 37 percent for radio and 32 percent for television. Yet while there appears to be good communication effect, and the cost is reasonable, the overall revenue is still only 1 percent of the TV advertising revenue per year. Part of the problem is that the reach is still limited, only 3.6 million per month for Cineplex Odeon, for example.[9]

STRENGTHS OF MOVIE THEATRES AS A MEDIA

No Control for Selective Exposure The viewers constitute a captive audience who cannot avoid the ad messages unless they are in another part of the theatre.

Cost The cost of advertising in a theatre varies from one setting to the next. However, it is low in terms of both absolute and relative costs per exposure.

Clutter Lack of clutter is another advantage offered by advertising in movie theatres. Most theatres limit the number of ads.

Target Audience Selectivity The movie titles and ratings enable advertisers to place their commercials to reach specific target audiences. Furthermore, moviegoers are generally above average in income and education.

Target Audience Coverage Coverage is positive for most advertisers as all cities and larger towns have theatres and the chains can accommodate the placement in various locations.

Geographic Coverage Certain cities or towns can be featured in a campaign depending upon the needs of an advertiser.

Creativity for Processing Responses Movie ads tend to be repeats of those in other media to launch a brand new campaign. In either case, advertisers expect similar response to what is found, for example, on television. However, the special mood created in the movie theatre compared to at-home consumption makes the experience richer and advertisers use theatre ads as an emotional spike that can transfer to the product more readily, especially if the theatre is located next to a mall or store where the product may be sold.

Attention and Involvement The larger screen and the fact that consumers are facing the screen with little opportunity to avoid the ads deliver strong attention and involvement.

LIMITATIONS OF MOVIE THEATRES AS A MEDIA

Media Image Perhaps the major disadvantage is that many people do not wish to see advertising in this media. A number of studies suggest that these ads may create a high degree of annoyance.[10] This dissatisfaction may carry over to the product itself, to the movies, or to the theatres. Mike Stimler, president of the specialty video label Water Bearer Films, says, "People boo in movie theatres when they see product advertising."[11] Anne-Marie Marcus, vice president of sales for Screenvision, contends that the furor has died down.[12]

In a study by Michael Belch and Don Sciglimpaglia, many moviegoers stated that not only would they not buy the product advertised, but also they would consider boycotting it. So advertisers should be cautious in their use of this medium. If they want to use movies, they may want to consider an alternative—placing products in the movies.

Cost While the cost of advertising in local theatres has been cited as a strength because of the low rates charged, ads exposed nationally can be expensive, with a corresponding high CPM compared to other media.

Reach and Frequency As suggested in the introduction for this section, while the number of people attending movies is substantial, the ability to reach substantial numbers of consumers with repeated messages is limited. In this sense, some advertisers would view this exposure as support to other media used.

Scheduling Flexibility Placement for ads generally requires eight weeks and category exclusivity in certain distribution outlets further limits the availability and scheduling ease with this media option.

Amount of Processing Time Similar to television ads, we see short fleeting messages, however, considerable research suggests that the environment of the theatre and the large screen contributes to strong recall.

POINT-OF-PURCHASE MEDIA

In-store communication is a specific form of place-based media that has existed for some time. Advertisers promote their products in supermarkets and other stores with a number of different "media" options. In the preceding sentence, we put media in quotation marks because often the tools used do not appear to be typical media. However, we use media as a general term to describe a method of transmitting an advertising message. It should be noted that some of these media are also thought of as sales promotions because some messages include a sales promotion (e.g., discount). Furthermore, some require the participation of retailers, which necessitates a payment that is often recorded as a trade promotion expense in the budget.

Point-of-purchase media includes tools such as wall signs, displays, banners, shelf signs, video displays on shopping carts, kiosks that provide recipes and beauty tips, coupons at counters and cash registers, LED (light-emitting diode) boards, and ads that broadcast over in-house screens.

Much of the attraction of point-of-purchase media is based on figures from Point of Purchase Advertising International (POPAI), which state that approximately two-thirds of consumers' purchase decisions are made in the store; some impulse categories demonstrate an 80-percent rate.[13] Many advertisers are spending more of their dollars where decisions are made now that they can reach consumers at the point of purchase, providing additional product information while reducing their own efforts

STRENGTHS OF POINT-OF-PURCHASE MEDIA

Target Audience Selectivity The main purpose of point-of-purchase media is to reach the target audience while making the purchase decision.

Absolute Cost and Cost Efficiency The absolute cost and CPM are generally reasonable compared to other media options.

Creativity for Cognitive Responses Key or deterministic benefits can be communicated just prior to purchase. These benefits may only become salient during the final choice decision.

Creativity for Emotional Responses Recent innovations in point-of-purchase media such as video screens at cash registers, attempt to bring the emotion of television commercials to the store environment so that consumers feel the same way just prior to purchasing the product.

Target Audience and Geographic Coverage Distributing point-of-purchase material across the country is simplified through retail chains. For example, a brand could have displays in virtually all grocery stores at the same time with placement agreed upon by personnel at head office.

Reach A key strength of point-of-sale media is that it is communicating to virtually all people who are considering purchasing in a particular category except for those going directly to the Internet or catalogues.

Attention Since consumers are in the process of shopping, point-of-sale media has a tremendous opportunity for attracting the attention of the target audience. In general, consumers are seeking additional information or sensory experience as they consider the product selection.

Amount of Processing Time and Involvement It may be difficult to universally classify point-of-purchase media as having strength with these two factors. It appears reasonable to suggest that if the target audience has not avoided a certain part of the store and also paid attention to a display, then there is the strong potential that the relevant messages will resonate such that a sufficient amount of consideration will be given.

LIMITATIONS OF POINT-OF-PURCHASE MEDIA

Media Image One source of discontent for a consumer may be that the shopping experience is hindered in some manner with too many commercial messages.

Scheduling Flexibility A marketer may be reliant on a third-party service provider who may not install or set up the tool correctly.

Clutter If you want to be there, so does the competition. The clutter that consumers feel while watching television or reading a magazine may also be felt in the purchase environment.

Frequency Processing of a point-of-sale media requires a consumer's presence in the retail environment. So except for those circumstances where a consumer is entering an establishment repeatedly, the likelihood of an advertiser achieving sufficient frequency through this media is quite limited.

Selective Exposure Consumers have complete control on where they want to look in a store, how much time they prefer to stay in one area, and whether they want to even bother looking at any form of in-store communication.

PROMOTIONAL PRODUCTS

According to the Promotional Products Association International (PPA), **promotional products marketing** is "the advertising or promotional medium or method that uses promotional products, such as ad specialties, premiums, business gifts, awards, prizes, or commemoratives." Promotional products marketing is the more up-to-date name for what used to be called specialty advertising. **Specialty advertising** has now been provided with a new definition:

> A medium of advertising, sales promotion, and motivational communication employing imprinted, useful, or decorative products called advertising specialties, a subset of promotional products.
>
> Unlike premiums, with which they are sometimes confused (called advertising specialties), these articles are always distributed free—recipients don't have to earn the specialty by making a purchase or contribution.[14]

As you can see from these descriptions, specialty advertising is often considered both an advertising and a sales promotion medium. In our discussion, we treat it as a supportive advertising medium in the IMC program (Exhibit 12–7).

There are over 15,000 *advertising specialty* items, including ballpoint pens, coffee mugs, key rings, calendars, T-shirts, and matchbooks. Unconventional specialties such as plant holders, wall plaques, and gloves with the advertiser's name printed on them are also used to promote a company or its product; so are glassware, trophies, awards, and vinyl products. If you stop reading for a moment and look around your desk (or wherever you are), you'll probably find some specialty advertising item nearby. It may be the pen you are using or even a book cover with the campus bookstore name on it.

The promotional products industry in Canada is substantial. Distributor revenue topped $2.1 billion in 2001, up from $1.1 billion in 1998 and $800 million in 1993. While inflation grew 16 percent over that nine-year period, distributor revenue climbed 160 percent. Clearly, many companies are looking to promotional products as a way of communicating to their customers, suppliers, employees, and the general public. Figure 12–4 shows the percentage of sales by product category. Wearables/Apparel accounted for the bulk at 37 percent while the next highest, writing instruments clipped in at 9 percent. Figure 12–5 shows the percentage of sales by program type. Business gifts, public relations, and employee relations and events account for nearly half of all revenue.[15]

Specialty items are used for many promotional purposes: to thank a customer for patronage, keep the name of the company in front of consumers, introduce new products, or reinforce the name of an existing company, product, or service. Advertising specialties are often used to support other forms of product promotions.

Exhibit 12–7
Promotional products can be a valuable contributor to the IMC program

STRENGTHS OF PROMOTIONAL PRODUCTS

Target Audience Selectivity and Coverage Because specialty advertising items are generally distributed directly to target customers, the medium offers a high degree of selectivity. The communication is distributed to the desired recipient, reducing waste coverage.

Creativity for Cognitive Responses As the variety of specialty items in Figure 12–4 demonstrates, this medium offers a high degree of flexibility. A message as simple as a logo or as long as is necessary can be distributed through a number of means. Both small and large companies can employ this medium, limited only by their own creativity.

FIGURE 12–4
Distributor product
category breakdown
☐☐☐☐☐

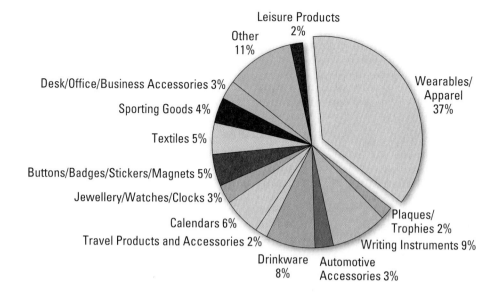

Leisure Products 2%
Other 11%
Desk/Office/Business Accessories 3%
Sporting Goods 4%
Textiles 5%
Buttons/Badges/Stickers/Magnets 5%
Jewellery/Watches/Clocks 3%
Calendars 6%
Travel Products and Accessories 2%
Drinkware 8%
Automotive Accessories 3%
Writing Instruments 9%
Plaques/Trophies 2%
Wearables/Apparel 37%

FIGURE 12–5
Distributor sales by
program type
☐☐☐☐☐

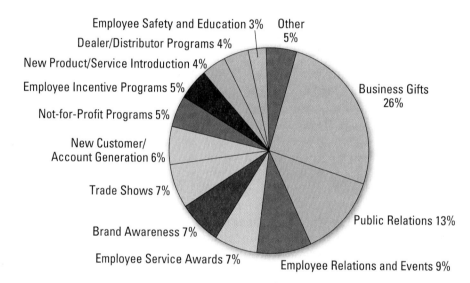

Employee Safety and Education 3%
Dealer/Distributor Programs 4%
New Product/Service Introduction 4%
Employee Incentive Programs 5%
Not-for-Profit Programs 5%
New Customer/Account Generation 6%
Trade Shows 7%
Brand Awareness 7%
Employee Service Awards 7%
Other 5%
Business Gifts 26%
Public Relations 13%
Employee Relations and Events 9%

Frequency Most forms of specialty advertising are designed for retention. Key chains, calendars, and pens remain with the potential customer for a long time, providing repeat exposures to the advertising message at no additional cost.

Absolute Cost and Cost Efficiency Some specialty items are rather expensive (for example, leather goods), but most are affordable to almost any size organization. While they are costly on a CPM basis when compared with other media, the high number of repeat exposures drives down the relative cost per exposure of this advertising medium.

Creativity for Emotional Responses Promotional products are perhaps the only medium that generates goodwill in the receiver. Because people like to receive gifts and many of the products are functional (key chains, calendars, etc.), consumers are grateful to receive them. In a recent study of users of promotional products, goodwill was cited as the number 1 reason for use.

Attention, Involvement, Amount of Processing Time These would all be considered strengths of promotional products assuming the recipient appreciates the actual item whether it is clothing or some kind of office product. Certainly the selection of the item in question will heavily influence consumer reaction.

LIMITATIONS OF PROMOTIONAL PRODUCTS

Media Image While most forms of specialty advertising are received as friendly reminders of the store or company name, the firm must be careful choosing the specialty item. The company image may be cheapened by a chintzy or poorly designed advertising form.

Clutter With so many organizations now using this advertising medium, the marketplace may become saturated. While you can always use another ballpoint pen or book of matches, the value to the receiver declines if replacement is too easy, and the likelihood that you will retain the item or even notice the message is reduced. The more unusual the specialty, the more value it is likely to have to the receiver.

Scheduling Flexibility The lead time required to put together a promotional products message is significantly longer than that for most other media.

Reach An advertiser hoping to expand the market through wider reach would likely find promotional products a weaker choice. As a support media, it thrives on assisting existing media that has reach as its strength.

Geographic Coverage While promotional products can be distributed essentially anywhere, the cost implications would severely curtail this as a feasible feature for most advertisers.

Selective Exposure Recipients of promotional products are in complete control as to whether they choose to display or show the item. It is entirely possible that a tremendous investment could receive very minimal exposure to the intended target audience.

AUDIENCE MEASUREMENT IN PROMOTIONAL PRODUCTS MARKETING

Owing to the nature of the industry, specialty advertising has no established ongoing audience measurement system. Research has been conducted in an attempt to determine the impact of this medium, however, including the following reports.

A study by Schreiber and Associates indicated 39 percent of people receiving advertising specialties could recall the name of the company as long as six months later, and a study conducted by A. C. Nielsen found that 31 percent of respondents were still using at least one specialty they had received a year or more earlier.[16]

A study by Gould/Pace University found the inclusion of a specialty item in a direct-mail piece generated a greater response rate and 321 percent greater dollar purchases per sale than mail pieces without such items.[17] Studies at Baylor University showed that including an ad specialty item in a thank-you letter can improve customers' attitudes toward a company's sales reps by as much as 34 percent and toward the company itself by as much as 52 percent.[18] Finally, Richard Manville Research reported the average household had almost four calendars; if they had not been given such items free, two-thirds of the respondents said they would purchase one, an indication of the desirability of this particular specialty item.[19] Figure 12–6 demonstrates how promotional products can be used effectively in an IMC program.

The Promotional Products Association International (www.ppai.org) is the trade organization of the field. The PPAI helps marketers develop and use specialty advertising forms. It also provides promotional and public relations support for specialty advertising and disseminates statistical and educational information. The Canadian association is Promotional Products Association of Canada (www.promocan.com).

FIGURE 12–6
The impact of promotional products in an IMC program
□ □ □ □ □

Combining Promotional Products with:	Effect
Advertising	Including direct mail with a promotional product increased response to a print ad to 4.2%, versus 2.3% with direct mail only and .7% with an ad only.
Personal selling	Customers receiving a promotional product expressed more goodwill toward the company than did those receiving a letter. They rated the company more positively in 52% of the cases and rated the salespeople more proficient (34%) and more capable (16%). Business-to-business customers receiving a promotional product were 14% more likely to provide leads, while salespersons who gave gifts to customers received 22% more leads than those who did not.
Trade shows	Responses to invitations to visit a booth were higher when a promotional product was enclosed.
Direct	Responses to direct-mail sales pieces were 1.9% with only a letter but 3.3% with a promotional product (75% higher). Other studies have shown increases of 50 to 66%.

YELLOW PAGES MEDIA

While most of us use the **Yellow Pages** frequently, we tend to forget they are advertising. The Yellow Pages are often referred to as a **directional medium** because the ads do not create awareness or demand for products or services; rather, once consumers have decided to buy, the Yellow Pages point them in the direction where their purchases can be made.[20]

STRENGTHS OF YELLOW PAGES MEDIA

Reach and Target Audience Coverage Directories are usually delivered to every home and business within a given geographic area, ensuring wide availability.

Attention, Involvement, and Processing Time Consumers use the Yellow Pages when they are considering, or have decided to take, action. Thus, by its very purpose, readers give the Yellow Pages their full attention and examine the information thoroughly.

Cost Efficiency and Absolute Cost Ad space and production costs are relatively low compared to other media.

Frequency Because of their longevity (Yellow Pages are published yearly), consumers return to the directories time and again. The average adult refers to the Yellow Pages about twice a week.[21]

Media Image Because consumers choose to use the Yellow Pages, they are not considered an intrusion. Studies show that most consumers rate the Yellow Pages very favourably.[22]

LIMITATIONS OF YELLOW PAGES MEDIA

Geographic Coverage Since Yellow Pages are essentially local media, they tend to be very localized. Add to this the increasing number of specialized directories, and the net result is a very specific offering.

Creativity for Cognitive and Emotional Responses While the Yellow Pages are somewhat flexible, their creative aspects are limited.

Scheduling Flexibility Printing schedules require that ads be placed a long time before the publications appear. It is impossible to get an ad in after the deadline, and advertisers need to wait a long time before the next edition. Further, because Yellow Pages are printed only once a year, they become outdated. Companies may relocate, go out of business, or change phone numbers in the period between editions.

Clutter A recent study by Avery Abernethy indicates that the Yellow Pages (like other media) experience problems with clutter.

Target Audience Selectivity The broad distribution of Yellow Pages makes selectivity impossible. A firm's information is exposed to many more consumers than it realistically strives to reach.

Selective Exposure The directional media characteristics of Yellow Pages puts the reader in complete control as to when the message will be exposed to the target audience.

PRODUCT PLACEMENT

An increasingly common way to promote a product is by showing the actual product or an ad for it as part of a movie or TV show. While such **product placement** does not constitute a major segment of the advertising and promotions business, it has proved effective for some companies. (Note: Like specialty advertising, product placement is sometimes considered a promotion rather than an advertising form. This distinction is not a critical one, and we have decided to treat product placement as a form of advertising.)

A number of companies pay to have their products used in movies and music videos. Exhibit 12–8 shows how BMW was able to get its product featured in the movie *The World Is Not Enough*. Avis, Ericcson, and BMW were all in the James Bond movie *Tomorrow Never Dies*. The movie had its own website with links to the companies with placements, and the companies, in turn, had links on their websites to the movie site. The financial results of product placement can be significant. Sales of Ray-Ban Wayfarer sunglasses tripled after Tom Cruise wore them in the movie *Risky Business*, and Ray-Ban Aviator sales increased 40 percent after he wore them in *Top Gun*.[23]

PRODUCT PLACEMENT DECISIONS

With up to $4 billion in North American revenue and up to 50 percent of all movies and television shows using product placement, advertising through this promotional media is certainly big business. Assuming a marketer selected the right vehicle for exposure, product placement contributes to higher awareness by its sheer volume of exposure. More successful product placement contributes to its brand position and requires a number of decisions.[24]

A primary issue to resolve concerns the source as represented by the plot, scenes, or characters of the movie or TV show. The creative use of the product profoundly impacts the experience ranging from a central role in the scene to a mere showing of the product to having a central character use or talk about the product.[25] Some recent examples of product placement occurring in Canada or as a result of movie or television production being filmed in Canada include:

- Canadian Club gate bottle, circa 1908, in the film *Chicago*, which was used by actress Queen Latifa to pour a drink from in one of her prison scenes[26]
- Two Visa decals, which were placed on the front window of the travel agency where Toula worked in *My Big Fat Greek Wedding*[27]
- People in the reality television show *Star Académie*, used a Rogers AT&T cellphone at the end of each episode to call their family and friends after being away for a long time.[28]
- Frito Lay products have been in 40 movies or shows in one year including Ruffles potato chips on *Degrassi: The Next Generation* and Lays potato chips in *Slapshot 2*.[29]
- Each cast member of the television show *Train 48* used a Fido cellphone, with one talking about the feature of a new Sony Ericcson phone.[30]

Related to the above two issues is the amount of time the product is featured and how many different vehicles a marketer wants to be exposed in. While a marketer and its agent obviously try to negotiate the

Exhibit 12–8
Many companies use movies to promote their products

most favourable situation on all these issues, they are also dependent upon the director's final artistic decision.[31] For example, product placement moved to animated shows with the placement of the Reach 400 Max toothbrush on the TV sitcom *Bob and Margaret* in the form of a five-to-10 second virtual placement that was blended into the show's program about a dentist. Reach managers felt the placement balanced the requirements of not too blatant, but noticed. Placement support included a tune-in spot for the show that featured the toothbrush along with the Reach commercial in the promotion schedule, and closed captioning sponsorship of the show. Reach toothbrush's placement offered more control than usual since the program already existed with an established time slot and the virtual placement material (i.e., logo, product visual) provided by Reach fit appropriately into established scenes.[32]

Finally, as a support medium, product placement needs to work with other marketing communication tools to achieve its maximum contribution. Much of the product placement in Quebec reality television shows are linked with sponsorship arrangements. For example, GM Canada sponsors *Le Grand blond avec un show surnois*—a late night talk show and *Testostérone*—a men's show in addition to having product placement as an important element. Similarly, *Ma Maison Rona* is a sponsored reality television show based on renovating someone else's home that naturally included trips to Rona for material.[33] Rona goes one step further as this product placement occurs during its mass media campaign.[34]

As promising as product placement appears, research indicates that its greatest strength lies in maintaining existing loyalty of current customers who see the product they consume actually consumed in a realistic situation by a character they can relate to or identify with. Furthermore, consumers indicate that real products are expected and preferred compared to some kind of generic unrecognizable brand.[35]

STRENGTHS OF PRODUCT PLACEMENT

Reach A large number of people see movies each year. The average film is estimated to have a life span of three and one-half years, and most of these moviegoers are very attentive audience members. When this is combined with the increasing home video rental market and network and specialty channels, the potential exposure for a product placed in a movie is enormous.

Frequency Depending on how the product is used in the movie (or program), there may be ample opportunity for repeated exposures (many, for those who like to watch a program or movie more than once).

Creativity for Emotional Responses We previously discussed the advantages of source identification that occurs with a creative message. When consumers see their favourite movie star wearing Oakleys, drinking Gatorade, or driving a Mercedes, this association may lead to a favourable product image. Most of those involved in product placement believe that association with the proper source is critical for success.

Cost Efficiency While the cost of placing a product may range from free samples to $1 million, these are extremes. The CPM for this form of advertising can be very low, owing to the high volume of exposures it generates.

Geographic Coverage The potential for geographic coverage is substantial as a top movie or television show could have national or international coverage. We emphasize the importance of this qualifying aspect as entertainment viewers can be fickle.

Selective Exposure It is very difficult for a theatre audience member to physically avoid the product placement through some form of zipping or zapping!

Clutter With category exclusivity rights within a vehicle and the fact that any show or movie only has a few product placements, the potential for clutter is very low. However, the plot, scenes, and dialogue act as a form of clutter that can be overcome with creative use of product placement.

Involvement A product placement done properly has direct relevance for the character or situation and is almost a transformational experience for the audience member that is paying full attention to the entertainment.

LIMITATIONS OF PRODUCT PLACEMENT

Absolute Cost While the CPM may be very low for product placement in movies, the absolute cost of placing the product may be very high, pricing some advertisers out of the market.

Amount of Processing Time and Attention While the way some products are exposed to the audience has an impact, there is no guarantee viewers will notice the product. Some product placements are more conspicuous than others. When the product is not featured prominently, the advertiser runs the risk of not being seen (although, of course, the same risk is present in all forms of media advertising). Furthermore, some product placements only last for a few seconds.

Exhibit 12–9
Ads often appear in the strangest places

Creativity for Cognitive Responses The appeal that can be made in this media form is limited. There is no potential for discussing product benefits or providing detailed information. Rather, appeals are limited to source association, use, and enjoyment. The endorsement of the product is indirect, and the flexibility for product demonstration is subject to its use in the film.

Scheduling Flexibility In many movies, the advertiser has no say over when and how often the product will be shown. Fabergé developed an entire Christmas campaign around its Brut cologne and its movie placement, only to find the movie was delayed until February.

Media Image Many TV viewers and moviegoers are incensed at the idea of placing ads in programs or movies. These viewers want to maintain the barrier between program content and commercials. If the placement is too intrusive, they may develop negative attitudes toward the brand.

Target Audience Selectivity By its very nature of being cast in a movie, the potential for exposure beyond a brand's target audience is enormous. Although a certain amount of selectivity is viable through the type of movie or show, there is likely considerable wasted coverage.

Target Audience Coverage Movie attendance is historically strong, however, in many cases it will be difficult to reach a substantial portion of one's audience with a single movie. Similarly, even a hit television show may only reach a portion of a brand's target audience.

AUDIENCE MEASUREMENT FOR PRODUCT PLACEMENT

To date, no audience measurement is available except from the providers. Potential advertisers often have to make decisions based on their own creative insights (see Exhibit 12–9) or rely on the credibility of the source. However, at least two studies have demonstrated the potential effectiveness of product placements. Research provided by Pola Gupta and Kenneth Lord showed that prominently displayed placements led to strong recall.[36] A study by Pola Gupta and Stephen Gould indicated that viewers are accepting of promotional products and in general evaluate them positively, though some products (alcohol, guns, cigarettes) are perceived as less acceptable.[37]

SUMMARY

This chapter introduced you to the vast number of out-of-home and support media available to marketers. Out-of-home media include outdoor, transit, place-based, and point-of-purchase. Support media include promotional products, Yellow Pages, and product placement. While these constitute many examples and options for a marketer, it seems the choices are quite endless at times.

Collectively, these media offer a variety of strengths. Cost, ability to reach the target audience, and flexibility are just a few of those cited in this chapter. In addition, many of the media discussed here have effectively demonstrated the power of their specific medium to get results.

But each of these media has limitations. Perhaps the major weakness with most is the lack of audience measurement and veri-

fication. The advertiser is forced to make decisions without hard data or based on information provided by the media. As the number and variety of media continue to grow, it is likely the major weaknesses will be overcome.

KEY TERMS

out-of-home media, *344*
support media, *344*
posters, *344*
backlit posters, *345*
bulletins, *345*
superboards, *345*
spectaculars, *345*

street-level posters, *345*
mobile signage, *346*
showing, *348*
transit advertising, *349*
interior transit cards, *349*
interior door cards, *349*
exterior posters, *349*

station posters, *350*
transit shelters, *350*
subway online, *350*
in-flight advertising, *353*
airport displays, *353*
promotional products
    marketing, *359*

specialty advertising, *359*
Yellow Pages, *362*
directional medium, *362*
product placement, *363*

DISCUSSION QUESTIONS

1. What are promotional products? List some of the advantages and disadvantages of this medium. Provide examples where the use of this medium would be appropriate.

2. Discuss some of the merits of in-flight advertising. What types of products might most effectively use this medium?

3. Explain how various support media might be used as part of an IMC program. Take any three of the media discussed in the chapter and explain how they might be used in an IMC program for automobiles, cellular telephones, and Internet services.

4. A prevalent strategy among advertisers is to get themselves into television shows and movies. Discuss the possible advantages and disadvantages that might result from such exposures.

5. The Yellow Pages has been proven to be an extremely effective advertising medium for some firms. Explain why the Yellow Pages are so effective. Are there any limitations associated with this medium? If so, what are they?

6. Discuss advantages and disadvantages associated with advertising in movie theatres. For what types of products and/or services might these media be most effective?

7. What are place-based media? Explain what type of advertisers would most benefit from their use.

Sales Promotion

CHAPTER OBJECTIVES

- To understand the role of sales promotion in a company's integrated marketing communications program and to examine why it is increasingly important.

- To examine the objectives, strategy, and tactical components of a sales promotion plan.

- To examine the consumer and trade sales promotion strategy options and the factors to consider in using them.

- To understand key IMC issues related to sales-promotion decisions.

Kraft and Crayola Draw Up a Winning Promotion

Kraft, Crayola, YTV, and grocery retailers illustrate the importance of partnership for the success of joint consumer and trade promotional programs. Consumers found a unique PIN/prize code stamped on a game piece in the shape of a school bus in specially marked Kraft or Christie product packages. Consumers then could go online to play a game and claim a prize at ytv.com/kraft. Kraft then sent a prize that featured a new Crayola product (e.g., crayon markers). The promotion ran from July to December 2003 with ads featured on TV, in *What's Cooking* and *Not for Adults* magazines, with in-store displays, and on Kraft Canada's website. Redemptions exceeded initial expectations as Kraft and Crayola gave away more than 500,000 Crayola products.

With multiple partners, it was imperative that each participant perceives strategic value.

Kraft saw Crayola as a perfect partner for a back-to-school promotion right when consumers were buying such products. Crayola received excellent imagery exposure in grocery stores where it considered its presence weak historically. Grocery stores enjoyed the combination of two significant brands with a very creative point-of-sale display—a giant school bus. YTV increased its media consumption through its television spots and online execution. And received a free premium from Crayola, or in Crayola's eyes a cost efficient and communication effective method of distributing a sample.

The Kraft and Crayola promotion signals a growing trend of brands taking a more strategic orientation towards sales promotion that builds the brand with a positive brand experience, which reinforces the brand positioning strategy. Advertisers are looking towards going beyond the "one-off" promotion that tried to move volumes of product and did not lend itself to build the brand successfully (i.e., brand position). In fact, once the significant promotional campaign is established, many believe it is important to continue in subsequent years or to maintain the consistent theme with promotions occurring throughout the year. For example, after the Kraft–Crayola promotion, both partners planned to continue the relationship with an additional promotion in the next year. Thus reinforcing another key principle of the strategic approach of sales promotion—significant management of important partner relationships.

Sources: Matthew Diamond, "Leveraging the Big Idea," *Marketing Magazine*, October 6, 2003; Fawzia Sheikh, "Casting Off the One-Off," *Marketing Magazine*, May 10, 2004.

As discussed in the opening vignette, marketers recognize that advertising alone is not always enough to move their products off store shelves and into the hands of consumers. Companies also use sales promotion methods targeted at both consumers and the wholesalers and retailers that distribute their products to stimulate demand. Most companies' integrated marketing communications programs include consumer and trade promotions that are coordinated with advertising, direct marketing, and publicity/public relations campaigns as well as sales force efforts.

This chapter focuses on the role of sales promotion in a firm's IMC program. We examine how marketers use both consumer- and trade-oriented promotions to influence the purchase behaviour of consumers as well as wholesalers and retailers. We explore the objectives of sales promotion programs and the various types of sales promotion tools that can be used at both the consumer and trade level. We also consider how sales promotion can be integrated with other elements of the promotional mix and look at problems that can arise when marketers become overly dependent on consumer and trade promotions, especially the latter.

SALES PROMOTION
PLANNING

CHARACTERISTICS AND TYPES OF SALES PROMOTION

Sales promotion has been defined as "a direct inducement that offers an extra value or incentive for the product to the sales force, distributors, or the ultimate consumer with the primary objective of creating an immediate sale."[1] Keep in mind several important aspects of sales promotion as you read this chapter.

First, sales promotion involves some type of inducement that provides an *extra incentive* to buy. This incentive is usually the key element in a promotional program; it may be a coupon or price reduction, the opportunity to enter a contest or sweepstakes, a money-back refund or rebate, or an extra amount of a product. The incentive may also be a free sample of the product, given in hopes of generating a future purchase, or a premium that serves as a reminder of the brand and reinforces its image. Most sales promotion offers attempt to add some value to the product or service. While advertising appeals to the mind and emotions to give the consumer a reason to buy, sales promotion appeals more to the pocketbook and provides an incentive for purchasing a brand.

Sales promotion can also provide an inducement to marketing intermediaries such as wholesalers and retailers. A trade allowance or discount gives retailers a financial incentive to stock and promote a manufacturer's products. A trade contest directed toward wholesalers or retail personnel gives them extra incentive to perform certain tasks or meet sales goals.

A second point is that sales promotion is essentially an *acceleration tool*, designed to speed up the selling process and maximize sales volume.[2] By providing an extra incentive, sales promotion techniques can motivate consumers to purchase a larger quantity of a brand or shorten the purchase cycle of the trade or consumers by encouraging them to take more immediate action.

Companies also use limited-time offers such as price-off deals to retailers or a coupon with an expiration date to accelerate the purchase process.[3] Sales promotion attempts to maximize sales volume by motivating customers who have not responded to advertising. The ideal sales promotion program generates sales that would not be achieved by other means. However, as we shall see later, many sales promotion offers end up being used by current users of a brand rather than attracting new users.

A final point regarding sales promotion activities is that they can be *targeted to different parties* in the marketing channel. As shown in Figure 13–1, sales promotion can be broken into two major categories: consumer-oriented and trade-oriented promotions. Activities involved in **consumer sales promotion** include sampling, couponing, premiums, contests and sweepstakes, refunds and rebates, bonus packs,

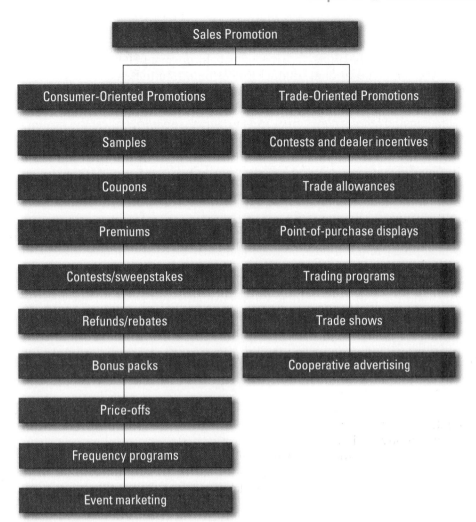

FIGURE 13–1
Types of sales promotion activities

□ □ □ □ □

price-offs, and event marketing. These promotions are directed at consumers, the end purchasers of goods and services, and are designed to induce them to purchase the marketer's brand. Consumer promotions are also used by retailers to encourage consumers to shop in their particular stores. **Trade sales promotion** includes dealer contests and incentives, trade allowances, point-of-purchase displays, sales training programs, trade shows, cooperative advertising, and other programs designed to motivate distributors and retailers to carry a product and make an extra effort to push it to their customers.

Many marketing programs include both trade- and consumer-oriented promotions, since motivating both groups maximizes the effectiveness of the promotional program. Programs designed to persuade the trade to stock, merchandise, and promote a manufacturer's products are part of a **promotional push strategy**. The goal of this strategy is to push the product through the channels of distribution by aggressively selling and promoting the item to the resellers, or trade. A push strategy tries to convince resellers they can make a profit on a manufacturer's product and to encourage them to order the merchandise and push it through to their customers. Promotion to the trade includes all the elements of the promotional mix. Company sales representatives call on resellers to explain the product, discuss the firm's plans for building demand among ultimate consumers, and describe special programs being offered to the trade, such as introductory discounts, promotional allowances, and cooperative ad programs. The company may use **trade advertising** to interest wholesalers and retailers and motivate them to purchase its products for resale to

371

their customers. Trade advertising usually appears in publications that serve the particular industry.

Sometimes manufacturers face resistance from channel members who do not want to take on an additional product line or brand. In these cases, companies may turn to a **promotional pull strategy**, spending money on advertising and sales promotion efforts directed toward the ultimate consumer. The goal of a pull strategy is to create demand among consumers and encourage them to request the product from the retailer. Seeing the consumer demand, retailers will order the product from wholesalers (if they are used), which in turn will request it from the manufacturer. Thus, stimulating demand at the end-user level pulls the product through the channels of distribution.

Whether to emphasize a push or a pull strategy depends on a number of factors, including the company's relations with the trade, its promotional budget, and demand for the firm's products. Companies that have favourable channel relationships may prefer to use a push strategy and work closely with channel members to encourage them to stock and promote their products. A firm with a limited promotional budget may not have the funds for advertising and sales promotion that a pull strategy requires and may find it more cost effective to build distribution and demand by working closely with resellers. When the demand outlook for a product is favourable because it has unique benefits, is superior to competing brands, or is very popular among consumers, a pull strategy may be appropriate. Companies often use a combination of push and pull strategies, with the emphasis changing as the product moves through its life cycle.

GROWTH OF SALES PROMOTION

While sales promotion has been part of the marketing process for a long time, its role and importance in a company's integrated marketing communications programs has increased by an annual growth rate of 5 to 7 percent. Consumer-package-goods firms continue to be the core users of sales promotion programs and tools. However, sales promotion activity is also increasing in new categories, including health care, computer hardware and software, electronics, and deregulated utilities.[4]

Not only has the total amount of money spent on sales promotion increased, but the percentage of marketers' budgets allocated to promotion has grown as well. For many years advertising was the major component in the promotional mix of most consumer-product companies. Until the 1980s, nearly half of marketers' promotional dollars was spent on advertising campaigns designed to create or reinforce brand awareness and build long-term loyalty. However by the mid- to late 80s, a fundamental change had occurred in the way most consumer-product companies were marketing their products. The proportion of the marketing budget allocated to sales promotion rose sharply, while the amount spent on media advertising declined. The increase in spending on sales promotion at the expense of media advertising continued throughout the decade of the 90s and into the new millennium. Currently, estimates are that marketers spend between 60 and 75 percent of their promotional budgets on sales promotion, with the remainder being allocated to media advertising.[5]

Many factors have led to the shift in marketing dollars to sales promotion from media advertising. Among them are the strategic importance of sales promotion, the growing power of retailers, declining brand loyalty, increased promotional sensitivity, brand proliferation, fragmentation of the consumer market, short-term focus, increased accountability, competition, clutter, and reaching a specific target audience.

Strategic Importance of Sales Promotion   A major reason for the increase in spending on sales promotion is that the promotion industry has matured over the past several decades. Increased sophistication and a more strategic role and focus have elevated the discipline and its role in the IMC program of many companies.[6] In the past, sales promotion specialists would be brought in after key strategic branding decisions were made. Promotional agencies were viewed primarily as tacticians whose role was to develop a promotional program such as a contest or sweepstakes or a coupon or sampling program that could create a short-term increase in sales. However, many companies are now making promotional specialists part of their strategic brand-building team, a move that puts sales promotion on par with media advertising. Promotional agencies have expanded their integrated marketing capabilities as well as their expertise in branding and helping their clients build relationships with their customers.

Growing Power of Retailers One reason for the increase in sales promotion is the power shift in the marketplace from manufacturers to retailers. For many years, manufacturers of national brands had the power and influence; retailers were just passive distributors of their products. Consumer products manufacturers created consumer demand for their brands by using heavy advertising and some consumer-oriented promotions, such as samples, coupons, and premiums, and exerted pressure on retailers to carry the products. Retailers did very little research and sales analysis; they relied on manufacturers for information regarding the sales performance of individual brands.

In recent years, however, several developments have helped to transfer power from the manufacturers to the retailers. With the advent of optical checkout scanners and sophisticated in-store computer systems, retailers gained access to data concerning how quickly products turn over, which sales promotions are working, and which products make money.[7] Retailers use this information to analyze sales of manufacturers' products and then demand discounts and other promotional support from manufacturers of lagging brands. Companies that fail to comply with retailers' demands for more trade support often have their shelf space reduced or even their product dropped.

Another factor that has increased the power of retailers is the consolidation of the grocery store industry, which has resulted in larger chains with greater buying power and clout. These large chains have become accustomed to trade promotions and can pressure manufacturers to provide deals, discounts, and allowances. Consolidation has also given large retailers more money for advancing already strong private label initiatives, and sales promotion is the next step in the marketing evolution of private label brands. Private label brands in various package-good categories such as foods, drugs, and health and beauty care products are giving national brands more competition for retail shelf space and increasing their own marketing, including the use of traditional sales promotion tools. Well-marketed private label products are forcing national brand leaders, as well as second-tier brands, to develop more innovative promotional programs and to be more price-competitive.[8]

Declining Brand Loyalty Another major reason for the increase in sales promotion is that consumers have become less brand loyal to one brand. Some consumers are always willing to buy their preferred brand at full price without any type of promotional offer. However, many consumers are loyal coupon users and/or are conditioned to look for deals when they shop. They may switch back and forth among a set of brands they view as essentially equal. These brands are all perceived as being satisfactory and interchangeable, and favourable brand switches (discussed in Chapter 2) purchase whatever brand is on special or for which they have a coupon.

Increased Promotional Sensitivity Marketers are making greater use of sales promotion in their marketing programs because consumers respond favourably to the incentives it provides. A major research project completed by Promotion Decisions, Inc., in 1999 tracked the purchase behaviour of over 33,000 consumers and their response to both consumer and trade promotions. The results showed that 42 percent of the total unit volume of the 12 package-good products analyzed was purchased with some type of incentive while 58 percent was purchased at full price. Coupons were particularly popular among consumers, as 24 percent of the sales volume involved the use of a coupon.[9]

373

Exhibit 13–1
Sales promotion tools such as coupons are often used to encourage trial of a new brand

An obvious reason for consumers' increased sensitivity to sales promotion offers is that they save money. Another reason is that many purchase decisions are made at the point of purchase by consumers who are increasingly time-sensitive and facing too many choices. Some studies have found that up to 70 percent of purchase decisions are made in the store, where people are very likely to respond to promotional deals.[10] Buying a brand that is on special or being displayed can simplify the decision-making process and solve the problem of overchoice.

Brand Proliferation A major aspect of many firms' marketing strategies has been the development of new products. Consumer-product companies are launching more new products each year. The market has become saturated with new brands, which often lack any significant advantages that can be used as the basis of an advertising campaign. Thus, companies increasingly depend on sales promotion to encourage consumers to try these brands. Marketers are relying more on samples, coupons, rebates, premiums, and other innovative promotional tools to achieve trial usage of their new brands and encourage repeat purchase (Exhibit 13–1).

Promotions are also important in getting retailers to allocate some of their precious shelf space to new brands. The competition for shelf space for new products in stores is enormous. Supermarkets carry an average of 30,000 products (compared with 13,067 in 1982). Retailers favour new brands with strong sales promotion support that will bring in more customers and boost their sales and profits. Many retailers require special discounts or allowances from manufacturers just to handle a new product. These slotting fees or allowances, which are discussed later in the chapter, can make it expensive for a manufacturer to introduce a new product.

Fragmentation of the Consumer Market As the consumer market becomes more fragmented and traditional mass-media–based advertising less effective, marketers are turning to more segmented, highly targeted approaches. Many companies are tailoring their promotional efforts to specific regional markets. Sales promotion tools have become one of the primary vehicles for doing this, through programs tied into local flavour, themes, or events. For example, in an effort to increase traffic during lunch and dinner, a major western Canadian franchisee of 25 Denny's Restaurants used advertising (e.g., radio, newspaper), sales promotion (e.g., featured menu prices, guarantee), and public relations (e.g., sponsorship of junior hockey) to increase sales by 15 percent during 2001.[11]

Marketers are also shifting more of their promotional efforts to direct marketing, which often includes some form of sales promotion incentive. Many marketers use information they get from premium offers, trackable coupons, rebates, and sweepstakes to build databases for future direct-marketing efforts. As marketers continue to shift from media advertising to direct marketing, promotional offers will probably be used even more to help build databases. The technology is already in place to enable marketers to communicate individually with target consumers and transform mass promotional tools into ways of doing one-to-one marketing.[12]

Short-Term Focus Many businesspeople believe the increase in sales promotion is motivated by marketing plans and reward systems geared to short-term performance and the immediate generation of sales volume. Some think the package-goods brand management system has contributed to marketers' increased dependence on sales promotion. Brand managers use sales promotions routinely, not only to introduce new products or defend against the competition but also to meet quarterly or yearly sales and market share goals. The sales force, too, may have short-term quotas or goals to meet and may also receive requests from retailers and wholesalers for promotions. Thus, reps may pressure marketing or brand managers to use promotions to help them move the products into the retailers' stores.

Many managers view consumer and trade promotions as the most dependable way to generate short-term sales, particularly when they are price related. The reliance on sales promotion is particularly high in mature and slow-growth markets, where it is difficult to stimulate consumer demand through advertising. This has led to concern that managers have become too dependent on the quick sales fix that can result from a promotion and that the brand franchise may be eroded by too many deals.

Increased Accountability In addition to pressuring their marketing or brand managers and sales force to produce short-term results, many companies are demanding to know what they are getting for their promotional expenditures. Sales promotion is more economically accountable than advertising. In companies struggling to meet their sales and financial goals, top management is demanding measurable, accountable ways to relate promotional expenditures to sales and profitability.

Managers who are being held accountable to produce results often use price discounts or coupons, since they produce a quick and easily measured jump in sales. It takes longer for an ad campaign to show some impact and the effects are more difficult to measure. Marketers are also feeling pressure from the trade as powerful retailers demand sales performance from their brands. Real-time data available from computerized checkout scanners make it possible for retailers to monitor promotions and track the results they generate on a daily basis.

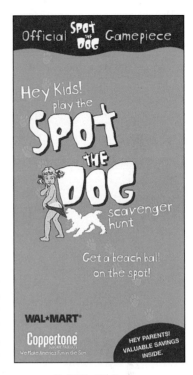

Exhibit 13–2
Coppertone developed an account-specific promotion for Wal-Mart

375

Competition Another factor that led to the increase in sales promotion is manufacturers' reliance on trade and consumer promotions to gain or maintain competitive advantage. The markets for many products are mature and stagnant, and it is increasingly difficult to boost sales through advertising. Exciting, breakthrough creative ideas are difficult to come by, and consumers' attention to mass media advertising continues to decline. Rather than allocating large amounts of money to run dull ads, many marketers have turned to sales promotion.

Many companies are tailoring their trade promotions to key retail accounts and developing strategic alliances with retailers that include both trade and consumer promotional programs. A major development in recent years is **account-specific marketing** (also referred to as *comarketing*), whereby a manufacturer collaborates with an individual retailer to create a customized promotion that accomplishes mutual objectives (see Exhibit 13–2).

Retailers may use a promotional deal with one company as leverage to seek an equal or better deal with its competitors. Consumer and trade promotions are easily matched by competitors, and many marketers find themselves in a promotional trap where they must continue using promotions or be at a competitive disadvantage. (We discuss this problem in more detail later in the chapter.)

Clutter A promotional offer in an ad can break through the clutter that is prevalent in most media today. A premium offer may help attract consumers' attention to an ad, as will a contest or sweepstakes. Some studies have shown that readership scores are higher for print ads with coupons than for ads without them.[13] However, more recent studies by Starch INRA Hooper suggest that magazine ads with coupons do not generate higher readership.[14]

Reaching a Specific Target Audience Most companies focus their marketing efforts on specific market segments and are always looking for ways to reach their target audiences. Many marketers are finding that sales promotion tools such as contests and sweepstakes, events, coupons, and samplings are very effective ways to reach specific geographic, demographic, psychographic, and ethnic markets. Sales promotion programs can also be targeted to specific user-status groups such as nonusers or light versus heavy users.

SALES PROMOTION VERSUS ADVERTISING

Marketing and advertising executives are concerned about how the shift in the allocation of the promotional budget from advertising to sales promotion affects brand equity. As noted in Chapter 1, *brand equity* is an intangible asset of added value or goodwill that results from consumers' favourable image, impressions of differentiation, and/or strength of attachment to a brand.

Some critics argue that sales promotion increases come at the expense of brand equity and every dollar that goes into promotion rather than advertising devalues the brand.[15] They say trade promotions in particular contribute to the destruction of brand franchises and equity as they encourage consumers to purchase primarily on the basis of price. Proponents of advertising argue that marketers must maintain strong equity if they want to differentiate their brands and charge a premium price for them. They say advertising is still the most effective way to build the long-term value of a brand: it informs consumers of a brand's features and benefits, creates an image, and helps build and maintain brand loyalty. This may not be universally true as the following example demonstrates.

Cadbury Trebor Allan communicated the crunch benefit of Crispy Crunch and Crunchie chocolate bars with a novel approach. It connected the "crunch" of the brands' names with the idea that the Toronto Raptors' Vince Carter "delivered in the crunch." Clearly a clever play on words, the campaign featured a special event called "Crunch Time" for the Raptors' home opener where fans received a poster and enjoyed various activities during the game. Print and TV ads communicated a contest to win tickets to the basketball game or a year's supply of bars. Special packaging and an employee tie-in with Vince Carter were other key connections between the brands and the star.[16]

Marketing experts generally agree that advertising plays an important role in building and maintaining a brand's image and position, which are core components of its equity. Many are concerned that if the trend toward spending more on sales promotion at the expense of media advertising continues, brands may lose the equity that advertising helped create and be forced to compete primarily on the basis of price. Many of these concerns are justified, but not all sales promotion activities detract from the value of a brand as this next example illustrates.

Coors Canada has used sales promotion to build its brand equity in the face of stiff sales promotion competition from other brands. Just a few years ago, Coors was offering only one sales promotion per year, its famous "Talking Can & Cap" campaign. Now Coors Canada spends 25 percent of its marketing budget on sales promotions, and 25 percent of its $4.8-million media budget is allocated to support the sales promotions. In 2001, it offered four in-case promotions in Western Canada, one in Quebec, and at least one in Ontario. Says one Coors Canada executive, "We are trying to make our in-case promotions build equity as much as they can for what they are, (but) we also have promotions that we're primarily trying to drive image with." Coors Canada's "Tracker" campaign for Coors Light in Quebec is an example of this. When a consumer opens a "tracker" bottle, the Coors Light/Musique Plus Tracker team greets the lucky winner with trip to a Los Angeles party. The opened bottle triggers a Global Positioning System transmitter that facilitates the search![17]

SALES PROMOTION
PLAN

In this section, we examine the various parts of a sales promotion plan. First, we consider some objectives marketers have for sales promotion programs. Next, we illustrate why the various sales promotion decisions are strategic options. Finally, we discuss the key tactics that are critical for all sales promotions. We focus on the consumer market to illustrate these ideas. Application to the trade market is readily done once the concept is understood.

OBJECTIVES OF CONSUMER SALES PROMOTION

As the use of sales promotion techniques continues to increase, companies must consider what they hope to accomplish through their consumer promotions and how they interact with other promotional activities such as advertising, direct marketing, and personal selling. When marketers implement sales promotion programs without considering their long-term cumulative effect on the brand's image and position in the marketplace, they often do little more than create short-term spikes in the sales curve.

Not all sales promotion activities are designed to achieve the same objectives. As with any promotional mix element, marketers must plan consumer promotions by conducting a situation analysis and determining sales promotion's specific role in the integrated marketing communications program. They must decide what the promotion is designed to accomplish and to whom it should be targeted. Setting clearly defined objectives and measurable goals for their sales promotion programs forces managers to think beyond the short-term sales fix (although this can be one goal).

While the basic goal of most consumer sales promotion programs is to induce purchase of a brand, the marketer may have a number of different objectives for both new and established brands. We use the ideas developed in Chapter 4 to highlight how sales promotions can help achieve behavioural and communication objectives.

Trial Purchase   One of the most important uses of sales promotion techniques is to encourage consumers to try a new product or service. While thousands of new products are introduced to the market every year, as many as 90 percent of them fail within the first year. Many of these failures are due to the fact that the new product or brand lacks the promotional support needed to encourage initial trial by enough consumers. Many new brands are merely new versions of an existing product without unique benefits, so advertising alone cannot induce trial. Sales promotion tools have become an important part of new brand introduction strategies; the level of initial trial can be increased through techniques such as sampling, couponing, and refund offers.

A trial purchase objective is also relevant for an established brand that uses a sales promotion to attract nonusers of the product category. Attracting nonusers of the product category can be very difficult, as consumers may not see a need for the product. Sales promotions can appeal to nonusers by providing them with an extra incentive to try the product, but a more common strategy for increasing sales of an established brand is to attract consumers who use a competing brand. This can be done by giving them an incentive to switch, such as a coupon, premium offer, bonus pack, or price deal. Marketers can also get users of a competitor to try their brand through sampling or other types of promotional programs.

Repeat Purchase   The success of a new brand depends not only on getting initial trial but also on inducing a reasonable percentage of people who try the brand to repurchase it and establish ongoing purchase patterns. Promotional incentives such as coupons or refund offers are often included with a sample to encourage repeat purchase after trial. For example, when Lever Brothers introduced its Lever 2000 brand of bar soap, it distributed millions of free samples along with a 75-cent coupon. The samples allowed consumers to try the new soap, while the coupon provided an incentive to purchase it.

A company can use sales promotion techniques in several ways to retain its current customer base through continued repeat purchases. One way is to load them with the product, taking them out of the market for a certain time. Special price promotions, coupons, or bonus packs can encourage consumers to stock up on the brand. This not only keeps them using the company's brand but also reduces the likelihood they will switch brands in response to a competitor's promotion.

Increasing Consumption   Many marketing managers are responsible for established brands competing in mature markets, against established competitors, where consumer purchase patterns are often well set. Awareness of an established brand is generally high as a result of cumulative advertising effects, and many consumers have probably tried the brand. These factors can create a challenging situation for the brand manager. Sales promotion can generate some new interest in an established brand to help increase sales or defend market share against competitors.

Marketers attempt to increase sales for an established brand in several ways, and sales promotion can play an important role in each. One way to increase product consumption is by identifying new uses for the brand. Sales promotion tools like recipe books or calendars that show various ways of using the product often can accomplish this.

Support IMC Program/Build Brand Equity   A final objective for consumer-oriented promotions is to enhance or support the integrated marketing communications effort for a brand or company. Building brand equity and image has traditionally been done through advertising. However, sales promotion techniques such as contests or sweepstakes and premium offers are often used to draw attention to an ad, increase involvement with the message and product/service, and help build relationships with consumers.

Marketers often turn to sales promotion in the fall to reach students of all ages who are going back to school. For example, DaimlerChrysler displayed its new PT Cruiser and Neon RT to university students at nine campuses across Canada during frosh week in September 2001 as part of its "Coolest car on campus" campaign. A contest allowed students to paint a PT Cruiser with water-based paint, with the winning university receiving the car for a campus drive-safe program. In addition, students dressed up in costumes in front of the car, and photos were sent to their parents as part of the "I'll be graduating before you know it" campaign.[18]

CONSUMER SALES PROMOTION STRATEGY DECISIONS

Strategic decisions for sales promotions fall into three broad categories: sales promotion tool decision, application across product lines, and application in geographic markets.

Sales Promotion Strategy Options   Our view of sales promotions is that the options identified in Figure 13–1 are important strategic choices for a marketer. Essentially, the key strategic decision for a marketer concerns the most appropriate sales promotion option(s) that will best achieve the behavioural objective(s) for the target audience(s). Two characteristics of sales promotions help guide the strategic direction of the sales promotion plan: the degree to which the sales promotion is "franchise building" and whether the incentive of the sales promotion is immediate or delayed.

Franchise-Building Characteristic   Sales promotion activities that communicate distinctive brand attributes and contribute to the development and reinforcement of brand identity are **consumer franchise-building (CFB) promotions**.[19] Consumer sales promotion efforts cannot make consumers loyal to a brand that is of little value or does not provide them with a specific benefit. But they can make consumers aware of a brand and, by communicating its specific features and benefits, contribute to the development of a favourable brand attitude. Consumer franchise-building promotions are designed to build long-term brand preference and help the company achieve the ultimate goal of full-price purchases that do not depend on a promotional offer.

For years, franchise or image building was viewed as the exclusive realm of advertising, and sales promotion was used only to generate short-term sales increases. But now marketers are recognizing the image-building potential of sales promotion and paying attention to its CFB value. A survey of senior marketing executives found that 88 percent believe consumer promotions can help build a brand's equity, and 58 percent think trade promotions can contribute.[20]

By using sales promotion to contribute to franchise building, companies develop an offer consistent with the image of the brand. An example of a successful consumer brand-building promotion is the Search for 2000 Uses Sweepstakes promotion for WD-40, shown in Exhibit 13–3. The WD-40 Company positions its brand as the leading multipurpose problem solver that cleans, protects, penetrates, lubricates, and displaces moisture like no other product on earth. The marketing strategy for WD-40 is to continually promote the myriad of uses for the product. The Search for 2000 Uses Sweepstakes, which was launched to coincide with the new millennium, asked consumers to suggest their use for WD-40 in order to be entered for a chance to win various prizes, such as WD-40 can radios, T-shirts, baseball caps, and a grand prize of $10,000 in company stock. The sweepstakes reinforced WD-40's image as a multipurpose problem solver and also encouraged consumers to visit the company's website to enter their use.

Exhibit 13–3
WD-40's Search for 2000 Uses Sweepstakes is an excellent example of a consumer brand-building promotion

Nonfranchise-Building Characteristic **Nonfranchise-building (non-FB) promotions** are designed to accelerate the purchase decision process and generate an immediate increase in sales. These activities do not communicate information about a brand's unique features or the benefits of using it, so they do not contribute to the building of brand identity and image. Price-off deals, bonus packs, and rebates or refunds are examples of non-FB sales promotion techniques. Trade promotions receive the most criticism for being nonfranchise building—for good reason. First, many of the promotional discounts and allowances given to the trade are never passed on to consumers. Most trade promotions that are forwarded through the channels reach consumers in the form of lower prices or special deals and lead them to buy on the basis of price rather than brand equity.

Many specialists in the promotional area stress the need for marketers to use sales promotion tools to build a franchise and create long-term continuity in their promotional programs. Whereas non-FB promotions merely borrow customers from other brands, well-planned CFB activities can convert consumers to loyal customers. Short-term non-FB promotions have their place in a firm's promotional mix, particularly when competitive developments call for them. But their limitations must be recognized when a long-term marketing strategy for a brand is developed.

Incentive Characteristic As noted, sales promotions provide consumers with an extra incentive or reward for engaging in a certain form of behaviour, such as purchasing a brand. For some sales promotion tools, the incentive that the consumer receives is immediate, while for others the reward is delayed and not realized immediately. Using their situation analysis as an input, marketers decide the relative balance between immediate or delayed incentives. The decision is based on the target audience(s) and the intended behavioural objective(s). The chart in Figure 13–2 outlines which sales promotion tools can be used to accomplish various behavioural objectives and identifies whether the extra incentive or reward is immediate or delayed.[21]

It should be noted that in Figure 13–2 some of the sales promotion techniques are listed more than once because they can be used to accomplish more than one objective with both immediate and delayed incentives. For example, loyalty programs

379

FIGURE 13–2 ☐☐☐☐ Consumer sales promotion tools for various objectives

Communication and Behavioural Objectives

Consumer Reward Incentive	Trial purchase	Repeat purchase/ customer loading	Support IMC program/ build brand equity
Immediate	• Sampling • Instant coupons • In-store coupons • In-store rebates	• Price-off deals • Bonus packs • In- and on-package free premiums • Loyalty programs	• Events • In- and on-package free premiums
Delayed	• Media- and mail-delivered coupons • Mail-in refunds and rebates • Free mail-in premiums • Scanner- and Internet-delivered coupons	• In- and on-package coupons • Mail-in refunds and rebates • Loyalty programs	• Self-liquidating premiums • Free mail-in premiums • Contests and sweepstakes • Loyalty programs

can be used to retain customers by providing both immediate and delayed rewards. Shoppers who belong to loyalty programs sponsored by supermarkets, and who receive discounts every time they make a purchase, are receiving immediate rewards that are designed to retain them as customers. Some loyalty promotions, such as frequency programs used by airlines, car rental companies, and hotels, offer delayed rewards by requiring that users accumulate points to reach a certain level or status before the points can be redeemed. Loyalty programs can also be used by marketers to help build brand equity. For example, when an airline or car rental company sends its frequent users upgrade certificates, the practice helps build relationships with these customers and thus contributes to brand equity.

One explanation for how sales promotion incentives work lies in the theory of **operant conditioning**. The individual must actively *operate* or act on some aspect of the environment for learning to occur. Operant conditioning is sometimes referred to as *instrumental conditioning* because the individual's response is instrumental in getting a positive reinforcement (reward) or negative reinforcement (punishment). **Reinforcement**, the reward or favourable consequence associated with a particular response, is an important element of instrumental conditioning. Behaviour that is reinforced strengthens the bond between a stimulus and a response. Thus, if a consumer buys a product with a sales promotion and experiences a positive outcome, the likelihood that the consumer will use this product again increases. If the outcome is not favourable, the likelihood of buying the product again decreases. Note that sales promotion have both immediate and delayed reinforcements that must fit with the particular target audience and the accompanying objectives desired.

Two aspects of reinforcement that are particularly relevant to sales promotion strategies are schedules of reinforcement and shaping. Different **schedules of reinforcement** result in varying patterns of learning and behaviour. Learning occurs most rapidly under a *continuous reinforcement schedule,* in which every response is rewarded—but the behaviour is likely to cease when the reinforcement stops. Marketers must provide continuous reinforcement to consumers or risk their switching to brands that do.

Learning occurs more slowly but lasts longer when a *partial* or *intermittent reinforcement schedule* is used and only some of the individual's responses are rewarded. Promotional programs have partial reinforcement schedules. A firm may offer consumers an incentive to use the company's product. The firm does not want to offer the incentive every time (continuous reinforcement), because consumers might become dependent on it and stop buying the brand when the incentive is withdrawn. A study that examined the effect of reinforcement on bus ridership found that discount coupons given as rewards for riding the bus were as effective when given on a partial schedule as when given on a continuous schedule.[22] The cost of giving the discount coupons under the partial schedule, however, was considerably less.

Reinforcement schedules can also be used to influence consumer learning and behaviour through a process known as **shaping**, the reinforcement of successive acts that lead to a desired behaviour pattern or response.[23] In a promotional context, shaping procedures are used as part of the introductory program for new products. Figure 13–3 provides an example of how samples and discount coupons can be used to introduce a new product and take a consumer from trial to repeat purchase. Marketers must be careful in their use of shaping procedures: If they drop the incentives too soon, the consumer may not establish the desired behaviour; but if they overuse them, the consumer's purchase may become contingent on the incentive rather than the product or service.

Application across Product Lines   Another part of the strategic sales promotion decision is the degree to which each sales promotion tool is applied to the range of sizes, varieties, models, or products. Overall, there are three important product decisions for sales promotions. The first concerns whether the sales promotion should be run on the entire line or on individual items. If the latter option is selected (i.e., selective application), the second decision concerns which specific items. The marketer could run a promotion on either the more or less popular items. Similarly, the marketer could focus on higher or lower price points. Sometimes, a sales promotion is offered on a unique product format or size instead of the regular product. For example, Kellogg's bundled three brands of cereal with plastic in one sales promotion in which each size was not the standard size typically distributed. Thus, the third strategic issue concerns whether the sales promotion is run on the "regular" stock or some other special version.

Terminal Goal: Repeat Purchase Behaviour

Approximation Sequence	Shaping Procedure	Reinforcement Applied
Induce product trial	Free samples distributed; large discount coupon	Product performance; coupon
Induce purchase with little financial obligation	Discount coupon prompts purchase with little cost; coupon good for small discount on next purchase enclosed	Product performance; coupon
Induce purchase with moderate financial obligation	Small discount coupon prompts purchase with moderate cost	Product performance
Induce purchase with full financial obligation	Purchase occurs without coupon assistance	Product performance

FIGURE 13–3

Application of shaping procedures in marketing

Application across Geographic Markets   Sales promotions can be run nationally or in select markets. Local or regional market conditions, with respect to consumer demand and competitive intensity, tend to dictate the degree of tailoring sale promotions for each geographic market. Intuitively, it appears that many marketers would be faced with situations where offering unique sales promotions for each geographic market would achieve optimal communication and behavioural effects; however, there are three factors that marketers need to consider. First, a regional focus requires additional managerial commitment in planning and implementation. Second, achieving objectives more specifically may result in greater expense, thus necessitating a cost-benefit analysis. Finally, national accounts may not be too receptive with different types of sales promotions in one province versus another.

CONSUMER SALES PROMOTION TACTICS DECISIONS

You can receive a coupon with a value anywhere from 50¢ to $2.00 for many consumer products, early in the year or later in the year, often or not so often, or from any number of outlets (e.g., direct mail, magazine). As this implies, for each sales promotion option, the marketer faces a number of key tactical decisions: value of the incentive, timing, and distribution. We briefly describe each of these so that you can put together a comprehensive sales promotion plan.

Value of Incentive   Whether the marketer is offering some sort of price discount or a consumer franchise-building sales promotion such as a premium, eventually the marketer has to decide the value of the sales promotion. For example, should the coupon be the equivalent of a 10- or a 20-percent discount? This decision is contingent upon the threshold at which consumers will respond to a sales promotion and the number of potential consumer responses; each will contribute to the total cost of the sales promotion. Similarly, if a beer company is offering a premium, a strategic decision has to be made as to the relative value of the premium: for example, a T-shirt worth $10 to $15 or perhaps a "cozy" worth a couple of dollars.

A non-economic interpretation of value is also possible. Hostess Frito-Lay (HFL) has used various in-pack collectables (e.g., stickers) of well-known entertainment or pop-culture icons (e.g., *The Simpsons, Star Wars*) that attract young impulse-purchase consumers. The focus of these sales promotions transfer well to point-of-sale displays to attract consumer's attention and to meet retailers' need for innovative merchandising to move product off the shelves. In 2001, HFL used Marvel comic-book characters on packaging and convenience-store point-of-sale displays, and offered limited-edition comic books as part of a trivia challenge in association with Teletoon.[24]

Timing   The time element of the sales promotion is important in a few directions that are mutually dependent. A marketer has to decide during which months, weeks, or days the sales promotion will be offered. Seasonal or some other consumption pattern discovered through market research, or the situation analysis, may guide this choice. Secondly, sales promotions can be offered for one day, one week, a few weeks, or even a few months. Target audience and behavioural objectives typically guide this duration decision. Finally, the frequency of the sales promotion is a final timing consideration. If coupons have been decided, the marketer needs to decide whether one will be offered every six months or perhaps two every six months.

Distribution   For most sales promotions, there is a logistical consideration as to how the promotion will get to the consumer or how the consumer will get to the sales promotion. There are many choices for sales promotions such as coupons (e.g., direct mail, in-ad), while for others, such as premiums, the choices may be limited. We discuss some of the distribution options for each sales promotion in the next section, where we describe each sales promotion and their strengths and limitations.

CONSUMER SALES PROMOTION STRATEGY OPTIONS

Marketers use various sales promotion techniques to meet the objectives just discussed. Figure 13–4 shows the extent to which these consumer promotions are used by package-goods companies. We now review a number of these options.

SAMPLING

Sampling involves a variety of procedures whereby consumers are given some quantity of a product for no charge to induce trial. Sampling is generally considered the most effective way to generate trial, although it is also the most expensive. As a sales promotion technique, sampling is often used to introduce a new product or brand to the market. However, as Figure 13–4 shows, sampling is also used for established products as well. Some companies do not use sampling for established products, reasoning that samples may not induce satisfied users of a competing brand to switch and may just go to the firm's current customers, who would buy the product anyway. This may not be true when significant changes (new and improved) are made in a brand.

Manufacturers of package-goods products such as food, health care items, cosmetics, and toiletries are heavy users of sampling since their products meet the three criteria for an effective sampling program:

1. The products are of relatively low unit value, so samples do not cost too much.
2. The products are divisible, which means they can be broken into small sample sizes that are adequate for demonstrating the brand's features and benefits to the user.

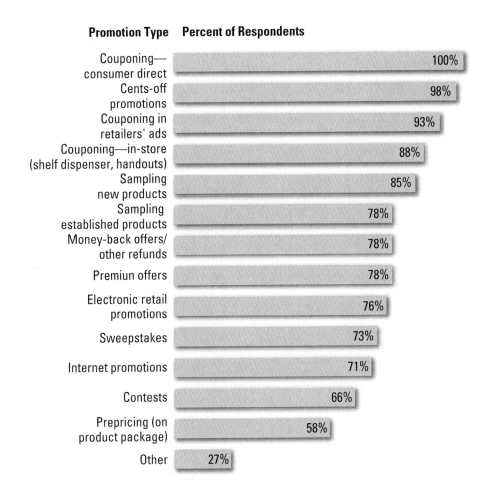

Promotion Type | **Percent of Respondents**

- Couponing—consumer direct: 100%
- Cents-off promotions: 98%
- Couponing in retailers' ads: 93%
- Couponing—in-store (shelf dispenser, handouts): 88%
- Sampling new products: 85%
- Sampling established products: 78%
- Money-back offers/other refunds: 78%
- Premiun offers: 78%
- Electronic retail promotions: 76%
- Sweepstakes: 73%
- Internet promotions: 71%
- Contests: 66%
- Prepricing (on product package): 58%
- Other: 27%

FIGURE 13–4

Types of consumer promotions used by package-goods manufacturers

□ □ □ □ □

383

3. The purchase cycle is relatively short, so the consumer will consider an immediate purchase or will not forget about the brand before the next purchase occasion.

Strengths and Limitations of Sampling   Samples are an excellent way to induce a prospective buyer to try a product or service. A major study conducted by the Promotion Marketing Association in 2002 found that the vast majority of consumers receiving a sample either use it right away or save it to use sometime later.[25] Sampling generates much higher trial rates than advertising or other sales promotion techniques.

Getting people to try a product leads to a second benefit of sampling: consumers experience the brand directly, gaining a greater appreciation for its benefits. This can be particularly important when a product's features and benefits are difficult to describe through advertising. Many foods, beverages, and cosmetics have subtle features that are most appreciated when experienced directly. Nearly 70 percent of the respondents in the PMA survey indicated that they have purchased a product they did not normally use after trying a free sample. The study also found that samples are even more likely to lead to purchase when they are accompanied with a coupon.

While samples are an effective way to induce trial, the brand must have some unique or superior benefits for a sampling program to be worthwhile. Otherwise, the sampled consumers revert back to other brands and do not become repeat purchasers. The costs of a sampling program can be recovered only if it gets a number of consumers to become regular users of the brand at full retail price.

Another possible limitation to sampling is that the benefits of some products are difficult to gauge immediately, and the learning period required to appreciate the brand may require supplying the consumer with larger amounts of the brand than are affordable. An example would be an expensive skin cream that is promoted as preventing or reducing wrinkles but has to be used for an extended period before any effects are seen.

Sampling Methods   One basic decision the sales promotion or brand manager must make is how the sample will be distributed. The sampling method chosen is important not only in terms of costs but also because it influences the type of consumer who receives the sample. The best sampling method gets the product to the best prospects for trial and subsequent repurchase. Some basic distribution methods include door-to-door, direct-mail, in-store, and on-package approaches.

Door-to-door sampling, in which the product is delivered directly to the prospect's residence, is used when it is important to control where the sample is delivered. This distribution method is very expensive because of labor costs, but it can be cost-effective if the marketer has information that helps define the target audience and/or if the prospects are located in a well-defined geographic area.

Sampling through media, some companies have samples delivered directly to consumers' homes by including them with newspapers or magazines. There are a number of newspapers that can now distribute a sample into a subscriber segment as small as 250 households with little increase in costs to marketers.[26]

Sampling through the mail is common for small, lightweight, nonperishable products. A major advantage of this method is that the marketer has control over where and when the product will be distributed and can target the sample to specific market areas. Many marketers are using information from geodemographic target marketing programs such as Claritas's Prizm or Microvision to better target their sample mailings. The main drawbacks to mail sampling are postal restrictions and increasing postal rates.

In-store sampling is increasingly popular, especially for food products. The marketer hires temporary demonstrators who set up a table or booth, prepare small samples of the product, and pass them out to shoppers. The in-store sampling approach can be very effective for food products, since consumers get to taste the item and the demonstrator can give them more information about the product while it is being sampled. Demonstrators may also give consumers a cents-off coupon for the sampled item to encourage immediate trial purchase. While this sampling method can be very effective, it can also be expensive and requires a great deal of planning, as well as the cooperation of retailers.

On-package sampling, where a sample of a product is attached to another item, is another common sampling method (see Exhibit 13–4). This procedure can be very cost-effective, particularly for multiproduct firms that attach a sample of a new product to an existing brand's package. A drawback is that since the sample is distributed only to consumers who purchase the item to which it is attached, the sample will not reach nonusers of the carrier brand. Marketers can expand this sampling method by attaching the sample to multiple carrier brands and including samples with products not made by their company.

Event sampling has become one of the fastest-growing and most popular ways of distributing samples. Many marketers are using sampling programs that are part of integrated marketing programs that feature events, media tie-ins, and other activities that provide consumers with a total sense of a brand rather than just a few tastes of a food or beverage or a trial size of a package-goods product. Event sampling can take place in stores as well as at a variety of other venues such as concerts, sporting events, and other places.

Direct sampling is when, with the advancement of technology, marketers can deliver samples directly. Some companies send samples to consumers who call toll-free numbers to request them or mail in sample request forms. As discussed in Chapter 15, these sampling methods are becoming popular because they can help marketers build a database for direct marketing.

Location sampling allows many companies to use specialized sample distribution services who help the company identify consumers who are nonusers of a product or users of a competing brand and develop appropriate procedures for distributing a sample to them. Many college students receive sample packs at the beginning of the semester that contain trial sizes of such products as mouthwash, toothpaste, headache remedies, and deodorant.

The Internet is yet another way companies are making it possible for consumers to sample their products, and it is adding a whole new level of targeting to the mix by giving consumers the opportunity to choose the samples they want. Schick Canada created a three-page mini-site to let consumers order a free sample of its new unisex razor, Xtreme III, in the fall of 2000. The home page (www.schick.ca) showed uncluttered images of the product and a couple indicating its unisex feature. The second page described a couple of features, while the third page permitted consumers to request the sample. A link on www.canadianfreestuff.com directed users to the site in addition to a viral e-mail. In the first three months, Schick Canada had received about 9,000 requests for samples.

Sampling Application With the decline of wet cat food in a can category, Effem looked to samples to launch its Whiskas Flavour Lock pouch and its Temptations treat cat food in two new product formats—wet cat food in a convenient pouch and tasty treats as a cat snack. Using a database, Effem delivered samples to a total of 250,000 households in less than four months. Print ads, online ads, and retail point-of-sale supported the direct contact. Consumers also responded with an online request and received one of three samples through the mail. Consumers requested about 20 percent of the samples online making this Canadian site the second most visited international site owned by Effem's parent, Mars Corporation. Whiskas' market share in the wet pouch category increased by 1.5 percent and volume by weight rose 20 percent with Whiskas as the only brand growing in the declining wet cat food category. Temptations increased its share by 7 percent and maintained its lead in the treat category.[27]

Exhibit 13–4
Armor All uses on-package samples for related products

COUPONS

The oldest, most widely used, and most effective sales promotion is the cents-off coupon. Research indicates that, on average, Canadians used about eight coupons per person, and that 85 percent of Canadians used coupons in 2003. In fact, about one-third of all Canadians used coupons in the past week during 2003.[28] And more than half of all Canadian households claim that coupons influence their brand purchase decision.

Figure 13–5 summarizes recent statistics indicating the scope of coupons in Canada. The number of coupons distributed by consumer package goods marketers reached 2.6 billion in 2003. Distribution peaked to 3.3 billion in 1996, however, except for 2002, the past five years produced fairly steady consistency. Except for 2003, the number of coupons redeemed exceeded 100 million over the past few years. In 2003, marketers used a greater percentage of less targeted media that have lower redemption rates to distribute coupons. The value of an average redeemed coupon approximated $1.00 and saved Canadians over $100 million each year!

Strengths and Limitations of Coupons Coupons have a number of strengths that make them popular sales promotion tools for both new and established products. First, coupons make it possible to offer a price reduction only to those consumers who are price-sensitive. Such consumers generally purchase because of coupons, while those who are not as concerned about price buy the brand at full value. Coupons also make it possible to reduce the retail price of a product without relying on retailers for cooperation, which can often be a problem. Coupons are generally regarded as second only to sampling as a promotional technique for generating trial. Since a coupon lowers the price of a product, it reduces the consumer's perceived risk associated with trial of a new brand. Coupons can encourage repurchase after initial trial. Many new products include a cents-off coupon inside the package to encourage repeat purchase. Coupons can also be useful promotional devices for established products. They can encourage nonusers to try a brand, encourage repeat purchase among current users, and get users to try a new, improved version of a brand. Coupons may also help coax users of a product to trade up to more expensive brands.

But there are a number of problems with coupons. First, it can be difficult to estimate how many consumers will use a coupon and when. Response to a coupon is rarely immediate; it typically takes anywhere from two to six months to redeem one. A study of coupon redemption patterns by Inman and McAlister found that many coupons are redeemed just before the expiration date rather than in the period following the initial coupon drop.[29] Many marketers are attempting to expedite redemption by shortening the time period before expiration. The average length of time from issue date to expiration date for coupons in 2001 was 234 days. However, coupons remain less effective than sampling for inducing initial product trial in a short period.

A problem associated with using coupons to attract new users to an established brand is that it is difficult to prevent the coupons from being used by consumers who already use the brand. For example, General Foods decided to reduce its use of coupons for Maxwell House coffee when research revealed the coupons were being

FIGURE 13–5
Coupon redemption rates

	1999	2002	2001	2002	2003
Quantity distributed	2.50 billion	2.52 billion	2.67 billion	2.32 billion	2.60 billion
Quantity redeemed	115 million	112 million	122 million	110 million	97 million
Average face value coupons *distributed*	97¢	$1.08	$1.25	$1.25	$1.23
Average face value coupons *redeemed*	99¢	$1.10	$1.05	$1.07	$1.08
Average valid period	232 days	270 days	234 days	219 days	214 days
Consumer savings	$115 million	$120 million	$128 million	$118 million	$105 million

FIGURE 13–6
Calculating
couponing costs
☐ ☐ ☐ ☐ ☐

	Cost per Coupon Redeemed: An Illustration	
1.	Distribution cost 5,000,000 circulation $\times$ $15/M	$75,000
2.	Redemptions at 2%	100,000
3.	Redemption cost 100,000 redemptions $\times$ $.75 face value	$75,000
4.	Retailer handling cost and processor fees 100,000 redemptions $\times$ $.10	$10,000
5.	Total program cost Items 1 + 3 + 4	$160,000
6.	Cost per coupon redeemed Cost divided by redemption	$1.60
7.	Actual product sold on redemption (misredemption estimated at 20%) 100,000 $\times$ 80%	80,000
8.	Cost per product moved Program cost divided by amount of product sold	$2.00

redeemed primarily by current users. Rather than attracting new users, coupons can end up reducing the company's profit margins among consumers who would probably purchase the product anyway.

Other problems with coupons include low redemption rates and high costs. Couponing program expenses include the face value of the coupon redeemed plus costs for production, distribution, and handling of the coupons. Figure 13–6 shows the calculations used to determine the costs of a couponing program using an FSI (freestanding insert) in the Saturday newspaper and a coupon with an average face value of 75 cents. The marketer should track costs closely to ensure the promotion is economically feasible.

Recent research on coupon face value indicates that testing for the most appropriate level is important for determining the most efficient (i.e., cost per coupon redeemed) coupon program. Since a coupon program combines redemption, printing, distribution, and handling costs, the face value and corresponding redemption rate can influence the overall efficiency of the program. The research tested a number of direct mail and FSI offers from various firms selling major grocery brands with different face values and consistent communication elements across all offers. The results indicate that moving from $.50 to $1.00 off nearly doubles the redemption rate (e.g., 2 percent to 4 percent) while moving from $1.00 to $1.50 off improves the redemption rate at a slower rate (e.g., 4 percent to 5 percent). Overall, this curvilinear relationship between face value and redemption rate made the $1.00 offer 20 percent and 12 percent more cost efficient versus the $.50 and $1.50 offers respectively. Conclusions from the research suggest the choice of face value should not make the program go over budget, the face value and redemption rate connection will vary by brand, lower face values may not be the most cost efficient program, higher face values are good for brand trial, and lower face values good for brand retrial.[30]

Another problem with coupon promotions is misredemption, or the cashing of a coupon without purchase of the brand. Coupon misredemption or fraud occurs in a number of ways, including:

- Redemption of coupons by consumers for a product or size not specified on the coupon.
- Redemption of coupons by salesclerks in exchange for cash.
- Gathering and redemption of coupons by store managers or owners without the accompanying sale of the product.
- Gathering or printing of coupons by criminals who sell them to unethical merchants, who in turn redeem them.

FIGURE 13–7
Coupon distribution
across all media
□ □ □ □ □

Media type	1999	2000	2001	2002	2003
FSI	52%	55%	55%	64%	65%
In-store	17%	17%	16%	13%	11%
In/on package	16%	13%	12%	8%	9%
Direct mail	8%	5%	5%	6%	5%
Magazine	2%	5%	6%	6%	6%
Charity	2%	2%	2%	2%	1%
Other	3%	3%	4%	1%	3%

Many manufacturers hold firm in their policy to not pay retailers for questionable amounts or suspicious types of coupon submissions. However, some companies are less aggressive, and this affects their profit margins. Marketers must allow a certain percentage for misredemption when estimating the costs of a couponing program. Ways to identify and control coupon misredemption, such as improved coding, are being developed, but it still remains a problem.

Coupon Distribution Coupons can be disseminated to consumers in a number of ways, including freestanding inserts in Saturday newspapers, direct mail, newspapers (either in individual ads or as a group of coupons in a cooperative format), magazines, and packages. Figure 13–7 summarizes the percentage distributed across all avenues.

Distribution through newspaper *freestanding inserts* (FSIs) is by far the most popular method for delivering coupons to consumers, accounting for over 65 percent of all coupons distributed in 2003. There are a number of reasons why FSIs are the most popular way of delivering coupons, including their high-quality four-colour graphics, competitive distribution costs, national same-day circulation, market selectivity, and the fact that they can be competition-free due to category exclusivity (by FSI company). Because of their consumer popularity and predictable distribution, coupons distributed in FSIs are also a strong selling point with the retail trade. On the other hand, FSIs suffer from a low redemption rate of 1 or 2 percent, and their widespread distribution may lead to a clutter problem.

Direct mail accounts for about 5 percent of all coupons distributed. Most are sent by local retailers or through co-op mailings where a packet of coupons for many different products is sent to a household (Exhibit 13–5). Direct-mail couponing has several advantages. First, the mailing can be sent to a broad audience or targeted to specific geographic or demographic segments. Firms that mail their own coupons can be quite selective about recipients. Another important advantage of direct-mail couponing is a redemption rate of nearly 6 percent, much higher than for FSIs.[31] Direct-mail couponing can also be combined with a sample, which makes it a very effective way to gain the attention of consumers. The major disadvantage of direct-mail coupon delivery is the expense relative to other distribution methods. The cost per thousand for distributing coupons through co-op mailings ranges from $10 to $15, and more targeted promotions can cost $20 to $25 or even more. Also, the higher redemption rate of mail-delivered coupons may result from the fact that many recipients are already users of the brand who take advantage of the coupons sent directly to them.

Exhibit 13–5
Valpak coupons are also now available online

The use of *newspapers* and *magazines* as couponing vehicles is similar to direct mail, accounting for 6 percent of the total distributed in 2003. The advantages of newspapers as a couponing vehicle include market selectivity, shorter lead times with timing to the day, cooperative advertising opportunities that can lead to cost efficiencies, and promotional tie-ins with retailers. Other advantages of newspaper-delivered coupons are the broad exposure and consumer receptivity. Many consumers actively search the newspaper for coupons, especially on Saturdays or "food day" (when grocery stores advertise their specials). This enhances the likelihood of the consumer at least noticing the coupon. Distribution of coupons through magazines can take advantage of the selectivity of the publication to reach specific target audiences, along with enhanced production capabilities and extended copy life in the home. One feature of these print options is that the distribution cost is not a factor if the advertiser was planning to run a print ad in the first place. However, clearly there is a significant limitation with a 1 percent redemption rate.

Placing coupons either *inside* or on the *outside* of the package is a distribution method that accounted for about 19 percent of the coupons distributed in 2003. The in/on package coupon has virtually no distribution costs and a much higher redemption rate than other couponing methods, nearing 6 percent. An in/on pack coupon that is redeemable for the next purchase of the same brand is known as a **bounce-back coupon**. This type of coupon gives consumers an inducement to repurchase the brand.

Bounce-back coupons are often used with product samples to encourage the consumer to purchase the product after sampling. They may be included in or on the package during the early phases of a brand's life cycle to encourage repeat purchase, or they may be a defensive manoeuvre for a mature brand that is facing competitive pressure and wants to retain its current users. The main limitation of bounce-back coupons is that they go only to purchasers of the brand and thus do not attract nonusers. A bounce-back coupon placed on the package for Kellogg's Eggo brand waffles is shown in Exhibit 13–6.

Another type of in/on pack coupon is the **cross-ruff coupon**, which is redeemable on the purchase of a different product, usually one made by the same company but occasionally through a tie-in with another manufacturer. Cross-ruff coupons have a redemption rate of about 5 percent and can be effective in encouraging consumers to try other products or brands. Companies with wide product lines, such as cereal manufacturers, often use these coupons.

Yet another type of package coupon is the **instant coupon**, which is attached to the outside of the package so that the consumer can rip it off and redeem it immediately at the time of purchase. Instant coupons have redemption levels of around 36 percent and give consumers an immediate point-of-purchase incentive. They can be selectively placed in terms of promotion timing and market region. Some companies prefer instant coupons to price-off deals because the latter require more cooperation from retailers and can be more expensive, since every package must be reduced in price.

Another distribution method that has experienced strong growth over the past 10 years or so is **in-store couponing**, which includes all co-op couponing programs distributed in a retail store environment. This medium now accounts for around 11 percent of total coupon distribution. Coupons are distributed to consumers in stores in several ways, including tear-off pads, handouts in the store (sometimes as part of a sampling demonstration), on-shelf dispensers, and electronic dispensers, with an 8-percent redemption rate. These in-store coupons have several advantages: They can reach consumers when they are ready to

Exhibit 13–6
Kellogg's uses an on-package coupon to encourage repurchase

make a purchase, increase brand awareness on the shelf, generate impulse buying, and encourage product trial. They also provide category exclusivity. In-store couponing removes the need for consumers to clip coupons from FSIs or print ads and then remember to bring them to the store.

Innovations for Coupons   Earlier we noted that coupon distribution has dropped by about 20 percent in recent years. However, despite the growing sentiment among major marketers that coupons are inefficient and costly, very few companies are likely to abandon them entirely. Although most coupons never get used, consumers use some of them and have come to expect them. More than 80 percent of consumers use coupons and nearly one-quarter say they use them every time they shop. With so many consumers eager for coupons, marketers will continue to accommodate them. However, companies as well as the coupon industry are looking for ways to improve on their use.

Marketers are continually searching for more effective couponing techniques. General Mills, Kellogg, and Post recently replaced brand-specific coupons with universal coupons good for any of their cereal brands. For example, to make its couponing spending more efficient, Post began using universal coupons worth $1.50 off two boxes (matching the average cereal-coupon discount of 75 cents) and cut coupon distribution in half. Even though Post dropped only half as many coupons, redemption rates reached 6 percent, far exceeding the FSI average of less than 2 percent.[32]

Some marketers are broadening their use of account-specific direct-mail couponing, in which coupons are cobranded with individual retailers but can be used by consumers at any retail store. Procter & Gamble began using account-specific couponing with Tide detergent and has broadened the program to include mailings for a number of other brands.[33]

While many marketers are using the Internet for online promotions, online coupons account for about 5 percent of all coupons distributed. One of the major problems that has kept marketers away from "e-couponing" is the risk of fraud, as it is too easy for consumers or unscrupulous retailers to mass-duplicate online coupons by printing out several, or by photocopying the black-and-white prints. There are ways to deal with this problem such as coding coupons and verifying them in-store when they are redeemed. However, this is time-consuming and not very popular with retailers. Two alternatives are now on the scene in Canada. Two websites, coupons.com and save.ca, allow consumers to print or receive coupons in the mail respectively. Currently, the fraud problem is not a significant concern in Canada.[34]

PREMIUMS

Premiums are a sales promotion device used by many marketers. A **premium** is an offer of an item of merchandise or service either free or at a low price that is an extra incentive for purchasers. Many marketers are eliminating toys and gimmicks in favor of value-added premiums that reflect the quality of the product and are consistent with its image and positioning in the market. The two basic types of offers are the free premium and the self-liquidating premium.

Free Premiums   Free premiums are usually small gifts or merchandise included in the product package or sent to consumers who mail in a request along with a proof of purchase. In/on package free premiums include toys, balls, trading cards, or other items included in cereal packages, as well as samples of one product included with another. Surveys have shown that in/on package premiums are consumers' favourite type of promotion.[35]

Package-carried premiums have high impulse value and can provide an extra incentive to buy the product. However, several problems are associated with their use. First, there is the cost factor, which results from the premium itself as well as from extra packaging that may be needed. Finding desirable premiums at reasonable costs can be difficult, particularly for adult markets, and using a poor premium may do more harm than good.

Since most free mail-in premium offers require the consumer to send in more than one proof of purchase, they encourage repeat purchase and reward brand loyalty. But a major drawback of mail-in premiums is that they do not offer immediate reinforcement or reward to the purchaser, so they may not provide enough incentive to purchase the brand. Few consumers take advantage of mail-in premium offers; the average redemption rate is only 2 to 4 percent.[36]

Free premiums have become very popular in the restaurant industry, particularly among fast-food chains such as McDonald's and Burger King, which use premium offers in their kids' meals to attract children.[37] McDonald's has become the world's largest toymaker on a unit basis, commissioning about 750 million toys per year for its Happy Meals (Exhibit 13–7). Many of the premium offers used by the fast-food giants have cross-promotional tie-ins with popular movies and can be very effective at generating incremental sales. McDonald's gained a major competitive advantage with movie tie-in premiums in 1996 when it signed an agreement with Disney giving McDonald's exclusive rights to promotional tie-ins with Disney movies for 10 years.[38]

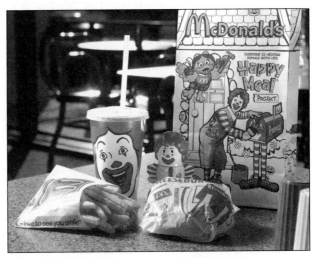

Exhibit 13–7
McDonald's Happy Meals use toys to help attract children

Labatt's had a winner with the Labatt Blue NHL Crazy Coldie Program during the 2002 Stanley Cup Playoffs. Each case of Double Blue (i.e., 12 Blue and 12 Blue Light) had a coldie (e.g., holder to keep beer cold) in the shape of the jersey of one of the 30 teams. While the in-pack premium is relatively inexpensive, it resonated with the 19–34 male market that pushed sales to a 300-percent market share growth during the promotional program. Success can be partly attributed to the promotion's ads where three humourous spots showed consumers trying to wear the "coldie jersey" despite its obvious small size and a host of other promotional support activities such as a contest and special events.[39]

Perhaps the most successful in-package premium in Canada in 2001 was a General Mills giveaway of six CD-ROM computer games such as Monopoly Junior and Clue. Modelled after a similar premium offer in the U.S., the Canadian division worked with only one games supplier, Hasbro, versus a couple of partners used south of the border. Hasbro was selected because both it and General Mills represent quality and heritage. The premium was so popular that store employees witnessed consumers searching through cases to find the game they wanted, as well as some consumers who left the store with only the CD-ROM, after purchasing the cereal. For competitive reasons, executives at General Mills were not willing to reveal any results but did admit that the consumer reaction was beyond belief given the empty shelves.[40] IMC Perspective 13–1 shows another cereal premium to a different target audience.

One of the fastest-growing types of incentive offers being used by marketers is Air Miles, which have literally become a promotional currency. Consumers are now choosing credit-card services, phone services, hotels, and many other products and services on the basis of mileage premiums for Air Miles. Even the Liquor Control Board of Ontario gives Air Miles!

Self-Liquidating Premiums **Self-liquidating premiums** require the consumer to pay some or all of the cost of the premium plus handling and mailing costs. The marketer usually purchases items used as self-liquidating premiums in large quantities and offers them to consumers at lower-than-retail prices. The goal is not to make a profit on the premium item but rather just to cover costs and offer a value to the consumer.

In addition to cost savings, self-liquidating premiums offer several advantages to marketers. Offering values to consumers through the premium products can create

Walking with Special K

Many of us start the New Year off with a resolution or two and Special K tried to help those who desired to lose weight or live a healthier lifestyle when the calendar showed January 2004 by offering a free pedometer (i.e., a device that measures how far one walks) in boxes of Special K.

Historically, Kellogg Canada had always associated Special K with various types of messages emphasizing good diet, a healthy balanced lifestyle, and the like. Advertising had often shown women exercising or living life to the fullest with Special K as an important part of their nutrition and diet. Its most recent brand positioning strategy, "Keep it Simple," stressed the need for consumers to maintain a healthy weight level.

As part of this strategy, Kellogg saw the pedometer as a natural fit to reinforce the brand in a positive light. In fact, consumer research prior to the launch of the sales promotion demonstrated considerable acceptance. Thus, a natural connection of healthy eating and living through exercise was communicated, something that the managers at Kellogg firmly believed in.

The value of the promotion represented significant value to consumers as each pedometer was worth approximately

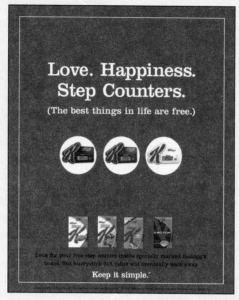

$15, and the expense would be substantial for Kellogg as it planned to give away 800,000 inside Special K boxes and 200,000 others would be distributed through mail-in offers. As a national program, the pedometer would be available until quantities lasted, presumably for the first few months of 2004, just in time for the spring walking season!

Television advertising and public relations supported the sales promotion to ensure maximum awareness and to enhance the overall perception of the brand. The TV spot featured the decades-old Nancy Sinatra song, "These Boots are Made for Walkin'," which was obviously connected to the pedometer. A voice-over suggested to consumers to increase the amount of walking they do in everyday life, like taking the stairs instead of the elevator. With a suggestion to walk an extra 20 minutes per day, consumers would feel better about themselves and the pedometer helped in that regard.

Source: Lesley Young, "Special K Walks Its Talk," *Marketing Magazine*, January 12, 2004.

interest in the brand and goodwill that enhances the brand's image. These premiums can also encourage trade support and gain in-store displays for the brand and the premium offer. Self-liquidating premiums are often tied directly to the advertising campaign, so they extend the advertising message and contribute to consumer franchise building for a brand.

General Mills Canada was at it again with a successful self-liquidating premium during Christmas of 2001. Customers received a beanbag version of the Pillsbury Doughboy for $2.99 with the purchase of two refrigerated-dough products. This marked the first time the brand icon had ever been directly merchandised! Pillsbury had the perfect opportunity because the Doughboy is the second-most recognized icon in North America, after Coca-Cola's Polar Bears. Even more impressive was the retailer participation and consumer acceptance. All retailers in Canada ran with the deal, and more than 200,000 Doughboys found a new home. And just to make sure that consumers liked the idea even more, the Doughboy came in three models: one holding a candy cane, another, a stocking, and the third, gifts.[41]

Self-liquidating premium offers have the same basic limitation as mail-in premiums: a very low redemption rate. Low redemption rates can leave the marketer with a large supply of items with a logo or some other brand identification that makes them hard to dispose of. Thus, it is important to test consumers' reaction to a premium incentive and determine whether they perceive the offer as a value. Another option is to use premiums with no brand identification, but that detracts from their consumer franchise-building value.

CONTESTS AND SWEEPSTAKES

Contests and sweepstakes are an increasingly popular consumer sales promotion. These promotions seem to have an appeal and glamour that tools like cents-off coupons lack. Contests and sweepstakes are exciting because, as one expert has noted, many consumers have a "pot of gold at the end of the rainbow mentality" and think they can win the big prizes being offered.[42] Marketers are attracted to contests and sweepstakes as a way of generating attention and interest among a large number of consumers. IMC Perspective 13–2 describes Canadian Tire's foray into contests.

There are differences between contests and sweepstakes. A **contest** is a promotion where consumers compete for prizes or money on the basis of skills or ability. The company determines winners by judging the entries or ascertaining which entry comes closest to some predetermined criteria. Contests usually provide a purchase incentive by requiring a proof of purchase to enter or an entry form that is available from a dealer or advertisement. Some contests require consumers to read an ad or package or visit a store display to gather information needed to enter. Marketers must be careful not to make their contests too difficult to enter, as doing so might discourage participation among key prospects in the target audience.

A **sweepstakes** is a promotion where winners are determined purely by chance; it cannot require a proof of purchase as a condition for entry. Entrants need only submit their names for the prize drawing. While there is often an official entry form, handwritten entries must also be permitted. One form of sweepstakes is a **game**, which also has a chance element or odds of winning. Scratch-off cards with instant winners are a popular promotional tool. Some games occur over a longer period and require more involvement by consumers. Promotions where consumers must collect game pieces are popular among retailers and fast-food chains as a way to build store traffic and repeat purchases. For example, McDonald's has used promotions based on the game *Monopoly* several times in recent years.

Because they are easier to enter, sweepstakes attract more entries than contests. They are also easier and less expensive to administer, since every entry does not have to be checked or judged. Choosing the winning entry in a sweepstakes requires only the random selection of a winner from the pool of entries or generation of a number to match those held by sweepstakes entrants. Experts note that the costs of mounting a sweepstakes are also very predictable. Companies can buy insurance to indemnify them and protect against the expense of awarding a big prize. In general, sweepstakes present marketers with a fixed cost, which is a major advantage when budgeting for a promotion.

Strengths of Contests and Sweepstakes A recent study suggests that sales can be enhanced by trial and repeat purchases through a sweepstakes advertised via in-store ad pads. A 12-week experiment of 20 mass-merchandiser outlets—10 test and 10 control stores—revealed that a major household product increased its sales by 70 percent in the test stores during the four-week test period compared to the previous four-week period that featured no advertising or promotion. Furthermore, during the posttest four-week period that had no ad-pad, sales hit a 30-percent increase.[43] Clearly, non-customers either recalled the sales promotion and ad message, or new or existing customers returned for a repeat purchase. In either case, the improved communication and behavioural effects of the promotion make it useful for both manufacturers and retailers.

A New Twist on an Established Sales Promotion

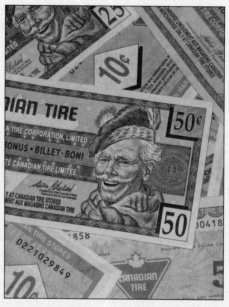

Look into any Canadian's wallet, or glove compartment, and you're sure to find a wad of Canadian Tire "money" stashed away somewhere. That same promotional tool, which was introduced in 1958 to launch Canadian Tire's entry into the retail gasoline industry, provided the needed inspiration to launch their "Big Spender" ad campaign, and also their first-ever integrated in-store and online national "Big Spender Giveaway" contest in late 2001.

Canadian Tire is a brand icon these days, with a number of things going well for them. About 90 percent of Canadians have shopped at their locations. It equally attracts men and women, and it has loyal following from young to retired people. Ninety-nine percent of Canadians recognize the Canadian Tire name, one of the five most-recognized brands in Canada. And a Canadian Tire "money" is in fact one of the country's most successful and popular customer rewards program, boasting a 90 percent redemption and participation level.

The "Big Spender" campaign marked the first time that Canadian Tire "money" was communicated in a broadcast ad that featured the song, "Big Spender," and showed many people buying various items at Canadian Tire with the Canadian Tire "money" that they had won. "We knew that putting Canadian Tire 'money' front and centre in our advertising and promotional programs would hold tremendous appeal for customers because it is such an important part of the Canadian Tire shopping experience today," writes Eymbert Vaandering, vice president of marketing at Canadian Tire in Toronto. "Customers love Canadian Tire 'money' because it's simple to use, it's earned in dollars and cents, it can be used anytime, in any quantity and to buy any item."

From an IMC perspective, the "Big Spender" contest was cutting edge, using a multi-channel media campaign that included TV and radio, an in-store contest supported by flyers, card-member statement inserts, POP at stores and in gas bars, and an online contest featuring a total of $350,000 in Canadian Tire "money" and merchandising prizes. The online part of the contest included a scavenger hunt to create greater excitement for consumers. Overall, the IMC approach drove traffic to the store, gas bars, and the website and strongly increased sales.

Source: "Hey, Big Spender," *Marketing Magazine*, January 14, 2002.

Contests and sweepstakes can get the consumer involved with a brand by making the promotion product relevant. For example, contests that ask consumers to suggest a name for a product or to submit recipes that use the brand can increase involvement levels. Nabisco developed an "Open a box, make up a snack," promotional contest for its three top cracker brands—Ritz, Triscuit, and Wheat Thins. Consumers sent in their favourite recipes, which were then made available on a dedicated website and at a toll-free number.

Marketers can use contests and sweepstakes to build brand equity by connecting the prizes to the lifestyle, needs, or interests of the target audience. Procter & Gamble teamed up with MuchMusic for two contests to promote its Cover Girl brand of make-up. In January 2001, seven lucky winners received a live, on-air makeover with celebrity hair and makeup artists. Another contest, "Prom Night 2001," featured one winner and nine friends receiving a makeover and a limousine ride to their prom, among other prizes.[44]

Contests can be designed to be consistent with the brand positioning strategy used in advertising. Axe deodorant body spray used an unusual skill or ability in its recent contest in Quebec. It sent camera teams to popular clubs and asked men to recite their best "pick-up" lines. Winners received dinner and a shopping spree and their victorious efforts were shown on Musique Plus. While this is certainly provocative, it is quite fitting with the sexual allurement communicated in Axe's recent television commercials.[45]

Limitations of Contests and Sweepstakes While the use of contests and sweepstakes continues to increase, there are some limitations associated with these types of promotions. Many sweepstakes and/or contest promotions do little to contribute to consumer franchise building for a product or service and may even detract from it. The sweepstakes or contest often becomes the dominant focus rather than the brand, and little is accomplished other than giving away substantial amounts of money and/or prizes. Many promotional experts question the effectiveness of contests and sweepstakes. Some companies have cut back or even stopped using them because of concern over their effectiveness and fears that consumers might become dependent on them.[46]

Despite this challenge it is possible to overcome this limitation. O.K. Tire connected to the local community where its dealers are located with a positive consumer-franchise building contest to launch its re-branding strategy. O.K. Tire offered 40 prizes totalling $50,000 to local community groups that were identified on ballots entered at one of the 230 dealerships. Results included current customers filling out many ballots while visiting a dealership for service, new customers acting upon the television and radio ads to try O.K. Tire, increased word-of-mouth communication in many locales, and enhanced personal communication with an emphasis on the dealer as a trusted neighbourhood business.[47]

Numerous legal considerations affect the design and administration of contests and sweepstakes.[48] But companies must still be careful in designing a contest or sweepstakes and awarding prizes. Most firms use consultants that specialize in the design and administration of contests and sweepstakes to avoid any legal problems, but they may still run into problems with promotions.

A final problem with contests and sweepstakes is participation by professionals or hobbyists who submit many entries but have no intention of purchasing the product or service. Because it is illegal to require a purchase as a qualification for a sweepstakes entry, consumers can enter as many times as they wish. Professional players sometimes enter one sweepstakes several times, depending on the nature of the prizes and the number of entries the promotion attracts. Newsletters are even available that inform them of all the contests and sweepstakes being held, the entry dates, estimated probabilities of winning for various numbers of entries, how to enter, and solutions to any puzzles or other information that might be needed. The presence of these professional entrants not only defeats the purpose of the promotion but may also discourage entries from consumers who think their chances of winning are limited.

REFUNDS AND REBATES

Refunds (also known as rebates) are offers by the manufacturer to return a portion of the product purchase price, usually after the consumer supplies some proof of purchase. Consumers are generally very responsive to rebate offers, particularly as the size of the savings increases. Rebates are used by makers of all types of products, ranging from package goods to major appliances, cars, and computer software.

Package-goods marketers often use refund offers to induce trial of a new product or encourage users of another brand to switch. Consumers may perceive the savings offered through a cash refund as an immediate value that lowers the cost of the item, even though those savings are realized only if the consumer redeems the refund or rebate offer. Redemption rates for refund offers typically range from 1 to 3 percent for print and point-of-purchase offers and 5 percent for in/on package offers.

Refund offers can also encourage repeat purchase. Many offers require consumers to send in multiple proofs of purchase. The size of the refund offer may even increase as the number of purchases gets larger. Some package-goods companies are switching away from cash refund offers to coupons or cash/coupon combinations. Using coupons in the refund offer enhances the likelihood of repeat purchase of the brand.

Rebates have become a widely used form of promotion for consumer durables. Products such as cameras, sporting goods, appliances, televisions, audio and video equipment, computers, and cars frequently use rebate offers to appeal to price-conscious consumers. The use of rebates for expensive items like cars was begun by Chrysler Corp. in 1981 to boost sales and generate cash for the struggling company. Rebates are now common not only in the auto industry and other durable products but for package-goods products as well.

Strengths and Limitations of Refunds and Rebates Rebates can help create new users and encourage brand switching or repeat purchase behaviour, or they can be a way to offer a temporary price reduction. The rebate may be perceived as an immediate savings even though many consumers do not follow through on the offer. This perception can influence purchase even if the consumer fails to realize the savings, so the marketer can reduce price for much less than if it used a direct price-off deal.

Some limitations are associated with refunds and rebates. Many consumers are not motivated by a refund offer because of the delay and the effort required to obtain the savings. They do not want to be bothered saving cash register receipts and proofs of purchase, filling out forms, and mailing in the offer.[49] A study of consumer perceptions found a negative relationship between the use of rebates and the perceived difficulties associated with the redemption process.[50] The study also found that consumers perceive manufacturers as offering rebates to sell products that are not faring well. Nonusers of rebates were particularly likely to perceive the redemption process as too complicated and to suspect manufacturers' motives. This implies that companies using rebates must simplify the redemption process and use other promotional elements such as advertising to retain consumer confidence in the brand.

When small refunds are being offered, marketers may find other promotional incentives such as coupons or bonus packs more effective. They must be careful not to overuse rebate offers and confuse consumers about the real price and value of a product or service. Also, consumers can become dependent on rebates and delay their purchases or purchase only brands for which a rebate is available. Many retailers have become disenchanted with rebates and the burden and expense of administering them.[51]

Exhibit 13–8
Bonus packs provide more value for consumers

BONUS PACKS

Bonus packs offer the consumer an extra amount of a product at the regular price by providing larger containers or extra units (Exhibit 13–8). Bonus packs result in a lower cost per unit for the consumer and provide extra value as well as more product for the money. There are several advantages to bonus pack promotions. First, they give marketers a direct way to provide extra value without having to get involved with complicated coupons or refund offers. The additional value of a bonus pack is generally obvious to the consumer and can have a strong impact on the purchase decision at the time of purchase.

Bonus packs can also be an effective defensive manoeuvre against a competitor's promotion or introduction of a new brand. By loading current users with large amounts of its product, a marketer can often remove these consumers from the market and make them less susceptible to a competitor's promotional efforts. Bonus packs may result in larger purchase orders and favourable display space in the store if relationships with retailers are good.

They do, however, usually require additional shelf space without providing any extra profit margins for the retailer, so the marketer can encounter problems with bonus packs if trade relationships are not good. Another problem is that bonus packs may appeal primarily to current users who probably would have purchased the brand anyway or to promotion-sensitive consumers who may not become loyal to the brand.

PRICE-OFF DEALS

Exhibit 13–9
Examples of price-off packages

Another consumer sales promotion tool is the direct **price-off deal**, which reduces the price of the brand. Price-off reductions are typically offered right on the package through specially marked price packs, as shown in Exhibit 13–9. Typically, price-offs range from 10 to 25 percent off the regular price, with the reduction coming out of the manufacturer's profit margin, not the retailer's. Keeping the retailer's margin during a price-off promotion maintains its support and cooperation.

Marketers use price-off promotions for several reasons. First, since price-offs are controlled by the manufacturer, it can make sure the promotional discount reaches the consumer rather than being kept by the trade. Like bonus packs, price-off deals usually present a readily apparent value to shoppers, especially when they have a reference price point for the brand and thus recognize the value of the discount.[52] So price-offs can be a strong influence at the point of purchase when price comparisons are being made. Price-off promotions can also encourage consumers to purchase larger quantities, preempting competitors' promotions and leading to greater trade support.

Price-off promotions may not be favourably received by retailers, since they can create pricing and inventory problems. Most retailers will not accept packages with a specific price shown, so the familiar X amount off the regular price must be used. Also, like bonus packs, price-off deals appeal primarily to regular users instead of attracting nonusers. Finally, the federal government has regulations regarding the conditions that price-off labels must meet and the frequency and timing of their use.

FREQUENCY PROGRAMS

One of the fastest growing areas of sales promotion is the use of **frequency programs** (also referred to as *continuity* or *loyalty programs*). Frequency programs have become commonplace in a number of product and service categories, particularly travel and hospitality, as well as among retailers. Virtually every airline, car rental company, and hotel chain has some type of frequency program. Loyalty programs are also used by a variety of retailers, including grocery stores, department stores, home centres, bookstores, and even local bagel shops.

Many package-goods companies are also developing frequency programs. Pillsbury, Nestlé, Kraft, and others have recently introduced continuity programs that offer consumers the opportunity to accumulate points for continuing to purchase their brands; the points can be redeemed for gifts and prizes. For example, Gerber Baby Foods has developed a frequency program known as Gerber Rewards, in which consumers who purchase 16 or more Gerber products at one time automatically receive a game-piece coupon carrying a unique PIN number and an 800 phone number.[53] Customers call the phone number, punch in the PIN number, and receive points for entry into a sweepstakes giving away a $250,000 college scholarship. Consumers earn more points with subsequent purchases of Gerber products.

There are a number of reasons why frequency programs have become so popular. Marketers view these programs as a way of encouraging consumers to use their products or services on a continual basis and as a way of developing strong customer loyalty. Many companies are also realizing the importance of customer retention and understand that the key to retaining and growing market share is building

397

relationships with loyal customers. Frequency programs also provide marketers with the opportunity to develop databases containing valuable information on their customers that can be used to better understand their needs, interests, and characteristics as well as to identify and track a company's most valuable customers. These databases can also be used to target specific programs and offers to customers to increase the amount they purchase and/or to build stronger relationships with them. For example, as part of the Gerber Rewards program discussed above, the company developed a database on those entering the sweepstakes that includes the ages of their children. Participants in the program periodically receive direct mail offers of discounts and deals on Gerber products that are based on the ages of their children.

As frequency programs become more common, marketers will be challenged to find ways to use them as a means of differentiating their product, service, business, or retail store. Marketers must find ways to make them true loyalty programs rather than just frequent-buyer programs. This will require the careful management of databases to identify and track valuable customers and their purchase history and the strategic use of targeted loyalty promotions.

EVENT MARKETING

Event marketing has become very popular in recent years. It is important to make a distinction between *event marketing* and *event sponsorships*, as the two terms are often used interchangeably yet they refer to different activities. **Event marketing** is a type of promotion where a company or brand is linked to an event or where a themed activity is developed for the purpose of creating experiences for consumers and promoting a product or service. Event marketing has become very popular in recent years as marketers develop integrated marketing programs including a variety of promotional tools that create experiences for consumers in an effort to associate their brands with certain lifestyles and activities. Marketers use events to distribute samples as well as information about their products and services or to actually let consumers experience the product.

An **event sponsorship** is an integrated marketing communications activity where a company develops actual sponsorship relations with a particular event (e.g., concert, art exhibition, cultural activity, social change, sports) and provides financial support in return for the right to display a brand name, logo, or advertising message and be identified as a supporter of the event. Part of the confusion between these two promotions arises from the fact that event marketing often takes place as part of a company's event sponsorship. We discuss the former concept here and address the latter in the next chapter as it more relates to public relations activities.

Two recent events to distribute samples in situations that reinforced their brand positioning strategy achieved great success. Aveeno, a marketer of skin care and moisturizer products, launched its 2004 Snowfest tour with product sampling, a contest, and an "Après Ski" party at 16 ski hills across Canada. Activities such as these can enhance the post-event advertising or can benefit from pre-event advertising. For instance, Aveeno used print and online ads to round out its IMC campaign.[54] An event run by Coffee-Mate was almost an anti-event with a "tease, taste and reveal" approach. It distributed 800,000 free cups of coffee with Coffee-Mate liquid at high-traffic locations (e.g., offices, commuter hubs, arenas) in six Canadian cities. To overcome the Coffee-Mate equals powder association, it did not disclose the brand until after the consumer had tasted the product.[55]

Subaru wanted to get consumers, sales consultants, and media representatives to be familiar with its new brands, Impreza WRX and Outback H6, so it developed the "2001 Subaru National Ride & Drive," its first event-marketing program. Members of each target audience in six Canadian cities (Quebec City, Montreal, Toronto, Calgary, Edmonton, and Vancouver) could test-drive the vehicles and talk to key Subaru employees.

Subaru enlisted over 5,000 candidates through auto-show response cards and their website. From that enlistment, 3,000 qualified individuals received a direct-mail invitation to the event, of which 77 percent responded positively versus a 50- to 60-percent objective. The event included a classroom-style seminar, a vehicle and course walk-around, the test-drive, and a demonstration by professional drivers with participants in the car. Subaru obtained enthusiastic written and verbal feedback on the event, especially the demonstration, and gave a thank-you card to all participants, which directed them to a dedicated website that had photos of the event.

The information received continued in the selling process. All information was passed on to the respective dealerships along with highlights of the event (e.g., statistics, photos). The program resulted in a 3 percent participant-to-sales conversion rate in the first six weeks; given the nature of car purchases, additional sales may be forthcoming to improve this ratio. Other statistics show the value of event marketing as post-event purchasing desires increased over the pre-event numbers, and 61 percent of all participants claimed that they would visit a Subaru dealership.[56]

OBJECTIVES OF TRADE SALES PROMOTION

TRADE SALES PROMOTION

Like consumer promotions, sales promotion programs targeted to the trade should be based on well-defined objectives and measurable goals and a consideration of what the marketer wants to accomplish. Typical objectives for promotions targeted to marketing intermediaries such as wholesalers and retailers include obtaining distribution and support for new products, maintaining support for established brands, encouraging retailers to display established brands, and building retail inventories.

Obtain Distribution for New Products   Trade promotions are often used to encourage retailers to give shelf space to new products. Essentially, this translates into a trial purchase objective like we saw with consumer promotions. Manufacturers recognize that only a limited amount of shelf space is available in supermarkets, drugstores, and other major retail outlets. Thus, they provide retailers with financial incentives to stock new products. For example, Lever Brothers used heavy sampling and high-value coupons in the successful introduction of Lever 2000 bar soap. However, in addition to these consumer promotions, the company used discounts to the trade to encourage retailers to stock and promote the new brand.

While trade discounts or other special price deals are used to encourage retailers and wholesalers to stock a new brand, marketers may use other types of promotions to get them to push the brand. Merchandising allowances can get retailers to display a new product in high-traffic areas of stores, while incentive programs or contests can encourage wholesale or retail store personnel to push a new brand.

Maintain Trade Support for Established Brands   Trade promotions are often designed to maintain distribution and trade support for established brands. Clearly, this objective is akin to a repeat purchase objective that we saw with consumer sales promotion. Brands that are in the mature phase of their product life cycle are vulnerable to losing wholesale and/or retail distribution, particularly if they are not differentiated or face competition from new products. Trade deals induce wholesalers and retailers to continue to carry weaker products because the discounts increase their profit margins. Brands with a smaller market share often rely heavily on trade promotions, since they lack the funds required to differentiate themselves from competitors through media advertising.

Even if a brand has a strong market position, trade promotions may be used as part of an overall marketing strategy. As discussed previously, Heinz has relied heavily on trade promotions to hold its market share position for many of its brands. Many consumer-package-goods companies count on trade promotions to maintain retail distribution and support.

Build Retail Inventories   Manufacturers often use trade promotions to build the inventory levels of retailers or other channel members, another form of repeat purchasing. There are several reasons manufacturers want to load retailers with their products. First, wholesalers and retailers are more likely to push a product when they have high inventory levels rather than storing it in their warehouses or back rooms. Building channel members' inventories also ensures they will not run out of stock and thus miss sales opportunities.

Some manufacturers of seasonal products offer large promotional discounts so that retailers will stock up on their products before the peak selling season begins. This enables the manufacturer to smooth out seasonal fluctuations in its production schedule and passes on some of the inventory carrying costs to retailers or wholesalers. When retailers stock up on a product before the peak selling season, they often run special promotions and offer discounts to consumers to reduce excess inventories.

Encourage Retailers to Display Established Brands Another objective of trade-oriented promotions is to encourage retailers to display and promote an established brand. This could be analogous to increased consumption as seen with consumer sales promotion objectives since the retailer demonstrates increased commitment. Marketers recognize that many purchase decisions are made in the store and promotional displays are an excellent way of generating sales. An important goal is to obtain retail store displays of a product away from its regular shelf location. A typical supermarket has approximately 50 display areas at the ends of aisles, near checkout counters, and elsewhere. Marketers want to have their products displayed in these areas to increase the probability shoppers will come into contact with them. Even a single display can increase a brand's sales significantly during a promotion.

Manufacturers often use multifaceted promotional programs to encourage retailers to promote their products at the retail level. For example, manufacturers will combine its advertising and consumer sales promotions and offer them at the same time as the trade promotion.

TRADE SALES PROMOTION STRATEGY OPTIONS

Manufacturers use a variety of trade promotion tools as inducements for wholesalers and retailers. Next we examine some of the most often used types of trade promotions and some factors marketers must consider in using them. These promotions include contests and incentives, trade allowances, displays and point-of-purchase materials, sales training programs, trade shows, and co-op advertising.

Contests and Incentives Manufacturers may develop contests or special incentive programs to stimulate greater selling effort and support from reseller management or sales personnel. Contests or incentive programs can be directed toward managers who work for a wholesaler or distributor as well as toward store or department managers at the retail level. Manufacturers often sponsor contests for resellers and use prizes such as trips or valuable merchandise as rewards for meeting sales quotas or other goals.

Contests or special incentives are often targeted at the sales personnel of the wholesalers, distributors/dealers, or retailers. These salespeople are an important link in the distribution chain because they are likely to be very familiar with the market, more frequently in touch with the customer (whether it be another reseller or the ultimate consumer), and more numerous than the manufacturer's own sales organization. Manufacturers often devise incentives or contests for these sales personnel. These programs may involve cash payments made directly to the retailer's or wholesaler's sales staff to encourage them to promote and sell a manufacturer's product. These payments are known as **push money** (pm) or *spiffs*. For example, an appliance manufacturer may pay a $25 spiff to retail sales personnel for selling a certain model or size. In sales contests, salespeople can win trips or valuable merchandise for meeting certain goals established by the manufacturer. As shown in Figure 13–8, these incentives may be tied to product sales, new account placements, or merchandising efforts.

- **Product or Program Sales**
  Awards are tied to the selling of a product, for example:
     Selling a specified number of cases
     Selling a specified number of units
     Selling a specified number of promotional programs

- **New Account Placements**
  Awards are tied to:
     The number of new accounts opened
     The number of new accounts ordering a minimum number of cases or units
     Promotional programs placed in new accounts

- **Merchandising Efforts**
  Awards are tied to:
     Establishing promotional programs (such as theme programs)
     Placing display racks, counter displays, and the like

FIGURE 13–8

Three forms of promotion targeted to reseller salespeople

☐ ☐ ☐ ☐ ☐

While contests and incentive programs can generate reseller support, they can also be a source of conflict between retail sales personnel and management. Some retailers want to maintain control over the selling activities of their sales staff. They don't want their salespeople devoting an undue amount of effort to trying to win a contest or receive incentives offered by the manufacturer. Nor do they want their people becoming too aggressive in pushing products that serve their own interests instead of the product or model that is best for the customer.

Events Often event marketing or event sponsorship programs directed to consumers are also linked to the trade as a way to foster good relationships among channel members and to enhance merchandising activities. For example, a tour of famous figure skaters— Kurt Browning, Elvis Stojko, Brian Orser, Isabelle Brasseur, Lloyd Eisler, Jose Chouinard, and Shae-Lynn Bourne—performed in many small Canadian cities with sponsorship from Procter and Gamble's Nice'n Easy brand of hair colouring for women. Usually, people in many of these towns did not have the opportunity to see such shows and P&G felt a need to more directly connect with markets that had strong consumer acceptance for this product. As part of the sponsorship, P&G ran various promotions with its retail distributors and customized the programs to meet their respective needs in addition to the usual contests and incentives. Zellers, Loblaws, and Shoppers Drug Mart hosted in-store autograph sessions. Wal-Mart organized tickets for the Children's Miracle Network and skating seminars for local clubs.[57]

Trade Allowances Probably the most common trade promotion is some form of **trade allowance**, a discount or deal offered to retailers or wholesalers to encourage them to stock, promote, or display the manufacturer's products. Types of allowances offered to retailers include buying allowances, promotional or display allowances, and slotting allowances.

Buying Allowances A buying allowance is a deal or discount offered to resellers in the form of a price reduction on merchandise ordered during a fixed period. These discounts are often in the form of an **off-invoice allowance**, which means a certain per-case amount or percentage is deducted from the invoice. A buying allowance can also take the form of *free goods*; the reseller gets extra cases with the purchase of specific amounts (for example, 1 free case with every 10 cases purchased).

Buying allowances are used for several reasons. They are easy to implement and are well accepted, and sometimes expected, by the trade. They are also an effective way to encourage resellers to buy the manufacturer's product, since they will want to take advantage of the discounts being offered during the allowance period. Manufacturers offer trade discounts expecting wholesalers and retailers to pass the price reduction through to consumers, resulting in greater sales. However, as discussed shortly, this is often not the case.

Promotional Allowances Manufacturers often give retailers allowances or discounts for performing certain promotional or merchandising activities in support of their brands. These merchandising allowances can be given for providing special displays away from the product's regular shelf position, running in-store promotional programs, or including the product in an ad. The manufacturer generally has guidelines or a contract specifying the activity to be performed to qualify for the promotional allowance. The allowance is usually a fixed amount per case or a percentage deduction from the list price for merchandise ordered during the promotional period.

Slotting Allowances Retailers often demand a special allowance for agreeing to accept a new product. *Slotting allowances*, also called *stocking allowances, introductory allowances,* or *street money*, are fees retailers charge for providing a slot or position to accommodate the new product. Retailers justify these fees by pointing out the costs associated with taking on so many new products each year, such as redesigning store shelves, entering the product into their computers, finding warehouse space, and briefing store employees on the new product.[58] They also note they are assuming some risk, since so many new product introductions fail.

Slotting fees can range from a few hundred dollars per store to $50,000 or more for an entire retail chain. Manufacturers that want to get their products on the shelves nationally can face several million dollars in slotting fees. Many marketers believe slotting allowances are not appropriate and say some 70 percent of these fees go directly to retailers' bottom lines. Retailers can continue charging slotting fees because of their power and the limited availability of shelf space in supermarkets relative to the large numbers of products introduced each year. Large manufacturers with popular brands are less likely to pay slotting fees than smaller companies that lack leverage in negotiating with retailers.

A recent study by Paul Bloom, Gregory Gundlach, and Joseph Cannon examined the views of manufacturers, wholesalers, and grocery retailers regarding the use of slotting fees. Their findings suggest that slotting fees shift the risk of new product introductions from retailers to manufacturers and help apportion the supply and demand of new products. They also found that slotting fees lead to higher retail prices, are applied in a discriminatory fashion, and place small marketers at a disadvantage.[59]

Problems with Trade Allowances Many companies are concerned about the abuse of trade allowances by wholesalers, retailers, and distributors. Marketers give retailers these trade allowances so that the savings will be passed through to consumers in the form of lower prices, but companies such as Procter & Gamble claim that only 30 percent of trade promotion discounts actually reach consumers because 35 percent is lost in inefficiencies and another 35 percent is pocketed by retailers and wholesalers. Moreover, many marketers believe that the trade is taking advantage of their promotional deals and misusing promotional funds.

For example, many retailers and wholesalers engage in a practice known as **forward buying**, where they stock up on a product at the lower deal or off-invoice price and resell it to consumers after the marketer's promotional period ends. Another common practice is **diverting**, where a retailer or wholesaler takes advantage of the promotional deal and then sells some of the product purchased at the low price to a store outside its area or to a middleperson who resells it to other stores.

Forward buying and diverting are widespread practices. Industry studies show that nearly 40 percent of wholesalers' and retailers' profits come from these activities. In addition to not passing discounts on to consumers, forward buying and diverting create other problems for manufacturers. They lead to huge swings in demand that cause production scheduling problems and leave manufacturers and retailers always building toward or drawing down from a promotional surge.

Marketers also worry that the system leads to frequent price specials, so consumers learn to make purchases on the basis of what's on sale rather than developing any loyalty to their brands.

The problems created by retailers' abuse led Procter & Gamble, one of the country's most powerful consumer products marketers, to adopt **everyday low pricing (EDLP)**, which lowers the list price of over 60 percent of its product line by 10 to 25 percent while cutting promotional allowances to the trade. The price cuts leave the overall cost of the product to retailers about the same as it would have been with the various trade allowance discounts.

P&G argues that EDLP eliminates problems such as deal buying, leads to regular low prices at the retail level, and helps build brand loyalty among consumers. Yet the EDLP strategy has caused great controversy in the trade, which depends heavily on promotions to attract consumers. Some retailers took P&G products off the shelf; others cut their ads and displays of the company's brands. Retailers prefer to operate on a *high/low strategy* of frequent price specials and argue that EDLP puts them at a disadvantage against the warehouse stores and mass merchandisers that already use everyday low pricing. They also say that some products, such as those that are bought on impulse, thrive on promotions and don't lend themselves to EDLP. Retailers rely on promotions like end-of-aisle displays and price discounts to create excitement and generate incremental sales and profits.[60]

Critics of EDLP also note that while the strategy may work well for market leaders whose brands enjoy high loyalty, it is not effective for marketers trying to build market share or prop up lagging products. Moreover, many consumers are still motivated more by promotional deals and specials than by advertising claims from retailers promoting everyday low prices.

Despite the criticism, P&G says EDLP is paying off and volume is growing faster in its brands that have switched to the new pricing strategy. And it claims that market share in two-thirds of these product categories has increased. P&G recently extended its use of everyday low pricing to international markets.[61]

Displays and Point-of-Purchase Materials The next time you are in a store, take a moment to examine the various promotional materials used to display and sell products. Point-of-purchase displays are an important promotional tool because they can help a manufacturer obtain more effective in-store merchandising of products. Companies in Canada spend a lot of money on point-of-purchase materials, including end-of-aisle displays, banners, posters, shelf cards, motion pieces, and stand-up racks, among others. Exhibit 13–10 shows an award-winning point-of-purchase display for Wilson baseball gloves.

Many manufacturers help retailers use shelf space more efficiently through **planograms**, which are configurations of products that occupy a shelf section in a store. Some manufacturers are developing computer-based programs that allow retailers to input information from their scanner data and determine the best shelf layouts by experimenting with product movement, space utilization, profit yields, and other factors.[62]

Sales Training Programs Another form of manufacturer-sponsored promotional assistance is sales training programs for reseller personnel. Many products sold at the retail level require knowledgeable salespeople who can provide consumers with information about the features, benefits, and advantages of various brands and models. Cosmetics, appliances, computers, consumer electronics, and sporting equipment are examples of products for which consumers often rely on well-informed retail sales personnel for assistance.

Manufacturers provide sales training assistance to retail salespeople in a number of ways. They may conduct classes or training sessions that retail personnel can attend to increase their knowledge of a product or a product line. These training sessions present information and ideas on how to sell the manufacturer's product and

403

Exhibit 13–10
This award-winning point-of-purchase display plays an important role in the merchandising of Wilson baseball gloves

may also include motivational components. Sales training classes for retail personnel are often sponsored by companies selling high-ticket items or complex products such as personal computers, cars, or ski equipment.

Another way manufacturers provide sales training assistance to retail employees is through their own sales force. Sales reps educate retail personnel about their product line and provide selling tips and other relevant information. The reps can provide ongoing sales training as they come into contact with retail sales staff on a regular basis and can update them on changes in the product line, market developments, competitive information, and the like.

Manufacturers also give resellers detailed sales manuals, product brochures, reference manuals, and other material. Many companies provide videocassettes for retail sales personnel that include product information, product-use demonstrations, and ideas on how to sell their product. These selling aids can often be used to provide information to customers as well.

Trade Shows Another important promotional activity targeted to resellers is the **trade show**, a forum where manufacturers can display their products to current as well as prospective buyers. According to the Trade Show Bureau, nearly 100 million people attend the 5,000 trade shows each year in the United States and Canada, and the number of exhibiting companies exceeds 1.3 million. In many industries, trade shows are a major opportunity to display one's product lines and interact with customers. They are often attended by important management personnel from large retail chains as well as by distributors and other reseller representatives.

A number of promotional functions can be performed at trade shows, including demonstrating products, identifying new prospects, gathering customer and competitive information, and even writing orders for a product. Trade shows are particularly valuable for introducing new products, because resellers are often looking for new merchandise to stock. Shows can also be a source of valuable leads to follow up on through sales calls or direct marketing. The social aspect of trade shows is also important. Many companies use them to entertain key customers and to develop and maintain relationships with the trade. A recent academic study demonstrated that trade shows generate product awareness and interest and can have a measurable economic return.[63]

Cooperative Advertising The final form of trade-oriented promotion we examine is **cooperative advertising**, where the cost of advertising is shared by more than one party. There are three types of cooperative advertising. Although the first two are not trade-oriented promotion, we should recognize their objectives and purpose.

Horizontal cooperative advertising is advertising sponsored in common by a group of retailers or other organizations providing products or services to the market. For example, automobile dealers who are located near one another in an auto park or along the same street often allocate some of their ad budgets to a cooperative advertising fund. Ads are run promoting the location of the dealerships and encouraging car buyers to take advantage of their close proximity when shopping for a new automobile.

Ingredient-sponsored cooperative advertising is supported by raw materials manufacturers; its objective is to help establish end products that include the company's materials and/or ingredients. Companies that often use this type of advertising include Du Pont, which promotes the use of its materials such as Teflon, Thinsulate, and Kevlar in a variety of consumer and industrial products, and NutraSweet, whose artificial sweetener is an ingredient in many food products and beverages. Perhaps the best-known, and most successful, example of this type of cooperative advertising is the "Intel Inside" program, sponsored by Intel Corporation.

The most common form of cooperative advertising is the trade-oriented form, **vertical cooperative advertising**, in which a manufacturer pays for a portion of the advertising a retailer runs to promote the manufacturer's product and its

DISCUSSION QUESTIONS

1. What are the differences between consumer and trade sales promotion? Discuss the role of each in a marketer's IMC program.

2. Discuss how sales promotion can be used as an acceleration tool to speed up the sales process and maximize sales volume.

3. Discuss the various reasons marketers have been shifting their marketing dollars to sales promotion from media advertising. Discuss the pros and cons of this reallocation of marketers' advertising and promotion budgets.

4. What are the differences between consumer franchise-building and nonfranchise-building promotions? Find an example of a promotional offer you believe contributes to the equity of a brand and explain why.

5. Discuss how the Internet can be used for the distribution of various promotional offers such as samples, coupons, premiums, contests, and sweepstakes.

6. What is meant by a sales promotion trap? Find an example of an industry where a promotional war is currently taking place. What are the options for a marketer involved in such a situation?

7. Canadian Tire and Pillsbury used an aspect of their brand for a sales promotion for the first time ever. Does this damage the brand at all in light of some concerns about sales promotion raised in this chapter? What other brand has a long-standing icon that could be used for a sales promotion?

14

Public Relations

CHAPTER OBJECTIVES

- To recognize the role of public relations in the promotional mix.

- To understand public relations and its strengths and limitations.

- To understand the reasons for corporate advertising and its strengths and limitations.

- To know how to compile a public relations plan.

- To understand how public relations is obtained partly through publicity generated through news media.

The World is Drinking Canadian Iceberg Vodka

Established in 1994, Canadian Iceberg Vodka, a small firm based in St. John's, Newfoundland, captured 1 percent of the Canadian market of 3.3 million cases in 2002. Moreover, it has expanded to 14 other countries including the U.S., Japan, European countries, and even Russia, the home of vodka. In 2001, *Wine Access* magazine named it the best vodka in the world and during the 1998 World Spirits Championships, Iceberg Vodka received second place and garnered a best-buy rating.

And the key to their success is not just the name Iceberg Vodka, but rather the water used in the distilling process. It is actually pure water from harvested icebergs drifting from the Arctic to the north Atlantic each spring. With such a unique product characteristic that no other vodka can claim, Iceberg Vodka can position their product as cool and pure—cool from the icebergs, and pure from the water since the ice contains no mineral content as it was formed prior to pollution.

With a minimal budget, Iceberg Vodka relied on direct communication to the consumer market through shows like the Toronto Wine and Cheese Show, the Canadian International Food & Beverage Show, the Gourmet Food and Wine Show, and similar shows in other countries.

Voting on Vodka
A Blind Tasting of International Premium Vodkas

In 2004 the #1 Premium Vodka is...
ICEBERG VODKA

RANK
1. **ICEBERG** (Canada)
2. Ciroc (France)
   Ketel One (Holland)
4. Citadelle (France)
   Stolichnaya (Russia)
6. Finlandia (Finland)
   Zyr (Russia)
8. Pearl (Canada)
   Vincent Van Gogh (Holland)
   Three Olives (Great Britain)
11. Wyborowa (Poland)
   Grey Goose (France)
13. Absolut (Sweden)
   Jewel of Russia (Russia)
15. Chopin (Poland)
16. Belvedere (Poland)
   Vox (Netherlands)

Note: This represents a sampling of the 25 vodkas tested.
Source: The Greater New York Chapter of Tasters Guild International - Jan 26, 2004

Please drink responsibly.
www.icebergvodka.com
12,000 Years in the making
Naturally pure and smooth
from 100% pure icebergs

Essentially, Iceberg Vodka selected these and related venues to allow consumers to taste the vodka since many tasters switched brands once they experienced the full-flavour effect. Print and radio ads supported the taste-test initiative, but publicity through news stories provided a tremendous boost that could not have been attained with the firm's limited budget.

With the story of fishermen going out in their boats each spring to harvest the icebergs, the media had a natural angle to present to their readers, listeners, or viewers. Articles featuring Iceberg Vokda appeared in magazines such as *Canadian Business*, *Atlantic Progress*, *Atlantic Business*, *Wine Spectator*, and *Wine Access*. Television crews from European countries covered recent spring harvestings, and Iceberg Vodka received followup e-mails requesting information on where to purchase. The publicity has been so impressive that consumers are going directly to their local liquour board for distribution. Increased sales have given Iceberg Vodka the opportunity to expand its horizons with a new print campaign for the North American market.

Source: Heleana Katz, "Tip of the Iceberg," *Marketing Magazine*, March 24, 2003.

Public relations, publicity, and corporate advertising all have promotional program elements that may be of great benefit to marketers. They are integral parts of the overall promotional effort that must be managed and coordinated with the other elements of the promotional mix. However, these three tools do not always have the specific objectives of product and service promotion, nor do they always involve the same methods you have become accustomed to as you have read this text. Typically, these activities are designed more to change attitudes toward an organization or issue than to promote specific products or affect behaviours directly (though you will see that this role is changing in some organizations). This chapter explores the role of public relations, its related topic of publicity generated by news media, corporate advertising, the strengths and limitations of each, and the process by which they are employed. Examples of such efforts—both successful and unsuccessful—are also included.

PUBLIC RELATIONS

What is public relations? How does it differ from other elements of marketing discussed thus far? Perhaps a good starting point is to define what the term *public relations* has traditionally meant and then to introduce its new role.

THE TRADITIONAL DEFINITION OF PR

A variety of books define **public relations**, but perhaps the most comprehensive definition is that offered by the *Public Relations News* (the weekly newsletter of the industry):

> the management function which evaluates public attitudes, identifies the policies and procedures of an organization with the public interest, and executes a program of action (and communication) to earn public understanding and acceptance.[1]

Public relations is indeed a management function. The term *management* should be used in its broadest sense; it is not limited to business managements but extends to other types of organizations, including nonprofit institutions. In this definition, public relations requires a series of stages, including:

- The determination and evaluation of public attitudes.
- The identification of policies and procedures of an organization with a public interest.
- The development and execution of a communications program designed to bring about public understanding and acceptance.

This definition reveals that public relations involves much more than activities designed to sell a product or service. The PR program may involve some of the promotional program elements previously discussed but use them in a different way. For example, press releases may be mailed to announce new products or changes in the organization, special events may be organized to create goodwill in the community, and advertising may be used to state the firm's position on a controversial issue.

THE NEW ROLE OF PR

In an increasing number of marketing-oriented companies, new responsibilities have been established for public relations. It takes on a much broader (and more marketing-oriented) perspective, designed to promote the organization as well as its products and/or services.

The way that companies and organizations use public relations might best be viewed as a continuum. On one end of the continuum is the use of PR from a traditional perspective. In this perspective public relations is viewed as a nonmarketing function whose primary responsibility is to maintain mutually beneficial relationships between the organization and its publics. In this case, customers or potential customers are only part of numerous publics—employees, investors, neighbours, special-interest groups, and so on. Marketing and public relations are separate departments; if external agencies are being used, they are separate agencies. At the other end of the continuum, public relations is considered primarily a marketing communications function. All noncustomer relationships are perceived as necessary only in a marketing context.[2] In these organizations, public relations reports to marketing. As the book by the Rieses clearly indicates, for many companies the PR function is moving more and more toward a "new role," which is much closer to a marketing function than a traditional one.

The new role of public relations envisions both strong marketing and strong PR departments. Rather than each department operating independently, the two work closely together, blending their talents to provide the best overall image of the firm and its product or service offerings. Toyota Canada took this one step further by recently merging its advertising and public relations departments.[3]

Writing in *Advertising Age*, William N. Curry notes that organizations must use caution in establishing this relationship because PR and marketing are not the same thing, and when one becomes dominant, the balance required to operate at maximum efficiency is lost.[4] He says losing sight of the objectives and functions of public relations in an attempt to achieve marketing goals may be detrimental in the long run. Others take an even stronger view that if public relations and marketing distinctions continue to blur, the independence of the PR function will be lost and it will become much less effective.[5] In fact, as noted by Cutlip, Center, and Broom, marketing and public relations are complementary functions, "with each making unique but complementary contributions to building and maintaining the many relationships essential for organizational survival and growth. To ignore one is to risk failure in the other."[6] This position is consistent with our perception that public relations is an important part of the IMC process, contributing in its own way but also in a way consistent with marketing goals.

Exhibit 14–1
Firestone responds to negative publicity

417

PUBLICITY: ONE EFFECT OF PUBLIC RELATIONS

Publicity refers to the generation of news about a person, product, service, or organization that appears in broadcast or print media. In some instances, it appears that publicity and public relations occur at the same time or in close proximity of one another. For example, a string of SUV accidents led to major problems for 102-year-old Bridgestone/Firestone. In response to the problem, Firestone replaced nearly 900,000 tires and implemented a communications program to counter the negative publicity, a program including television commercials, personal visits to dealers, and print advertising such as that shown in Exhibit 14–1. As a result of the campaign, Firestone lost none of its 10,000 independent tire dealers and two years later was on the road to recovery. In this case, consumers were exposed to both publicity and public relations at varying stages of the identification and solution to the problem.

In other instances, it seems that publicity is the end result or effect of the public relations effort. Because marketers like to have as much control as possible over

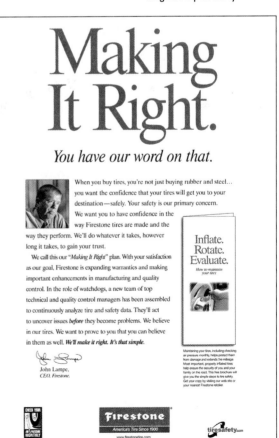

the time and place where information is released, they often provide the news media with pre-packaged material. One way to do this is with the **video news release (VNR)**, a publicity piece produced by publicists so that stations can air it as a news story. The videos almost never mention that they are produced by the subject organization, and most news stations don't mention it either.

Another example is when a firm uses the media effectively for product launches. The firm, Hill and Knowlton, was faced with the task of generating publicity for Microsoft Canada's launch of Windows 2000 through the media. A concern was that the media might treat it as a non-event because of previous reports of early reviews and the like. The solution was to focus on key customer benefits in all communications to those that would provide third-party endorsements and all media players. The launch featured a presence on *Canada AM* (e.g., interview and demonstration), a CIO breakfast in Toronto, a speech by the president of Microsoft Canada, press conferences, interviews with Microsoft representatives, and a partner/customer reception. The results over the next six weeks saw Microsoft receive 28 million media impressions.

There are at least three complications that contribute to these two examples. First is the fact that publicity typically lasts for a short period of time. The communication effect of an article in the newspaper about a new product may last for a few weeks. Alternatively, public relations is a concerted program with many exposures extending over a period of time that has a lasting communication effect. A second complication is that public relations is designed to provide positive information about a firm and is usually controlled by the firm or its agent. Publicity, on the other hand, is not always positive and is not always under the control of, or paid for by, the organization. One factor that distinguishes publicity from the other IMC program elements is its sheer power as a form of communication, which gives rise to the final complication. Some of the more powerful incidents of publicity are unplanned by the corporation, and the focus is on the successful and unsuccessful reactions of the organization to positive or negative events.

Perhaps the most famous example of publicity and public relations occurring at the same time is Tylenol. Many years ago, seven people in the Chicago area died after taking Extra Strength Tylenol capsules that had been laced with cyanide (after the product reached the store). Within one week of the poisonings, Tylenol's market share fell from 35 to only 6.5 percent after extensive media coverage of the tampering. Strong public relations efforts combined with an already strong product and corporate image helped the product rebound (despite the opinions of many experts that it had no chance of recovering). The Johnson & Johnson marketing efforts designed to aid recovery are a model in proficiency and have been studied by students of marketing (in both the classroom and the boardroom) for many years. A brand or firm with a lesser image would never have been able to come back. Tylenol regained almost 100 percent of its original brand share in just a few months.

STRENGTHS OF PUBLIC RELATIONS

Credibility Because public relations communications are not perceived in the same light as advertising—that is, the public does not realize the organization either directly or indirectly paid for them—they tend to have more credibility. The fact that the media are not being compensated for providing the information may lead receivers to consider the news more truthful and credible. For example, an article in newspapers or magazines discussing the virtues of aspirin may be perceived as much more credible than an ad for a particular brand of aspirin.

Automotive awards presented in magazines such as *Motor Trend* have long been known to carry clout with potential car buyers. Now marketers have found that even lesser media mean a lot as well. General Motors' Pontiac division played up an award given to Pontiac as "the best domestic sedan" by *MotorWeek* in a

30-minute program carried by about 300 public broadcasting stations. Likewise, Chrysler trumpeted the awards given to its Jeep Cherokee by *4-Wheel & Off Road* magazine.[7] It has become a common practice for car companies to promote their achievements.

News about a product may in itself serve as the subject of an ad. Exhibit 14–2 demonstrates how Olympus used favourable publicity from a variety of sources to promote its digital camera. A number of auto manufacturers have also taken advantage in their ads of high customer satisfaction ratings reported by J. D. Powers & Associates, an independent research firm specializing in automotive research.

Cost In both absolute and relative terms, the cost of public relations is very low, especially when the possible effects are considered. While a firm can employ public relations agencies and spend millions of dollars on PR, for smaller companies this form of communication may be the most affordable alternative available.

Many public relations programs require little more than the time and expenses associated with putting the program together and getting it distributed, yet they still accomplish their objectives.

Avoidance of Clutter Because they are typically perceived as news items, public relations messages are not subject to the clutter of ads. A story regarding a new product introduction or breakthrough is treated as a news item and is likely to receive attention.

Lead Generation Information about technological innovations, medical breakthroughs, and the like results almost immediately in a multitude of inquiries. These inquiries may give the firm some quality sales leads.

Reach Specific Audiences Because some products appeal to only small market segments, it is not feasible to engage in advertising and/or promotions to reach them. If the firm does not have the financial capabilities to engage in promotional expenditures, the best way to communicate to these groups is through public relations.

Image Building Effective public relations helps to develop a positive image for the organization. The examples discussed thus far have indicated strong image building capabilities with proactive public relations.

Exhibit 14–2
Olympus capitalizes on positive publicity in its advertising

419

LIMITATIONS OF PUBLIC RELATIONS

Weaker Brand or Corporate Identification Effect Perhaps the major disadvantage of public relations is the potential for not completing the communications process. While public relations messages can break through the clutter of commercials, the receiver may not make the connection to the source. Many firms' PR efforts are never associated with their sponsors in the public mind.

Inconsistent Message Public relations may also misfire through mismanagement and a lack of coordination with the marketing department. When marketing and PR departments operate independently, there is a danger of inconsistent communications, redundancies in efforts, and so on.

PUBLIC RELATIONS PLAN

Public relations is an ongoing process requiring formalized policies and procedures for dealing with problems and opportunities. Just as you would not develop an advertising and/or promotions program without a plan, you should not institute public relations efforts haphazardly. Moreover, the public relations plan needs to be integrated into the overall marketing communications program. A public relations plan can be structured like the other IMC tools we have discussed thus far. It starts with a situation analysis and includes decisions with respect to target audiences, behavioural objectives, communication objectives, strategy, and tactics. Once the plan is written, marketers should ask themselves some of the questions in Figure 14–1 to determine whether their public relations plan is complete. Given the broad nature of public relations, there are many options for each part of the plan that we now discuss.

SITUATION ANALYSIS

Some elements of the situation analysis from the marketing plan or IMC plan are reviewed. An additional key piece of information is a current assessment of people's attitudes toward the firm, its product or service, or specific issues beyond those directed at a product or service. Why are firms so concerned with the public's attitudes?

One reason is that these attitudes may affect sales of the firm's products. A number of companies have experienced sales declines as a result of consumer boycotts. Procter & Gamble, Coors, and Nike are just a few companies that responded to organized pressures. Second, no one wants to be perceived as a bad citizen. Corporations exist in communities, and their employees may both work and live there. Negative attitudes carry over to employee morale and may result in a less-than-optimal working environment internally and in the community.

Due to their concerns about public perceptions, many privately held corporations, publicly held companies, utilities, and the media survey public attitudes. The reasons for conducting this research are many:

- *It provides input into the planning process.* Once the firm has determined public attitudes, they become the starting point in the development of programs designed to maintain favourable positions or change unfavourable ones.
- *It serves as an early warning system.* Once a problem exists, it may require substantial time and money to correct. By conducting research, the firm may be able to identify potential problems and handle them effectively before they become serious issues.
- *It secures support internally.* If research shows that a problem or potential problem exists, it will be much easier for the public relations arm to gain the support it needs to address this problem.
- *It increases the effectiveness of the communication.* The better it understands a problem, the better the firm can design communications to deal with it.[8]

FIGURE 14–1

Ten questions for evaluating public relations plans

1. Does the plan reflect a thorough understanding of the company's business situation?
2. Has the PR program made good use of research and background sources?
3. Does the plan include full analysis of recent editorial coverage?
4. Do the PR people fully understand the product's strengths and weaknesses?
5. Does the PR program describe several cogent, relevant conclusions from the research?
6. Are the program objectives specific and measurable?
7. Does the program clearly describe what the PR activity will be and how it will benefit the company?
8. Does the program describe how its results will be measured?
9. Do the research, objectives, activities, and evaluations tie together?
10. Has the PR department communicated with marketing throughout the development of the program?

DETERMINE RELEVANT TARGET AUDIENCES

The targets of public relations efforts may vary, with different objectives for each. Some may be directly involved in selling the product; others may affect the firm in a different way (e.g., they may be aimed at stockholders or legislators). These audiences may be internal or external to the firm.

Internal audiences may include the employees of the firm, stockholders and investors, members of the local community, suppliers, and current customers. Why are community members and customers of the firm considered internal rather than external? According to John Marston, it's because these groups are already connected with the organization in some way and the firm normally communicates with them in the ordinary routine of work.[9]

External audiences are those people who are not closely connected with the organization (e.g., the public at large). It may be necessary to communicate with both groups on an ongoing basis for a variety of reasons.

McGraw-Hill Ryerson Limited
2001 Annual Report
www.mcgrawhill.ca

Exhibit 14–3
Annual reports serve a variety of purposes

Employees of the Firm   Maintaining morale and showcasing the results of employees' efforts are often prime objectives of the public relations program. Organizational newsletters, notices on bulletin boards, paycheck envelope stuffers, direct mail, and annual reports are some of the methods used to communicate with these groups. Personal methods of communicating may be as formal as an established grievance committee or as informal as an office Christmas party. Other social events, such as corporate sports teams or picnics, are also used to create goodwill.

Stockholders and Investors   You may think an annual report like the one in Exhibit 14–3 just provides stockholders and investors with financial information regarding the firm. While this is one purpose, annual reports are also a communications channel for informing this audience about why the firm is or is not doing well, future plans, and other information that goes beyond numbers.

For example, McDonald's has successfully used annual reports to fend off potential PR problems. One year the report described McDonald's recycling efforts to alleviate consumers' concerns about waste; another report included a 12-page spread on food and nutrition. Other companies use similar strategies, employing shareholders' meetings, video presentations, and other forms of direct mail. General Motors' annual public interest report is sent to shareholders and community members to detail the company's high standards of corporate responsibility. Companies have used these approaches to generate additional investments, to bring more of their stocks "back home" (i.e., become more locally controlled and managed), and to produce funding to solve specific problems, as well as to promote goodwill.

Community Members   People who live and work in the community where a firm is located or doing business are often the target of public relations efforts. Such efforts may involve ads informing the community of activities that the organization is engaged in—for example, reducing air pollution, cleaning up water supplies, or, as shown in Exhibit 14–4, protecting turtles. (As you can see, the community can be defined very broadly.) Demonstrating to people that the organization is a good citizen with their welfare in mind may also be a reason for communicating to these groups.

Racing To
The Moon.

Chevron
People Do.
www.peopledo.com

Exhibit 14–4
Chevron demonstrates
concern for the public

Suppliers and Customers   An organization wishes to maintain *goodwill* with its suppliers as well as its consuming public. If consumers think a company is not socially conscious, they may take their loyalties elsewhere. Suppliers may be inclined to do the same. Indirect indications of the success of PR efforts may include more customer loyalty, less antagonism, or greater cooperation between the firm and its suppliers or consumers. Historically, most people viewed public relations as a communications strategy to maintain customers. Cisco, Novell, and Sony recently used public relations effectively to attract new Canadian customers in their distribution channels. Each firm experienced substantial sales increases with specific tools to reach particular audiences that had not perceived the benefits offered.[10]

The Media   Perhaps one of the most critical external publics is the media, which determine what you will read in your newspapers or see on TV, and how this news will be presented. Because of the media's power, they should be informed of the firm's actions. Companies issue press releases and communicate through conferences, interviews, and special events. The media are generally receptive to such information so long as it is handled professionally; reporters are always interested in good stories.

Educators   A number of organizations provide educators with information regarding their activities. The Canadian Marketing Association and the Promotional Products Association of Canada, among others, keep educators informed in an attempt to generate goodwill as well as exposure for their causes. These groups and major corporations provide information regarding innovations, state-of-the-art research, and other items of interest.

Educators are a target audience because, like the media, they control the flow of information to certain parties—in this case, people like you. Magazines such as *Canadian Business* and *The Economist* attempt to have professors use them in their classes. In addition to selling more magazines, such usage would also lend credibility to the mediums.

Civic and Business Organizations   The local nonprofit civic organizations also serve as gatekeepers of information. Companies' financial contributions to these groups, speeches at organization functions, and sponsorships are all designed to create goodwill. Corporate executives' service on the boards of nonprofit organizations also generates positive public relations.

Governments   Public relations often attempts to influence government bodies directly at both local and national levels. Successful lobbying may mean immediate success for a product, while regulations detrimental to the firm may cost it millions.

Financial Groups   In addition to current shareholders, potential shareholders and investors may be relevant target markets. Financial advisors, lending institutions, and others must be kept abreast of new developments as well as financial information, since they offer the potential for new sources of funding. Press releases and corporate reports play an important role in providing information to these publics.

BEHAVIOURAL OBJECTIVES

The framework for behavioural objectives discussed in Chapter 4 is readily applicable for public relations. Recall that behavioural objectives are trial purchase, repeat purchase, purchase-related action, or consumption. No matter what target audiences are selected in the prior step, an astute marketer will know that it is important to understand the type of behaviour desired as a result of the communication. The idea of a "purchase" seems incongruous for some public relations situations, so the marketer may have to view this as the target audience "buying into the idea" or some other specific behaviour in order to carefully define the objectives.

COMMUNICATION OBJECTIVES

Similarly, the communication objectives of Chapter 4 can be used for public relations. Communication objectives include category need, brand awareness, brand attitude, purchase intention, and purchase facilitation. Each of these can be the focus of the public relations plan, although slight modifications are needed. For example, the "brand" may in fact be the corporation itself or a new product that is talked about in a press release. In addition, the notion of a "category" has to be adjusted. Some target audiences want to be affiliated with "good corporate citizens" that are responsible to the community, the environment, or some other issue. Often then, the "category" will be related to the particular topic or focus of the public relations message.

Awareness is critical for a brand and is important for the organization. Many organizations engage in various social causes because the exposure of their name will enhance the general public's recall and recognition at a later point in time.

We started off by highlighting the importance of existing attitudes of the target audiences. Clearly then, the public relations plan should have a specific section that outlines the attitude change or modification desired. It should also illustrate the key motives addressed and what attributes or benefits of the firm or product that the message should focus on.

STRATEGY

The strategy decisions for public relations are twofold, as we saw with advertising: message and media. The primary message decisions concern the degree to which the message will have a marketing or corporation focus, and the creative associated with the message. We will briefly describe some issues related to this decision in this section. Like advertising, there are a number of options to disseminate the message, news media, advertising media, and events. We will discuss these in more detail in the next major section.

Focus of the Message   Thomas L. Harris has referred to public relations activities designed to support marketing objectives as **marketing public relations (MPR)** functions.[11] Marketing objectives that may be aided by public relations activities include raising awareness, informing and educating, gaining understanding, building trust, giving consumers a reason to buy, and generating consumer acceptance. These points are consistent with the behavioural and communication objective of our framework. Marketing public relations can be used effectively in the following ways:

- Building marketplace excitement before media advertising breaks.
- Creating news about a new advertising or promotional campaign.
- Introducing a product with little or no advertising.
- Influencing the influentials—that is, providing information to opinion leaders.
- Defending products at risk with a message of reassurance.
- Constructively promoting a product.

Ikea Canada's innovative activities successfully increase media exposure and exemplify marketing public relations. In fact, a key source of many zany ideas originated from its consumer surveys—shopping at Ikea was seen as a bit stressful for some couples so it hosted relationship seminars on Valentine's Day. Ikea's Relax event noticed the fact that many Canadians found relaxing to be naughtier than sex. This prompted Ikea to issue instructions for making a restful home along with an "Ikea Adrenaline Index" on their website featuring humourous questions to assess people's stress levels. Store openings and catalogue launches both receive ambitious events to ensure that the media covers the story. Ikea sees the value of these activities and they invest heavily with a 50-percent budget increase as well as each event receiving a $500,000 allotment. IMC Perspective 14–1 shows a few other examples of MPR in action to generate strong word-of-mouth communication.

The historic role of public relations is one of communicating a favourable image of the corporation as a whole. The domain of this image, or reputation management, concerns every facet of how the organization interacts with its many social, economic, political, and charitable constituents, in addition to the general public locally, nationally, and internationally.

Given the two broad directions of the actual message, marketing versus corporate, an organization has to decide the relative degree of the messages' impact over the course of a year or even longer, as public relations tends to have a lasting communication effect. Too much of a focus in either direction and the organization loses the opportunity to communicate fully.

Creative of the Message We will discuss the many tools for public relations shortly; however, in deciding what message to communicate, the marketer is faced with the decision as to whether the creative strategy of advertising or other IMC tools should be adopted for public relations. On the one hand, there is the argument that all communications should have a common look and feel to them. To counter this, one could argue that unique target audiences with a specific message should have an appropriate creative associated with it.

Delivery of the Message In the course of defining public relations and publicity, and explaining the content of a public relations plan, we have generally described two mechanisms for the delivery of the message. Various news media outlets are available and the media has the choice of publishing or not publishing the materials that organizations submit for their consideration. Alternatively, organizations can turn to other options where they control the dissemination of the message through different types of corporate advertising opportunities in which the organization is responsible for the costs, much like regular product advertising we have covered thus far. These two topics are quite involved, have their respective strengths and limitations, and will be discussed in their respective sections subsequently.

TACTICS

The choice of news media or corporate advertising dictates the types of tactics employed. When using news media, a marketer would need to know how to make a media presentation, whom to contact, how to issue a press release, and what to know about each medium addressed, including TV, radio, newspapers, magazines, and direct-response advertising. In addition, decisions regarding alternative media such as news conferences, seminars, events, and personal letters, as well as insights on how to deal with government and other legislative bodies have to be made. Because this information is too extensive to include as a single chapter in this text, we suggest you peruse one of the many books available on this subject for additional insights. For corporate advertising, many tactical considerations have been addressed in Chapter 7. We briefly touch on a few more shortly.

What's the Buzz?

Have you ever wondered why something was all of a sudden popular, like a new brand of shoes or clothing, even though you've never seen any advertising or marketing for it? Ever wonder how you came to simply agree that "this is the in thing" now?

This is "buzz," a strategic meshing of public relations and word of mouth that work together to create awareness and stimulate sales of a product of service. In a *Harvard Business Review* article titled "The Buzz of Buzz" (November/December 2000), author Renée Dye wrote: "Word-of-mouth promotion has become an increasingly potent force, capable of catapulting products from obscurity into runaway commercial success." Innovative companies are using the promotional and brand power of public relations as a competitive advantage to reach you, the consumer, in this cluttered marketplace. For example:

- Lingerie retailer La Senza staged fashion shows on the streets of Toronto.
- Greeting-card retailer Hallmark invited men to watch a movie marathon of *Love Story* to celebrate Father's Day.
- Orange-juice maker Tropicana launched an on-pack tie-in with the movie *Monsters Inc.* to the delight of many kids screaming like monsters.

Marketing public relations programs appears useful for all communications situations: emerging brands, public launches, brand repositioning, and the rejuvenation of mature brands. In all cases, PR can spark perceptual and attitudinal change and result in new positive consumer support for new users, current customers, and competitor's customers. One reason for the recent growth of PR appears to be the weakness of traditional media to reach their target audience effectively. Indeed, some successful PR programs are online as marketers try to attract new customers who are younger.

It seems that word of mouth is still the most trusted form of communication, and PR is the right kind of exposure to generate the kind of communication effects that marketers love: awareness and positive attitude that results in more people spreading the word and presenting the brand within a relevant context. And PR's ability to do this less expensively than other IMC tools makes it a vital part of a marketer's communications plans.

Source: Judy Lewis, "Building Buzz," *Marketing Magazine*, January 28, 2002.

PUBLIC RELATIONS EFFECTIVENESS

As with the other promotional program elements, it is important to evaluate the effectiveness of the public relations efforts. In addition to determining the contribution of this program element to attaining communications objectives, the evaluation tells management:

- How to assess what has been achieved through public relations activities;
- How to measure public relations achievements quantitatively;
- How to judge the quality of public relations achievements and activities.

As shown in Figure 14–2, a number of exposure measures may be used to assess the effects of PR programs through news media. Raymond Simon suggests additional managerial approaches and research methods for accomplishing this evaluation process, including the following:[12]

- *Management by objectives.* Executives and their managers act together to identify communication objectives to be attained and the responsibilities of the managers. These objectives are then used as a standard to measure accomplishments.
- *Matching objectives and results.* Specific communications objectives should be related to actions, activities, or media coverage.
- *Personal observation and reaction.* Personal observation and evaluation by one's superiors should occur at all levels of the organization.

FIGURE 14–2

Criteria for measuring the effectiveness of PR

□ □ □ □ □

A system for measuring the effectiveness of the public relations program has been developed by Lotus HAL. The criteria used in the evaluation process follow:

- Total number of impressions over time
- Total number of impressions on the target audience
- Total number of impressions on specific target audiences
- Percentage of positive articles over time
- Percentage of negative articles over time
- Ratio of positive to negative articles
- Percentage of positive/negative articles by subject
- Percentage of positive/negative articles by publication or reporter
- Percentage of positive/negative articles by target audience

- *Public opinion and surveys.* Research in the form of public opinion surveys may be used to gather data to evaluate program goal attainment.
- *Internal and external audits.* Internal audits involve evaluations by superiors or peers within the firm to determine the performance of the employee (or his or her programs). External audits are conducted by consultants or other parties outside the organization.

Others suggest comprehensive approaches like we have seen with advertising. Walter Lindenmann says three levels of measures are involved: (1) the basic, which measures the actual PR activities undertaken; (2) the intermediate, which measures audience reception and understanding of the message; and (3) the advanced, which measures the perceptual and behavioral changes that result.[13] We remind you that this approach is entirely consistent with the exposure, processing, communications effects model described in Chapter 3. An application of these concepts is conveyed in Figure 14–3, which is a model developed by Ketchum Public Relations for tracking the effects of public relations. Some organizations may use a combination of measures, depending on their specific needs. For example, Hewlett-Packard uses impression counts, awareness and preference studies, in-house assessments, press clippings counts, and tracking studies.[14]

PUBLIC RELATIONS

In this section, we discuss how organizations can acheive public relations communication objectives through publicity generated through news media and consider the strengths and limitations of this option.

NEWS MEDIA OPTIONS

A number of news media options are available for communicating with various target audiences, including press releases, press conferences, exclusives, interviews, and community involvement.

The Press Release One of the most important publics is the press. To be used by the press, information must be factual, true, and of interest to the medium as well as to its audience. The source of the **press release** can do certain things to improve the likelihood that the "news" will be disseminated (see Exhibit 14–5).

Jonathan Schenker of Ketchum Public Relations, New York, suggests four technological methods to make life easier for the press and to increase the likelihood that the media will use your story:

- *Telephone press conferences.* Since reporters cannot always get to a press conference, use the telephone to call them for coverage.
- *In-studio media tours.* Satellite communications providing a story, and a chance to interview, from a central location such as a TV studio save broadcast journalists time and money by eliminating their need to travel.

426

FIGURE 14–3 ☐☐☐☐   The Ketchum Effectiveness Yardstick (KEY); a strategic approach to the measurement of public relations results

At Ketchum, we believe strongly that it is possible to measure public relations effectiveness. We also believe strongly that measuring public relations results can be done in a timely and cost-efficient manner.

Our strategic approach to public relations measurement involves a two-step process:

1. Setting in advance very specific and clearly defined public relations goals and objectives, and,

2. Pinpointing those levels of measurement that are crucial to the organization in determining to what extent those specific public relations goals and objectives have been met.

In the model, there are three levels for measuring PR effectiveness:

- Level #1—the Basic level for measuring public relations OUTPUTS. This measures the amount of exposure an organization receives in the media, the total number of placements, the total number of impressions, and/or the likelihood of having reached specific target audience groups. Research tools often used when conducting Level #1 measurement include content analysis or publicity tracking studies, secondary analysis, segmentation analysis, and basic public opinion polls.

- Level #2—the Intermediate level for measuring public relations OUTGROWTHS. Outgrowths measure whether or not target audience groups actually received the messages directed at them, paid attention to them, understood the messages, and retained those messages in any shape or form. Research tools often used when conducting Level #2 measurement include focus groups; in-depth interviews; telephone, mail, face-to-face, or mall intercept surveys; testing techniques; and recall studies.

- Level #3—the Advanced level for measuring public relations OUTCOMES. This measures opinion, attitude, and/or behaviour change to determine if there has been a shift in views and/or how people act when it comes to an organization, its products, or its services. Research tools often used when conducting Level #3 measurement include before-and-after studies, experimental and quasi-experimental research, ethnographic studies, communications audits, and multivariate analyses of data.

- The different levels of measuring public relations impact can be plotted on a yardstick in a hierarchial fashion. Here is a graphic displaying the KETCHUM EFFECTIVENESS YARDSTICK (KEY), which summarizes from left to right these levels of public relations measurement:

Level #1	Level #2	Level #3
Basic—Measuring	Intermediate—Measuring	Advanced—Measuring
OUTPUTS	OUTGROWTHS	OUTCOMES
Media placements	Receptivity	Opinion change
Impressions	Awareness	Attitude change
Targeted	Comprehension	Behaviour change
Audiences	Retention	

More detailed information about Ketchum's strategic approach to measuring public relations effectiveness may be obtained by contacting Graham Hueber, Vice President and Director of Research at Ketchum.

- *Multicomponent video news releases (VNR).* A five-component package consisting of a complete script in print and on tape, a video release with a live reporter, a local contact source at which to target the video, and a silent video news release that allows the station to fill in with its own news reporter lend an advantage by saving the media money.

- *Targeted newswire stories.* When the sender targets the public relations message, reporters are spared the need to read through volumes of news stories to select those of interest to their target audiences.

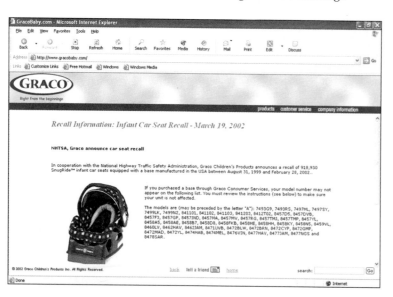

Exhibit 14–5

A Graco press release

The information in a press release won't be used unless it's of interest to the readers of the medium it's sent to. For example, financial institutions may issue press releases to business trade media and to the editor of the business section of a general-interest newspaper. Information on the release of a new rock album is of more interest to radio disk jockeys than to TV newscasters; sports news also has its interested audiences.

Press Conferences We are all familiar with **press conferences** held by political figures. While used less often by organizations and corporations, this form of delivery can be very effective. The topic must be of major interest to a specific group before it is likely to gain coverage. Usually major accomplishments (such as a profit announcement), major breakthroughs (such as medical cures), emergencies, or catastrophes warrant a national press conference. On a local level, community events, local developments, and the like may receive coverage. Companies often call press conferences when they have significant news to announce, such as the introduction of a new product or advertising campaign. Sports teams use this tool to attract fan attention and interest when a new star is signed. TV3, a Malaysian broadcast system, held an international press conference to announce its introduction of an interactive TV service.

A medium sized Canadian company, Atelier America, used media relations to announce its innovative method of reproducing oil on canvas masterpieces. All major U.S. media organizations covered the press conference in New York City. The story circulated through all major U.S. cities and Europe and peaked with coverage on ABC's *World News Tonight* with Peter Jennings. Almost immediately, telephone orders emerged that could be tracked accurately with the media coverage. Previously weak Internet orders reversed overwhelmingly.[15]

Exclusives Although most public relations efforts seek a variety of channels for distribution, an alternative strategy is to offer one particular medium exclusive rights to the story if that medium reaches a substantial number of people in the target audience. Offering an **exclusive** may enhance the likelihood of acceptance. As you watch television over the next few weeks, look for the various networks' and local stations' exclusives. Notice how the media actually use these exclusives to promote themselves.

Interviews When you watch TV or read magazines, pay close attention to the personal interviews. Usually someone will raise specific questions, and a spokesperson provided by the firm will answer them. Ted Rogers often gives interviews pertaining to the many technological divisions that exist in the Rogers communications conglomerate. IMC Perspective 14–2 shows effective use of media interviews by Labatt.

Community Involvement Many corporations enhance their public images through involvement in the local community that are often covered by the media. This involvement may take many forms, including membership in local organizations and contributions to or participation in community events. For example, Rogers' employees work throughout many neighbourhoods on Halloween evening to promote community safety. It also includes organizations participating in emergencies.

A Clear PR Message for Labatt Sterling

The content of a message is a critical advertising decision as well as a significant public relations decision as seen by the recent launch of Labatt Sterling, a beer containing just 2.5 grams of carbohydrates. The increasing health concerns of consumers and the introduction of specialized, brand name diets has resulted in low-carbohydrate niche products in a variety of food categories and beer was no exception in the latter part of 2003.

According to Ipsos-Reid, a leading market research firm, 80 percent of all Canadians believed a low-carb diet could be part of their efforts towards weight reduction, and 61 percent indicated that they tried to minimize their carbohydrate consumption to avoid gaining weight. One expert believed this research signalled a fundamental change in the diets of Canadian consumers, not just a passing fad, and that marketers needed to approach the marketing and communication appropriately.

Labatt was up for the challenge for its new brand. Since most brands of premium domestic beer contained between 11 to 17 grams of carbohydrates, Labatt recognized the importance of finding the right message. Labatt did not want to focus on the health issues of carbohydrates, nor did they want to address the issue of good/bad carbohydrates. Instead, they made it clear that most beers did not have high carbohydrate levels to begin with and that consumers now had a choice on the level of carbohydrates they could

consume. This approach appeared better than claiming carbohydrates are a problem and Sterling is a low-carbohydrate solution.

To communicate this critical message, Labatt turned to public relations through many media interviews that generated over 20 million impressions across Canada. A television spot supported the public relations a few months later, but success had already been achieved with the initial part of the campaign. With only public relations communicating its message, Labatt sold 85,000 six-packs in the first week, causing shortages in three provinces. It obtained 1 percent of the overall beer market and likely converted those who had stopped drinking beer in order to avoid the carbohydrates completely.

Labatt received additional message support from the Brewers Association of Canada that conducted a media and public relations campaign at the same time. It communicated that many of the dietary concerns associated with beer were due to the food consumed while drinking beer, not the beer itself. The association's plan of a dietician explaining that a glass of orange juice has more carbohydrates than beer on shows like *Canada AM* complemented Labatt's public relations message perfectly.

Source: Chris Daniels, "Carb-Charged Communications," *Marketing Magazine*, March 1, 2004.

STRENGTHS OF NEWS MEDIA

Highly Credible Unlike advertising and sales promotion, publicity is not usually perceived as being sponsored by the company. So consumers perceive this information as more objective and place more confidence in it. Ethical Perspective 14–3, featuring Nestlé, shows this point clearly.

Endorsement Publicity information may be perceived as endorsed by the medium in which it appears. For example, an article on the durability of a new golf ball reported by *Golf* magazine reflects its authentication. *Car & Driver*'s award for car of the year reflects the magazine's perception of the quality of the auto selected.

Nestlé Listens to Its Customers and Does the Right Thing

Nestlé Canada's quick reversal in 2001 of its plans to stop manufacturing its chocolate bars in a peanut-and nut-free environment is a smart business decision. It was an all-too-rare instance where a company actually listened to consumer feedback and acted in a way that, in the short term, probably limits its flexibility. In the long term, though, Nestlé's bold move will likely pay off in spades in terms of consumer goodwill, and the whole experience appears to have given it a leg up in developing, and in fact cornering, an unexplored market segment and marketing proposition.

When Nestlé announced in late April 2001 that, as of January 2002, it would no longer guarantee that Smarties, Aero, Kit Kat, Coffee Crisp, and Mirage chocolates would be produced in a nut-free environment, there was an air of inevitability to it. Consumer demand for chocolate products containing nuts is, in fact, on the rise, and the company wanted the flexibility to be able to use the same facility to produce them as is used for the non-nut products. But once you have nuts running through the machinery, and nut particles floating in the air, it's virtually impossible to ensure that trace elements of nuts aren't in something. An estimated 150 to 200 people die each year in North America because of anaphylaxis, in essence of severe asthmatic reaction to foods, most notably nuts. And unlike, say, the risks of tobacco smoke, which can take decades to do its damage, contact with even a particle of a nut can trigger an attack.

So, better safe than sorry, Nestlé embarked on a PR and outreach effort to alert the public of the change. It was just one of the realities of business these days. For the sake of competitive advantage and efficiencies, the consumer loses some choices, and we're all a bit diminished by the reduction in options. But, hey, it's only a candy bar and who can argue the business logic?

But as Nestlé almost instantly began to hear in literally thousands of phone calls, letters, and e-mails that it received in the wake of its announcement, while the portion of the population directly affected by nut allergies is small—maybe 2.5 percent, or 600,000 to 700,000 Canadians—the universe of those impacted by the problem is huge and growing. It learned that just about every place where kids congregate, such as schools, day care centres, summer camps, and clubs such as Scouts and Guides, is becoming increasingly sensitized to the dangers and is restricting foods with peanuts.

Nestlé was also surprised to learn from those that were contacting it that their products had, in fact, been the only

major chocolate brands still offering safety for those with nut allergies. In effect, a move in the name of internal efficiency and production flexibility was mushrooming into a situation where the company was snatching candy from allergic kids. Further, the company was contacted by people who hadn't realized that Nestlé's products were nut-free, and now that they did know, would love to be able to buy them.

Still, the public reaction was so far under the radar that it was a surprise, albeit a pleasant one, to hear that the company was changing its plans after just three weeks—a decision so sudden that it was unable to keep off store shelves the new packaging warning that products were no longer nut-free.

The lobbying effort, such as it was, was more a wave of simultaneous personal reactions rather than any orchestrated assault. Yes, one Toronto man set up a website (www.savethesmarties.com) to rally opposition to the move, and spokespeople for various allergy bodies publicly urged the company to change its mind; but for the most part, the company was inundated with individuals telling stories about how the decision would impact family and friends.

"We have been truly overwhelmed by the emotional chord that our original decision struck with consumers," said Graham Lute, Nestlé's senior vice president of consumer communications, meals, beverages and dairy, corporate affairs, and market intelligence, in a May 14 release announcing the change of heart. "We've listened to consumers and moved quickly to reverse our original decision. We will pursue other options to satisfy the growing segment of consumers who want peanut/nut chocolate products."

The media reaction to the move was downright glowing. Positive pieces appeared in all the major papers and the leader of the Anaphylaxis Network could be heard on CBC Radio praising Nestlé for its sensitivity and urging people to buy its products.

Nestlé clearly will have to incur unplanned-for costs to set up a new facility to produce products with nuts, but if it can tastefully capitalize on the consumer goodwill and awareness generated by its adept handling of the peanut problem, it may well come out ahead of the game. But even if there is no huge payback, the company deserves high praise for simply doing the right thing at the right time.

Source: Adapted from Stan Sutter, "Not Just Peanuts," *Marketing Magazine*, June 11, 2001. Used with permission.

Frequency Potential Still another reason for publicity's power is the frequency of exposure it generates. For example, a successful public relations activity could generate exposure in multiple media (i.e., broadcast, print, Internet).

LIMITATIONS OF NEWS MEDIA

Timing Timing of the publicity through news media is not always completely under the control of the marketer. Unless the press thinks the information has very high news value, the timing of the press release is entirely up to the media—if it gets released at all. Thus, the information may be released earlier than desired or too late to make an impact.

Accuracy The information contained in the press release sometimes gets lost in translation—that is, it is not always reported the way the provider wishes it to be. As a result, inaccurate information, omissions, or other errors may result. Sometimes when you see a publicity piece that was written on the basis of a press release, you wonder if the two are even about the same topic.

CORPORATE ADVERTISING

The term **corporate advertising** tends to be used as a catchall for any type of advertising run for the direct benefit of the corporation rather than its products or services. For purposes of this text we use it to describe any type of advertising designed to promote the organization itself rather than its products or services. Corporate advertising is targeted at both internal and external audiences and involves the promotion of the organization as well as its ideas. Marketers seek attainment of corporate advertising's objectives by implementing image, advertising, cause-related advertising, and sponsorship. We cover these three topics in this section, but first we look at the reason for corporate advertising, namely the management of corporate reputation and the concerns of corporate advertising.

CORPORATE REPUTATION

Earlier in this text we suggested that the communications framework described for advertising can be applied to other communication tools, and previously in this chapter we highlighted that it can be used for various public relations tools. This thought is echoed with a summary of the planning process used by executives of a leading public relations firm, Fleishman-Hillard Canada, in its efforts to assist clients with reputation management:[16]

- Gain a detailed, forward-looking understanding of corporate business objectives, competitive positioning, and the desired corporate reputation or corporate brand. This is best accomplished through interviews with senior corporate and business unit executives.
- Define the key audience, derive audience-specific behavioural and attitudinal objectives, and audience-specific corporate positioning attributes.
- Assess current perceptions of the company held by each key stakeholder group or audience on each of the key reputational attributes.
- Implement reputation-management programs throughout the corporation.
- Establish an ongoing plan to measure and monitor corporate reputation, and use reputation measurement to refine communications programs.

We highlight the issue of corporate reputation, a term that is used in public relations to convey the idea of corporate image, since a key outcome of corporate advertising is to influence overall perceptions of the organization. Clearly, the notion of corporate reputation is attitudinal thus indicating that the general framework suggested in this text can be applied to all IMC tools. Furthermore, all methods described in Chapter 8 (e.g., focus groups, interviews, surveys) are readily applied for measuring corporate advertising effectiveness

It is clear that many believe corporate reputation to be a very important characteristic as shown by an annual survey of Canadian CEOs, sponsored by KPMG, which ranks many of Canada's top firms (Figure 14–4). RBC Financial Group reached the top recently in this evaluation of corporations along nine key attributes: best long-term investment value, innovation and product/service development, human resource management, financial performance, corporate social responsibility, high quality service/product, corporate governance, customer service, and overall most respected.

Shell Canada improved its reputation with its current communications program that emphasized its sustainable development policies. After it launched the initial ads in the winter of 2002, Shell Canada's internal "favourability index" improved by several percentage points. A more recent campaign initiated in the fall of 2003 continued the theme of Shell Canada employees talking about their jobs in relation to the environment. In addition, print ads accentuated the importance of balancing profit and principles and portrayed Shell Canada as a company of ethical employees.[17] The contrast between KPMG's rankings and Shell Canada's own results indicates the difficulty in carefully managing corporate advertising and that the results are dependent upon the criteria used to assess its effectiveness.

CONCERNS

Corporate advertising is one of the more controversial forms of advertising. Since it is designed to promote the firm overall—by enhancing its image, assuming a position on a social issue or cause, or seeking direct involvement in something—there appears to be multiple interpretations as to its purpose which gives rise to a few concerns.

Minimal Consumer Interest A Gallup and Robinson study reported in *Advertising Age* found consumers were 35 percent less interested in corporate ads than in product-oriented advertising.[18] This may be because consumers do not understand the reasons behind such ads.

Rank				Score *		
2003	2002	2001	Company	2003	2002	2001
1	1	2	RBC Financial Group	983	1106	589
2	7	147	WestJet Airlines Ltd.	357	217	6
3	3	3	BCE Inc.	344	320	413
4	5	7	Loblaw Companies Ltd.	251	266	136
5	2	1	Bombardier Inc.	227	463	841
6	8	6	Research in Motion Ltd.	196	199	149
7	12	24	The Bank of Nova Scotia	179	170	49
8	19	-	EnCana Corporation	151	147	-
9	20	14	BMO Financial Group	150	148	77
10	4	8	Magna International Inc.	145	271	114
11	23	30	Canadian Tire Corporation Ltd.	141	114	43
12	17	18	Suncor Energy Inc.	140	149	60
13	16	10	Canadian Imperial Bank of Commerce	135	155	104
14	22	-	Four Seasons Hotels and Resorts	133	129	-
15	18	41	Manulife Financial Corporation	129	151	34
16	6	23	Dofasco Inc.	106	230	51
17	11	38	Wal-Mart Canada Corp.	104	173	38
18	9	5	TD Bank Financial Group/TD Canada Trust	103	183	209
19	24	21	GE Canada Inc.	99	113	54
20	15	25	Microsoft Canada Co.	92	157	48
20	13	29	Canadian National Railway Co.	92	44	52
21	41	4	Nortel Networks Ltd.	90	43	373
22	10	13	IBM Canada Ltd.	88	176	81
23	33	245	Enbridge Inc.	82	60	1
24	35	51	TransCanada PipeLines Ltd.	81	57	15
25	30	24	Petro-Canada	75	75	49

Source: Ninth annual survey of Canada's most respected corporations, KPMG, 2003.

FIGURE 14–4

The 25 most admired and respected Canadian corporations as ranked by Canadian CEOs

Costly Form of Self-Indulgence Firms have been accused of engaging in corporate image advertising only to satisfy the egos of top management. This argument stems from the fact that corporate ads are not easy to write. The message to be communicated is not as precise and specific as one designed to position a product, so the top managers often dictate the content of the ad, and the copy reflects their ideas and images of the corporation.

The Firm Must be in Trouble Some critics believe the only time firms engage in corporate advertising is when they are in trouble—either in a financial sense or in the public eye—and are advertising to attempt to remedy the problem.

Poor Expenditure Given that the ads do not directly appeal to anyone, are not understood, and do not promote anything specific, critics say the monies could be better spent in other areas. Again, much of this argument has its foundation in the fact that corporate image ads are often intangible. They typically do not ask directly for a purchase; they do not ask for investors. Rather, they present a position or try to create an image. Because they are not specific, many critics believe their purpose is lost on the audience and these ads are not a wise investment of the firm's resources.

IMAGE ADVERTISING

One form of corporate advertising is devoted to promoting the organization's overall image. **Image advertising** may accomplish a number of objectives, including

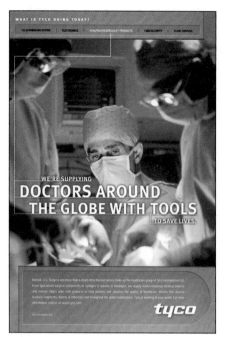

Exhibit 14–6
Tyco uses image advertising to avoid confusion

creating goodwill both internally and externally, creating a position for the company, specifying a firm's perspective on an issue, and generating resources, both human and financial.

Positioning As shown in Exhibit 14–6, ads are often designed to create an image of the firm in the public mind. The exhibit shows how Tyco is attempting to create an image of itself as a market leader and health care expert, not a toy company.

This type of advertising also occurs when a company changes its name. In 2001, Andersen Consulting became Accenture, while Mutual Life Insurance became Clarica. Accenture was part of a worldwide makeover of 178 offices costing $263 million with 50 separate marketing teams. The Canadian team used public relations, direct mail to clients, and consumer print and TV ads created by an American agency. Clarica is the Latin root word for "clear" and that became the focus of all advertising messages, both print and television, as consumers truly wanted clear financial choices. Naturally, Clarica created a clear image of the "new" company through its corporate advertising efforts.[19]

Television Sponsorship A firm often runs corporate image advertising on TV programs or specials. For example, the Hallmark or IBM specials and documentaries on network TV are designed to promote the corporation as a good citizen. By associating itself with high-quality or educational programming, the firm hopes for a carryover effect that benefits its own image.

According to John Bennett, senior VP for international marketing communications, the sponsorships are designed to fulfill specific business objectives while providing support for the recipients.[20] Exhibit 14–7 shows a few organizations that decided a Juno Awards sponsorship would be good for them.

Exhibit 14–7
Some Juno Awards sponsors

Recruitment The promotional piece presented in Exhibit 14–8 is a good example of corporate image advertising designed to attract new employees. If you are a graduating senior considering a career in the new Internet economy, this ad, promoting a corporate image for the company, will interest you.

The employment section of most major metropolitan newspapers is an excellent place to see this form of corporate image advertising at work. Notice the ads in these papers and consider the images the firms are presenting.

Financial Support Some corporate advertising is designed to generate investments in the corporation. By creating a more favourable image, the firm makes itself attractive to potential stock purchasers and investors. More investments mean more working capital, more monies for research and development, and so on. In this instance, corporate image advertising is almost attempting to make a sale; the product is the firm.

Advocacy Firms often take positions on certain social, business, or environmental issues that influence its image and the public's perception. Such **advocacy advertising** is concerned with propagating ideas and elucidating controversial social issues of public importance in a manner that supports the interests of the sponsor.[21]

While still portraying an image for the company or organization, advocacy advertising does so indirectly, by adopting a position on a particular issue rather than promoting the organization itself. The ads may be sponsored by a firm or by a trade association and are designed to tell readers how the firm operates or management's position on a particular issue.

The reason for the advertising can be due to the firm's negative publicity, the firm's inability to place an important message through public relations channels, or the firm just wants to get certain ideas accepted or have society understand its concerns.

CAUSE-RELATED ADVERTISING

An increasingly popular method of image building is **cause-related marketing**, in which companies link with charities or nonprofit organizations as contributing sponsors. The company benefits from favourable publicity, while the charity receives much-needed funds. Spending on cause-related marketing has increased considerably in the past decade. Proponents of cause marketing say that association with a cause may differentiate one brand or store from another, increase consumer acceptance of price increases, generate favourable publicity, and even win over skeptical officials who may have an impact on the company.[22]

Cause marketing relationships can take a variety of forms. Making outright donations to a nonprofit cause, having companies volunteer for the cause, donating materials or supplies, running public service announcements, or even providing event refreshments are some of the ways companies get involved. KitchenAid found a unique way to get involved with the Canadian Breast Cancer Foundation. Its consumers hosted at-home parties and their guests donated money instead of bringing the host a gift (e.g., bottle of wine, flowers). Hosts could browse "cookforthecure.ca" for recipes, etc. and submit the funds that were raised (see Exhibit 14–9). Success for this program is attributed to thorough competitive and consumer analysis that indicated it would resonate with its customers.[23]

While companies receive public relations benefits from their association with causes, with 80 percent of consumers saying they have a more positive impression of companies that support a cause, they sometimes receive financial rewards as well.[24] An Ipsos-Reid poll illustrated the current benefits that Canadians regard as socially responsible activities:

- 76 percent of Canadians think Canadian companies are doing a good job in terms of doing business in a socially responsible way (14 percent say companies are doing a "very good" job, while 62 percent say companies are doing a "somewhat good" job).
- 23 percent give Canadian companies poor marks (16 percent say companies are doing a "somewhat poor" job and 6 percent say they are doing a "very poor" job).
- 55 percent say they have consciously decided to buy a product or service from one company over another because they felt the company was a good corporate citizen, while 52 percent have consciously refused to buy a product or a service from a company not conducting business in a socially responsible way.
- While Canadians want to see companies operate in a socially responsible manner, they do question the motives of companies who

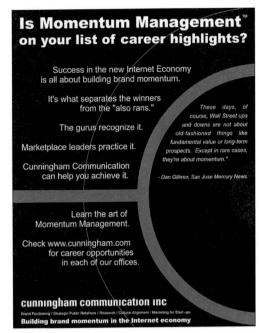

Exhibit 14–8
An ad designed to attract new employees

Exhibit 14–9
KitchenAid supports the fight against breast cancer

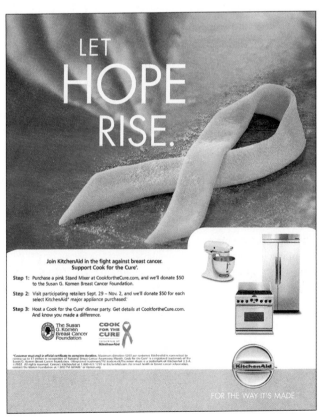

undertake socially responsible activities (68 percent think companies are motivated by their bottom line, while 29 percent say companies care about being socially responsible).

- However, Canadians like good news (68 percent say that a corporate social responsibility news story about a company being singled out for a very positive action is more likely to grab their attention than a story about a company being highlighted for a very negative action).
- Women are more likely than men to want to read about a company's positive action (71 percent versus 64 percent).[25]

At the same time, not all cause marketing is a guarantee of success. Cause marketing requires more than just associating with a social issue, and it takes time and effort. Companies can get into trouble by misleading consumers about their relationships. It is also possible to waste money by hooking up with a cause that offers little connection or relation to their brand. Firms need to avoid picking the wrong cause—finding that their customers and potential customers either have little interest in or don't like the cause. Finally, the results of cause-marketing efforts can sometimes be hard to quantify. IMC Perspective 14–4 describes Canon Canada's efforts for an important cause.

SPONSORSHIP

Corporate sponsorships of charities and causes has become a popular form of public relations. While some companies sponsor specific events and/or causes with primarily traditional public relations objectives in mind, a separate and more marketing-oriented use of sponsorships is also on the increase. Such **event sponsorships** take on a variety of forms, as shown in Figure 14–5. In response to the growth of sponsorship, industry members recently established the Sponsorship Marketing Council of Canada to demonstrate sponsorship as a valuable communication tool by establishing practices and measurement tools to validate the investment.[26]

Sports receives the majority of event sponsorship monies. Among the most popular sporting events for sponsorship are auto racing, golf and tennis tournaments, and running events. Professional sports leagues and teams as well as Olympic teams and competitions also receive large amounts of sponsorship money. Bicycle racing, beach volleyball, skiing, and various water sports are also attracting corporate sponsorship. Traditionally, tobacco, beer, and car companies have been among the largest sports event sponsors. Now a number of other companies have become involved in event sponsorships, including beverage companies, airlines, telecommunications and financial services companies, and high-tech firms.

As expected, there are a number of specific decisions associated with event sponsorship including the types of sponsorship, target audience fit, target audience exposure, and brand positioning. We explore these important sponsorship decisions in the context of sports sponsorship for illustrative purposes since it is the dominant

FIGURE 14–5

Annual sponsorship spending in North America by property ($ millions)

☐ ☐ ☐ ☐ ☐

	1996	1997	1998	1999	2002
Sports	$3,540	$3,840	$4,556	$5,100	$6,430
Entertainment tours and attractions	566	650	680	756	865
Festivals, fairs, events	512	558	612	685	834
Causes	485	535	544	630	828
Arts	323	354	408	460	610
Total	$5,426	$5,937	$6,800	$7,631	$9,567

Source: Adapted from *Promo*, June 1, 2002.

Canon Helps Child Find

One of the most important aids for parents when searching for their missing child is a recent, high quality photograph. With that in mind, Canon Canada and Child Find Ontario, an agency with a tremendous achievement in keeping children safe and helping locate them when missing, teamed up to provide parents the opportunity to protect their child's safety.

To help the cause, Canon Canada donated six high-resolution digital cameras, six Bubble Jet direct photo printers, printing supplies, and $15,000 for financial support. Parents could visit a KidCheck I.D. location throughout Ontario and receive a package that included the picture produced from Canon's equipment. And with approximately 66,000 cases of missing children reported to police each year, the recorded information and photograph could help locate the children faster or improve upon the 90-percent recovery rate.

An impetus for this community involvement in Canada was Canon USA's work with the National Center for Missing and Exploited Children in the United States. As part of the process, Canon Canada met with many different agencies but chose Child Find Ontario and its strong record of successfully finding missing children.

The Canadian initiative connected with the very essence of Canon's corporate philosophy known as Kyosei, meaning "individuals and corporations working together for the common good." According to Stanley Skorayko, vice-president of corporate communications for Canon Canada, "We are extremely pleased and proud to be in a position to provide assistance to families in such a meaningful way, even though we hope and pray that they never have to be used to locate a missing child."

Source: Wayne Doyle, "Pictures To Put Away," *Marketing Magazine*, July 28, 2003.

expenditure and is projected to hit over $10 billion in North America in 2004. Each of these ideas can be readily adapted to other events (i.e., entertainment, festivals, or arts). Sport sponsorship can be successful with clear objectives, a good positioning strategy, adequate budget, appropriate sporting vehicle, and key tactical implementation, similar characteristics that we have seen in other types of promotional plans.[27]

Types of Sponsorship Sport sponsorship involves endorsement deals or sponsoring a team, league, event, athlete or organization, along with stadium naming or broadcast rights. The goal is to associate a brand with its target audience's entertainment consumption or lifestyle, thus enriching the overall brand experience. One thought on the topic suggested three levels of sponsorship.[28] Proprietary has little or no external sanctioning or partnerships. Nike's RunTO featured a running event throughout the entire city of Toronto. Affiliated advertising utilizes the assets of a sponsorship or association. For example, the Esso Legends of Hockey brings together the Hockey Hall of Fame, NHL, NHLPA, and NHL Alumni. Programming lives within a larger event or sponsorship, for example, Powerade's "Thirst for Soccer" that visits youth soccer tournaments across Canada.

Sole sponsorship of a team is not a priority for every sponsorship arrangement. The Toronto Rock, a member of the National Lacrosse League (NLL) since 1998, represents one unique recent success story since many brands were involved right from the start. Sports sponsorship contributed to its early success for the team since the high profile brands provided much needed financial support and credibility. More recently, the team listens to the marketing and communication goals of the sponsor and customizes the sponsorship package. Therefore, it is no surprise to see that the Toronto Rock has many partners as shown in Figure 14–6.[29]

FIGURE 14–6

On a roll: The Toronto Rock's big-league sponsor list

□ □ □ □ □

- American Express
- Bic
- BMO Nesbitt Burns
- Bosch
- Brine
- Budget Car Rental
- Colgate
- Fitness Depot
- Future Shop
- Gait/Debeer
- Gatorade
- GO Transit
- Hotcool Wear
- Jetsgo

- Joe Badali's
- Loblaws
- Mazda
- Molson
- Mr. Sub
- Music World
- Nike
- Pennzoil
- Pizza Pizza
- Playstation
- Power Water
- Proline
- Sportsnet
- The Armadillo

- The FAN 590
- The Score Television Network
- The Westin Harbour Castle
- Tim Hortons
- *Toronto Sun*
- Toshiba
- Toyota
- Universal Home Video
- Wendy's
- Woodbine Entertainment
- Yamaha

Working with an athletic sponsorship is similar to sponsorship with a team, but we see a few unique issues. Foremost is ensuring a fit between the athlete and the company or brand. Exposure arrangements regarding an athlete's identity (e.g., name, image, and likeness), amount and type of service, and corporate logo placement need to be established. The strategic communication use of an athlete in advertising, public relations, or sales promotion and conditions such as investment protection (e.g., ethics clause) rounds out the arrangement.[30]

Brand Positioning Many companies are attracted to event sponsorships because effective IMC programs can be built around them and promotional tie-ins can be made to local, regional, national, and even international markets. Companies are finding event sponsorships an excellent platform from which to build equity and gain affinity with target audiences as well as a good public relations tool for the corporation in general.

While the overall market position of the brand may be well established throughout the marketing plan, sport sponsorship permits a brand positioning strategy to a unique and well-defined target audience that the brand has specific communication and behavioural objectives. For example, a sports sponsorship could enable a brand to establish awareness and new brand associations as it reaches new customers to develop trial purchases.

However, brands should be prepared to spend accordingly to achieve their objectives, as the initial sponsorship investment requires additional advertising or sales promotion expenditures. As the foundation is critical, brands should ensure that the rights and benefits of the sports sponsorship allow the brand to achieve its objectives and positioning. For example, sponsorship in hockey can have limits without the clearance from various stakeholders (e.g., NHL, NHLPA, and Hockey Canada). Finally, picking the right sponsorship that has the right profile at the right time and a partner that is receptive to making the deal work is paramount for successful implementation.

Target Audience Fit Most companies focus their marketing efforts on specific market segments and are always looking for ways to reach these target audiences. Many marketers are finding that event sponsorships are very effective ways to reach specific target audiences based on geographic, demographic, psychographic, and ethnic characteristics. For example, golf tournaments are a popular event for sponsorship by marketers of luxury automobiles and other upscale products and services. The golf audience is affluent and highly educated, and marketers believe that golfers care passionately about the game, leading them to form emotional attachments to brands they associate with the sport.

In 2001, Clairol Canada signed a one-year, six-figure deal with the Canadian Football League to help launch their new hair colouring products for men. As one executive points out, "We're using the CFL and the Grey Cup to create excitement around hair colour and to make it more appealing to men, who may look at hair colour as something completely feminine. Also, Herbal Essences is targeted at men 15 to 25, and that's very much the target audience of the CFL and the Grey Cup." The deal includes national consumer promotion with in-store and media support. Other communications include on-field signage and in-stadium commercial messages during all playoff games, including the Grey Cup.[31]

Target Audience Exposure Many marketers are attracted to event sponsorship because it gets their company and/or product names in front of consumers. By choosing the right events for sponsorship, companies can get visibility among their target market. Canadian amateur athletes and semi-pro sports organizations have been working with marketers to develop sponsorships that benefit both parties. Alpine Canada Alpin (ACA), the governing body for the Canadian alpine ski racing, generated $1.9 million in sponsorship deals representing 25 percent of its annual budget compared to 16 percent from the public sector for the 2000–01 season. It signed deals with Wrigley Canada, General Motors, and Fido cellphones. The key success factor in landing these deals is the fact that World Cup ski races had TV audiences of over 30 million.[32]

Measuring Sponsorship Effectiveness As we have seen with other communication tools, sponsorship planning follows a general framework of performing a situation analysis with relevant consumer and competitive research, establishing objectives (i.e., marketing, communication, behavioural), developing strategy and tactics, and outlining the criteria and measures of effectiveness to assess if objectives have been met. A major issue that faces the event sponsorship industry is incomplete research. As marketers become interested in targeted audiences, they will want more evidence that event sponsorship is effective and a good return on their investment.

Despite this concern, the growth in sponsorship investments has led to a corresponding emergence of measuring the effectiveness of sponsorships. Essentially, measures of sponsorship effectiveness can be categorized as exposure-based methods or tracking measures:[33]

- *Exposure methods.* Exposure methods can be classified as those that monitor the quantity and nature of the media coverage obtained for the sponsored event and those that estimate direct and indirect audiences. While commonly employed by corporations, scholars have heavily criticized these measures. Pham argues that media coverage is not the objective of sponsorships and should not be considered as a measure of effectiveness. He argues that the measures provide no indication of perceptions, attitude change, or behavioural change and should therefore not be considered as measures of effectiveness.[34]
- *Tracking measures.* These measures are designed to evaluate the awareness, familiarity, and preferences engendered by sponsorship based on surveys. A number of empirical studies have measured recall of sponsors' ads, awareness of and attitudes toward the sponsors and their products, and image effect including brand and corporate images. Moreover, the tracking measures could be done for current customers, potential customers, and the general public before, during, and after the event to get a complete picture of the sponsorship.[35]

While each of these measures has its advantages and disadvantages, we suggest using several in assessing the impact of sponsorships. In fact, the selection of appropriate measures is so critical that some recommend that they may have to be customized for each sponsorship activity.[36] In addition to those mentioned here, the eight-step process suggested in Figure 14–7 could be used to guide these evaluations.

439

FIGURE 14–7
Eight steps to measuring event sponsorship
☐ ☐ ☐ ☐ ☐

1. Narrowly define objectives with specifics.
2. Establish solid strategies against which programming will be benchmarked and measure your programming and effectiveness against the benchmark.
3. Set measurable and realistic goals; make sure everything you do supports them.
4. Enhance, rather than just change, other marketing variables.
5. Programming should be crafted to reflect the particulars of your company's constituencies and target audiences.
6. Define the scope of your involvement. Will it involve multiple areas within the company? Who internally and externally comprises the team?
7. Think "long term." It takes time to build brand equity. Also, think of leveraging your sponsorship through programming for as long as possible, before and after the event.
8. Build evaluation and a related budget into your overall sponsoring program. Include items such as pre- and post-event attitude surveys, media analysis, and sales results.

STRENGTHS OF CORPORATE ADVERTISING

Positioning Firms, like products, need to establish an image or position in the marketplace. Corporate advertising activities are one way to accomplish this objective. A well-positioned product is much more likely to achieve success than is one with a vague or no image. The same holds true of the firm. Companies with strong positive corporate images have an advantage over competitors that may be enhanced when they promote any aspect of their organization or products.

Control of Message Exposure As the PR efforts of firms have increased, the attention paid to these events by the media has lessened (not because they are of any less value, but because there are more events to cover). The net result is that when a company engages in a public relations effort, there is no guarantee it will receive press coverage and publicity. Corporate advertising gets the message out, and though consumers may not perceive it as positively as information from an objective source, the fact remains that it can communicate what has been done.

Reach a Select Target Audience Corporate advertising should not be targeted to the general public. It is often targeted to investors and managers of other firms rather than to the general public. It doesn't matter if the general public does not appreciate this form of communication, as long as the target audience does. In this respect, this form of advertising may be accomplishing its objectives.

LIMITATIONS OF CORPORATE ADVERTISING

Questionable Effectiveness There is no strong evidence to support the belief that corporate advertising works. A study by Bozell & Jacobs Advertising of 16,000 ads concluded that corporate advertising contributed to only 4 percent of the variability in the company's stock price, compared with a 55 percent effect attributable to financial factors.[37] A second study also casts doubts on earlier studies that concluded that corporate advertising worked.[38]

Constitutionality and/or Ethics Some critics contend that since larger firms have more money, they can control public opinion unfairly. This point was resolved in the courts in favour of the advertisers. Nevertheless, many consumers still see such advertising as unfair and immediately take a negative view of the sponsor.

SUMMARY

This chapter examined the role of the promotional elements of public relations. Public relations is typically done through publicity generated through news media and corporate advertising. We noted that these areas are all significant to the marketing and communications effort and are usually considered differently from the other promotional elements. The reasons for this special treatment stem from the facts that (1) they are typically not designed to promote a specific product or service and (2) in many instances it is harder for the consumer to make the connection between the communication and its intent.

Public relations was shown to be useful in its traditional responsibilities as well as in a more marketing-oriented role. In many firms, PR is a separate department operating independently of marketing; in others, it is considered a support system. Many large firms have an external public relations agency, just as they have an outside ad agency.

In the case of publicity, another factor enters the equation: lack of control over the communication the public will receive. In corporate advertising, the organization remains the source and retains much more control. Publicity often takes more of a reactive than a proactive approach, yet it may be more instrumental (or detrimental) to the success of a product or organization than all other forms of promotion combined.

While not all publicity can be managed, the marketer must nevertheless recognize its potential impact. Press releases and the management of information are just two of the factors under the company's control. Proper reaction and a strategy to deal with uncontrollable events are also responsibilities.

Corporate advertising was described as controversial, largely because the source of the message is top management, so the rules for other advertising and promoting forms are often not applied. This element of communication definitely has its place in the promotional mix. But to be effective, it must be used with each of the other elements, with specific communications objectives in mind.

Finally, in this chapter we tried to illustrate that the public relations plan is put together much like the advertising or sales promotion plans.

441

KEY TERMS

public relations, *416*
publicity, *417*
video news release (VNR), *418*
internal audiences, *421*

external audiences, *421*
marketing public relations, *423*
press release, *426*
press conference, *428*

exclusive, *428*
corporate advertising, *431*
image advertising, *433*
advocacy advertising, *434*

cause-related marketing, *435*
event sponsorships, *436*

DISCUSSION QUESTIONS

1. Discuss some of the advantages associated with the use of marketing public relations (MPRs). What are some of the disadvantages?

2. Explain why traditional public relations practitioners might be unhappy with the organization's use of MPRs. Take a position as to whether this criticism is justified.

3. List and describe the advantages and disadvantages of the use of public relations in an IMC program. Provide an example of an appropriate use of public relations in this mix.

4. What is a video news release (VNR)? Provide an example of a situation in which a company might employ the use of a VNR. Discuss some of the ethical implications (if any) in using this tool.

5. Many companies are now taking the position that their charitable contributions should lead to something in return—for example, sales or increased visibility. Discuss the pros and cons of this position.

6. Many companies are now trying to generate as much free publicity as they can. Cite some examples of this, and discuss the advantages and disadvantages associated with this strategy.

7. Describe some criteria used by firms to measure public relations effectiveness.

Direct Marketing

CHAPTER OBJECTIVES

- To recognize the purpose of direct marketing as a communications tool.

- To appreciate the strategies and tactics involved in direct marketing.

- To demonstrate the use of direct-marketing media.

- To determine the scope and effectiveness of direct marketing.

Direct-Response Television Fundraising

Place of Miracles: Inside the Hospital for Sick Children aired November 2002 and ushered in the era of direct-response television to raise funds for the eminent facility located in downtown Toronto. As the drama continued throughout the one-hour show, viewers naturally felt they were watching an episode of a television show and not a plea for more money as they witnessed the heart-felt story of young Olivia and her quest for a new heart. And more importantly, viewers observed and identified with the parents of Olivia who related their experiences and explained their gratitude for the health-care service Olivia received. At the end of the film, Olivia received her transplanted heart and the requests for donations and a phone number were shown on the screen.

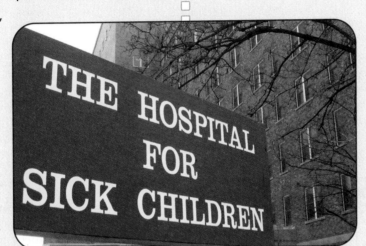

Pledges from direct-response television average about 45 percent of all callers, but *Place of Miracles* struck it rich with 61 percent. And direct-response television was part of the many direct-marketing tools that the foundation responsible for fundraising implements each year. With an annual goal of $54 million for 2003, the foundation also planned to use telemarketing, direct mail, door-to-door solicitation, radio, and a telethon. But the direct-response television played a key role because of its extensive reach and its ability to target those aged 35–50 who have children, a group the foundation did not reach with direct mail, which often reached those over age 55. Overall, the initial foray into this new direct-marketing alternative raised $850,000, double the expected target.

In choosing direct-response television, the hospital also recognized its value in building the overall brand, something unheard of previously. However, health-care facilities and other non-profit institutions face competition from all organizations and causes that seek funds from the general public. In fact, one advertising agency executive suggested that the fundraising in the not-for-profit world faced stronger competition than for the for-profit firms.

Source: Michelle Warren, "Sick Kids' Direct Drama," *Marketing Magazine*, February 10, 2003.

In this chapter, we discuss direct marketing and its role as a communications tool. Direct marketing includes programs such as direct mail, catalogues, telemarketing, and infomercials. In essence, it is communication in each of the media we have discussed thus far, but with a more immediate sales objective. Direct marketing is one of the fastest-growing forms of promotion in terms of dollar expenditures, and for many marketers it is rapidly becoming the medium of choice for reaching consumers. Stan Rapp and Thomas Collins, in their book *Maximarketing*, propose that direct marketing be the driving force behind the overall marketing program.[1] They present a nine-step model that includes creating a database, reaching prospects, developing the sale, and developing the relationship. We begin with an overview of direct marketing and then examine direct-marketing programs. The chapter concludes with a discussion of the strengths and limitations of this marketing tool.

DIRECT MARKETING

While most companies continue to rely primarily on the other promotional mix elements to move their products and services through intermediaries, an increasing number are going directly to the consumer. These companies believe that while the traditional promotional mix tools such as advertising, and sales promotion, are effective in creating brand image, conveying information, and/or creating awareness. However, going direct with these same tools can generate an immediate behavioural response which makes direct marketing a valuable tool in the integrated communications program.

DEFINING DIRECT MARKETING

As noted in Chapter 1, **direct marketing** is a system of marketing by which organizations communicate directly with target customers to generate a response or transaction. This response may take the form of an inquiry, a purchase, or even a vote. In his *Dictionary of Marketing Terms*, Peter Bennett defines direct marketing as:

> The total of activities by which the seller, in effecting the exchange of goods and services with the buyer, directs efforts to a target audience using one or more media (direct selling, direct mail, telemarketing, direct-action advertising, catalogue selling, cable TV selling, etc.) for the purpose of soliciting a response by phone, mail, or personal visit from a prospect or customer.[2]

Direct marketing uses a set of **direct-response media**, including direct mail, telemarketing, interactive TV, print, the Internet, and other media. These media are the tools by which direct marketers implement the communications process. As you can see in Figure 15–1, direct marketing is an aspect of total marketing—that is, it involves marketing research, segmentation, evaluation, and the like, just as our planning model in Chapter 1 did.

The purchases of products and services through direct-response advertising $51 billion in Canada during 2000.[3] Firms that use this marketing method range from major retailers to publishing companies to computer retailers to financial services. Business-to-business and industrial marketers have also significantly increased their direct-marketing efforts.

THE GROWTH OF DIRECT MARKETING

Direct marketing has been around since the invention of the printing press in the 15th century. However, the major impetus behind the growth of direct marketing may have been the development and expansion of the postal service, which made catalogues available to both urban and rural dwellers so that consumers could

	Ad Spending ($ 000s)	Sales Impact ($ 000s)
All media	9,369,259	51,192,316
Direct mail	1,872,507	16,050,887
Telephone marketing	2,837,118	16,146,281
Newspaper	1,109,262	7,182,170
Magazine	487,503	3,048,530
Television	1,579,419	4,349,055
Radio	549,256	1,806,043
Other	934,192	2,609,349

Source: CMA 2001 Market Fact Book.

FIGURE 15–1

2000 Direct marketing statistics

☐ ☐ ☐ ☐ ☐

access goods that were otherwise unavailable during the late 1800s and early 1900s. More recently, catalogues revolutionized North American buying habits; consumers could now shop without ever leaving their homes.

But catalogues alone do not account for the rapid growth of direct marketing. A number of factors in our society have led to the increased attractiveness of this medium for both buyer and seller:

- *Consumer credit cards.* There are a significant number of credit cards—bank, oil company, retail, and so on—in circulation in Canada. This makes it feasible for consumers to purchase both low- and high-ticket items through direct-response channels and assures sellers that they will be paid. Of course, not all of this will be through direct marketing, but a high percentage of direct purchases do use this method of payment, and companies such as American Express, MasterCard, and Visa are among the heaviest direct advertisers.
- *Direct-marketing syndicates.* Companies specializing in list development, statement inserts, catalogues, and sweepstakes have opened many new opportunities to marketers. The number of these companies continues to expand, creating even more new users.
- *Structure of North American society.* One of the major factors contributing to the success of direct marketing is that so many of us are now "money-rich and time-poor."[4] with the rapid increase in dual-income families At the same time, the increased popularity of physical fitness, do-it-yourself crafts and repairs, and home entertainment have reduced the time available for shopping and have increased the attractiveness of direct purchases.
- *Technological advances.* The rapid technological advancement of the electronic media and of computers has made it easier for consumers to shop and for marketers to be successful in reaching the desired target markets. The majority of the 11 million households in Canada receive home shopping programs.
- *Miscellaneous factors.* A number of other factors have contributed to the increased effectiveness of direct marketing, including changing values, more sophisticated marketing techniques, and the industry's improved image. These factors will also ensure the success of direct marketing in the future. Figure 15–2 shows us just how much direct marketing is growing in Canada.[5] Of the various advertising methods shown in this chart, all but direct-response television and transit advertising have a positive net projected increase in usage. Notice that website usage, direct mail, and e-mail advertising are all on a steep growth rate.

While some organizations rely on direct marketing solely to generate consumer response, in many others, direct marketing is an integral part of the IMC program. They use direct marketing to achieve goals other than sales goals and to integrate it with other program elements. We first examine the role of direct marketing in the IMC program and then consider its more traditional role.

445

FIGURE 15–2
Direct marketing growth
in Canada
☐☐☐☐☐

Projected change in frequency of using various media (% of advertisers)			
	More	Less	About the Same	Net Projected Increase
Website	65	4	22	+61
Addressed direct mail	37	7	41	+30
E-mail advertising/messages	33	9	30	+24
Newspapers	23	12	58	+11
Magazines	25	17	49	+ 8
Radio	21	14	54	+ 7
Television	17	12	57	+ 5
Banner ads	18	11	45	+ 7
Telemarketing	18	14	39	+ 4
Free standing inserts in newspapers	17	14	50	+ 3
Transit	10	13	49	– 3
Direct response television	5	11	47	– 6

Source: Canadian Facts, 2000.

THE ROLE OF DIRECT MARKETING IN THE IMC PROGRAM

Direct marketing is now an important component in the integrated marketing programs of many organizations. In fact, direct-marketing activities support and are supported by other elements of the promotional mix.

Combining Direct Marketing with Advertising Obviously, direct marketing is in itself a form of advertising. Whether through mail, print, or TV, the direct-response offer is an ad. It usually contains a 1-800 or 1-900 number or a form that requests mailing information. Sometimes the ad supports the direct-selling effort. For example, Victoria's Secret runs image ads to support its store and catalogue sales. Direct-response ads or infomercials are also referred to in retail outlet displays.

Combining Direct Marketing with Public Relations As you will see later in this text, public relations activities often employ direct-response techniques. Private companies may use telemarketing activities to solicit funds for charities or cosponsor charities that use these and other direct-response techniques to solicit funds. Likewise, corporations and/or organizations engaging in public relations activities may include 1-800 numbers or website addresses in their ads or promotional materials.

Combining Direct Marketing with Personal Selling Telemarketing and direct selling are two methods of personal selling. Non-profit organizations such as charities often use telemarketing to solicit funds. For-profit companies are also using telemarketing with much greater frequency to screen and qualify prospects (which reduces selling costs) and to generate leads. Direct-mail pieces are often used to invite prospective customers to visit auto showrooms to test-drive new cars; the salesperson then assumes responsibility for the selling effort.

Combining Direct Marketing with Sales Promotions How many times have you received a direct-mail piece notifying you of a sales promotion or event or inviting you to participate in a contest or sweepstakes? Ski shops regularly mail announcements of special end-of-season sales. Whistler Ski Resort and Intrawest constantly mail out promotions to their customer database announcing promotional and seasonal vacation packages, room rates, and lift ticket specials. The Bay, Sears, and other retail outlets call their existing customers to notify them of special sales promotions. Each of these is an example of a company using direct-marketing tools to inform customers of sales promotions. In turn, the sales promotion event may support the direct-marketing effort. Databases are often built from the names and addresses acquired from a promotion, and direct mail and/or telemarketing calls follow.

DIRECT-MARKETING PROGRAM PLAN

To successfully implement direct-marketing programs, companies must make a number of decisions. As in other marketing programs, they must determine (1) what the program's objectives will be; (2) who to target by using a database; (3) what direct-marketing media strategy will be employed; and (4) how to measure direct-marketing effectiveness.

DIRECT-MARKETING OBJECTIVES

The direct marketer seeks a direct response. The objectives of the program are normally behaviours—for example, test-drives, votes, contributions, and/or sales. A typical objective is defined through a set response, perhaps a 2 to 3 percent response rate.

Not all direct marketing seeks a behavioural response, however. Many organizations use direct marketing to build an image, maintain customer satisfaction, and inform and/or educate customers that may lead to future actions. Exhibit 15–1 shows how the province of Saskatchewan uses direct mail to encourage travel.

DEVELOPING A DATABASE

As we have discussed throughout this text, market segmentation and targeting are critical components of any promotional program. Direct-marketing programs employ these principles even more than others, since the success of a direct-marketing program is in large part tied to the ability to reach a very significant target audience. To segment and target their audiences, direct marketers use a **database**, a listing of customers and/or potential customers. This database is a tool for **database marketing**—the use of specific information about individual customers and/or prospects to implement more effective and efficient marketing communications.[6]

Exhibit 15–1
Saskatchewan encourages visits through direct mail

Figure 15–3 demonstrates how database marketing works. As you can see, the database marketing effort must be an integral part of the overall IMC program. At the very least, this list contains names, addresses, and postal codes; more sophisticated databases include information on demographics and psychographics, purchase transactions and payments, personal facts, neighbourhood data, and even credit histories (see Figure 15–4). The new privacy legislation introduced in 2004 places greater limitations on what marketers can do with information stored in their databases. We refer you to www.privcom.gc.ca for a complete guide.

This database serves as the foundation from which the direct-marketing programs evolve. Databases are used to perform the following functions:[7]

* *Improving the selection of market segments.* Some consumers are more likely to be potential purchasers, users, voters, and so on than others. By analyzing the characteristics of the database,

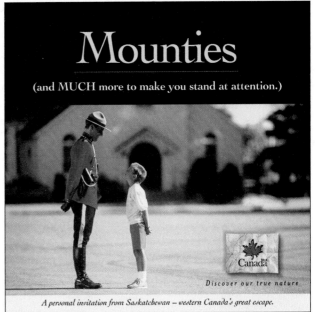

Mounties
(and MUCH more to make you stand at attention.)

Canada
Discover our true nature

A personal invitation from Saskatchewan – western Canada's great escape.

447

FIGURE 15–3
How database marketing works
☐ ☐ ☐ ☐ ☐

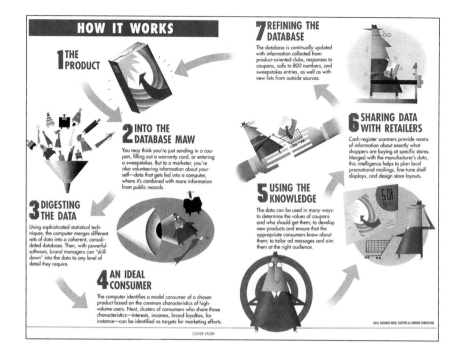

a marketer can target a greater potential audience. For example, catalogue companies have become very specialized. Companies such as Lands' End, Sears, and The Gap, have culled their lists and become much more efficient, targeting only those who are most likely to purchase their products.

- *Stimulate repeat purchases.* Once a purchase has been made, the customer's name and other information are entered into the database. These people are proven direct-marketing users who offer high potential for repurchase. Magazines, for example, routinely send out renewal letters and/or call subscribers before the expiration date. Blockbuster Entertainment helps its video-rental customers select movies, locate additional Blockbuster locations, or renew their membership (Exhibit 15–2). Companies from window cleaners to carpet cleaners to car dealers build a base of customers and contact them when they are "due" to repurchase.

FIGURE 15–4
Contents for a comprehensive database
☐ ☐ ☐ ☐ ☐

Consumer Database	Business-to-Business Database
Name	Name of company/contact/decision maker(s)
Address/postal code	Title of contact
Telephone number	Telephone number
Length of residence	Source of order/inquiry or referral
Age	Credit history
Gender	Industrial classification
Marital status	Size of business
Family data (number of children, etc.)	Revenues
Education	Number of employees
Income	Time in business
Occupation	Headquarters location
Transaction history	Multiple locations
Promotion history	Purchase history
Inquiring history	Promotion history
Unique identifier	Inquiry history
	Unique identifier

- *Cross-sell.* Customers who demonstrate a specific interest also constitute strong potential for other products of the same nature. For example, the National Geographic Society has successfully sold globes, maps, videos, travel magazines, and an assortment of other products to subscribers who obviously have an interest in geography and/or travel. Likewise, Victoria's Secret has expanded its clothing lines primarily through sales to existing customers, and Kraft–General Foods has successfully cross-sold products in its varied food line. Upon responding to the direct-mail piece sent by Hertz (Exhibit 15–3), you are asked for your permission for Hertz to provide your name to its parent company, Ford, and others, and to allow Hertz to send you information on other products and services.

Exhibit 15–2
Blockbuster uses mailers to cross promote

- *Customer relationship management.* Customer relationship management (CRM), described in Chapter 1, requires that the marketer develop and maintain a significant amount of information about its clients. The aim of CRM is to establish a relationship with one's customers through affinities, personalized communications, and product/service offerings. For CRM to work effectively, a database is required. While CRM relies on technology specifically designed for managing customer relationships, there are overlapping characteristics of CRM and database marketing. Suffice it to say at this point that many of the techniques employed in database marketing are necessary to develop an effective CRM program.

Numerous other companies have established comprehensive databases on existing and potential customers both in North America and internationally. Database marketing has become so ubiquitous that many people are concerned about invasion of privacy. Direct marketers are concerned as well. The Canadian Marketing Association (CMA) and the Canadian Advertising Foundation (CAF) have asked its members to adhere to ethical rules of conduct in their marketing efforts. They point out that if the industry does not police itself, the government will.

Sources of Database Information   There are many sources of information for direct-marketing databases:

- *Statistics Canada.* Census data provide information on almost every household in Canada. Data include household size, demographics, income, and other information.
- *Canada Post.* Postal codes provide information on both household and business locations.

Exhibit 15–3
Hertz seeks permission to use receivers' names

- *List services.* Many providers of lists are available. The accuracy and timeliness of the lists vary.
- *Info Canada.* Provincial Business Directory provides information regarding business lists. Published by province, Direct Mail List Rates and Data contains thousands of list selections
- *Marketing research houses.* Large research houses conduct annual studies of customers who buy at home via

Shoppers Drug Mart's Optimum Loyalty Program

Four years ago, Canada's largest pharmacy launched Optimum, its highly successful loyalty program, and attained 8 million members by the spring of 2004. Similar to other programs, consumers accumulate points based on the volume of their purchases in exchange for discounts or other rewards. And like other programs, the implementation is predicated on the maintenance of a database of information for all its members. However, unlike other loyalty programs, Shoppers developed a program for pharmaceutical and packaged goods brands that would latch onto the sophisticated database, which tracks customers' purchases by product category and brand.

Schering Canada took advantage of this opportunity by sending a direct-mail offer for its Claritin product to 180,000 allergy sufferers in April and August of 2003. Based on the historic purchase patterns of consumers contained in the database, Claritin's message and promotion targeted exactly those who would be considering switching brands or considering not purchasing Claritin again. The direct-mail offer contained information about allergies and an offer of 3,000 Optimum points towards the next purchase of Claritin. Although the benefit of such precise targeting impressed Schering, the reasonable initial cost dropped considerably when other companies like Procter & Gamble joined. And to top it off, Claritin enjoyed category exclusivity, as the direct-mail inserts had no other allergy medication featured. Even though Schering kept the results confidential, it claimed success and planned another execution in 2004.

For L'Oréal Canada, the feature of tracking actual sales from Shoppers sales receipts added even stronger reasons for launching a direct-mail piece to launch its hair colouring product, Couleru Experte. Women within a certain age range who had a particular purchasing history received an interactive, game-like insert to deliver the message and an offer for Optimum points towards a purchase. Point-of-sale displays also supported the program. L'Oreal tracked the sales results and determined who bought with and without the Optimum points offer and claimed the results were better than any other programs implemented previously.

A sample and an Optimum points offer for Dove Face Care impressed its brand manager who noted above-average performance through positive trial and repurchase compared to usual direct-marketing initiatives. Despite the success of these brands, one expert cautioned Shoppers that some of its members would not enjoy receiving so many direct-mail pieces, which would ultimately diminish the value of the loyalty program.

Source: Chris Daniels, "Vendor Bender," *Marketing Magazine*, April 5, 2004.

mail or telephone. They compile information on total orders placed, types of products purchased, demographics, and purchase satisfaction, among others.

- *Loyalty programs.* Continuity programs designed to enhance loyalty are a new source of consumers with precise purchase patterns. IMC Perspective 15–1 provides an example of the Optimum Loyalty Program.
- *Others.* The Canadian Marketing Association, Dunn and Bradstreet, Fortune 500, *The Book of Lists*, and other published periodicals of this nature all contain listed information that can be used for these purposes.

Consumer-goods manufacturers, banks, credit bureaus, retailers, charitable organizations, and other business operations also sell lists and other selected information. Companies can build their own databases through completed warranty cards, surveys, and so on.

Determining the Effectiveness of the Database   While many companies maintain a database, many do not use them effectively. Collecting names and information is not enough; the list must be kept current, purged of old and/or inactive customers, and updated frequently. The more information about customers that can be contained in the database, the more effective it will be. An **RFM scoring method** is often used for this purpose. RFM stands for the recency, frequency, and monetary transactions between the company and the customer. More specifically, data need to be entered each time there is a transaction so that the company can track how recently purchases have been made, how often they are made, and what amounts of money are being spent. In addition, tracking which products and/or services are used increases the ability for databases to conduct the activities previously mentioned in this section. By analyzing the database on a regular basis, the company or organization can identify trends and buying patterns that will help it establish a better relationship with its customers by more effectively meeting their needs.

DIRECT-MARKETING MEDIA STRATEGY

As with all other communications programs discussed in this text, marketers must decide the message to be conveyed, the size of the budget, and so on. Perhaps the major difference between direct-marketing programs and other promotional mix programs regards the use of media.

As shown in Figure 15–1, direct marketing employs a number of media, including direct mail, telemarketing, direct-response broadcasting, the Internet, and print. Each medium is used to perform specific functions, although they generally follow a one- or two-step approach.

In the **one-step approach**, the medium is used directly to obtain an order. You've probably seen TV commercials for products such as wrench sets, workout equipment, or magazine subscriptions in which the viewer is urged to phone a toll-free number to place an order immediately. Usually these ads accept credit cards or cash on delivery and give an address. Their goal is to generate an immediate sale when the ad is shown.

The **two-step approach** may involve the use of more than one medium. The first effort is designed to screen, or qualify, potential buyers. The second effort generates the response. For example, many companies use telemarketing to screen on the basis of interest, then follow up to interested parties with more information designed to achieve an order or use personal selling to close the sale.

A variation of the two-step approach emerged with the advent of the Internet. Many companies run direct-response television commercials to encourage website visits. For example, in its effort to move from a soup company to a food company, the Campbell Company of Canada ran nine ads with a celebrity chef demonstrating different cooking methods that directed consumers to a website, www.power2cook.ca, and followed up with extensive direct-mail pieces to 2 million Canadians.[8]

Direct Mail   Direct mail is often called junk mail—the unsolicited mail you receive. However, more advertising dollars continue to be spent in direct mail than in almost any other advertising medium—an estimated $1.9 billion in 2000.[9] Mail-order sales exceeded $16 billion in 2000 ($10 billion in the consumer market).[10] Statistics show that 64 percent of Canadians read addressed direct mail right away when it arrives. Another 23 percent of Canadians keep it to review later at a time more convenient to them.[11] IMC Perspective 15–2 shows how direct mail is used to deliver more creative messages with new electronic media.

Consider a CD-ROM as Part of a Direct-Mail Campaign

More and more marketers who produce direct mail are leveraging the power of the Internet to employ a drive-to-Web strategy: using hard-copy direct mail as a catalyst for dialogue that takes place online. And while no one seems to disagree that online is a great place to generate dialogue, marketers continue to search for the Holy Grail of drive-to-Web. How can people move from the envelope to the keyboard?

One of the most overlooked tactics to achieve this transition is the CD-ROM. CD-ROMs came into fashion years ago. At the time, they were expensive to produce, and when consumers took to their computers, the payoff was marginal at best. And there was no Web beyond the CD to fully engage the customer. So the CD-ROM has become almost an afterthought in the wired world, conjuring up images of stick-figure animations and installation nightmares for consumers.

Nothing could be further from the truth. First, computing technology has grown exponentially, with more than 70-percent penetration rates across Canada for consumers. For business people, it's virtually 100 percent. And the horsepower in those computers has delivered the promise of an easy-loading, fully engaging multimedia experience.

But too often marketers don't fully explore CD-ROMs, for two reasons:

1. *Too much focus on cost per piece.* Not enough focus is placed on return per piece. CD-ROMs are viewed as an expensive per-piece addition to a direct-mail campaign. The reality is that the inclusion of a CD-ROM can deliver significant lifts in response. When compared on an ROI

basis, a CD-ROM can be one of the most cost-effective ways to lift response.

2. *Timeline pressure.* It takes time to think through and create a CD-ROM production. Even with existing content, the development of a CD-ROM is often longer than the relatively fast turnaround that printers are able to deliver these days.

VHS video is another method used by direct marketers to generate a lift in response, but the CD-ROM has its advantages over video. First, it has inherent interactivity that allows a customer to browse a catalogue, search for topics by interest, or make calculations. It is an easy-to-access, non-linear resource and is therefore more likely to be kept and used again. It can be easily outfitted with Web links to ensure that the dialogue continues, and those links can more easily be measured when directed to a specific URL. And it has the potential to save a bundle in postage.

Source: Adapted from John Peloza, "The CD-ROM as a Direct Tool," *Marketing Magazine*, April 29, 2002. Used with permission.

Direct mail is not restricted to small companies seeking our business. Respected large companies such as RBC (Royal Bank of Canada) and Air Miles have increased their expenditures in this area, as have many others. Canada 2000 Facts statistics show that the overall opinions of companies that use direct mail are more positive than for companies that use other direct marketing media. Sales through direct mail in the business-to-business market reached $6 billion in 2000.[12] Figure 15–5 shows how Canada Post views the advantages of using direct mail to promote your business.

Market with direct mail

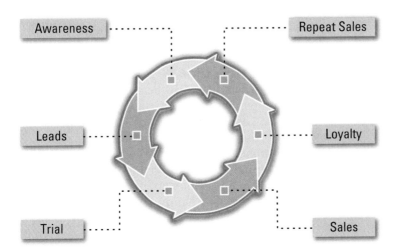

Many advertisers shied away from direct mail in the past, fearful of the image it might create or harbouring the belief that direct mail was useful only for low-cost products. But this is no longer the case. For example, Porsche Cars North America, Inc., uses direct mail to target high-income, upscale consumers who are most likely to purchase its expensive sports cars (Exhibit 15–4). In one example, Porsche developed a direct-mail piece that was sent to a precisely defined target market: physicians in specialties with the highest income levels. This list was screened to match the demographics of Porsche buyers and narrowed further to specific geographic areas. The direct-mail piece was an x-ray of a Porsche 911 Carrera 4 written in the language of the medical audience. This creative campaign generated one of the highest response rates of any mailing Porsche has done in recent years.[13] The materials shown in Exhibit 15–5 are just some of the ones sent by Mercedes to introduce its new sports utility vehicle.

Exhibit 15–4
Porsche targets direct mail to upscale audiences

Keys to the success of direct mail are the **mailing list**, which constitutes the database from which names are generated, and the ability to segment markets. Lists have become more current and more selective, eliminating waste coverage. Segmentation on the basis of geography (usually through postal codes), demographics, and lifestyles has led to increased effectiveness. The most commonly used lists are of individuals who have already purchased direct-mail products.

The importance of the list has led to a business of its own. It has been estimated that there are over 38 billion names on lists in North America, and many companies have found it profitable to sell the names of purchasers of their products and/or services to list firms. There are also a growing number of list-management companies springing up on the Internet. Canadian mailing lists by association or type of vocation are common. Canadian companies such as www.interactdirect.com, based in London, Ontario, are more common now.

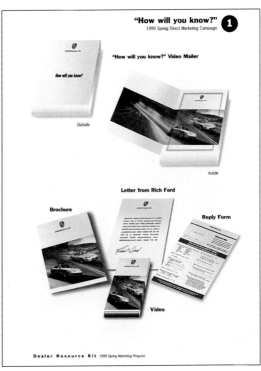

Catalogues Major participants in the direct-marketing business include catalogue companies. The number of catalogues mailed and the number of catalogue shoppers have increased significantly.

453

Exhibit 15–5
Mercedes used direct mail to introduce its new SUV

Many companies use catalogues in conjunction with their more traditional sales and promotional strategies. For example, companies such as Ikea, Canadian Tire, and Sears sell directly through catalogues but also use them to inform consumers of product offerings available in the stores. Some companies rely solely on catalogue sales. For example, Yves Rocher is a firm that markets botanical beauty care products for women. It expanded into Canada with its small catalogues.

Lee Valley Tools of Ottawa started out as a mail order catalogue company 20 years ago, but has branched out to retail stores across the country and online sales (Exhibit 15–6).

Home Depot started out as the headquarters for contractors and handy home renovators, but in Canada it started a decorating catalogue "The Home Depot DreamBook" to inspire women looking to improve their homes. Thus, catalogues can be used as a direct-marketing tool to attract a new target audience while not alienating the original loyal customer.[14]

In addition to the traditional hard copies, catalogues are now available on the Internet for both consumer and business-to-business customers. In some instances in the consumer market, the catalogue merchandise is available in retail stores as well. In others, the catalogue and retail divisions are treated as separate entities. For example, if you purchase through the Eddie Bauer catalogue, you can exchange or return the merchandise to the retail stores. At The Gap, the catalogue is used to supplement the inventory in stock, and phone orders for different sizes and so on can be made from the store and shipped for free.

Broadcast Media The success of direct marketing in the broadcast industry has been truly remarkable. Direct-response TV generated around $4.4 billion in sales in 2000. Advertising expenditures amounted to $1.6 billion in 2000.[15] Two broadcast media are available to direct marketers: television and radio. While radio was used quite extensively in the 1950s, its use and effectiveness have dwindled substantially in recent years. Thus, the majority of direct-marketing broadcast advertising now occurs on TV, which receives the bulk of our attention here.

Direct marketing in the broadcast industry involves both direct-response advertising and support advertising. In **direct-response advertising**, the product or service is offered and a sales response is solicited, through either the one- or two-step approach previously discussed. Examples include ads for magazine subscriptions, CDs, and tips on football or basketball betting. Toll-free phone numbers are included so that the receiver can immediately call to order. It should be pointed out, however, that the two-step approach is still very common on the radio, particularly with local companies. **Support advertising** is designed to do exactly that—support other forms of advertising. Ads for Publishers Clearing House or *Reader's Digest* or other companies telling you to look in your mailbox for a sweepstakes entry are examples of support advertising.

Direct-response TV encompasses a number of media, including direct-response TV spots like those just mentioned, infomercials, and home shopping shows (teleshopping). And Internet-TV has recently been introduced.

Exhibit 15–6
Lee Valley uses catalogues to communicate and sell directly

Infomercials The lower cost of commercials on cable and satellite channels has led advertisers to a new form of advertising. An **infomercial** is a long commercial that ranges from 3 to 60 minutes.

Exhibit 15–7
Volvo uses an infomer-
cial to attract buyers

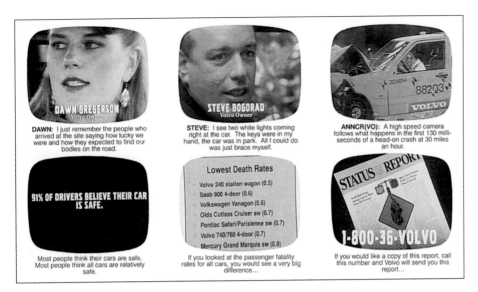

(Most are 30 minutes long, though the 5-minute format is gaining in popularity.) Many infomercials are produced by the advertisers and are designed to be viewed as regular TV shows. Consumers dial a 1-800 or 1-900 number to place an order. IMC Perspective 15–3 highlights the best practices of direct-response TV from the view of an industry practitioner. This form of show is popular with small firms and infomercials have been adopted by many big, mainstream marketers. Apple Computer, Microsoft, Sony, Volvo, and Philips Electronics are just some of the many others now employing this method of communication (Exhibit 15–7).

As to their effectiveness, studies indicate that infomercials get watched and sell products. One study profiling infomercial viewers and buyers demonstrated that this advertising medium is indeed effective with a broad demographic base, not significantly different from the infomercial non-shopper in age, education, income, or gender. There are also a number of differences between infomercial shoppers and non-shoppers.[16]

TV Advertorials   In 1999, Peugeot took its first step into TV programming by developing a series of **advertorials** to show the public its entire model range. Peugeot is the first auto manufacturer to use TV advertorials. The company developed eight 5-minute films positioning the autos as "The Drive of Your Life" while providing comprehensive information on test-drives, technical specifications, and demonstrations. In addition, the auto company developed advertorials for its website, with each advertorial targeted to different target audiences.[17]

Teleshopping   The development of toll-free telephone numbers, combined with the widespread use of credit cards, has led to a dramatic increase in the number of people who shop via their TV sets. Jewellery, kitchenware, fitness products, electronics, and a variety of items are now promoted (and sold) this way. The Shopping Channel (TSC) is Canada's broadcast retailer available on all delivery formats (cable, satellite) across the country. And, of course, the lines of communication get blurred even more as TSC is available in catalogue and on the Internet.

Print Media   Magazines and newspapers are difficult media to use for direct marketing. Because these ads have to compete with the clutter of other ads and because the space is relatively expensive, response rates and profits may be lower than in other media. This does not mean these media are not used (as evidenced by the fact that expenditures total almost $2 billion in 2000).[18] You're more likely to find them in specific interest areas such as financial newspapers or sports, sex, or hobby

The ABCs of Direct-Response TV

Direct-response television (DRTV) is hot. More and more advertisers, including a large number of blue-chip companies, are using short-form DRTV and infomercials to market their products and services. That's the good news.

The bad news is that a lot of what passes for DRTV is not DRTV at all. They are more like brand commercials with a 1-900 number stuck on the end. That's fine for those who are satisfied with generating a couple of phone calls. However, for those advertisers interested in producing DRTV commercials that make the phones sit up and sing, here are some rules to making powerful, profitable direct-response commercials and infomercials.

- *The more you tell, the more you sell.* The most important thing to understand about DRTV is that each commercial needs to function as a complete, stand-alone sales presentation. That means that by the end of your spot, the viewer must have enough information to feel comfortable making a purchasing decision. It's your job to give them that information. That means presenting as many features and benefits, answering as many questions, and overcoming as many objections as possible in the allotted time. Don't cheat yourself out of a sale by leaving valuable information out of your spot.
- *The product is King, Queen, and Supreme Ruler.* Don't waste a second of precious air time talking about anything except your product or service. Creative concepts that are not about extolling the virtues of your product or service are a waste of time.
- *Focus groups will kill your commercial.* Focus groups will happily tell you what they like or don't like about your DRTV commercial. Unfortunately, what they like or don't like in a commercial has nothing to do with what makes them buy from a commercial. Never confuse what a viewer likes with what makes them pick up the phone and buy. Save your money and skip the focus groups.
- *Show your product.* TV is not a store or a showroom. The viewer can't reach up and squeeze the Charmin and then take that shiny new SUV out for a test drive. You're going to have to show how beautiful and irresistible your product

really is. And by the way, with a little imagination you can also "show" intangible products or services, such as long distance, financial planning, or even political ideas.
- *Demonstrate your product.* Beauty shots are critical, but the viewer also needs to see your product or service in action. Remember this: Dynamite demonstrations have sold more products than any other DRTV technique. They captivate an audience and fuel the desire to purchase.
- *Use graphics to reinforce key selling messages.* Study after study has concluded that people understand and recall information better when they hear it and see it. Therefore, make sure that all the key selling points are also written on the screen as graphics at the exact same time as they are being spoken by the talent.
- *Include a powerful offer.* It is not absolutely essential to have an offer, but keep in mind that a good offer can transform an okay commercial into a runaway bestseller. Offers work because they make the viewer think about the cost of not acting, and nobody wants to miss out on a great deal. The better the offer, the better the response.
- *Value is in the mind of the viewer.* The effectiveness of your offer depends upon its perceived rather than its real value. That is why so many effective DRTV offers include inexpensive bonus items that boost the perceived value of the offer.
- *Testimonials work.* Consumers respond to hearing other consumers talk about how wonderful a product or service is and how much they love it. Especially if they happen to mention how skeptical they were before they tried it. To find out how well testimonials work, just try doing a successful infomercial without them.
- *The script is everything.* If you haven't already noticed, DRTV is a scriptwriter's medium. If the script is written properly, using proven, time-tested DR principles, the phones will sing. If the script is not written properly, your commercial will die a silent death.

Source: Adapted from Ian French, "Twenty-Four Ways to Dynamic DRTV", *Marketing Magazine*, February 11, 2002. Used with permission.

magazines. Exhibit 15–8 shows a direct ad that appeared in a magazine. You can find many more in specific interest areas like sports or hobby magazines.

Direct-to-consumer magazines hit Canada recently when the Hudson's Bay Company launched Canada's first publication, *Lifestyle*, to the 500,000 members within its HBC Rewards database. HBC planned to measure the consumer response to specific promotions and advertisers within the magazine could also join in so that they too could track their results.[19]

Telemarketing If you have a telephone, you probably do not have to be told about the rapid increase in the use of **telemarketing**, or sales by telephone. Combined telemarketing sales (consumer and business-to-business) totalled over $16 billion in 2000—with $7 billion in the consumer market.[20] Telemarketing expenditures reached almost $3 billion for 2000. There are two types of telemarketing used by businesses. Outbound telemarketing refers to calls made by a company or its sponsor to a potential buyer or client, soliciting the sale of products, services, donations, votes, or any other "value" issue. Inbound telemarketing occurs when a company has advertised its 1-800 number or its website address, for example, asking the customer to call the number, visit the store, or log on to the website. Both profit and charitable organizations have employed this medium effectively in both one- and two-step approaches.

As telemarketing continues to expand in scope, a new dimension referred to as **audiotex** or **telemedia** has evolved. Tom Eisenhart defines telemedia as the "use of telephone and voice information services (900, 800, and 976 numbers) to market, advertise, promote, entertain, and inform."[21] Many telemedia programs are interactive. Figure 15–6 shows more specifically how 800/900 numbers are used as marketing tools.[22]

Problems associated with telemarketing include its potential for fraud and deception and its potential for annoyance. However, data on call centres in Canada show that most call centres are well managed. The majority communicate clearly if the interaction is recorded, follow the laws governing telemarketing, and work with their employees to ensure appropriate interactions.[23] Those in the telemarketing and telemedia industry have responded to public criticisms. As more and more large companies use telemedia, its tarnished image will likely brighten up. However, the potential legislation of a national opt-out phone list, as currently done in the United States, would certainly limit the number of outbound calls.

Exhibit 15–8
A direct-response print ad

457

FIGURE 15–6 ☐☐☐☐ The use of 800, 900, and 976 numbers in marketing

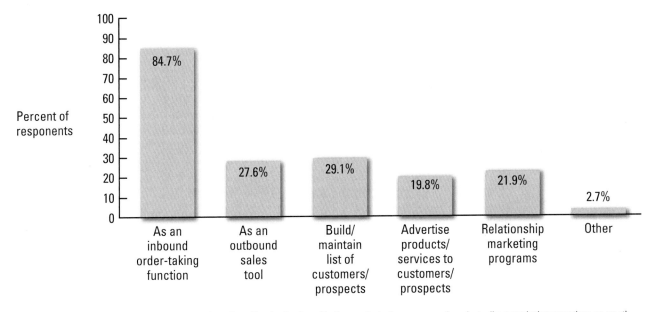

Note: *Direct* forecast survey was conducted by Jacobson Consulting Applications. The firms mailed a four-page questionnaire to direct-marketing executives, on an *n*th name basis from *Direct's* circulation list. There were 565 responses.

DIRECT-MARKETING EFFECTIVENESS

For direct-marketing programs that do not have an objective of generating an immediate behavioural response, traditional measures of advertising effectiveness can be applied. In those situations requiring a direct response, measuring the effectiveness should include some specific behavioural measure in addition to the communication measures. Using the cost per order (CPO), advertisers can evaluate the relative effectiveness of an ad in only a few minutes based on the number of calls generated. By running the same ad on different stations, a direct marketer can determine the relative effectiveness of the medium itself. For example, if the advertiser targets a $5 return per order and a broadcast commercial (production and print) costs $2,500, the ad is considered effective if it generates 500 orders. Similar measures have been developed for print and direct-mail ads.

Tracking the behavioural effects is exactly what Sprint Canada emphasized during the launch of its new "Red is Smarter" campaign. Each creative execution contained a unique toll-free number in a controlled region so that it could gauge the impact of different persuasive messages when the call centre received the inbound consumer response. Sprint Canada used the same idea for different promotional offers.[24]

EVALUATION OF DIRECT MARKETING

Many of the strengths and limitations of direct marketing have already been presented. As we have done with other media, we now summarize these factors in a concluding section.

STRENGTHS OF DIRECT MARKETING

Selective Reach Direct marketing lets the advertiser reach a large number of people and reduces or eliminates waste coverage. Intensive coverage may be obtained through broadcast advertising or through the mail. While not everyone drives on highways where there are billboards or pays attention to TV commercials, virtually everyone receives mail. A good list allows for minimal waste, as only those consumers with the highest potential are targeted. For example, a political candidate can direct a message at a very select group of people (those living in a certain postal code, or members of McGill University Alumni, or the Royal Vancouver Yacht Club say); in the same vein, a music club can target recent purchasers of CD players, or a medical software supplier can target all M.D.s in the medical association directories.

Segmentation Capabilities Marketers can purchase lists of recent product purchasers, car buyers, bankcard holders, and so on. These lists may allow segmentation on the basis of geographic area, occupation, demographics, and job title, to mention a few. Combining this information with the geocoding capabilities of Prizm or Vals (discussed in Chapter 2), marketers can develop effective segmentation strategies.

Frequency Depending on the medium used, it may be possible to build frequency levels. The program vehicles used for direct-response TV advertising are usually the most inexpensive available, so the marketer can afford to purchase repeat times. Frequency may not be so easily accomplished through the mail, since consumers may be annoyed to receive the same mail repeatedly.

Flexibility Direct marketing can take on a variety of creative forms. For example, the Discovery Network sent 17-inch TV sets to media buyers through the mail. The only message accompanying the TV sets was one on the cord that said "Plug me in" and another on a videotape that read "Play me." Upon doing so, the recipient was greeted with a 7-minute promotional video. Direct-mail pieces also allow for detailed copy that provides a great deal of information. The targeted mailing of videotapes containing product information has increased dramatically, as companies have found this a very effective way to provide potential buyers with product information.

Timing While many media require long-range planning and have long closing dates, direct-response advertising can be much more timely. Direct mail, for example, can be put together very quickly and distributed to the target population. TV programs typically used for direct-response advertising are older, less sought programs that are likely to appear on the station's list of available spots. Another common strategy is to purchase available time at the last possible moment to get the best price.

Personalization No other advertising medium can personalize the message as well as direct media. Parents with children at different age levels can be approached, with their child's name included in the appeal. Car owners are mailed letters congratulating them on their new purchase and offering accessories. Computer purchasers are sent software solicitations. Graduating college and university students receive very personalized information that recognizes their specific needs and offers solutions (such as credit cards).

Costs While the CPM for direct mail may be very high on an absolute and a relative basis, its ability to specifically target the audience and eliminate waste coverage reduces the actual CPM. The ads used on TV are often among the lowest-priced available, and a video can be delivered for less than $1 (including postage). A second factor contributing to the cost effectiveness of direct-response advertising is the cost per customer purchasing. Because of the low cost of media, each sale generated is very inexpensive.

Measures of Effectiveness No other medium can measure the effectiveness of its advertising efforts as well as direct response. Feedback is often immediate and always accurate.

LIMITATIONS OF DIRECT MARKETING

Image Factors Many people believe unsolicited mail promotes junk products, and others dislike being solicited. Likewise, direct-response ads on TV are often low-budget ads for lower-priced products, which contributes to the image that something less than the best products are marketed in this way. (Some of this image is being overcome by the home shopping channels, which promote some very expensive products.) Using the fax machine as a direct-response promotional media choice is unwelcome with most businesses.

Accuracy One of the advantages cited for direct mail and telemarketing was targeting potential customers specifically. But the effectiveness of these methods depends on the accuracy of the lists used. People move, change occupations, and so on, and if the lists are not kept current, selectivity will decrease. Computerization has greatly improved the currency of lists and reduced the incidence of bad names; however, the ability to generate lists is becoming a problem.[25]

Content Support In our discussion of media strategy objectives in Chapter 9, we said that the ability of magazines to create mood contributes to the overall effectiveness of the ads they carry. In direct-response advertising, mood creation is limited to the surrounding program and/or editorial content. Direct mail, telephone, and online services are unlikely to create a desirable mood.

SUMMARY

This chapter introduced you to the rapidly growing field of direct marketing, which involves a variety of methods and media beyond direct mail and telemarketing. The versatility of direct marketing offers many different types of companies and organizations a powerful promotional and selling tool.

Direct marketing continues to outpace other advertising and promotional areas in growth; many of the Fortune 500 companies now use sophisticated direct-marketing strategies. Database marketing has become a critical component of many marketing programs.

Advantages of direct marketing include its selective reach, segmentation, frequency, flexibility, and timing. Personalized and custom messages, low costs, and the ability to measure program effectiveness are also advantages of direct-marketing programs.

At the same time, a number of disadvantages are associated with the use of direct marketing. Image problems, the proliferating sale and use of databases (some of them based on inaccurate lists), lack of content support, and the intrusive nature of the medium make some marketers hesitant to use direct-marketing tools. However, self-policing of the industry and involvement by large, sophisticated companies have led to significant improvements. As a result, the use of direct marketing will continue to increase.

KEY TERMS

direct marketing, *444*
direct-response
   media, *444*
database, *447*
database marketing, *447*

RFM scoring method, *451*
one-step approach, *451*
two-step approach, *451*
mailing list, *453*

direct-response
   advertising, *454*
support advertising, *454*
infomercial, *454*

advertorial, *455*
telemarketing, *457*
audiotex, *457*
telemedia, *457*

DISCUSSION QUESTIONS

1. Identify some of the factors that have contributed to the growth of direct marketing. Do you see these factors being as relevant today? Discuss why or why not, and the impact they will have on direct marketing in the future.

2. Explain how a consumer goods company might employ database marketing. A business-to-business company? A service company?

3. The catalogue has become an important part of the shopping lives of many consumers. Describe different groups that you think might find catalogues useful in the consumer market, and explain what aspects of catalogues would attract them to this medium.

4. One of the disadvantages associated with direct-marketing media is the high cost per exposure. Some marketers feel that this cost is not really as much of a disadvantage as is claimed. Argue for or against this position.

5. Why have companies such as Volvo, Cadillac, and General Motors increased their use of infomercials? Is this a wise strategy?

6. Give an example of how companies might use direct marketing as part of an IMC program. Provide examples of both consumer and business marketers.

7. Direct marketing has been beset by a number of problems that have tarnished its image. Discuss some of these and what might be done to improve direct marketing's image.

8. How might business-to-business marketers use telemarketing effectively?

461

Internet and Interactive Media

CHAPTER OBJECTIVES

- To explore the different ways the Internet is used to communicate.

- To review the strengths and limitations of the Internet and interactive media.

- To understand the role of the Internet and interactive media in an IMC program.

- To evaluate the effectiveness of communications through the Internet.

General Mills Discovers the Internet

Consumer packaged goods companies have tried to figure out how to use the Internet to their advantage. While a general corporate information site tells the story of the organization and its products, brand managers for everyday food products looked to find a way to build their brands on this new medium. With decades of history advertising on radio and television, most consumer packaged goods companies considered moving advertising dollars to the Internet a risky move. In fact, one large company with many popular brand names declared itself a television advertising company while others waded into the Internet waters with tremendous trepidation.

The executives at General Mills Canada were no exception as they brainstormed how to seize the opportunity of the Internet and they eventually found a solution for a brand extension of their Nature Valley granola bar called Chewy Trail Mix. Using its experience with television, General Mills made a number of conclusions. It decided that it would not build a website since it would not build its own television channel. It did not make sense to advertise on niche websites since it would never advertise on community television channels. And, it would not focus on the General Mills logo since it did not plan to do this for its commercials.

The natural conclusion was to use the Internet as a medium to reach a wide audience and the most logical choice was the Sympatico.ca portal that received 5 million visitors per month. A Nature Valley/Sympatico microsite emerged when users selected certain subject sections. The repackaged look of the website provided links to various outdoor activities like hiking, golfing, and skiing. These links informed users about these recreational activities, provided recommendations on how to enjoy their experiences, and gave suggestions on what to eat, i.e., Nature Valley Chewy Trail Mix. The microsite featured an advergame that was tied to receiving a free sample delivered to the user's home. Executives believed in promotions targeted to adults aged 25–49 who enjoyed an active lifestyle but were not health-obsessed. Post-promotion results appeared impressive. The Nature Valley brand received an 18-percent increase in message association scores, a 35-percent increase in unaided brand awareness, and 20,000 unique visitors played the advergame.

Source: Chris Daniels, "Off to a Flying Start," *Marketing Magazine*, February 3, 2003.

Anyone who has followed the Internet industry over the last decade has seen an amazing series of events. Moving from a medium with almost no presence in the marketing environment to one that was the centre of attention, the Internet experienced a boom and eventually became a puzzle waiting to be solved, as many marketers tried to discover what role the Internet would assume in their communication program.

What the lead-in to this chapter illustrates, however, is that some companies have apparently solved the puzzle and have effectively integrated the Internet into their marketing communications programs. As you will see in this chapter, others have been successful as well, particularly when they view the Internet as a component of the integrated marketing communications program and not as the only tool required for success.

In this chapter we will discuss the Internet and interactive media, marketers' objectives for using these media, and ways to measure their effectiveness. As you will see, the Internet and interactive media are valuable components of the integrated marketing communications program and, like other components, are most effective when used in conjunction with other program elements. We will begin our discussion with the Internet.

DEFINING THE INTERNET

Before beginning our discussion, it may be useful to establish some common ground. While all of us are familiar with the Internet, the degree to which we are familiar varies. Understanding the material presented in this chapter will be easier if you are familiar with the terms used in the discussion. In this section, we briefly explain the basic parts of the Internet and related concepts.

INTERNET

The **Internet** is a worldwide means of exchanging information and communicating through a series of interconnected computers. It was started as a U.S. Defense Department project, but it is now accessible to anyone with a computer and a modem. While the most popular component of the Internet is the **World Wide Web (WWW)**, there are other features as well, as shown in Figure 16–1. For marketers, a number of these features offer potential, but it is the Web that has developed as the commercial component. For that reason, the following discussion will focus on

FIGURE 16–1
Features of the Internet
☐ ☐ ☐ ☐ ☐

Feature	Use
Electronic mail (e-mail)	Allows users to send electronic mail anywhere in the world
Usenet	Discussion groups, newsgroups, and electronic bulletin boards, similar to those offered by online services
Telnet	Online databases, library catalogues, and electronic journals at hundreds of colleges and public libraries
File transfer protocol (ftp) or hypertext transfer protocol (http)	The ability to transfer files from one mainframe computer to another
Client server	Allows for the transfer of files from one mainframe computer to another
Gopher	A document retrieval system used to search for information
Wide Area Information Server (WAIS)	Enables one to use keywords in specific databases and retrieve full text information
World Wide Web (WWW)	Does much the same thing as gopher and WAIS, but combines sound, graphic images, video, and hypertext on a single page; the commercial arm of the Internet

464

FIGURE 16–2
Internet terminology

☐ ☐ ☐ ☐ ☐

Term	Definition
Ad clicks	Number of times users click on an ad banner.
Ad click rate	Often referred to as "click-through," the percentage of ad views that result in an ad click.
Ad views (impressions)	Number of times an ad banner is downloaded (and presumably seen by viewers).
Banner	An ad on a Web page that may be "hot-linked" to the advertiser's site.
Button	An advertisement smaller than a traditional banner ad. Buttons are usually square in shape and located down the left or right side of the site; sometimes referred to as "tiles."
CPC	Cost per click—a marketing formula used to price ad banners. Some advertisers pay on the basis of the number of clicks a specific ad banner gets.
CPM	Cost per thousand for a site.
Domain name	The unique name of an Internet site. The top-level domain name for Canada is .ca and registrations are managed by the Canadian Internet Registration Authority (CIRA).
Hit	Each instance in which a server sends a file to a browser. Hits are used to measure the traffic on a site.
Interstitial	An advertisement that appears in a window on your screen while you are waiting for a Web page to load.
Link	An electronic connection between two websites.
Opt-in-e-mail	List of Internet users who have voluntarily signed up to receive commercial e-mail about topics of interest.
Page views	Number of times a user requests a page that contains a particular ad; used to indicate the number of times an ad was potentially seen, or "gross impressions."
Rich media	Advanced technology used in Internet ads, such as streaming video, which allows interaction and special effects.
Sponsorships	The sponsoring of a site's content by an advertiser.
Unique users	Number of different individuals who visit a site within a specific time period.
Valid hits	Number of hits that deliver all the information to a user (excludes error messages, redirects, etc.)
Visits	A sequence of requests made by one user at one site.

using the Web as a communications and sales tool. Before reading further, however, please take a few minutes to examine Figure 16–2 to familiarize yourself with some of the terms that we will be using. In reality, there are many more words that have been added to our language as a result of the growth of the Internet (you can also purchase a dictionary of Internet terms), but space permits only a small inclusion here. Thus, we have stayed away from the technical jargon, concentrating primarily on marketing communications terms.

E-BUSINESS

E-business encompasses all business activities conducted electronically, which can include incorporating Internet technologies but also includes other forms of electronic means. The focus of e-business is to use the technology to manage day-to-day business processes such as online sales and marketing, manufacturing, inventory control, employees, distributors, vendors and partners, to name a few. The intent is to improve communication to better manage a company's value *chain*.

E-COMMERCE

Many people think that electronic commerce, or **e-commerce**, is exclusively the domain of the Internet. It is not! E-commerce is simply a term for any kind of commercial activity that is electronically facilitated. Therefore, electronic commerce may include fax machines, banking machines, credit-card readers, or point-of-sale (POS) retail systems as well as the Internet to conduct transactions. According to U.S. Federal Standard 1032C from the Institute for Telecommunication Sciences, the term electronic commerce refers to "business transactions conducted by electronic means other than conventional telephone service, e.g., facsimile or electronic mail (e-mail)."

I-COMMERCE

Now that you can see from the above, that if all *financial transactions*, whether buying or selling, whether focused on the business-to-consumer market or the business-to-business market using electronic technology is called e-commerce, we can now define **i-commerce** as all those transactions done via the Internet. Many companies use the term e-commerce to define their Internet commerce, so don't be confused. The Internet and its terminology are evolving every day; by the time you read this textbook, much more will have evolved!

And this evolution will be seen in a number of new technologies. Take a look at the following examples of new gadgets out on the market today that are Internet-enabled: handheld PCs, PDAs (personal digital assistants), pen devices, palmtops, wallet PCs, Net phones and Web phones, Net printers, and more. By the year 2003, the number of handheld devices connected to the Internet surpassed the number of personal computers connected to the Internet.

INTERNET MARKETING

Picture all of the marketing functions that you have learned so far conducted on the Internet. If you were the Internet marketing director of a company, you would be responsible for the planning and implementation of an Internet marketing plan that would include goals for sales and market growth. This plan would have a target audience strategy, a product assortment and service strategy, pricing strategies for the various market segments, distribution strategies that maximize the Internet customer's purchasing and delivery satisfaction, and of course, a communications strategy to reach those sales and market share goals. This, in a nutshell, is what **Internet marketing** encompasses.

INTERNET MARKETING COMMUNICATION

As with other media discussed earlier in this text, businesses that have websites require the development of an IMC (integrated marketing communications) plan that uses the Internet to help fulfill their marketing communication goals. This plan should consider target audiences (users of the Net), specific objectives and strategies, and methods for measuring effectiveness. To develop a successful Internet marketing communications strategy, all of the lessons learned so far in this text apply to the Internet as well.

INTERNET PARTICIPANTS

The Internet, like all other media, has both customers (users) and those trying to reach these users (advertisers, sponsors, e-commerce). As with other media, the message can be targeted to consumer markets and business markets. We briefly identify these two to further explain the scope of the Internet as communication media.

Consumer Market During 2003, approximately 7.9 million of the 12.3 Canadian households (64 percent) had at least one person who used the Internet regularly.[1]

This represented a 5-percent increase over 2002, however the growth dropped significantly from 19 percent and 24 percent experienced in 2000 and 2001, respectively. A number of reasons have been offered to explain the initial adoption. A long period of economic prosperity, Internet innovation, heavy investments by companies, and changing lifestyles of the consumer (some consumers are now "money rich and time poor") have all contributed. However, the recent slowing of the growth signals that an eventual peak of adoption will be less than predictions of previous years.

The demographic profile of Internet users has evolved over time. The principal characteristic is the well-documented fact that Internet use is greatly influenced by the socio-economic status of the household; that is, the households with higher incomes and higher levels of education are much more likely to own a computer and use the Internet. For example, in Canada, only 35 percent of individuals with household incomes under $23,000 in 2004 had used the Internet from any location, compared to 90 percent of individuals in households with incomes of $70,000 or more. Thirty-two percent of adults 20 and over with less than a high school diploma used the Internet, whereas 88 percent of those with a university degree did so.[2] Figure 16–3 summarizes the types of usage ranging from online purchases to searches of various types of information to entertainment activities for households that have Internet access.

Business Market Internet usage for business reached higher levels than households in 2003. About 78 percent of all private-sector enterprises used the Internet compared to a 100-percent usage for public-sector organizations. About one-third of all business enterprises have a website and over 90 percent of all public-sector organizations have a website.[3] Although one-third adoption of a website may appear low,

	Regular home-use households (%)				
	1999	2000	2001	2002	2003
Purpose of use					
E-mail	91.7	93.3	94.7	95.2	95.7
Electronic banking	27.7	36.6	44.4	51.0	56.6
Purchasing goods/services	19.0	23.8	26.0	30.5	34.2
Medical/health information	54.2	57.1	61.8	63.9	65.3
Formal education/training	32.0	47.3	47.0	47.3	45.7
Government information	44.1	47.1	52.5	56.7	59.1
Search for employment	-	30.5	33.2	35.0	36.1
General browsing	84.7	90.1	91.0	89.6	89.1
Playing games	42.7	45.3	50.1	50.0	51.3
Chat groups	26.2	27.4	28.0	27.2	26.5
Obtaining/saving music	27.1	44.3	47.9	47.3	37.8
Listening to radio	17.5	23.2	25.3	24.0	24.1
Find sports-related information	—	43.2	45.3	46.3	45.2
Financial information	—	46.1	46.8	45.7	46.0
View the news	—	50.8	53.8	52.9	55.5
Travel information/arrangements	—	54.6	56.3	59.1	61.8
Other Internet services	34.7	44.1	43.3	48.1	43.1

FIGURE 16–3
Households using the Internet from home, by purpose of use
☐ ☐ ☐ ☐ ☐

Source: Statistics Canada, CANSIM, table 358-0006 and Catalogue no. 56F0004MIE.

these organizations accounted for 85 percent of all gross business income. Moreover, the vast majority of Canadian businesses are very small—businesses with 20 or more employees represent only 5 percent of all enterprises.

Many large business-to-business marketers use the Internet in a variety of ways. Hewlett-Packard has budgeted over $100 million to target B2B users of its equipment.[4] Cisco and Dell use the Web to track and distribute sales leads in real time, while others such as Scientific International train their sales representatives and host sales meetings via the Web as well as sell.[5] Cisco estimates that it saves $1 million per month by having sales meetings on the Web.[6] One of the main benefits for business-to-business marketers is the ability to acquire information about products and services. In today's Internet world, a company can immediately pull up the product and service offerings of a provider, without having to make a phone call or wait for a salesperson to visit. In turn, the same company can reach thousands of potential customers that it would not have been possible to reach without a website—at a significantly reduced cost.

INTERNET COMMUNICATION

The role of the **website** is to act as the place where information is made available by the website provider to Internet users (see IMC Perspective 16–1). Developing and maintaining a successful website requires significant time and effort. To attract visitors to the site and have them return to it requires a combination of creativity, effective marketing, continual updating of the site, and the use of other media to direct consumers.

When major corporations first began to conduct business on the Internet, they put up websites primarily for information purposes. Companies had sites that were really not much more than online catalogues designed for information purposes only. The role of the website quickly changed, however; sites have become much more creative and with technological advances it is possible to create fancier graphics, audio, and animation online.

Thus, the Internet is a communications medium, allowing companies to create awareness, provide information, and influence attitudes, as well as pursue other communications objectives. But it is also in part a direct-response medium, allowing the user to both purchase and sell products through e-commerce (Figure 16–4). Let's first look at some of the communication objectives these companies want to achieve.

WEBSITE COMMUNICATION OBJECTIVES

From a purely communication standpoint, websites typically attempt to acheive three broad communication objectives; awareness, information, and brand building.

FIGURE 16–4
Focus of online marketing efforts—by customer base
☐ ☐ ☐ ☐ ☐

% Focusing on...	TOTAL	Customer Base		
		Business to Consumer	Business to Business	Both
Brand/Image building	52	46	65	60
Customer acquisition	43	54	39	47
Direct response	32	34	19	43
Promotion	42	49	39	51
Sales	38	39	40	47

BASE: Those doing online marketing (n=279)

Source: Canadian Marketing Association 2005 Fact Book.

The Dot-CA Revolution!

Marketers are increasingly reaching to the Internet to support marketing campaigns by including websites as part of the marketing mix. The selection of a domain name enabling visitors to reach a specific site is an important decision, as it has to be memorable and connected to the brand or company.

Up until the late 1990s, dot-com domain names were often chosen by default. But now, Canadian businesses have a new alternative the Canadian Internet Registration Authority (CIRA). CIRA is the not-for-profit corporation mandated to operate the dot-ca top-level domain for all Canadians. It is responsible for setting policy and managing the dot-ca domain database as well as registering domain names through its network of certified registrars. The Ottawa-based dot-ca governing body has recently experienced 500 percent growth in dot-ca registrations between December 2000 (60,000 names) and July 2002 (300,000 names).

Previously, dot-ca domain names had been registered on a volunteer basis at the University of British Columbia. With the recent usage and rapid commercialization of the Internet, the Internet community agreed that the original rules and mode of operation had to be changed. A representative committee recommended that a not-for-profit, private-sector corporation be incorporated to run the dot-ca registry. This occurred in December 1998, when the CIRA was incorporated.

In November 2001, CIRA commissioned a study by The Strategic Council, which reveals that Canadian Internet users:

- Know that dot-ca means Canada,
- Prefer visiting dot-ca sites for services and information (71 percent agreement),
- Prefer to shop online through a dot-ca web site if given a choice (77 percent agreement),
- Associate dot-com with American and international companies,
- Associate great patriotic and emotional appeal with dot-ca domain names.

An analysis carried out by Jupiter Media Metrix on behalf of CIRA corroborates the rising popularity of the dot-ca extension. Jupiter Media Metrix studied the traffic flow of ten popular websites with both dot-com and dot-ca extensions—AOL, eBay, foodtv, Ford, Google, MSN, Netscape, Sears, Ticketmaster, and Yahoo!—between January 2001 and April 2002. In eight of the ten sites, the results reveal that there is a greater traffic increase in the website with the dot-ca extension over those with dot-com.

In May 2002, another CIRA study performed by Impact Research, a member of the Cossette Communications Group—Canada's largest full service communications agency—revealed that Canadian companies perceive more value in dot-ca names for Canadian consumers and business development, and sites bearing dot-ca names are more trustworthy and honest than dot-com sites.

Marketers registering domain names for campaigns and promotions need to think of how they will manage their domain names after the campaigns or promotions have ended. Domain names can be registered for periods ranging from one to ten years. "Domain name poachers" are on the lookout for expired domain names that have been advertised and promoted. By registering expired names and directing them to other sites, poachers are able to increase their visitor traffic and charge higher advertising banner fees.

Create Awareness   Advertising on the Web can be useful in creating awareness of an organization as well as its specific product and service offerings. For small companies with limited budgets, the Web offers the opportunity to create awareness well beyond what might be achieved through traditional media. However, the Internet may not be the most optimal media for awareness in many situations due to its limited reach of a website without other communication to direct consumers.

Disseminate Information   One of the primary objectives for using the Web is to provide in-depth information about a company's products and services. In business-to-business markets, having a website has become a necessity, as more and more buyers expect that a company will have a site providing them with detailed information about its offerings. In the public sector, all levels of government use the Internet to provide its citizens with a wide range of information on its services and

Exhibit 16–1
Cheerios uses their package to send users to their home page

Exhibit 16–2
Sharp uses the Web to enhance its image

policies. For example, we cited Internet usage statistics in this chapter from research conducted by Statistics Canada. For many consumer companies, their websites serve as a means of communicating more information about their products and services. The Huggies site shows how a website can facilitate this objective, while the Cheerios box shown in Exhibit 16–1 demonstrates how General Mills refers users to its site for additional information.

Build a Brand Image Many websites are designed to reflect the image a company wants to portray. For example, when you have a few minutes to spare, check out the consumer sites at iam.ca and labattblue.ca or the business-to-business site at www.sharp.com (Exhibit 16–2). All of these are excellent examples of websites used for image building. Interestingly, one of the difficulties traditional marketers have experienced is that of creating a brand image on the Internet. While some of these companies have been successful, others have not fared as well and have come to realize that branding and image-creating strategies must be specifically adapted to this medium.

According to David Aaker, a well-renowned marketing expert, the Internet—as part of an integrated marketing communications program—can be a useful tool for branding.[7] Unfortunately, many companies have not yet figured out how to successfully brand through the Internet. A review of the literature over the past five years will lead to a number of articles discussing this very topic and the difficulties in achieving this objective. While space does not permit an in-depth review, let's discuss just a few of the many reasons why companies attempting to create branding through the Internet may not be achieving their goals.

Branding Is a Complicated Process While creating a strong brand is not easy in any communications effort, some marketers feel that it may be even more difficult to do on the Internet. As noted by Karen Benezra, editor of *Brandweek* magazine, many companies—dot-coms as well as traditional—have spent millions of dollars trying to brand by advertising on the Internet, with only lukewarm success. One reason behind this problem, Benezra notes, is the lack of a clear understanding of the role the Web should assume in the branding process. New or less well known brands may have to assume different strategies than those used by more established brands such as Volvo, BMW, or The Gap. Another reason is that many marketers mistakenly believe that simply creating awareness or attention will lead to a strong brand. Finally, notes Benezra, it takes a long time to establish a brand relationship with a customer, and the Internet hasn't been around long enough to prove its branding capabilities.[8]

Branding and Direct Response May Be Counter Objectives Noting the similarities between the Internet and other direct-response media like catalogues or interactive TV, some marketers feel that the Internet is best suited to be a direct-response medium. They contend that direct marketing requires a very targeted effort, searching for high-probability buyers.

Branding, on the other hand, is much less targeted and reaches out to numerous audiences. According to Erwin Ephron of *Advertising Age*, the Internet is somewhere in between, and trying to achieve both objectives at the same time has led to unsuccessful branding efforts.[9]

Costs Are Too High Successful branding does not take place overnight. Unfortunately, many marketers aren't willing, or feel that they can't afford, to wait. Such marketers may view the Internet as a "quick fix" that will allow them to instantly establish their brands. When they discover that the Internet is not able to provide instant identity, they may quickly return to their focus on ROI or the bottom line. Cutting advertising and brand identity efforts on the Internet will immediately reflect cost savings and a return to business as normal.[10]

The above are just a few of many reasons that can be offered as to why branding on the Internet has been less successful than many hoped. We believe that the Internet—as part of an integrated marketing communications program—can be used for branding purposes, as well as for other objectives. The opening vignette provides an example of a company that has used this medium effectively, by integrating media.

WEBSITE STRATEGY

Making a site work and having one work successfully are not the same thing, however, and whether a site is effective is determined by what it is that management hopes to achieve through the site. As already noted, some sites are offered for informational purposes only (this tends to be more common in the business-to-business market than the consumer market), while others approach the market much more aggressively. For example, Kimberly-Clark Corporation, the manufacturer of Huggies brand (diapers, Pull-Ups training pants, and Little Swimmers swim pants) has been extremely successful in its Internet marketing efforts. The Huggies home page (Exhibit 16–3) goes well beyond providing information. The site has additional objectives, such as developing a relationship with parents, establishing a brand image for the products through online campaigns, and supporting sales. For example, one campaign designed to develop one-on-one relationships offered a free sample to anyone who sent in his or her name, address, and e-mail address. Thousands of people responded to the offer, providing Kimberly-Clark with an enormous database useful for future marketing efforts. Another campaign targeted parents visiting other websites such as CTW.org (Children's Television Workshop, producer of *Sesame Street*), Women.com, iVillage.com, and BabyZone.com. In addition, anyone typing in the keywords *diapers* or *infant care* on portals Lycos and

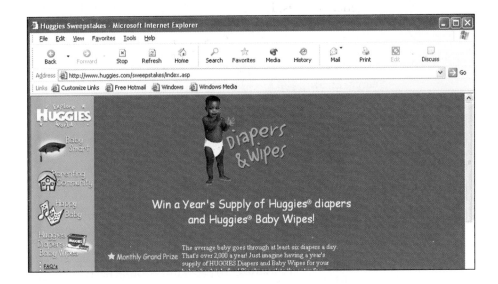

Exhibit 16–3
Huggies homepage

Excite was greeted with a Huggies banner ad. To bring visitors to the site, Huggies provided tips on baby care, chat with other parents, access to other baby links, and additional information about Huggies products. Finally, to support sales, the site directed customers to the nearest retail store that sells Huggies brands.

As the Huggies example demonstrates, a website can be an effective tool for the marketer. Depending on the nature of one's business and one's marketing objectives for the Internet, a website can range from being a very simple source of information about the company and its products to being a powerful tool for developing a brand image, communicating an advertising message, executing sales promotions, delivering public relations, and conducting direct marketing transactions.

INTERNET AND IMC

The Internet may be one of the strongest arguments yet for companies to adopt an integrated marketing communications perspective. Rather than hurting traditional media and reducing the expenditures therein, the Internet both complements and relies on other media in an effective IMC program. In this section, we discuss how the Internet can be used with other program elements.

ADVERTISING

Like broadcast or print, the Internet is also used as an advertising medium. Companies and organizations working to promote their products and services must consider this medium as they would television, magazines, outdoor, and so on. In 2003, the Interactive Advertising Bureau (IAB) of Canada estimated that online advertising reached $237 million (Figure 16–5). However, this is still drastically lower than the almost $3 billion spent on television. The types of online advertising used by companies is shown in Figure 16–6. We now discuss these various options.

Banners Nearly every website that incorporates *third-party advertising* as part of their *revenue model* displays **banner ads**. It is the most common form of advertising on the Web, accounting for approximately 53 percent of advertising expenditures. The number of online ad impressions listed in the 4th quarter of 2000 in Canada was 172 billion. The expected average number of banner ads that online users will see per day in 2005 are 950.[11] Banner ads may be used for creating awareness or recognition or for direct-marketing objectives. Banner ads that run vertically down the side of a Web page are often called *skyscrapers*, or *inline ads*. While banner ads can be useful for driving traffic to a website, they can often be more useful for branding purposes—making Internet users aware of a brand or positioning a brand in the minds of users.

FIGURE 16–5
2003 revenue, segmented ($ millions)

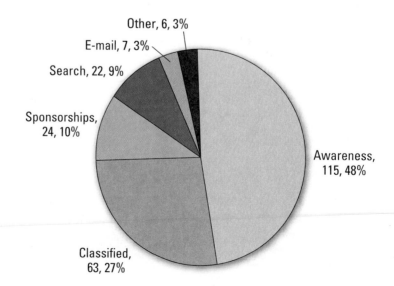

Other, 6, 3%
E-mail, 7, 3%
Search, 22, 9%
Sponsorships, 24, 10%
Awareness, 115, 48%
Classified, 63, 27%

% using...	Customer Base			
	TOTAL	B2C	B2B	Both
E-mail marketing	75	78	77	84
Banner or tower ads on a third party website	52	62	58	56
Banner or tower ads on your company's website	42	58	44	43
Search engine optimization	41	45	52	44
Affiliate program	25	25	23	36
Pop-ups on your company's website	15	15	6	20
Pop-ups on a third party website	9	15	6	10
Other	8	10	4	13

BASE: Those doing online marketing

Source: Canadian Marketing Association 2005 Fact Book.

FIGURE 16–6

Types of online advertising used— by company revenue ☐ ☐ ☐ ☐ ☐

Sponsorship   Another common form of advertising is **sponsorship**, of which there are two types. Regular sponsorship occurs when a company pays to sponsor a section of a site. A more involved agreement is the **content sponsorship**, in which the sponsor not only provides dollars in return for name association but also participates in providing the content itself. In some cases, the site is responsible for providing content and having it approved by the sponsor; in other instances, the sponsor may contribute all or part of the content. Due in part to the decline in the effectiveness of banner ads and to the desire for more enrollment and exposure, sponsorships have been increasing in popularity.

Pop-Ups/Pop-Unders   When you access the Internet, have you ever seen a small window appear with an advertising message? Such windows are known as **pop-ups**, and they often appear when you access a certain site. Pop-ups are usually larger than a banner ad but smaller than a full screen. **Pop-unders** are ads that appear underneath the Web page and become visible only when the user leaves the site. For example, if you ever visited a travel website, you probably were hit with a pop-under ad for Orbitz—one of the heaviest users of this form of Web advertising.

While some companies like Orbitz believe that pop-ups and pop-unders are effective forms of advertising, others disagree. Consumer complaints have led Google.com, iVillage.com, and Earthlink (among others) to no longer accept these advertising forms. (According to iVillage, its research indicates that as many as 90 percent of its users dislike such ads.) Nevertheless, indications are that despite the annoying qualities of pop-ups and pop-unders, more and more websites are offering this type of advertising.

Interstitials   **Interstitials** are ads that pop up on your screen while you are waiting for a site's content to download. Although some advertisers believe that interstitials are irritating and more of a nuisance than a benefit, a study conducted by Grey Advertising found that only 15 percent of those surveyed felt that the ads were irritating (versus 9 percent for banner ads) and that 47 percent liked the ads (versus 38 percent for banners). Perhaps more importantly, while ad recall of banner ads was approximately 51 percent, recall of interstitials was much higher, at 76 percent.

Push Technologies   **Push technologies**, or **webcasting** technologies, also called intermercials, allow companies to "push" a message to consumers rather than waiting for them to find it. Push technologies dispatch Web pages and news updates and may have sound and video geared to specific audiences and even individuals. For example, a manager whose job responsibilities involve corporate finance might log on to his or her computer and find that new stories are automatically there on the economy, stock updates, or a summary of a speech. Companies such as Pointcast provide screen savers that automatically "hook" the viewer to their sites for sports, news, weather reports, and/or other information that the viewer has specified. Users can use **personalization**— that is, they can personalize their sites to request the kinds of specific information they are most interested in viewing. For example, if you are into sports, you can have updates sent to you through sites providing sports information. The service is paid for by advertisers who flash their messages on the screen.

Links   While considered by some as not a type of advertising, **links** serve many of the same purposes as are served by the types discussed above. Links come in two types, text and logos. A visitor to one site may click on a logo that provides additional information and/or related materials at another site. Thus someone on TSN.ca may link to Nike.com and find information on sports-related products. Other forms of advertising, such as ads placed in chat rooms, are also available. Given the limited use of many of these alternatives, we suggest the reader consult additional resources for more information.

Sales Promotion on the Internet   Companies have found the Internet to be a very effective medium for delivering sales promotions. Contests can be communicatied and executed on a website. We noted the advent of coupons in Chapter 13. Essentially we have witnessed every single sales promotion evolve digitally.

PERSONAL SELLING ON THE INTERNET

The Internet has been both a benefit and a detriment to many of those involved in personal selling—particularly those in the business-to-business market. For some, the Internet has been a threat that might take away job opportunities. Companies have found that they can remain effective—even increase effectiveness—by building a strong Web presence. The high-cost and poor-reach limitations of personal selling are allowing these companies to reduce their sales force.

On the positive side, websites have been used quite effectively to enhance and support the selling effort. As noted earlier, the Web has become a primary source of information for millions of customers in the consumer and business-to-business markets. Visitors to websites can gain volumes of information about a company's products and services. In return, the visitors become a valuable resource for leads that both internal and external salespersons can follow up, and they become part of a prospect database. Not only can potential customers learn about the company's offerings, but the selling organization can serve and qualify prospects more cost-effectively.

Some companies have used the Internet to improve their one-on-one relationships with customers. By providing more information in a more timely and efficient manner, a company enables customers to learn more about what it has to offer. This increases the opportunity for cross-selling and customer retention. For example, Neoforma.com links hospitals and medical supply vendors with listings of 300,000 medical products, with pages describing separate product categories.[12] For those interested in medical products, the site has become a one-stop shopping centre. In addition, by providing a website, companies can improve their response times to inquiries as well as complaints, thereby improving customer service.

PUBLIC RELATIONS ON THE INTERNET

As with other media, the Internet is a useful medium for conducting public relations activities. Many sites devote a portion of their content to public relations activities, including the provision of information about the company, its philanthropic activities, and annual reports. Companies have used the Web to establish media, government, investor, and community relationships; deal with crises; and even perform corporate image, advocacy, and cause-related advertising. Companies have used their websites to address issues as well as to provide information about products and services, archive press releases, link to other articles and sites, and provide lists of activities and events. Other Internet tools, including e-mails and e-mail newsletters, have also been used effectively.

Shel Holtz, in his book *Public Relations on the Internet*, notes that the Internet offers a number of opportunities to public relations practitioners, including: (1) the development of media relations websites, (2) the ability to provide customized information dissemination, and (3) the development of positive e-mail relationships. Shel Holtz notes that while there are many similarities between public relations activities conducted in traditional media and those conducted on the Internet, three main elements account for the differences between the two:

- The Internet offers a more limited opportunity to gain attention due to short exposure times.
- The Internet offers the opportunity to build internal links that provide the media with instant access to additional sources of information on the issue.
- The Internet offers the ability to provide much more substantial information. Print and broadcast materials are confined by time and space limitations, while the Internet can literally provide volumes of information at a fingertip—or click of a mouse.[13]

One example of the use of public relations on the Internet is provided by Chrysler. Working with reporters, Chrysler developed a one-stop information source for the media (the public could also use the site, but reporters would have to register to use the "newsroom"). News stories and other forms of content, photo images, and cross-references to other sites or media were included on the site, as were press kits and a calendar of upcoming events (Exhibit 16–4). The objective of the site was to improve relations with the press, and Chrysler was quite effective in doing so.

At the same time, many philanthropic and non-profit organizations have found the Internet to be a useful way to generate funds. Several sites have developed to perform the functions that are required in traditional fund-raising programs. Other sites have been formed to handle public relations activities for charitable organizations, provide information regarding the causes the charity supports, collect contributions, and so on.

DIRECT MARKETING ON THE INTERNET

Our discussion of direct marketing and the Internet will approach the topic from the perspective of e-mail and short-message services.

Exhibit 16–4
Chrysler provides public relations information on its site

E-Mail Direct mail on the Internet is essentially an electronic version of regular mail. Like regular mail it is highly targeted, relies heavily on lists, and attempts to reach consumers with specific needs through targeted messages. As we discussed earlier under personalization, consumers can opt to have specific types of e-mail sent to them and other types not sent. For example, if you permit, media firms and Web portals will e-mail you information about specific promotions, articles that will appear, books on sale, and other items that you may purchase.

Alternatively companies can use e-mail for different purposes. For example, Bell Sympatico uses e-mail for customer stages. It sends e-mail to new consumers who sign-up with Sympatico as their Internet service provider in order to obtain personal information and make the new user comfortable with the Internet. Later, when the data analysis of usage behaviour indicates a high probability of a customer leaving, Bell Sympatico sends out a customized e-mail to encourage the customer to stay. The results have been impressive as the firm has noted a substantial drop in its percentage of customers leaving, also known in the industry as churn. Finally, subsequent data analysis identifies customers who may be using services that do not fully meet their needs, and Bell Sympatico sends out an e-mail communicating a more appropriate service level. In some cases, it has sent direct mail, but it received a substantially less response rate.[14]

Sometimes, users may also receive less targeted and unwanted e-mails. The electronic equivalent of junk mail, these messages are referred to as **SPAM**. However, legitimate and enlightened marketers accept the practice of permission-based marketing where consumers register to willingly receive e-mail communications from organizations. Figure 16–7 summarizes the different types of advertising and promotion messages that Canadian consumers are most interested in receiving via e-mail and Figure 16–8 indicates Canadian consumers' typical behavioural responses after receiving an e-mail.

FIGURE 16–7
Registering to receive
e-mail/types of sites
registered
□ □ □ □ □

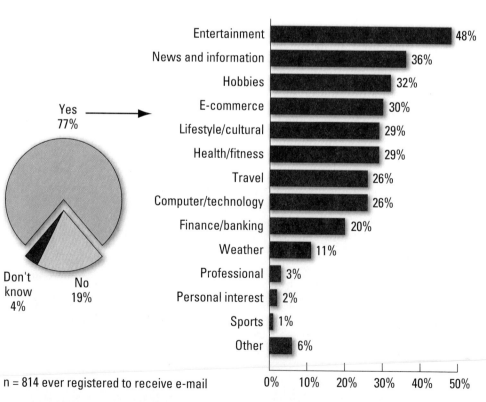

Yes → Entertainment 48%
77%

News and information 36%

Hobbies 32%

E-commerce 30%

Lifestyle/cultural 29%

Health/fitness 29%

Travel 26%

Computer/technology 26%

Finance/banking 20%

Weather 11%

Professional 3%

Personal interest 2%

Sports 1%

Other 6%

Don't know 4%   No 19%

0%   10%   20%   30%   40%   50%

n = 814 ever registered to receive e-mail

Source: Ipsos-Reid, 2004 E-mail Marketing Study

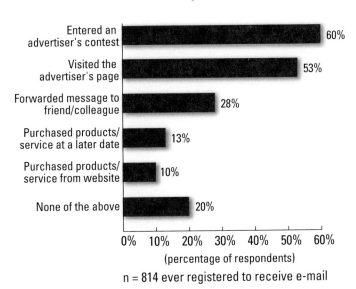

FIGURE 16–8
Activities resulting from permission-based commercial e-mail
☐ ☐ ☐ ☐ ☐

Source: Ipsos-Reid, 2004 E-mail Marketing Study

Short-Message Service With recent wireless technology advances, instant text messages sent to cellphone users emerged as a new way to communicate via the Internet. In 2002, Canadian cellphone carriers agreed to connect their networks so that text messages could be sent to any cellphone hand-set, regardless of the carrier used. For example, instead of only being able to send messages from one Telus user to another, Telus customers could send messages to a friend who used Rogers, Bell Mobility, or Fido.[15]

This technological evolution paved the way for marketers to develop innovative two-way communication. Rather than send text messages one-way like e-mail, marketers conceived of the idea of creating short-code as part of a short-message service (SMS) so that consumers could immediately respond to relevant ads through their cellphone hand-set. For example, if "24BLUE" is seen on a billboard, the consumer could type this in and receive whatever promotional offer or information Labatt wanted to send as part of their overall promotional program. Overall, the SMS becomes a permission-based pull communication as only those interested in the promotional messages respond accordingly. Moreover, the marketer can reach any cellphone user with the technology standardization.[16]

With 7 million SMS functional cellphones sold in Canada each year, the future of SMS is explosive. Two years after the standardization across carriers, Canadians sent 37 million messages per month. However, this is light compared to what is happening in Europe and Asia. For example, the U.K. has double the population of Canada, yet 1.9 billion messages are sent each month.[17]

And companies also will likely find innovative ways to interact with their current customers, going beyond promotional incentives to attract switchers. For example, pharmaceutical company Janssen-Ortho, manufacturer of a contraceptive patch for women, sends weekly reminders to change their patch to women who have provided the request.[18]

MEASURING INTERNET EFFECTIVENESS

Measuring the effectiveness of the Internet is done by variety of methods, most of which can be done electronically. Audience information (demographics, psychographics, and so on) and exposure were the initial measures of effectiveness; however, fully measuring communication effects is an emerging trend.

AUDIENCE MEASURES

You will see that while the Internet industry has developed its own measures of effectiveness, there are some problems with these measures that must be considered

FIGURE 16–9

IAB Guidelines for
Internet measurement

□ □ □ □ □

Ad impression. This is a measurement of responses from an ad delivery system to an ad request from the user's browser.

Click. This measure includes three forms: click-through, in-unit click and mouse-over. A *click-through* occurs when the viewer clicks on the ad to have information sent to him or her. The in-unit click and the mouse-over are ad interactions without the content being sent to the viewer.

Visit. A visit is defined as "one or more text and/or graphics downloads from a site qualifying as at least one page, without 30 consecutive minutes of inactivity, which can be reasonably attributed to a single browser for a single session." The browser must "pull" text or graphic content to be considered a visit.

Unique measurement (browsers, visitors, and users). This is the number of actual individual people, within a designated reporting timeframe, with activity consisting of one or more visits to a site or the delivery of pushed content. A unique user can be either (1) an actual individual who accesses a site (unique visitor) or (2) an actual individual who is pushed content and/or ads such as e-mail, newsletters, interstitials, and pop-up or pop-under ads. Each individual is counted only once in the unique-user or visitor measure for the reporting period. When no attempt is made to estimate the number of unique users based on the number of unique cookies received, the measure should be referred to as unique browsers.

Page impression. This is a measurement of the responses from a Web server to a page request from the user's browser. Pagelike items should be counted as follows:

- Pop-ups—ad impressions
- Interstitials—ad impressions
- Pop-unders—ad impressions
- HTML newsletters (if opened)—page impressions (if ad only—ad impressions)
- Auto-refreshed pages—page impressions
- Frames—page impressions

when employing them. In an attempt to respond to criticism of the audience metrics employed, as well as to standardize some of the measures used to gauge effectiveness of the Internet, the Internet Advertising Bureau (IAB)—the largest and most influential trade group—conducted research on these methods. In their 2002 report, the group created voluntary guidelines intended to make uniform the various incompatible systems that evaluate effectiveness of Internet advertisements. The guidelines included five measures that would allow for independent auditing and verification (Figure 16–9). It is believed that the adoption of these guidelines, along with objective auditing, will make the Internet a more attractive medium for many of those who advertise in traditional media.

The measures suggested do not include a commonly employed method referred to as *hits*—the number of times that a specific component of a site is requested. Hits could include 100 people making one request each or one person making 100 requests. As a measure of communication effectiveness, hits have generally been considered a weak metric. Thus, while some may still track hits, many companies have abandoned this measure or place little emphasis on it.

This information is typically collected by a cookie, an electronic device attached to your file (usually without your knowing it) that collects information on where you visit, how many times you visit, where you click, and the like. A new technology goes beyond "cookies" by tracking what sites are on the Internet and where, as well as who, goes to them. The technology collects data on all Web activity by any user who signs up for it and measures how much traffic a site gets, where they go next are all reported. The limitation of these measures (i.e., exposure only) and the need of advertisers' desire for additional information have resulted in further investigation for comprehensive effective measures to more fully track processing or communication effects in terms of awareness or attitude.

PROCESSING AND COMMUNICATION EFFECTS MEASURES

The movement for comprehensive communication effects measurement reveals that the Internet has its own set of criteria for measuring effectiveness and it is also borrowing from traditional measures—for example, brand recall is becoming a major area of focus.[19] Many companies that provide research information in traditional media are now extending their reach into the Internet world. Academics are also beginning to publish articles related to measuring effectiveness on the Internet. Studies on consumers' attitudes toward a site, response variations in e-mail surveys, and similarities between brick-and-mortar retailing and e-commerce are just a few of the many articles being published in academic journals to advance the measurement of the Internet.[20] We now summarize a few emerging communication effects measures.

Online Measuring   Firms are developing methods similar to those found in other media (i.e. PMB study) to measure demographics, psychographics, location of Web access, media usage, and buying habits. Clients can determine who saw their ads, determine reach, and ascertain whether the right target audience was reached. Advertisers can test the impact of their messages, receiving a report detailing impressions and clicks by time of day and day of the week.

Recall and Retention   Traditional interviews with Web users help determine recall and whether viewers remember the ads they see, as well as whether there is a "halo-effect" among ads.

Surveys   Survey research, conducted both online and through traditional methods, is employed to determine everything from site usage to attitudes toward a site.

Panels   Adapting traditional panel research is the focus of some firms that provide information on demographics, unique users, frequency of visitors, pages viewed, and how long a viewer stays at a site ("stickiness").

Sales   Of course, for the e-commerce marketers, a prime indicator of effectiveness is the number of sales generated. Adding information regarding demographics, user behaviours, and so on, can increase the effectiveness of this measure.

Tracking   Some companies now provide information on specific communication measures like brand awareness, message association, brand attitude, and purchase intention.

SOURCES OF MEASUREMENT DATA

The number of sources available that provide information about the Internet is enormous. Below we provide a partial list just to give you some indication of the types of information available. Most of the companies listed are the largest and/or most cited sources, and the list is by no means intended to be exhaustive:

- *Arbitron*. Arbitron provides demographic, media usage, and lifestyle data on users of the Internet as well as other interactive media.
- *MRI and SMRB*. Both of these companies now provide information regarding viewership profiles for the Internet and other interactive media. Nielsen offers similar data.
- *Audit Bureau of Circulations*. This print agency is developing a product called WebFacts to certify Web counts.
- *Internet Advertising Bureau (IAB)*. A trade organization of the Internet, IAB provides information on statistics, usage, and strategies regarding the Internet.

479

- *eMarketer.* This company publishes comparative data from various research sources and explains the different methods used to arrive at the projections. It also publishes its own projections.
- *Nielson Net Ratings.* Nielson provides audience information and analysis based on click-by-click Internet behaviour through a meter installed on users' computers at home and work.
- *Jupiter MediaMetrics.* This large merged firm provides statistics and website information, including data on users, projections, trends, and so on.
- *Business 2.0* and *Fast Company.* Each of these business-to-business magazines targets those interested in the Internet, from a technological as well as a business perspective, with emphasis on the latter.
- *Internet Advertising Report* and *office.com.* Both these organizations provide an online newsletter containing information on trends, statistics, and other articles of interest to Internet users in the business community.

EVALUATION OF INTERNET MARKETING

As we have dome for other media thus far in the text, we summarize the various strengths and limitations of the Internet as media for delivering a message. IMC Perspective 16–2 shows how Saturn has successfully applied the strengths of the Internet.

STRENGTHS OF INTERNET MARKETING

Target Marketing A major strength of the Web is the ability to target very specific groups of individuals with a minimum of waste coverage. For those in the business-to-business market, the Internet resembles a combination trade magazine and trade show, as only those most interested in the products and/or services that a site has to offer will visit the site (others have little or no reason to do so). In the consumer market, through personalization and other targeting techniques, sites are becoming more tailored to meet one's needs and wants.

Message Tailoring As a result of precise targeting, messages can be designed to appeal to the specific needs and wants of the target audience. The interactive capabilities of the Net make it possible to carry on one-to-one marketing with increased success in both the business and the consumer markets.

Interactive Capabilities Because the Internet is interactive, it provides strong potential for increasing customer involvement and satisfaction and almost immediate feedback for buyers and sellers. A recent study indicated that as many as 47 percent of Internet users multitask. [21] As multitasking increases, the interactive capabilities of the Internet will make this medium even more attractive.

Information Access Perhaps the greatest strength of the Internet is its availability as an information source. Internet users can find a plethora of information about almost any topic of their choosing merely by conducting a search through one of the search engines. Once they have visited a particular site, users can garner a wealth of information regarding product specifications, costs, purchase information, and so on. Links will direct them to even more information if it is desired.

Sales Potential The numbers provided earlier in this chapter demonstrate the incredible sales numbers being generated in both the business-to-business and the consumer segments. Forecasts are for almost exponential growth in the future.

Creativity Creatively designed sites can enhance a company's image, lead to repeat visits, and positively position the company or organization in the consumer's mind.

Saturn Sets a Virtual Scene

A young guy cruising down a deserted highway spots in his rear-view mirror a UFO that's chasing his vehicle. As cool as 007, the driver steps on the accelerator and smoothly outpaces the spacecraft.

No, it's not a scene from the sequel to *Independence Day*. The almost-cheesy animated film, called *Intergalactic Getaway*, is one of four short clips currently showing on the SaturnCanada.com website. The mini-movies, which run no longer than 30 seconds each, are essentially animated ads for the automaker's new Ion, a vehicle Saturn is hoping to peddle to a younger, more image-conscious audience.

According to Eric LeBlanc, advertising and promotions manager at Saturn Canada, a launch campaign for its new vehicle "wouldn't be complete without the Internet." That's why the online efforts, which also encompass banner advertising and innovative e-mail marketing, is the driving force behind a new integrated campaign for the Ion.

And it is truly integrated. The campaign includes television, direct mail, outdoor, cinema, and newspaper. But unlike the integrated campaigns of many other marketers, in this case the digital component is not an afterthought.

"The Internet is often thought of as a secondary or peripheral medium," says LeBlanc. "We think of it as a primary medium like everything else."

It is not surprising that a player in the automotive industry is enthusiastically embracing the Internet. Daniel Taras, vice-president, i-business and sector specialist at iPerceptions, a business intelligence company headquartered in New York with offices in Toronto and Montreal, says automotive sites have the highest frequency of repeat visitors compared with the sites of other sectors.

Taras says Canadian data shows that 45 percent of all visitors to primary automotive sites have already visited the site at least six times before in the previous six months (just 20 percent of visitors are first timers). "That is a huge validation of the Internet and has resulted in all of the car companies trying to leverage that fact by building a community around the Web," he says. Taras adds that conducting research is the main reason people visit automotive sites.

For Saturn Canada, a division of General Motors based in Oshawa, Ontario, the Internet is especially important. "Our target markets are the largest users of the Internet in the automotive industry, so as part of a launch campaign we need to keep the Web front and centre," says LeBlanc, who says up to 75 percent of Saturn's drivers surf the Web. "Consumers

arm themselves with so much information from the online medium before they go into a retail facility. It isn't like in the past when they shopped from dealership to dealership."

Saturn's long-time ad agency, Cossette Communication-Marketing in Toronto, knew the Internet would be a key component of the campaign. A year prior to the launch of the Ion, Cossette's various divisions, including Blitz, its data, direct and promotional arm, and Nucleus, its planning division, as well as Cossette Interactive and the traditional side, brainstormed together as one marketing team.

The goal, irrespective of the agency division, was to target the new Ion, which comes in both a Sedan and Quad Coupe, at single urban dwellers. These potential customers are roughly between the ages of 18 and 40 with a university education and an average household income of $35,000 and over. (The Ion Sedan starts at just over $15,000, while pricing for the Quad Coupe will be released in the spring.)

"Everyone is involved at the very beginning, because that's how you get great ideas, by throwing them around," explains Kate Tutlys, account director at Cossette and the account lead on the Ion launch. "We wanted to come up with a promotion that we could say in three words, and would also be understood in three words."

Those three words were "Movies for Life," a sweepstakes that offers consumers a chance to win four movie passes a month for 25 years. Research showed that the target demographic "went to the movies at least once or twice a month," says LeBlanc. "Plus, I am always challenging the agency to come up with something that we haven't done before, which is a good differentiator in the marketplace."

It made sense to promote the sweepstakes in theatres across Canada via a 60-second cinema spot, as well as through backlit posters, in-lobby banners, and theatre magazine ads. Direct mail, including an insert in GM Visa card statements, is being dropped to 40,000 drivers, including current Saturn owners. Although not advertising the promotion directly, television ads were picked up from Goodby Silverstein & Partners in San Francisco, Saturn's U.S. agency, and included a tag directing viewers to the Saturn Canada website.

And the website is where the promotion really plays out. All the advertising drives to saturncanada.com, where consumers can register to win movies for life. The contest entries provide a database of drivers Saturn can talk to in the future, but also offers an immediate way of targeting consumers potentially in the market for a Saturn.

Based on learning from previous campaigns, Saturn knew that the Internet was great for detecting "hot leads"—people who are currently or about to be in the market for a new car, as well as those fitting the target demographic. According to iPerceptions, 20 percent of visitors to automotive sites are planning to buy a car in the next three months and 11 percent within just a month. Says Taras, "There is a huge opportunity for conversion there."

To sift out those hot leads, the Saturn site asks entrants to answer questions about their car-buying plans, in addition to filling in personal information. Depending on their answers, a pop-up window or e-mail then informs users that they have qualified for a free test drive and two free movie passes, which can be redeemed at the dealership.

"The strategy is to only drive to the retailers people who are qualified to be taking a test drive and not open that message up and get a special premium to just everybody," explains Melanie North, group account director at Cossette Interactive.

But the site isn't just a way to gather market intelligence. It also acts as a mini-destination site by showing the product's hip features in an interactive way. That is why the movies, with titles including *The Cluster Conspiracy*, *First Expressions* and *The Quad Coupe Equation*, have a B-movie quality to them. They were created to show how the vehicles could be personalized to the driver, such as the option of leopard skin dashboard interior.

"I thought that was an exceptional idea. I actually pushed the agency to look at something in that area," says LeBlanc. "I wanted to get a sitelet that was fun, interactive, and played upon the idea of movies for life. The little featurettes are a different way to deliver a message in an interactive manner."

It is too early to tell how successful the campaign has been—it officially wraps at the end of May—but so far the entry count has exceeded those of previous contests. For LeBlanc, it proves yet again the value of incorporating the online medium into an integrated ad campaign.

Source: Chris Daniels, "Saturn Sets a Virtual Scene," *Marketing Magazine*, April 21, 2003.

Exposure For many smaller companies, with limited budgets, the Web enables them to gain exposure to potential customers that heretofore would have been impossible. For a fraction of the investment that would be required using traditional media, companies can gain national and even international exposure in a timely manner.

Speed For those requesting information on a company, its products, and/or its service offerings, the Internet is the quickest means of acquiring this information.

LIMITATIONS OF INTERNET MARKETING

Measurement Problems One of the greatest limitations of the Internet is the lack of reliability of the research numbers generated. A quick review of forecasts, audience profiles, and other statistics offered by research providers will demonstrate a great deal of variance—leading to a serious lack of validity and reliability. One company, eMarketer, has attempted to reconcile such differences and explain the reasoning for the discrepancies (differences in methodologies employed), but the problem still exists. Many have stressed concerns over the fact that most site's figures are not audited, which may lead to rampant cheating in respect to the numbers reported.[22]

Websnarl At times, downloading information from the Net takes a long time. When there are a number of users, the time increases and some sites may be inaccessible due to too many visitors. For many users who expect speed, this is a major disadvantage. Recent technological advancements are helping to reduce this problem.

Clutter As the number of ads proliferates, the likelihood of one ad's being noticed drops accordingly. The result is that some ads may not get noticed, and some consumers may become irritated by the clutter. Some studies already show that banner ads may be losing effectiveness for this very reason.

Potential for Deception Attempts of advertisers to target children with subtle advertising messages has proven to be a significant concern. In addition, data collection without consumers' knowledge and permission, hackers, and credit card theft are a number of problems confronting the Internet.

Limited Production Quality Although it is improving, Net advertising does not offer the capabilities of many competitive media from a production standpoint. While the advent of advanced technologies and rich media is narrowing the gap, the Net still lags behind some traditional media in this area.

Poor Reach While the Internet numbers are growing in leaps and bounds, its reach is still far behind that of television. As a result, as discussed earlier, Internet companies have turned to traditional media to achieve reach and awareness goals. In addition, statistics show that only a small percentage of sites on the Internet are captured by search engines and that the top 50 sites listed account for 95 percent of the sites visited.[23]

Media Image Numerous studies have reported on the irritating aspects of some Internet tactics like clutter, e-mail, SPAM, and pop-ups and pop-unders that deter visitors from repeat visits.

Overall, the Internet offers marketers some very definite limitations over traditional media. At the same time, its limitations render this medium as less than a one-stop solution. However, as part of an IMC program, the Internet is a very valuable tool.

ADDITIONAL INTERACTIVE MEDIA

While the Internet has captured most of the attention of marketers, additional interactive media are also available and can be used as a contributor to an IMC program. Interactive CD-ROMs, kiosks, and interactive phones have been used by marketers to provide information to their audiences. Interactive television advertising was recently introduced in Canada and the U.S. a few years ago and wireless communication offers even more interactive media opportunities.

In the U.S., one of the more attention-getting and promising of the new interactive media is WebTV. A wholly owned subsidiary of Microsoft, WebTV (now called MSN TV) had more than 1 million subscribers in 2000.[24] Another interactive TV company, OpenTV, has over 300,000 subscribers.[25] Multitasking will allow television viewers to watch an event—for example, a football game—and pull up information on players, history of the matchups between the teams, and other statistics without ever leaving the couch or the game. (The numbers will appear in a window.) WebTV's "Personal TV" service allows viewers complete control over what they watch and when they watch it. In addition, viewers can pause the live program, digital video record, and instant replay. The service also allows for fast forwarding, rewinding, skipping ahead, and/or searching for one's favourite scene.

Interactive television, emerged in Canada during October of 2001 when Rogers Cable launched Enhanced Television for its 27,000 digital cable customers who have digital set-top boxes connected to the televisions. This technology, developed by Wink Communications of California, is similar to WebTV described above. Canadian consumers can now interact with programs and commercials by pushing the select button of their remote control when the flashing "i" appears periodically on the screen. If the results previously found in the U.S. are any indication, then we may see extensive advertising dollars invested in this media. For example, Wink executives cite a financial services firm that had half its users who interacted with the ad request a new account kit.[26]

The technology behind interactive television is predicated on three important features. Addressability is achieved since each box has a unique IP address much like computers have when connecting to the Internet. Thus, the exact time and location of an advertising message is known which gives exact precision on the nature of the audience exposed to the message. Personalization software and program viewership of will allow advertisers to deliver a tailored message to a precisely defined target audience. The implication of this is that an advertiser of a children's product can reach households with children with a specific ad. Finally, consumers interact with the advertiser by requesting coupons, samples or product information (i.e., location).[27]

While interactive television is making a splash in North America the past few years, campaigns have been flourishing in Europe and Asia. For example, Procter and Gamble has adapted this technolog in the U.K. and Hong Kong as a key part of their marketing mix for some brands. In France, Honda has had success with using responses to bring consumer further along in the decision-making process of buying a car as consumers requested information or arranged a test drive.[28]

The future of interactive television in Canada appears promising. Early results show that 30 percent of the households have interacted with Enhanced TV, a figure substantially higher than the average response rate found in the U.S. However, media industry observers note that while the technology is interesting, they will be cautious about purchasing media time until it appears to be a vital part of the media mix.[29]

SUMMARY

This chapter introduced you to the Internet and interactive media. It explained some of the objectives for these media and how they can be used in an IMC program.

The discussion of the Internet focused on understanding the key terms used in the industry, the objectives sought when using the Internet, and Internet communications strategies. In addition, the role of the Internet in an IMC program was discussed, with an explanation of how all the IMC program elements can be used with the Internet. Strengths of the Internet—including the ability to target markets, interactive capabilities, and relationship building—were discussed. In addition, limitations—including high costs, unreliable measurements and statistics, and relatively low reach (compared to that of traditional media)—were reviewed. Sources of Internet measurement data were also provided.

The Internet has been the most rapidly adopted medium of our time. It holds great potential for both business-to-business and consumer marketers. However, contrary to popular belief, the Internet is not a stand-alone medium. Its role in an integrated marketing communications program strengthens the overall program as well as the effectiveness of the Internet itself.

Interactive media has not yet fulfilled its promise. While still in its infancy, the medium has not received the acceptance and use expected. Test market indications are that the medium still needs improvements—particularly in content—before reaching mass acceptance.

KEY TERMS

Internet, *464*
World Wide Web (WWW), *464*
e-business, *465*
e-commerce, *465*

i-commerce, *466*
Internet marketing, *466*
website, *468*
banner ads, *472*
sponsorship, *473*

content sponsorship, *473*
pop-ups/pop-unders, *473*
interstitials, *473*
push technologies, *473*
webcasting, *473*

personalization, *474*
links, *474*
SPAM, *476*

DISCUSSION QUESTIONS

1. While some believe that the Internet poses a threat to traditional media, others disagree, arguing that it is just another medium to marketers. Explain some of the arguments on both sides. What is your conclusion?

2. The Internet is growing at an extremely rapid pace. At the same time, there are indications that this growth will slow. Discuss some factors that may lead to decreased growth of the use of this medium.

3. Discuss the objectives marketers may be seeking in their use of the Internet. Which is the Internet best suited for?

4. Explain the different forms that advertisers might use to advertise on the Internet. Discuss some of the advantages and disadvantages associated with each.

5. What is meant by personalization? Give an example of how a consumer company might use personalization.

6. A number of Internet marketers have been criticized as engaging in unethical practices. Discuss some of the practices that might be considered unethical. What should be done to curtail these practices?

7. Discuss some of the ways that marketers attempt to measure the effectiveness of their programs on the Internet. How do these measures relate to more traditional measures? Describe the advantages and disadvantages of traditional versus Internet measures.

8. Discuss some of the advantages of using the Internet. For which types of companies is the Internet best suited? Why?

9. What is interactive TV? Explain how interactive television differs from traditional television. Give an example of how a company might employ this medium.

10. Many marketers feel that the Internet offers much more potential to business-to-business marketers than it does to consumer marketers. Detail some of the reasons they feel this way and draw a conclusion as to the merits of this argument.

17

Organizing for Integrated Marketing Communication

CHAPTER OBJECTIVES

- To understand how companies organize for advertising and other aspects of integrated marketing communications.

- To examine methods for selecting, compensating, and evaluating advertising agencies.

- To explain the role and functions of specialized marketing communications organizations.

- To examine various perspectives on the use of integrated services and responsibilities of advertisers versus agencies.

Get a Grip on Advertising

In 2001, Labatt Brewing Co. fired its advertising agency of eight years, Ammirati Puris. Frustrated with the agency's inability to deliver sufficient value for Labatt's advertising investments and dissatisfied with the agency model where clients paid too much money for the work and received far too little attention, Labatt decided to associate itself with a new stripped-down agency that would only have a few clients.

Industry participants believed the comments to be a bit off base since Labatt seemed to describe the existing creative boutique. Moreover, even the smallest of agencies required staff to do background research, develop strategies, and take care of clients' needs, not to mention staff to handle basic accounting and information technology services. Finally, creative people thrive on a variety of work and many wondered how a small agency would be able to keep highly skilled creative employees fulfilled. Irrespective of these concerns, Labatt believed a creative-first organization that produced advertising more inexpensively was possible.

It announced its new agency, Grip Limited, in January of 2002. Grip would be 100 percent employee-owned and its sole client would be Labatt. Grip claimed that it would be responsible to its clients and not its shareholders and that it would have greater efficiency in the advertising development process. When announced, the model almost sounded as if the agency would be Labatt's advertising department, however, clients would eventually sit on the board and play an active management role.

Two years later, Labbatt renewed the initial two-year contract for another year. The "Cheers to Friends" campaign designed by Grip proved to Labatt that the new model had future potential. Labatt experienced stronger trust with Grip versus other agencies as it continually worked with senior creative talent. And the original intention of Grip having other clients emerged. In 2004, Grip won the $50-million Bell Canada English creative account and had many other clients as well such as Honda Canada, Parmalat Canada, and Cadbury Adams Canada. And three years after starting, *Marketing Magazine* named Grip the Advertising Agency of the Year for 2004.

Sources: "If They Build It, Will Anyone Come?" *Marketing Magazine*, December 10, 2001; "Labatt Grips its New Agency Model," *Marketing Magazine*, January 14, 2002; Angela Kryhul, "Canada's Independence Movement," *Marketing Magazine*, June 23, 2003; Michelle Warren, "Labatt Keeps a Promise with Grip as 'La-Boys' Build Their Client Base," *Marketing Magazine*, January 12, 2004.

Developing and implementing an integrated marketing communications program is usually a complex and detailed process involving the efforts of many persons from both the marketing firm and the advertising and other types of agencies. The advertising and promotions business is changing as marketers search for better ways to communicate with their customers. These changes are impacting the way marketers organize for marketing communications, as well as their relationships with advertising agencies and other communication specialists.

This chapter discusses how companies organize internally for advertising and promotion. For most companies, advertising is planned and executed by an outside ad agency. Many large agencies offer a variety of other IMC capabilities, including public relations, sales promotion, and direct marketing. Thus, we will devote particular attention to the ad agency's role and the overall relationship between company and agency.

Other participants in the promotional process (such as direct-response, sales promotion, and interactive agencies and public relations firms) are becoming increasingly important as more companies take an integrated marketing communications approach to promotion. We examine the role of these specialized marketing communications organizations in the promotional process as well. The chapter concludes with a discussion of whether marketers are best served by using the integrated services of one large agency or the separate services of a variety of communications specialists.

ORGANIZING FOR ADVERTISING AND PROMOTION IN THE FIRM

Virtually every business organization uses some form of marketing communications. However, the way a company organizes for these efforts depends on several factors, including its size, the number of products it markets, the role of advertising and promotion in its marketing mix, the advertising and promotion budget, and its marketing organization structure. Many individuals throughout the organization may be involved in the promotions decision-making process. Marketing personnel have the most direct relationship with advertising and are often involved in many aspects of the decision process, such as providing input to the campaign plan, agency selection, and evaluation of proposed programs. Top management is usually interested in how the advertising program represents the firm, and this may also mean being involved in advertising decisions even when the decisions are not part of its day-to-day responsibilities.

While many people both inside and outside the organization have some input into the advertising and promotion process, direct responsibility for administering the program must be assumed by someone within the firm. Many companies have an advertising department headed by an advertising or communications manager operating under a marketing director. An alternative used by many large multiproduct firms is a decentralized marketing (brand management) system.

THE CENTRALIZED SYSTEM

In many organizations, marketing activities are divided along functional lines, with advertising placed alongside other marketing functions such as sales, marketing research, and product planning, as shown in Figure 17–1. The **advertising manager** is responsible for all promotions activities except sales. In the most common example of a **centralized system**, the advertising manager controls the entire promotions operation, including budgeting, coordinating creation and production of ads, planning media schedules, and monitoring and administering the sales promotions programs for all the company's products or services.

The specific duties of the advertising manager depend on the size of the firm and the importance it places on promotional programs. Basic functions the manager and staff perform include the following.

488

FIGURE 17–1 □□□□ The advertising department under a centralized system

Planning and Budgeting   The advertising department is responsible for developing advertising and promotions plans that will be approved by management and recommending a promotions program based on the overall marketing plan, objectives, and budget. Formal plans are submitted annually or when a program is being changed significantly, as when a new campaign is developed. While the advertising department develops the promotional budget, the final decision on allocating funds is usually made by top management.

Administration and Execution   The manager must organize the advertising department and supervise and control its activities. The manager also supervises the execution of the plan by subordinates and/or the advertising agency. This requires working with such departments as production, media, art, copy, and sales promotion. If an outside agency is used, the advertising department is relieved of much of the executional responsibility; however, it must review and approve the agency's plans.

Coordination with Other Departments   The manager must coordinate the advertising department's activities with those of other departments, particularly those involving other marketing functions. For example, the advertising department must communicate with marketing research and/or sales to determine which product features are important to customers and should be emphasized in the company's communications. Research may also provide profiles of product users and nonusers for the media department before it selects broadcast or print media. The advertising department may also be responsible for preparing material the sales force can use when calling on customers, such as sales promotion tools, advertising materials, and point-of-purchase displays.

Coordination with Outside Agencies and Services   Many companies have an advertising department but still use many outside services. For example, companies may develop their advertising programs in-house while employing media buying services to place their ads and/or use collateral services agencies to develop brochures, point-of-purchase materials, and so on. The department serves as liaison between the company and any outside service providers and also determines which ones to use. Once outside services are retained, the manager will work with other marketing managers to coordinate their efforts and evaluate their performances.

A centralized organizational system is often used when companies do not have many different divisions, product or service lines, or brands to advertise. Many companies prefer a centralized advertising department because developing and coordinating advertising programs from one central location facilitates communication regarding the promotions program, making it easier for top management to participate in decision making. A centralized system may also result in a more efficient operation because fewer people are involved in the program decisions, and as their experience in making such decisions increases, the process becomes easier.

At the same time, problems are inherent in a centralized operation. First, it is difficult for the advertising department to understand the overall marketing strategy for the brand. The department may also be slow in responding to specific needs and problems of a product or brand. As companies become larger and develop or acquire new products, brands, or even divisions, the centralized system may become impractical.

THE DECENTRALIZED SYSTEM

In large corporations with multiple divisions and many different products, it is very difficult to manage all the advertising, promotional, and other functions through a centralized department. These types of companies generally have a **decentralized system**, with separate manufacturing, research and development, sales, and marketing departments for various divisions, product lines, or businesses. Many companies that use a decentralized system, such as Procter & Gamble, Gillette Co., and Nestlé, assign each product or brand to a **brand manager** who is responsible for the total management of the brand, including planning, budgeting, sales, and profit performance. (The term *product manager* is also used to describe this position.) The brand manager, who may have one or more assistant brand managers, is also responsible for the planning, implementation, and control of the marketing program.[1]

Under this system, the responsibilities and functions associated with advertising and promotions are transferred to the brand manager, who works closely with the outside advertising agency and other marketing communications specialists as they develop the promotional program.[2] In a multiproduct firm, each brand may have its own ad agency and may compete against other brands within the company, not just against outside competitors. For example, Exhibit 17–1 shows ads for Cheer and Tide, which are both Procter & Gamble products that compete for a share of the laundry detergent market.

As shown in Figure 17–2, the advertising department is part of marketing services and provides support for the brand managers. The role of marketing services is to assist the brand managers in planning and coordinating the integrated marketing communications program. In some companies, the marketing services group may include sales promotion. The brand managers may work with sales promotion

Exhibit 17–1
Many of Procter & Gamble's brands compete against each other

FIGURE 17–2 ☐☐☐☐ A decentralized brand management system

people to develop budgets, define strategies, and implement tactical executions for both trade and consumer promotions. Marketing services may also provide other types of support services, such as package design and merchandising.

Some companies may have an additional layer(s) of management above the brand managers to coordinate the efforts of all the brand managers handling a related group of products. An example is the organizational structure of Procter & Gamble, shown in Figure 17–3. This system—generally referred to as a **category management system**—includes category managers as well as brand and advertising managers. The category manager oversees management of the entire product category and focuses on the strategic role of the various brands in order to build profits and market share.[3]

The advertising manager may review and evaluate the various parts of the program and advise and consult with the brand managers. This person may have the authority to override the brand manager's decisions on advertising. In some multi-product firms that spend a lot on advertising, the advertising manager may coordinate the work of the various agencies to obtain media discounts for the firm's large volume of media purchases.

An advantage of the decentralized system is that each brand receives concentrated managerial attention, resulting in faster response to both problems and opportunities. The brand manager system is also more flexible and makes it easier to adjust various aspects of the advertising and promotional program, such as creative platforms and media and sales promotion schedules.[4]

There are some drawbacks to the decentralized approach. Brand managers often lack training and experience. The promotional strategy for a brand may be

FIGURE 17–3
A Procter & Gamble
division, using the
category management
system
□ □ □ □ □

developed by a brand manager who does not really understand what advertising or sales promotion can and cannot do and how each should be used. Brand managers may focus too much on short-run planning and administrative tasks, neglecting the development of long-term programs.

Another problem is that individual brand managers often end up competing for management attention, marketing dollars, and other resources, which can lead to unproductive rivalries and potential misallocation of funds. The manager's persuasiveness may become a bigger factor in determining budgets than the long-run profit potential of the brands. These types of problems were key factors in Procter & Gamble's decision to switch to a category management system.

Finally, the brand management system has been criticized for failing to provide brand managers with authority over the functions needed to implement and control the plans they develop.[5] Some companies have dealt with this problem by expanding the roles and responsibilities of the advertising and sales promotion managers and their staff of specialists. The staff specialists counsel the individual brand managers, and advertising or sales promotion decision making involves the advertising and/or sales promotion manager, the brand manager, and the marketing director.

ADVERTISING AGENCIES

The use of an advertising agency is unique for each advertiser. And as you might expect, there are many different types. In this section we provide a general overview that describes the situation. We review the advertising agency decision, describe the activities of a full-service agency, and identify other types of agencies.

ADVERTISING AGENCY DECISION

Irrespective of whether an advertiser uses a centralized or decentralized organizational structure, there remains the choice of whether a firm will have its own in-house agency or whether it will employ an external advertising agency. We now briefly discuss the relative merits and concerns of both options.

In-House Agency Option   Some companies, in an effort to reduce costs and maintain greater control over agency activities, have set up their own advertising agencies internally. An **in-house agency** is an advertising agency that is set up, owned, and operated by the advertiser. Some in-house agencies are little more than advertising departments, but in other companies they are given a separate identity and are responsible for the expenditure of large sums of advertising dollars. Large advertisers that use in-house agencies include Calvin Klein, Avon, Revlon, and Benetton. Many companies use in-house agencies exclusively; others combine in-house efforts with those of outside agencies. For example, No Fear handles most of its advertising in-house, but it does use an outside agency for some of its creative work (Exhibit 17–2). (The specific roles performed by in-house agencies will become clearer when we discuss the functions of outside agencies.)

A major reason for using an in-house agency is to reduce advertising and promotion costs. Companies with very large advertising budgets pay a substantial amount to outside agencies in the form of media commissions. With an internal structure, these commissions go to the in-house agency. An in-house agency can also provide related work such as sales presentations and sales force materials, package design, and public relations at a lower cost than outside agencies. A study by M. Louise Ripley found that creative and media services were the most likely functions to be performed outside, while merchandising and sales promotion were the most likely to be performed in-house.[6]

Saving money is not the only reason companies use in-house agencies. Time savings, bad experiences with outside agencies, and the increased knowledge and understanding of the market that come from working on advertising and promotion for the product or service day by day are also reasons. Companies can also maintain tighter control over the process and more easily coordinate promotions with the firm's overall marketing program. Some companies use an in-house agency simply because they believe it can do a better job than an outside agency could.[7]

Opponents of in-house agencies say they can give the advertiser neither the experience and objectivity of an outside agency nor the range of services. They argue that outside agencies have more highly skilled specialists and attract the best creative talent and that using an external firm gives a company a more varied perspective on its advertising problems and greater flexibility. In-house personnel may become narrow or grow stale while working on the same product line, but outside agencies may have different people with a variety of backgrounds and ideas working on the account. Flexibility is greater because an outside agency can be dismissed if the company is not satisfied, whereas changes in an in-house agency could be slower and more disruptive.

The cost savings of an in-house agency must be evaluated against these considerations. For many companies, high-quality advertising is critical to their marketing success and should be the major criterion in determining whether to use in-house services. Companies like Rockport and Redken Laboratories have moved their in-house work to outside agencies in recent years. Redken cited the need for a "fresh look" and objectivity as the reasons, noting that management gets too close to the product to come up with different creative ideas. Companies often hire outside agencies as they grow and their advertising budgets and needs increase. For example, the fast-growing personal computer company Gateway hired an outside agency a few years ago to handle all of its advertising.[8]

493

Exhibit 17–2
Most of the advertising for No Fear is done by an in-house agency

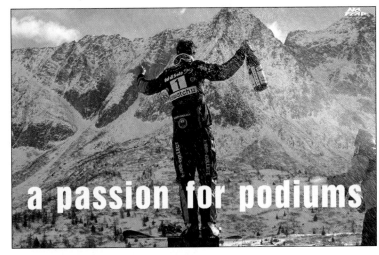

Advertising Agency Option   Many major companies use an advertising agency to assist them in developing, preparing, and executing their promotional programs. An ad agency is a service organization that specializes in planning and executing advertising programs for its clients. Probably the main reason outside agencies are used is that they provide the client with the services of highly skilled individuals who are specialists in their chosen fields. An advertising agency staff may include artists, writers, media analysts, researchers, and others with specific skills, knowledge, and experience who can help market the client's products or services. Many agencies specialize in a particular type of business and use their knowledge of the industry to assist their clients.

An outside agency can also provide an objective viewpoint of the market and its business that is not subject to internal company policies, biases, or other limitations. The agency can draw on the broad range of experience it has gained while working on a diverse set of marketing problems for various clients. For example, an ad agency that is handling a travel-related account may have individuals who have worked with airlines, cruise ship companies, travel agencies, hotels, and other travel-related industries. The agency may have experience in this area or may even have previously worked on the advertising account of one of the client's competitors. Thus, the agency can provide the client with insight into the industry (and, in some cases, the competition).

The Canadian advertising agency industry is similar to others—there is a combination of domestic firms and international organizations, especially from the U.S. Many of the latter have extensive sales in Canada, however recent legal changes pertaining to accounting practices do not permit the release of sales revenue for its subsidiaries. Consequently, it is impossible to fully describe the size and scope of the industry as a whole for 2003. This problem has persisted for the past two years, however data from 2001 indicates that the Canadian industry is highly concentrated. For example, the top 20 firms combined for total revenue of $1 billion while the total revenue for the top 50 firms amounted to almost $1.4 billion. Given the limited data, we still present the top five Canadian-based advertising agencies in Figure 17–4 for reference. Nurun and Cossette had the highest foreign revenues of Canadian agencies with $20 million and $18 million respectively. Figure 17–5 puts the context of the Canadian revenue into perspective compared to the large multinational firms. The data recognizes that MDC Partners' foreign sales mark them as the Canadian leader.

The strong presence of international ad agencies in Canada reflects a global trend. The advertising industry underwent major changes as large agencies merged with or acquired other agencies and support organizations. These **superagencies** were formed so that agencies could provide clients with integrated marketing communications services worldwide. Some advertisers became disenchanted with the superagencies and moved to smaller agencies that were flexible and more responsive.[9] However, the agency business consolidated again as medium-size agencies were acquired and became part of large advertising organizations such as Omnicom Group, WPP Group, and the Interpublic Group of Cos. Many of the mid-size agencies were acquired by or forged alliances with larger agencies because their clients

FIGURE 17–4
Domestic revenue of Canada's top 5 communications services companies
□ □ □ □ □

Ranking	Company	2003 Revenues ($C M)
1	Cossette Communication Group	145.7
2	MDC Partners	65.6
3	Maritz Canada	49.3
4	Carlson Marketing Group Canada	40.0
5	Nurun	24.5

Source: *Marketing Magazine*, June 24, 2002.

Rank 2003	2002	Company	Headquarters	Worldwide revenue ($US M) 2003	% change
1	1	Omnicom Group	New York	8,621.4	14.4
2	3	WPP Group	London	6,756.1	16.9
3	2	Interpublic Group of Companies	New York	5,863.4	-5.5
4	4	Publicis Groupe	Paris	4,408.9	7.3
5	5	Dentsu	Tokyo	2,545.0	11.0
6	6	Havas	Suresnes, France	1,877.5	-0.6
7	7	Grey Global Group	New York	1,307.3	9.0
8	NA	Hakuhodo DY Holdings	Tokyo	1,208.1	N/A
9	9	Aegis Group	London	1,067.4	21.9
10	10	Asatsu-DK	Tokyo	413.9	16.8
Canadian-based organizations in the top 30					
16	17	MDC Partners	Toronto	193.7	12.8
26	27	Cossette Communication Group	Quebec City	115.9	15.4

Source: *Marketing Magazine*, June 21, 2004.

FIGURE 17–5
World's top ad organizations

wanted an agency with international communications capabilities and their alignment with larger organizations gave them access to a network of agencies around the world.[10] Recent merger and acquisition activity concerns has seen major agencies acquiring companies specializing in areas such as interactive communications, direct marketing, and sales promotion so that they can offer their clients an ever-broader range of integrated marketing communication services.[11]

FULL-SERVICE ADVERTISING AGENCIES

Since ad agencies can range in size from a one- or two-person operation to large organizations with over 1,000 employees, the services offered and functions performed will vary. In order to understand the variety of agencies, we focus on the largest and most complex. Many companies employ what is known as a **full-service agency**, which offers its clients a full range of marketing, communications, and promotions services, including planning, creating, and producing the advertising; performing research; and selecting media. A full-service agency may also offer nonadvertising services such as strategic market planning; sales promotions, direct marketing, and interactive capabilities; package design; and public relations and publicity.

The full-service agency is made up of departments that provide the activities needed to perform the various advertising functions and serve the client, as shown in Figure 17–6.

Account Services Account services, or account management, is the link between the ad agency and its clients. Depending on the size of the client and its advertising budget, one or more account executives serve as liaison. The **account executive** is responsible for understanding the advertiser's marketing and promotions needs and interpreting them to agency personnel. He or she coordinates agency efforts in planning, creating, and producing ads. The account executive also presents agency recommendations and obtains client approval.

As the focal point of agency–client relationships, the account executive must know a great deal about the client's business and be able to communicate this to specialists in the agency working on the account.[12] The ideal account executive has a strong marketing background as well as a thorough understanding of all phases of the advertising process.

FIGURE 17–6 ☐☐☐☐ Full-service agency organizational chart

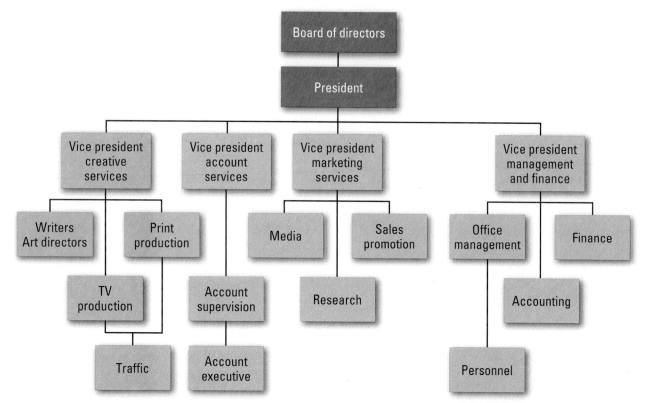

Marketing Services Over the past two decades, use of marketing services has increased dramatically. One service gaining increased attention is research, as agencies realize that to communicate effectively with their clients' customers, they must have a good understanding of the target audience. As shown in Chapter 1, the advertising planning process begins with a thorough situation analysis, which is based on research and information about the target audience.

Most full-service agencies maintain a *research department* whose function is to gather, analyze, and interpret information that will be useful in developing advertising for their clients. This can be done through primary research—where a study is designed, executed, and interpreted by the research department—or through the use of secondary (previously published) sources of information. Sometimes the research department acquires studies conducted by independent syndicated research firms or consultants. The research staff then interprets these reports and passes on the information to other agency personnel working on that account.

The research department may also design and conduct research to pretest the effectiveness of advertising the agency is considering. For example, copy testing is often conducted to determine how messages developed by the creative specialists are likely to be interpreted by the receiving audience.

The *media department* of an agency analyzes, selects, and contracts for space or time in the media that will be used to deliver the client's advertising message. The media department is expected to develop a media plan that will reach the target audience and effectively communicate the message. Since most of the client's ad budget is spent on media time and/or space, this department must develop a plan that both communicates with the right audience and is cost-effective.

Media specialists must know what audiences the media reach, their rates, and how well they match the client's target audience. The media department reviews information on demographics, magazine and newspaper readership, radio listenership, and consumers' TV viewing patterns to develop an effective media plan. The media buyer implements the media plan by purchasing the actual time and space. The media department is becoming an increasingly important part of the agency business as many large advertisers consolidate their media buying with one or a few agencies to save money and improve media efficiency. An agency's strategic ability to negotiate prices and effectively use the vast array of media vehicles available is becoming as important as its ability to create ads.

The research and media departments perform most of the functions that full-service agencies need to plan and execute their clients' advertising programs. Some agencies offer additional marketing services to their clients to assist in other promotional areas. An agency may have a sales promotion department, or merchandising department, that specializes in developing contests, premiums, promotions, point-of-sale materials, and other sales materials. It may have direct-marketing specialists and package designers, as well as a PR/publicity department. Many agencies have developed interactive media departments to create websites for their clients. The growing popularity of integrated marketing communications has prompted many full-function agencies to develop capabilities and offer services in these other promotional areas.

Creative Services   The creative services department is responsible for the creation and execution of advertisements. The individuals who conceive the ideas for the ads and write the headlines, subheads, and body copy (the words constituting the message) are known as **copywriters**. They may also be involved in determining the basic appeal or theme of the ad campaign and often prepare a rough initial visual layout of the print ad or television commercial.

While copywriters are responsible for what the message says, the *art department* is responsible for how the ad looks. For print ads, the art director and graphic designers prepare *layouts*, which are drawings that show what the ad will look like and from which the final artwork will be produced. For TV commercials, the layout is known as a *storyboard*, a sequence of frames or panels that depict the commercial in still form.

Members of the creative department work together to develop ads that will communicate the key points determined to be the basis of the creative strategy for the client's product or service. Writers and artists generally work under the direction of the agency's creative director, who oversees all the advertising produced by the organization. The director sets the creative philosophy of the department and may even become directly involved in creating ads for the agency's largest clients.

Once the copy, layout, illustrations, and mechanical specifications have been completed and approved, the ad is turned over to the *production department.* Most agencies do not actually produce finished ads; they hire printers, engravers, photographers, typographers, and other suppliers to complete the finished product. For broadcast production, the approved storyboard must be turned into a finished commercial. The production department may supervise the casting of people to appear in the ad and the setting for the scenes as well as choose an independent production studio. The department may hire an outside director to turn the creative concept into a commercial. Copywriters, art directors, account managers, people from research and planning, and representatives from the client side may all participate in production decisions, particularly when large sums of money are involved.

Creating an advertisement often involves many people and takes several months. In large agencies with many clients, coordinating the creative and production processes can be a major problem. A *traffic department* coordinates all phases of production to see that the ads are completed on time and that all deadlines for submitting the ads to the media are met. The traffic department may be located in the creative services area of the agency, or be part of media or account management, or be separate.

Management and Finance   Like any other business, an advertising agency must be managed and perform basic operating and administrative functions such as accounting, finance, and human resources. It must also attempt to generate new business.

Large agencies employ administrative, managerial, and clerical people to perform these functions. The bulk of an agency's income (approximately 64 percent) goes to salary and benefits for its employees. Thus, an agency must manage its personnel carefully and get maximum productivity from them.

Structure Full-function advertising agencies must develop an organizational structure that will meet their clients' needs and serve their own internal requirements. Most medium-size and large agencies are structured under either a departmental or a group system. Under the **departmental system**, each of the agency functions shown in Figure 17–6 is set up as a separate department and is called on as needed to perform its specialty and serve all of the agency's clients. Ad layout, writing, and production are done by the creative department, marketing services is responsible for any research or media selection and purchases, and the account services department handles client contact. Some agencies prefer the departmental system because it gives employees the opportunity to develop expertise in servicing a variety of accounts.

Many large agencies use the **group system**, in which individuals from each department work together in groups to service particular accounts. Each group is headed by an account executive or supervisor and has one or more media people, including media planners and buyers; a creative team, which includes copywriters, art directors, artists, and production personnel; and one or more account executives. The group may also include individuals from other departments such as marketing research, direct marketing, or sales promotion. The size and composition of the group varies depending on the client's billings and the importance of the account to the agency. For very important accounts, the group members may be assigned exclusively to one client. In some agencies, they may serve a number of smaller clients. Many agencies prefer the group system because employees become very knowledgeable about the client's business and there is continuity in servicing the account.

498

Exhibit 17–3
This popular Coca-Cola spot was done by the company's in-house creative boutique

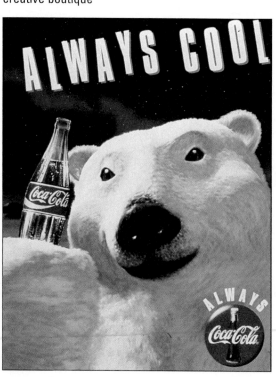

OTHER TYPES OF AGENCIES AND SERVICES

Not every agency is a large full-service agency. Many smaller agencies expect their employees to handle a variety of jobs. For example, account executives may do their own research, work out their own media schedule, and coordinate the production of ads written and designed by the creative department. Many advertisers, including some large companies, are not interested in paying for the services of a full-service agency but are interested in some of the specific services agencies have to offer. Over the past few decades, several alternatives to full-service agencies have evolved, including creative boutiques and media buying services.

Creative Boutiques A **creative boutique** is an agency that provides only creative services. These specialized companies have developed in response to some clients' desires to use only the creative talent of an outside provider while maintaining the other functions internally. The client may seek outside creative talent because it believes an extra creative effort is required or because its own employees do not have sufficient skills in this regard. For example, a few years ago Coca-Cola created an in-house agency called Edge Creative. The agency created several commercials for Coca-Cola's flagship brand, including the popular polar bears spot (Exhibit 17–3).

Full-service agencies often subcontract work to creative boutiques when they are very busy or want to avoid adding full-time employees to their payrolls. Creative boutiques by a reward based on the degree of achieving mutually agreed upon objectives between the client and the agency. Another focus of the study is to view the remuneration as a part of a system of linking performance, its measurement, and reward within the client–agency relationship, something that has been characteristic of supply relationships in other industries. The benefits of the PBR system are:

- Greater efficiency and accountability
- Achievement of cost efficiencies
- Higher productivity
- Fewer barriers of self-interest
- Stronger mutual understanding
- Improved retention of creative talent
- Increased agency strategic input
- Improved client–agency communication

Performance measures are a key element of the PBR system and the study highlights three general groups that should comprise the evaluation; overall business performance, marketing communication effectiveness, and agency process evaluation. Measures from the first two groups are familiar to us (see Chapter 4). Business measures include sales, market share, profitability, and margins. Marketing communication effectiveness measures include brand awareness and brand image ratings (i.e., brand attitude). This group also includes likability of advertising and advertising impact (i.e., emotional responses), two measures that are more processing related. This group also includes four objectives that are more behavioural: intent to purchase, trial, repeat purchase, and brand loyalty. The final group concerns the various services the agency provides and its overall management process.

The PBR system recognizes that there is no standard formula in applying these measures. The relative importance of each measure needs to be investigated for each brand and its marketing situation. Furthermore, the measures should take into account the role of promotion in the marketing mix and how promotion contributes to business results for the brand and within the product category or industry. In addition, the PBR study provides the following suggestions. Objectives can be short term and long term. An appropriate number of objectives should be used to focus the organization. The objectives should be consistent with other performance measures used in the organization. Objectives should be periodically re-evaluated by the client and the agency. Although some of these recommendations may be intuitive, the Canadian PBR study is the most thorough, published examination of the PBR system in the world. Another remarkable achievement for our marketing communication industry![18]

EVALUATION OF AGENCIES

Given the substantial amounts of money being spent on advertising and promotion, demand for accountability of the expenditures has increased. Regular reviews of the agency's performance are necessary. The agency evaluation process usually involves two types of assessments, one financial and operational and the other more qualitative. The **financial audit** focuses on how the agency conducts its business. It is designed to verify costs and expenses, the number of personnel hours charged to an account, and payments to media and outside suppliers. The **qualitative audit** focuses on the agency's efforts in planning, developing, and implementing the client's advertising programs and considers the results achieved. Sometimes it may appear that an evaluation is not required when the advertiser publicly praises its agency (Exhibit 17–5).

Exhibit 17–5
IBM congratulates its agency for developing an award-winning campaign

503

THE BOOK OF *e* BUSINESS

"IF IT DOESN'T SELL, IT ISN'T CREATIVE."

–David Ogilvy

Touffou–the Ogilvy castle. "Just throw those Clios and Lions in the basement."

WE WOULD LIKE to congratulate Ogilvy & Mather for this year's Grand EFFIE–winning e-business Infrastructure campaign and the Silver-winning "Easy to Buy" campaign. The work was impressive. The numbers, staggering. Your friends and partners at IBM thank you for a year of incredible success.

IBM.

The agency evaluation is often done on a subjective, informal basis, particularly in smaller companies where ad budgets are low or advertising is not seen as the most critical factor in the firm's marketing performance. Some companies have developed formal, systematic evaluation systems, particularly when budgets are large and the advertising function receives much emphasis. As advertising costs continue to rise, the top management of these companies wants to be sure money is being spent efficiently and effectively.

As part of its mandate as an industry resource, the Institute of Communications and Advertising, provides a Guide to Best Practice that includes information to facilitate agency evaluation (the Guide and the PBR study are both available at www.ica-ad.com). The document provides guidelines on the client–agency relationship and includes many forms that can be used as a basis for evaluating an agency in all areas of performance such as account management, creative, planning and research, production, media planning and buying, budget and financial, agency management, direct marketing, interactive marketing, and public relations.

One example of a formal agency evaluation system is that used by Whirlpool, which markets a variety of consumer products. Whirlpool management meets once a year with the company's agencies to review their performance. Whirlpool managers complete an advertising agency performance evaluation, part of which is shown in Exhibit 17–6. These reports are compiled and reviewed with the agency

Exhibit 17–6
Whirlpool's ad agency
performance evaluation

504

CREATIVE SERVICES

Always 4	Often 3	Occasionally 2	Seldom 1	Never 0	NA	Marks Scored
1. Agency produces fresh ideas and original approaches						
2. Agency accurately interprets facts, strategies and objectives into usable advertisements and plans						
3. Creative group is knowledgeable about company's products, markets and strategies						
4. Creative group is concerned with good advertising communications and develops campaigns and ads that exhibit this concern						
5. Creative group produces on time						
6. Creative group performs well under pressure						
7. Creative group operates in a businesslike manner to control production costs and other creative charges						
8. Agency presentations are well organized with sufficient examples of proposed executions						
9. Creative group participates in major campaign presentations						
10. Agency presents ideas and executions not requested but felt to be good opportunities						
11. Agency willingly accepts ideas generated by other locations/agency offices vs. being over-protective of its own creative product						
12. Other areas not mentioned						
13. Agency demonstrates commitment to client's business						
14. Agency creative proposals are relevant and properly fulfill creative brief						

Value—(marks)

	Rating:		Total marks scored
Excellent	90–100%		
Good	80–89%		
Average	70–79%		Total possible marks
Fair	60–69%		
Poor	below 60%		Score

ACCOUNT REPRESENTATION & SERVICE

Always 4	Often 3	Occasionally 2	Seldom 1	Never 0	NA	Marks Scored
1. Account representatives act with personal initiative						
2. Account representatives anticipate needs in advance of direction by client (ie: are proactive)						
3. Account group takes direction well						
4. Agency is able to demonstrate results of programs implemented						
5. Account representatives function strategically rather than as creative advisors only						
6. Account representatives are knowledgeable about competitive programs and share this information along with their recommendations in a timely manner						
7. Account representatives respond to client requests in a timely fashion						
8. Account group operates in a business-like manner to control costs						
9. Agency recommendations are founded on sound reasoning and supported factually, and appropriately fit within budget constraints						
10. Agency is able to advise the client on trends and developments in technology						
11. Account representatives demonstrate a high degree of professionalism in both written and oral communication						
12. Agency presents ideas and executions not requested by felt to be good opportunities						
13. Agency makes reasoned recommendations on allocation of budgets						
14. Agency demonstrates commitment to client's business						
15. There is a positive social relationship between client and agency						

Value—(marks)

	Rating:		Total marks scored
Excellent	90–100%		
Good	80–89%		
Average	70–79%		Total possible marks
Fair	60–69%		
Poor	below 60%		Score

at each annual meeting. Whirlpool's evaluation process covers six areas of performance. The company and the agency develop an action plan to correct areas of deficiency.

REASONS FOR AGENCIES LOSING CLIENTS

The evaluation process described above provides valuable feedback to both the agency and the client, such as indicating changes that need to be made by the agency and/or the client to improve performance and make the relationship more productive. Many agencies have had very long-lasting relationships with their clients (see Exhibit 17–7); however, long-term relationships are becoming less common.

Agency-of-record (AOR) is the term used to describe those situations where a client works with an exclusive agency for a number of years. It is the very foundation on which the advertising agency business exists—a service provider whose foremost interest is in building the client's brand. A recent trend is that some advertisers do not have a specific AOR, but work with different agencies at once, or in succession, depending upon their communication needs. In essence, agencies engage in project-like work for a client by developing a short campaign or performing creative work only. For example, a client

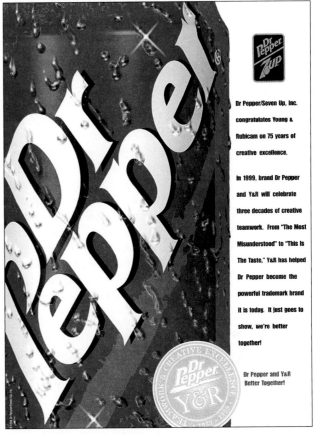

Exhibit 17–7
Young & Rubicam has been the agency for Dr Pepper for more than three decades

can contract the creative work to an agency but rely on its own market research resources. Advertisers believe they are saving money, finding the best ideas for an assignment, and putting pressure on agencies to perform. Critics believe this allows marketing investments to gravitate away from advertising and limit brand development, minimizes consistency across multiple campaigns, or constrains creativity to position the brand effectively.[19]

While the debate continues, many Canadian campaigns such as Coors, Shoppers Drug Mart, Mr. Sub, Budget, Apple, and WestJet are the result of project work. In some cases, the brand had an AOR status but the client decided to use a smaller or different agency for a particular assignment. Advertisers cite the need to remain flexible and the desire to test out new agencies for future relationships. In fact, a considerable amount of the project work went to smaller independent agencies or creative boutiques, which suggests longer-term relationships could be in the future.[20]

There are a number of reasons why clients switch agencies. Some of the more common reasons that agencies lose clients are as follows:

* *Poor performance or service.* The client becomes dissatisfied with the quality of the advertising and/or the service provided by the agency.
* *Poor communication.* The client and agency personnel fail to develop or maintain the level of communication necessary to sustain a favourable working relationship.
* *Unrealistic demands by the client.* The client places demands on the agency that exceed the amount of compensation received and reduce the account's profitability.
* *Personality conflicts.* People working on the account on the client and agency sides do not have enough rapport to work well together.
* *Personnel changes.* A change in personnel at either the agency or the advertiser can create problems. New managers may wish to use an agency with which they have established ties. Agency personnel often take accounts with them when they switch agencies or start their own.

- *Changes in size of the client or agency.* The client may outgrow the agency or decide it needs a larger agency to handle its business. If the agency gets too large, the client may represent too small a percentage of its business to command attention.
- *Conflicts of interest.* A conflict may develop when an agency merges with another agency or when a client is part of an acquisition or merger.
- *Changes in the client's corporate and/or marketing strategy.* A client may change its marketing strategy and think a new agency is needed to carry out the new program.
- *Declining sales.* When sales of the client's product or service are stagnant or declining, advertising may be seen as contributing to the problem. A new agency may be sought for a new creative approach.
- *Conflicting compensation philosophies.* Disagreement may develop over the level or method of compensation. As more companies move toward incentive-based compensation systems, disagreement over compensation is becoming more commonplace.
- *Changes in policies.* Policy changes may result when either party reevaluates the importance of the relationship, the agency acquires a new (and larger) client, or either side undergoes a merger or acquisition.

If the agency recognizes these warning signs, it can try to adapt its programs and policies to make sure the client is satisfied. Some of the situations discussed here are unavoidable, and others are beyond the agency's control. But to maintain the account, problems within the agency's control must be addressed.

The time may come when the agency decides it is no longer in its best interest to continue to work with the client. Personnel conflicts, changes in management philosophy, and/or insufficient financial incentives are just a few of the reasons for such a decision. Then the agency may terminate the account relationship.

SPECIALIZED SERVICES

Many companies assign the development and implementation of their promotional programs to an advertising agency. But several other types of organizations provide specialized services that complement the efforts of ad agencies. Direct-response agencies, sales promotion agencies, and public relations firms are important to marketers in developing and executing IMC programs. Let us examine the functions these organizations perform.

SALES PROMOTION AGENCIES

Developing and managing sales promotion programs such as contests, sweepstakes, refunds and rebates, premium and incentive offers, and sampling programs is a very complex task. Most companies use a **sales promotion agency** to develop and administer these programs. Some large ad agencies have created their own sales promotion department or acquired a sales promotion firm. However, most sales promotion agencies are independent companies that specialize in providing the services needed to plan, develop, and execute a variety of sales promotion programs.

Sales promotion agencies often work in conjunction with the client's advertising and/or direct-response agencies to coordinate their efforts with the advertising and direct-marketing programs. Services provided by large sales promotion agencies include promotional planning, creative, research, tie-in coordination, fulfillment, premium design and manufacturing, catalogue production, and contest/sweepstakes management. Many sales promotion agencies are also developing direct/database marketing and telemarketing to expand their integrated marketing services capabilities. Sales promotion agencies are generally compensated on a fee basis. Exhibit 17–8 shows an ad for DVC, which was selected as the promotional agency of the decade a few years ago by *Promo* magazine.

PUBLIC RELATIONS FIRMS

Many large companies use both an advertising agency and a PR firm. The **public relations firm** develops and implements programs to manage the organization's publicity, image, and affairs with consumers and other relevant publics, including employees, suppliers, stockholders, government, labour groups, citizen action groups, and the general public. The PR firm analyzes the relationships between the client and these various publics, determines how the client's policies and actions relate to and affect these publics, develops PR strategies and programs, implements these programs using various public relations tools, and evaluates their effectiveness.

The activities of a public relations firm include planning the PR strategy and program, generating publicity, conducting lobbying and public affairs efforts, becoming involved in community activities and events, preparing news releases and other communications, conducting research, promoting and managing special events, and managing crises. As companies adopt an IMC approach to promotional planning, they are coordinating their PR activities with advertising and other promotional areas. Many companies are integrating public relations and publicity into the marketing communications mix to increase message credibility and save media costs.[21]

Exhibit 17–8
DVC is one of the leading promotional agencies

DIRECT-RESPONSE AGENCIES

One of the fastest-growing areas of IMC is direct marketing, where companies communicate with consumers through telemarketing, direct mail, and other forms of direct-response advertising. As this industry has grown, numerous direct-response agencies have evolved that offer companies their specialized skills in both consumer and business markets.

Direct-response agencies provide a variety of services, including database management, direct mail, research, media services, and creative and production capabilities. While direct mail is their primary weapon, many direct-response agencies are expanding their services to include such areas as infomercial production and database management. Database development and management is becoming one of the most important services provided by direct-response agencies. Many companies are using database marketing to pinpoint new customers and build relationships and loyalty among existing customers.[22]

A typical direct-response agency is divided into three main departments: account management, creative, and media. Some agencies also have a department whose function is to develop and manage databases for their clients. The account managers work with their clients to plan direct-marketing programs and determine their role in the overall integrated marketing communications process. The creative department consists of copywriters, artists, and producers. Creative is responsible for developing the direct-response message, while the media department is concerned with its placement.

Like advertising agencies, direct-response agencies must solicit new business and have their performance reviewed by their existing clients, often through formal assessment programs. Most direct-response agencies are compensated on a fee basis, although some large advertisers still prefer the commission system.

INTERACTIVE AGENCIES

With the rapid growth of the Internet and other forms of interactive media, a new type of specialized marketing communications organization has evolved—the interactive agency. Many marketers are using **interactive agencies** that specialize in the development and strategic use of various interactive marketing tools such as websites for the Internet, banner ads, CD-ROMs, and kiosks.[23] They recognize that the development of successful interactive marketing programs requires expertise in technology as well as areas such as creative website design, database marketing, digital media, and customer relationship management. Many traditional advertising agencies have established interactive capabilities, ranging from a few specialists within the agency to an entire interactive division.

While many agencies have or are developing interactive capabilities, a number of marketers are turning to more specialized interactive agencies to develop websites and interactive media. They feel these companies have more expertise in designing and developing websites as well as managing and supporting them. Interactive agencies range from smaller companies that specialize in website design and creation to full-service interactive agencies that provide all the elements needed for a successful Internet/interactive marketing program. These services include strategic consulting regarding the use of the Internet and online branding, technical knowledge, systems integration, and the development of electronic commerce capabilities.

As the Internet becomes an increasingly important marketing tool, more companies will be turning to interactive agencies to help them develop successful interactive marketing programs. The number of interactive agencies will continue to grow, as will their importance in the development and implementation of Internet-based strategies and initiatives.

INTEGRATED MARKETING COMMUNICATIONS SERVICES

As noted in Chapter 1, during the 1980s many of the large agencies began developing IMC capabilities when they realized that their clients were shifting their promotional dollars away from traditional advertising to other forms of promotion. Some did this through mergers and acquisitions and became superagencies consisting of advertising, public relations, sales promotion, and direct-response agencies. Many large agencies are continuing to expand their IMC capabilities by acquiring specialists in various fields. All the major agency holding companies either own or have substantial investments in interactive and direct-response agencies.

Currently, marketers can choose from a variety of specialized organizations to assist them in planning, developing, and implementing an integrated marketing communications program. But companies must decide whether to use a different organization for each marketing communications function or consolidate them with a large advertising agency that offers all of these services under one roof. In this final section, we discuss the issue as to whether an advertiser would want to use an integrated services agency or not, assess the agency–client responsibilities for IMC, and summarize the current situation regarding the agency–client relationship in the context of an IMC environment.

PROS AND CONS OF INTEGRATED SERVICES

It has been argued that the concept of integrated marketing is nothing new, particularly in smaller companies and communication agencies that have been coordinating a variety of promotional tools for years. And larger advertising agencies have been trying to gain more of their clients' promotional business for over 20 years. However, in the past, the various services were run as separate profit centres. Each was motivated to push its own expertise and pursue its own goals rather than develop truly integrated marketing programs. Moreover, the creative specialists in many agencies resisted becoming involved in sales promotion or direct marketing. They preferred to concentrate on developing magazine ads or television commercials rather than designing coupons or direct-mail pieces.

Proponents of the integrated marketing services agency (the one-stop shop) contend that past problems are being solved and the various individuals in the agencies and subsidiaries are learning to work together to deliver a consistent message to the client's customers. They argue that maintaining control of the entire promotional process achieves greater synergy among each of the communications program elements. They also note that it is more convenient for the client to coordinate all of its marketing efforts—media advertising, direct mail, special events, sales promotions, and public relations—through one agency. An agency with integrated marketing capabilities can create a single image for the product or service and address everyone, from wholesalers to consumers, with one voice.

But not everyone wants to turn the entire IMC program over to one agency. Opponents say the providers become involved in political wrangling over budgets, do not communicate with each other as well and as often as they should, and do not achieve synergy. They also claim that agencies' efforts to control all aspects of the promotional program are nothing more than an attempt to hold on to business that might otherwise be lost to independent providers. They note that synergy and economies of scale, while nice in theory, have been difficult to achieve and competition and conflict among agency subsidiaries have been a major problem.[24] Many companies use a variety of vendors for communication functions, choosing the specialist they believe is best suited for each promotional task, be it advertising, sales promotion, or public relations.

Compounding these concerns is the opinion that advertising agencies are neither sufficiently staffed to ensure complete integration, nor are they fully cognizant of multiple target audiences. Advertising agency personnel are trained in particular aspects of the process and are less inclined to consider many marketing variables in their decisions. Furthermore, they tend to consider only the end user or consumer rather than all the parties in the marketing process who are connected to the results of the communications plan. It is recommended that marketers ensure that the agencies consider the needs of all (e.g., customer service staff, sales representatives, distributors, and retailers) in their communication plans.[25]

RESPONSIBILITY FOR IMC: AGENCY VERSUS CLIENT

Surveys of advertisers and agency executives have shown that both groups believe integrated marketing is important to their organizations' success and that it will be even more important in the future.[26] However, marketers and agency executives have very different opinions regarding who should be in charge of the integrated marketing communications process. Many advertisers prefer to set strategy for and coordinate their own IMC campaigns, but most agency executives see this as their domain.

While agency executives believe their shops are capable of handling the various elements an integrated campaign requires, many marketers, particularly larger firms, disagree. Marketing executives say the biggest obstacle to implementing IMC is the lack of people with the broad perspective and skills to make it work. Agencies are felt to lack expertise in database marketing, marketing research, and information technology. Internal turf battles, agency egos, and fear of budget reductions are also cited as major barriers to successful integrated marketing campaigns.[27]

Many ad agencies are adding more resources to offer their clients a full line of services. They are expanding their agencies' capabilities in interactive and multimedia advertising, database management, direct marketing, public relations, and sales promotion. However, many marketers still want to set the strategy for their IMC campaigns and seek specialized expertise, more quality and creativity, and greater control and cost efficiency by using multiple providers.

Most marketers do recognize that ad agencies will no longer stick primarily to advertising and will continue to expand their IMC capabilities. There is an opportunity for agencies to broaden their services beyond advertising—but they will have to develop true expertise in a variety of integrated marketing communications areas. They will also have to create organizational structures that make it possible for individuals with expertise in a variety of communications areas to work well together

509

both internally and externally. One thing is certain: as companies continue to shift their promotional dollars away from media advertising to other IMC tools, agencies will continue to explore ways to keep these monies under their roofs.

AGENCY–CLIENT RELATIONSHIPS WITH IMC

In a series of interviews, an executive from each of BMO Financial Group, Levi Strauss & Co., Nestlé Canada, and Moosehead Breweries offered his or her opinion on broad questions surrounding agency–client relations. What do marketers (i.e., clients) want from their agency partners? Are agencies meeting these needs? What can marketers do to forge stronger relations with agency partners?[28]

The needs of marketers are broad and varied, including more integrated plans using a range of communication tools, constant messages across many tools, greater understanding of the marketer's brand, overall good quality, more precise measurement of communication effects, insight into market positioning strategies, and of course, very creative ads.

Agencies appear to be performing very well in some areas, but there appears to be room for improvement. While there have been increased attempts at integration, there may be certain biases of individuals towards one tool versus another. Improved creative planning has emerged, however, concern regarding full accountability currently exists. Agencies offer greater services with larger multinationals, although this has not always been completely beneficial for clients. The creative planning process has become very efficient, but the process has not changed significantly to reflect evolution of IMC. Although measurement of communication effects is recognized as a priority, there remains a need to find innovative ways to know if communication dollars have been invested properly. Finally, clients prefer to have more strategic thinking along with the outstanding creative ads that agencies continue to deliver!

Marketers believe they can help agencies in the relationship by being better clients through good personnel, clear decision-making, sufficient budgets and lead times, and solid market research. In addition, clients should provide clear direction of their needs at the start of the creative process and involve the agency completely. This also includes sharing sensitive and confidential information so that the agency understands the client's business, marketing, and market positioning objectives. In the end, the agency and client must be viewed as one team not two organizations.

Some of these and other findings emerged from a recent survey of agency and clients conducted in both Canada and the U.S. In partnership, *Marketing Magazine* and *Brandweek* administered over 10,000 addressed e-mail questionnaires. A highlight of this research is that it tried to obtain a balanced perspective on many advertising industry issues by having an independent research organization design the study and collect the data rather than industry associations.[29]

A survey of the marketers reported the following:

- 45 percent maintained a primary relationship with an ad agency, while many preferred working on a project basis or with multiple specialty agencies.
- Agencies from all disciplines were used; advertising (79 percent), public relations (59 percent), direct marketing (54 percent), sales promotion (54 percent), events (46 percent), and interactive marketing (46 percent).
- Clients valued creativity, strategic insights, and excellence in execution fairly equally.
- Agencies tended to have poor performance in multidisciplined thinking (31 percent), strategic depth (30 percent), creative breadth (26 percent), and resource availability (26 percent).
- Additional services deemed important were independent ROI audits and training of agency staff with respect to marketing versus advertising only.

A survey of the agencies revealed a few noteworthy facts:

- About half focused on multiple disciplines while the other half specialized on one.
- Agencies tended to have one or two dominant clients and only one-third had 15 or more clients.
- Business of the AOR and the project was split roughly equally.
- Approximately 60 percent of all relationships lasted three years or more.
- Agencies viewed client relationships, client loyalty, and strategic involvement as the most important factors compared to profits or performance based rewards.

In reviewing the two perspectives of the agency–client relationship, some issues for future collaboration appear relevant. Some divergence on the type of partnership between agency and client is emerging. A different view regarding performance-based remuneration is a challenge for agreement. Long-term relationships appear to be more difficult to maintain. The degree to which claimed and actual integration across disciplines occur is at odds. The ability of agencies to deliver independent marketing ideas and focus on ROI may be a limitation that clients will desire with increased frequency.

SUMMARY

Companies use two basic systems to organize internally for advertising and promotion. Centralized systems offer the advantages of facilitated communications, lower personnel requirements, continuity in staff, and more top-management involvement. Disadvantages include a lower involvement with overall marketing goals, longer response times, and difficulties in handling multiple product lines.

Decentralized systems offer the advantages of concentrated managerial attention, more rapid responses to problems, and increased flexibility, though they may be limited by ineffective decision making, internal conflicts, misallocation of funds, and a lack of authority. Firms have to decide if they will hire an external advertising agency or use an in-house service to create their ads and purchase media. In-house agencies, while offering the advantages of cost savings,

control, and increased coordination, have the disadvantage of less experience, objectivity, and flexibility.

Many firms use advertising agencies to help develop and execute their programs. These agencies may take on a variety of forms, including full-service agencies, creative boutiques, and media buying services. The first offers the client a full range of services (including creative, account, marketing, and financial and management services); the other two specialize in creative services and media buying, respectively. Agencies are compensated through commission systems, percentage charges, and fee- and cost-based systems. Recently, the emphasis on agency accountability has increased. Agencies are being evaluated on both financial and qualitative aspects, and some clients are using incentive-based compensation systems that tie agency

compensation to performance measures such as sales and market share.

In addition to using ad agencies, marketers use the services of other marketing communication specialists, including direct marketing agencies, sales promotion agencies, public relations firms, and interactive agencies. A marketer must decide whether to use a different specialist for each promotional function or have all of its integrated marketing communications done by an advertising agency that offers all of these services under one roof.

Recent studies have found that most marketers believe it is their responsibility, not the ad agency's, to set strategy for and coordinate IMC campaigns. The lack of a broad perspective and specialized skills in nonadvertising areas is seen as the major barrier to agencies' increased involvement in integrated marketing communications.

512

KEY TERMS

advertising manager, *488*
centralized system, *488*
decentralized system, *490*
brand manager, *490*
category management
    system, *491*
in-house agency, *493*
superagencies, *494*

full-service agency, *495*
account executive, *495*
copywriters, *497*
departmental system, *498*
group system, *498*
creative boutique, *498*
media buying services, *499*
commission system, *499*

negotiated commission, *501*
fixed-fee method, *502*
fee-commission
    combination, *502*
cost-plus system, *502*
percentage charges, *502*
incentive-based system, *502*
financial audit, *503*

qualitative audit, *503*
sales promotion agency, *506*
public relations firm, *507*
direct-response agency, *507*
interactive agencies, *507*

DISCUSSION QUESTIONS

1. What are some of the specific responsibilities and duties of an advertising manager under a centralized advertising department structure? Why is an advertising manager needed if a company uses an outside agency?

2. Discuss the pros and cons of using an in-house advertising agency. What are some of the reasons why companies might change from using an in-house agency and hire an outside agency?

3. Discuss the various functions a full-service advertising agency performs for its clients. Might any one of these functions be more important than another?

4. Discuss some of the reasons why traditional advertising agencies have been developing more IMC capabilities. What changes might these agencies have to make to improve their service?

5. Discuss the various methods by which advertising agencies are compensated. What factors will determine the type of compensation arrangement a company uses with an agency?

6. Why are many companies moving away from the traditional commission system and using incentive-based compensation for their advertising agencies? Why might an ad agency be reluctant to accept an incentive-based compensation system?

7. Discuss the various reasons why marketers often choose to switch advertising agencies. Find an example of a company that has recently changed advertising agencies and analyze the reasons given for the change.

8. Why might a company choose to use a creative boutique rather than a larger full-service agency?

9. Discuss the reasons why a company might want to have all its integrated marketing communication activities performed versus having these activities performed by several different agencies who specialize in various areas of IMC, like public relations, direct marketing, sales promotion, and Internet marketing.

Regulatory, Ethical, and Social Issues for Integrated Marketing Communications

CHAPTER OBJECTIVES

- To be familiar with the advertising regulation system in Canada.

- To evaluate the ethical perspectives of advertising.

- To understand the social effects of advertising.

- To examine the economic role of advertising and its effects on consumer choice, competition, and product costs and prices.

De Facto's De-Normalization Campaign

The Association régionale sport étudiant du Québec et Chaudière-Appalaches, a regional group funded by the Quebec government with a mandate of promoting a balance of studies, sports, and healthy living to young people, launched its De Facto brand to counter the problem of smoking with an extensive French-language communication campaign during the fall of 2003.

A TV and cinema ad featured the primary message. A group of executives in a boardroom, presumably from the tobacco industry, witness a teen girl smoking on a television screen and then congratulate themselves for their success at converting another non-smoker. The ad claimed that 475,000 Canadian youth provide profits to the tobacco industry through their purchase of cigarettes. It ends with the tag line "The truth...unfiltered" and identification of the brand De Facto despite being funded $690,000 from Health Canada. This de-normalization campaign targeted 12- to 17-year-olds and intended to encourage the belief that it is not normal to smoke. Other media included radio, a website (defacto.ca), sports sponsorship, events, and promotional products. The campaign represented a test case to determine if it should be continued nationally.

The origin of the campaign centred on research indicating that 23 percent of Quebec youth smoke, nearly 20 percent of all Canadian youth smoke, and 85 percent of all smokers begin before the age of 18, as well as the recent tobacco industry

activities occurring in the U.S. Accidentally released information of youth marketing practices of American tobacco firms led to the industry paying billions of dollars in damages. Of which, some money financed a de-normalization "Truth" campaign that dramatized the industry's manipulation tactics and successfully presented the youth smoking problem according to the creators of the De Facto campaign.

Immediately following the start of the campaign, Imperial Tobacco Canada stated that its marketing activities did not and never would target children and considered such activities as deplorable. The company claimed that the campaign contained erroneous allegations or out-of-context information to hurt the tobacco industry's image. However, the agency responsible for the campaign claimed it based the message on information from Statistics Canada and the World Health Organization. Imperial also reminded the public that the industry spends $500,000 per year to train employees of small stores on how to keep minors from purchasing their product. Towards the end of 2003, the three major firms of the tobacco industry accused the creators of the campaign with libel. Subsequently, media ads stopped and some website content ceased to exist.

In response, the Quebec Coalition for Tobacco Control in Montreal claimed the De Facto campaign merely expressed the analysis of public health experts and the ruling of a Quebec Superior Court Justice who stated that the court did not believe that tobacco firms aimed their advertising to smokers over 19 years of age. Further, it claimed the industry's legal actions intended to curtail the future freedom of other organizations to communicate their views since challenging the tobacco industry would mean extensive and expensive legal battles.

The debate raged on as the tobacco industry countered the free speech argument and stated that free speech did not permit "distortions, falsehoods and outright lies" through the use of old documents, misrepresented quotes, and libellous ads. It noted that the government investigated 20 years of JTI-Macdonald's marketing documents and found no record of any youth marketing programs. It also suggested that such activities are clearly illegal and any public accusation was negligent and defamatory. Finally, it cited research that questioned whether the de-normalization campaign in the U.S. lowered youth smoking.

Posttests of the campaign provided evidence of extensive communication effects. Unaided and aided awareness totalled 94 percent, surpassing the objective of 75 percent. Also, 81 percent of all respondents rated the campaign credible (i.e., rating 4, 5, 6 on a 6-point scale) while respondents who smoke indicated 74 percent credibility. Organizers planned for a continued $5-million campaign over two years and submitted funding requests to provincial and federal governments.

Sources: Danny Kucharsky, "Tobacco Firms Fire Back at De Facto," *Marketing Magazine*, December 8, 2003; Danny Kucharsky, "Youth Targeted by Tobacco's Tricks in De Facto Anti-Smoking Effort," *Marketing Magazine*, September 22, 2003; Danny Kucharsky, "Imperial Objects to 'demonization'," *Marketing Magazine*, September 29, 2003; Paul Bleau, "Redefining Normal," *Marketing Magazine*, January 19, 2004; Louis Gauvin, "All for Free Speech-But Only for Themselves," *Marketing Magazine*, January 26, 2004; Christian Guay, "Distortions, Falsehoods and Outright Lies," *Marketing Magazine*, February 23, 2004; Danny Kucharsky, "Clearing the Smoke," *Marketing Magazine*, May 3, 2004.

If I were to name the deadliest subversive force within capitalism, the single greatest source of its waning morality—I would without hesitation name advertising. How else should one identify a force that debases language, drains thought, and undoes dignity?[1]

The primary focus of this text has been on the role of advertising and other promotional variables as marketing activities used to convey information to, and influence the behaviour of, consumers. We have been concerned with examining the advertising and promotion function in the context of a business and marketing environment and from a perspective that assumes these activities are appropriate. However, as you can see in this quote from economist Robert Heilbroner, not everyone shares this viewpoint. Advertising and promotion are the most visible of all business activities and are prone to scrutiny by those who are concerned about the methods marketers use to sell their products and services.

Proponents of advertising argue that it is the lifeblood of business—it provides consumers with information about products and services and encourages them to improve their standard of living. They say advertising produces jobs and helps new firms enter the marketplace. Companies employ people who make the products and provide the services that advertising sells. Free market economic systems are based on competition, which revolves around information, and nothing delivers information better and at less cost than advertising.

Not everyone, however, is sold on the value of advertising. Critics argue that most advertising is more propaganda than information; it creates needs and faults consumers never knew they had. Ads suggest that children won't succeed without a computer, that our bodies should be leaner, our faces younger, and our houses cleaner. They point to the sultry, scantily clad bodies used in ads to sell everything from perfume to beer to power tools and argue that advertising promotes materialism, insecurity, and greed.

Because of its high visibility and pervasiveness, along with its persuasive character, advertising has been the subject of a great deal of controversy and criticism. Numerous books are critical of not only advertising's methods and techniques but also its social consequences. Various parties—including scholars, economists, politicians, sociologists, government agencies, social critics, special-interest groups, and consumers—have attacked advertising for a variety of reasons, including its excessiveness, the way it influences society, the methods it uses, its exploitation of consumers, and its effect on our economic system.

Advertising is a very powerful force, and this text would not be complete without a look at the criticisms regarding its ethical, social, and economic effects as well as some defences against these charges. Before we entertain this debate, we will review the regulations affecting advertising in Canada. As you read this chapter, remember that the various perspectives presented reflect judgments of people with different backgrounds, values, and interests. You may see nothing wrong with the ads for cigarettes or beer or sexually suggestive ads. Other students, however, may oppose these actions on moral and ethical grounds. While we attempt to present the arguments on both sides of these controversial issues, you will have to draw your own conclusions as to who is right or wrong.

ADVERTISING REGULATION IN CANADA

Regulation of advertising in Canada occurs through both government regulation and self-regulation. In this section, we review both of these topics. With respect to government regulation, we focus on three prevalent domains. The Canadian Radio-television and Telecommunications Commission (CRTC) is responsible for laws and regulations concerning broadcasting and telecommunications, so its role in advertising is relevant. Health Canada has placed stringent laws for tobacco promotion. Finally, the Quebec government has strong regulations with respect to advertising to children. In the other direction, the Advertising Standards Council (ASC) acts as the self-regulation body for the advertising industry. Responsibility for many of the federal laws regarding the content of advertising messages for specific product categories has been transferred to ASC by the request of the federal government.

CANADIAN RADIO-TELEVISION AND TELECOMMUNICATIONS COMMISSION (CRTC)

The mandate of the CRTC is to ensure that the *Broadcasting Act of 1991* and the *Telecommunications Act of 1993* are upheld throughout Canada. The broad objective of both acts is to make certain that all Canadians can receive broadcasting and telecommunications services. In attaining its mandate, the CRTC is required to delicately balance the needs of citizens, industries, and various interest groups with respect to programming and costs. For purposes of advertising, we will concentrate on the broadcasting side.

The CRTC regulates over 5,900 media organizations (i.e., television, cable distribution, AM and FM radio, pay and specialty television, direct-to-home satellite systems, multipoint distribution systems, subscription television and pay audio). The CRTC is responsible for granting the licences for these media and ensuring that they comply with the *Broadcasting Act*. Within the context of the *Broadcasting Act*, the CRTC focuses on a number of relevant issues (i.e., content, competition, technology).

As a regulator, the CRTC recently evaluated two highly topical applications that would have changed the advertising industry substantially in Canada. The Canadian Cable Television Association requested that cable operators be allowed to carry a digital feed of U.S. specialty services (e.g., HBO, ESPN). The Canadian Association of Broadcasters countered with a defence that such services were not necessary since the programming was available on existing channels.[2] A marketing firm with the support of the Canadian Association of Advertisers wanted to insert Canadian ads during the feed of U.S. specialty services (e.g., TBS, A&E). Once again the Canadian Association of Broadcasters argued against this change suggesting that sufficient advertising capacity existed in Canada, and that increased capacity would reduce advertising revenue.[3] In both cases, the CRTC denied the application.

As you may expect, advertising is one area in which the CRTC plays a role. We now turn to a few of the more topical or interesting aspects of advertising that are regulated by the CRTC:

- *Advertising limits.* The CRTC ensures that TV stations and specialty services carry 12 minutes of advertising during the broadcast day, which lasts 18 hours beginning at 6:00 a.m. However, public service announcements or "ads" for Canadian TV shows are not counted in this total.
- *Infomercials.* An infomercial is a program lasting more than 12 minutes that combines the promotion of a product in an engaging entertainment-like style. The CRTC approves all infomercials for any television station, network, or specialty service.
- *900 numbers.* The CRTC has guidelines for advertising adult-oriented phone services by restricting the number of times they are advertised and the hour in which they are aired. Implementation of this occurs through the Television Bureau of Canada.
- *Alcohol and drugs.* There are regulations for advertising these products, but the CRTC has disbanded the screening process of the ads. This is now the responsibility of the ASC, and we will summarize this later in this section.

There are two areas for which you might expect the CRC to be involved in, but thus far, it has no responsibility:

- *False or misleading ads.* The CRTC does not address complaints of these types of ads and refers complaints to the Competition Bureau of the Federal Government. The CRTC has left this for the ASC as well.
- *Internet.* For the time being, the CRTC has not provided any regulations on the content of the Internet, although the Federal Government provides extensive guideline booklets.

REGULATION OF TOBACCO ADVERTISING

Tobacco products are severely restricted by Health Canada regulations on their use of traditional advertising media. One avenue that tobacco companies turned to fairly quickly when the restrictions were enacted many years ago was to sponsor various arts, cultural, and sporting events; however, this option will be discontinued in 2003. Print ads communicating these sponsorships were the only permitted advertising, so the new restriction appears to present even greater limits. Presently, tobacco firms also face significant packaging requirements such as presenting graphic images of the consequences of tobacco use, disallowing any reference to "light," and including a full list of ingredients. With such limited options to attract new users or retain existing consumers, the tobacco companies have been very creative with interesting media choices recently.

Underground marketing has emerged where communication of the brands occurs through exclusive distribution in select bars, pubs, and nightclubs. Through mechanisms such as these, the tobacco companies can get customers to register so that direct marketing techniques can take place, such as contest offers. And 1-800 numbers on tobacco packaging get customers to engage with the tobacco firms directly using creative angles. Point-of-sale communication has also been a competitive tactic that the companies aggressively pursue. Some companies have begun to use the Internet, but thus far, mostly as a means of communicating sponsorship deals. Currently, all of these IMC tools are legal, and we will find out whether the future looks bright for tobacco manufacturers, as they continue to innovate, or cloudy if the government steps in even further.[4]

QUEBEC REGULATIONS ON ADVERTISING TO CHILDREN

According to the *Consumer Protection Act of Quebec*, it is illegal to direct commercial advertising messages to persons younger than 13 years of age. Provisions are in place to determine whether or not an ad is directed to children. Specifically, the provisions concern the product, the way the ad is presented, and the time and place the ad is shown. One exception to the law is a regularly published magazine that is for sale. These magazines, however, have 16 guidelines with respect to their advertising claims; the types of products; the portrayal of people's behaviour, motivation, or attitude reflected in the ad; and the source of the message (i.e., person or character).

To apply the law, the Quebec government provides summary guidelines for advertisers to follow, and it also provides screening services for advertisers if they are uncertain whether it contravenes the law. The purpose of the guidelines is to ensure that advertisers fully understand and correctly interpret the law. The guidelines pertain to precisely describing the types of advertising appeals that are not permitted, clearly defining what is meant by a children's TV program, and exactly stating the percentage of children in the audience that constitutes a children's TV program. The guidelines include the degree to which messages can be directed towards children depending upon whether the product is exclusively for children (i.e., candy), partially for children (i.e., cereal), or not for children. There are also specific guidelines for public service announcements directed to children, even though there is no commercial message.

ADVERTISING STANDARDS COUNCIL (ASC)

The ASC is a not-for-profit, self-regulatory, industry body with a mandate to create and maintain community confidence in advertising. The ASC represents advertisers, media organizations, and advertising industry suppliers and has more than 200 corporate members. Its Standards Division administers the industry's self-regulatory codes (i.e., *Canadian Code of Advertising Standards*, *Gender Portrayal Guidelines*), handles complaints about advertising, and administers any disputes that arise between advertisers. Its Advertising Clearance Division previews advertisements in five industry categories, as well as ads directed towards children, ensuring that advertisers will follow applicable legislation, regulatory codes, and industry standards.

Canadian Code of Advertising Standards   The Code, as it is known, describes what is not acceptable advertising. According to the ASC, "Advertising is defined as any message (the content of which is controlled directly or indirectly by the advertiser) expressed in any language and communicated in any medium to Canadians with the intent to influence their choice, opinion or behaviour." The Code pertains to the content of ads only. It does not limit the promotion of legal products or the demonstration of products for their intended purpose. The intention of the Code is to provide standards so that responsible and effective adverting results without minimizing the right of firms to advertise. It does not supersede any other laws or regulations.

The Code is used as the criteria to assess whether a complaint is legitimate or not, and the ASC is very clear in how it uses the Code to resolve complaints. "The context and content of the advertisement and the audience actually, or likely to be, or intended to be, reached by the advertisement, and the medium/media used to deliver the advertisement, are relevant factors in assessing its conformity with the Code."

The Code is supported by all member organizations as it sets the standard for advertising with respect to honesty, truth, accuracy, fairness, and propriety. Members are expected to follow the Code both in letter and in spirit and are expected to substantiate any advertised claims when requested. The Code contains fourteen clauses.

1. Accuracy and Clarity	9. Imitation
2. Disguised Advertising Techniques	10. Safety
3. Price Claims	11. Superstitions and Fears
4. Bait and Switch	12. Advertising to Children
5. Guarantees	13. Advertising to Minors
6. Comparative Advertising	14. Unacceptable Depictions and
7. Testimonials	Portrayals
8. Professional or Scientific Claims	

In 2003, ASC updated clauses 6, 10, and 14 as part of its ongoing mandate to ensure that the Code reflects current practices and fairness. While on the surface the changes were just a few words for each clause, the meaning permitted a more reasonable and flexible interpretation. As part of the change, ASC began posting "interpretive guidelines" so that members could understand the code more thoroughly.[5]

Gender Portrayal Guidelines The Guidelines, based on a previous CRTC task force, attempts to ensure that women and men are portrayed appropriately and equally in advertising. The ASC presents the Guidelines as the direction of areas or topics from which complaints or issues have arisen over the past 30 years. Overall, there are six clauses pertaining to authority, decision making, sexuality, violence, diversity, and language.

When interpreting the Guidelines, ASC has four suggestions that advertisers should consider. The overall impression of the ad should not violate the spirit of gender equality. There are clauses specifically addressed towards women, as men are at less risk of being negatively portrayed. History and art should not be used as an excuse for violating a clause. Finally, certain products and how they are advertised are amenable to more appropriate media.

Complaint Process The Standards Division handles complaints in three streams. **Consumer complaints** are those from ordinary citizens who believe that an ad is unacceptable. The ASC receives these complaints directly as well as through government departments and agencies of all levels, the Better Business Bureau, the CRTC, and the Canadian Broadcast Standards Council. **Special interest group complaints** are those from a demonstrated organization that expresses a unified viewpoint. This is a new stream first recognized in the spring of 2002. Complaints from other advertisers are known as **trade disputes**. While there is a distinct complaint process for consumers and special interest groups, the general procedures for each have a degree of similarity that we will touch upon. A summary of all consumer complaints is published in an annual report.

The initial complaint is authenticated to make sure that it is, in fact, a consumer or special interest group complaint and not a trade dispute. From there, the complaint is evaluated to determine whether it legitimately violates a Code provision. This initial assessment occurs at the national (i.e., Toronto) or regional (i.e., Alberta, Atlantic, British Columbia) Consumer Response Councils for English ads, and le Conseil des normes in Montreal for French ads. If the complaint is valid, the advertiser is contacted and has an opportunity to respond to the complaint before the Council makes a formal ruling. On the other hand, the advertiser can take an appropriate action to remedy the complaint as part of the response. In these cases, the advertiser would not be identified in the ASC complaints report. An advertiser who responds and does not remedy the situation can be identified in the report if the Council upholds the complaint.

Complaints Report   The ASC has published a more comprehensive annual report since 1997. This format includes the identification of advertisers and the details of all complaints. Previously the annual report provided global statistics. Figure 18–1 shows a capsule summary of the past 3 years, in which the number of complaints and ads has experienced an unusual spike for 2002. The ratio of the number of complaints to the number of ads indicates that the number of complaints per ad is less than two. This underscores the fact that the number of complaints is not a factor, but rather the content of the complaint is justification for investigating an ad. The percentage of complaints upheld has seen some modest movement, as expressed by the number of complaints received, pursued, and evaluated by council. Each of these ratios have been relatively consistent the past three years. In general, about half of all complaints originate from television, but 2001 saw an interesting change with the second highest number of complaints coming from out-of-home media. Finally, the complaints-by-product category does not seem to indicate a discernable pattern. We now briefly review some ads that received the most complaints during the past few years.

In 2001, two complaints stood out as having substantially more complaints than the average. A magazine ad for an Yves Saint Laurent fragrance allegedly had a photo that was sexually exploitive of women, showing a woman apparently in the throes of ecstasy. This ad received 12 complaints, and the Council upheld the complaint, citing Clause 14 of the *Code* and principles of the Guideline. It seems while some amount of sensuality is acceptable for advertising fragrances, this ad had crossed the line a bit too far.

During 2001, a Ford Motor Company TV ad showed a young female shoving a male store clerk into the hatchback of her car and driving away with him. This ad received nine complaints, and the Council upheld the complaint, citing Clause 14 as the ad depicted an abduction, which is an unlawful activity. Ford appealed the decision; however, the Appeal Panel confirmed the original decision. Ford's post-appeal statement makes this example an interesting debate:

> "Ford of Canada did not intend to offend any segment of the population in this particular advertisement; rather the aim of the ad was to show the attributes of the Focus. The identical advertisement shown in Quebec (both in English and in French) was determined not to contravene the *Code* by the Consumer Response Council and Appeal Panel in Quebec. Particulars of this complaint were provided to the press by a consumer complainant even though this process is intended to be confidential. Subsequent to the Appeal Decision,

	2003	2002	2001
Number of complaints (ads)			
Received	1,133 (716)	1,828 (870)	1,164 (815)
Pursued	860 (493)	1,026 (602)	833 (540)
Evaluated by Council	226 (109)	341 (97)	321 (155)
Upheld by Council	131 (57)	206 (51)	161 (75)
Upheld Complaints %			
Received	12%	11%	14%
Pursued	15%	18%	19%
Evaluated by Council	58%	60%	50%
Leading *Code* Clause	Clause 14	Clause 14	Clause 14
	Clause 1	Clause 1	Clause 1
Leading Product Category	Retail	Media	Personal/Proprietary
	Food/Supermarkets	Retail	Food/Supermarkets
	Personal/Proprietary	Food/Supermarkets	Automotive
Leading Media	Television	Out-of-Home	Television
	Newspaper	Television	Out-of-Home

FIGURE 18–1

Summary of complaints from the Advertising Standards Council's annual Complaints Report

Margaret Wente, in a lengthy *Globe and Mail* article dated January 31, 2002, gave strong positive support for the ad. However, in light of the decision of the ASC Appeal Panel, Ford of Canada will withdraw the current English advertisement."

In 2002, nudity was an issue in a K-Rock 97.3 out-of-home ad. Billboard ads showed three apparently nude men with nutshells placed strategically across their anatomy. The campaign received 115 complaints and seven petitions totalling 455 signatures. Although Council recognized the display was consistent with the unusual personalities of the hosts, it nevertheless deemed that nudity was gratuitously exploited. A 2002 television ad for an alcohol beverage manufacturer showed women reacting aggressively to personal slights. Council judged the reaction to be excessive to the perceived offence.

During 2003, another radio station, The Wolf 104.9, featured a mostly nude woman in a billboard ad that received 36 complaints. The image taken from behind focused on her buttocks and showed her hand resting on a guitar with a caption reading "Now turn us on." After the initial complaints, the word "censored" was used to cover the woman. In both cases, Council deemed the ads offensive and demeaning to women. Council received 19 complaints of an out-of-home ad illustrating a religious figure dressed in unorthodox attire that denigrated and disparaged an identifiable group.

In early 2004, a television ad for an alcohol beverage depicted two women engaging in a passionate kiss. The 113 complaints indicated that the scene was inappropriate for family viewing programming. Council upheld this complaint stating, "the commercial displayed obvious indifference to conduct or attitudes that offended standard of public decency prevailing among a significant segment of the population." Council concluded that the ad in question did not contravene the code providing it was shown later than 9:30 in the evening.

Clearance Process   The ASC provides clearance services for ads for many product categories and ads directed towards children for all jurisdictions except Quebec. IMC Perspective 18–1 highlights a successful campaign directed towards children.

- *Alcohol.* The ASC adheres to the CRTC *Code for Broadcast Advertising of Alcoholic Beverages.* The CRTC disbanded the clearance services in 1997. This code gives 17 precise guidelines on what is not permitted in alcohol ads. Some of the guidelines pertain to not attracting under-age drinkers, non-drinkers, or problem drinkers. Many other guidelines focus on the message with respect to the type of consumption motivation, consumption situation, source, and appeal. The ASC will review all TV and radio ads across the country as well as print and out-of-home ads in British Columbia.
- *Cosmetics.* Health Canada transferred the clearance for cosmetic products ads to the ASC in 1992, although clearance is not an absolute requirement. The ASC follows the *Guidelines for Cosmetic Advertising and Labelling Claims.* The most recent version is a joint publication of the ASC, Health Canada, and the Canadian Cosmetic, Toiletry and Fragrance Association, and was published in 2000. The guidelines list acceptable and unacceptable claims for two types of hair care products, nail products, and five types of skin care products. Another set of guidelines list unacceptable and acceptable claims for toothpaste, deodorant, mouthwash, perfumes/fragrances/colognes, sun-care products, vitamins, and aromatherapy products. Finally, the same is done for different benefit claims such as anti-wrinkle, healthy, ingredients, nourishment, relaxation, respiration, revitalization, therapy/treatment and lifting.
- *Non-prescription drugs.* Health Canada also transferred the clearance of non-therapeutic aspects of non-prescription drug ads directed towards consumers to the ASC in 1992. The ASC ensures that broadcast and print copy comply with Health Canada's *Consumer Drug Advertising Guidelines* and *The Food and Drugs Act and Regulations.* Health Canada has also given to the ASC the responsibility for resolving any complaints of advertising for this category.

Tastes Great—Can't Wait

What do you get when you combine a VIA Rail train, some kids, and the fun marketing of Kool-Aid? How about the "Kool-Train," an award-winning campaign that won the Best of Show at *Marketing Magazine*'s Media Innovation Awards and a spot in the Media Lions competition at the International Advertising Festival in Cannes.

In 1998 and 1999, Kraft Canada launched the "Face" campaign, where the Kool-Aid Smile was seen on interesting and non-traditional venues like the Toronto Island Ferry and the bottom of public swimming pools. The success of the campaign presented a challenge for the media team that was looking for the next "wow!" idea for spring/summer 2000. The idea had to be fresh and captivating for kids, one that would build on the unique "Pointable Media" theme, and yet not alienate the moms with purchasing power.

The result of strategic media thinking and creativity was the "Kool-Train" concept, ten VIA train engines wrapped in fun and wacky Kool-Aid imagery. The Media Edge developed the concept of the Kool-Train and approached various partners to incorporate integrated campaigns to build on the theme. VIA Rail Canada, *Kidsworld Magazine*, *TV Guide*, and YTV all jumped on board. So, Kool-Aid and its partners created a totally integrated campaign that was completely relevant for kids and moms alike in giving them an ethical and socially responsible brand experience.

Kidsworld Magazine developed a Kool-Train curriculum. It provided teachers and students with an original and fun learning experience through a history-based program. YTV tied in and featured a Kool-Train contest that asked kids to use visual arts to show how the railroad affected Canada. It was communicated nicely with the help of two popular YTV hosts, Sam and Aaron. *TV Guide*, in the meantime, was approached with a unique contest idea to "Spot the Kool-Train" within its listing pages over a 4-week period, integrating VIA Rail and Holiday Inn prizes to attract the mom as another key target audience.

From Kool-Aid's perspective, the campaign was a success with increased awareness and a three-year record-high volume share during a cool and rainy summer. From a kids consumer behaviour perspective, it appears Kool-Aid hit the mark too. It offered an IMC program that spoke to kids of a certain age with the media and sales promotion that fits them precisely.

Sources: Helen Kang, "A Kool Way to Target Kids/Moms," *Marketing Magazine*, July 30, 2001; Kraft Foods Newsroom, "All Aboard the Kool-Train," Kraft Foods, May 1, 2000, www.kraft.com/newsroom.

To facilitate this change, Health Canada has published a document that describes its role, the ASC's role, and the claims that can be made in ads directed to consumers. Most of the guidelines in this document focus on the need for advertisers to provide factual information of the product's attributes and benefits and that the claims are scientifically valid.

- *Ads directed to children.* The ASC uses the *Broadcast Code for Advertising to Children (Children's Code)*, published by the Canadian Association of Broadcasters in cooperation with the ASC, to assess whether ads directed towards children are appropriate. The code takes into account the unique characteristics of children to ensure adequate safety and has nine guidelines concerning factual presentation, product prohibitions, avoiding undue pressure, scheduling, source or endorser of the message, price, comparison claims, safety, and social values. The code also gives seven instructions on clearance procedures, such as when clearance is required or not, when ads can be directed to children, and during which programs ads can be directed to children. Ethical Perspective 18–2 illustrates some other mechanisms for protecting children.
- *Food.* The ASC evaluates broadcast ads with respect to *The Food and Drugs Act and Regulations* and the *Guide to Food Labelling and Advertising.* Its policy guidelines make a distinction between food claims that are exempt from clearance and those that require clearance in four categories: general

Children's Views of Advertising

Media literacy of children is thriving in Canada thanks to some organizations devoted to ensuring that kids understand the media environment they live in. One such firm, Mediacs, provides workshops to children in their classrooms on many topics including how marketing and advertising influences perceptions of body image, sexual stereotypes, and the like. With media literacy a part of the core curriculum across Canada, it is not surprising to find many other organizations involved in similar work such as the Association for Media Literacy, the Media Awareness Network (MAN), Concerned Children's Advertisers (CCA), and the Canadian Teachers' Federation. And the goal is not to communicate that all advertising messages are inherently bad. But rather, to encourage children to think critically with a knowledge base and to ask themselves the right kinds of questions as they process each message.

To further these objectives, each organization delivers media literacy with their own specialized approach. For example, the CCA offers curriculum-based lesson plans for all grade levels, and additional information for teachers and parents that support its public service announcements. And in Nova Scotia, part of the training set by the Department of Education is to allow children the opportunity to create ads on computers so they can understand the significance of some advertising techniques. The MAN provides research reports to assess the degree to which media literacy is delivered across the country.

As these activities take hold, the question arises as to how literate children are these days. One market research firm invited 200 children from its online panel of 2,000 that it regularly surveys to participate in an impromptu evaluation of clothing ads featuring both sexual (e.g., Guess) and non-sexual (e.g., The Gap) content. An interesting trend of three groups emerged; anti-brand, comfort, and high fashion. The anti-brand children recognized the clothing ads but clearly rejected all of them on principle and were offended by sexually suggestive clothing ads. Comfort consumers claim their purchase decision is not affected by their like or dislike of advertising but were offended by ads with sex. The final group often buy brands that use sex in advertising, however, these consumers claim they enjoy the style and fashion, and are receptive to the advertising but still not overly fond of it. Overall, the three groups claim the major influences for their purchase are peers, displays, and price, not advertising. However, the researchers found some indication of stronger ad recognition of the sexual content ads versus the non-sexual content ads.

Sources: Kelly Lynne Ashton, "Wise to the Game," *Marketing Magazine*, August 11, 2003; Kathleen Martin, "Building Critical Consumers," *Marketing Magazine*, January 19, 2004.

---

advertising, occasion-greeting advertising (i.e., Christmas), promotional advertising, and sponsorship advertising. In addition, the ASC guidelines for the use of comparative advertising in food commercials outline six principles of appropriate executions of this presentation style. Finally, the ASC guidelines on claims based on research and survey data have requirements pertaining to all aspects of the research design (i.e., sample, data collection).

ETHICAL EFFECTS OF ADVERTISING

While many laws and regulations determine what advertisers can and cannot do, not every issue is covered by a rule. Marketers must often make decisions regarding appropriate and responsible actions on the basis of ethical considerations rather than on what is legal or within industry guidelines. **Ethics** are moral principles and values that govern the actions and decisions of an individual or group.[6]

Ethical issues must be considered in integrated marketing communications decisions. And advertising and promotion are areas where a lapse in ethical standards or judgment can result in actions that are highly visible and often very damaging to a company. For example, many organizations and individuals have been critical of advertisers such as Calvin Klein for promoting sexual permissiveness and objectifying women in their ads (Exhibit 18–1). The company was heavily criticized and even boycotted over the controversial "kiddie porn" ads it ran a few years ago featuring intimate snapshots of teenagers in provocative states of undress.[7]

Much of the controversy over advertising stems from the ways many companies use it as a selling tool and from its impact on society's tastes, values, and lifestyles (Exhibit 18–2). Specific techniques used by advertisers are criticized as deceptive or untruthful, offensive or in bad taste, and exploitative of certain groups, such as children. We discuss each of these criticisms, along with advertisers' responses.

ADVERTISING AS UNTRUTHFUL OR DECEPTIVE

One of the major complaints against advertising is that many ads are misleading or untruthful and deceive consumers. A number of studies have shown a general mistrust of advertising among consumers.[8] A study by Banwari Mittal found that consumers felt that less than one-quarter of TV commercials are honest and believable.[9] Sharon Shavitt, Pamela Lowery, and James Haefner recently conducted a major national survey of over 1,000 adult consumers to determine the general public's current attitudes toward and confidence in advertising. They found that Americans generally do not trust advertising, although they tend to feel more confidence in advertising claims when focused on their actual purchase decisions.[10]

Advertisers should have a reasonable basis for making a claim about product performance and may be required to provide evidence to support their claims. However, deception can occur more subtly as a result of how consumers perceive the ad and its impact on their beliefs.[11] The difficulty of determining just what constitutes deception, along with the fact that advertisers have the right to use puffery and make subjective claims about their products, tends to complicate the issue. **Puffery** has been legally defined as "advertising or other sales presentations which praise the item to be sold with subjective opinions, superlatives, or exaggerations, vaguely and generally, stating no specific facts."[12] But a concern of many critics is the extent to which advertisers are *deliberately* untruthful or misleading.

Sometimes advertisers have made overtly false or misleading claims or failed to award prizes promoted in a contest or sweepstakes. However, these cases usually involve smaller companies and a tiny portion of the hundreds of billions of dollars spent on advertising and promotion each year. Most advertisers do not design their messages with the intention to mislead or deceive consumers or run sweepstakes with no intention of awarding prizes. Not only are such practices unethical, but the culprits would damage their reputation and risk prosecution by regulatory groups or government agencies. National advertisers in particular invest large sums of money to develop loyalty to, and enhance the image of, their brands. These companies are not likely to risk hard-won consumer trust and confidence by intentionally deceiving consumers.

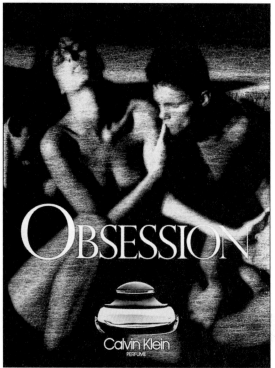

Exhibit 18–1
Ads by Calvin Klein have been the target of criticism by women's groups and others

525

Exhibit 18–2
Benetton's "Death Row" ads created a major controversy

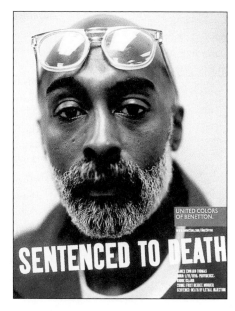

The problem of untruthful or fraudulent advertising and promotion exists more at the local level and in specific areas such as mail order, telemarketing, and other forms of direct marketing. Yet there have been many cases where large companies were accused of misleading consumers with their ads or promotions. Some companies test the limits of industry and government rules and regulations to make claims that will give their brands an advantage in highly competitive markets.

Periodically, we find unusual advertising that some may claim as deceptive. Labatt Breweries of Canada advertised in newspapers and communicated information about Carlsberg beer. However, upon reading the ad, it was not entirely clear that Labatt was the sponsor of the ad, especially when it no longer sells the beer! Labatt had sold Danish Carlsberg beer under licence for 15 years and lost the contract to Moosehead and yet, somehow, Labatt felt compelled to explain that Carlsberg was not exactly the same as it was before because it had a new brewer. It seems part of the motivation for such an ad arose from ads that Molson ran a few years before noting that even though Labatt gave the impression that its Kokanee beer was made with glacial mountain water from B.C., it was in fact brewed in London, Ontario, using the city's water supply.[13]

While many critics of advertising would probably agree that most advertisers are not out to deceive consumers deliberately, they are still concerned that consumers may not be receiving enough information to make an informed choice. They say advertisers usually present only information that is favourable to their position and do not always tell consumers the whole truth about a product or service.

Many believe advertising should be primarily informative in nature and should not be permitted to use puffery or embellished messages. Others argue that advertisers have the right to present the most favourable case for their products and services and should not be restricted to just objective, verifiable information.[14] They note that consumers can protect themselves from being persuaded against their will and that the various industry and government regulations suffice to keep advertisers from misleading consumers. Figure 18–2 shows the advertising principles of the Association of Canadian Advertisers which advertisers may use as a guideline in preparing and evaluating their ads.

ADVERTISING AS OFFENSIVE OR IN BAD TASTE

Another common criticism of advertising, particularly by consumers, is that ads are offensive, tasteless, irritating, boring, obnoxious, and so on. In the recent study by

FIGURE 18–2
Advertising principles of the Association of Canadian Advertisers
□ □ □ □ □

1. *Advertisers must behave responsibly.* ACA believes:
   - Industry self-regulation is in the best interests of all Canadians. Self-regulatory policy exists to ensure that Canadians' fundamental rights and social values are not only acknowledged, but also protected.
   - Advertisers already demonstrate their responsibility by endorsing the Canadian Code of Advertising Standards—the principal instrument of self-regulation for the advertising industry in Canada.
   - The Code of Advertising Standards is only one of many industry codes and guidelines. For example, there are guidelines for gender portrayal, advertising to children, and food labelling, to name just a few.

2. *Advertisers have a right to freedom of speech.* Specifically:
   - The ACA does not believe it is reasonable for a government to allow companies to manufacture and sell legal products, and collect taxes, and then restrict them from telling anyone about it.
   - The ACA remains vigilant in ensuring advertisers' commercial freedom of speech.
   - Advertising, including advertising of products we may not like, is an aspect of free speech, and that free speech is one of society's highest values.

3. *Advertisers make an important contribution to the Canadian economy and culture.* Specifically:

- Advertising is important to the economic and cultural life of Canadians.
- In all its forms, advertising is estimated to represent an annual $10-billion investment in the Canadian economy.
- Advertising revenues fuel the Canadian broadcasting system. Advertisers pay for the production and delivery into Canadian homes of programs that entertain, inform, and educate. It also funds newspapers, magazines, and even movies and Internet sites.
- Commercials reflect our life. They are a powerful tool and means of passing along our values, traditions, and lifestyles to new citizens and the next generation.
- Locally produced commercials contribute to our sense of identity and promote national unity.

4. *Advertisers support a vibrant, competitive economy.* The ACA believes:

- An increased reliance on market forces does not mean that a strong and enriched local and Canadian identity cannot be maintained.
- Our ability to protect culture by limiting access to communications vehicles is becoming increasingly difficult. A prime example is the Internet.
- In the rapidly changing world of communications, market conditions, not protectionism, should prevail.

Source: The Association of Canadian Advertisers, www.aca-online.com.

FIGURE 18–2
continued
☐ ☐ ☐ ☐ ☐

Shavitt and her colleagues, about half of the respondents reported feeling offended by advertising at least sometimes. A number of other studies have found that consumers feel most advertising insults their intelligence and that many ads are in poor taste.[15] Consumers can be offended or irritated by advertising in a number of ways, such as the type of product, fear appeals, sexual appeals, and shock appeals.

Product Type Some object when a product or service like contraceptives or personal hygiene products is advertised at all. Only in the last few years have media begun accepting ads for condoms, as the AIDS crisis forced them to reconsider their restrictions (Exhibit 18–3). A study of prime-time TV commercials found a strong product class effect with respect to the types of ads consumers perceived as distasteful or irritating. The most irritating commercials were for feminine hygiene products; ads for women's undergarments and hemorrhoid products followed.[16] Another study found that consumers are more likely to dislike ads for products they do not use and for brands they would not buy.[17] Ads for personal products have become more common on television and in print, and the public is more accepting of them.[18] However, advertisers must still be careful of how these products are presented and the language and terminology used. There are still many rules, regulations, and taboos advertisers must deal with to have their TV commercials approved by the networks.[19]

Fear Appeals Another way advertising can offend consumers is by the type of appeal or the manner of presentation. For example, many people object to appeals that exploit consumer anxieties. Fear appeal ads, especially for products such as deodorants, mouthwash, and dandruff shampoos, are criticized for attempting to create anxiety and using a fear of social rejection to sell these products. Some ads for home computers were also criticized for attempting to make parents think that if their young children couldn't use a computer, they would fail in school.

Exhibit 18–3
Many magazines and TV stations now accept ads for condoms

527

Exhibit 18–4
This Airwalk ad was criticized for being suggestive and symbolizing sexual submission

Sexual Appeals The advertising appeals that have received the most criticism for being in poor taste are those using sexual appeals and/or nudity. These techniques are often used to gain consumers' attention and may not even be appropriate to the product being advertised. Even if the sexual appeal relates to the product, people may be offended by it. Many people object to both nudity in advertising and sexually suggestive ads.

Advertising critics are particularly concerned about the use of sexual appeals to glorify the image of cigarettes, liquor, and beer or to suggest they can enhance one's own attractiveness. Some women's groups criticized the Airwalk ad shown in Exhibit 18–4, arguing that it showed a submissive and sexually available woman. A critic argued that the ad contains a number of symbolic cues that are sexually suggestive and combine to reinforce an image of the woman's sexual submission to the man.[20]

Another common criticism of sexual appeals is that they can demean women (or men) by depicting them as sex objects (Exhibit 18–5). This was clearly the reason the ASC upheld the complaint for the Yves Saint Laurent fragrance discussed in the previous section along with a few other examples.

Exhibit 18–5
Sexual appeals are often criticized for portraying women as sex objects

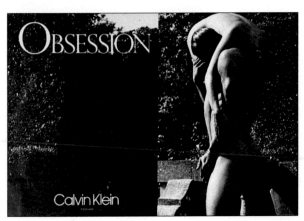

Shock Appeals With the increasing clutter in the advertising environment, advertisers continue to use sexual appeals that may offend some people but catch the attention of consumers and many even generate publicity for their companies. In recent years there has been an increase in what is often referred to as a shock appeal, in which marketers use nudity, sexual suggestiveness, or other startling images to get consumers' attention. A shock appeal is not new, as Calvin Klein and Benetton have used this approach in their ads for about 20 years. What is new is the pervasiveness of shock appeals in other domains as we have seen in some of the ASC rulings summarized earlier. Many advertising experts argue that what underlines the increased use of shock appeals is the pressure on marketers and their agencies to do whatever it takes to get their ads noticed. However, critics argue that the more advertisers use the appeal, the more shocking the ads have to be to get attention. How far advertisers can go with this appeal will probably depend on the public's reaction. When advertisers have gone too far, they are likely to pressure the advertisers to change their ads and the media to stop accepting them. Ethical Perspective 18–3 discusses how many marketers are using gender stereotypes to draw consumers' attention to their ads.

While marketers and ad agencies often acknowledge that their ads push the limits with regard to taste, they also complain about a double standard that exists for advertising versus editorial television program content. They argue that even the most suggestive commercials are bland compared with the content of many television programs.

Sex Role Stereotypes Still Alive and Well

It is, apparently, a particularly dirty fork. It is not just dirty, but dirty and compelling, attracting the attention of both the woman and her young daughter. "I hate leftovers!" declares the woman. "Yuck!" adds the daughter. Then the male voice-over for Dual Action Electrasol speaks, and we learn that with Electrasol the woman's problems will be solved. In fact, that same fork, now clean, powerfully draws mother and daughter back into the kitchen. The daughter triumphantly holds the fork and exclaims, "Hey! No more leftovers!"

It is an unimaginative television ad at best, one created years ago and being rerun now to promote the Reckitt Benckiser–owned brand. It is an ad, however, that illustrates what still plagues many advertisements for cleaning products: the notion that women are obsessed with dirt, or the notion that if anyone was to be obsessed with dirt, it would be a woman. The Electrasol ad is notable because it shows not one, but two generations, suggesting that either the mother is training her daughter to worry about dirt, or this worry is innate in all females, manifesting itself even at a young age.

While some advertisers are making attempts to portray men in more domestic roles, the fact that, in the 21st century, we are still seeing advertisements that primarily continue to target women as the cleaners and caretakers (think "Dr. Mom") says little about how hard women and men, although women in particular, have worked to break down these stereotypes. And, although historically pigeon-holing women in the "homemaker" role was a hot button for those angry about how women are portrayed in the media, it has become a lesser evil, explains Melanie Cishecki, executive director for MediaWatch, a Toronto–based organization that works to improve the portrayal of women and girls in the media. There are now, after all, other serious issues to contend with.

"Advertisers have made some changes in that kind of (domestic) portrayal of women," Cishecki notes. "Now, it may be a question of there being other issues that have emerged that seem to be more pressing in the public mind like violence, like sexualization of women, like the body image issue."

You don't have to look far to find examples of the latter issues. They're everywhere, from the recent breast-obsessed campaign in Toronto promoting the MOJO radio station to the controversial global ad created in-house by Yves Saint Laurent (YSL) to promote its Opium perfume, which features a naked woman (save high-heeled sandals and some jewelry) lying on a black satin cloth with her back arched, her mouth open, her left hand holding her left breast, her knees bent, and her thighs spread apart. Both are examples of the current trend towards "porno chic" that's causing a stir in Europe.

The buzz about the Opium ad in Canada, according to Leanne Delap, the editor of Toronto–based *Fashion* magazine, is that the model is a size 12, so "she pleases those who want to see more realistic dimensions of female beauty, but offends those who object to the nudity." Indeed, it caused enough of a flap that poster versions of it were banned in Britain late last year, although the magazine campaign is ongoing.

Though YSL's model may please those who look for more "realistic" female images, the Opium ad is certainly open to more disturbing interpretations: Not only is the model—Sophie Dahl, interestingly enough, the granddaughter of children's author Roald Dahl—nude, but she is presented as sexually available. She is clearly passive, despite her hand on her breast. And she sports a green circle around her eye that bears a much more striking resemblance to a bruise than to any eye-shadow/eye-liner combination. This could lead some consumers to see a connection between the clear sexual imagery in the ad and a subtle hint at violence toward women.

There are reasons why ads such as the Opium ad are created. "I don't believe that any male ad executive gets up on a Wednesday morning and says, 'I'm going to go into work today and make life hell for women,'" says Louise Ripley, a professor of marketing, women's studies, and environmental studies at York University in Toronto. "But they are so deeply socialized in anti-women thinking that it comes through without thinking about it."

Source: Adapted from Kathleen Martin, "How Far Really?" *Marketing Magazine*, July 2, 2001. Used with permission.

ADVERTISING AND CHILDREN

One of the most controversial topics advertisers must deal with is the issue of advertising to children. TV is a vehicle through which advertisers can reach children easily. Children between the ages of 2 and 11 watch an average of 15.5 hours of TV a week. Studies show that television is an important source of information for children about products.[21] Concern has also been expressed about marketers' use of other promotional vehicles and techniques such as radio ads, point-of-purchase displays, premiums in packages, and the use of commercial characters as the basis for TV shows.

Critics argue that children, particularly young ones, are especially vulnerable to advertising because they lack the experience and knowledge to understand and evaluate critically the purpose of persuasive advertising appeals. Research has shown that preschool children cannot differentiate between commercials and programs, do not perceive the selling intent of commercials, and cannot distinguish between reality and fantasy.[22] Research has also shown that children need more than a skeptical attitude toward advertising; they must understand how advertising works in order to use their cognitive defenses against it effectively.[23] Because of children's limited ability to interpret the selling intent of a message or identify a commercial, critics charge that advertising to them is inherently unfair and deceptive and should be banned or severely restricted.

At the other extreme are those who argue that advertising is a part of life and children must learn to deal with it in the **consumer socialization process** of acquiring the skills needed to function in the marketplace.[24] They say existing restrictions are adequate for controlling children's advertising. A recent study by Tamara Mangleburg and Terry Bristol provided support for the socialization argument. They found that adolescents developed skeptical attitudes toward advertising that were learned through interactions with socialization agents such as parents, peers, and television. They also found that marketplace knowledge plays an important role in adolescents' skepticism toward advertising. Greater knowledge of the marketplace appears to give teens a basis by which to evaluate ads and makes them more likely to recognize the persuasion techniques used by advertisers.[25]

The *Children's Code* discussed earlier recognizes the above debate explicitly, in the background section, to find a balance between these two points of view. A study comparing the attitudes of business executives and consumers regarding children's advertising found that marketers of products targeted to children believe advertising to them provides useful information on new products and does not disrupt the parent–child relationship. However, the general public did not have such a favourable opinion. Older consumers and those from households with children had particularly negative attitudes toward children's advertising.[26]

It is important to many companies to communicate directly with children. However, only by being sensitive to the naiveté of children as consumers will they be able to do so freely and avoid potential conflict with those who believe children should be protected from advertising.

Finally, while we have been concerned with ads directed towards children, advertisers need to be careful not to unwillingly produce ads directed towards adults that make an impression upon children. For example, ASC published a bulletin, consistent with CRTC regulations, stating that marketers of alcoholic beverages could not use a spokesperson that is perceived as a role model for children. This arose from Molson's use of Don Cherry for its "Bubba" beer ads.[27]

SOCIAL EFFECTS OF ADVERTISING

Concern is often expressed over the impact of advertising on society, particularly on values and lifestyles. While a number of factors influence the cultural values, lifestyles, and behaviour of a society, the overwhelming amount of advertising and its prevalence in the mass media lead many critics to argue that advertising plays a major role in influencing and transmitting social values. In his book *Advertising and Social Change*, Ronald Berman says:

The institutions of family, religion, and education have grown noticeably weaker over each of the past three generations. The world itself seems to have grown more complex. In the absence of traditional authority, advertising has become a kind of social guide. It depicts us in all the myriad situations possible to a life of free choice. It provides ideas about style, morality, behavior.[28]

While there is general agreement that advertising is an important social influence agent, opinions as to the value of its contribution are often negative. Advertising is criticized for encouraging materialism, manipulating consumers to buy things they do not really need, perpetuating stereotypes, and controlling the media.

ADVERTISING ENCOURAGES MATERIALISM

Many critics claim advertising has an adverse effect on consumer values by encouraging **materialism**, a preoccupation with material things rather than intellectual or spiritual concerns. Many critics believe that advertising:

* Seeks to create needs rather than merely showing how a product or service fulfills them.
* Surrounds consumers with images of the good life and suggests the acquisition of material possessions leads to contentment and happiness and adds to the joy of living.
* Suggests material possessions are symbols of status, success, and accomplishment and/or will lead to greater social acceptance, popularity, sex appeal, and so on.

The ad shown in Exhibit 18–6 for Rolls-Royce automobiles is an example of how advertising can promote materialistic values.

This criticism of advertising assumes that materialism is undesirable and is sought at the expense of other goals. But many believe materialism is an acceptable part of the **Protestant ethic**, which stresses hard work and individual effort and initiative and views the accumulation of material possessions as evidence of success. Others argue that the acquisition of material possessions has positive economic impact by encouraging consumers to keep consuming after their basic needs are met. Many believe economic growth is essential and materialism is both a necessity and an inevitable part of this progress.

Economist John Kenneth Galbraith, often a vocal critic of advertising, describes the role advertising plays in industrialized economies by encouraging consumption:

> Advertising and its related arts thus help develop the kind of man the goals of the industrial system require—one that reliably spends his income and works reliably because he is always in need of more. In the absence of the massive and artful persuasion that accompanies the management of demand, increasing abundance might well have reduced the interest of people in acquiring more goods. Being not pressed by the need for these things, they would have spent less reliably to get more. The consequence—a lower and less reliable propensity to consume—would have been awkward for the industrial system.[29]

It has also been argued that an emphasis on material possessions does not rule out interest in intellectual, spiritual, or cultural values. Defenders of advertising say consumers can be more interested in higher-order goals when basic needs have been met. Raymond Bauer and Stephen Greyser point out that consumers may purchase material things in the pursuit of nonmaterial goals.[30] For example, a person may buy an expensive stereo system to enjoy music rather than simply to impress someone or acquire a material possession.

Even if we assume materialism is undesirable, there is still the question of whether advertising is responsible for creating and encouraging it. While many critics argue that advertising is a major

531

Exhibit 18–6
Rolls-Royce appeals to consumers' materialism

contributing force to materialistic values, others say advertising merely reflects the values of society rather than shaping them.[31] They argue that consumers' values are defined by the society in which they live and are the results of extensive, long-term socialization or acculturation.

The argument that advertising is responsible for creating a materialistic and hedonistic society is addressed by Stephen Fox in his book *The Mirror Makers: A History of American Advertising and Its Creators*. Fox concludes advertising has become a prime scapegoat for our times and merely reflects society. Regarding the effect of advertising on cultural values, he says:

> To blame advertising now for those most basic tendencies in American history is to miss the point. It is too obvious, too easy, a matter of killing the messenger instead of dealing with the bad news. The people who have created modern advertising are not hidden persuaders pushing our buttons in the service of some malevolent purpose. They are just producing an especially visible manifestation, good and bad, of the American way of life.[32]

The ad shown in Exhibit 18–7 was developed by the American Association of Advertising Agencies and suggests that advertising is a reflection of society's tastes and values, not vice versa. The ad was part of a campaign that addressed criticisms of advertising.

Advertising does contribute to our materialism by portraying products and services as symbols of status, success, and achievement and by encouraging consumption. As Richard Pollay says, "While it may be true that advertising reflects cultural values, it does so on a very selective basis, echoing and reinforcing certain attitudes, behaviours, and values far more frequently than others."[33]

ADVERTISING MAKES PEOPLE BUY THINGS THEY DON'T NEED

A common criticism of advertising is that it manipulates consumers into buying things they do not need. Many critics say advertising should just provide information useful in making purchase decisions and should not persuade. They view information advertising (which reports price, performance, and other objective criteria) as desirable but persuasive advertising (which plays on consumers' emotions, anxieties, and psychological needs and desires such as status, self-esteem, and attractiveness) as unacceptable. Persuasive advertising is criticized for fostering discontent among consumers and encouraging them to purchase products and services to solve deeper problems. Critics say advertising exploits consumers and persuades them to buy things they don't need. Ethical Perspective 18–4 raises this issue for discussion.

Defenders of advertising offer a number of rebuttals to these criticisms. First, they point out that a substantial amount of advertising is essentially informational in nature.[34] Also, it is difficult to separate desirable informational advertising from undesirable persuasive advertising. Shelby Hunt, in examining the *information-persuasion dichotomy*, points out that even advertising that most observers would categorize as very informative is often very persuasive.[35] He says, "If advertising critics really believe that persuasive advertising should not be permitted, they are actually proposing that no advertising be allowed, since the purpose of all advertising is to persuade."[36]

Defenders of advertising also take issue with the argument that it should be limited to dealing with basic functional needs. In our society, most lower-level needs recognized in Maslow's hierarchy, such as the need for food, clothing, and shelter, are satisfied for most people. It is natural to move from basic needs

Exhibit 18–7
The advertising industry argues that advertising reflects society

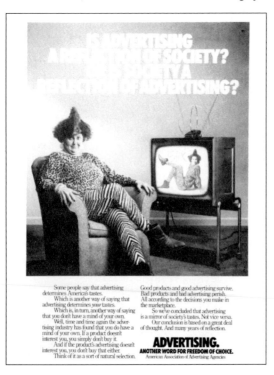

Canadian Direct-to-Consumer (DTC) Prescription Drug Advertising

Firms advertising prescriptions drugs in Canada may either communicate the brand name but not the disease or communicate the disease but not the brand name according to Health Canada DTC regulations. A consequence of the first regulation is that consumers are able to recognize or recall a brand but are limited in connecting the brand name to the proper product category. A consequence of the second regulation is that advertisers are building the overall product category but limited in letting consumers know that their brand is available to fulfill a need.

In contrast, spillover DTC ads from the United States do not face these regulations so most Canadian consumers receive two types of ads. In Canada, a study published in the *Canadian Medical Association Journal* suggests that a high percentage of all patients who requested DTC advertised drugs from their doctors received prescriptions. The study looked at physicians and patients from Sacramento, California, and Vancouver. In the former city, 7.2 percent of the patients requested advertised drugs with physicians fulfilling 72 percent of the requests, while in the latter city, 3.3 percent of the patients requested with physicians fulfilling 78 percent.

Recently, a handful of Canadian DTC advertising campaigns received notable media coverage. As described in the opening vignette for Chapter 6, Viagra captured the biggest impression with its light-hearted creative strategy for erectile dysfunction. However, competitors for Viagra entered the market later and their ads portrayed the problem and or the brand in a different light. Intensive advertising for birth control prescriptions emerged as well. Finally, vaccination medicine, one type of DTC advertising that can communicate the brand name and its disease, continued the trend of increased DTC prescription advertising.

On St. Valentine's Day 2004, Eli Lilly Canada launched its first two DTC television commercials for its erectile dysfunction drug, Cialis, to compete with Viagra. The first showed scenes of a man turning off the televised hockey game while the other showed a man putting a record on a turntable.

Both 10-second closed-captioned sponsorship messages contained a super "The Weekend is Here" indicating that the weekend is a time for relaxation and an opportunity for couples to be more romantic. It also picked up on "le weekender" nickname of the brand in Europe indicating the staying power of its users after consumption! The ads ended with the logo and suggestion to ask your doctor.

A campaign for the birth control pill Marvelon found an interesting approach to work within the Health Canada regulations. It had a branded transit poster that showed a blister pack of pills with the brand name and a headline saying "Duh." It also had unbranded washroom posters and doorknob hangers at university campuses that showed two images: an intimate couple with a headline saying "Good Time," and a woman and a baby with a headline saying "Life Time." It concluded with a message "For every action, there is an equal and opposite reaction. Be prepared." The same ads were used to communicate to doctors and they facilitated discussions in the doctor's office as both groups had been exposed to both types of ads. Overall sales of oral contraceptives had risen during the two years the brand was advertised.

Prevnar, a vaccine to prevent pneumococcal meningitis in children, continued with its second DTC ad campaign in the winter of 2004. Unlike the drugs mentioned above, ads for vaccines like Wyeth's Prevnar can mention both the brand name and the associated disease since it falls under different Health Canada regulations as the treatment is administered by a health-care professional. Wyeth worked with Health Canada and Advertising Standards Canada prior to running the campaign to ensure it complied with the regulations.

Sources: Lesley Young, "DTC Ads a Hit with Patients," *Marketing Magazine*, September 8, 2003; Lesley Young, "Pill Ads Reach Doctors, Patients," *Marketing Magazine*, December 8, 2003; Lesley Young, "Wyeth's Prevnar Appeals to Parents," *Marketing Magazine*, February 16, 2004; Lesley Young, "Cialis Debuts in Valentine's Setting," *Marketing Magazine*, February 23, 2004.

to higher-order ones such as self-esteem and status or self-actualization. Consumers are free to choose the degree to which they attempt to satisfy their desires, and wise advertisers associate their products and services with the satisfaction of higher-order needs.

Proponents of advertising offer two other defences against the charge that advertising makes people buy things they do not really need. First, this criticism attributes too much power to advertising and assumes consumers have no ability to defend themselves against it.

DESPITE WHAT SOME PEOPLE THINK, ADVERTISING CAN'T MAKE YOU BUY SOMETHING YOU DON'T NEED.

Some people would have you believe that you are putty in the hands of every advertiser in the country.

They think that when advertising is put under your nose, your mind turns to oatmeal.

It's mass hypnosis. Subliminal seduction. Brain washing. Mind control. It's advertising.

And you are a pushover for it.

It explains why your kitchen cupboard is full of food you never eat. Why your garage is full of cars you never drive.

Why your house is full of books you don't read, TV's you don't watch, beds you don't use, and clothes you don't wear.

You don't have a choice. You are forced to buy.

That's why this message is a cleverly disguised advertisement to get you to buy land in the tropics.

Got you again, didn't we? Send in your money.

ADVERTISING
ANOTHER WORD FOR FREEDOM OF CHOICE.
American Association of Advertising Agencies

Exhibit 18–8
The AAAA responds to the claim that advertising makes consumers buy things they do not need

534

Second, it ignores the fact that consumers have the freedom to make their own choices when confronted with persuasive advertising. While they readily admit the persuasive intent of their business, advertisers are quick to note it is extremely difficult to make consumers purchase a product they do not want or for which they do not see a personal benefit. For example, the "green" marketing movement has not gotten consumers to forgo low prices in favour of products that make environmental claims. The market research firm of Roper Starch Worldwide conducted an extensive study of 300 green ads that appeared in magazines between 1991 and 1994 and found that most were not effective. The study concluded that too many green ads failed to make the connection between what the company is doing for the environment and how it affects individual consumers.[37]

If advertising were as powerful as the critics claim, we would not see products with multimillion-dollar advertising budgets failing in the marketplace. The reality is that consumers do have a choice, and they are not being forced to buy. Consumers ignore ads for products and services they do not really need or that fail to interest them (see Exhibit 18–8).

ADVERTISING AND STEREOTYPING

Advertising is often accused of creating and perpetuating stereotypes through its portrayal of women and ethnic minorities.

Women   The portrayal of women in advertising is an issue that has received a great deal of attention through the years.[38] Advertising has received much criticism for stereotyping women and failing to recognize the changing role of women in our society. Critics have argued that advertising often depicts women as preoccupied with beauty, household duties, and motherhood or shows them as decorative objects or sexually provocative figures. The various research studies conducted through the years show a consistent picture of gender stereotyping that has varied little over time. Portrayals of adult women in American television and print advertising have emphasized passivity, deference, lack of intelligence and credibility, and punishment for high levels of efforts. In contrast, men have been portrayed as constructive, powerful, autonomous, and achieving.[39]

Research on gender stereotyping in advertising targeted to children has found a pattern of results similar to that reported for adults. A recent study found sex-role stereotyping in television advertising targeted at children in the United States as well as in Australia.[40] Boys are generally shown as being more knowledgeable, active, aggressive, and instrumental than girls. Nonverbal behaviours involving dominance and control are associated more with boys than girls. Advertising directed toward children has also been shown to feature more boys than girls, to position boys in more dominant, active roles, and to use male voiceovers more frequently than female ones.[41]

Feminist groups such as MediaWatch argue that advertising that portrays women as sex objects contributes to violence against women. MediaWatch and its supporters often communicate to advertisers and their agencies about ads they find insulting to women and have even called for boycotts against offending advertisers. MediaWatch has also been critical of advertisers for the way they portray women in advertising for clothing, cosmetics, and other products. The organization feels that many of these ads contribute to the epidemic of eating disorders and smoking among women and girls who hope such means will help them control their weight.[42]

In a recent annual report, MediaWatch gave "thumbs-down awards" to Vichy, Browns Shoes, Calvin Klein, and Kahlúa Black Russian. Positive recognition went to "Cam's Breast Exam," a TV ad showing eager lads ready to do a breast exam for women to prevent cancer, and Body Shop for realistically portraying women. MediaWatch also effectively identifies advertisers who portray women inappropriately and offers tips for marketers to advertise more effectively and avoid controversy. For example, it noted that Terra Footwear stopped a national billboard campaign that showed "lingerie-clad female models holding construction tools in suggestive poses."[43]

While sexism and stereotyping still exist, advertising's portrayal of women is improving in many areas. Many advertisers have begun to recognize the importance of portraying women realistically. The increase in the number of working women has resulted not only in women having more influence in family decision making but also in more single-female households, which mean more independent purchasers.

Researchers Steven Kates and Glenda Shaw-Garlock argue that the transformed social positioning of women in North American society is perhaps the most important social development of this century.[44] They note that as women have crossed the boundary from the domestic sphere to the professional arena, expectations and representations of women have changed as well. For example, a number of magazines, such as MS and Working Woman, now incorporate and appeal to the sociocultural shifts in women's lives. Many advertisers are now depicting women in a diversity of roles that reflect their changing place in society. In many ads, the stereotypic character traits attributed to women have shifted from weak and dependent to strong and autonomous.[45]

Some advertisers have found that being more sensitive to women customers can influence their purchase behaviour. For example, a few years ago Maidenform began a campaign critical of negative stereotyping of women that significantly increased sales (Exhibit 18–9). Nike saw its sales to women increase 28 percent as a result of its "Empathy" campaign, which directly targeted women and issues that are relevant to them.[46]

Exhibit 18–9
Maidenform's campaign lamenting the stereotyping of women resulted in a significant increase in sales

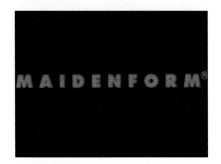

Somehow, women always seem to
   be portrayed like this.
Or like this.
Like this.

Or like this.
Like this.
Or like this.
While there are many stereotypes
   of women . . .

there aren't many women who
   fit them.
A simple truth known by all
   women . . . most men . . .
   and one lingerie company.

Exhibit 18–10
Ikea broke new ground with this ad showing an interracial couple shopping for furniture

Visible Minorities   Several U.S. academic studies in the late 1980s and early 90s examined the incidence of visible minorities in advertising. A study conducted in 1987 found that 11 percent of the people appearing in commercials were African-Americans.[47] Another study conducted two years later found that African-Americans appeared in 26 percent of all ads on network TV that used live models but Hispanics appeared in only 6 percent of the commercials with live models. The researchers also found that TV ads in which blacks appeared were overwhelmingly integrated (Exhibit 18–10) and the blacks were likely to have played either minor or background roles in the majority of the ads.[48] A study conducted in 1995 found that 17 percent of prime-time network TV ads featured African-Americans as dominant characters and the majority of commercials featured them in minor roles.[49] A recent study by Corliss L. Green found that ads targeting African-Americans through racially targeted media, especially with race-based products, benefit from featuring African-American models with a dominant presence in the ad.[50]

A recent study of U.S. prime-time TV commercials found that Asian male and female models are overrepresented in terms of their proportion of the U.S. population (3.6 percent), appearing in 8.4 percent of the commercials. However, Asian models were more likely than members of other minority groups to appear in background roles, and Asian women were rarely depicted in major roles. The study also found that portrayals of Asian-Americans put more emphasis on the work ethic and less on other aspects of their lives.[51]

It may be difficult to generalize these findings to Canada, however; we should keep in mind that Canadians are exposed to these ads when watching U.S. television programs that do not simulcast Canadian commercials or when reading American magazines. So to a degree, Canadian consumers will experience and perceive some amount of imbalance through this exposure.

Visible minorities comprise about 18 percent of Canada's population, of which 23 percent are Chinese, 19 percent are South Asians, and 19 percent are black. Recent Canadian trends and commentary by practitioners suggest that the portrayal of visible minorities can be improved in Canadian advertising, even though there has been significant improvement over the past 5 years. For example, a recent study suggests that 45 percent of all Canadians feel that advertising is directed to whites, and 48 percent feel that visible minorities are under-represented.[52]

Perhaps following on the success of Budweiser's award-winning "Whassup" campaign, many Canadian beer companies were including many visible minorities in their ads in 2001. Although the beer companies do not have specific guidelines, they encourage the casting of their TV commercials to have a full representative selection of actors. However, there are some who contend that the casting does not always specify that visible minorities are welcome and that this problem carries over to other media such as print, Internet, and direct mail.[53]

ADVERTISING AND THE MEDIA

The fact that advertising plays such an important role in financing the media has led to concern that advertisers may influence or even control the media (Exhibit 18–11). It is well documented that *economic censorship* occurs, whereby the media avoid certain topics or even present biased news coverage, in acquiescence to advertiser demands.[54] In fact, Professors Lawrence Soley and Robert Craig say, "The assertion that advertisers attempt to influence what the public sees, hears, and reads in the mass media is perhaps the most damning of all criticisms of advertising, but this criticism isn't acknowledged in most advertising textbooks."[55] We will address this important issue in this book by considering arguments on both sides.

Arguments Supporting Advertiser Control   Some critics charge the media's dependence on advertisers' support makes them susceptible to various forms of influence, including exerting control over the editorial content of magazines and newspapers; biasing editorial opinions to favour the position of an advertiser; limiting coverage of a controversial story that might reflect negatively on a company; and influencing the program content of television.

Newspapers and magazines receive nearly 70 percent of their revenue from advertising; commercial TV and radio derive virtually all their income from advertisers. Small, financially insecure newspapers, magazines, or broadcast stations are the most susceptible to pressure from advertisers, particularly companies that account for a large amount of the media outlet's advertising revenue. A local newspaper may be reluctant to print an unfavourable story about a car dealer or supermarket chain on whose advertising it depends. For example, a few years ago more than 40 car dealers cancelled their ads in the *San Jose Mercury News* when the paper printed an article titled "A Car Buyer's Guide to Sanity." The dealers objected to the tone of the article, which they felt implied consumers should consider car dealers unethical adversaries in the negotiation process.[56] A survey of 147 daily newspapers found that more than 90 percent of editors have been pressured by advertisers and more than one-third of them said advertisers had succeeded in influencing news at their papers.[57]

Individual TV stations and even the major networks also can be influenced by advertisers. Programming decisions are made largely on the basis of what shows will attract the most viewers and thus be most desirable to advertisers. Critics say this often results in lower-quality television as educational, cultural, and informative programming is usually sacrificed for shows that get high ratings and appeal to the mass markets.

Arguments Against Advertiser Control   The commercial media's dependence on advertising means advertisers can exert influence on their character, content, and coverage of certain issues. However, media executives offer several reasons why advertisers do not exert undue influence over the media.

First, they point out it is in the best interest of the media not to be influenced too much by advertisers. To retain public confidence, they must report the news fairly and accurately without showing bias or attempting to avoid controversial issues. Media executives point to the vast array of topics they cover and the investigative reporting they often do as evidence of their objectivity. They want to build a large audience for their publications or stations so that they can charge more for advertising space and time.

Media executives also note that an advertiser needs the media more than they need any individual advertiser, particularly when the medium has a large audience or does

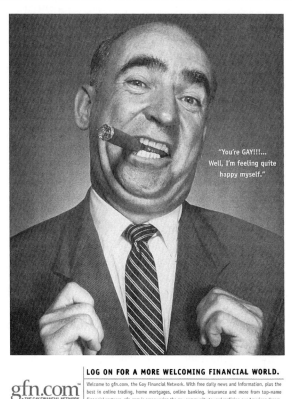

"You're GAY!!!... Well, I'm feeling quite happy myself."

LOG ON FOR A MORE WELCOMING FINANCIAL WORLD.

gfn.com™
► THE GAY FINANCIAL NETWORK

Welcome to gfn.com, the Gay Financial Network. With free daily news and information, plus the best in online trading, home mortgages, online banking, insurance and more from top-name financial partners, gfn.com is empowering the gay community toward realizing our American dream.

free daily financial news and information │ banking ► mortgages ► insurance ► investing

Exhibit 18–11
The Gay Financial Network broke barriers by becoming the first gay-oriented company to advertise in the mainstream media

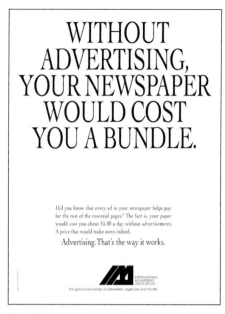

WITHOUT ADVERTISING, YOUR NEWSPAPER WOULD COST YOU A BUNDLE.

Did you know that every ad in your newspaper helps pay for the rest of the essential pages? The fact is, your paper would cost you about $5.00 a day without advertisements. A price that would make news indeed.

Advertising. That's the way it works.

INTERNATIONAL ADVERTISING ASSOCIATION

The global partnership of advertisers, agencies and media.

Exhibit 18–12
This ad points out how advertising lowers the cost of newspapers for consumers

a good job of reaching a specific market segment. Many publications and stations have a very broad base of advertising support and can afford to lose an advertiser that attempts to exert too much influence. This is particularly true for the larger, more established, financially secure media. For example, a consumer products company would find it difficult to reach its target audience without network TV and could not afford to boycott a network if it disagreed with a station's editorial policy or program content. Even the local advertiser in a small community may be dependent on the local newspaper, since it may be the most cost-effective media option available.

The media in Canada are basically supported by advertising; this means we can enjoy them for free or for a fraction of what they would cost without advertising. The alternative to an advertiser-supported media system is support by users through higher subscription costs for the print media and a fee or pay-per-view system with TV. The ad in Exhibit 18–12, part of a campaign by the International Advertising Association, explains how advertising lowers the cost of print media for consumers. Another alternative is government-supported media like those in many other countries, but this runs counter to most people's desire for freedom of the press. Although not perfect, our system of advertising-supported media provides the best option for receiving information and entertainment.

SUMMARIZING SOCIAL EFFECTS

We have examined a number of issues and have attempted to analyze the arguments for and against them. Many people have reservations about the impact of advertising and promotion on society. The numerous rules, regulations, policies, and guidelines marketers comply with do not cover every advertising and promotional situation. Moreover, what one individual views as distasteful or unethical may be acceptable to another.

Negative opinions regarding advertising and other forms of promotion have been around almost as long as the field itself, and it is unlikely they will ever disappear. However, the industry must address the various concerns about the effects of advertising and other forms of promotion on society. Advertising is a very powerful institution, but it will remain so only as long as consumers have faith in the ads they see and hear every day. Many of the problems discussed here can be avoided if individual decision makers make ethics an important element of the IMC planning process.

The primary focus of this discussion of social effects has been on the way advertising is used (or abused) in the marketing of products and services. It is important to note that advertising and other IMC tools, such as direct marketing and public relations, are also used to promote worthy causes and to deal with problems facing society (drunk driving, drug abuse, and the AIDS crisis, among others). Campaigns for nonprofit organizations and worthy causes are often developed pro bono by advertising agencies, and free advertising time and space are donated by the media.

ECONOMIC EFFECTS OF ADVERTISING

Advertising plays an important role in a free-market system like ours by making consumers aware of products and services and providing them with information for decision making. Advertising's economic role goes beyond this basic function, however. It is a powerful force that can affect the functioning of our entire economic system.

Advertising can encourage consumption and foster economic growth. It not only informs customers of available goods and services but also facilitates entry into markets for a firm or a new product or brand; leads to economies of scale in production, marketing, and distribution, which in turn lead to lower prices; and hastens the acceptance of new products and the rejection of inferior products.

Critics of advertising view it as a detrimental force that not only fails to perform its basic function of information provision adequately but also adds to the cost of products and services and discourages competition and market entry, leading to industrial concentration and higher prices for consumers.

In their analysis of advertising, economists generally take a macroeconomic perspective: they consider the economic impact of advertising on an entire industry or on the economy as a whole rather than its effect on an individual company or brand. Our examination of the economic impact of advertising focuses on these broader macro-level issues. We consider its effects on consumer choice, competition, and product costs and prices.

EFFECTS ON CONSUMER CHOICE

Some critics say advertising hampers consumer choice, as large advertisers use their power to limit our options to a few well-advertised brands. Economists argue that advertising is used to achieve (1) **differentiation**, whereby the products or services of large advertisers are perceived as unique or better than competitors', and (2) brand loyalty, which enables large national advertisers to gain control of the market, usually at the expense of smaller brands.

Larger companies often end up charging a higher price and achieve a more dominant position in the market than smaller firms that cannot compete against them and their large advertising budgets. When this occurs, advertising not only restricts the choice alternatives to a few well-known, heavily advertised brands but also becomes a substitute for competition based on price or product improvements.

Heavily advertised brands dominate the market in certain product categories, such as soft drinks, beer, and cereals.[58] But advertising generally does not create brand monopolies and reduce the opportunities for new products to be introduced to consumers. In most product categories, a number of different brands are on the store shelves and thousands of new products are introduced every year. The opportunity to advertise gives companies the incentive to develop new brands and improve their existing ones. When a successful new product such as a personal computer is introduced, competitors quickly follow and use advertising to inform consumers about their brand and attempt to convince them it is superior to the original. Companies like Virgin Atlantic Airways recognize that advertising has been an important part of their success (Exhibit 18–13).

"We spent over 40 million dollars to kill a rubber chicken."

Richard Branson, Chairman, Virgin Atlantic Airways.

Exhibit 18–13
Virgin Atlantic Airways chair Richard Branson acknowledges the importance of advertising

539

EFFECTS ON COMPETITION

One of the most common criticisms economists have about advertising concerns its effects on competition. They argue that power in the hands of large firms with huge advertising budgets creates a **barrier to entry**, which makes it difficult for other firms to enter the market. This results in less competition and higher prices. Economists note that smaller firms already in the market find it difficult to compete against the large advertising budgets of the industry leaders and are often driven out of business. For example, the Canadian beer industry is dominated by two national brewers, Molson and Labatts, who account for over 90 percent of the market. With their high advertising and promotion expenditures, these companies are spending much less per barrel than smaller firms, making it very difficult for the latter to compete.

Large advertisers clearly enjoy certain competitive advantages. First, there are **economies of scale** in advertising, particularly with respect to factors such as media costs. Firms such as Procter & Gamble, which spends millions of dollars per year on advertising and promotion, are able to make large media buys at a reduced rate and allocate them to their various products.

Large advertisers usually sell more of a product or service, which means they may have lower production costs and can allocate more monies to advertising, so they can afford the costly but more efficient media like network television. Their large advertising outlays also give them more opportunity to differentiate their products and develop brand loyalty. To the extent that these factors occur, smaller competitors are at a disadvantage and new competitors are deterred from entering the market.

While advertising may have an anticompetitive effect on a market, there is no clear evidence that advertising alone reduces competition, creates barriers to entry, and thus increases market concentration. Lester Telser noted that high levels of advertising are not always found in industries where firms have a large market share. He found an inverse relationship between intensity of product class advertising and stability of market share for the leading brands.[59] These findings run contrary to many economists' belief that industries controlled by a few firms have high advertising expenditures, resulting in stable brand shares for market leaders.

Defenders of advertising say it is unrealistic to attribute a firm's market dominance and barriers to entry solely to advertising. There are a number of other factors, such as price, product quality, distribution effectiveness, production efficiencies, and competitive strategies. For many years, Hershey chocolate bar was a dominant brand even though it spent little on advertising. Hershey did not advertise at all until 1970. For 66 years, the company relied on the quality of its products, its favourable reputation and image among consumers, and its extensive channels of distribution to market its brands. Industry leaders often tend to dominate markets because they have superior product quality and the best management and competitive strategies, not simply the biggest advertising budgets.[60]

EFFECTS ON PRODUCT COSTS AND PRICES

A major area of debate among economists, advertisers, consumer advocates, and policymakers concerns the effects of advertising on product costs and prices. Critics argue that advertising increases the prices consumers pay for products and services. First, they say the large sums of money spent advertising a brand constitute an expense that must be covered and the consumer ends up paying for it through higher prices. This is a common criticism from consumer advocates. Several studies show that firms with higher relative prices advertise their products more intensely than do those with lower relative prices.[61]

A second way advertising can result in higher prices is by increasing product differentiation and adding to the perceived value of the product in consumers' minds. Paul Farris and Mark Albion note that product differentiation occupies a central position in theories of advertising's economic effects.[62] The fundamental premise is that advertising increases the perceived differences between physically homogeneous products and enables advertised brands to command a premium price without an increase in quality.

Critics of advertising generally point to the differences in prices between national brands and private-label brands that are physically similar, such as aspirin or tea bags, as evidence of the added value created by advertising. They see consumers' willingness to pay more for heavily advertised national brands rather than purchasing the lower-priced, nonadvertised brand as wasteful and irrational. However, consumers do not always buy for rational, functional reasons. The emotional, psychological, and social benefits derived from purchasing a national brand are important to many people. Moreover, say Albion and Farris,

> Unfortunately there seems to be no single way to measure product differentiation, let alone determine how much is excessive or attributable to the effects of advertising . . . Both price insensitivity and brand loyalty could be created by a number of factors such as higher product quality, better packaging, favorable use experience and market position. They are probably related to each other but need not be the result of advertising.[63]

Exhibit 18–14
This ad refutes the argument that reducing advertising expenditures will lead to lower prices

Proponents of advertising offer several other counterarguments to the claim that advertising increases prices. They acknowledge that advertising costs are at least partly paid for by consumers. But advertising may help lower the overall cost of a product more than enough to offset them. For example, advertising may help firms achieve economies of scale in production and distribution by providing information to and stimulating demand among mass markets. These economies of scale help cut the cost of producing and marketing the product, which can lead to lower prices—if the advertiser chooses to pass the cost savings on to the consumer. The ad in Exhibit 18–14, from a campaign sponsored by the American Association of Advertising Agencies, emphasizes this point.

Advertising can also lower prices by making a market more competitive, which usually leads to greater price competition. A study by Lee Benham found that prices of eyeglasses were 25 to 30 percent higher in states that banned eyeglass advertising than in those that permitted it.[64] Robert Steiner analyzed the toy industry and concluded that advertising resulted in lower consumer prices. He argued that curtailment of TV advertising would drive up consumer prices for toys.[65] Finally, advertising is a means to market entry rather than a deterrent and helps stimulate product innovation, which makes markets more competitive and helps keep prices down.

Overall, it is difficult to reach any firm conclusions regarding the relationship between advertising and prices. After an extensive review of this area, Farris and Albion concluded, "The evidence connecting manufacturer advertising to prices is neither complete nor definitive . . . consequently, we cannot say whether advertising is a tool of market efficiency or market power without further research."[66]

Economist James Ferguson argues that advertising cannot increase the cost per unit of quality to consumers because if it did, consumers would not continue to respond positively to advertising.[67] He believes advertising lowers the costs of information about brand qualities, leads to increases in brand quality, and lowers the average price per unit of quality.

SUMMARIZING ECONOMIC EFFECTS

Albion and Farris suggest that economists' perspectives can be divided into two principal schools of thought that make different assumptions regarding the influence of advertising on the economy.[68] Figure 18–3 summarizes the main points of the "advertising equals market power" and "advertising equals information" perspectives.

Advertising Equals Market Power   The belief that advertising equals market power reflects traditional economic thinking and views advertising as a way to change consumers' tastes, lower their sensitivity to price, and build brand loyalty among buyers

FIGURE 18–3 ☐☐☐☐ Two schools of thought on advertising's role in the economy

Advertising = Market Power		Advertising = Information
Advertising affects consumer preferences and tastes, changes product attributes, and differentiates the product from competitive offerings.	Advertising	Advertising informs consumers about product attributes but does not change the way they value those attributes.
Consumers become brand loyal and less price sensitive and perceive fewer substitutes for advertised brands.	Consumer buying behaviour	Consumers become more price sensitive and buy best "value." Only the relationship between price and quality affects elasticity for a given product.
Potential entrants must overcome established brand loyalty and spend relatively more on advertising.	Barriers to entry	Advertising makes entry possible for new brands because it can communicate product attributes to consumers.
Firms are insulated from market competition and potential rivals; concentration increases, leaving firms with more discretionary power.	Industry structure and market power	Consumers can compare competitive offerings easily and competitive rivalry increases. Efficient firms remain, and as the inefficient leave, new entrants appear; the effect on concentration is ambiguous.
Firms can charge higher prices and are not as likely to compete on quality or price dimensions. Innovation may be reduced.	Market conduct	More informed consumers pressure firms to lower prices and improve quality; new entrants facilitate innovation.
High prices and excessive profits accrue to advertisers and give them even more incentive to advertise their products. Output is restricted compared with conditions of perfect competition.	Market performance	Industry prices decrease. The effect on profits due to increased competition and increased efficiency is ambiguous.

of advertised brands. This results in higher profits and market power for large advertisers, reduces competition in the market, and leads to higher prices and fewer choices for consumers. Proponents of this viewpoint generally have negative attitudes regarding the economic impact of advertising.

Advertising Equals Information The belief that advertising equals information takes a more positive view of advertising's economic effects. This model sees advertising as providing consumers with useful information, increasing their price sensitivity (which moves them toward lower-priced products), and increasing competition in the market. Advertising is viewed as a way to communicate with consumers and tell them about a product and its major features and attributes. More informed and knowledgeable consumers pressure companies to provide high-quality products at lower prices. Efficient firms remain in the market, whereas inefficient firms leave as new entrants appear. Proponents of this model believe the economic effects of advertising are favourable and think it contributes to more efficient and competitive markets.

To me it means that if we believe to any degree whatsoever in the economic system under which we live, in a high standard of living and in high employment, advertising is the most efficient known way of moving goods in practically every product class.

My proof is that millions of businessmen have chosen advertising over and over again in the operations of their business. Some of their decisions may have been wrong, but they must have thought they were right or they wouldn't go back to be stung twice by the same kind of bee.

It's a pretty safe bet that in the next 10 years many Americans will be using products and devices that no one in this room has even heard of. Judging purely by past performance, American advertising can be relied on to make them known and accepted overnight at the lowest possible prices.

Advertising, of course, makes possible our unparalleled variety of magazines, newspapers, business publications, and radio and television stations.

It must be said that without advertising we would have a far different nation, and one that would be much the poorer—not merely in material commodities, but in the life of the spirit.

Leo Burnett

These excerpts are from a speech given by Leo Burnett on the American Association of Advertising Agencies' 50th anniversary, April 20, 1967.

FIGURE 18–4
This message describes the positive economic effects of advertising

☐ ☐ ☐ ☐ ☐

It is unlikely the debate over the economic effects and value of advertising will be resolved soon. Many economists will continue to take a negative view of advertising and its effects on the functioning of the economy, while advertisers will continue to view it as an efficient way for companies to communicate with their customers and an essential component of our economic system. The International Advertising Association has been running a campaign for several years to convince consumers around the world of the economic value of advertising. Ads like the one shown in Exhibit 18–15 are used in countries such as China and Russia, where consumers are unfamiliar with the concept of advertising. The goal of the campaign is to get consumers in these countries to recognize the role advertising plays in contributing to their economic well-being.[69]

Figure 18–4, excerpts from a speech given by famous adman Leo Burnett, summarizes the perspective of most advertising people on the economic effects of advertising. While many advertising and marketing experts agree that advertising and promotion play an important role in helping to expand consumer demand for new products, not everyone would agree that this is desirable.

WHEN ADVERTISING DOES ITS JOB, MILLIONS OF PEOPLE KEEP THEIRS.

Good advertising doesn't just inform. It sells. It helps move product and keep businesses in business. Every time an ad arouses a consumer's interest enough to result in a purchase, it keeps a company going strong. And it helps secure the jobs of the people who work there.

Advertising. That's the way it works.

INTERNATIONAL ADVERTISING ASSOCIATION

The global partnership of advertisers, agencies and media

Exhibit 18–15
This ad is part of a global campaign by the International Advertising Association to educate consumers about the economic value of advertising

543

SUMMARY

Various levels of government regulate different aspects of Canadian advertising; however, self-regulation of these laws is quite prominent in Canada. This self-regulation occurs through the Advertising Standards Council (ASC), a non-profit organization of advertising industry members. The ASC responds to all complaints with respect to advertising and publishes an annual report that summarizes the complaints it receives each year. The ASC is also responsible for clearing ads prior to their airing for a number of products. Some of the ASC's responsibilities have been given to it as the federal government has withdrawn services with the belief that industry is sufficiently responsible.

Even though there appears to be sufficient control of advertising, it is a very powerful institution that has been the target of considerable criticism regarding its ethical, social, and economic impact. The criticism of advertising concerns the specific techniques and methods

used as well as its effect on societal values, tastes, lifestyles, and behaviour. Critics argue that advertising is deceptive and untruthful; that it is often offensive, irritating, or in poor taste; and that it exploits certain groups. Many people believe advertising should be informative only and advertisers should not use subjective claims, puffery, embellishment, or persuasive techniques.

Advertising often offends consumers by the type of appeal or manner of presentation used; sexually suggestive ads and nudity receive the most criticism. Advertisers say their ads are consistent with contemporary values and lifestyles and are appropriate for the target audiences they are attempting to reach. Advertising to children is an area of particular concern, since critics argue that children lack the experience, knowledge, and ability to process and evaluate persuasive advertising messages rationally.

The pervasiveness of advertising and its prevalence in the

mass media have led critics to argue that it plays a major role in influencing and transmitting social values. Advertising has been charged with encouraging materialism, manipulating consumers to buy things they do not really want or need, perpetuating stereotypes through its portrayal of certain groups such as women and visible minorities.

Advertising has also been scrutinized with regard to its economic effects. The basic economic role of advertising is to give consumers information that helps them make consumption decisions. Some people view advertising as a detrimental force that has a negative effect on competition, product costs, and consumer prices. Economists' perspectives regarding the effects of advertising follow two basic schools of thought: the advertising equals market power model and the advertising equals information model. Arguments consistent with each perspective were considered in analyzing the economic effects of advertising.

SUMMARY

DISCUSSION QUESTIONS

1. Explain why you agree or disagree with the rulings of the ASC presented in this chapter regarding the Yves Saint Laurent fragrance ad and the Ford Focus automobile ad?

2. Discuss the role of ethics in advertising and promotion. How do ethical considerations differ from legal considerations?

3. What is meant by shock advertising? Evaluate the arguments for and against the use of shock advertising by marketers.

4. Evaluate the arguments for and against advertising to children.

Do you feel restrictions are needed for advertising and other forms of promotion targeted to children?

5. A common criticism of advertising is that it stereotypes women. Discuss the ways this might occur. Do you think the Airwalk ad shown in Exhibit 18–4 is suggestive and symbolizes sexual submission?

6. With which position do you agree: "Advertising determines Canadian consumers' tastes and values and is responsible for creating a materialistic society,"

or "Advertising is a reflection of society and mirrors its tastes and values"?

7. Discuss how advertising can impact consumer choice, as well as its impact on product costs and the prices paid for products and services.

8. Discuss the two major perspectives of the economic impact of advertising: "advertising equals market power" versus "advertising equals information."

Endnotes

CHAPTER ONE

1. "AMA Board Approves New Marketing Definition," *Marketing News*, March 1, 1985, p. 1.
2. Michael L. Ray, *Advertising and Communication Management* (Englewood Cliffs, NJ: Prentice Hall, 1982).
3. Ralph S. Alexander, ed., *Marketing Definitions* (Chicago: American Marketing Association, 1965), p. 9.
4. Clarence Poirier, "Making the Most of Magazines," *Marketing Magazine*, October 15, 2001.
5. Richard Lewis, "Absolut Vodka Case History," *A Celebration of Effective Advertising: 30 Years of Winning EFFIE Campaigns* (New York: American Marketing Association, 1999), pp. 20–23.
6. H. Frazier Moore and Bertrand R. Canfield, *Public Relations: Principles, Cases, and Problems*, 7th ed. (Burr Ridge, IL: Irwin, 1977), p. 5.
7. Karin Scott, "Beyond Press Coverage," *Marketing Magazine*, June 16, 2003.
8. Michelle Warren, "Pub Visits Lead Guinness Holiday Push," *Marketing Magazine*, January 27, 2003.
8. Lesley Young, "Kraft Dishes Taste Content to Rogers," *Marketing Magazine*, October 27, 2003.
10. Adrienne Ward Fawcett, "Integrated Marketing—Marketers Convinced: Its Time Has Arrived," *Advertising Age*, November 6, 1993, pp. S1–2.
11. "Do Your Ads Need a SuperAgency?" *Fortune*, April 27, 1991, pp. 81–85; Faye Rice, "A Cure for What Ails Advertising?" *Fortune*, December 16, 1991, pp. 119–22.
12. Don E. Schultz, "Integrated Marketing Communications: Maybe Definition Is in the Point of View," *Marketing News*, January 18, 1993, p. 17.
13. Harlan E. Spotts, David R. Lambert, and Mary L. Joyce, "Marketing Déjà Vu: The Discovery of Integrated Marketing Communications," *Journal of Marketing Education* 20, no. 3 (December 1998), pp. 210–18.
14. Kate Fitzgerald, "Beyond Advertising," *Advertising Age*, August 3, 1998, pp. 1, 14; Jane Smith, "Integrated Marketing," *Marketing Tools*, November/December 1995, pp. 63–70; Thomas R. Duncan and Stephen E. Everett, "Client Perception of Integrated Marketing Communications," *Journal of Advertising Research*, May/June 1993, pp. 30–39.
15. Lesley Young, "A Marketing Tale," *Marketing Magazine*, July 30, 2001.
16. Anthony J. Tortorici, "Maximizing Marketing Communications through Horizontal and Vertical Orchestration," *Public Relations Quarterly* 36, no. 1 (1991), pp. 20–22.
17. Robert H. Ducoffe, Dennis Sandler, and Eugene Secunda, "A Survey of Senior Agency, Advertiser, and Media Executives on the Future of Advertising," *Journal of Current Issues and Research in Advertising* 18, no. 1 (Spring 1996).
18. Sergio Zyman, *The End of Marketing As We Know It* (New York: HarperBusiness, 1999); Joe Cappo, "Agencies: Change or Die," *Advertising Age*, December 7, 1992, p. 26.
19. Leonard L. Berry, "Relationship Marketing of Services—Growing Interest, Emerging Perspectives," *Journal of the Academy of Marketing Science* 23, no. 4, 1995, pp. 236–45; Jonathan R. Capulsky and Michael J. Wolfe, "Relationship Marketing: Positioning for the Future," *Journal of Business Strategy*, July–August 1991, pp. 16–26.
20. B. Joseph Pine II, Don Peppers, and Martha Rogers, "Do You Want to Keep Your Customers Forever?" *Harvard Business Review*, March–April 1995, p. 103–14.
21. Don E. Schultz, "Integrated Marketing Communications: Maybe Definition Is in the Point of View."
22. Tom Duncan and Sandra E. Moriarty, "A Communication-Based Model for Managing Relationships," *Journal of Marketing* 62 (April 1998), pp. 1–13.
23. Angela Kryhul, "Shoppers Prestige Play," *Marketing Magazine*, January 19, 2004.
24. J. Paul Peter and Jerry C. Olson, *Consumer Behavior* (Burr Ridge, IL.: Richard D. Irwin, 1987), p. 505.
25. Michael R. Solomon, "The Role of Products as Social Stimuli: A Symbolic Interactionism Perspective," *Journal of Consumer Research*, December 1983, pp. 319–29.
26. Don E. Schultz, Stanley I. Tannenbaum, and Robert F. Lauterborn, *Integrated Marketing Communications: Putting It Together and Making It Work* (Lincolnwood, IL: NTC Publishing Group), p. 72.
27. "The Message Is in the Bottle," *Marketing Magazine*, October 8, 2001.
28. Peter and Olson, *Consumer Behavior*, p. 571.
29. Paul W. Farris and David J. Reibstein, "How Prices, Ad Expenditures, and Profits Are Linked," *Harvard Business Review*, November–December 1979, pp. 172–84.
30. Eric N. Berkowitz, Roger A. Kerin, and William Rudelius, *Marketing*, 6th ed. (Burr Ridge, IL: Irwin/McGraw-Hill, 2000).
31. David W. Stewart, Gary L. Frazier, and Ingrid Martin, "Integrated Channel Management: Merging the Communication and Distribution Functions of the Firm," in *Integrated Communication: Synergy of Persuasive Voices*, pp. 185–215, Esther Thorson & Jeri Moore (eds), Lawrence Earlbaum Associates, 1996, Mahwah, NJ.
32. Michelle Warren, "Sprint, Microcell Effort is in the Red," *Marketing Magazine*, September 22, 2003.

CHAPTER TWO

1. Russell W. Belk, "Possessions and the Extended Self," *Journal of Consumer Research*, September 1988, pp. 139–68.
2. Leon G. Schiffman and Leslie Lazar Kannuk, *Consumer Behavior*, 4th ed. (Englewood Cliffs, NJ: Prentice Hall, 1991), p. 192.
3. Eric N. Berkowitz, Roger A. Kerin, Steven W. Hartley, and William Rudelius, *Marketing*, 6th ed. (Burr Ridge, IL: Irwin/McGraw-Hill, 2000), p. 14.
4. A. H. Maslow, "'Higher' and 'Lower' Needs," *Journal of Psychology* 25 (1948), pp. 433–36.
5. For an excellent discussion of memory and consumer behaviour, see James R. Bettman, "Memory Factors in Consumer Choice: A Review," *Journal of Marketing* 43 (Spring 1979), pp. 37–53.
6. Gilbert Harrell, *Consumer Behavior* (San Diego: Harcourt Brace Jovanovich, 1986), p. 66.
7. Raymond A. Bauer and Stephen A. Greyser, *Advertising in America: The Consumer View* (Boston: Harvard Business School, 1968).
8. J. Paul Peter and Jerry C. Olson, *Consumer Behavior*, 2nd ed. (Burr Ridge, IL: Irwin/McGraw-Hill, 1990), p. 73.
9. Gordon W. Allport, "Attitudes," in *Handbook of Social Psychology*, ed. C. M. Murchison (Winchester, MA: Clark University Press, 1935), p. 810.
10. Robert B. Zajonc and Hazel Markus, "Affective and Cognitive Factors in Preferences," *Journal of Consumer Research* 9 (1982), pp. 123–31.
11. Alvin Achenbaum, "Advertising Doesn't Manipulate Consumers," *Journal of Advertising Research*, April 2, 1970, pp. 3–13.
12. William D. Wells, "Attitudes and Behavior: Lessons from the Needham Lifestyle Study," *Journal of Advertising Research*, February–March 1985, pp. 40–44; and Icek Ajzen and Martin Fishbein, "Attitude-Behavior Relations: A Theoretical Analysis and Review of Empirical Research," *Psychological Bulletin*, September 1977, pp. 888–918.

13. Joel B. Cohen, Paul W. Minniard, and Peter R. Dickson, "Information Integration: An Information Processing Perspective," in *Advances in Consumer Research*, vol. 7, ed. Jerry C. Olson (Ann Arbor, MI: Association for Consumer Research, 1980), pp. 161–70.

14. Peter and Olson, *Consumer Behavior*, p. 182.

15. Peter L. Wright and Fredric Barbour, "The Relevance of Decision Process Models in Structuring Persuasive Messages," *Communications Research*, July 1975, pp. 246–59.

16. James F. Engel, "The Psychological Consequences of a Major Purchase Decision," in *Marketing in Transition*, ed. William S. Decker (Chicago: American Marketing Association, 1963), pp. 462–75.

17. Richard L. Oliver, *Satisfaction: A Behavioral Perspective on the Consumer* (New York: McGraw-Hill, 1997).

18. John A. Howard and Jagdish N. Sheth, *The Theory of Consumer Behavior* (New York: John Wiley & Sons, 1969).

19. Lyman E. Ostlund, *Role Theory and Group Dynamics in Consumer Behavior: Theoretical Sources*, ed. Scott Ward and Thomas S. Robertson (Englewood Cliffs, NJ: Prentice Hall, 1973), pp. 230–75.

20. James Stafford and Benton Cocanougher, "Reference Group Theory," in *Perspective in Consumer Behavior*, ed. H. H. Kassarjian and T. S. Robertson (Glenview, IL: Scott, Foresman, 1981), pp. 329–43.

21. Jagdish N. Sheth, "A Theory of Family Buying Decisions," in *Models of Buying Behavior*, ed. Jagdish N. Sheth (New York: Harper & Row, 1974), pp. 17–33.

22. Larry Percy, John R. Rossiter, and Richard Elliot, *Strategic Advertising Management* (Oxford University Press, 2001).

23. Norma Ramage, "Educating the Young," *Marketing Magazine*, March 22, 2004.

24. Edward M. Tauber, "Research on Food Consumption Values Finds Four Market Segments: Good Taste Still Tops," *Marketing News*, May 15, 1981, p. 17; Rebecca C. Quarles, "Shopping Centers Use Fashion Lifestyle Research to Make Marketing Decisions," *Marketing News*, January 22, 1982, p. 18; and "Our Auto, Ourselves," *Consumer Reports*, June 1985, p. 375.

25. Judith Graham, "New VALS 2 Takes Psychological Route," *Advertising Age*, February 13, 1989, p. 24.

26. Norma Ramage, "Chinese Theme Added to Bell Effort," *Marketing Magazine*, February 2, 2004.

27. Celine Wong, "Can't Knock the Hustle," *Marketing Magazine*, May 3, 2004.

28. For an excellent discussion of social class and consumer behaviour, see

Richard P. Coleman, "The Continuing Significance of Social Class to Marketing," *Journal of Consumer Research* 10, no. 3 (December 1983), pp. 265–80.

29. Chris Daniels, "Almost Rich," *Marketing Magazine*, April 26, 2004.

30. Russell Belk, "Situational Variables and Consumer Behavior," *Journal of Consumer Research*, December 1975, pp. 157–64.

31. John Rossiter and Larry Percy, *Advertising Communications and Promotion Management* (New York: McGraw Hill, 1996).

32. Chris Powell, "TMN Puts Spotlight on Subscribers," *Marketing Magazine*, February 23, 2004.

33. Dave Scholz and Jean-Marc Leger, "The Fickle Beer Consumer," *Marketing Magazine*, May 10, 2004.

34. Ibid.

35. Sarah Dobson, "Coffee Crisp Targets Caffeine Crowd," *Marketing Magazine*, February 10, 2003.

36. John Rossiter and Larry Percy.

CHAPTER THREE

1. Wilbur Schram, *The Process and Effects of Mass Communications* (Urbana: University of Illinois Press, 1955).

2. Ibid.

3. Joseph Ransdell, "Some Leading Ideas of Peirce's Semiotic," *Semiotica* 19 (1977), pp. 157–78.

4. Michael Solomon, *Consumer Behavior*, 4th ed. (Upper Saddle River, NJ: Prentice-Hall, 1999), p. 17.

5. Nina Munk, "Levi's Ongoing Quest for Street Cred," *Fortune*, February 1, 1999, p. 40.

6. For an excellent article on the application of semiotics to consumer behaviour and advertising, see David G. Mick, "Consumer Research and Semiotics: Exploring the Morphology of Signs, Symbols, and Significance," *Journal of Consumer Research* 13, no. 2 (September 1986), pp. 196–213; see also Edward F. McQuarrie and David Glen Mick, "Figures of Rhetoric in Advertising Language," *Journal of Consumer Research* 22 (March 1996), pp. 424–38.

7. Barry L. Bayus, "Word of Mouth: The Indirect Effect of Marketing Efforts," *Journal of Advertising Research*, June/July 1985, pp. 31–39; Robert E. Smith and Christine A. Vogt, "The Effects of Integrating Advertising and Negative Word-of-Mouth Communications on Message Processing and Response," *Journal of Consumer Psychology*, 4 No. 2 (1995), pp. 133–51.

8. Jacob Jacoby and Wayne D. Hoyer, "Viewer Miscomprehension of Televised Communication: Selected Findings," *Journal of Marketing*, Fall

1982, pp. 12–26; Jacoby and Hoyer, "The Comprehension and Miscomprehension of Print Communications: An Investigation of Mass Media Magazines," Advertising Education Foundation study, New York, 1987.

9. E. K. Strong, *The Psychology of Selling* (New York: McGraw-Hill, 1925), p. 9.

10. Robert J. Lavidge and Gary A. Steiner, "A Model for Predictive Measurements of Advertising Effectiveness," *Journal of Marketing* 24 (October 1961), pp. 59–62.

11. Everett M. Rogers, *Diffusion of Innovations* (New York: Free Press, 1962), pp. 79–86.

12. William J. McGuire, "An Information Processing Model of Advertising Effectiveness," in *Behavioral and Management Science in Marketing*, ed. Harry J. Davis and Alvin J. Silk (New York: Ronald Press, 1978), pp. 156–80.

13. Michael L. Ray, "Communication and the Hierarchy of Effects," in *New Models for Mass Communication Research*, ed. P. Clarke (Beverly Hills, CA: Sage, 1973), pp. 147–75.

14. Herbert E. Krugman, "The Impact of Television Advertising: Learning without Involvement," *Public Opinion Quarterly* 29 (Fall 1965), pp. 349–56.

15. Scott A. Hawkins and Stephen J. Hoch, "Low-Involvement Learning: Memory without Evaluation," *Journal of Consumer Research* 19, no. 2 (September 1992), pp. 212–25.

16. Harold H. Kassarjian, "Low Involvement: A Second Look," in *Advances in Consumer Research*, vol. 8 (Ann Arbor: Association for Consumer Research, 1981), pp. 31–34; also see Anthony G. Greenwald and Clark Leavitt, "Audience Involvement in Advertising: Four Levels," *Journal of Consumer Research* 11, no. 1 (June 1984), pp. 581–92.

17. Judith L. Zaichkowsky, "Conceptualizing Involvement," *Journal of Advertising* 15, no. 2 (1986), pp. 4–14.

18. DeAnna S. Kempf and Russell N. Laczniak, "Advertising's Influence on Subsequent Product Trial Processing," *Journal of Advertising*, Vol. 30, No. 3, Fall 2001, pp. 27–38.

19. Jerry C. Olson, Daniel R. Toy, and Phillip A. Dover, "Mediating Effects of Cognitive Responses to Advertising on Cognitive Structure," in *Advances in Consumer Research*, vol. 5, ed. H. Keith Hunt (Ann Arbor, MI: Association for Consumer Research, 1978), pp. 72–78.

20. Anthony A. Greenwald, "Cognitive Learning, Cognitive Response to Persuasion and Attitude Change," in *Psychological Foundations of Attitudes*, ed. A. G. Greenwald, T. C. Brock, and T. W. Ostrom (New York: Academic Press, 1968); Peter L.

547

Wright, "The Cognitive Processes Mediating Acceptance of Advertising," *Journal of Marketing Research* 10 (February 1973), pp. 53–62; Brian Wansink, Michael L. Ray, and Rajeev Batra, "Increasing Cognitive Response Sensitivity," *Journal of Advertising* 23, no. 2 (June 1994), pp. 65–76.

21. Peter Wright, "Message Evoked Thoughts, Persuasion Research Using Thought Verbalizations," *Journal of Consumer Research* 7, no. 2 (September 1980), pp. 151–75.

22. Scott B. Mackenzie, Richard J. Lutz, and George E. Belch, "The Role of Attitude toward the Ad as a Mediator of Advertising Effectiveness: A Test of Competing Explanations," *Journal of Marketing Research* 23 (May 1986), pp. 130–43; and Rajeev Batra and Michael L. Ray, "Affective Responses Mediating Acceptance of Advertising," *Journal of Consumer Research* 13 (September 1986), pp. 234–49.

23. Tim Ambler and Tom Burne, "The Impact of Affect on Memory of Advertising," *Journal of Advertising Research* 29, no. 3 (March/April 1999), pp. 25–34; Ronald Alsop, "TV Ads That Are Likeable Get Plus Rating for Persuasiveness," *The Wall Street Journal*, February 20, 1986, p. 23.

24. David J. Moore and William D. Harris, "Affect Intensity and the Consumer's Attitude toward High Impact Emotional Advertising Appeals," *Journal of Advertising* 25, no. 2 (Summer 1996), pp. 37–50; Andrew A. Mitchell and Jerry C. Olson, "Are Product Attribute Beliefs the Only Mediator of Advertising Effects on Brand Attitude?" *Journal of Marketing Research* 18 (August 1981), pp. 318–32.

25. David J. Moore, William D. Harris, and Hong C. Chen, "Affect Intensity: An Individual Difference Response to Advertising Appeals," *Journal of Consumer Research* 22 (September 1995), pp. 154–64; Julie Edell and Marian C. Burke, "The Power of Feelings in Understanding Advertising Effects," *Journal of Consumer Research* 14 (December 1987), pp. 421–33.

26. Richard E. Petty and John T. Cacioppo, "Central and Peripheral Routes to Persuasion: Application to Advertising," in *Advertising and Consumer Psychology*, ed. Larry Percy and Arch Woodside (Lexington, MA: Lexington Books, 1983), pp. 3–23.

27. David A. Aaker, Rajeev Batra, and John G. Myers, *Advertising Management*, 5th ed. (Upper Saddle River, NJ: Prentice Hall, 1996).

28. Gerald J. Gorn, "The Effects of Music in Advertising on Choice: A Classical Conditioning Approach," *Journal of Marketing* 46 (Winter 1982), pp. 94–101.

29. James J. Kellaris, Anthony D. Cox, and Dena Cox, "The Effect of Background Music on Ad Processing: A Contingency Explanation," *Journal of Marketing*, 57, no. 4 (Fall 1993), p. 114.

30. Richard E. Petty, John T. Cacioppo, and David Schumann, "Central and Peripheral Routes to Advertising Effectiveness: The Moderating Role of Involvement," *Journal of Consumer Research* 10 (September 1983), pp. 135–46.

31. Demetrios Vakratsas and Tim Ambler, "How Advertising Works: What Do We Really Know?" *Journal of Marketing* 63 (January 1999), pp. 26–43.

32. Bruce F. Hall, "A New Model for Measuring Advertising Effects," *Journal of Advertising Research*, Vol. 42, No. 2, (March/April 2002) pp. 23–31.

33. William M. Weilbacher, "Point of View: Does Advertising Cause a 'Hierarchy of Effects'?," *Journal of Advertising Research*, 41, No. (6) (November/December 2001) pp. 19–26.

CHAPTER FOUR

1. Robert A. Kriegel, "How to Choose the Right Communications Objectives," *Business Marketing*, April 1986, pp. 94–106.

2. Paul-Marc Rendon, "rookie Effort for New Converse Shoe," *Marketing Magazine*, December 1, 2003.

3. Donald S. Tull, "The Carry-Over Effect of Advertising," *Journal of Marketing*, April 1965, pp. 46–53.

4. Darral G. Clarke, "Econometric Measurement of the Duration of Advertising Effect on Sales," *Journal of Marketing Research* 23 (November 1976), pp. 345–57.

5. Philip Kotler, *Marketing Decision Making: A Model Building Approach* (New York: Holt, Rinehart & Winston, 1971), ch. 5.

6. For a more detailed discussion of this, see William M. Weilbacher, *Advertising*, 2nd ed. (New York: Macmillan, 1984), p. 112.

7. Russell H. Colley, *Defining Advertising Goals for Measured Advertising Results* (New York: Association of National Advertisers, 1961).

8. Ibid., p. 21.

9. Michael L. Ray, "Consumer Initial Processing: Definitions, Issues, Applications," in *Buyer/Consumer Information Processing*, ed. G. David Hughes (Chapel Hill: University of North Carolina Press, 1974); David A. Aaker and John G. Myers, *Advertising Management*, 2nd ed. (Englewood Cliffs, NJ: Prentice Hall, 1982), pp. 122–23.

10. Sandra Ernst Moriarty, "Beyond the Hierarchy of Effects: A Conceptual Framework," in *Current Issues and Research in Advertising*, ed. Claude R. Martin, Jr., and James H. Leigh (Ann

Arbor, MI: University of Michigan, 1983), pp. 45–55.

11. Don E. Schultz, Dennis Martin, and William Brown, *Strategic Advertising Campaigns*, 2nd ed. (Lincolnwood, IL: Crain Books, 1984).

12. Courtland I. Bovee and William F. Arens, *Advertising*, 3rd ed. (Burr Ridge, IL: Richard D. Irwin, 1989).

13. Stewart H. Britt, "Are So-Called Successful Advertising Campaigns Really Successful?" *Journal of Advertising Research* 9, no. 2 (1969), pp. 3–9.

14. Steven W. Hartley and Charles H. Patti, "Evaluating Business-to-Business Advertising: A Comparison of Objectives and Results," *Journal of Advertising Research* 28 (April/May 1988), pp. 21–27.

15. Ibid., p. 25.

16. Study cited in Robert F. Lauterborn, "How to Know If Your Advertising Is Working," *Journal of Advertising Research* 25 (February/March 1985), pp. RC 9–11.

17. Don E. Schultz, "Integration Helps You Plan Communications from Outside-In," *Marketing News*, March 15, 1993, p. 12.

18. Thomas R. Duncan, "To Fathom Integrated Marketing, Dive!" *Advertising Age*, October 11, 1993, p. 18.

19. Chris Powell, "*Globe* Targets Circulation Gains, " *Marketing Magazine*, February 2, 2004.

20. Angela Scardillo, "Making Milk COOL," *Marketing Magazine*, August 11, 2003.

21. Paul Ferris, "CTC Hits the Road with Toyota," *Marketing Magazine*, September 15, 2003.

22. Eve Lazarus, "Taking on Goliath," *Marketing Magazine*, March 4, 2002.

23. Paul Ferris, "Ditching the Minivans," *Marketing Magazine*, March 15, 2004.

24. Danny Kucharsky, "French Transit Ads Tell Traffic Truths," *Marketing Magazine*, February 9, 2004.

25. Frank Dennis, "Selling Hidden Brands," *Marketing Magazine*, May 10, 2004.

26. Eve Lazarus, "Taking on Goliath," *Marketing Magazine*, March 22, 2002.

27. Brent Cuthbertson, and Grant Stockwell, "That Rings a Bell," *Marketing Magazine*, October 20, 2003.

28. Dave Scholz and Gilbert Paquette, "The Impact of Auto Advertising," *Marketing Magazine*, June 30, 2003.

29. Mark Higgins, "Smart Marketing," *Marketing Magazine*, April 2, 2001.

30. Lesley Young, "It Pays to Get Aggressive," *Marketing Magazine*, February 12, 2001.

CHAPTER FIVE

1. Dan Fost, "Growing Older, but Not Up," *American Demographics*, September 1998, pp. 58–65.

2. *Ayer's Dictionary of Advertising Terms* (Philadelphia: Ayers Press, 1976).

3. "WestJet Fuels Up Advertising Effort," *Marketing Magazine*, March 2001; "Flying the Cluttered Skies," *Marketing Magazine*, April 9, 2001.

4. Davis A. Aaker and John G. Myers, *Advertising Management*, 3rd ed. (Englewood Cliffs, NJ: Prentice Hall, 1987), p. 125.

5. Jack Trout and Al Ries, "Positioning Cuts through Chaos in the Marketplace," *Advertising Age*, May 1, 1972, pp. 51–53.

6. "Sleemans Brings Out the Truth," *Marketing Magazine*, May 28, 2001; "Sleeman Shifts Its Target," *Marketing Magazine*, April 16, 2001; "Sleeman Ads Bow Without Brewery Boss," *Marketing Magazine*, April 4, 2001; "Sleeman Touts Label-Free Brand," *Marketing Magazine*, April 15, 2002.

7. For a review of multiattribute models, see William L. Wilkie and Edgar A. Pessemier, "Issues in Marketing's Use of Multiattribute Models," *Journal of Marketing Research* 10 (November 1983), pp. 428–41.

8. David A. Aaker and J. Gary Shansby, "Positioning Your Product," *Business Horizons*, May–June 1982, pp. 56–62.

9. Lesley Young, "Harvey's Keeps An Eye on the Grill," *Marketing Magazine*, September 29, 2003.

10. Trout and Ries, "Positioning Cuts through Chaos."

11. Lesley Young, "An Order of Fries, with Attitude," *Marketing Magazine*, November 17, 2003.

12. Lesley Young, "Wireless Marketers Unleash Hounds," *Marketing Magazine*, December 8, 2003.

13. Norma Ramage, "WestJet Finds A Competitive Niche," *Marketing Magazine*, July 28, 2003.

14. Jeff Robillard and Phil Copithorne, "Big Idea Fits in Small Space," *Marketing Magazine*, February 23, 2004.

15. George Walton, "Appealingly Local," *Marketing Magazine*, May 5, 2003.

16. Michelle Warren, "*Fubar* Guys Light Up Anti-Smoking Ads," *Marketing Magazine*, January 19, 2004.

17. Sarah Dobson, "Sub Culture," *Marketing Magazine*, May 10, 2004.

18. Aaker and Myers, *Advertising Management*.

19. Elizabeth C. Hirschman, "Role-Based Models of Advertising Creation and Production," *Journal of Advertising* 18, no. 4 (1989), pp. 42–53.

20. Ibid., p. 51.

21. Cyndee Miller, "Study Says 'Likability' Surfaces as Measure of TV Ad Success," *Marketing News*, January 7, 1991, pp. 6, 14; and Ronald Alsop, "TV Ads That Are Likeable Get Plus Rating for Persuasiveness," *The Wall Street Journal*, February 20, 1986, p. 23.

22. Nicolas Massey, "Answer A Higher Calling," *Marketing Magazine*, March 22, 2004.

23. For an interesting discussion on the embellishment of advertising messages, see William M. Weilbacher, *Advertising*, 2nd ed. (New York: Macmillan, 1984), pp. 180–82.

24. David Ogilvy, *Confessions of an Advertising Man* (New York: Atheneum, 1963); and Hanley Norins, *The Compleat Copywriter* (New York: McGraw-Hill, 1966).

25. Hank Sneiden, *Advertising Pure and Simple* (New York: ANACOM, 1977).

26. Quoted in Valerie H. Free, "Absolut Original," *Marketing Insights*, Summer 1991, p. 65.

27. James Webb Young, *A Technique for Producing Ideas*, 3rd ed. (Chicago: Crain Books, 1975), p. 42.

28. Sandra E. Moriarty, *Creative Advertising: Theory and Practice* (Englewood Cliffs, NJ: Prentice Hall, 1986).

29. Brian Mills, "The Egg Man Cometh," *Marketing Magazine*, February 26, 2001.

30. Bruce MacDonald, "The Art of the Brief," *Marketing Magazine*, October 27, 2003.

CHAPTER SIX

1. John O'Toole, *The Trouble with Advertising*, 2nd ed. (New York: Random House, 1985), p. 131.

2. Rosser Reeves, *Reality in Advertising* (New York: Knopf, 1961), pp. 47, 48.

3. Ogilvy, *Confessions*.

4. Martin Mayer, *Madison Avenue, U.S.A.* (New York: Pocket Books, 1958).

5. Jack Trout and Al Ries, "The Positioning Era Cometh," *Advertising Age*, April 24, 1972, pp. 35–38; May 1, 1972, pp. 51–54; May 8, 1972, pp. 114–16.

6. Ingrid Button, "Turning the Export Ship Around," *Marketing Magazine*, August 27, 2001.

7. Lara Mills, "Campaigns with Legs," *Marketing Magazine*, May 15, 2000.

8. Danny Kucharsky, "Pepsi Guys Star in Quebec Ads," *Marketing Magazine*, March 17, 2003.

9. "Cows Cheer Olympic Athletes," *Marketing Magazine*, February 4, 2002.

10. Kate MacArthur, "BK flame-broils McCann," *Advertising Age*, October 1, 2001, pp. 1, 60.

11. Jean Halliday and Alice Z. Cuneo, "Nissan Reverses Course to Focus on the Product," *Advertising Age*, February 16, 1998, pp. 1, 39.

12. Jean Halliday, "Nissan Launches New Brand Campaign," August 21, 2002, http://www.adage.com/news.

13. Lara Mills, "Campaigns with Legs," *Marketing Magazine*, May 15, 2000.

14. Michael Adams, *Fire and Ice*, Penguin, 2003.

15. Nancy Evans and Bruce Maclellan, "The Risk of Frost Bite," *Marketing Magazine*, June 30, 2003.

16. David Macdonald and Michael Adams, "We Are What We Drive," *Marketing Magazine*, March 15, 2004.

17. Stan Sutter, "Canada's Ad Renascence," *Marketing Magazine*, March 29, 2004.

18. Stan Sutter, "Vive la difference," *Marketing Magazine*, January 26, 2004.

19. Chris Daniels, "Canucks vs. Yanks," *Marketing Magazine*, May 22, 2000.

20. Lesley Young, "RadioShack Corners New Ad Theme," *Marketing Magazine*, September 08, 2003.

21. *Marketing Magazine*, "Cannes-ada," July 3, 2000; "Cannes 2001," July 2, 2001; "Cannes Ad Festival Can be a Real Eye-Opener for Marketers," July 2, 2001; "The Bashful Beaver," November 26, 2001; "More Canuck Work Entered at Cannes," May 29, 2002; Jim McElgunn, "Canucks at Cannes," July 1, 2002; Angela Kryhul, "Where Big Ideas Rule," June 30, 2003; "Canada Arrives at Cannes," July 12, 2004.

22. Sandra E. Moriarty, *Creative Advertising: Theory and Practice*, 2nd ed. (Englewoods Cliffs, NJ: Prentice Hall, 1991), p. 76.

23. William M. Weilbacher, *Advertising*, 2nd ed. (New York: Macmillan, 1984), p. 197.

24. William Wells, John Burnett, and Sandra Moriarty, *Advertising* (Englewood Cliffs, NJ: Prentice Hall, 1989), p. 330.

25. William L. Wilkie and Paul W. Farris, "Comparative Advertising: Problems and Potential," *Journal of Marketing* 39 (1975), pp. 7–15.

26. For a review of comparative advertising studies, see Cornelia Pechmann and David W. Stewart, "The Psychology of Comparative Advertising," in *Attention, Attitude and Affect in Response to Advertising*, ed. E. M. Clark, T. C. Brock, and D. W. Stewart (Hillsdale, NJ: Lawrence Erlbaum, 1994), pp. 79–96; and Thomas S. Barry, "Comparative Advertising: What Have We Learned in Two Decades?" *Journal of Advertising Research* 33, no. 2 (1993), pp. 19–29.

27. Stuart J. Agres, "Emotion in Advertising: An Agency Point of View," in *Emotion in Advertising: Theoretical and Practical Explanations*, ed. Stuart J. Agres, Julie A. Edell, and Tony M. Dubitsky (Westport, CT: Quorom Books, 1991).

28. Francois Lacoursiere, "La Vie en Bleu," *Marketing Magazine*, February 02, 2004.

29. Edward Kamp and Deborah J. Macinnis, "Characteristics of Portrayed Emotions in Commercials: When Does What Is Shown in Ads Affect Viewers?" *Journal*

of Advertising Research, November/December 1995, pp. 19–28.

30. For a review of research on the effect of mood states on consumer behaviour, see Meryl Paula Gardner, "Mood States and Consumer Behavior: A Critical Review," *Journal of Consumer Research* 12, no. 3 (December 1985), pp. 281–300.

31. Cathy Madison, "Researchers Work Advertising into an Emotional State," *Adweek*, November 5, 1990, p. 30.

32. Joanne Caza, "From Destination to Journey," *Marketing Magazine*, September 8, 2003.

33. Michael L. Ray and William L. Wilkie, "Fear: The Potential of an Appeal Neglected by Marketing," *Journal of Marketing* 34 (January 1970), pp. 54–62.

34. Brian Sternthal and C. Samuel Craig, "Fear Appeals Revisited and Revised," *Journal of Consumer Research* 1 (December 1974), pp. 22–34.

35. Punam Anand Keller and Lauren Goldberg Block, "Increasing the Persuasiveness of Fear Appeals: The Effect of Arousal and Elaboration," *Journal of Consumer Research* 22, no. 4 (March 1996), pp. 448–60.

36. John F. Tanner, Jr., James B. Hunt, and David R. Eppright, "The Protection Motivation Model: A Normative Mode of Fear Appeals," *Journal of Marketing* 55 (July 1991), pp. 36–45.

37. Ibid.

38. Sternthal and Craig, "Fear Appeals Revisited and Revised."

39. Herbert Jack Rotfeld, "The Textbook Effect: Conventional Wisdom, Myth and Error in Marketing," *Journal of Marketing* 64 (April 2000), pp. 122–27.

40. For a discussion of the use of humour in advertising, see C. Samuel Craig and Brian Sternthal, "Humor in Advertising," *Journal of Marketing* 37 (October 1973), pp. 12–18.

41. Yong Zhang, "Response to Humorous Advertising: The Moderating Effect of Need for Cognition," *Journal of Advertising* 25, no. 1 (Spring 1996), pp. 15–32; Marc G. Weinberger and Charles S. Gulas, "The Impact of Humor in Advertising: A Review," *Journal of Advertising* 21 (December 1992), pp. 35–59.

42. Marc G. Weinberger and Leland Campbell, "The Use of Humor in Radio Advertising," *Journal of Advertising Research* 31 (December/January 1990–91), pp. 44–52.

43. Thomas J. Madden and Marc C. Weinberger, "Humor in Advertising: A Practitioner View," *Journal of Advertising Research* 24, no. 4 (August/September 1984), pp. 23–26.

44. David Ogilvy and Joel Raphaelson, "Research on Advertising Techniques That Work and Don't Work," *Harvard Business Review*, July/August 1982, p. 18.

45. Topline, no. 4 (September 1989), McCann-Erickson, New York.

46. Media Innovation Awards, *Marketing Magazine*, November 5, 2003.

47. Herbert C. Kelman, "Processes of Opinion Change," *Public Opinion Quarterly* 25 (Spring 1961), pp. 57–78.

48. William J. McGuire, "The Nature of Attitudes and Attitude Change," in *Handbook of Social Psychology*, 2nd ed., ed. G. Lindzey and E. Aronson (Cambridge, MA: Addison-Wesley, 1969), pp. 135–214; Daniel J. O'Keefe, "The Persuasive Effects of Delaying Identification of High- and Low-Credibility Communicators: A Meta-Analytic Review," *Central States Speech Journal* 38 (1987), pp. 63–72.

49. Roobina Ohanian, "The Impact of Celebrity Spokespersons' Image on Consumers' Intention to Purchase," *Journal of Advertising Research*, February/March 1991, pp. 46–54.

50. Erick Reidenback and Robert Pitts, "Not All CEOs Are Created Equal as Advertising Spokespersons: Evaluating the Effective CEO Spokesperson," *Journal of Advertising* 20, no. 3 (1986), pp. 35–50; Roger Kerin and Thomas E. Barry, "The CEO Spokesperson in Consumer Advertising: An Experimental Investigation," in *Current Issues in Research in Advertising*, ed. J. H. Leigh and C. R. Martin (Ann Arbor: University of Michigan, 1981), pp. 135–48; and J. Poindexter, "Voices of Authority," *Psychology Today*, August 1983.

51. A. Eagly and S. Chaiken, "An Attribution Analysis of the Effect of Communicator Characteristics on Opinion Change," *Journal of Personality and Social Psychology* 32 (1975), pp. 136–44.

52. For a review of these studies, see Brian Sternthal, Lynn Phillips, and Ruby Dholakia, "The Persuasive Effect of Source Credibility: A Situational Analysis," *Public Opinion Quarterly* 42 (Fall 1978), pp. 285–314.

53. Brian Sternthal, Ruby Dholakia, and Clark Leavitt, "The Persuasive Effects of Source Credibility: Tests of Cognitive Response," *Journal of Consumer Research* 4, no. 4 (March 1978), pp. 252–60; and Robert R. Harmon and Kenneth A. Coney, "The Persuasive Effects of Source Credibility in Buy and Lease Situations," *Journal of Marketing Research* 19 (May 1982), pp. 255–60.

54. For a review, see Noel Capon and James Hulbert, "The Sleeper Effect: An Awakening," *Public Opinion Quarterly* 37 (1973), pp. 333–58.

55. Darlene B. Hannah and Brian Sternthal, "Detecting and Explaining the Sleeper Effect," *Journal of Consumer Research* 11, no. 2 (September 1984), pp. 632–42.

56. H. C. Triandis, *Attitudes and Attitude Change* (New York: Wiley, 1971).

57. Lise Laguerre, "It's Respect in Either Language," *Marketing Magazine*, May 6, 2002.

58. J. Mills and J. Jellison, "Effect on Opinion Change Similarity between the Communicator and the Audience He Addresses," *Journal of Personality and Social Psychology* 9, no. 2 (1969), pp. 153–56.

59. Louisa Flinn, "Kings of the Road," *Marketing Magazine*, February 16, 2004.

60. "P&G smiles with Sale and Pelletier," *Marketing Magazine*, March 4, 2002.

61. Valerie Folkes, "Recent Attribution Research in Consumer Behavior: A Review and New Directions," *Journal of Consumer Research* 14 (March 1988), pp. 548–65; John C. Mowen and Stephen W. Brown, "On Explaining and Predicting the Effectiveness of Celebrity Endorsers," in *Advances in Consumer Research*, vol. 8 (Ann Arbor, MI: Association for Consumer Research, 1981), pp. 437–41.

62. Charles Atkin and M. Block, "Effectiveness of Celebrity Endorsers," *Journal of Advertising Research* 23, no. 1 (February/March 1983), pp. 57–61.

63. Ellen Neuborne, "Generation Y," *Business Week*, February 15, 1999, pp. 81–88.

64. Michael A. Kamins, "An Investigation into the 'Match-Up' Hypothesis in Celebrity Advertising," *Journal of Advertising* 19, no. 1 (1990), pp. 4–13.

65. Grant McCracken, "Who Is the Celebrity Endorser? Cultural Foundations of the Endorsement Process," *Journal of Consumer Research* 16, no. 3 (December 1989), pp. 310–21.

66. Ibid., p. 315.

67. B. Zafer Erdogan, Michael J. Baker and Stephen Tagg, "Selecting Celebrity Endorsers: The Practitioner's Perspective," *Journal of Advertising Research*, Vol. 41, No. 43 (May/June 2001), pp. 39–48.

68. For an excellent review of these studies, see Marilyn Y. Jones, Andrea J. S. Stanaland, and Betsy D. Gelb, "Beefcake and Cheesecake: Insights for Advertisers," *Journal of Advertising* 27, no. 2 (Summer 1998), pp. 32–51; and W. B. Joseph, "The Credibility of Physically Attractive Communicators," *Journal of Advertising* 11, no. 3 (1982), pp. 13–23.

69. Michael Solomon, Richard Ashmore, and Laura Longo, "The Beauty Match-Up Hypothesis: Congruence between Types of Beauty and Product Images in Advertising," *Journal of Advertising* 21, no. 4, pp. 23–34; M. J. Baker and Gilbert A. Churchill, Jr., "The Impact of Physically Attractive Models on Advertising Evaluations," *Journal of Marketing Research* 14 (November 1977), pp. 538–55.

70. Robert W. Chestnut, C. C. La Chance, and A. Lubitz, "The Decorative Female Model: Sexual Stimuli and the Recognition of the

Advertisements," *Journal of Advertising* 6 (Fall 1977), pp. 11–14; and Leonard N. Reid and Lawrence C. Soley, "Decorative Models and Readership of Magazine Ads," *Journal of Advertising Research* 23, no. 2 (April/May 1983), pp. 27–32.

71. Amanda B. Bower, "Highly Attractive Models in Advertising and the Women Who Loathe Them: The Implications of Negative Affect for Spokesperson Effectiveness," *Journal of Advertising*, Vol. 30, No. 3, (Fall 2001), pp. 51–63; Amanda B. Bower and Stacy Landreth, "Is Beauty Best? Highly Versus Normally Attractive Models in Advertising," *Journal of Advertising*, Vol. 30, No. 1, pp. 1–12.

CHAPTER SEVEN

1. Martin Mayer, *Madison Avenue, U.S.A.* (New York: Pocket Books, 1958), p. 64.
2. "Dove Revives Soap Litmus Test," *Marketing Magazine*, January 15, 2001.
3. Norma Ramage, "Toyota Owners Drive Prairie Effort, *Marketing Magazine*, March 17, 2003.
4. Danny Kucharsky, "Desjardins Interprets Life in New Ads," *Marketing Magazine*, September 22, 2003.
5. Sally Beatty, "P&G to Ad Agencies: Please Rewrite Our Old Formulas," *The Wall Street Journal*, November 5, 1998, pp. B1, 10; Alecia Swasy, "P&G Tries Bolder Ads—With Caution," *The Wall Street Journal*, May 7, 1990, pp. B1, 7.
6. Jeff Chatterton, "A Whole New Ball Game," *Marketing Magazine*, November 10, 2003.
7. Angela Kryhul, "The Great Canadian Icon," *Marketing Magazine*, June 26, 2000.
8. Danny Kucharsky, "Mega Bloks Target Kids at Retail," *Marketing Magazine*, November 12, 2001.
9. Barbara B. Stern, "Classical and Vignette Television Advertising: Structural Models, Formal Analysis, and Consumer Effects," *Journal of Consumer Research* 20, no. 4 (March 1994), pp. 601–15; and John Deighton, Daniel Romer, and Josh McQueen, "Using Drama to Persuade," *Journal of Consumer Research* 15, no. 3 (December 1989), pp. 335–43.
10. Karen Howe and Ian Mcintosh, "A Clever Parody," *Marketing Magazine*, January 12, 2004.
11. Herbert E. Krugman, "On Application of Learning Theory to TV Copy Testing," *Public Opinion Quarterly* 26 (1962), pp. 626–39.
12. C. I. Hovland and W. Mandell, "An Experimental Comparison of Conclusion Drawing by the Communicator and by the Audience," *Journal of Abnormal and Social Psychology* 47 (July 1952), pp. 581–88.
13. Alan G. Sawyer and Daniel J. Howard, "Effects of Omitting Conclusions in Advertisements to Involved and Uninvolved Audiences," *Journal of Marketing Research* 28 (November 1991), pp. 467–74.
14. George E. Belch, "The Effects of Message Modality on One- and Two-Sided Advertising Messages," in *Advances in Consumer Research*, vol. 10, ed. Richard P. Bagozzi and Alice M. Tybout (Ann Arbor, MI: Association for Consumer Research, 1983), pp. 21–26.
15. Robert E. Settle and Linda L. Golden, "Attribution Theory and Advertiser Credibility," *Journal of Marketing Research* 11 (May 1974), pp. 181–85; and Edmund J. Faison, "Effectiveness of One-Sided and Two-Sided Mass Communications in Advertising," *Public Opinion Quarterly* 25 (Fall 1961), pp. 468–69.
16. "Campaigns with Legs," *Marketing Magazine*, May 15, 2000.
17. Alan G. Sawyer, "The Effects of Repetition of Refutational and Supportive Advertising Appeals," *Journal of Marketing Research* 10 (February 1973), pp. 23–37; and George J. Szybillo and Richard Heslin, "Resistance to Persuasion: Inoculation Theory in a Marketing Context," *Journal of Marketing Research* 10 (November 1973), pp. 396–403.
18. Andrew A. Mitchell, "The Effect of Verbal and Visual Components of Advertisements on Brand Attitudes and Attitude toward the Advertisement," *Journal of Consumer Research* 13 (June 1986), pp. 12–24; and Julie A. Edell and Richard Staelin, "The Information Processing of Pictures in Advertisements," *Journal of Consumer Research* 10, no. 1 (June 1983), pp. 45–60; Elizabeth C. Hirschmann, "The Effects of Verbal and Pictorial Advertising Stimuli on Aesthetic, Utilitarian and Familiarity Perceptions," *Journal of Advertising* 15, no. 2 (1986), pp. 27–34.
19. Jolita Kisielius and Brian Sternthal, "Detecting and Explaining Vividness Effects in Attitudinal Judgments," *Journal of Marketing Research* 21, no. 1 (1984), pp. 54–64.
20. H. Rao Unnava and Robert E. Burnkrant, "An Imagery-Processing View of the Role of Pictures in Print Advertisements," *Journal of Marketing Research* 28 (May 1991), pp. 226–31.
21. Susan E. Heckler and Terry L. Childers, "The Role of Expectancy and Relevancy in Memory for Verbal and Visual Information: What Is Incongruency?" *Journal of Consumer Research* 18, no. 4 (March 1992), pp. 475–92.
22. Michael J. Houston, Terry L. Childers, and Susan E. Heckler, "Picture-Word Consistency and the Elaborative Processing of Advertisements," *Journal of Marketing Research*, November 1987, pp. 359–69.
23. William F. Arens, *Contemporary Advertising*, 6th ed. (Burr Ridge, IL: Irwin/McGraw-Hill, 1998), p. 284.
24. W. Keith Hafer and Gordon E. White, *Advertising Writing*, 3rd ed. (St. Paul, MN: West Publishing, 1989), p. 98.
25. Michelle Warren, "Press and Poster," *Marketing Magazine*, March 24, 2003.
26. Janet Kestin, "Reality Rules," *Marketing Magazine*, February 26, 2001.
27. Carol Marie Cooper, "Who Says Talk Is Cheap," *New York Times*, October 22, 1998, pp. C1, 5; and Wendy Brandes, "Star Power Leaves Some Voice-Over Artists Speechless," *The Wall Street Journal*, June 2, 1995, p. B6.
28. Linda M. Scott, "Understanding Jingles and Needledrop: A Rhetorical Approach to Music in Advertising," *Journal of Consumer Research* 17, no. 2 (September 1990), pp. 223–36.
29. Ibid., p. 223.
30. Russell I. Haley, Jack Richardson, and Beth Baldwin, "The Effects of Nonverbal Communications in Television Advertising," *Journal of Advertising Research* 24, no. 4, pp. 11–18.
31. Gerald J. Gorn, "The Effects of Music in Advertising on Choice Behavior: A Classical Conditioning Approach," *Journal of Marketing* 46 (Winter 1982), pp. 94–100.
32. Stephanie N. Mehta, "Northern Telecom Plays Down Phone Roots, Embraces 'I Word,'" *The Wall Street Journal*, April 14, 1999, p. B10.
33. "Bud Light Sells Spoof Soundtrack," *Marketing Magazine*, February 21, 2002.
34. "Follow the Bouncing Ball to P.E.I.," *Marketing Magazine*, March 22, 2004.
35. Angela Kryhul, "Name Your Tune," *Marketing Magazine*, October 14, 2002.
36. Angela Kryhul, "Name Your Tune," *Marketing Magazine*, October 14, 2002.
37. Eleftheria Parpis, "Creative: Best Campaign," *Adweek*, January 24, 2000, p. 1.
38. Richard Vaughn, "How Advertising Works: A Planning Model," *Journal of Advertising Research* 20, no. 5 (October 1980), pp. 27–33.
39. Richard Vaughn, "How Advertising Works: A Planning Model Revisited," *Journal of Advertising Research* 26, no. 1 (February/March 1986), pp. 57–66.
40. Christopher P. Puto and William D. Wells, "Informational and Transformational Advertising: The Different Effects of Time," in *Advances in Consumer Research*, Vol. 11, ed. Thomas C. Kinnear (Ann Arbor, MI: Association for Consumer Research, 1984), p. 638.

551

41. Eric LeBlanc and Kate Tutly, "The Heart of the Matter," *Marketing Magazine*, July 16, 2001.

CHAPTER EIGHT

1. Mary Tolan, "Holidays Are Here and So Is Ad Puzzle," *Advertising Age*, November 16, 1998, p. 36.
2. Ibid.
3. Laura Bird, "Loved the Ad. May (or May Not) Buy the Product," *The Wall Street Journal*, April 7, 1994, p. B1.
4. "What Is Good Creative?" *Topline*, no. 41 (New York: McCollum Spielman Worldwide, 1994), p. 4.
5. James R. Hagerty, "Tests Lead Lowe's to Revamp Strategy," *The Wall Street Journal*, March 11, 1999, p. B18.
6. "21 Ad Agencies Endorse Copy-Testing Principles," *Marketing News* 15, no. 17 (February 19, 1982), p. 1.
7. Ibid.
8. John M. Caffyn, "Telepex Testing of TV Commercials," *Journal of Advertising Research* 5, no. 2 (June 1965), pp. 29-37; Thomas J. Reynolds and Charles Gengler, "A Strategic Framework for Assessing Advertising: The Animatic vs. Finished Issue," *Journal of Advertising Research*, October/ November 1991, pp. 61-71; Nigel A. Brown and Ronald Gatty, "Rough vs. Finished TV Commercials in Telepex Tests," *Journal of Advertising Research* 7, no. 4 (December 1967), p. 21.
9. Charles H. Sandage, Vernon Fryburger, and Kim Rotzoll, *Advertising Theory and Practice*, 10th ed. (Burr Ridge, IL: Richard D. Irwin, 1979).
10. Lyman E. Ostlund, "Advertising Copy Testing: A Review of Current Practices, Problems and Prospects," *Current Issues and Research in Advertising*, 1978, pp. 87-105.
11. Jack B. Haskins, "Factual Recall as a Measure of Advertising Effectiveness," *Journal of Advertising Research* 4, no. 1 (March 1964), pp. 2-7.
12. John Philip Jones and Margaret H. Blair, "Examining 'Conventional Wisdoms' about Advertising Effects with Evidence from Independent Sources," *Journal of Advertising Research*, November/December 1996, pp. 37-52.
13. Paul J. Watson and Robert J. Gatchel, "Autonomic Measures of Advertising," *Journal of Advertising Research* 19 (June 1979), pp. 15-26.
14. Priscilla A. LaBarbera and Joel D. Tucciarone, "GSR Reconsidered: A Behavior-based Approach to Evaluating and Improving the Sales Potency of Advertising," *Journal of Advertising Research*, September/ October 1995, pp. 33-40.
15. Flemming Hansen, "Hemispheric Lateralization: Implications for Understanding Consumer Behavior," *Journal of Consumer Research* 8 (1988), pp. 23-36.
16. Kevin Lane Keller, Susan E. Heckler, and Michael J. Houston, "The Effects of Brand Name Suggestiveness on Advertising Recall," *Journal of Marketing*, January 1998, pp. 48-57.
17. Jan Stapel, "Recall and Recognition: A Very Close Relationship," *Journal of Advertising Research*, July/August 1998, pp. 41-45.
18. Hubert A. Zielske, "Does Day-after Recall Penalize 'Feeling Ads'?" *Journal of Advertising Research* 22, no. 1 (1982), pp. 19-22.
19. Arthur J. Kover, "Why Copywriters Don't Like Advertising Research—and What Kind of Research Might They Accept," *Journal of Advertising Research*, March/April 1996, pp. RC8-RC10; Gary Levin, "Emotion Guides BBDO's Ad Tests," *Advertising Age*, January 29, 1990, p.12.
20. Terry Haller, "Day-after Recall to Persist Despite JWT Study; Other Criteria Looming," *Marketing News*, May 18, 1979, p. 4.
21. Dave Kruegel, "Television Advertising Effectiveness and Research Innovations," *Journal of Consumer Marketing* 5, no. 3 (Summer 1988), pp. 43-52.
22. Gary Levin, "Tracing Ads' Impact," *Advertising Age*, November 12, 1990, p. 49.
23. John Philip Jones, "Single-source Research Begins to Fulfill Its Promise," *Journal of Advertising Research*, May/June 1995, pp. 9-16.
24. Jeffrey L. Seglin, "The New Era of Ad Measurement," *Adweek's Marketing Week*, January 23, 1988, p. 24.
25. James F. Donius, "Marketing Tracking: A Strategic Reassessment and Planning Tool," *Journal of Advertising Research* 25, no. 1 (February/March 1985), pp. 15-19.
26. Russell I. Haley and Allan L. Baldinger, "The ARF Copy Research Validity Project," *Journal of Advertising Research*, April/May 1991, pp. 11-32.

CHAPTER NINE

1. Bruce Grondin, "Building North-South Links," *Marketing Magazine*, March 15, 2004.
2. Vicki Blake, "Hitching a Ride," *Marketing Magazine*, January 26, 2004.
3. Chris Powell, "Youth Confound Traditional Media," *Marketing Magazine*, March 1, 2004.
4. Lesley Young, "Primus Takes Aim at Cable, Telcos," *Marketing Magazine*, January 19, 2004.
5. Chuck Ross, "Study Finds for Continuity vs. Flights," *Advertising Age*, April 19, 1999, p. 2.
6. Lesley Young, "Campbell Warms Up to Bad Weather," *Marketing Magazine*, February 16, 2004.
7. Michael J. Naples, *Effective Frequency: The Relationship between Frequency and Advertising Effectiveness* (New York: Association of National Advertisers, 1979).
8. Joseph W. Ostrow, "Setting Frequency Levels: An Art or a Science?" *Journal of Advertising Research* 24 (August/September 1984), pp. 9-11.
9. Naples, *Effective Frequency*.
10. Joseph W. Ostrow, "What Level Frequency?" *Advertising Age*, November 1981, pp. 13-18.
11. Jack Myers, "More Is Indeed Better," *Media Week*, September 6, 1993, pp. 14-18; and Jim Surmanek, "One-Hit or Miss: Is a Frequency of One Frequently Wrong?" *Advertising Age*, November 27, 1995, p. 46.
12. Ostrow, "What Level Frequency?"
13. David A. Aaker and John G. Myers, *Advertising Management*, 3rd ed. (Englewood Cliffs, NJ: Prentice Hall, 1987), p. 474.
14. Joel N. Axelrod, "Induced Moods and Attitudes toward Products," *Journal of Advertising Research* 3 (June 1963), pp. 19-24; Lauren E. Crane, "How Product, Appeal, and Program Affect Attitudes toward Commercials," *Journal of Advertising Research* 4 (March 1964), p. 15.
15. *McGraw-Hill Lap Report* no. 3151 (New York: McGraw-Hill, 1988); Alan D. Fletcher, *Target Marketing through the Yellow Pages* (Troy, MI: Yellow Pages Publishers Association, 1991), p. 23.
16. Frank M. Bass, "A Simultaneous Equation Regression Study of Advertising and Sales of Cigarettes," *Journal of Marketing Research* 6, no. 3 (August 1969), p. 291; David A. Aaker and James M. Carman, "Are You Overadvertising?" *Journal of Advertising Research* 22, no. 4 (August/September 1982), pp. 57-70.
17. Julian A. Simon and Johan Arndt, "The Shape of the Advertising Response Function," *Journal of Advertising Research* 20, no. 4 (1980), pp. 11-28.
18. Paul B. Luchsinger, Vernan S. Mullen, and Paul T. Jannuzzo, "How Many Advertising Dollars Are Enough?" *Media Decisions* 12 (1977), p. 59.
19. Paul W. Farris, *Determinants of Advertising Intensity: A Review of the Marketing Literature* (Report no. 77-109, Marketing Science Institute, Cambridge, MA, 1977).
20. John P. Jones, "Ad Spending: Maintaining Market Share," *Harvard Business Review*, January/February 1990, pp. 38-42; and James C. Schroer, "Ad Spending: Growing Market Share," *Harvard Business Review*, January/February 1990, pp. 44-48.

21. Randall S. Brown, "Estimating Advantages to Large-Scale Advertising," *Review of Economics and Statistics* 60 (August 1978), pp. 428–37.

22. Kent M. Lancaster, "Are There Scale Economies in Advertising?" *Journal of Business* 59, no. 3 (1986), pp. 509–26.

23. Johan Arndt and Julian Simon, "Advertising and Economics of Scale: Critical Comments on the Evidence," *Journal of Industrial Economics* 32, no. 2 (December 1983), pp. 229–41; Aaker and Carman, "Are You Overadvertising?"

24. George S. Low and Jakki J. Mohr, "The Budget Allocation between Advertising and Sales Promotion: Understanding the Decision Process," 1991 AMA Educators' Proceedings, Chicago, Summer 1991, pp. 448–57.

25. Melvin E. Salveson, "Management's Criteria for Advertising Effectiveness" (Proceedings 5th Annual Conference, Advertising Research Foundation, New York, 1959), p. 25.

26. Robert Settle and Pamela Alreck, "Positive Moves for Negative Times," *Marketing Communications*, January 1988, pp. 19–23.

27. James O. Peckham, "Can We Relate Advertising Dollars to Market Share Objectives?" in *How Much to Spend for Advertising*, ed. M. A. McNiven (New York: Association of National Advertisers, 1969), p. 30.

28. George S. Low and Jakki Mohr, "Setting Advertising and Promotion Budgets in Multi-Brand Companies," *Journal of Advertising Research*, January/February 1999, pp. 667–78.

CHAPTER TEN

1. Television Bureau of Canada website (www.tvb.ca).
2. 2001 Fall Survey, BBM Canada.
3. "Making the Most of Magazines," *Marketing Magazine*, October 15, 2001.
4. Laura Petrecca, "4A's: Production Costs for TV Spots Up by 6%," *Advertising Age*, August 18, 1997, p. 30.
5. Joe Flint, "Commercial Clutter on TV Networks Rises to Record," *The Wall Street Journal*, March 2, 2000, p. B18.
6. Lex van Meurs, "Zapp! A Study on Switching Behavior during Commercial Breaks," *Journal of Advertising Research*, January/February 1998, pp. 43–53; John J. Cronin, "In-Home Observations of Commercial Zapping Behavior," *Journal of Current Issues and Research in Advertising* 17, no. 2 (Fall 1995), pp. 69–75.
7. John J. Cronin and Nancy Menelly, "In-Home Observations of Commercial Zapping Behavior," *Journal of Advertising* 21, no. 2 (June 1992), pp. 1–7.

8. Carrie Heeter and Bradley S. Greenberg, "Profiling the Zappers," *Journal of Advertising Research*, April/May 1985, pp. 9–12; Fred S. Zufryden, James H. Pedrick, and Avu Sandaralingham, "Zapping and Its Impact on Brand Purchase Behavior," *Journal of Advertising Research* 33 (January/February 1993), pp. 58–66; and Patricia Orsini, "Zapping: A Man's World," Spring Television Report, *Adweek's Marketing Week*, April 8, 1991, p. 3.

9. Lex van Meurs, "Zapp! A Study on Switching Behavior during Commercial Breaks," *Journal of Advertising Research*, January/February 1998, pp. 43–53.

10. Christopher Kelly, "What They Want, When They Want It," *Marketing Magazine*, May 5, 2003.

11. Dennis Kneal, "Zapping of TV Ads Appears Pervasive," *The Wall Street Journal*, April 25, 1988, p. 27.

12. John J. Cronin and Nancy Menelly, "Discrimination vs. Avoidance: 'Zipping' of Television Commercials," *Journal of Advertising* 21, no. 2 (June 1992), pp. 1–7.

13. Linda F. Alwitt and Parul R. Prabhaker, "Identifying Who Dislikes Television Advertising: Not by Demographics Alone," *Journal of Advertising Research* 32, no. 5 (1992), pp. 30–42.

14. Banwari Mittal, "Public Assessment of TV Advertising: Faint Praise and Harsh Criticism," *Journal of Advertising Research* no. 34, 1 (1994), pp. 35–53; Ernest F. Larkin, "Consumer Perceptions of the Media and Their Advertising Content," *Journal of Advertising* 8 (1979), pp. 5–7.

15. Lucy L. Henke, "Young Children's Perceptions of Cigarette Brand Advertising Symbols: Awareness, Affect, and Target Market Identification," *Journal of Advertising* 24, no. 4 (Winter 1995), pp. 13–28.

16. Susanne Boyce, "Cooking with Gas," *Marketing Magazine*, May 10, 2004.

17. Janet Eastwood, "Specialty is Our Specialty" *Marketing Magazine*, November 10, 2003.

18. Rick White & Mary Kreuk, "Money Show Management," *Marketing Magazine*, May 3, 2004.

19. Tim Wilson, "Give Digital a Chance," *Marketing Magazine*, March 29, 2004.

20. Chris Powell, "Follow the Viewer," *Marketing Magazine*, May 17, 2004.

21. Bruce Grondin, "No More BBM vs. Nielsen," *Marketing Magazine*, October 15, 2001; Chris Powell, "CanWest picks BBM over Nielsen," *Marketing Magazine*, June 3, 2002; www.bbm.ca; www.nielsenmedia.ca; www.tvb.ca.

22. Suein L. Hwang, "Old Media Get a Web Windfall," *The Wall Street Journal*, September 17, 1999, p. B1.

23. Verne Gay, "Image Transfer: Radio Ads Make Aural History," *Advertising Age*, January 24, 1985, p. 1.

24. Avery Abernethy, "Differences Between Advertising and Program Exposure for Car Radio Listening," *Journal of Advertising Research* 31, no. 2 (April/May 1991), pp. 33–42.

25. Martin Peers, "Radio Produces Both Gains and Skeptics," *The Wall Street Journal*, January 1, 1999, p. B6.

26. Ibid.

CHAPTER ELEVEN

1. Herbert E. Krugman, "The Measurement of Advertising Involvement," *Public Opinion Quarterly* 30 (Winter 1966–67), pp. 583–96.

2. Chris Powell, "A Pro-Barf Buy," Marketing Magazine, April 5, 2004; Eve Lazarus, "The Luxe Approach," *Marketing Magazine*, March 29, 2004.

3. Barb Grant, "Getting the Right Balance," *Marketing Magazine*, September 22, 2003.

4. Chris Powell, "La différence" *Marketing Magazine*, May 10, 2004.

5. *The Magazine Handbook* (New York: Magazine Publishers of America, 1999).

6. *The Magazine Handbook*.

7. Ibid.

8. *A Study of Media Involvement*, Vol. 7 (New York: Magazine Publishers of America, 1996).

9. Mary Pompili and Janet Eger, "Power Tools," *Marketing Magazine*, April 19, 2004.

10. Christine Larson, "Made to Order," *Adweek*, October 25, 1999, pp. 64–70.

11. Study cited in Jim Surmanek, *Media Planning: A Practical Guide* (Lincolnwood, IL: Crain Books, 1985).

12. *How Advertising Readership Is Influenced by Ad Size*, Report no. 110.1, Cahners Advertising Research, Newton, MA; and *Larger Advertisements Get Higher Readership*, LAP Report no. 3102, McGraw-Hill Research, New York.

13. *Effect of Size, Color and Position on Number of Responses to Recruitment Advertising*, LAP Report no. 3116, McGraw-Hill Research, New York.

14. Junu Bryan Kim, "Cracking the Barrier of Two Dimensions," *Advertising Age*, October 6, 1991, pp. 32, 34.

15. Maureen Cavan, "Building Our Own," *Marketing Magazine*, April 14, 2003.

16. David Chilton, "The Lazarus Syndrome," *Marketing Magazine*, April 14, 2003.

17. Briefs, *Marketing Magazine*, April 14, 2003.

18. Lesley Young, "Magazines: Briefs," *Marketing Magazine*, September 22, 2003.

19. Paul-Mark Rendon, "Osprey Takes Flight," *Marketing Magazine*, August 11, 2003.
20. Norma Ramage, "Frisky Business," *Marketing Magazine*, May 3, 2004.
21. Randy Stein, "The Intimate Medium," *Marketing Magazine*, August 11, 2003.
22. Chris Powell, "When Push Comes to Shove It," *Marketing Magazine*, March 15, 2004.
23. Ann Marie Kerwin, "Print's Power Play," *Advertising Age: The Next Century*, special issue, 1999.

CHAPTER TWELVE

1. *Adweek*, August 25, 1997, p. 3.
2. Mukesh Bhargava and Naveen Donthu, "Sales Response to Outdoor Advertising," *Journal of Advertising Research*, August 1999, pp. 7–18.
3. Lynne Kilpatrick, "Taking a Retail Approach All the Way to the Bank," *Marketing Magazine*, September 22, 2003.
4. Chris Powell, "Hip to be Square," *Marketing Magazine*, March 10, 2003.
5. Maritz AmeriPoll, August 1998.
6. Tom Shepansky, "The Exotic Tuna," *Marketing Magazine*, March 10, 2003.
7. Danny Kucharsky, "Outdoor's Measurement Challenge," *Marketing Magazine*, May 17, 2004.
8. Sally Basmajian, "Walking the Talk," *Marketing Magazine*, September 15, 2003.
9. "Cinema Advertising Comes of Age," *Marketing Magazine*, May 6, 2002.
10. Michael A. Belch and Don Sciglimpaglia, "Viewers' Evaluations of Cinema Advertising," *Proceedings of the American Institute for Decision Sciences*, March 1979, pp. 39–43.
11. Adam Snyder, "Are Spots on Home Video Badvertising?" *Brandweek*, January 29, 1996, p. 40.
12. Alice Cuneo, "Now Playing: Gap, Target Take Retail to the Movies," *Advertising Age*, June 9, 1997, p. 14.
13 David Kalish, "Supermarket Sweepstakes," *Marketing & Media Decisions*, November 1988, p. 34.
14. Promotional Products Association International (Irving, TX), 1996.
15. 2003 Promotional Products Industry Sales Volume Study, Promotional Products Association of Canada, May 2003.
16. George L. Herpel and Steve Slack, *Specialty Advertising: New Dimensions in Creative Marketing* (Irving, TX: Specialty Advertising Association, 1983), pp. 76, 79–80.
17. Ibid., p. 78.
18. M. J. Caballero and J. B. Hunt, *Smilin' Jack: Measuring Goodwill*, unpublished research report from the Center for Professional Selling, Baylor University, 1989; M. J. Cooper and J. B. Hunt, *How Specialty Advertising Affects Goodwill*, research report of

Specialty Advertising Association International (now PPAI), Irving, TX, 1992.
19. Herpel and Slack, *Specialty Advertising*, p. 75.
20. Carol Hall, "Branding the Yellow Pages," *Marketing & Media Decisions*, April 1989, p. 3.
21. Ibid., p. 5.
22. Yellow Pages Publishers Association, 2000.
23. J. D. Reed, "Plugging Away in Hollywood," *Time*, January 2, 1998, p. 103.
24. Philip J. Hart, "Product Placement for Dummies," *Marketing Magazine*, May 5, 2003; Paul-Mark Rendon, "Casting Call," *Marketing Magazine*, May 5, 2003.
25. Philip J. Hart, "Product Placement for Dummies," *Marketing Magazine*, May 5, 2003.
26. Ibid.
27. Ibid.
28. Danny Kucharsky, "A New Brand of Show," *Marketing Magazine*, May 5, 2003.
29. Paul-Mark Rendon, "Casting Call," *Marketing Magazine*, May 5, 2003.
30. Rosanne Caron, "On the Right Track," *Marketing Magazine*, July 14, 2003.
31. Philip J. Hart, "Product Placement for Dummies," *Marketing Magazine*, May 5, 2003.
32. Wahjudi Harsono and Elizabeth Kan, "Reaching the Target," *Marketing Magazine*, May 5, 2003.
33. Danny Kucharsky, "A New Brand of Show," *Marketing Magazine*, May 5, 2003.
34. Danny Kucharsky, "Rona Wants to Build a Stronger Image," *Marketing Magazine*, March 24, 2003.
35. Paul-Mark Rendon, "Casting Call," *Marketing Magazine*, May 5, 2003.
36. Pola Gupta and Kenneth Lord, "Product Placement in Movies: The Effect of Prominence and Mode on Audience Recall," *Journal of Current Issues and Research in Advertising* 20, no. 1 (Spring 1998), pp. 1–29.
37. Pola B. Gupta and Stephen J. Gould, "Consumers' Perceptions of the Ethics and Acceptability of Product Placements in Movies: Product Category and Individual Differences," *Journal of Current Issues and Research in Advertising* 19, no. 1 (Spring 1997), pp. 40–49.

CHAPTER THIRTEEN

1. Louis J. Haugh, "Defining and Redefining," *Advertising Age*, February 14, 1983, p. M44.
2. Scott A. Nielsen, John Quelch, and Caroline Henderson, "Consumer Promotions and the Acceleration of Product Purchases," in *Research on Sales Promotion: Collected Papers*, ed. Katherine E. Jocz (Cambridge, MA:

Marketing Science Institute, 1984).
3. J. Jeffrey Inman and Leigh McAlister, "Do Coupon Expiration Dates Affect Consumer Behavior?" *Journal of Marketing Research* 31, August 1994, pp. 423–28.
4. "Promotion Trends 2000," *Promo*, May 2000, p. A5.
5. "Slow + Steady: Promo's Exclusive Annual Report of the U.S. Promotion Industry," *Promo*, April 2002.
6. Betsy Spethman, "Sudden Impact," *Promo*, April 1999, pp. 42–48; Betsy Spethman,"Is Advertising Dead?" *Promo*, September 1998, pp. 32–36.
7. Richard Sale, "Evaluation in Evolution," *Promo*, September 1998, pp. 63–68.
8. Richard Sale, "Attack," *Promo*, September 1999, pp. 79–84.
9. *The Effects of Promotion Stimuli on Consumer Purchase Behavior* (Glenview, IL: FSI Council, 1999).
10. "1996 Trend Report," Actmedia, Inc., Anaheim, CA.
11. Brent Armstrong, "The First Meal's Not Enough," *Marketing Magazine*, September 10, 2001.
12. Al Urbanski, "Techno Promo," *Promo*, August 1998, pp. 48–52, 146, 147.
13. NCH Reporter, no. 1 (Nielsen Clearing House, 1983).
14. *The Magazine Handbook*, no. 59 (New York: Magazine Publishers of America, 1991).
15. Judann Dagnoli, "Jordan Hits Ad Execs for Damaging Brands," *Advertising Age*, November 4, 1991, p. 47.
16. Peter Widdis, "Bringing Brands to Life," *Marketing Magazine*, January 15, 2001.
17. "Promo's New Prominence," *Marketing Magazine*, September 3, 2001.
18. "It's Elementary," *Marketing Magazine*, December 3, 2001.
19. R. M. Prentice, "How to Split Your Marketing Funds Between Advertising and Promotion Dollars," *Advertising Age*, January 10, 1977, pp. 41–42, 44.
20. Betsy Spethmann, "Money and Power," *Brandweek*, March 15, 1993, p. 21.
21. Adapted from Terrence A. Shimp, *Advertising, Promotion, and Supplemental Aspect of Integrated Marketing Communication*, 4th ed. (Fort Worth, TX: Dryden Press, 1997), p. 487.
22. Brian C. Deslauries and Peter B. Everett, "The Effects of Intermittent and Continuous Token Reinforcement on Bus Ridership," *Journal of Applied Psychology* 62 (August 1977), pp. 369–75.
23. Michael L. Rothschild and William C. Gaidis, "Behavioural Learning Theory: Its Relevance to Marketing and Promotions," *Journal of Marketing Research* 45, no. 2 (Spring 1981), pp. 70–78.

24. "Hostess' Heroes," *Marketing Magazine*, August 6, 2001.

25. "Trial and Conversion VI: Consumers' Reactions to Samples and Demonstrations," Promotional Marketing Association, Inc. 2002.

26. Peter Breen, "Sophisticated Sampling," *Promo*, September 1999, pp. 63–68.

27. Lesley Young, "Marketing Direct Briefs," *Marketing Magazine*, November 3, 2003.

28. Couponing Facts, www.couponscanada.org.

29. J. Jeffrey Inman and Leigh McAlister, "Do Coupon Expiration Dates Affect Consumer Behavior?"

30. Wayne Mouland, "Choosing the Right Face Value," *Marketing Magazine*, May 10, 2004.

31. Redemption rates for all coupons provided by Wayne Mouland of Resolve Corporation.

32. Betsy Spethmann, "A Wake-Up Call at Breakfastime," *Promo*, December 1996, pp. 27–28.

33. Jack Neff, "P&G Extends Co-branded Coupons," *Advertising Age*, June 3, 1996, p. 9.

34. Lesley Young, "Stores Remain Wary of Web Coupons," *Marketing Magazine*, September 29, 2003.

35. Survey by Oxtoby-Smith, Inc., cited in "Many Consumers View Rebates as a Bother," *The Wall Street Journal*, April 13, 1989, p. B1.

36. William R. Dean, "Irresistable But Not Free of Problems," *Advertising Age*, October 6, 1980, pp. S1–12.

37. Eric Schmuckler, "Two Action Figures to Go, Hold the Burger," *Brandweek*, April 1, 1996, pp. 38–39.

38. "Mickey May Be the Big Winner in Disney–McDonald's Alliance," *The Wall Street Journal*, May 24, 1996, p. B5.

39. Michelle Halpern, "Labatt's Big PROMO! Score," *Marketing Magazine*, October 6, 2003.

40. "Cereal Killer," *Marketing Magazine*, May 14, 2001.

41. "Doughboy Promo Pops Off the Shelf," *Marketing Magazine*, January 14, 2002.

42. "Sweepstakes Fever," *Forbes*, October 3, 1988, pp. 164–66.

43. Wayne Mouland, "Sweeping Up Additional Sales," *Marketing Magazine*, October 6, 2003.

44. "P&G and MuchMusic Head to the Prom," *Marketing Magazine*, February 23, 2001; "Much, P&G Team Up to Target Teens," *Marketing Magazine*, March 5, 2001.

45. Paul-Mark Rendon, "Axe Seeks Best Mating Calls," *Marketing Magazine*, July 28, 2003.

46. Bob Woods, "Picking a Winner," *Promo*, August 1998, pp. 57–62.

47. Bruce Hawley, "More Than Just O.K.," *Marketing Magazine*, July 28, 2003.

48. Maxine S. Lans, "Legal Hurdles Big Part of Promotions Game," *Marketing News*, October 24, 1994, pp. 15–16.

49. Survey by Oxtoby-Smith, Inc., "Many Consumers View Rebates."

50. Peter Tat, William A. Cunningham III, and Emin Babakus, "Consumer Perceptions of Rebates," *Journal of Advertising Research*, August/September 1988, pp. 45–50.

51. Martha Graves, "Mail-In Rebates Stirring Shopper, Retailer Backlash," *Los Angeles Times*, January 11, 1989, Pt. IV, p. 1.

52. Edward A. Blair and E. Lair Landon, "The Effects of Reference Prices in Retail Advertisements," *Journal of Marketing* 45, no. 2 (Spring 1981), pp. 61–69.

53. Richard Sale, "Not Your Mother's Coupon," *Promo*, April 1999, pp. 56–61.

54. Paul-Mark Rendon, "Aveeno Smoothes the Slopes," *Marketing Magazine*, February 16, 2004.

55. Paul-Mark Rendon, "Coffee-Mate Gets Street Smart," *Marketing Magazine*, February 23, 2004.

56. "Takin' It to the Streets," *Marketing Magazine*, September 10, 2001.

57. Michelle Warren, "P&G Celebrates Small Communities with Nice'n Easy Skating Tour," *Marketing Magazine*, February 2, 2004.

58. Frank Green, "Battling for Shelf Control," *San Diego Union*, November 19, 1996, pp. C1, 6, 7.

59. Paul N. Bloom, Gregory T. Gundlach, and Joseph P. Cannon, "Slotting Allowances and Fees: Schools of Thought and Views of Practicing Managers," *Journal of Marketing*, 64, April 2000, pp. 92–108.

60. Melissa Campanelli, "What's in Store for EDLP?" *Sales & Marketing Management*, August 1993, pp. 56–59; "Procter & Gamble Hits Back," *Business Week*, July 19, 1993, pp. 20–22.

61. Amy Barone and Laurel Wentz, "Artzt Steering Barilla into EDLP Strategy," *Advertising Age*, February 26, 1996, p. 10.

62. Tom Steinhagen, "Space Management Shapes Up with Planograms," *Marketing News*, November 12, 1990, p. 7.

63. Srinath Gopalakrishna, Gary L. Lilien, Jerome D. Williams, and Ian K. Sequeria, "Do Trade Shows Pay Off?" *Journal of Marketing* 59, July 1995, pp. 75–83.

64. Cynthia Rigg, "Hard Times Means Growth for Co-op Ads," *Advertising Age*, November 12, 1990, p. 24.

65. Edwin L. Artzt, "The Lifeblood of Brands," *Advertising Age*, November 4, 1991, p. 32.

66. "Everyone Is Bellying Up to This Bar," *Business Week*, January 27, 1992, p. 84.

67. Jack Neff, "The New Brand Management," *Advertising Age*, November 8, 1999, pp. S2, 18; Benson P. Shapiro, "Improved Distribution with Your Promotional Mix," *Harvard Business Review*, March/April 1977, p. 116; and Roger A. Strang, "Sales Promotion—Fast Growth, Faulty Management," *Harvard Business Review*, July/August 1976, p. 119.

68. Priya Raghubir and Kim Corfman, "When Do Price Promotions Affect Pretrial Brand Evaluations?" *Journal of Marketing Research* 36 (May 1999), pp. 211–22.

69. Alan G. Sawyer and Peter H. Dickson, "Psychological Perspectives on Consumer Response to Sales Promotion," in *Research on Sales Promotion: Collected Papers*, ed. Katherine E. Jocz (Cambridge, MA: Marketing Science Institute, 1984).

70. William E. Myers, "Trying to Get Out of the Discounting Box," *Adweek*, November 11, 1985, p. 2.

71. Leigh McAlister, "Managing the Dynamics of Promotional Change," in *Looking at the Retail Kaleidoscope*, Forum IX (Stamford, CT: Donnelley Marketing, April 1988).

72. "Promotions Blemish Cosmetic Industry," *Advertising Age*, May 10, 1984, pp. 22–23, 26.

73. Elizabeth Gardener and Minakshi Trivedi, "A Communications Framework to Evaluate Sales Promotion Strategies," *Journal of Advertising Research*, May/June 1998, pp. 67–71.

CHAPTER FOURTEEN

1. Raymond Simon, *Public Relations, Concept and Practices*, 2nd ed. (Columbus, OH: Grid Publishing, 1980), p. 8.

2. Scott M. Cutlip, Allen H. Center, and Glen M. Broom, *Effective Public Relations*, 8th ed., (Upper Saddle River, N.J.: Prentice Hall, 2000).

3. Richard E. Rotman, When Worlds Combine," *Marketing Magazine*, September 29, 2003.

4. William N. Curry, "PR Isn't Marketing," *Advertising Age*, December 18, 1991, p. 18.

5. Martha M. Lauzen, "Imperialism and Encroachment in Public Relations," *Public Relations Review* 17, (3) (Fall 1991), pp. 245–55.

6. Cutlip, Center, and Broom, *Effective Public Relations*.

7. Raymond Serafin, "Cars Squeeze Mileage from Awards," *Advertising Age*, June 4, 1990, p. 36.

8. Simon, Public Relations, p. 164.

9. John E. Marston, *Modern Public Relations* (New York: McGraw-Hill, 1979).

10. Karin Scott, "Beyond Press Coverage," *Marketing Magazine*, June 16, 2003.

11. Thomas L. Harris, "How MPR Adds Value to Integrated Marketing Communications," *Public Relations Quarterly*, Summer 1993, pp. 13–18.

12. Raymond Simon, *Public Relations, Concepts and Practices*, 3rd ed. (New York: John Wiley & Sons, 1984), p. 291.

13. Walter K. Lindenmann, "An Effectiveness Yardstick to Measure Public Relations Success," *Public Relations Quarterly* 38, no. 1 (Spring 1993), pp. 7–10.

14. Deborah Holloway, "How to Select a Measurement System That's Right for You," *Public Relations Quarterly* 37, no. 3 (Fall 1992), pp. 15–18.

15. Julie Rusciolelli, "PR Discovers Metrics," *Marketing Magazine*, March 29, 2004.

16. Linda Smith, "When the Trust Begins to Rust," *Marketing Magazine*, March 1, 2004.

17. Norma Ramage, "Shell Builds a Worldwide Reputation," *Marketing Magazine*, September 15, 2003.

18. Jaye S. Niefeld, "Corporate Advertising," *Industrial Marketing*, July 1980, pp. 64–74.

19. Lesley Young, "New Names, New Challenges," *Marketing Magazine*, March 19, 2001.

20. John Burnett, "Shopping for Sponsorships? Integration Is Paramount," *Brandweek*, February 14, 1994, p. 18.

21. Prakash Sethi, *Advertising and Large Corporations* (Lexington, MA: Lexington Books, 1977), pp. 7–8.

22. Harvey Meyer, "When the Cause Is Just," *Journal of Business Strategy*, November/December 1999, pp. 27–31.

23. Michelle Warren, "Cause Commotion," *Marketing Magazine*, October 6, 2003.

24. Harvey Meyer, "When the Cause is Just," p. 28.

25. Michelle Warren, "Cause Commotion," *Marketing Magazine*, October 6, 2003.

26. Sarah Dobson, "The Hucksters are Gone," *Marketing Magazine*, April 5, 2004.

27. Michelle Warren, "The Sporting Life," *Marketing Magazine*, February 23, 2004.

28. Mark Harrison, "Own Alone," *Marketing Magazine*, February 23, 2004.

29. Chad Richardson, "A Piece of the Rock," *Marketing Magazine*, February 23, 2004.

30. Dan Cimoroni, "Don't Just Wish Upon a Star," *Marketing Magazine*, February 23, 2004.

31. "Clairol Expands CFL Sponsor Roster," *Marketing Magazine*, July 30, 2001.

32. "The 'Bush Leagues,'" *Marketing Magazine*, May 14, 2001.

33. Bettina Cornwell and Isabelle Maignan, "An International Review of Sponsorship Research," *Journal of Advertising*, March 1998.

34. Michel Tuan Pham, "The Evaluation of Sponsorship Effectiveness: A Model and Some Methodological Considerations," *Gestion* 2000, pp. 47–65.

35. Sandra Iacobelli, "Harder-Working Sponsorships," *Marketing Magazine*, October 6, 2003.

36. Ian Malcolm, "Made to Measure," *Marketing Magazine*, February 23, 2004.

37. Karen Benezra, "Cause and Effects Marketing," *Brandweek*, April 22, 1996, p. 38.

38. Donath, "Corporate Communications," p. 52.

CHAPTER FIFTEEN

1. Stan Rapp and Thomas I. Collins, *Maximarketing* (New York: McGraw-Hill, 1987).

2. Peter D. Bennett, ed., *Dictionary of Marketing Terms* (Chicago: American Marketing Association, 1988), p. 58.

3. *Canadian Marketing Association 2001 Fact Book*. (Don Mills: Canadian Marketing Association, 2001).

4. Jagdish N. Sheth, "Marketing Megatrends," *Journal of Consumer Marketing* 1, no. 1 (June 1983), pp. 5–13.

5. *Canadian Facts 2000*, Canada Post website, March 25, 2002.

6. "A Potent New Tool for Selling: Database Marketing," *Business Week*, September 5, 1994, pp. 56–59.

7. Herbert Kanzenstein and William S. Sachs, *Direct Marketing*, 2nd ed. (New York: Macmillan, 1992).

8. Lesley Young, "Campbell Evolves from 'Soup to Food' with New Direct Campaigns," *Marketing Magazine*, November 3, 2003.

9. *Canadian Marketing Association 2001 Fact Book*, 2001.

10. Ibid.

11. *Canadian Facts 2000*, Canada Post website, March 25, 2002.

12. *Canadian Marketing Association 2001 Fact Book*, 2001.

13. Cleveland Horton, "Porsche 300,000: The New Elite," *Advertising Age*, February 5, 1990, p. 8.

14. Lesley Young, "Home Depot Unveils 'Dream Book'" *Marketing Magazine*, October 20, 2003.

15. *Canadian Marketing Association 2001 Fact Book*, 2001.

16. Profiling study by Naveen Donthu and David Gilliland.

17. Anne-Marie Crawford, "Peugeot Develops First TV Advertorials for Cars," *Marketing Magazine*, December 9, 1999, p. 9.

18. *Canadian Marketing Association 2001 Fact Book*, 2001.

19. Lesley Young, "HBC Custom Magazine *Living Spree* to Track Readers' Shopping Habits," *Marketing Magazine*, August 11, 2003.

20. *Canadian Marketing Association 2001 Fact Book*, 2001.

21. Tom Eisenhart, "Tele-media: Marketing's New Dimension," *Business Marketing*, February 1991, pp. 50–53.

22. Direct Marketing Association 2000.

23. *Canadian Marketing Association 2005 Fact Book*, 2005.

24. Michelle Warren, "Sprint Grows Up," *Marketing Magazine*, April 19, 2004.

25. "Bear Market," *Direct*, December 1999, p. 1+.

CHAPTER SIXTEEN

1. Statistics Canada, Household Internet Use Survey, *The Daily*, July 8, 2004.

2. http://www.statcan.ca, online data tables.

3. Statistics Canada, *The Daily*, April 16, 2004.

4. Laurie Freeman, "HP Gambles $100 M on Securing Its Net Position," *Business Marketing*, June 1999, pp. 1+.

5. Melinda Ligos, "Point, Click, Sell," *Sales and Marketing Management*, May 1999, pp. 51–55.

6. Ibid.

7. David A. Aaker, "Fast Brand Building in Slow-Growth Markets," *Strategy and Business*, third quarter 2002, pp. 48–57.

8. Karen Benezra, "Branding the Web," *Chief Executive*, January 2001, pp. 30–34.

9. Erwin Ephron, "Direct Response or Branding?" *Advertising Age*, November 5, 2001, p. 14.

10. Sean Callahan, "Branding: Is it worth it?" *B to B*, August 20, 2001, p. 1, 24.

11. Jupiter Media Metrix.

12. Chad Kaydo, "You've Got Sales," *Sales and Marketing Management*, October 1999, pp. 29–39.

13. Shel Holtz, *Public Relations on the Internet* (New York: American Management Association, 1998).

14. Sarah Dobson, "Taking the High Road," *Marketing Magazine*, April 7, 2003.

15. Gary Schwartz, "Mobile Marketing 101," *Marketing Magazine*, July 14, 2003.

16. Ibid.

17. Paul-Mark Rendon, "Does Text Sell?" *Marketing Magazine*, April 26, 2004.

18. Ibid.

19. Ellen Neuborne and Robert D. Hof, "Branding on the Net," *Business Week*, November 9, 1998, pp. 76–86.

20. Alexa Bezjian-Avery, "New Media Interactive Advertising vs. Traditional Advertising," *Journal of Advertising Research*, August 1998, pp. 23–32; Qimel Chen and William D. Wells, "Attitude toward the Site," *Journal of Advertising Research*, September 1999, pp. 27–38; Kim Bartel Sheehan and Sally J. McMillan, "Response Variation in E-Mail Surveys," *Journal of Advertising Research*, July 1999, pp. 45–54; and John Eighmey, "Profiling

User Responses to Commercial Websites," *Journal of Advertising Research*, May 1997, pp. 59–66.

21. "Pluggin' in and Logging on: Simultaneous TV and Internet Usage," *eMarketer* Issue 181, September 12, 2002, p. 1.

22. Joseph Menn, "Web Firms May Vastly Inflate Claims of 'Hits'," *Los Angeles Times*, April 17, 2000, pp. 1–8.

23. Beth Cox, "Top 50 Web Sites Get 95 Percent of All Ad Dollars," Internet News.com, June 17, 1999.

24. Teresa Buyikan and Angela Dawson, "Dropping RPA, Web TV Puts Account in Play—Adweek," Adweek.com, May 10, 1999.

25. Patrick Seitz, "Open TV Eyes an Opening in Interactive TV Market," *Investors Business Daily*, February 10, 2000, p. A6.

26. Chris Powell, "The Flashing 'i'," *Marketing Magazine*, December 10, 2001.

27. Mark Sherman, "TV Gets Personal," *Marketing Magazine*, May 7, 2001.

28. Carey Toane, "Tune In, Turn On, Buy Lots," *Marketing Magazine*, April 16, 2001.

29. Chris Powell, "Media Cautious about Enhanced TV," *Marketing Magazine*, May 20, 2002.

CHAPTER SEVENTEEN

1. Jack Neff, "P&G Redefines the Brand Manager," *Advertising Age*, October 13, 1997, pp. 1, 18, 20.

2. Thomas J. Cosse and John E. Swan, "Strategic Marketing Planning by Product Managers—Room for Improvement?" *Journal of Marketing* 47 (Summer 1983), pp. 92–102.

3. "Behind the Tumult at P&G," Fortune, March 7, 1994, pp. 74–82; "Category Management: New Tools changing Life for Manufacturers, Retailers," *Marketing News*, September 25, 1989, pp. 2, 19.

4. Cosse and Swan, "Strategic Marketing Planning by Product Managers—Room for Improvement?"

5. Victor P. Buell, *Organizing for Marketing/Advertising Success* (New York: Association of National Advertisers, 1982).

6. M. Louise Ripley, "What Kind of Companies Take Their Advertising In-House?" *Journal of Advertising Research*, October/November 1991, pp. 73–80.

7. Bruce Horovitz, "Some Companies Say the Best Ad Agency Is No Ad Agency at All," *Los Angeles Times*, July 19, 1989, Sec IV, p. 5.

8. Bradley Johnson and Alice Z. Cuneo, "Gatey 2000 Taps DMB&B," *Advertising Age*, March 24, 1997, p. 2.

9. "Do Your Ads Need a Superagency?" *Fortune*, April 27, 1987, p. 81.

10. Sally Goll Beatty, "Global Needs Challenge Midsize Agencies," The

Wall Street Journal, December 14, 1995, p. B9.

11. Gordon Fairclough, "Pace of Ad Mergers Is Expected to Continue," *The Wall Street Journal*, April 23, 1999, p. B2.

12. Bob Lammons, "A Good Account Exec Makes a Big Difference," *Marketing News*, June 3, 1996, p. 12.

13. "Call in the Specialists," *Marketing Magazine*, June 4, 2001.

14. Jeffery Thibodeau, "Better Ways to Get Paid," *Marketing Magazine*, March 22, 2004.

15. www.aca-online.com

16. Judann Pollack, "ANA Survey: Under 50% Pay Agency Commissions," *Advertising Age*, June 15, 1998.

17. Paul-Mark Rendron, "Pay As You Play," *Marketing Magazine*, June 21, 2004.

18. "The Benefits of PBR," Marketing Magazine, July 9, 2001; "Executive Summary," *Marketing Magazine*, July 9, 2001; "Finding the Right PBR Performance Measures," *Marketing Magazine*, July 16, 2001.

19. Chris Daniels, "Part-Time Partners," *Marketing Magazine*, June 23, 2003.

20. Michelle Warren, "Project Work," *Marketing Magazine*, April 19, 2004; Michelle Warren, "The Year of Treading Water," *Marketing Magazine*, November 24, 2003.

21. Prema Nakra, "The Changing Role of Public Relations in Marketing Communications," *Public Relations Quarterly*, 1 (1991) pp. 42–45.

22. "A Potent New Tool For Selling: Database Marketing," *Business Week*, September 5, 1994, pp. 56–62.

23. Mark Gleason and Debra Aho Williamson, "The New Interactive Agency," *Advertising Age*, February 2, 1996, pp. S1–11.

24. "Ad Firms Falter on One-Stop Shopping," *The Wall Street Journal*, December 1, 1988, p. 81; and "Do Your Ads Need a Superagency?" *Fortune*, April 27, 1987, p. 81.

25. Hy Haberman, "Walking the Talk on Integration," *Marketing Magazine*, February 9, 2004.

26. Philip J. Kitchen and Don E. Schultz, "A Multi-Country Comparison of the Drive for IMC," *Journal of Advertising Research*, January/February 1999, pp. 21–38.

27. David N. McArthur and Tom Griffin, "A Marketing Management View of Integrated Marketing Communications," *Journal of Advertising Research*, 37, no. 5 (September/October) 1997, pp. 19–26; and Adrienne Ward Fawcett, "Integrated Marketing—Marketers Convinced: Its Time Has Arrived," *Advertising Age*, November 6, 1993, pp. S1–2.

28. Michelle Warren, "What Marketers Want," *Marketing Magazine*, November 24, 2003.

29. Kevin Astle, "The Shaky State of Marketer–Agency Relations," *Marketing Magazine*, November 24, 2003.

CHAPTER EIGHTEEN

1. Robert L. Heilbroner, "Demand for the Supply Side," *New York Review of Books* 38 (June 11, 1981), p. 40.

2. Chris Powell, "Digital Dogfight," *Marketing Magazine*, September 8, 2003.

3. Chris Powell, "The Inventory Debate," *Marketing Magazine*, January 26, 2004.

4. "Fanning the Embers," *Marketing Magazine*, September 10, 2001.

5. Stan Sutter, "Common Sense Evolution," *Marketing Magazine*, June 9, 2003.

6. Eric N. Berkowitz, Roger A. Kerin, Steven W. Hartley, William Rudedius, et al., *Marketing*, 5th ed. (Burr Ridge, IL: Irwin/McGraw-Hill, 1997), p. 102.

7. "Calvin's World," *Newsweek*, September 11, 1995, pp. 60–66.

8. Stephanie O'Donohoe, "Attitudes to Advertising: A Review of British and American Research," *International Journal of Advertising* 14 (1995), pp. 245–61.

9. Banwari Mittal, "Public Assessment of TV Advertising: Faint Praise and Harsh Criticism," *Journal of Advertising Research* 34, no. 1 (1994), pp. 35–53.

10. Sharon Shavitt, Pamela Lowery, and James Haefner, "Public Attitudes toward Advertising; More Favorable Than You Might Think," *Journal of Advertising Research*, July/August 1998, pp. 7–22.

11. Gita Venkataramini Johar, "Consumer Involvement and Deception from Implied Advertising Claims," *Journal of Marketing Research* 32 (August 1995), pp. 267–79; J. Edward Russo, Barbara L. Metcalf, and Debra Stephens, "Identifying Misleading Advertising," *Journal of Consumer Research* 8 (September 1981), pp. 119–31.

12. Ivan L. Preston, *The Great American Blow-Up: Puffery in Advertising and Selling* (Madison: University of Wisconsin Press, 1975), p. 3.

13. David Menzies, "Carlsberg Conspiracy," *Marketing Magazine*, March 29, 2004.

14. Shelby D. Hunt, "Informational vs. Persuasive Advertising: An Appraisal," *Journal of Advertising*, Summer 1976, pp. 5–8.

15. Banwari Mittal, "Public Assessment of TV Advertising: Faint Praise and Harsh Criticism"; J. C. Andrews, "The Dimensionality of Beliefs toward Advertising in General," *Journal of Advertising* 18, no. 1 (1989), pp. 26–35; Ron Alsop, "Advertisers Find the Climate Less Hostile Outside the

U.S.," *The Wall Street Journal*, December 10, 1987, p. 29.

16. David A. Aaker and Donald E. Bruzzone, "Causes of Irritation in Advertising," *Journal of Marketing*, Spring 1985, p. 47–57.

17. Stephen A. Greyser, "Irritation in Advertising," *Journal of Advertising Research* 13 (February 1973), pp. 3–10.

18. Ron Alsop, "Personal Product Ads Abound as Public Gets More Tolerant," *The Wall Street Journal*, April 14, 1986, p. 19.

19. Joanne Lipman, "Censored Scenes: Why You Rarely See Some Things in Television Ads," *The Wall Street Journal*, August 17, 1987, p. 17.

20. For an interesting analysis of an interpretation of this ad from a literary theory perspective see Aaron C. Ahuvia, "Social Criticism of Advertising: On the Role of Literary Theory and the Use of Data," *Journal of Advertising* 27, no. 1 (Spring 1998), pp. 143–62.

21. Scott Ward, Daniel B. Wackman, and Ellen Wartella, *How Children Learn to Buy: The Development of Consumer Information Processing Skills* (Beverly Hills, CA: Sage, 1979).

22. Thomas S. Robertson and John R. Rossiter, "Children and Commercial Persuasion: An Attribution Theory Analysis," *Journal of Consumer Research* 1, no. 1 (June 1974), pp. 13–20; and Scott Ward and Daniel B. Wackman, "Children's Information Processing of Television Advertising," in *New Models for Communications Research*, ed. G. Kline and P. Clark (Beverly Hills, CA: Sage, 1974), pp. 81–119.

23. Merrie Brucks, Gary M. Armstrong, and Marvin E. Goldberg, "Children's Use of Cognitive Defenses against Television Advertising: A Cognitive Response Approach," *Journal of Consumer Research* 14, no. 4 (March 1988), pp. 471–82.

24. For a discussion on consumer socialization, see Scott Ward, "Consumer Socialization," *Journal of Consumer Research* 1, no. 2 (September 1974), pp. 1–14.

25. Tamara F. Mangleburg and Terry Bristol, "Socialization and Adolescents' Skepticism toward Advertising," *Journal of Advertising* 27, no. 3 (Fall 1998), pp. 11–21.

26. Robert E. Hite and Randy Eck, "Advertising to Children: Attitudes of Business vs. Consumers," *Journal of Advertising Research*, October/November 1987, pp. 40–53; Ann D. Walsh, Russell N. Laczniak, and Les Carlson, "Mother's Preferences for Regulating Children's Television," *Journal of Advertising*, 27, no. 3 (Fall 1998), pp. 23–36.

28. Ronald Berman, *Advertising and Social Change* (Beverly Hills, CA: Sage, 1981), p. 13.

29. John K. Galbraith, *The New Industrial State* (Boston: Houghton Mifflin, 1967), cited in Richard W. Pollay, "The Distorted Mirror: Reflections on the Unintended Consequences of Advertising," *Journal of Marketing*, August 1986, p. 25.

30. Raymond A. Bauer and Stephen A. Greyser, "The Dialogue That Never Happens," *Harvard Business Review*, January/February 1969, pp. 122–28.

31. Morris B. Holbrook, "Mirror Mirror on the Wall, What's Unfair in the Reflections on Advertising," *Journal of Marketing* 5 (July 1987), pp. 95–103; and Theodore Levitt, "The Morality of Advertising," *Harvard Business Review*, July/August 1970, pp. 84–92.

32. Stephen Fox, *The Mirror Makers: A History of American Advertising and Its Creators* (New York: Morrow, 1984), p. 330.

33. Richard W. Pollay, "The Distorted Mirror: Reflections on the Unintended Consequences of Advertising," *Journal of Marketing* 50 (April 1986), p. 33.

34. Jules Backman, "Is Advertising Wasteful?" *Journal of Marketing* 32 (January 1968), pp. 2–8.

35. Hunt, "Informational vs. Persuasive Advertising."

36. Ibid., p. 6.

37. Kevin Goldman, "Survey Asks Which 'Green' Ads Are Read," *The Wall Street Journal*, April 11, 1994, p. B5.

38. Alice E. Courtney and Thomas W. Whipple, *Sex Stereotyping in Advertising* (Lexington, MA: Lexington Books, 1984).

39. Daniel J. Brett and Joanne Cantor, "The Portrayal of Men and Women in U.S. Television Commercials: A Recent Content Analysis and Trends of 15 Years," *Sex Roles* 18, no. 9/10 (1998), pp. 595–608; John B. Ford and Michael La Tour, "Contemporary Perspectives of Female Role Portrayals in Advertising," *Journal of Current Issues and Research in Advertising* 28, no. 1 (1996), pp. 81–93; "Body Shop, Zig Ad Lauded by Report," *Marketing Magazine*, March 18, 2002; "How Far Really?" *Marketing Magazine*, July 2, 2001.

40. Beverly A. Browne, "Gender Stereotypes in Advertising on Children's Television in the 1990s: A Cross-National Analysis," *Journal of Advertising* 27, no. 1 (Spring 1998), pp. 83–96.

41. Richard H. Kolbe, "Gender Roles in Children's Advertising: A Longitudinal Content Analysis," in *Current Issues and Research in Advertising*, ed. James H. Leigh and Claude R. Martin, Jr. (Ann Arbor: University of Michigan, 1990), pp. 197–206.

42. "Body Shop, Zig Ad Lauded by Report," *Marketing Magazine*, March 18, 2002; "How Far Really?" *Marketing Magazine*, July 2, 2001.

44. Steven M. Kates and Glenda Shaw-Garlock, "The Ever Entangling Web: A Study of Ideologies and Discourses in Advertising to Women," *Journal of Advertising* 28, no. 2 (Summer 1999), pp. 33–49.

45. Basil Englis, Michael Solomon, and Richard Ashmore, "Beauty before the Eyes of Beholders: The Cultural Encoding of Beauty Types in Magazine Advertising and Music Television," *Journal of Advertising*, June 1994, pp. 49–64.

46. Cyndee Miller, "Liberation for Women in Ads," *Marketing News*, August 17, 1992, p. 1; Adrienne Ward-Fawcett, "Narrowcast in Past, Women Earn Revised Role in Advertising," *Advertising Age*, October 4, 1993, p. S1.

47. James Stearns, Lynette S. Unger, and Steven G. Luebkeman, "The Portrayal of Blacks in Magazine and Television Advertising," in *AMA Educator's Proceedings*, ed. Susan P. Douglas and Michael R. Solomon (Chicago: American Marketing Association, 1987).

48. Robert E. Wilkes and Humberto Valencia, "Hispanics and Blacks in Television Commercials," *Journal of Advertising* 18, no. 1 (1989), pp. 19–26.

49. Julia Bristor, Renee Gravois Lee, and Michelle Hunt, "Race and Ideology: African American Images in Television Advertising," *Journal of Public Policy and Marketing* 14 (Spring 1995), pp. 48–59.

50. Corliss Green, "Ethnic Evaluations of Advertising: Interaction Effects of Strength of Ethnic Identification, Media Placement, and Degree of Racial Composition," *Journal of Advertising* 28, no. 1 (Spring 1999), pp. 49–64.

51. Charles R. Taylor and Barbara B. Stern, "Asian-Americans: Television Advertising and the 'Model Minority' Stereotype," *Journal of Advertising* 26, no. 2 (Summer 1997), pp. 47–61.

52. Jo Marney, "Counting Ethnic Canadians In," *Marketing Magazine*, June 4, 2001.

53. "Including Visible Minorities," *Marketing Magazine*, June 4, 2001; "Counting Ethnic Canadians In," *Marketing Magazine*, June 4, 2001; "A Toast to More Colour in Beer Ads," *Marketing Magazine*, June 4, 2001.

54. Jef I. Richards and John H. Murphy, II, "Economic Censorship and Free Speech: The Circle of Communication between Advertisers, Media and Consumers," *Journal of Current Issues and Research in Advertising* 18, no. 1 (Spring 1996), pp. 21–33.

55. Lawrence C. Soley and Robert L. Craig, "Advertising Pressure on Newspapers: A Survey," *Journal of Advertising*, December 1992, pp. 1–10.

56. Mark Simon, "Mercury News Ad Dispute Cooling Off: Advertisers Return While Reporters Stew," *San Francisco Business Chronicle*, July 15, 1994, p. B1.

57. Soley and Craig, "Advertising Pressure on Newspapers."

58. For a discussion of monopolies in the cereal industry, see Paul N. Bloom, "The Cereal Industry: Monopolists or Super Marketers?" *MSU Business Topics*, Summer 1978, pp. 41–49.

59. Lester G. Telser, "Advertising and Competition," *Journal of Political Economy*, December 1964, pp. 537–62.

60. Robert D. Buzzell, Bradley T. Gale, and Ralph G. M. Sultan, "Market Share—A Key to Profitability,"

Harvard Business Review, January/February 1975, pp. 97–106.

61. Robert D. Buzzell and Paul W. Farris, *Advertising Cost in Consumer Goods Industries*, Marketing Science Institute, Report no. 76, August 1976, p. 111; and Paul W. Farris and David J. Reibstein, "How Prices, Ad Expenditures, and Profits Are Linked," *Harvard Business Review*, November/December 1979, pp. 173–84.

62. Paul W. Farris and Mark S. Albion, "The Impact of Advertising on the Price of Consumer Products," *Journal of Marketing* 44, no. 3 (Summer 1980), pp. 17–35.

63. Ibid., p. 19.

64. Lee Benham, "The Effect of Advertising on the Price of Eyeglasses," *Journal of Law and Economics* 15 (October 1972), pp. 337–52.

65. Robert L. Steiner, "Does Advertising Lower Consumer Price?" *Journal of Marketing* 37, no. 4 (October 1973), pp. 19–26.

66. Farris and Albion, "The Impact of Advertising," p. 30.

67. James M. Ferguson, "Comments on 'The Impact of Advertising on the Price of Consumer Products,'" *Journal of Marketing* 46, no. 1 (Winter 1982), pp. 102–5.

68. Farris and Albion, "The Impact of Advertising."

69. Cyndee Miller, "The Marketing of Advertising," *Marketing News*, December 7, 1992, pp. 1, 2.

Credits and Acknowledgements

CHAPTER 1

Opening Photo: Andrew Simpson. **Exhibit 1-1:** Courtesy of V&S Vin and Spirit AB. Imported by the Absolut Spirits Company, New York, NY. **Exhibit 1-2:** Used by permission of Eveready Battery Company, Inc. **Exhibit 1-3:** Courtesy of Dairy Farmers of Ontario. Photography: Joaquin Rivas. **Exhibit 1-4:** Courtesy Johnson & Johnson Consumer Products, Inc. **Exhibit 1-5:** Courtesy E.I. du Pont de Nemours and Company. **Exhibit 1-6:** Courtesy of Energy Speaker Systems. **Exhibit 1-7:** Reprinted with permission by Lands' End, Inc. **Exhibit 1-8:** Courtesy of WestJet. **Exhibit 1-9:** Canadian Blood Services. 1/800 Alta Vista, Ottawa ON K1G 4J5. **Exhibit 1-10:** Courtesy of Dell Computer Corporation. **IMC Perspective 1-2:** CP/Steve White. **Exhibit 1-11:** © James Leynse/CORBIS SABA. **Exhibit 1-12:** Courtesy of Rado Watch Company Ltd. **Exhibit 1-13:** Courtesy of Pfizer Consumer Healthcare. **Exhibit 1-14:** Designs copyrighted by Tiffany and Company. **Exhibit 1-15:** Courtesy of McNeil Consumer Healthcare, 1999. **Exhibit 1-16:** Acushnet Company ©. Photography © Francine Zaslow. **Exhibit 1-17:** Courtesy of Honeywell. **Global Perspective 1-3:** CP/Steve White.

CHAPTER 2

Opening Photo: Photodisc. **Exhibit 2-1:** Courtesy of Mountain Equipment Co-op. **Exhibit 2-2:** Courtesy John Paul Mitchell Systems. **Exhibit 2-3:** Courtesy of Del Pharmaceuticals, Inc., a subsidiary of Del Laboratories, Inc. **Exhibit 2-4:** Courtesy of Rogers Communications Inc. **Exhibit 2-5:** © The Procter & Gamble Company. Used by permission. **Exhibit 2-6:** Used with permission from DaimlerChrysler Corp. **IMC Perspective 2-1:** AP/Wide World Photos. **Exhibit 2-7:** Courtesy Tropicana Products, Inc. **Exhibit 2-8:** Courtesy of Callaway Golf Company. **Exhibit 2-9:** Reprinted with permission from Labatt Brewing Company Limited. **Exhibit 2-10:** Fidelity Investments. © 2002 FMR Corp. All rights reserved. Used with permission. **Exhibit 2-11:** Director General Public Affairs, Department of National Defence. **Exhibit 2-12:** Courtesy of MADD. **IMC Perspective 2-2:** Ryan McVay/Getty Images. **Exhibit 2-13:** Reproduced with the permission of McDonald's Restaurants of Canada Limited. **IMC Perspective 2-3:** CP/Steve White. **Exhibit 2-14:** Courtesy of Novartis.

CHAPTER 3

Opening Photo: CP/Jeff McIntosh. **Global Perspective 3-1:** Courtesy of Coast Forest and Lumber Association. **Exhibit 3-1:** Courtesy Estee Lauder. **Exhibit 3-2:** © 1999 Time Inc. Reprinted by permission. **Exhibit 3-3:** Courtesy Johnson & Johnson Consumer Products, Inc. **Exhibit 3-4:** Courtesy of Zenith Electronics Corp. **Exhibit 3-5:** Courtesy Xerox Corp. **Exhibit 3-6:** Courtesy of Michelin North America. **Exhibit 3-7:** © H. J. Heinz Company, L.P. Used with permission. **Exhibit 3-8:** © The Procter & Gamble Company. Used by permission. **Global Perspective 3-2:** Courtesy of Whirlpool Corp. **Exhibit 3-9:** CP/Ryan Remiorz. **Exhibit 3-10:** Courtesy of Lancome, Paris. **IMC Perspective 3-3:** CP/Jeff McIntosh.

CHAPTER 4

Opening Photo: Courtesy of British Columbia Lottery Corporation. **Exhibit 4-1:** Courtesy of Toyota Motor North America, Inc. **Exhibit 4-2:** Courtesy of FPAC. **Exhibit 4-3:** Courtesy of Saputo Dairy. **Exhibit 4-4:** Courtesy of Hitachi America, Ltd. **IMC Perspective 4-2:** Courtesy of Maple Leaf Foods Inc.

CHAPTER 5

Opening Photo: Courtesy of the Toronto Blue Jays. **Exhibit 5-1:** Courtesy of Wolverine World Wide, Inc. **IMC Perspective 5-1:** Courtesy of Labatt Brewing Company Limited. **Exhibit 5-2:** Courtesy of Panasonic. **Exhibit 5-3:** Courtesy of The Pillsbury Company. **Exhibit 5-4:** © The Coca-Cola Company. "PowerAde," "PowerAde Light," the design of the stylized "P" and "Andean Chill" are trademarks of The Coca-Cola Company. **Exhibit 5-5:** Courtesy of Taxi/Cara Foods Ltd. **Exhibit 5-6:** © 2002 Lands' End, Inc. Used with permission. **Exhibit 5-7:** Courtesy Black & Decker. **Exhibit 5-8:** Courtesy The Valvoline Company, a division of Ashland Inc. **Exhibit 5-9:** Courtesy Fallon-McElligott for Rolling Stone. **Exhibit 5-10:** Courtesy America's Dairy Farmers, National Dairy Board. **IMC Perspective 5-2:** Courtesy of Savin. **Exhibit 5-11:** Courtesy Westin Hotels & Resorts. **Exhibit 5-12:** Courtesy of Polaroid Corp.

CHAPTER 6

Opening Photo: Courtesy of Taxi. **Exhibit 6-1:** © 2002 BMW of North America, LLC. Used with permission. The BMW name and logo are registered trademarks. **Exhibit 6-2:** Courtesy of Pfizer Canada Inc., Adams Division. **Exhibit 6-3:** Courtesy No Fear. **Exhibit 6-4:** Courtesy Leo Burnette Company, Inc. as agent for Hallmark Cards,

Incorporated. **Exhibit 6-5:** Courtesy 3M. **Exhibit 6-6:** Courtesy of Nissan North America, Inc. **IMC Perspective 6-1:** CP/Kevin Frayer. **IMC Perspective 6-2:** Courtesy of Hockey Canada. **Exhibit 6-7:** Courtesy of Nordica. **Exhibit 6-8:** Jeep. Used with permission from DaimlerChrysler Corp. **Exhibit 6-9:** Casey's is a registered trade-mark of PRC Trademarks Inc. **Exhibit 6-10:** Courtesy Bristol-Myers Squibb Co. **IMC Perspective 6-3:** Courtesy of Irving Oil Ltd. **Exhibit 6-11:** Courtesy Team One Advertising for LEXUS. **Exhibit 6-12:** Courtesy of Leo Burnett Company, Inc. for Callard & Bowser-Suchard, Inc. **Exhibit 6-13:** Courtesy MasterCard International Incorporated. **Exhibit 6-14:** Courtesy of Porsche Cars North America, Inc. **Exhibit 6-15:** Courtesy of HEAD/Penn Racquet Sports. **Exhibit 6-16:** Courtesy of Lever Brothers Company. **Exhibit 6-17:** Used with permission of General Motors Corp. **Exhibit 6-18:** Courtesy The Coca-Cola Company. **Exhibit 6-19:** Courtesy of PowerBar. **Exhibit 6-20:** Courtesy Revlon Consumer Products Corporation.

CHAPTER 7

Opening photo: Familiprix. **Exhibit 7-1:** © 1999 Castrol North America Inc. **Exhibit 7-2:** The DERMASIL print ad was reproduced courtesy Cheesebrough-Pond's USA Co. **Exhibit 7-3:** Courtesy DuPont. Teflon® is a registered trademark of DuPont. **IMC Perspective 7-1:** Home Hardware. **Exhibit 7-4:** Courtesy of Apple Computer, Inc. **Exhibit 7-5:** Courtesy of BASF Corp. **Exhibit 7-6:** Courtesy of White Wave, Inc. **Exhibit 7-7:** Courtesy W.K. Buckley Limited. **Exhibit 7-8:** Courtesy CamelBak Products, Inc. **Exhibit 7-9:** Courtesy Thomson Multimedia. Product photography by Thomas Card. Model photography by Dominik Guillemot. **Exhibit 7-10:** Courtesy of Team One Advertising for LEXUS. Photo by Martin Oort. **Exhibit 7-11:** Courtesy of Cambridge SoundWorks. **Exhibit 7-12:** Courtesy Sims. **IMC**

Perspective 7-2: Andrew Simpson. **IMC Perspective 7-3:** Courtesy of Sleeman Breweries. **Exhibit 7-13:** Courtesy of Volkswagen of America, Inc. and Arnold Worldwide. **Figure 7-3:** From the work of Richard Vaughn of Foote, Cone & Belding Advertising Agency. **Exhibit 7-14:** Courtesy of Norwegian Cruise Line. **Exhibit 7-15:** Courtesy of Apple Computer, Inc.

CHAPTER 8

Opening photo: Courtesy of Weston Bakeries Ltd. **Exhibit 8-1:** Churchill & Klehr/Liaison Agency, Inc. **IMC Perspective 8-1:** Andrew Simpson. **Exhibit 8-2:** Courtesy Roper Starch Worldwide. **Exhibit 8-3:** Courtesy Ipsos-ASI, Inc. **Exhibit 8-4:** Decision Analyst, Inc. **IMC Perspective 8-2:** Courtesy Molson Canada.

CHAPTER 9

Opening photo: Courtesy of General Motors Canada. **IMC Perspective 9-1:** McGraw-Hill Archive. **IMC Perspective 9-2:** Getty Images. **Figure 9-6:** Reprinted with permission from *Sales & Marketing Management*, © 2001, VNU Business Publications, USA. **Figure 9-7:** Reprinted with permission from *Sales & Marketing Management*, © 2001, VNU Business Publications, USA. **Figure 9-8:** Reprinted with permission from *Sales & Marketing Management*, © 2001, VNU Business Publications, USA. **Figure 9-11:** Who watches ads? December-January ratings in New York Market R.C. Percy & Company.

CHAPTER 10

Opening photo: Courtesy of Pfizer Canada Inc., Adams Division. **Exhibit 10-1:** Courtesy of Porsche Cars North America, Inc. **IMC Perspective 10-1:** CP/Patti Gower. **IMC Perspective 10-2:** Courtesy of Nielsen. **Exhibit 10-2:** Courtesy of Nielsen Media Research. **IMC Perspective 10-3:** CP/Fred Lummber. **Exhibit 10-3:** Banana

Boat of California, Inc. **Exhibit 10-4:** 2000-2001 BBM Television Data Book. Television Summer Drop-off. Used with permission.

CHAPTER 11

Opening photo: Courtesy of *UMM*. **Exhibit 11-1:** Courtesy of *Outpost* Magazine. **Exhibit 11-2:** Courtesy *Alberta Beef Magazine*. **IMC Perspective 11-1:** Courtesy of *Elle* Magazine. **Exhibit 11-3:** Courtesy of *Toronto Life* Magazine. **Exhibit 11-4:** Photography by Sharon Hoogstraten. **Exhibit 11-5:** Used by permission of WD-40 Company. **Exhibit 11-6:** Courtesy Newsweek, Inc. All rights reserved. **Exhibit 11-7:** Reprinted from 5/1/2000 BusinessWeek online by special permission, copyright © 2000 by the McGraw-Hill Companies, Inc. **IMC Perspective 11-2:** CP/Steve White. **Exhibit 11-8:** Courtesy Cathay Pacific Airways and McCann-Erickson. **IMC Perspective 11-3:** Andrew Simpson.

CHAPTER 12

Opening photo: Trident. **Exhibit 12-1:** Andrew Simpson. **Exhibit 12-2:** Andrew Simpson. **Exhibit 12-3:** Courtesy of Outdoor Advertising Association of America, Inc. **Exhibit 12-4:** Courtesy of Vert, Inc. **Exhibit 12-5:** Courtesy of Outdoor Advertising Association of America, Inc. **IMC Perspective 12-1:** Andrew Simpson. **Exhibit 12-6:** Courtesy of WestJet. **IMC Perspective 12-2:** Andrew Simpson. **Exhibit 12-7:** Courtesy of Promotional Products Association International. **Exhibit 12-8:** AP Photo/BMW, Stuart Ramson. **Exhibit 12-9:** AP photo/Adam Butler.

CHAPTER 13

Opening photo: Kraft Canada Ltd. **Exhibit 13-1:** KELLOGG'S POP-TARTS PASTRY SWIRLS™ and POP-TARTS SNACK-STIX™ are trademarks of Kellogg Company. All rights reserved. Used with permission. **Exhibit 13-2:** Courtesy of DVC Worldwide. **Exhibit 13-3:** Courtesy of WD-40 Company.

Exhibit 13-4: ArmorAll Products Corporation. **Exhibit 13-5:** Courtesy of Valpak Direct Marketing Systems, Inc. **Exhibit 13-6:** Courtesy Kellogg Company. Eggo®, Common Sense®, and Kellogg's® are registered trademarks of Kellogg Company. All rights reserved. **Exhibit 13-7:** Used with permission from McDonald's Corp. **IMC Perspective 13-1:** Courtesy of Kellogg Canada Inc. **IMC Perspective 13-2:** Andrew Simpson. **Exhibit 13.8:** ArmorAll Products Corporation. **Exhibit 13-9:** Courtesy Bristol-Myers Company. **Exhibit 13-10:** Courtesy of Wilson Sporting Goods Co. and Great Northern Corp. Display Group. **Exhibit 13-11:** Courtesy New Balance Athletic Shoes, Inc. **IMC Perspective 13-3:** McGraw-Hill Archive. **Exhibit 13-12:** Courtesy WD-40 Company. **Exhibit 13-13:** Courtesy Lever Brothers Company. **Exhibit 13-14:** © Dell Computer Corp.

CHAPTER 14

Opening photo: Courtesy of Iceberg Vodka. **Exhibit 14-1:** Courtesy of Bridgestone/Firestone Americas Holding, Inc. **Exhibit 14-2:** CLIENT: Olympus America, Inc. AGENCY: McCaffrey & Ratner Gottlieb Lane. **Exhibit 14-3:** McGraw-Hill Ryerson 2001 Annual Report. **Exhibit 14-4:** Reprinted with permission of Chevron Corporation. **Figure 14-3:** Reprinted courtesy of Ketchum Public Relations. **Exhibit 14-5:** Graco. **IMC Perspective 14-2:** Courtesy of Grip/Labatt Brewing Company Limited. **Ethical Perspective 14-3:** Adapted from Stan Sutter, "Not Just Peanuts," *Marketing Magazine*, June 11, 2001. Reprinted with permission of *Marketing Magazine*; photo: © Nestle Canada Inc. **Exhibit 14-6:** Courtesy Tyco International. **Exhibit 14-7:** Design: Alana

Roso/Silver Samba Design Co. **Exhibit 14-8:** Courtesy Cunningham Communications. **Exhibit 14-9:** Courtesy of KitchenAid Home Appliances.

CHAPTER 15

Opening photo: Andrew Simpson. **Exhibit 15-1:** Courtesy Tourism Saskatchewan, www.sasktourism.com. **Exhibit 15-2:** BLOCKBUSTER name, design and related marks are trademarks of Blockbuster, Inc. © 2003 Blockbuster, Inc. All rights reserved. **Exhibit 15-3:** © 1999 Hertz System, Inc. Hertz is a registered service mark and trademark of Hertz System, Inc. **IMC Perspective 15-1:** CP/Boris Spremo. **IMC Perspective 15-2:** Courtesy Newfoundland and Labrador Tourism. **Exhibit 15-4:** Courtesy Porsche Cars North America, Inc. **Exhibit 15-5:** Photograph by Sharon Hoogstraten. **Exhibit 15-6:** Courtesy of Lee Valley Hardware. **Exhibit 15-7:** Courtesy Volvo Cars of North America. **Exhibit 15-8:** Courtesy of Lenox, Inc. **Figure 15-6:** Direct Marketing Association, 1996 Statistical Fact Book, p. 146.

CHAPTER 16

Opening photo: Courtesy of General Mills Canada. **Exhibit 16-1:** Courtesy General Mills, Inc. "Cheerios" is a registered trademark of General Mills. Used with permission. **Exhibit 16-2:** Sharp. **Exhibit 16-3:** Huggies. **Exhibit 16-4:** Courtesy DaimlerChrysler Corporation.

CHAPTER 17

Opening photo: Courtesy of Grip Limited. **Exhibit 17-1:** © The Proctor & Gamble Company. **Exhibit 17-2:** Courtesy of No Fear. **Exhibit 17-3:** Courtesy The Coca-

Cola Company. "Coca-Cola" and the Dynamic Ribbon device are registered trademarks of The Coca-Cola Company. **Exhibit 17-4:** Courtesy of Rethink. **IMC Perspective 17-1:** Courtesy of Rethink. **Exhibit 17-5:** Used by permission of Association of National Advertisers: Trend in Compensation Survey: 2000. **Exhibit 17-6:** Courtesy of Whirlpool. **Exhibit 17-7:** DR PEPPER® is a registered trademark of Dr Pepper/Seven Up, Inc. © 2000 Dr Pepper/Seven Up Inc. **Exhibit 17-8:** Courtesy of DVC.

CHAPTER 18

Opening photo: CP/Jacques Boissinot. **Ethical Perspective 18-2:** Courtesy of Mediacs. **Exhibit 18-1:** Courtesy of Calvin Klein. **Exhibit 18-2:** Concept: O. Toscani. Courtesy of United Colors of Benetton. **Exhibit 18-3:** Courtesy Ansell. **Exhibit 18-4:** Courtesy Airwalk. **Exhibit 18-5:** Used by permission of Calvin Klein. **Exhibit 18-6:** Reprinted by permission of Rolls Royce Motor Cars Inc. **Exhibit 18-7:** © American Association of Advertising Agencies. **Exhibit 18-8:** © American Association of Advertising Agencies. **Exhibit 18-9:** Courtesy Maidenform Inc./Agency—Levine, Huntley, Schmidt & Beaver; Creative—Rochell Klein, Michael Vitello; Director—Mark Coppos, Coppos Films. **Exhibit 18-10:** Courtesy IKEA and Deutsch Inc. **Exhibit 18-11:** Courtesy gfn.com, the Gay Financial Network, Inc. **Exhibit 18-12:** Courtesy of International Advertising Association. **Exhibit 18-13:** © American Association of Advertising Agencies. **Exhibit 18-14:** © American Association of Advertising Agencies. **Exhibit 18-15:** Courtesy International Advertising Agency.

Name and Company Index

Subject Index

574

Subject Index

transformational motives, 130–131
transit advertising, 349
transit media
    airline transit options, 353–354
    commuter transit options, 349
    copy limitations, 351
    costs, 351, 353
    creative limitations, 351
    exposure, 351
    exterior posters, 349
    fake transit ads, 354
    frequency, 350
    geographic selectivity, 350
    image factors, 351
    in-flight advertising, 353
    interior door cards, 349
    interior transit cards, 349
    limitations of, 351, 353
    reach, 350
    select market, 350
    station posters, 350
    strengths of, 350, 353
    subway online, 350
    super-bus, 350
    timeliness, 351
    waste coverage, 351
transit shelter, 350
transit-shelter posters, 346–347
trial purchase, 377
trustworthiness, 171
two-sided message, 189
two-step approach, 451

U

undifferentiated marketing, 59
unduplicated reach, 257
unique selling proposition, 149
untruthful advertising, 525–526
usage, 58

V

VALS (values and lifestyles) program, 55, 59
vehicle option source effect, 215
verbal message, 189–190
vertical cooperative advertising, 404–405
video news release (VNR), 418, 427
video portion of commercial, 194–195
visible minorities, 536
visual elements, 193
visual image personality (VIP), 78
visual message, 189–190
voiceover, 196

W

wants, 38
waste coverage, 252, 351
webcasting technologies, 473
website
    communication objectives, 468
    development, 471–472
    role of, 471
websnarl, 482
women
    marketing communications industry, in, 507
    offensive advertising and, 526–528
    portrayals of, 534–535
    sex role stereotypes, 529
    sexism, 535
    sexual appeals, 526–528

stereotyping and advertising, 534–535
word-of-mouth communication, 70
World Wide Web (WWW), 464

Y

Yellow Pages media
    directional medium, 362
    limitations, 362–363
    strengths, 362

Z

zapping/zipping, 288
zero-based communications planning, 105

577